YOUR ACCOMPLISHMENTS ARE SUSPICIOUSLY HARD TO VERIFY

Other DILBERT® books from Andrews McMeel Publishing

Problem Identified and You're Probably Not Part of the Solution
ISBN: 978-0-7407-8534-4

I'm Tempted to Stop Acting Randomly
ISBN: 978-0-7407-7806-3

14 Years of Loyal Service in a Fabric-Covered Box
ISBN: 978-0-7407-7365-5

Freedom's Just Another Word for People Finding Out You're Useless
ISBN: 978-0-7407-7815-5

Dilbert 2.0: 20 Years of Dilbert
ISBN: 978-0-7407-7735-6

This Is the Part Where You Pretend to Add Value
ISBN: 978-0-7407-7227-6

Cubes and Punishment
ISBN: 978-0-7407-6837-8

Positive Attitude
ISBN: 978-0-7407-6379-3

Try Rebooting Yourself
ISBN: 978-0-7407-6190-4

What Would Wally Do?
ISBN: 978-0-7407-5769-3

Thriving on Vague Objectives
ISBN: 978-0-7407-5533-0

The Fluorescent Light Glistens Off Your Head
ISBN: 978-0-7407-5113-4

It's Not Funny If I Have to Explain It
ISBN: 978-0-7407-4658-1

Don't Stand Where the Comet Is Assumed to Strike Oil
ISBN: 978-0-7407-4539-3

Words You Don't Want to Hear During Your Annual Performance Review
ISBN: 978-0-7407-3805-0

When Body Language Goes Bad
ISBN: 978-0-7407-3298-0

What Do You Call a Sociopath in a Cubicle? Answer: A Coworker
ISBN: 978-0-7407-2663-7

Another Day in Cubicle Paradise
ISBN: 978-0-7407-2194-6

When Did Ignorance Become a Point of View?
ISBN: 978-0-7407-1839-7

Excuse Me While I Wag
ISBN: 978-0-7407-1390-3

Dilbert—A Treasury of Sunday Strips: Version 00
ISBN: 978-0-7407-0531-1

Random Acts of Management
ISBN: 978-0-7407-0453-6

Dilbert Gives You the Business
ISBN: 978-0-7407-0003-3

Don't Step in the Leadership
ISBN: 978-0-8362-7844-6

Journey to Cubeville
ISBN: 978-0-8362-6745-7

I'm Not Anti-Business, I'm Anti-Idiot
ISBN: 978-0-8362-5182-1

Seven Years of Highly Defective People
ISBN: 978-0-8362-3668-2

Casual Day Has Gone Too Far
ISBN: 978-0-8362-2899-1

Fugitive from the Cubicle Police
ISBN: 978-0-8362-2119-0

It's Obvious You Won't Survive by Your Wits Alone
ISBN: 978-0-8362-0415-5

Still Pumped from Using the Mouse
ISBN: 978-0-8362-1026-2

Bring Me the Head of Willy the Mailboy!
ISBN: 978-0-8362-1779-7

Shave the Whales
ISBN: 978-0-8362-1740-7

Dogbert's Clues for the Clueless
ISBN: 978-0-8362-1737-7

Always Postpone Meetings with Time-Wasting Morons
ISBN: 978-0-8362-1758-2

Build a Better Life by Stealing Office Supplies
ISBN: 978-0-8362-1757-5

For ordering information, call 1-800-223-2336.

YOUR ACCOMPLISHMENTS ARE SUSPICIOUSLY HARD TO VERIFY

by SCOTT ADAMS

Andrews McMeel
Publishing, LLC
Kansas City • Sydney • London

Your Accomplishments Are Suspiciously Hard to Verify copyright © 2011 by Scott Adams, Inc.
All rights reserved. Printed in the United States of America.
No part of this book may be used or reproduced in any manner whatsoever without written permission
except in the case of reprints in the context of reviews.
Andrews McMeel Publishing, LLC
an Andrews McMeel Universal company
1130 Walnut Street, Kansas City, Missouri 64106
www.andrewsmcmeel.com

11 12 13 14 15 BAM 10 9 8 7 6 5 4 3 2 1

ISBN: 978-1-4494-0102-3

Library of Congress Control Number: 2010937748

www.dilbert.com

For Shelly

Introduction

Have you noticed that people aren't good at comparing things? That works to your advantage. It's easy to mask your incompetence as long as you're free to pick your own points of reference. For example, if you reduce expenses at your workplace, you can claim success even if any moron easily could have reduced expenses by twice as much. The trick is to compare your results with the hypothetical results of an imaginary person who wasn't even trying. Keep your boss focused on the important thing—that you reduced expenses, dang it. Case closed. No more questions. Moving on.

Another time-honored approach for making your accomplishments difficult to verify is to work on projects that aren't expected to bear fruit until some undefined day in the future. In the window of time between initiating your deception and the moment you are unmasked as a fraud, you can be gaining experience, padding your resume, and job-hopping faster than a tiny cowboy in a porcupine rodeo. (I will pause now while you savor that excellent analogy.)

Perceived success is a numbers game. Don't be afraid to bounce from project to project. If you come in contact with enough random situations, sooner or later, by pure chance, you'll end up working with someone competent. Then you can call that person your partner and claim coauthorship of every idea that comes out of his or her mouth. Try to use the phrase "I forget which one of us thought of that idea" whenever you get a chance. That way you're not lying; you're simply forgetting details that aren't important. You're a Big Picture person.

At meetings, when one of your coworkers describes an actual accomplishment, do the slow clap and say, "FINALLY, you listened to my advice." Then change the subject.

If software is your thing, claim you removed a thousand lines of code and made the system 20 percent faster. Be sure to point out that the improvement is hard to notice because more people are using the system now.

People have bad memories. You can use that to your advantage, too. Speak of your project in glowing, hypothetical terms, under the guise of making some larger point, and hope that repetition makes it stick. For example, you could say, "Suppose my project saves $10 million. That would be twice as good as Carl's project, right?" If you throw around the $10 million figure often enough people will remember it as a fact.

These are but a few of the many ways you can make your accomplishments difficult to verify. For more, study this book and pay special attention to any strip featuring Wally.

Good luck.

S. Adams

Scott Adams

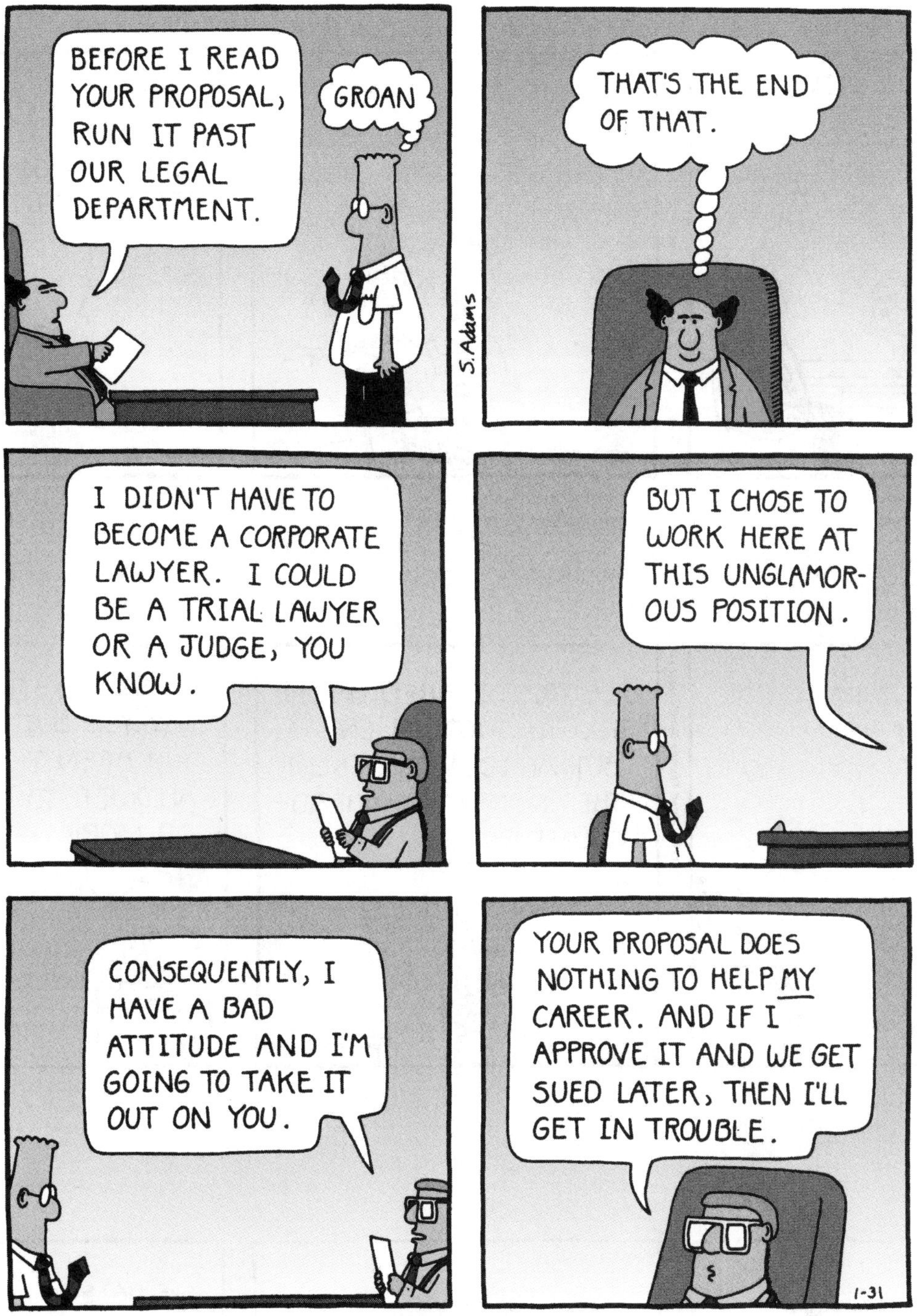
BEFORE I READ YOUR PROPOSAL, RUN IT PAST OUR LEGAL DEPARTMENT.
GROAN
S. Adams
THAT'S THE END OF THAT.
I DIDN'T HAVE TO BECOME A CORPORATE LAWYER. I COULD BE A TRIAL LAWYER OR A JUDGE, YOU KNOW.
BUT I CHOSE TO WORK HERE AT THIS UNGLAMOROUS POSITION.
CONSEQUENTLY, I HAVE A BAD ATTITUDE AND I'M GOING TO TAKE IT OUT ON YOU.
YOUR PROPOSAL DOES NOTHING TO HELP MY CAREER. AND IF I APPROVE IT AND WE GET SUED LATER, THEN I'LL GET IN TROUBLE.
1-31

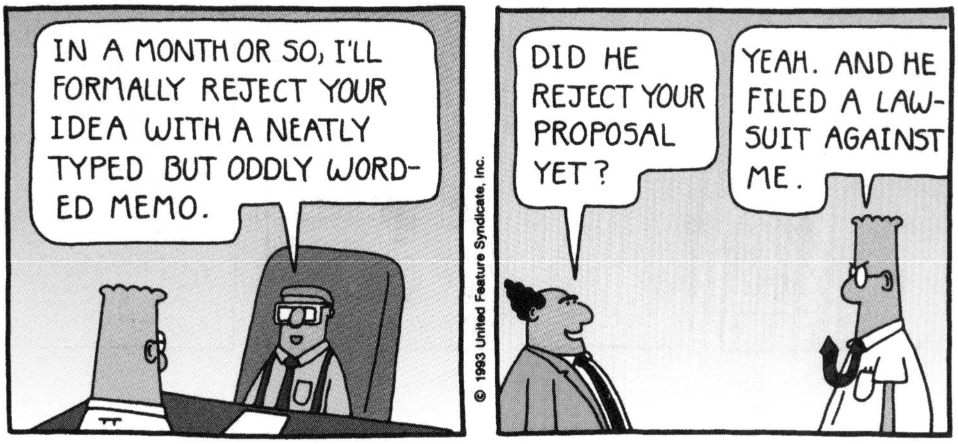
IN A MONTH OR SO, I'LL FORMALLY REJECT YOUR IDEA WITH A NEATLY TYPED BUT ODDLY WORDED MEMO.
© 1993 United Feature Syndicate, Inc.
DID HE REJECT YOUR PROPOSAL YET?
YEAH. AND HE FILED A LAWSUIT AGAINST ME.

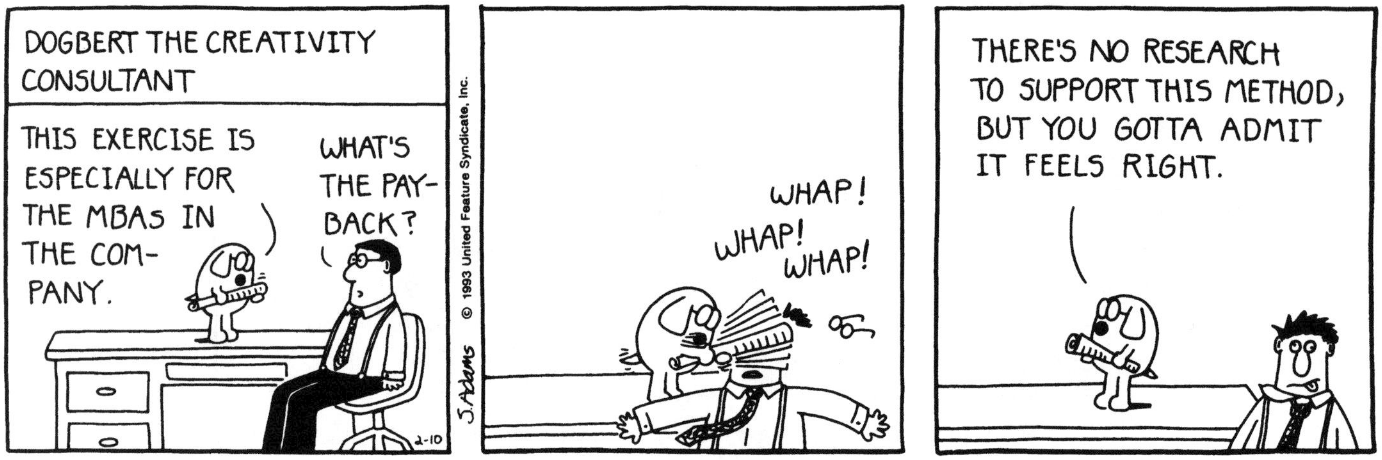
DOGBERT THE CREATIVITY CONSULTANT
THIS EXERCISE IS ESPECIALLY FOR THE MBAs IN THE COMPANY.
WHAT'S THE PAYBACK?
© 1993 United Feature Syndicate, Inc.
S. Adams
2-10
WHAP!
WHAP!
WHAP!
THERE'S NO RESEARCH TO SUPPORT THIS METHOD, BUT YOU GOTTA ADMIT IT FEELS RIGHT.

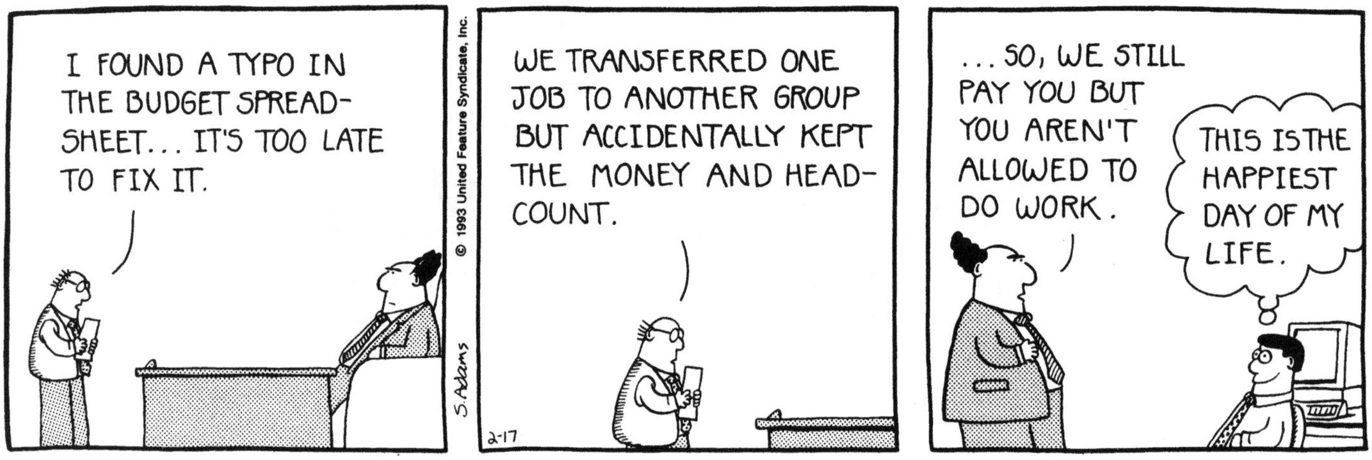
I FOUND A TYPO IN THE BUDGET SPREADSHEET... IT'S TOO LATE TO FIX IT.
© 1993 United Feature Syndicate, Inc.
S. Adams
2-17
WE TRANSFERRED ONE JOB TO ANOTHER GROUP BUT ACCIDENTALLY KEPT THE MONEY AND HEADCOUNT.
...SO, WE STILL PAY YOU BUT YOU AREN'T ALLOWED TO DO WORK.
THIS IS THE HAPPIEST DAY OF MY LIFE.

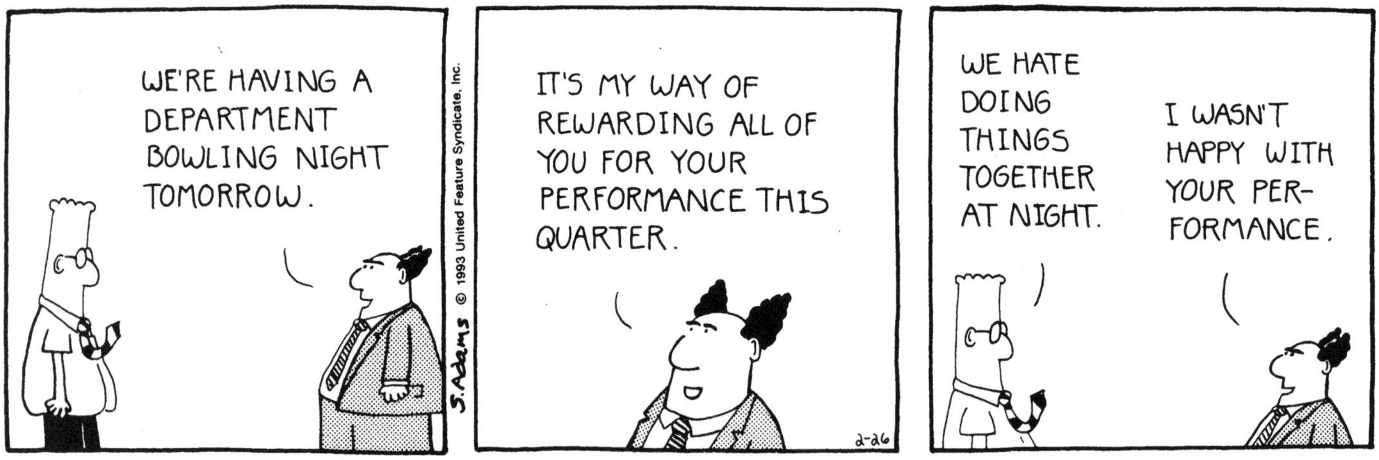
WE'RE HAVING A DEPARTMENT BOWLING NIGHT TOMORROW.
© 1993 United Feature Syndicate, Inc.
S. Adams
IT'S MY WAY OF REWARDING ALL OF YOU FOR YOUR PERFORMANCE THIS QUARTER.
2-26
WE HATE DOING THINGS TOGETHER AT NIGHT.
I WASN'T HAPPY WITH YOUR PERFORMANCE.

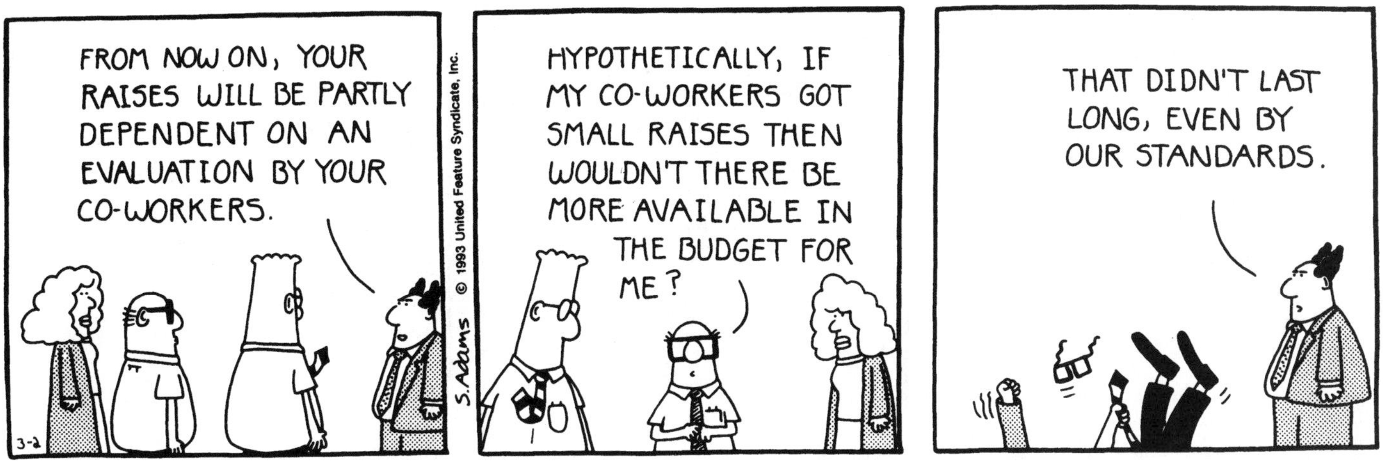
FROM NOW ON, YOUR RAISES WILL BE PARTLY DEPENDENT ON AN EVALUATION BY YOUR CO-WORKERS.
HYPOTHETICALLY, IF MY CO-WORKERS GOT SMALL RAISES THEN WOULDN'T THERE BE MORE AVAILABLE IN THE BUDGET FOR ME?
THAT DIDN'T LAST LONG, EVEN BY OUR STANDARDS.
© 1993 United Feature Syndicate, Inc.
S. Adams
3-2

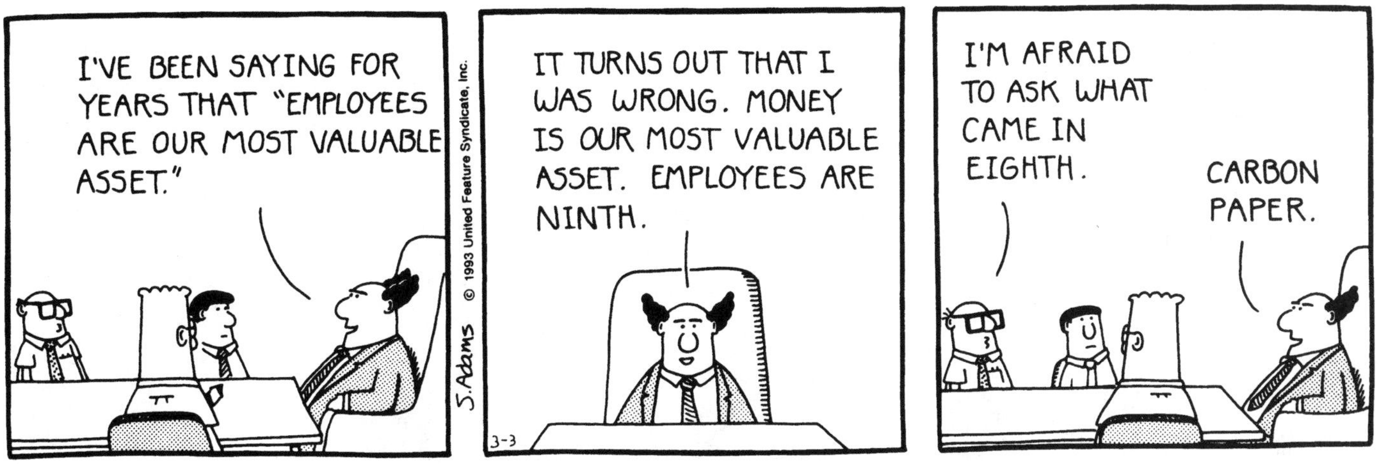
I'VE BEEN SAYING FOR YEARS THAT "EMPLOYEES ARE OUR MOST VALUABLE ASSET."
IT TURNS OUT THAT I WAS WRONG. MONEY IS OUR MOST VALUABLE ASSET. EMPLOYEES ARE NINTH.
I'M AFRAID TO ASK WHAT CAME IN EIGHTH.
CARBON PAPER.
© 1993 United Feature Syndicate, Inc.
S. Adams
3-3

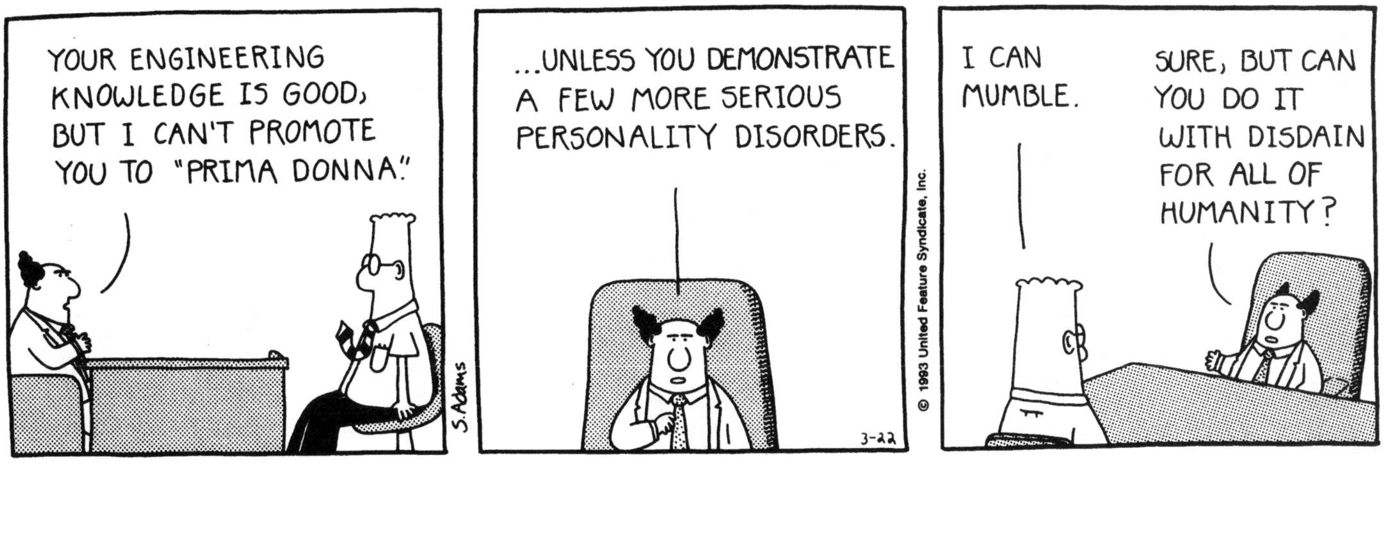
YOUR ENGINEERING KNOWLEDGE IS GOOD, BUT I CAN'T PROMOTE YOU TO "PRIMA DONNA."
...UNLESS YOU DEMONSTRATE A FEW MORE SERIOUS PERSONALITY DISORDERS.
I CAN MUMBLE.
SURE, BUT CAN YOU DO IT WITH DISDAIN FOR ALL OF HUMANITY?
S. Adams
3-22
© 1993 United Feature Syndicate, Inc.

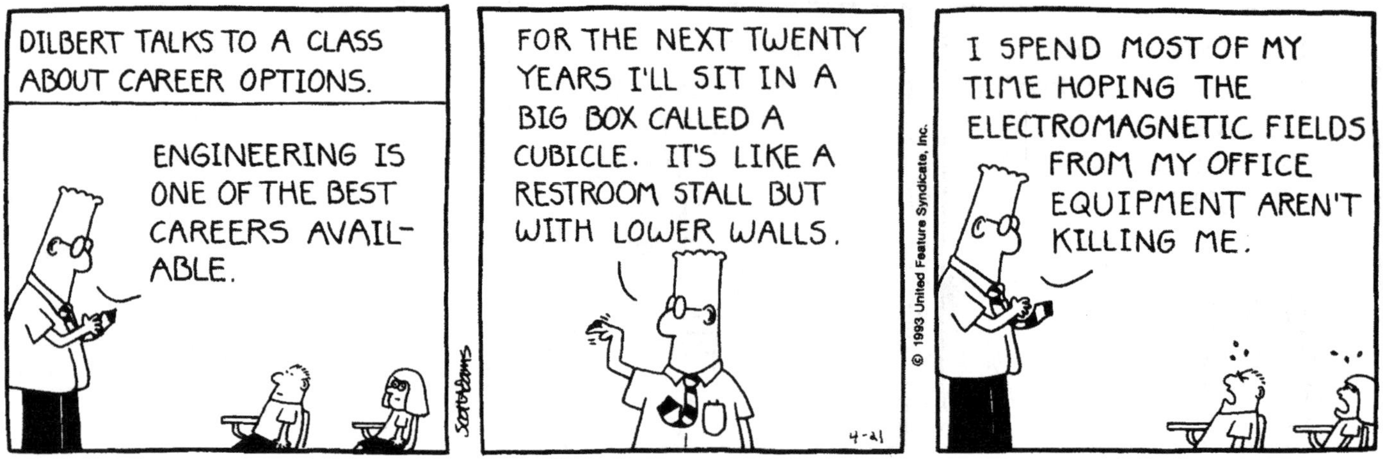
DILBERT TALKS TO A CLASS ABOUT CAREER OPTIONS.
ENGINEERING IS ONE OF THE BEST CAREERS AVAILABLE.
FOR THE NEXT TWENTY YEARS I'LL SIT IN A BIG BOX CALLED A CUBICLE. IT'S LIKE A RESTROOM STALL BUT WITH LOWER WALLS.
4-21
© 1993 United Feature Syndicate, Inc.
I SPEND MOST OF MY TIME HOPING THE ELECTROMAGNETIC FIELDS FROM MY OFFICE EQUIPMENT AREN'T KILLING ME.

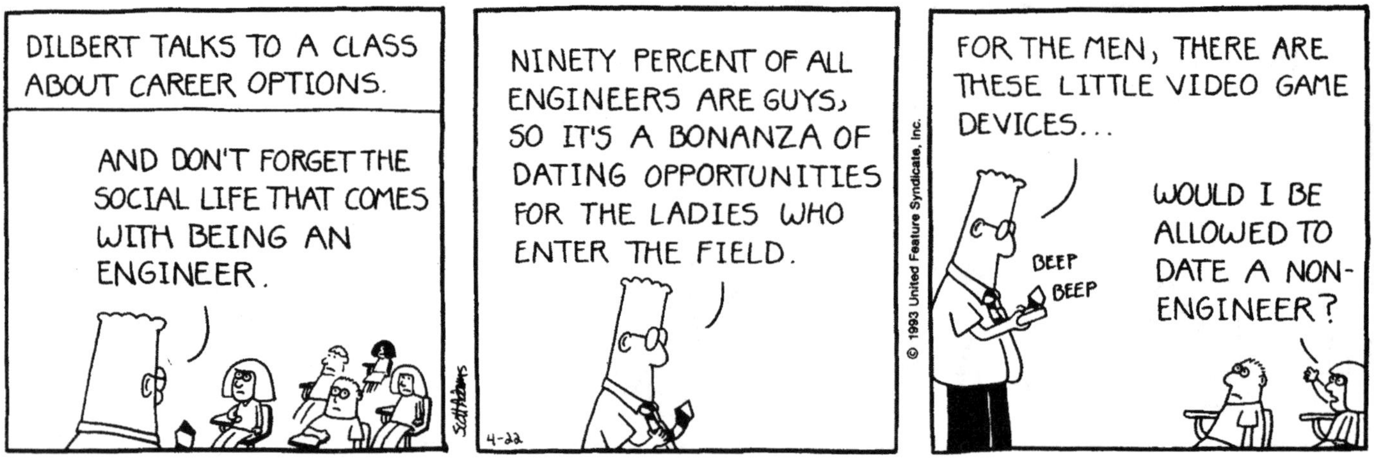
DILBERT TALKS TO A CLASS ABOUT CAREER OPTIONS.
AND DON'T FORGET THE SOCIAL LIFE THAT COMES WITH BEING AN ENGINEER.
NINETY PERCENT OF ALL ENGINEERS ARE GUYS, SO IT'S A BONANZA OF DATING OPPORTUNITIES FOR THE LADIES WHO ENTER THE FIELD.
4-22
© 1993 United Feature Syndicate, Inc.
FOR THE MEN, THERE ARE THESE LITTLE VIDEO GAME DEVICES...
BEEP BEEP
WOULD I BE ALLOWED TO DATE A NON-ENGINEER?

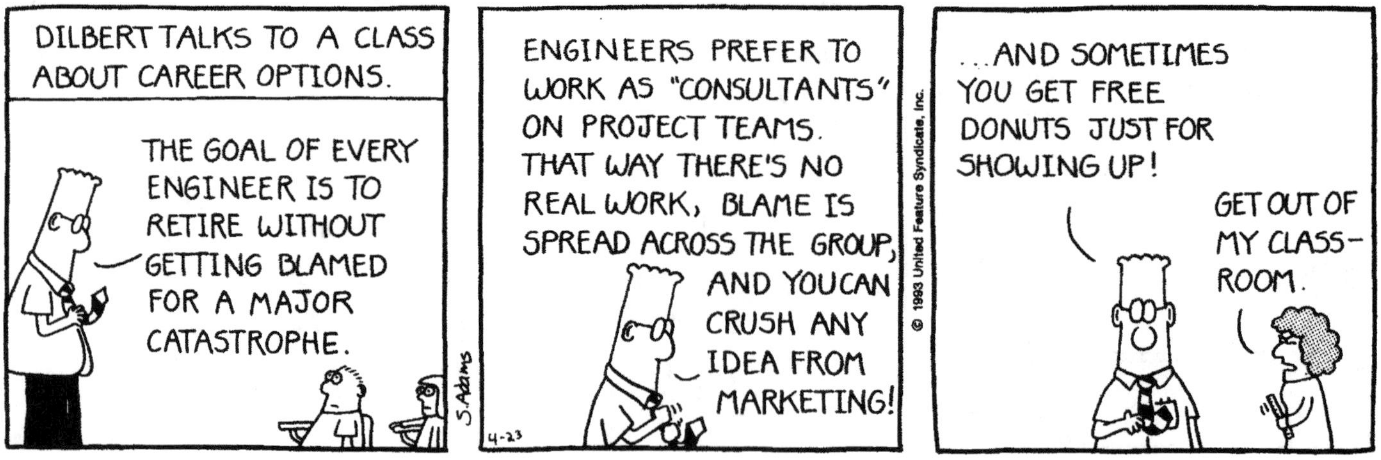
DILBERT TALKS TO A CLASS ABOUT CAREER OPTIONS.
THE GOAL OF EVERY ENGINEER IS TO RETIRE WITHOUT GETTING BLAMED FOR A MAJOR CATASTROPHE.
S. Adams
4-23
ENGINEERS PREFER TO WORK AS "CONSULTANTS" ON PROJECT TEAMS. THAT WAY THERE'S NO REAL WORK, BLAME IS SPREAD ACROSS THE GROUP,
AND YOU CAN CRUSH ANY IDEA FROM MARKETING!
© 1993 United Feature Syndicate, Inc.
...AND SOMETIMES YOU GET FREE DONUTS JUST FOR SHOWING UP!
GET OUT OF MY CLASSROOM.

GOVERNMENT STATISTICS SHOW THAT OFFICE PRODUCTIVITY WENT <u>DOWN</u> AS COMPUTERS BECAME WIDELY USED.

© 1993 United Feature Syndicate, Inc.

BUT I DIDN'T BELIEVE IT.

SO I WROTE A LITTLE SOFTWARE PROGRAM TO TEST THAT CONCLUSION.

IT ONLY TOOK A MONTH, BUT IT PRODUCED SOME IMPRESSIVE DATA.

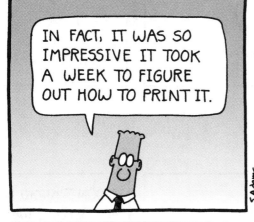

IN FACT, IT WAS SO IMPRESSIVE IT TOOK A WEEK TO FIGURE OUT HOW TO PRINT IT.

BUT BEFORE I COULD PRINT, MY COMPUTER CRASHED AND I DIDN'T HAVE BACKUP COPIES.

S.Adams

4-25

SO, IT SEEMS THE GOVERNMENT WAS RIGHT; COMPUTERS ARE TO BLAME FOR THE DECLINE IN PRODUCTIVITY.

DO YOU THINK THE EMPLOYEES COULD BE PARTLY RESPONSIBLE?

SURE, FIND A SCAPEGOAT.

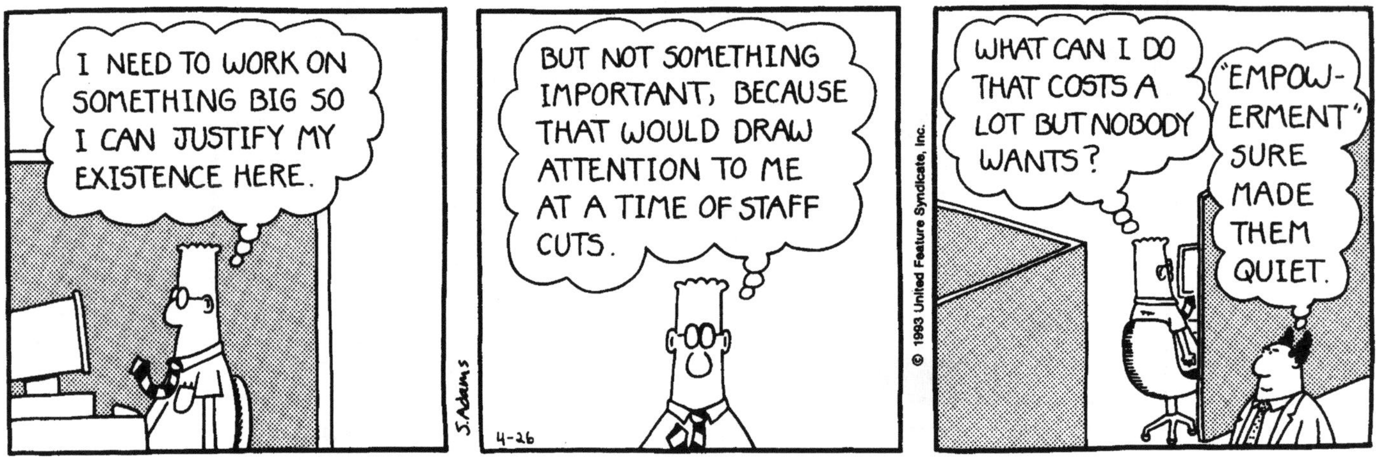
I NEED TO WORK ON SOMETHING BIG SO I CAN JUSTIFY MY EXISTENCE HERE.
S. Adams
BUT NOT SOMETHING IMPORTANT, BECAUSE THAT WOULD DRAW ATTENTION TO ME AT A TIME OF STAFF CUTS.
4-26
WHAT CAN I DO THAT COSTS A LOT BUT NOBODY WANTS?
"EMPOWERMENT" SURE MADE THEM QUIET.
© 1993 United Feature Syndicate, Inc.

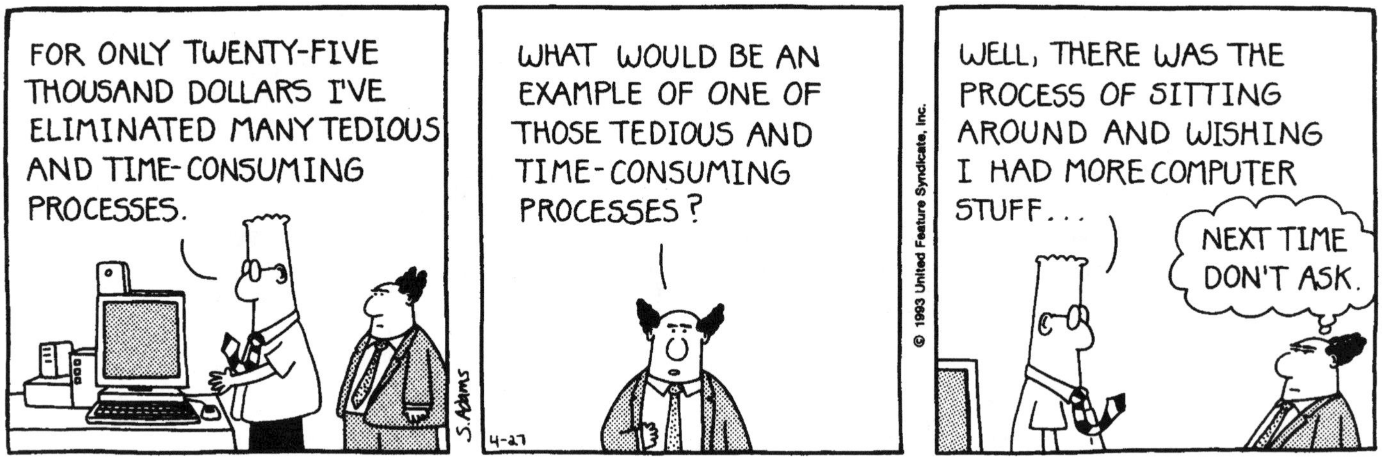
FOR ONLY TWENTY-FIVE THOUSAND DOLLARS I'VE ELIMINATED MANY TEDIOUS AND TIME-CONSUMING PROCESSES.
S. Adams
WHAT WOULD BE AN EXAMPLE OF ONE OF THOSE TEDIOUS AND TIME-CONSUMING PROCESSES?
4-27
WELL, THERE WAS THE PROCESS OF SITTING AROUND AND WISHING I HAD MORE COMPUTER STUFF...
NEXT TIME DON'T ASK.
© 1993 United Feature Syndicate, Inc.

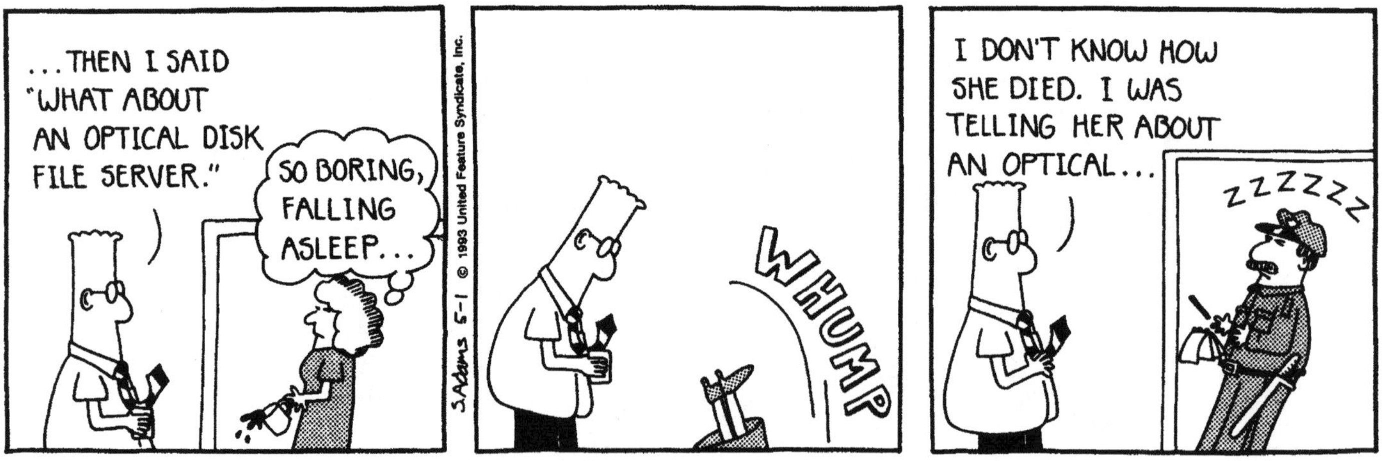
...THEN I SAID "WHAT ABOUT AN OPTICAL DISK FILE SERVER."
SO BORING, FALLING ASLEEP...
S. Adams 5-1 © 1993 United Feature Syndicate, Inc.
WHUMP
I DON'T KNOW HOW SHE DIED. I WAS TELLING HER ABOUT AN OPTICAL...
ZZZZZZ

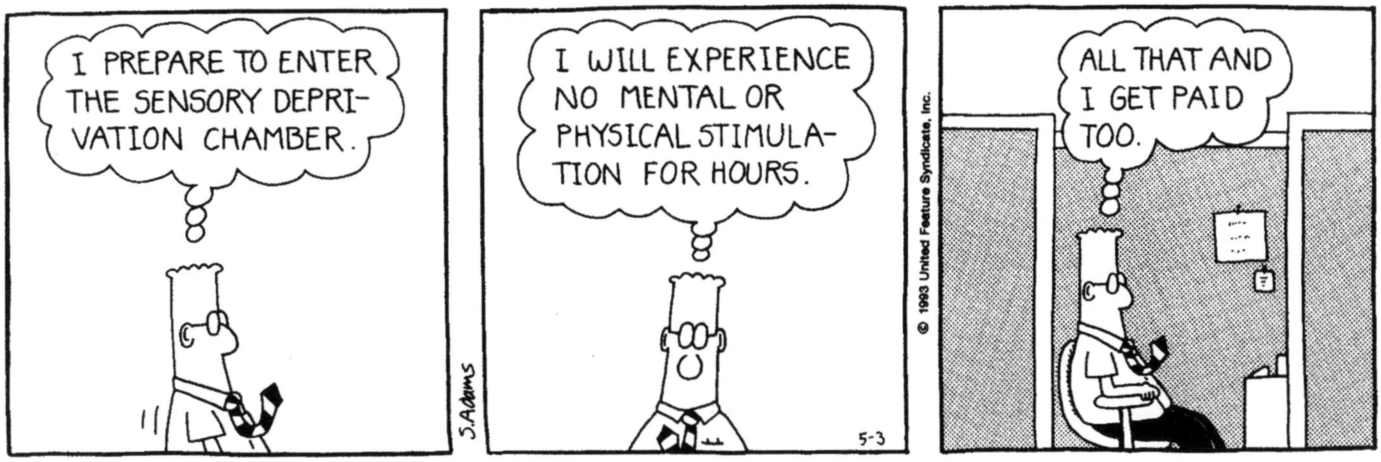
I PREPARE TO ENTER THE SENSORY DEPRIVATION CHAMBER.
S. Adams
I WILL EXPERIENCE NO MENTAL OR PHYSICAL STIMULATION FOR HOURS.
5-3
© 1993 United Feature Syndicate, Inc.
ALL THAT AND I GET PAID TOO.

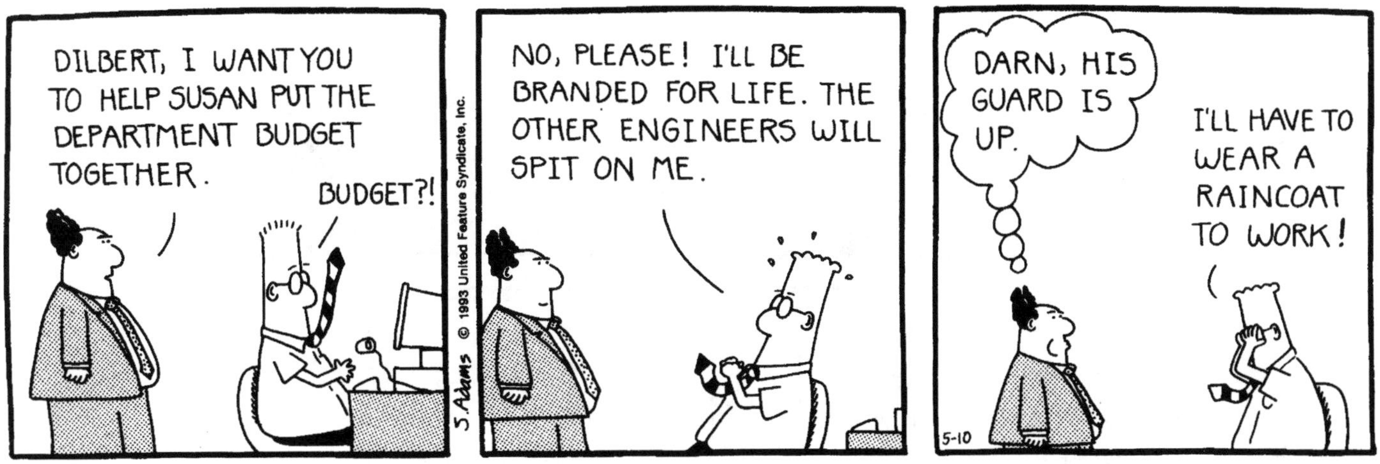
DILBERT, I WANT YOU TO HELP SUSAN PUT THE DEPARTMENT BUDGET TOGETHER.
BUDGET?!
S. Adams © 1993 United Feature Syndicate, Inc.
NO, PLEASE! I'LL BE BRANDED FOR LIFE. THE OTHER ENGINEERS WILL SPIT ON ME.
DARN, HIS GUARD IS UP.
I'LL HAVE TO WEAR A RAINCOAT TO WORK!
5-10

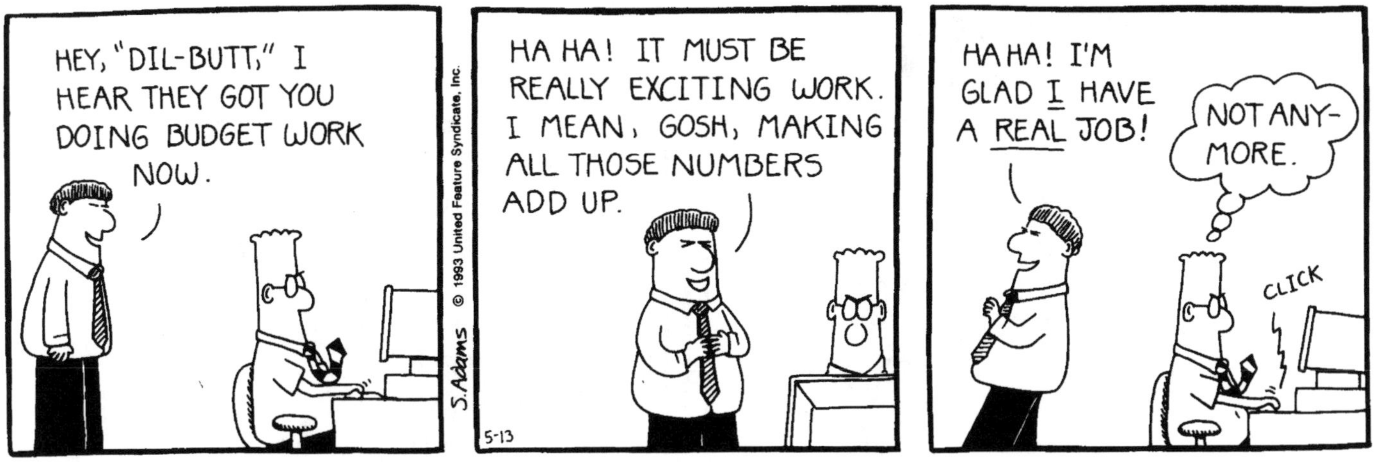
HEY, "DIL-BUTT," I HEAR THEY GOT YOU DOING BUDGET WORK NOW.
S. Adams © 1993 United Feature Syndicate, Inc.
HA HA! IT MUST BE REALLY EXCITING WORK. I MEAN, GOSH, MAKING ALL THOSE NUMBERS ADD UP.
5-13
HA HA! I'M GLAD I HAVE A REAL JOB!
NOT ANYMORE.
CLICK

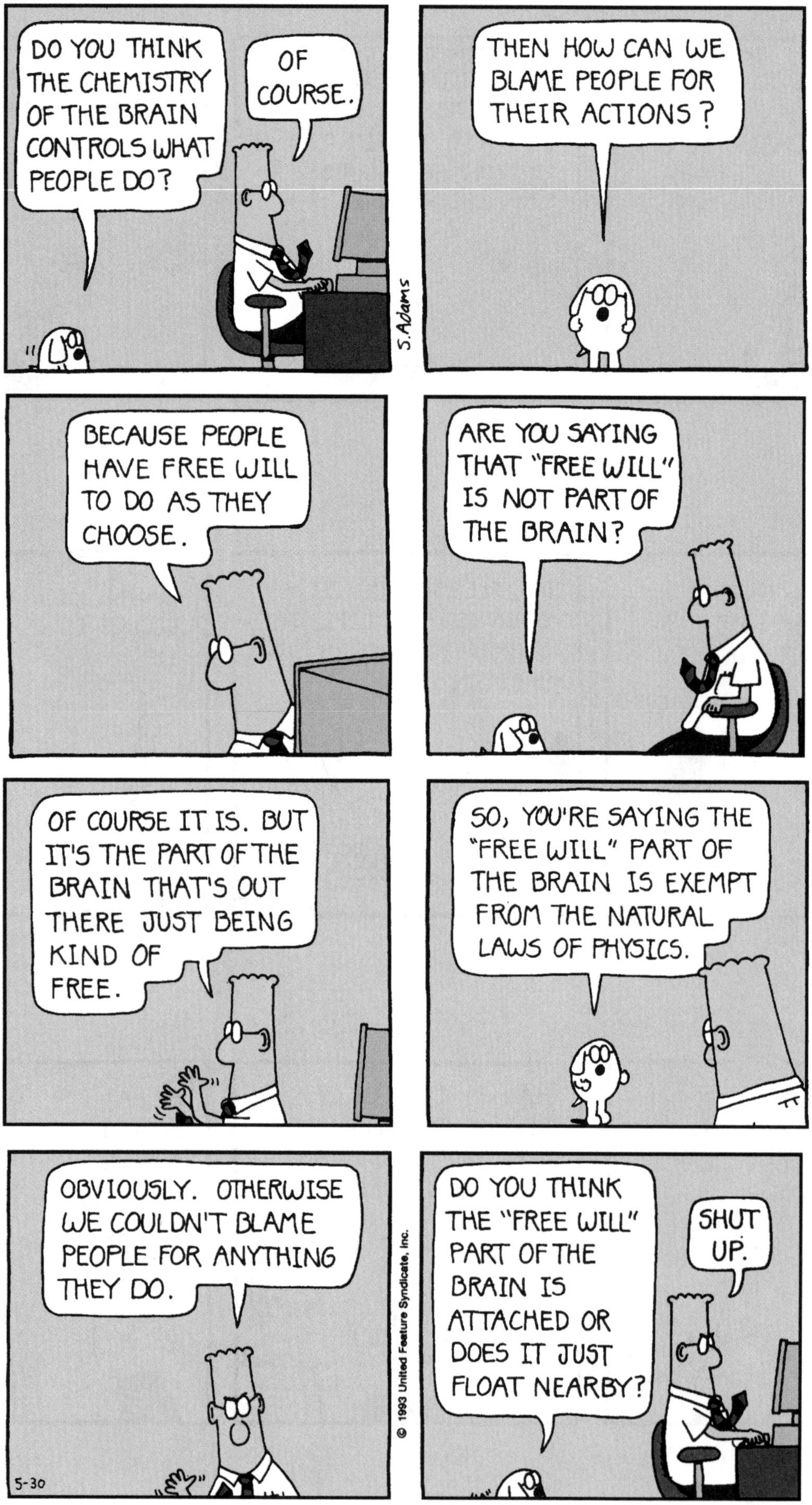
DO YOU THINK THE CHEMISTRY OF THE BRAIN CONTROLS WHAT PEOPLE DO?
OF COURSE.
S. Adams
THEN HOW CAN WE BLAME PEOPLE FOR THEIR ACTIONS?
BECAUSE PEOPLE HAVE FREE WILL TO DO AS THEY CHOOSE.
ARE YOU SAYING THAT "FREE WILL" IS NOT PART OF THE BRAIN?
OF COURSE IT IS. BUT IT'S THE PART OF THE BRAIN THAT'S OUT THERE JUST BEING KIND OF FREE.
SO, YOU'RE SAYING THE "FREE WILL" PART OF THE BRAIN IS EXEMPT FROM THE NATURAL LAWS OF PHYSICS.
OBVIOUSLY. OTHERWISE WE COULDN'T BLAME PEOPLE FOR ANYTHING THEY DO.
5-30
© 1993 United Feature Syndicate, Inc.
DO YOU THINK THE "FREE WILL" PART OF THE BRAIN IS ATTACHED OR DOES IT JUST FLOAT NEARBY?
SHUT UP.

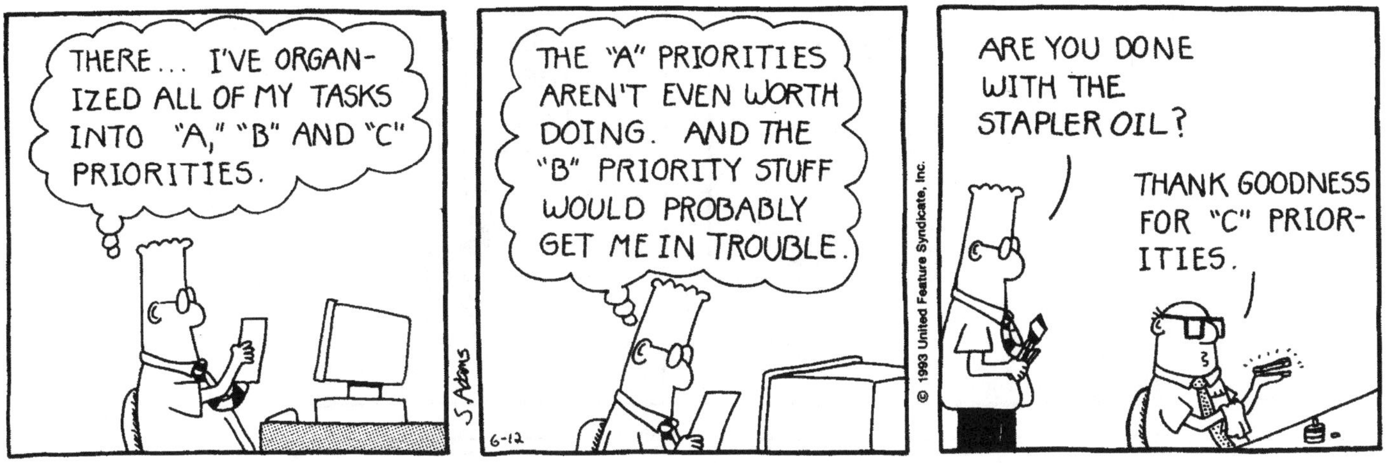
THERE... I'VE ORGANIZED ALL OF MY TASKS INTO "A," "B" AND "C" PRIORITIES.
S. Adams
6-12
THE "A" PRIORITIES AREN'T EVEN WORTH DOING. AND THE "B" PRIORITY STUFF WOULD PROBABLY GET ME IN TROUBLE.
© 1993 United Feature Syndicate, Inc.
ARE YOU DONE WITH THE STAPLER OIL?
THANK GOODNESS FOR "C" PRIORITIES.

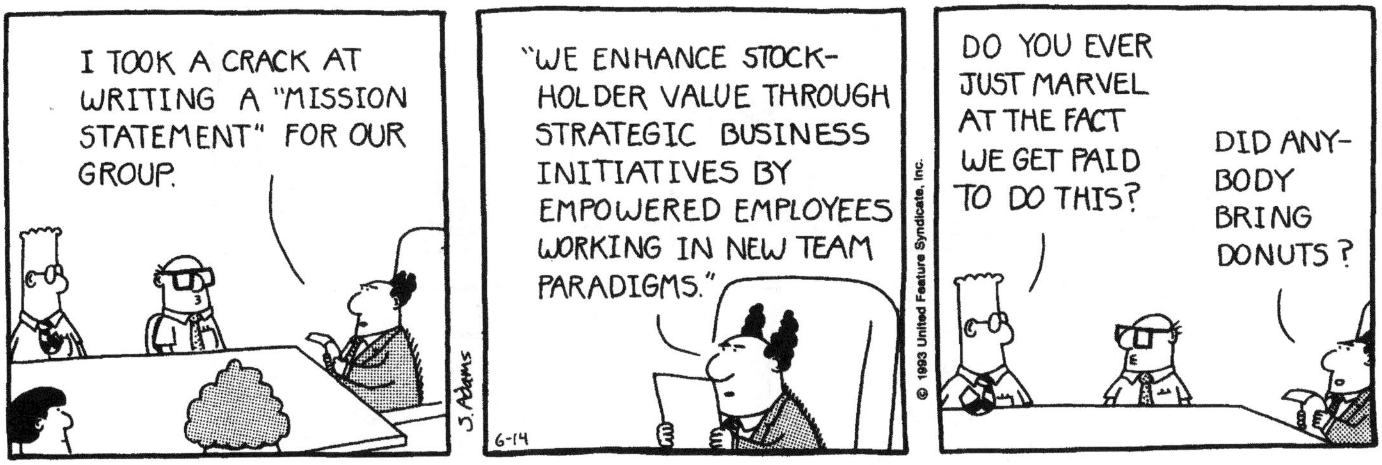
I TOOK A CRACK AT WRITING A "MISSION STATEMENT" FOR OUR GROUP.
S. Adams
6-14
"WE ENHANCE STOCKHOLDER VALUE THROUGH STRATEGIC BUSINESS INITIATIVES BY EMPOWERED EMPLOYEES WORKING IN NEW TEAM PARADIGMS."
© 1993 United Feature Syndicate, Inc.
DO YOU EVER JUST MARVEL AT THE FACT WE GET PAID TO DO THIS?
DID ANYBODY BRING DONUTS?

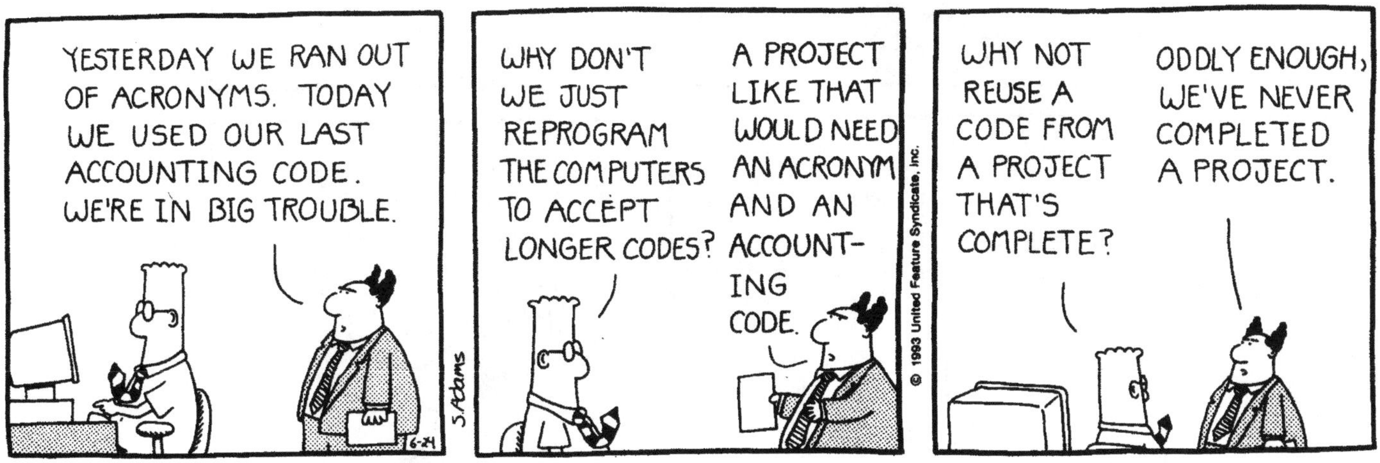
YESTERDAY WE RAN OUT OF ACRONYMS. TODAY WE USED OUR LAST ACCOUNTING CODE. WE'RE IN BIG TROUBLE.
6-24
S. Adams
WHY DON'T WE JUST REPROGRAM THE COMPUTERS TO ACCEPT LONGER CODES?
A PROJECT LIKE THAT WOULD NEED AN ACRONYM AND AN ACCOUNTING CODE.
© 1993 United Feature Syndicate, Inc.
WHY NOT REUSE A CODE FROM A PROJECT THAT'S COMPLETE?
ODDLY ENOUGH, WE'VE NEVER COMPLETED A PROJECT.

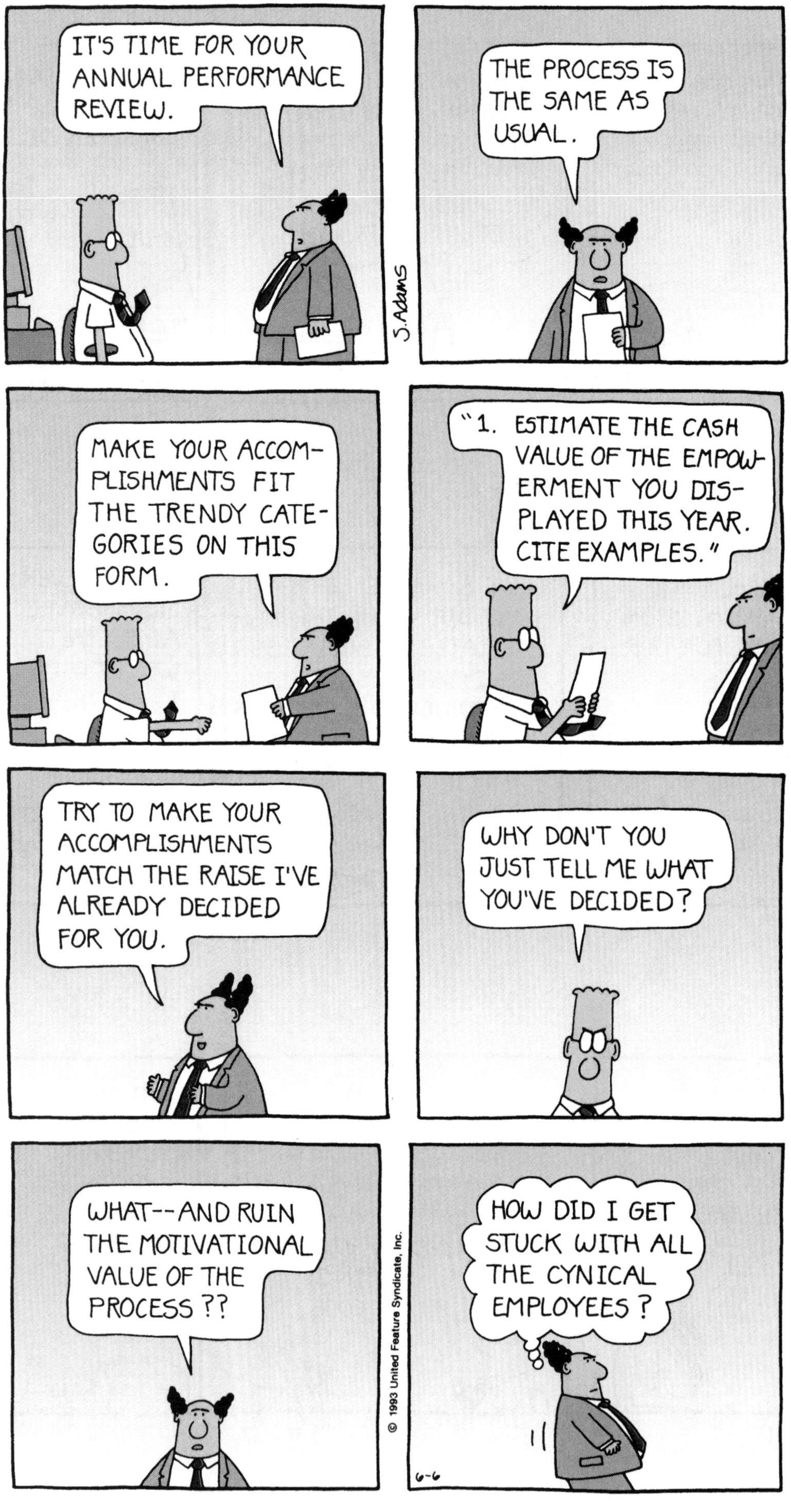
IT'S TIME FOR YOUR ANNUAL PERFORMANCE REVIEW.
S.Adams
THE PROCESS IS THE SAME AS USUAL.
MAKE YOUR ACCOMPLISHMENTS FIT THE TRENDY CATEGORIES ON THIS FORM.
"1. ESTIMATE THE CASH VALUE OF THE EMPOWERMENT YOU DISPLAYED THIS YEAR. CITE EXAMPLES."
TRY TO MAKE YOUR ACCOMPLISHMENTS MATCH THE RAISE I'VE ALREADY DECIDED FOR YOU.
WHY DON'T YOU JUST TELL ME WHAT YOU'VE DECIDED?
WHAT--AND RUIN THE MOTIVATIONAL VALUE OF THE PROCESS??
© 1993 United Feature Syndicate, Inc.
HOW DID I GET STUCK WITH ALL THE CYNICAL EMPLOYEES?
6-6

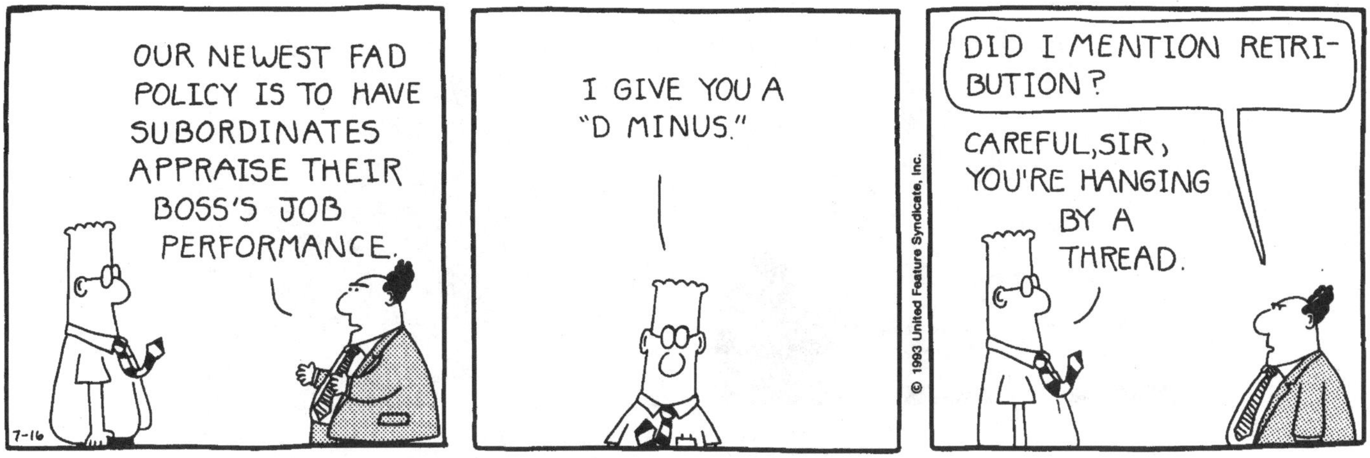
OUR NEWEST FAD POLICY IS TO HAVE SUBORDINATES APPRAISE THEIR BOSS'S JOB PERFORMANCE.
I GIVE YOU A "D MINUS."
DID I MENTION RETRIBUTION?
CAREFUL, SIR, YOU'RE HANGING BY A THREAD.
© 1993 United Feature Syndicate, Inc.

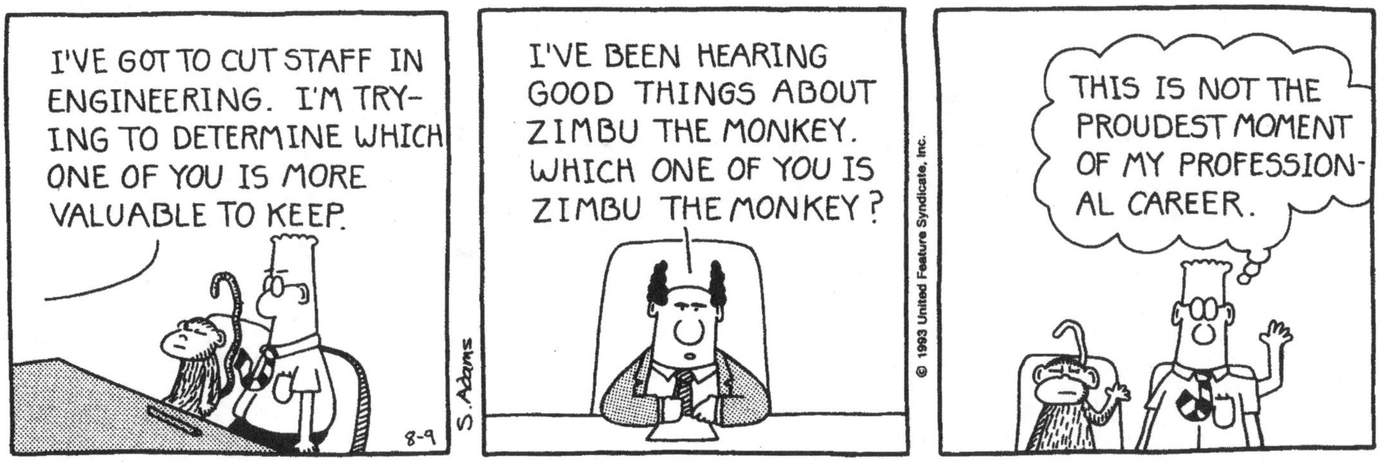
I'VE GOT TO CUT STAFF IN ENGINEERING. I'M TRYING TO DETERMINE WHICH ONE OF YOU IS MORE VALUABLE TO KEEP.
I'VE BEEN HEARING GOOD THINGS ABOUT ZIMBU THE MONKEY. WHICH ONE OF YOU IS ZIMBU THE MONKEY?
THIS IS NOT THE PROUDEST MOMENT OF MY PROFESSIONAL CAREER.
© 1993 United Feature Syndicate, Inc.

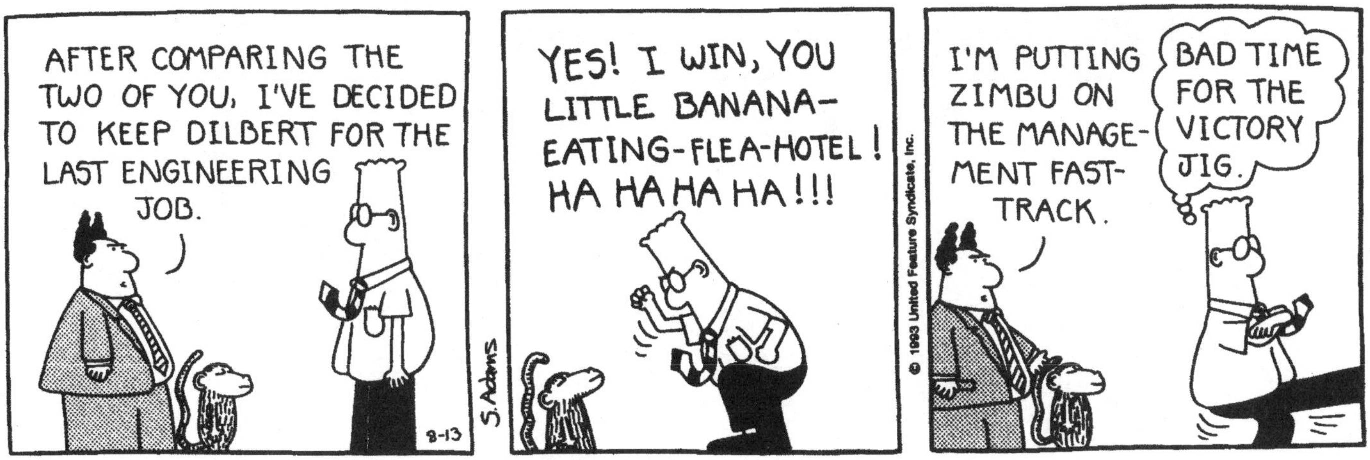
AFTER COMPARING THE TWO OF YOU, I'VE DECIDED TO KEEP DILBERT FOR THE LAST ENGINEERING JOB.
YES! I WIN, YOU LITTLE BANANA-EATING-FLEA-HOTEL! HA HA HA HA!!!
I'M PUTTING ZIMBU ON THE MANAGEMENT FAST-TRACK.
BAD TIME FOR THE VICTORY JIG.
© 1993 United Feature Syndicate, Inc.

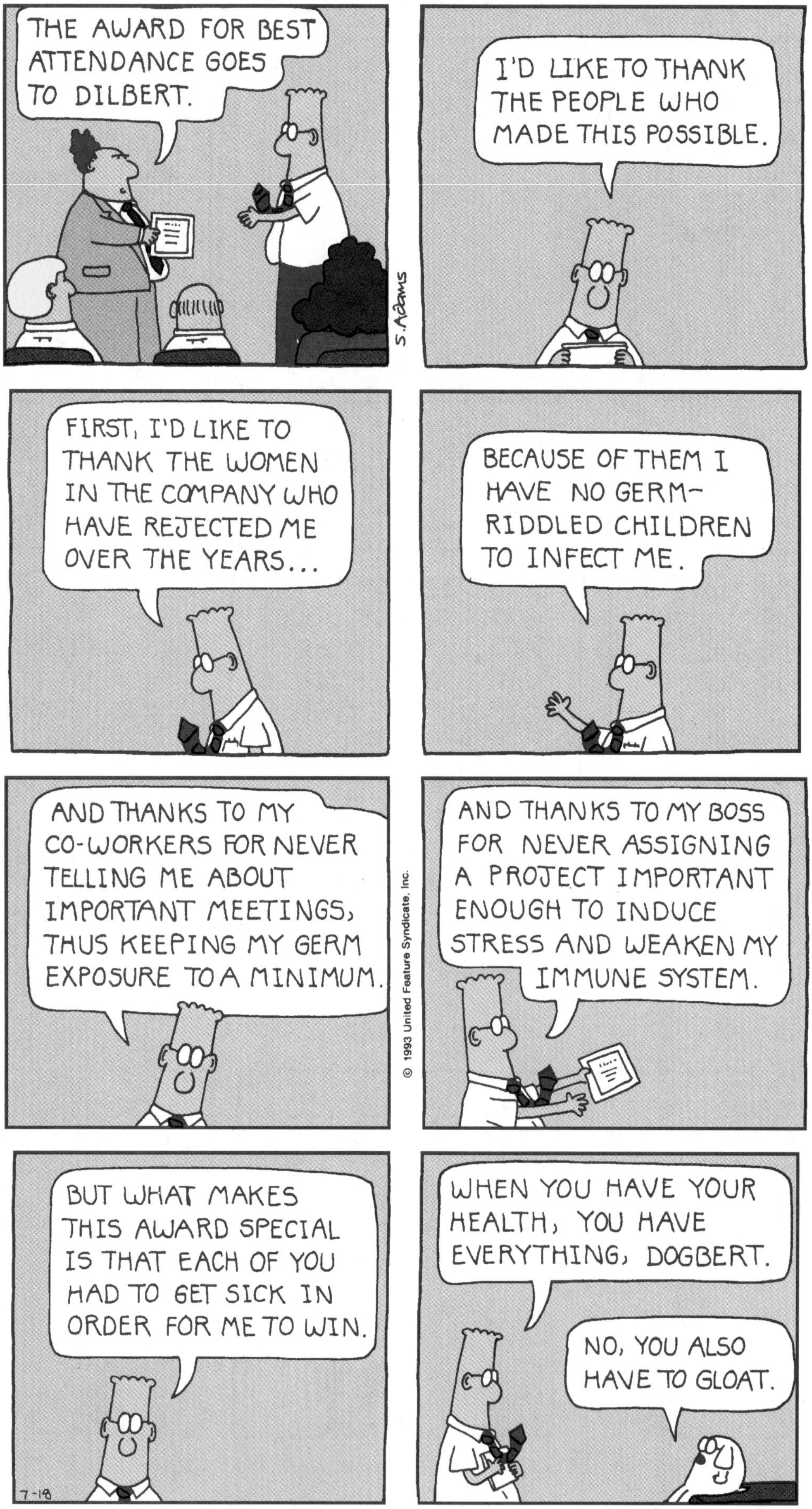
THE AWARD FOR BEST ATTENDANCE GOES TO DILBERT.
S. Adams
I'D LIKE TO THANK THE PEOPLE WHO MADE THIS POSSIBLE.
FIRST, I'D LIKE TO THANK THE WOMEN IN THE COMPANY WHO HAVE REJECTED ME OVER THE YEARS...
BECAUSE OF THEM I HAVE NO GERM-RIDDLED CHILDREN TO INFECT ME.
AND THANKS TO MY CO-WORKERS FOR NEVER TELLING ME ABOUT IMPORTANT MEETINGS, THUS KEEPING MY GERM EXPOSURE TO A MINIMUM.
© 1993 United Feature Syndicate, Inc.
AND THANKS TO MY BOSS FOR NEVER ASSIGNING A PROJECT IMPORTANT ENOUGH TO INDUCE STRESS AND WEAKEN MY IMMUNE SYSTEM.
BUT WHAT MAKES THIS AWARD SPECIAL IS THAT EACH OF YOU HAD TO GET SICK IN ORDER FOR ME TO WIN.
7-18
WHEN YOU HAVE YOUR HEALTH, YOU HAVE EVERYTHING, DOGBERT.
NO, YOU ALSO HAVE TO GLOAT.

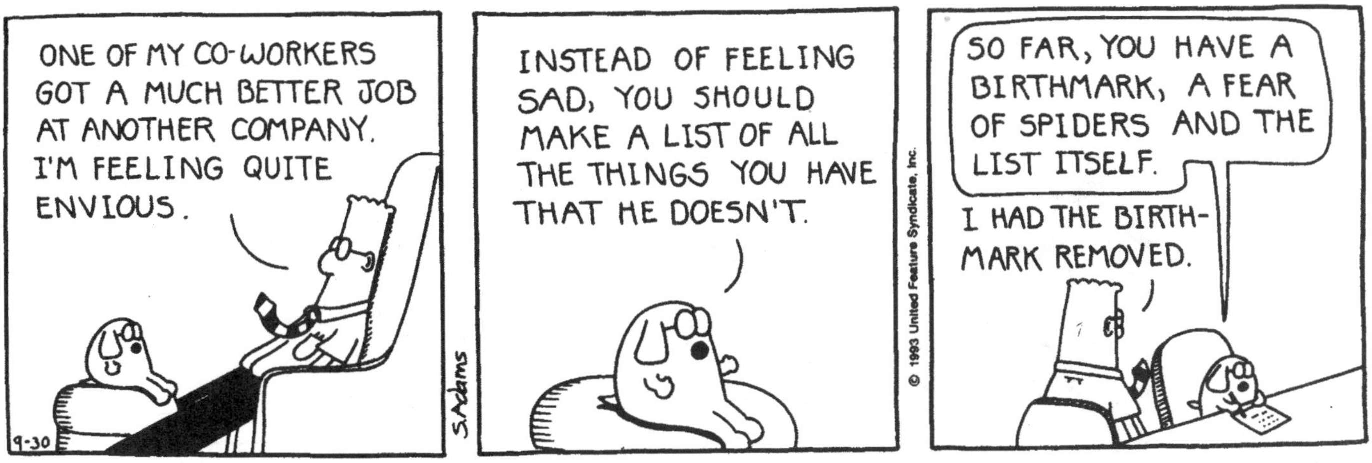
ONE OF MY CO-WORKERS GOT A MUCH BETTER JOB AT ANOTHER COMPANY. I'M FEELING QUITE ENVIOUS.
INSTEAD OF FEELING SAD, YOU SHOULD MAKE A LIST OF ALL THE THINGS YOU HAVE THAT HE DOESN'T.
SO FAR, YOU HAVE A BIRTHMARK, A FEAR OF SPIDERS AND THE LIST ITSELF.
I HAD THE BIRTH-MARK REMOVED.
© 1993 United Feature Syndicate, Inc.

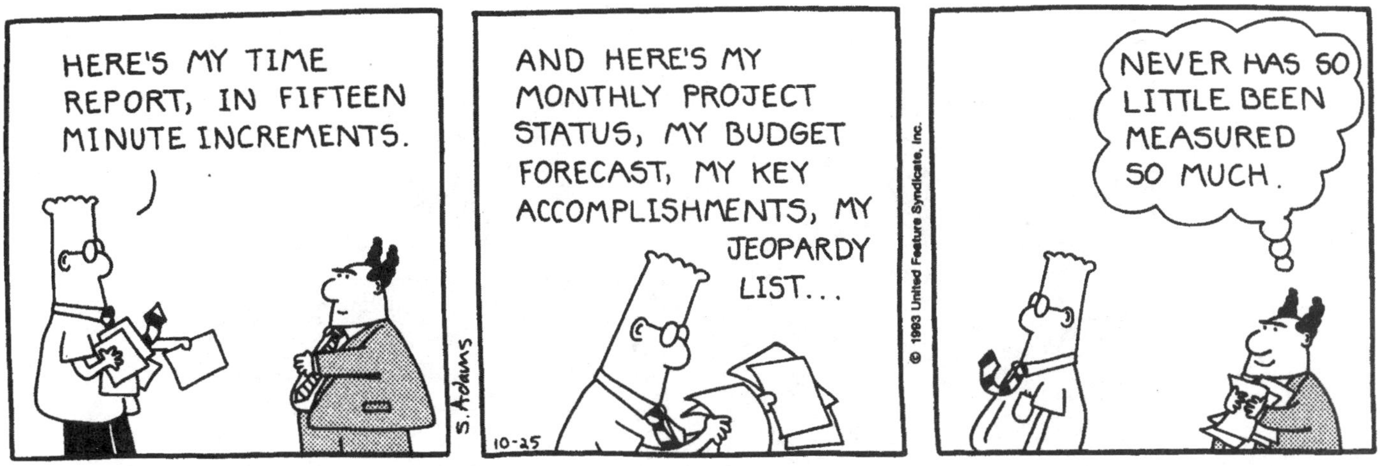
HERE'S MY TIME REPORT, IN FIFTEEN MINUTE INCREMENTS.
AND HERE'S MY MONTHLY PROJECT STATUS, MY BUDGET FORECAST, MY KEY ACCOMPLISHMENTS, MY JEOPARDY LIST...
NEVER HAS SO LITTLE BEEN MEASURED SO MUCH.
© 1993 United Feature Syndicate, Inc.

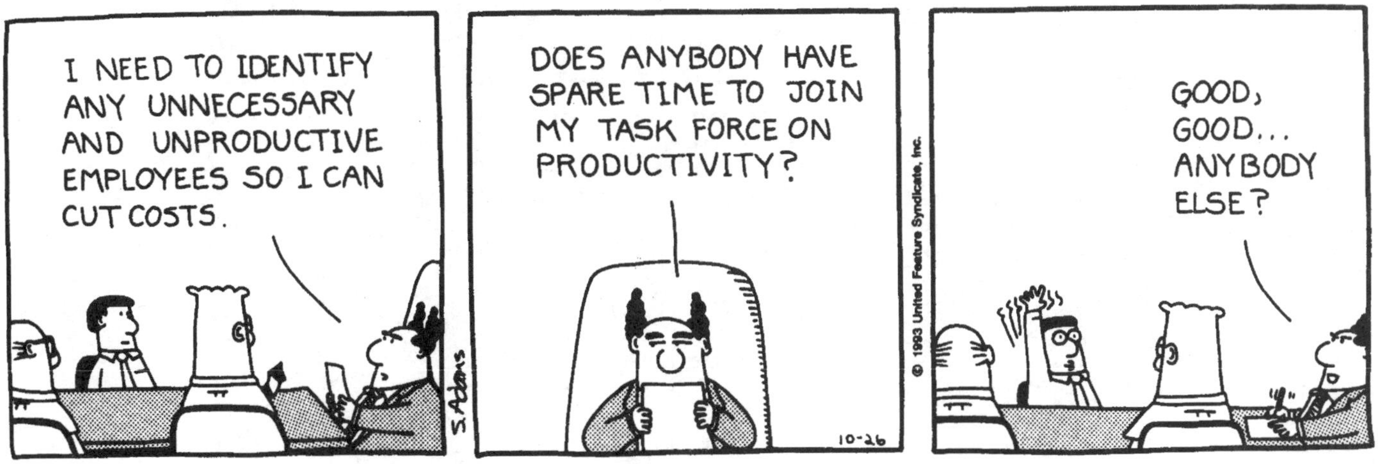
I NEED TO IDENTIFY ANY UNNECESSARY AND UNPRODUCTIVE EMPLOYEES SO I CAN CUT COSTS.
DOES ANYBODY HAVE SPARE TIME TO JOIN MY TASK FORCE ON PRODUCTIVITY?
GOOD, GOOD... ANYBODY ELSE?
© 1993 United Feature Syndicate, Inc.

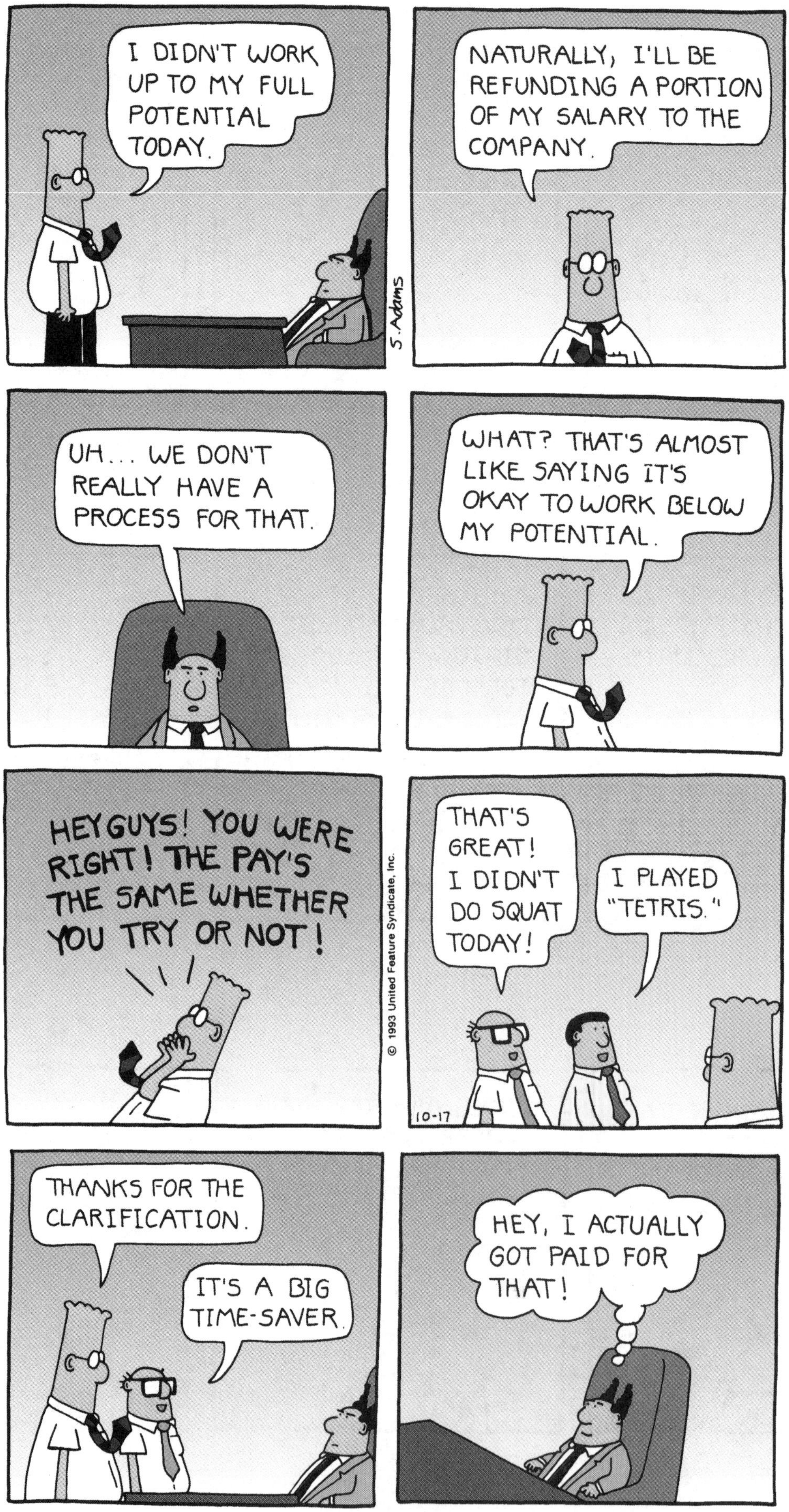
I DIDN'T WORK UP TO MY FULL POTENTIAL TODAY.
S. Adams
NATURALLY, I'LL BE REFUNDING A PORTION OF MY SALARY TO THE COMPANY.
UH... WE DON'T REALLY HAVE A PROCESS FOR THAT.
WHAT? THAT'S ALMOST LIKE SAYING IT'S OKAY TO WORK BELOW MY POTENTIAL.
HEY GUYS! YOU WERE RIGHT! THE PAY'S THE SAME WHETHER YOU TRY OR NOT!
© 1993 United Feature Syndicate, Inc.
THAT'S GREAT! I DIDN'T DO SQUAT TODAY!
I PLAYED "TETRIS."
10-17
THANKS FOR THE CLARIFICATION.
IT'S A BIG TIME-SAVER.
HEY, I ACTUALLY GOT PAID FOR THAT!

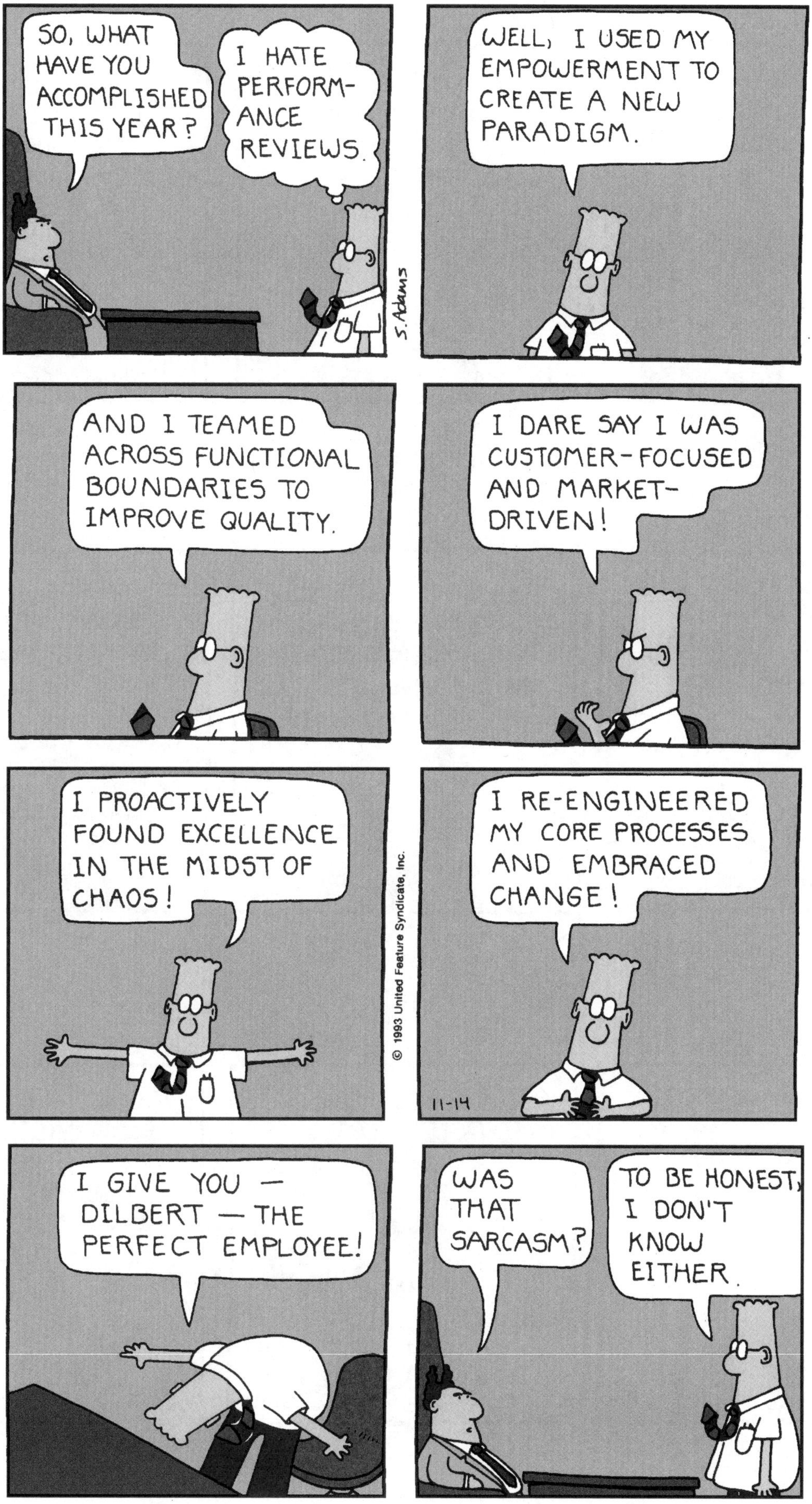
SO, WHAT HAVE YOU ACCOMPLISHED THIS YEAR?
I HATE PERFORM-ANCE REVIEWS.
S. Adams
WELL, I USED MY EMPOWERMENT TO CREATE A NEW PARADIGM.
AND I TEAMED ACROSS FUNCTIONAL BOUNDARIES TO IMPROVE QUALITY.
I DARE SAY I WAS CUSTOMER-FOCUSED AND MARKET-DRIVEN!
I PROACTIVELY FOUND EXCELLENCE IN THE MIDST OF CHAOS!
© 1993 United Feature Syndicate, Inc.
I RE-ENGINEERED MY CORE PROCESSES AND EMBRACED CHANGE!
11-14
I GIVE YOU — DILBERT — THE PERFECT EMPLOYEE!
WAS THAT SARCASM?
TO BE HONEST, I DON'T KNOW EITHER.

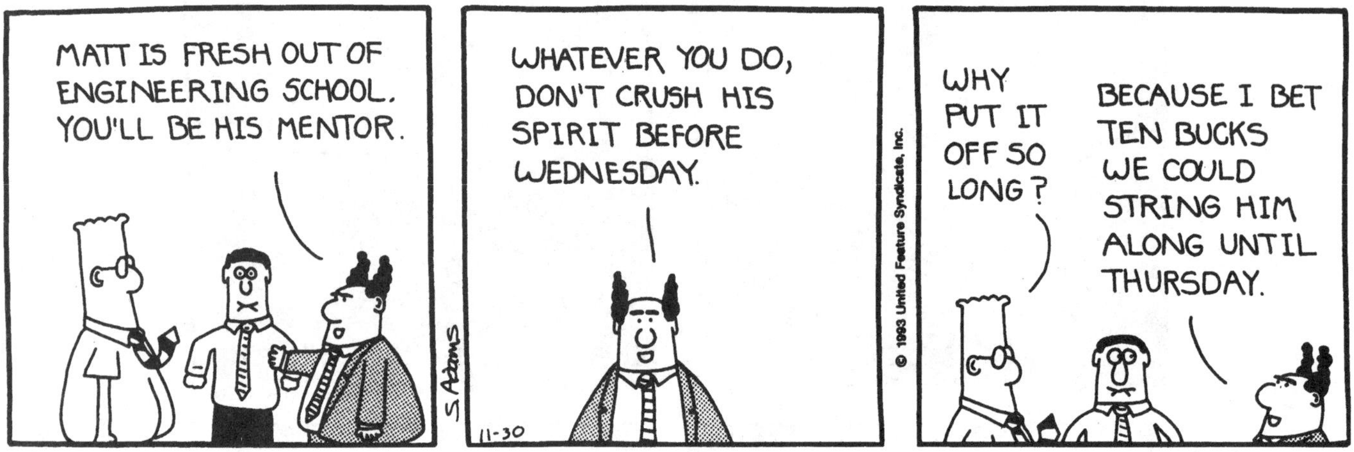
MATT IS FRESH OUT OF ENGINEERING SCHOOL. YOU'LL BE HIS MENTOR.
S. Adams
WHATEVER YOU DO, DON'T CRUSH HIS SPIRIT BEFORE WEDNESDAY.
11-30
© 1993 United Feature Syndicate, Inc.
WHY PUT IT OFF SO LONG?
BECAUSE I BET TEN BUCKS WE COULD STRING HIM ALONG UNTIL THURSDAY.

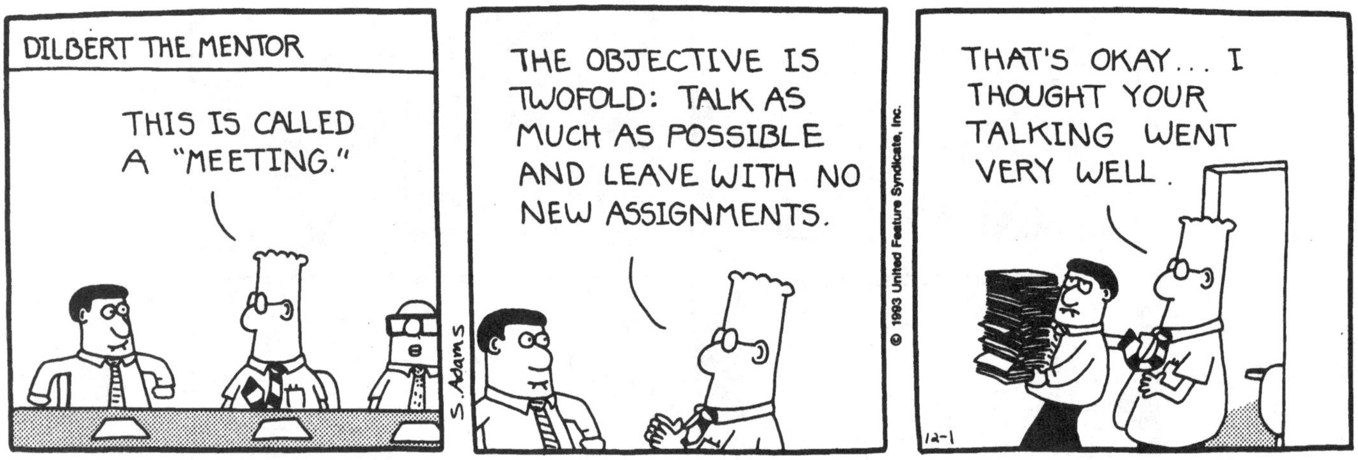
DILBERT THE MENTOR
THIS IS CALLED A "MEETING."
S. Adams
THE OBJECTIVE IS TWOFOLD: TALK AS MUCH AS POSSIBLE AND LEAVE WITH NO NEW ASSIGNMENTS.
© 1993 United Feature Syndicate, Inc.
THAT'S OKAY... I THOUGHT YOUR TALKING WENT VERY WELL.
12-1

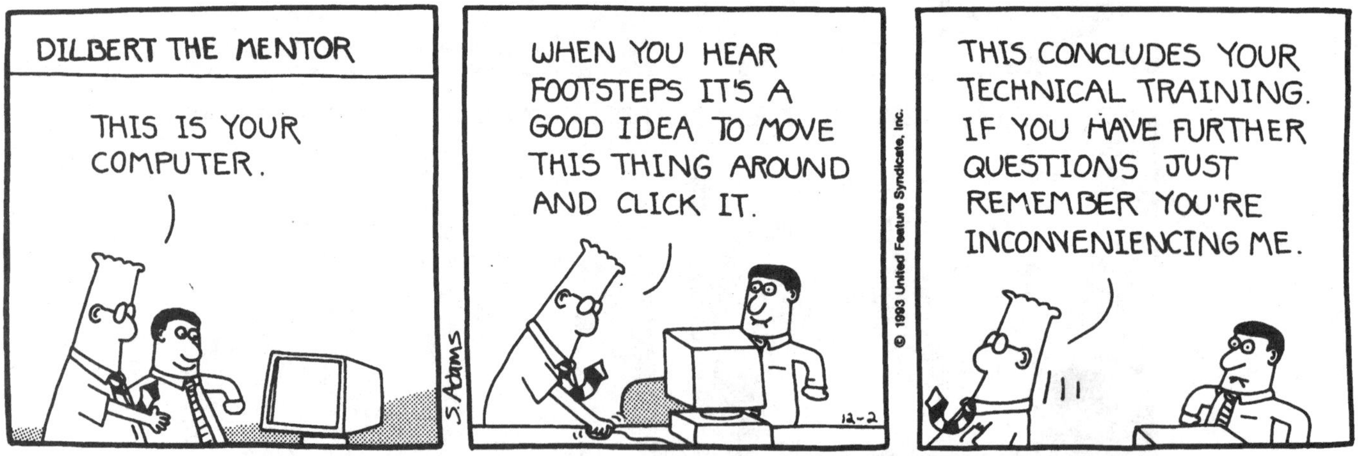
DILBERT THE MENTOR
THIS IS YOUR COMPUTER.
S. Adams
WHEN YOU HEAR FOOTSTEPS IT'S A GOOD IDEA TO MOVE THIS THING AROUND AND CLICK IT.
12-2
© 1993 United Feature Syndicate, Inc.
THIS CONCLUDES YOUR TECHNICAL TRAINING. IF YOU HAVE FURTHER QUESTIONS JUST REMEMBER YOU'RE INCONVENIENCING ME.

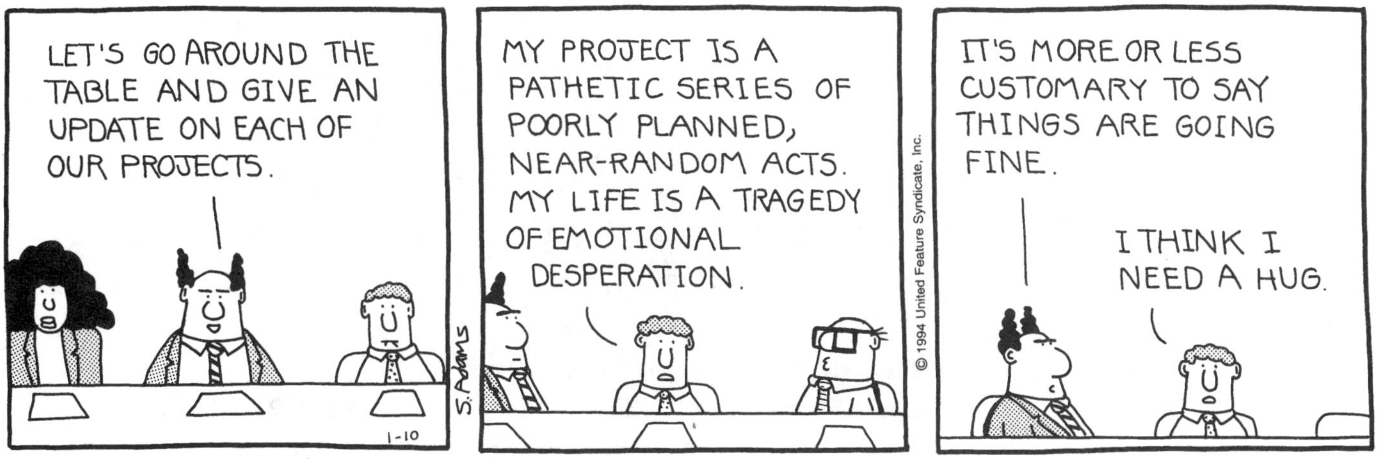
LET'S GO AROUND THE TABLE AND GIVE AN UPDATE ON EACH OF OUR PROJECTS.
1-10
S. Adams
MY PROJECT IS A PATHETIC SERIES OF POORLY PLANNED, NEAR-RANDOM ACTS. MY LIFE IS A TRAGEDY OF EMOTIONAL DESPERATION.
© 1994 United Feature Syndicate, Inc.
IT'S MORE OR LESS CUSTOMARY TO SAY THINGS ARE GOING FINE.
I THINK I NEED A HUG.

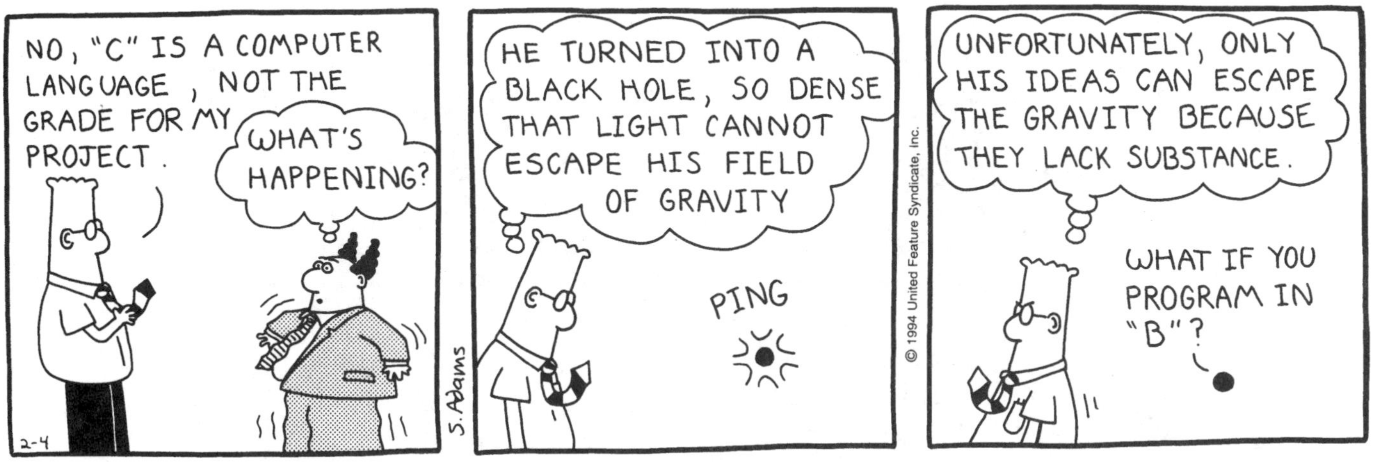
NO, "C" IS A COMPUTER LANGUAGE, NOT THE GRADE FOR MY PROJECT.
WHAT'S HAPPENING?
2-4
S. Adams
HE TURNED INTO A BLACK HOLE, SO DENSE THAT LIGHT CANNOT ESCAPE HIS FIELD OF GRAVITY
PING
© 1994 United Feature Syndicate, Inc.
UNFORTUNATELY, ONLY HIS IDEAS CAN ESCAPE THE GRAVITY BECAUSE THEY LACK SUBSTANCE.
WHAT IF YOU PROGRAM IN "B"?

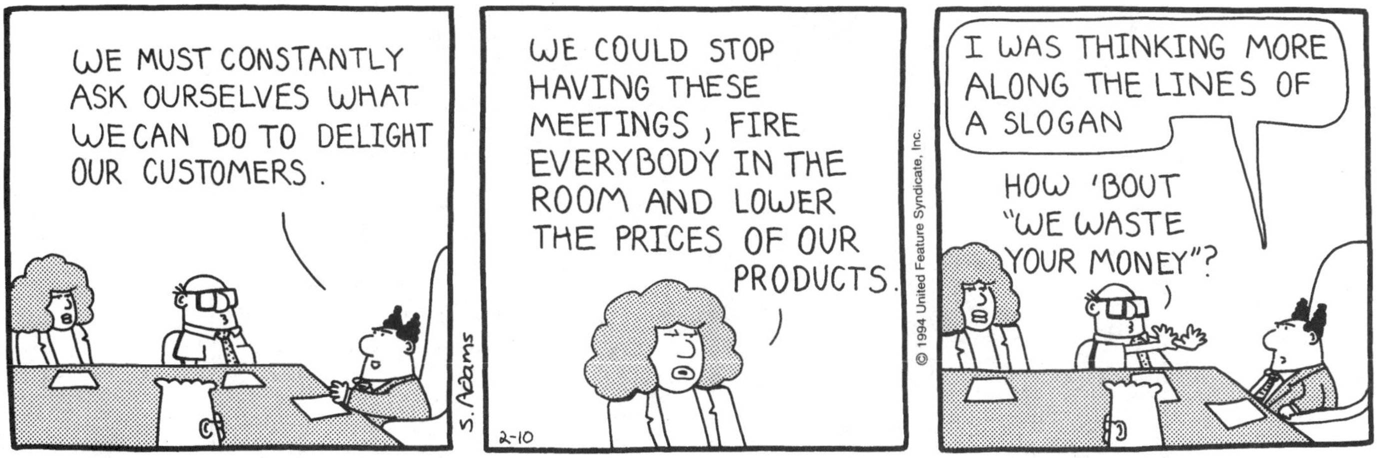
WE MUST CONSTANTLY ASK OURSELVES WHAT WE CAN DO TO DELIGHT OUR CUSTOMERS.
S. Adams
WE COULD STOP HAVING THESE MEETINGS, FIRE EVERYBODY IN THE ROOM AND LOWER THE PRICES OF OUR PRODUCTS.
2-10
© 1994 United Feature Syndicate, Inc.
I WAS THINKING MORE ALONG THE LINES OF A SLOGAN
HOW 'BOUT "WE WASTE YOUR MONEY"?

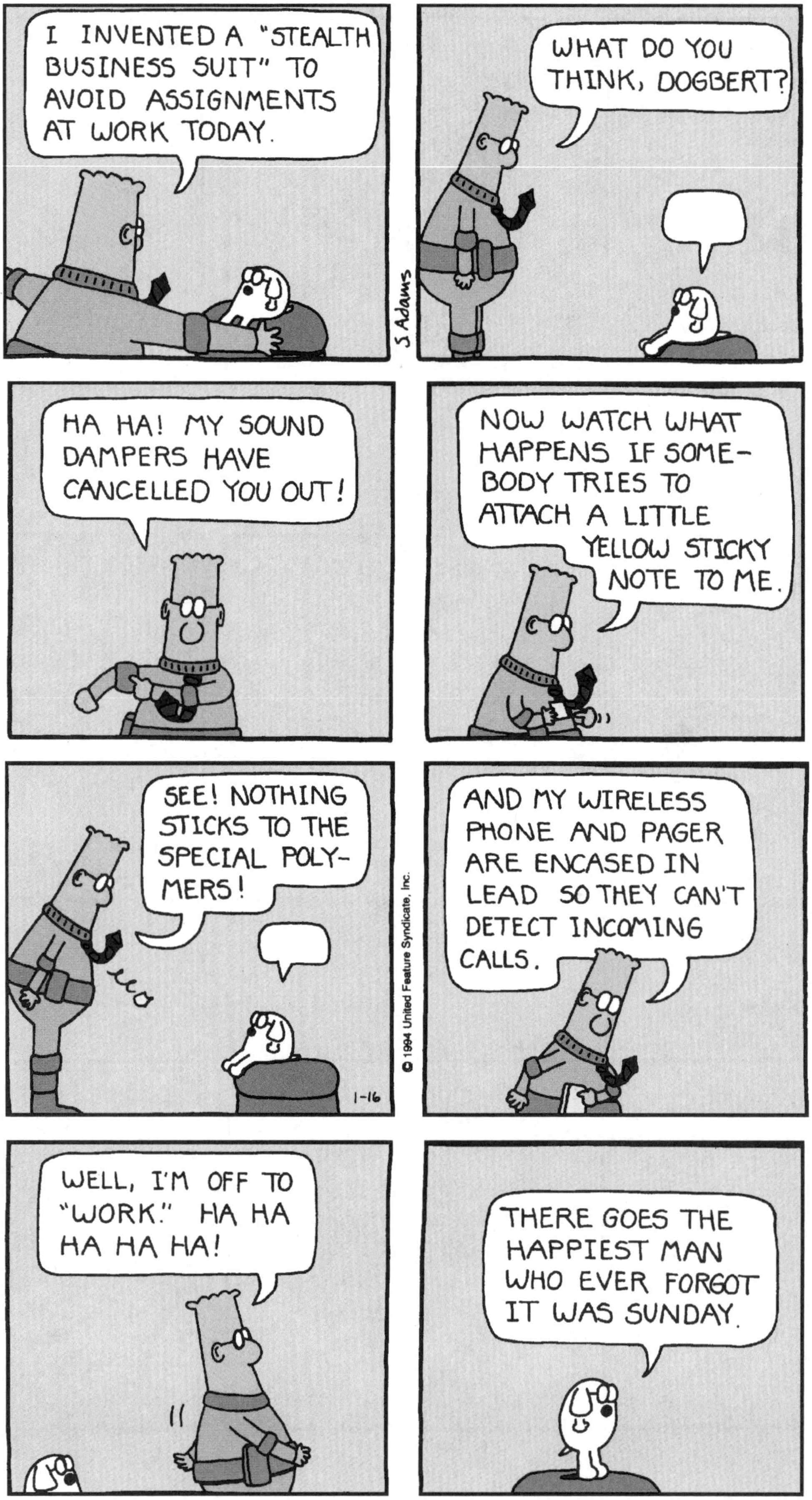
I INVENTED A "STEALTH BUSINESS SUIT" TO AVOID ASSIGNMENTS AT WORK TODAY.
S Adams
WHAT DO YOU THINK, DOGBERT?
HA HA! MY SOUND DAMPERS HAVE CANCELLED YOU OUT!
NOW WATCH WHAT HAPPENS IF SOMEBODY TRIES TO ATTACH A LITTLE YELLOW STICKY NOTE TO ME.
SEE! NOTHING STICKS TO THE SPECIAL POLYMERS!
1-16
© 1994 United Feature Syndicate, Inc.
AND MY WIRELESS PHONE AND PAGER ARE ENCASED IN LEAD SO THEY CAN'T DETECT INCOMING CALLS.
WELL, I'M OFF TO "WORK." HA HA HA HA HA!
THERE GOES THE HAPPIEST MAN WHO EVER FORGOT IT WAS SUNDAY.

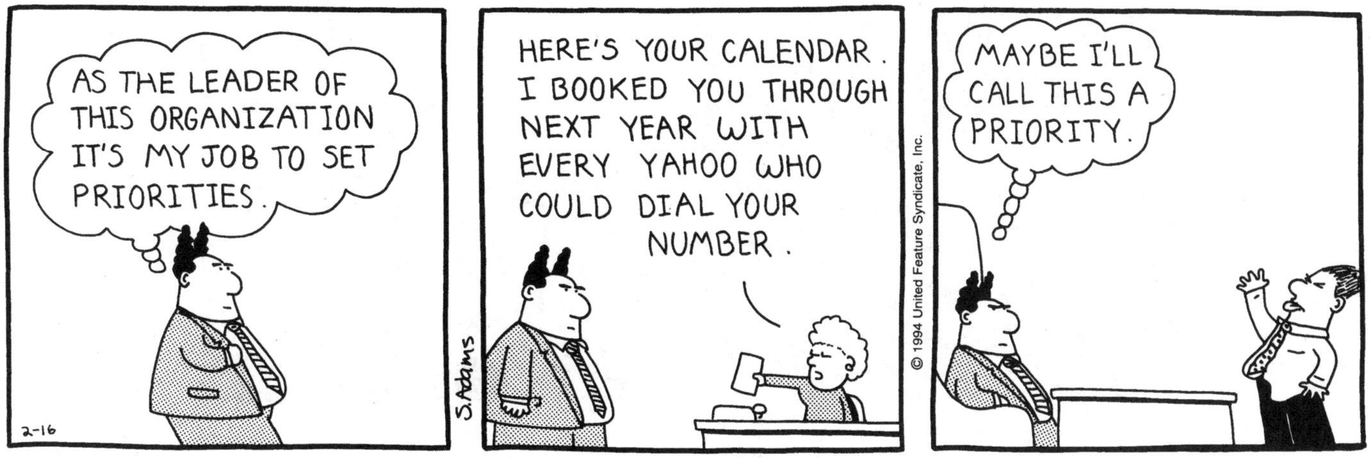
AS THE LEADER OF THIS ORGANIZATION IT'S MY JOB TO SET PRIORITIES.
2-16
HERE'S YOUR CALENDAR. I BOOKED YOU THROUGH NEXT YEAR WITH EVERY YAHOO WHO COULD DIAL YOUR NUMBER.
S. Adams
MAYBE I'LL CALL THIS A PRIORITY.
© 1994 United Feature Syndicate, Inc.

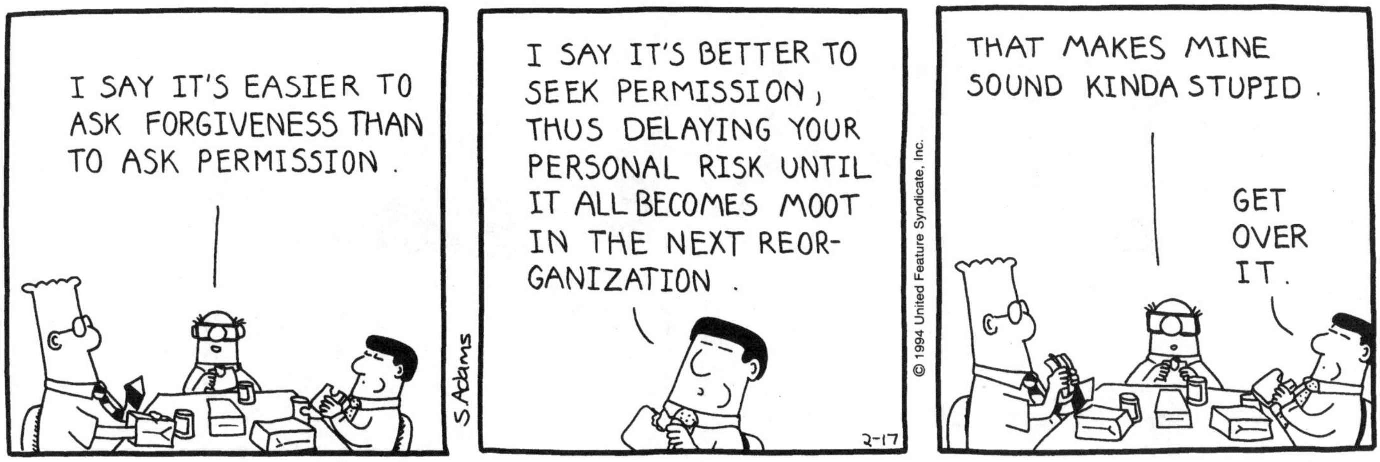
I SAY IT'S EASIER TO ASK FORGIVENESS THAN TO ASK PERMISSION.
I SAY IT'S BETTER TO SEEK PERMISSION, THUS DELAYING YOUR PERSONAL RISK UNTIL IT ALL BECOMES MOOT IN THE NEXT REORGANIZATION.
S. Adams
2-17
THAT MAKES MINE SOUND KINDA STUPID.
GET OVER IT.
© 1994 United Feature Syndicate, Inc.

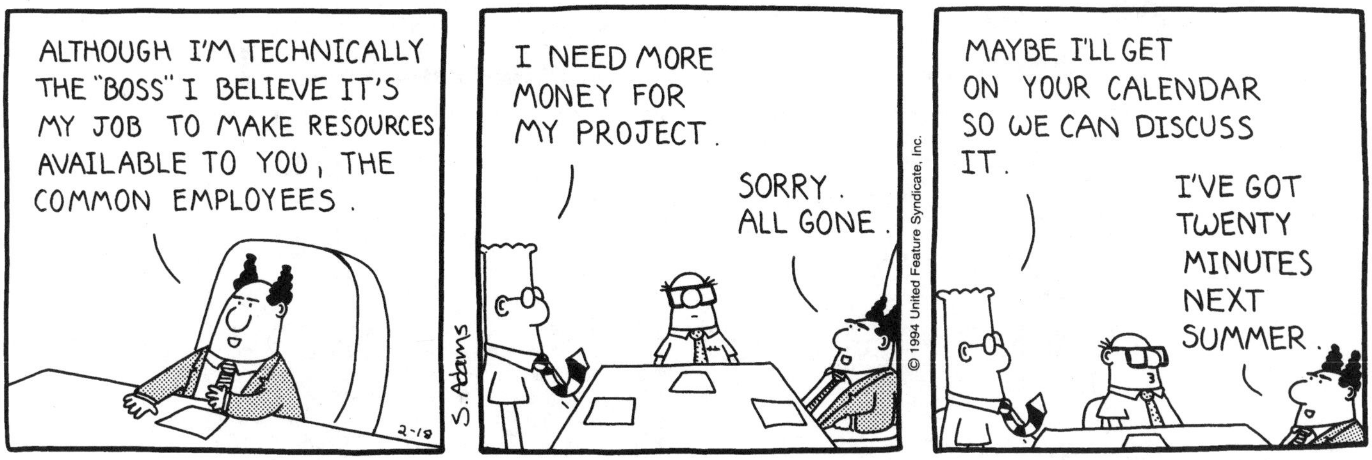
ALTHOUGH I'M TECHNICALLY THE "BOSS" I BELIEVE IT'S MY JOB TO MAKE RESOURCES AVAILABLE TO YOU, THE COMMON EMPLOYEES.
2-18
I NEED MORE MONEY FOR MY PROJECT.
SORRY. ALL GONE.
S. Adams
MAYBE I'LL GET ON YOUR CALENDAR SO WE CAN DISCUSS IT.
I'VE GOT TWENTY MINUTES NEXT SUMMER.
© 1994 United Feature Syndicate, Inc.

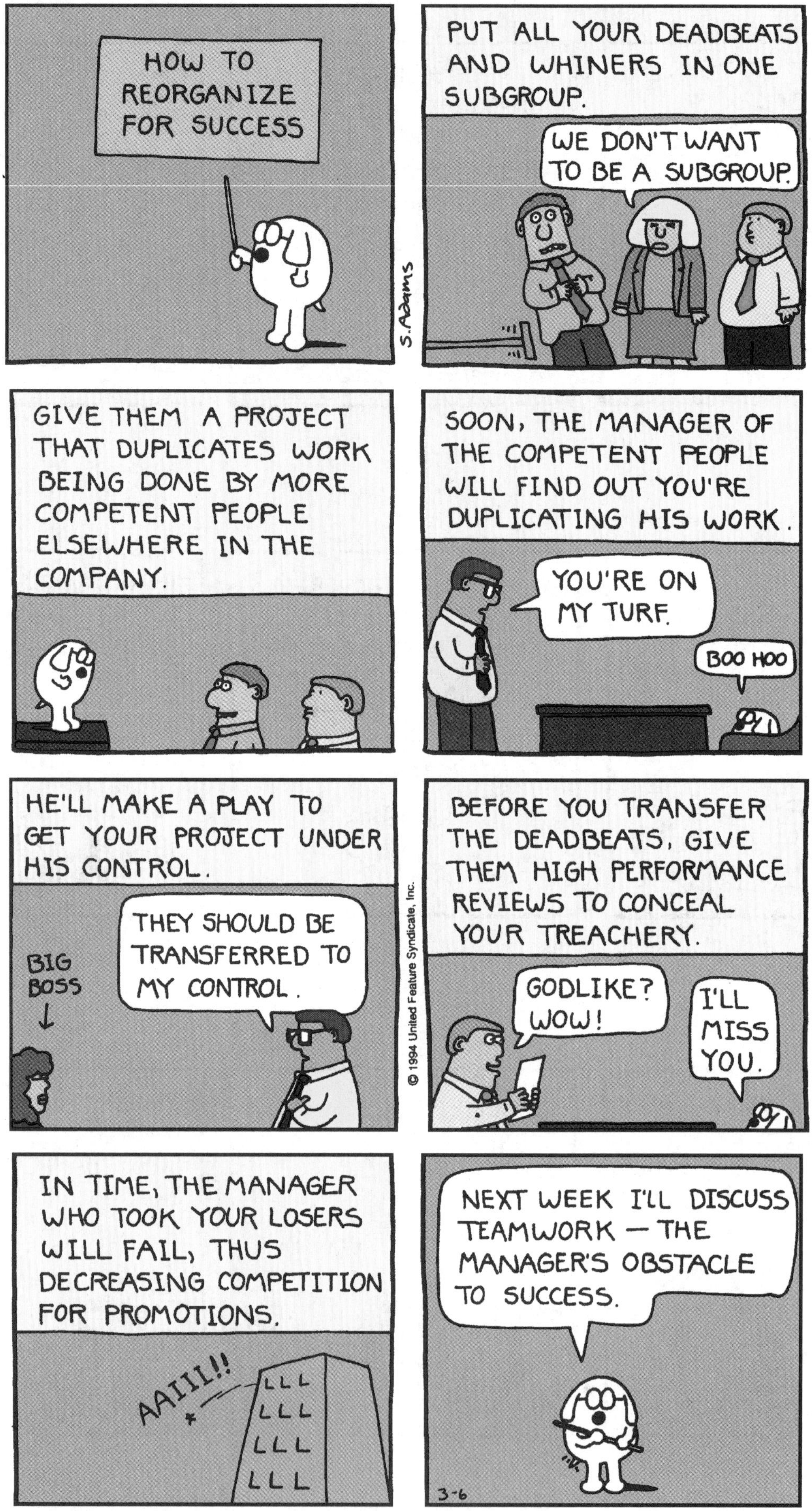
HOW TO REORGANIZE FOR SUCCESS
S. Adams
PUT ALL YOUR DEADBEATS AND WHINERS IN ONE SUBGROUP.
WE DON'T WANT TO BE A SUBGROUP.
GIVE THEM A PROJECT THAT DUPLICATES WORK BEING DONE BY MORE COMPETENT PEOPLE ELSEWHERE IN THE COMPANY.
SOON, THE MANAGER OF THE COMPETENT PEOPLE WILL FIND OUT YOU'RE DUPLICATING HIS WORK.
YOU'RE ON MY TURF.
BOO HOO
HE'LL MAKE A PLAY TO GET YOUR PROJECT UNDER HIS CONTROL.
BIG BOSS
THEY SHOULD BE TRANSFERRED TO MY CONTROL.
© 1994 United Feature Syndicate, Inc.
BEFORE YOU TRANSFER THE DEADBEATS, GIVE THEM HIGH PERFORMANCE REVIEWS TO CONCEAL YOUR TREACHERY.
GODLIKE? WOW!
I'LL MISS YOU.
IN TIME, THE MANAGER WHO TOOK YOUR LOSERS WILL FAIL, THUS DECREASING COMPETITION FOR PROMOTIONS.
AAIII!!
NEXT WEEK I'LL DISCUSS TEAMWORK — THE MANAGER'S OBSTACLE TO SUCCESS.
3-6

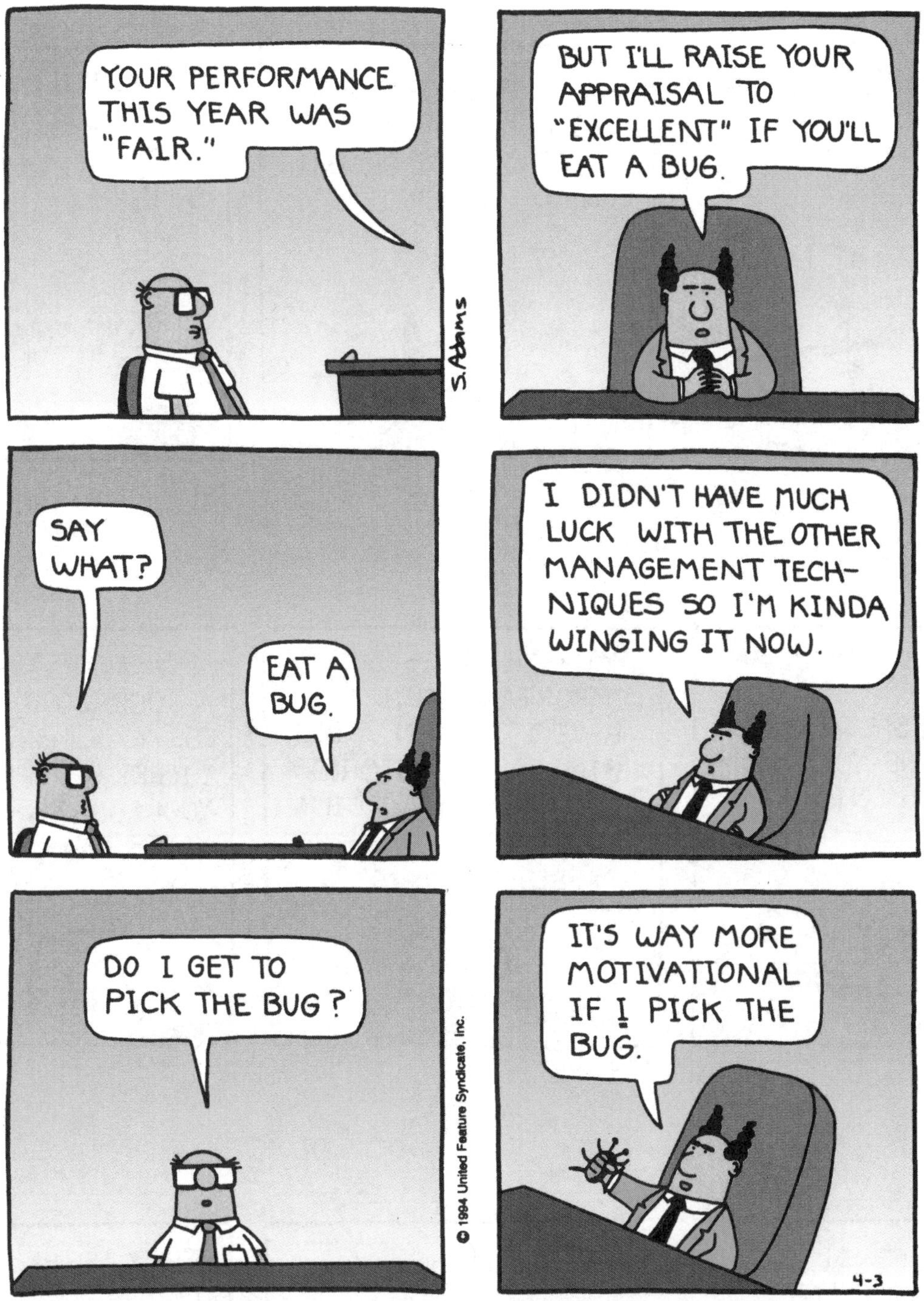
YOUR PERFORMANCE THIS YEAR WAS "FAIR."
S. Adams
BUT I'LL RAISE YOUR APPRAISAL TO "EXCELLENT" IF YOU'LL EAT A BUG.
SAY WHAT?
EAT A BUG.
I DIDN'T HAVE MUCH LUCK WITH THE OTHER MANAGEMENT TECH-NIQUES SO I'M KINDA WINGING IT NOW.
DO I GET TO PICK THE BUG?
© 1994 United Feature Syndicate, Inc.
IT'S WAY MORE MOTIVATIONAL IF I PICK THE BUG.
4-3

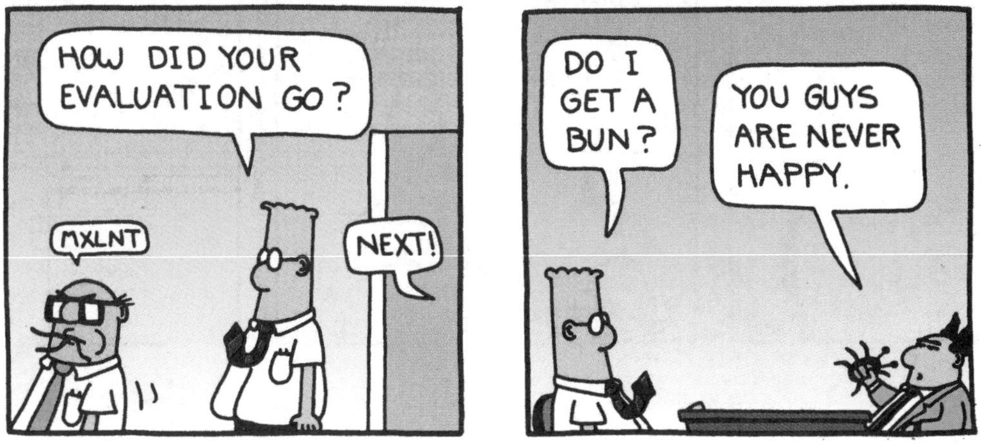
HOW DID YOUR EVALUATION GO?
MXLNT
NEXT!
DO I GET A BUN?
YOU GUYS ARE NEVER HAPPY.

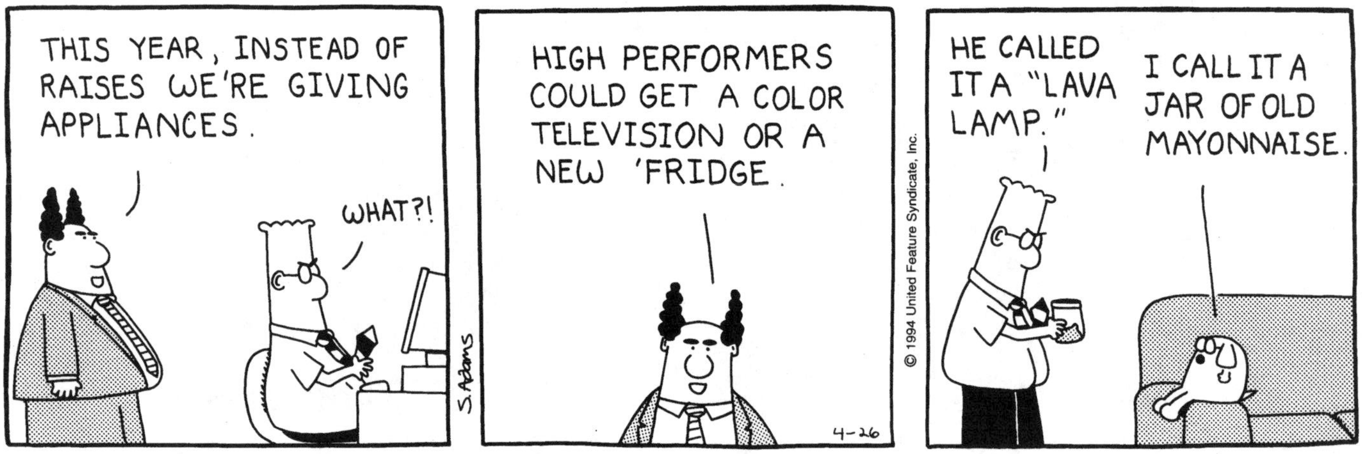
THIS YEAR, INSTEAD OF RAISES WE'RE GIVING APPLIANCES.
WHAT?!
HIGH PERFORMERS COULD GET A COLOR TELEVISION OR A NEW 'FRIDGE.
HE CALLED IT A "LAVA LAMP."
I CALL IT A JAR OF OLD MAYONNAISE.
© 1994 United Feature Syndicate, Inc.

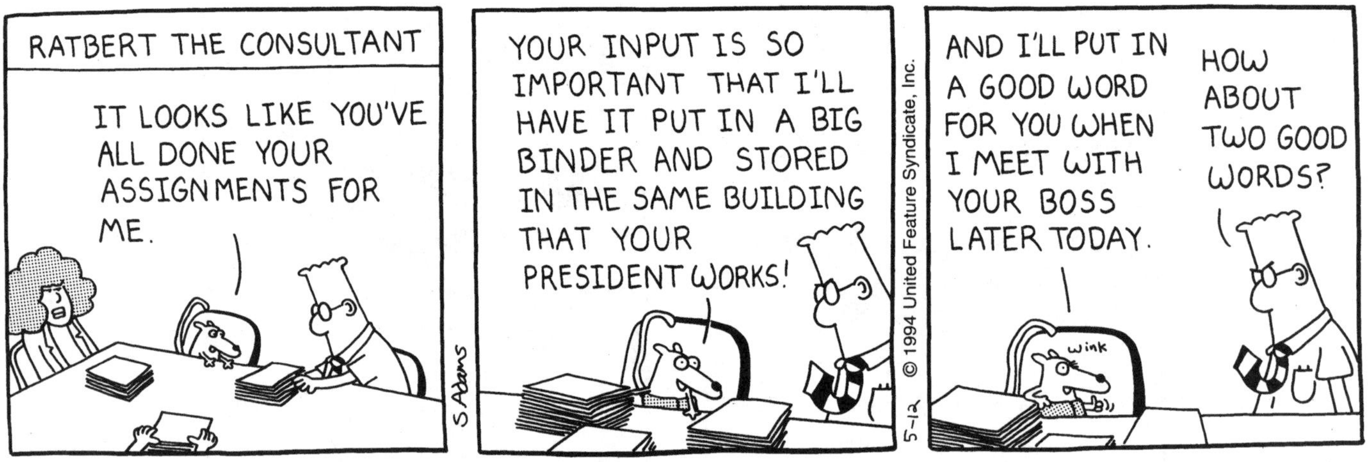
RATBERT THE CONSULTANT
IT LOOKS LIKE YOU'VE ALL DONE YOUR ASSIGNMENTS FOR ME.
YOUR INPUT IS SO IMPORTANT THAT I'LL HAVE IT PUT IN A BIG BINDER AND STORED IN THE SAME BUILDING THAT YOUR PRESIDENT WORKS!
AND I'LL PUT IN A GOOD WORD FOR YOU WHEN I MEET WITH YOUR BOSS LATER TODAY.
wink
HOW ABOUT TWO GOOD WORDS?
© 1994 United Feature Syndicate, Inc.

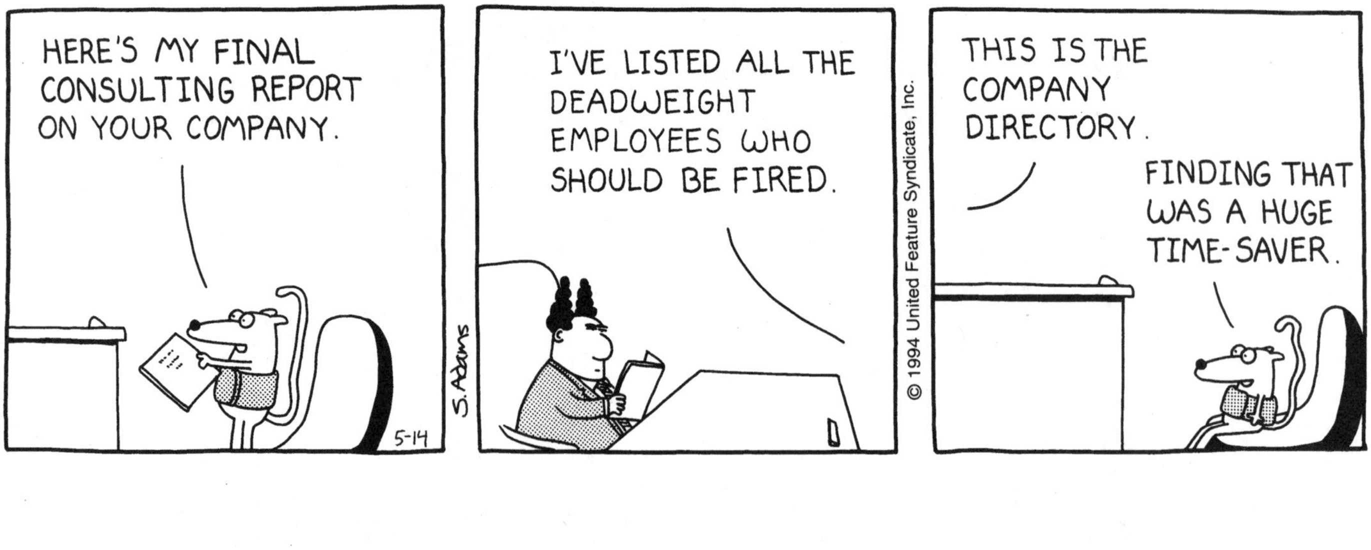
HERE'S MY FINAL CONSULTING REPORT ON YOUR COMPANY.
I'VE LISTED ALL THE DEADWEIGHT EMPLOYEES WHO SHOULD BE FIRED.
THIS IS THE COMPANY DIRECTORY.
FINDING THAT WAS A HUGE TIME-SAVER.
© 1994 United Feature Syndicate, Inc.

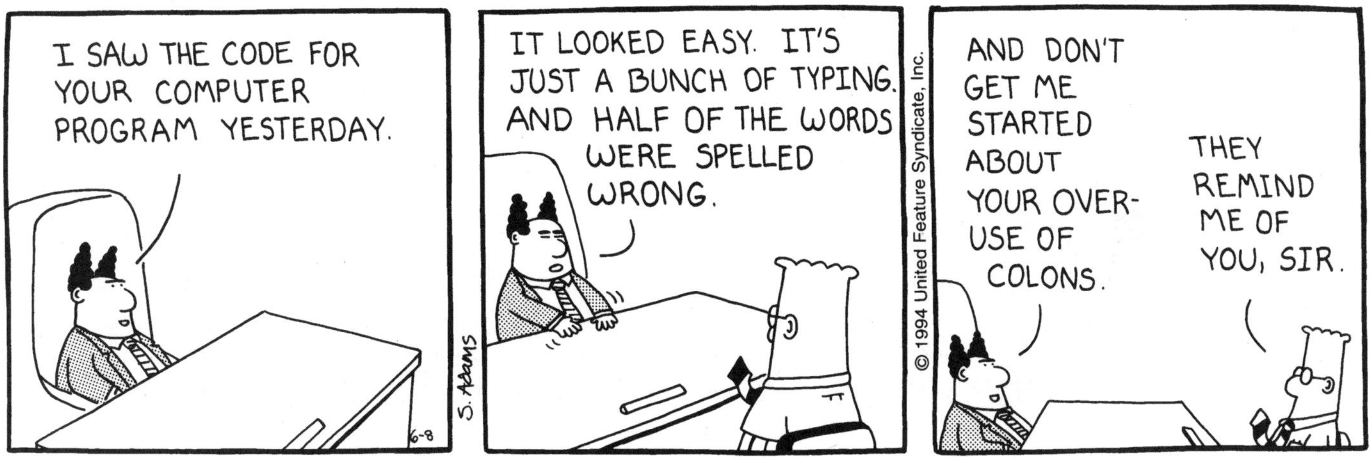
I SAW THE CODE FOR YOUR COMPUTER PROGRAM YESTERDAY.
IT LOOKED EASY. IT'S JUST A BUNCH OF TYPING. AND HALF OF THE WORDS WERE SPELLED WRONG.
AND DON'T GET ME STARTED ABOUT YOUR OVER-USE OF COLONS.
THEY REMIND ME OF YOU, SIR.
S. Adams
6-8
© 1994 United Feature Syndicate, Inc.

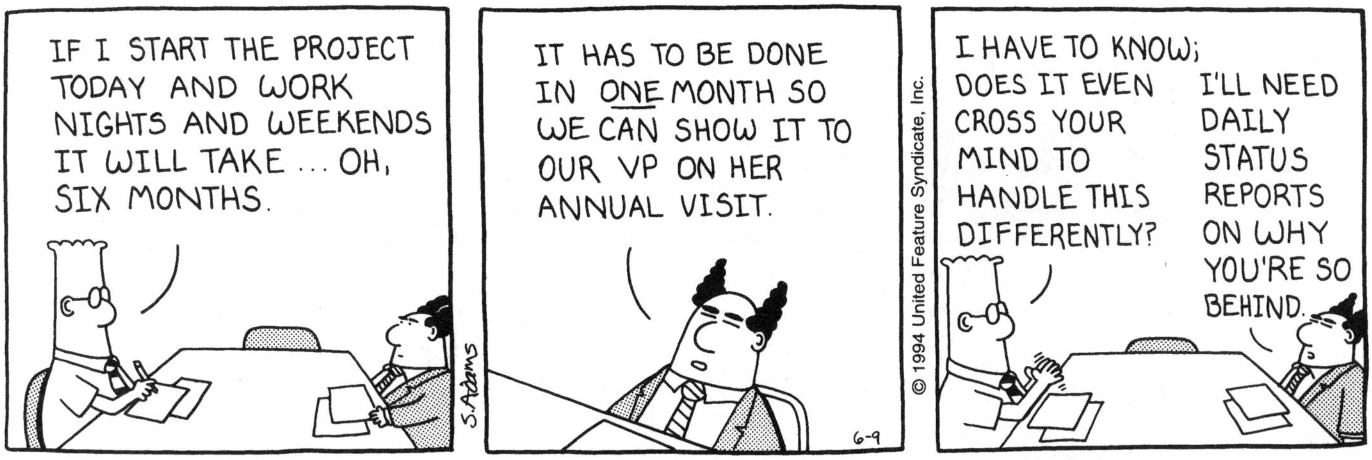
IF I START THE PROJECT TODAY AND WORK NIGHTS AND WEEKENDS IT WILL TAKE ... OH, SIX MONTHS.
IT HAS TO BE DONE IN ONE MONTH SO WE CAN SHOW IT TO OUR VP ON HER ANNUAL VISIT.
I HAVE TO KNOW; DOES IT EVEN CROSS YOUR MIND TO HANDLE THIS DIFFERENTLY?
I'LL NEED DAILY STATUS REPORTS ON WHY YOU'RE SO BEHIND.
S. Adams
6-9
© 1994 United Feature Syndicate, Inc.

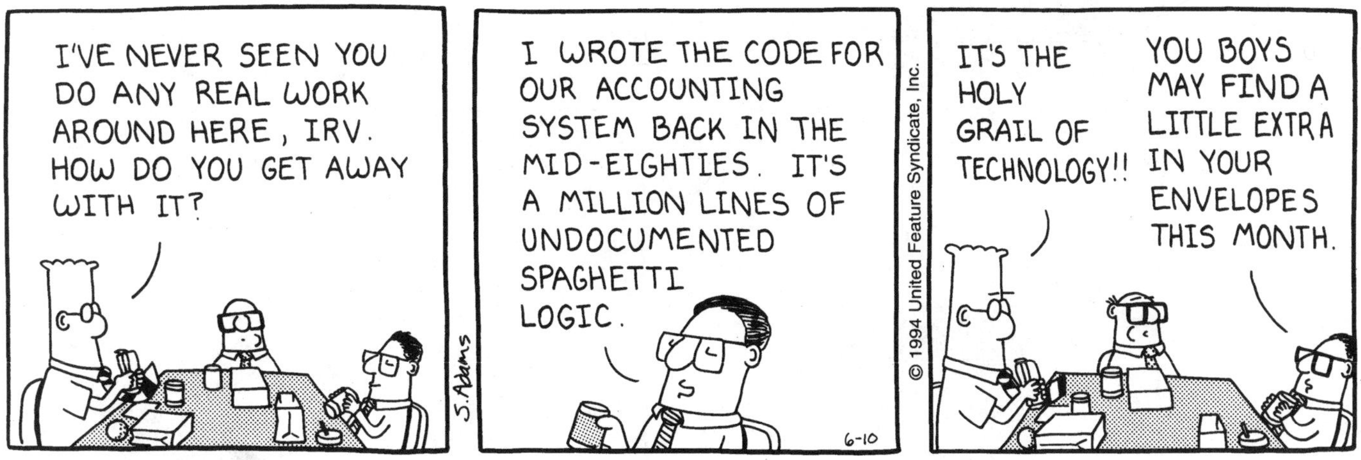
I'VE NEVER SEEN YOU DO ANY REAL WORK AROUND HERE, IRV. HOW DO YOU GET AWAY WITH IT?
I WROTE THE CODE FOR OUR ACCOUNTING SYSTEM BACK IN THE MID-EIGHTIES. IT'S A MILLION LINES OF UNDOCUMENTED SPAGHETTI LOGIC.
IT'S THE HOLY GRAIL OF TECHNOLOGY!!
YOU BOYS MAY FIND A LITTLE EXTRA IN YOUR ENVELOPES THIS MONTH.
S. Adams
6-10
© 1994 United Feature Syndicate, Inc.

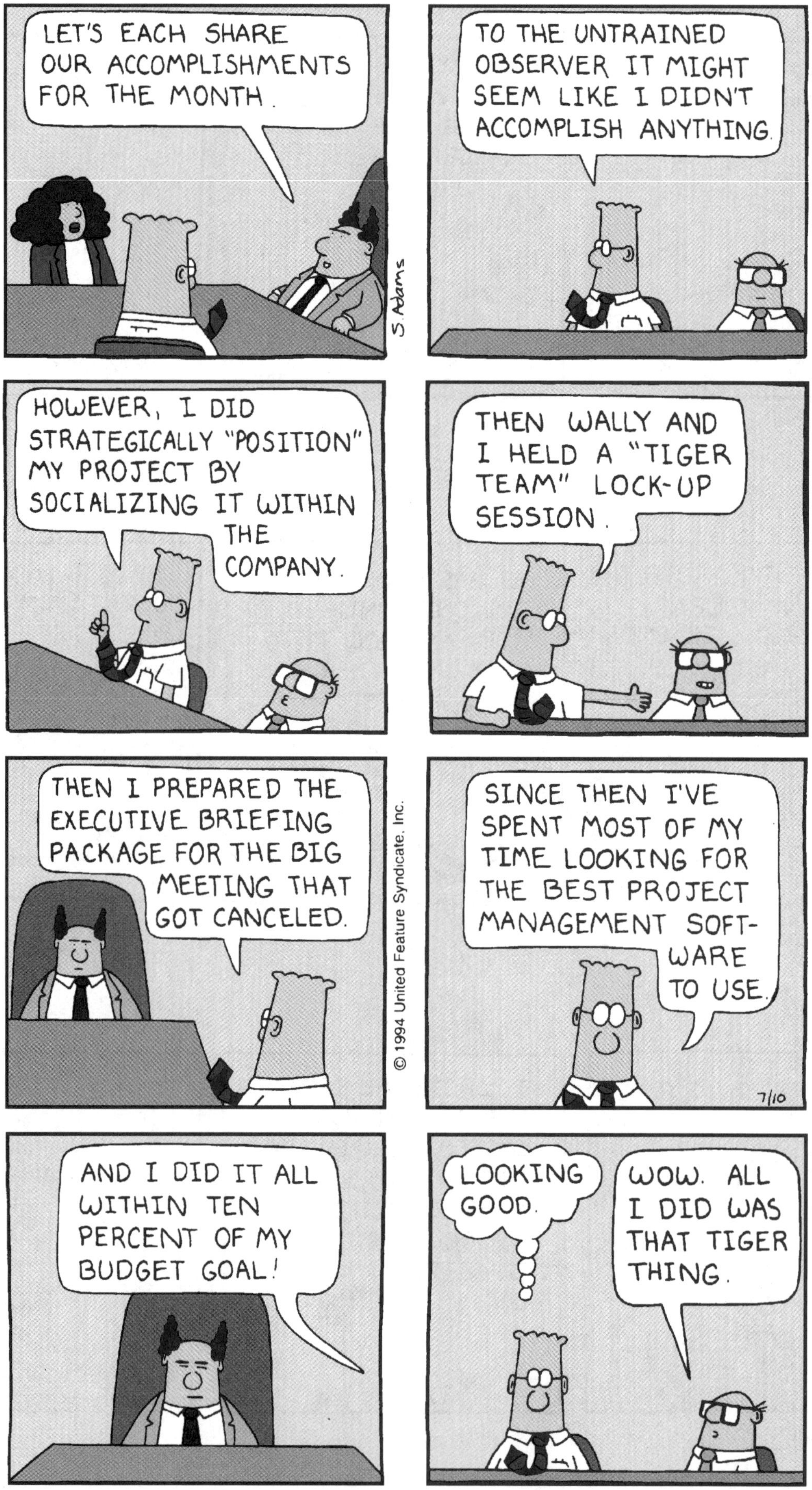
LET'S EACH SHARE OUR ACCOMPLISHMENTS FOR THE MONTH.
S. Adams
TO THE UNTRAINED OBSERVER IT MIGHT SEEM LIKE I DIDN'T ACCOMPLISH ANYTHING.
HOWEVER, I DID STRATEGICALLY "POSITION" MY PROJECT BY SOCIALIZING IT WITHIN THE COMPANY.
THEN WALLY AND I HELD A "TIGER TEAM" LOCK-UP SESSION.
THEN I PREPARED THE EXECUTIVE BRIEFING PACKAGE FOR THE BIG MEETING THAT GOT CANCELED.
© 1994 United Feature Syndicate, Inc.
SINCE THEN I'VE SPENT MOST OF MY TIME LOOKING FOR THE BEST PROJECT MANAGEMENT SOFT-WARE TO USE.
7/10
AND I DID IT ALL WITHIN TEN PERCENT OF MY BUDGET GOAL!
LOOKING GOOD.
WOW. ALL I DID WAS THAT TIGER THING.

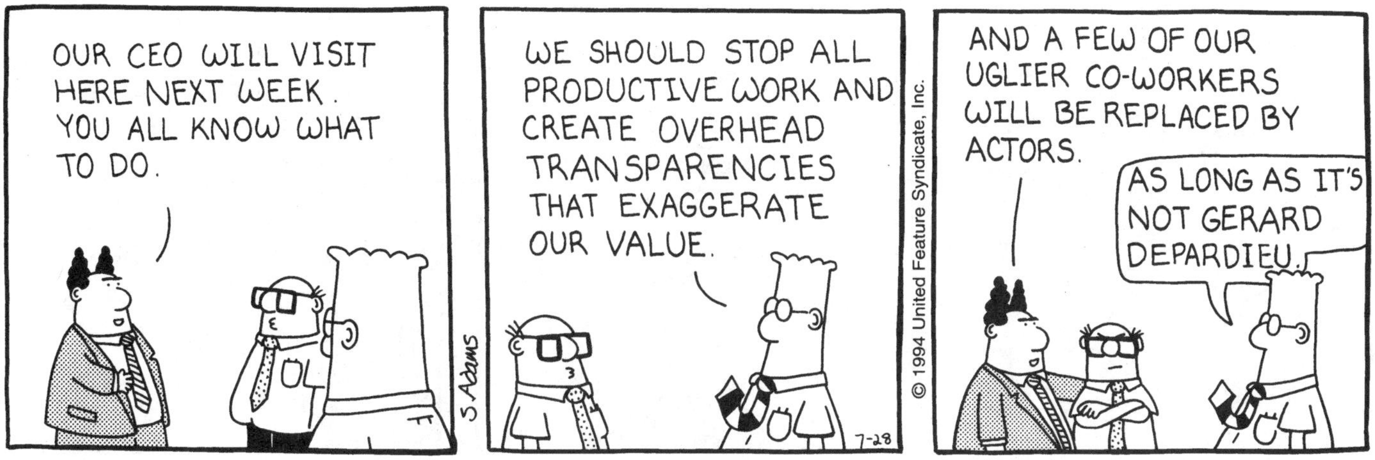
OUR CEO WILL VISIT HERE NEXT WEEK. YOU ALL KNOW WHAT TO DO.
WE SHOULD STOP ALL PRODUCTIVE WORK AND CREATE OVERHEAD TRANSPARENCIES THAT EXAGGERATE OUR VALUE.
AND A FEW OF OUR UGLIER CO-WORKERS WILL BE REPLACED BY ACTORS.
AS LONG AS IT'S NOT GERARD DEPARDIEU.
S. Adams
7-28
© 1994 United Feature Syndicate, Inc.

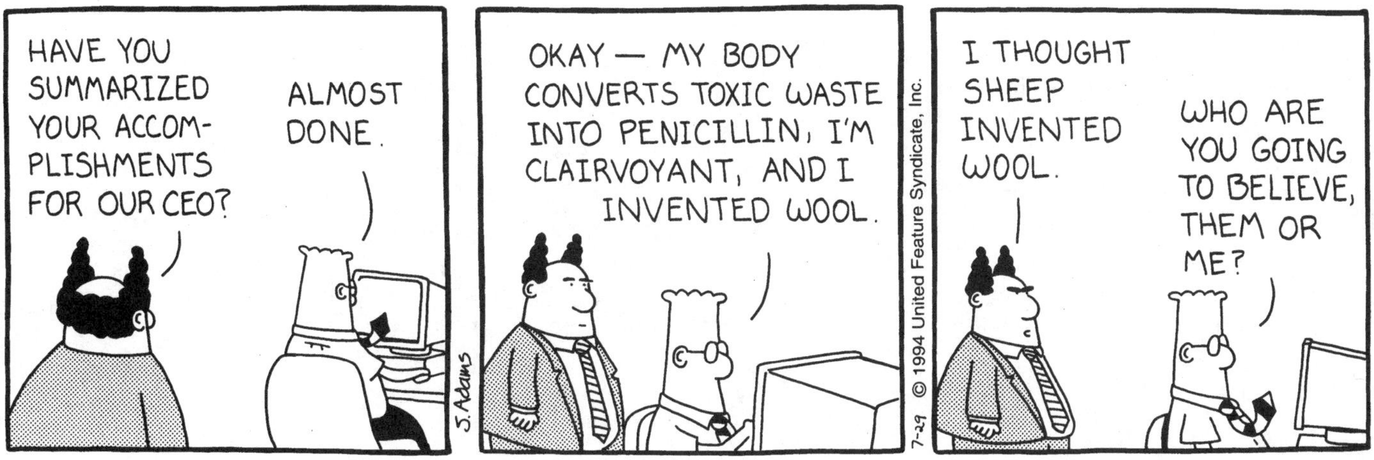
HAVE YOU SUMMARIZED YOUR ACCOM-PLISHMENTS FOR OUR CEO?
ALMOST DONE.
OKAY — MY BODY CONVERTS TOXIC WASTE INTO PENICILLIN, I'M CLAIRVOYANT, AND I INVENTED WOOL.
I THOUGHT SHEEP INVENTED WOOL.
WHO ARE YOU GOING TO BELIEVE, THEM OR ME?
S. Adams
7-29
© 1994 United Feature Syndicate, Inc.

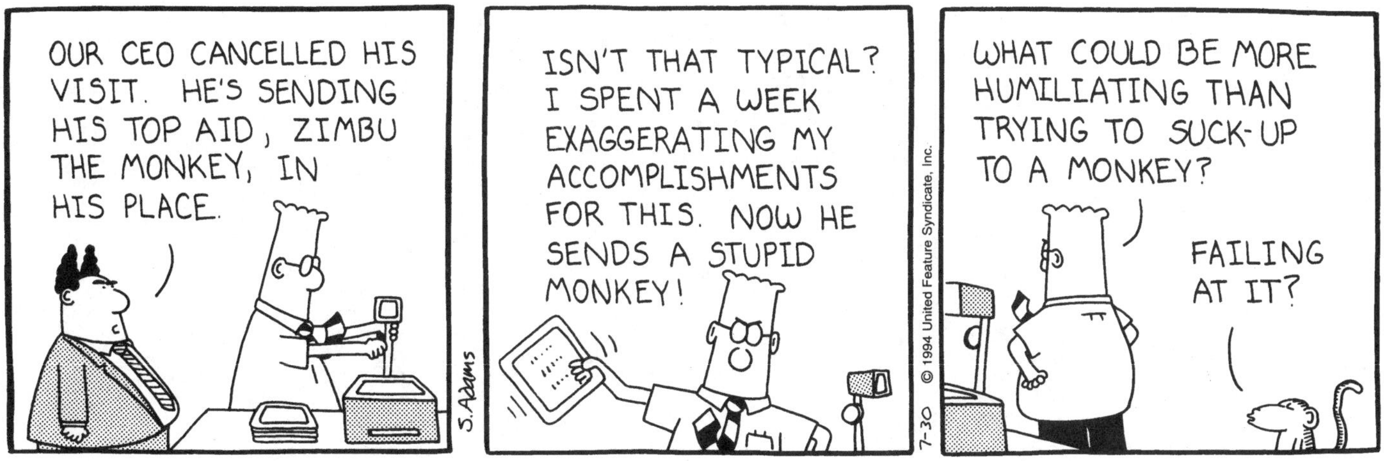
OUR CEO CANCELLED HIS VISIT. HE'S SENDING HIS TOP AID, ZIMBU THE MONKEY, IN HIS PLACE.
ISN'T THAT TYPICAL? I SPENT A WEEK EXAGGERATING MY ACCOMPLISHMENTS FOR THIS. NOW HE SENDS A STUPID MONKEY!
WHAT COULD BE MORE HUMILIATING THAN TRYING TO SUCK-UP TO A MONKEY?
FAILING AT IT?
S. Adams
7-30
© 1994 United Feature Syndicate, Inc.

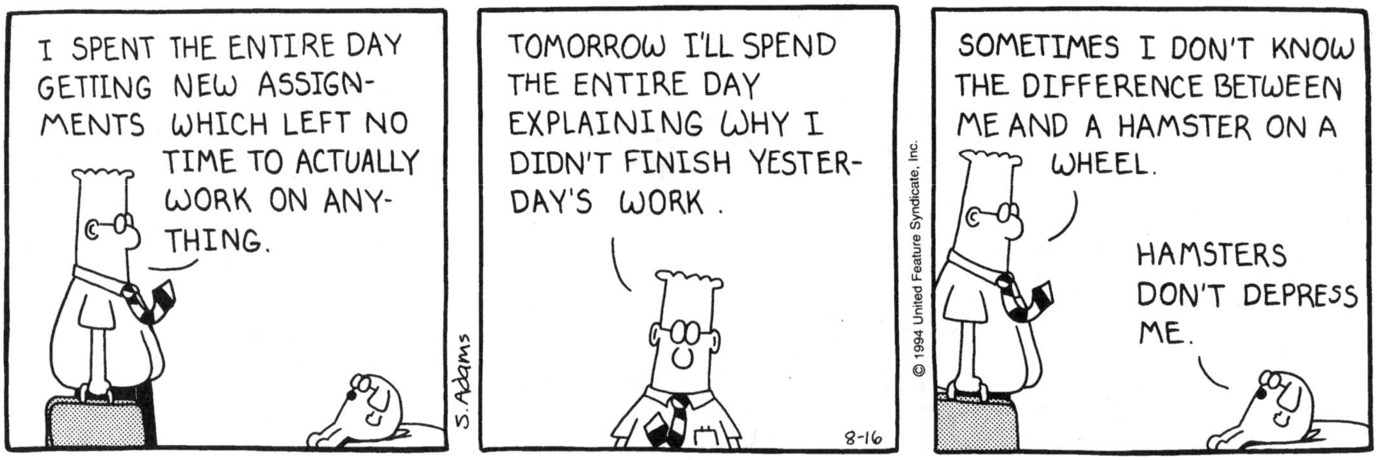
I SPENT THE ENTIRE DAY GETTING NEW ASSIGNMENTS WHICH LEFT NO TIME TO ACTUALLY WORK ON ANYTHING.
S. Adams
TOMORROW I'LL SPEND THE ENTIRE DAY EXPLAINING WHY I DIDN'T FINISH YESTERDAY'S WORK.
8-16
© 1994 United Feature Syndicate, Inc.
SOMETIMES I DON'T KNOW THE DIFFERENCE BETWEEN ME AND A HAMSTER ON A WHEEL.
HAMSTERS DON'T DEPRESS ME.

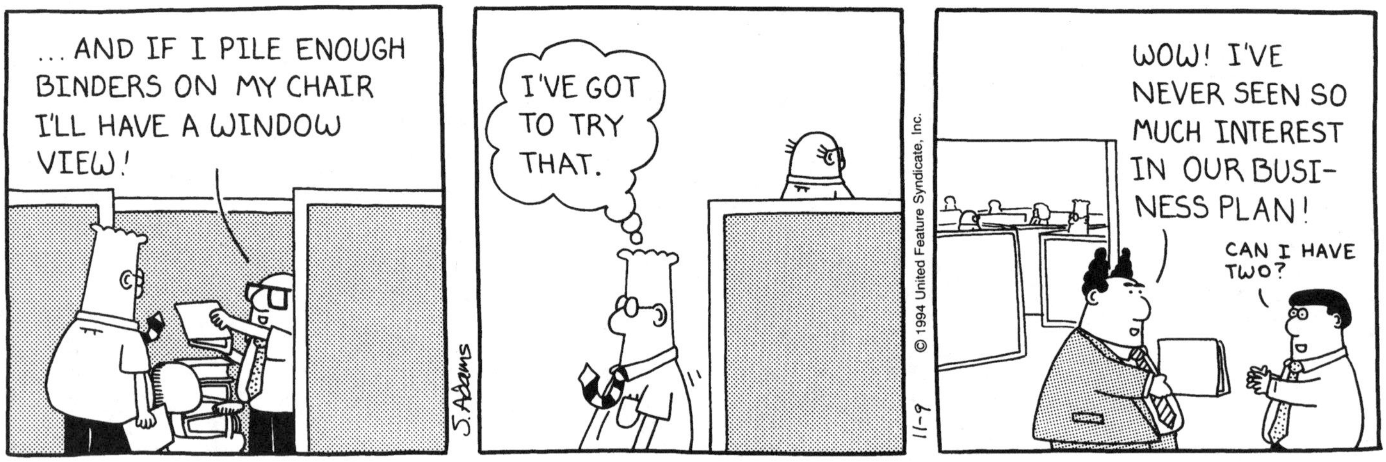
... AND IF I PILE ENOUGH BINDERS ON MY CHAIR I'LL HAVE A WINDOW VIEW!
S. Adams
I'VE GOT TO TRY THAT.
11-9
© 1994 United Feature Syndicate, Inc.
WOW! I'VE NEVER SEEN SO MUCH INTEREST IN OUR BUSINESS PLAN!
CAN I HAVE TWO?

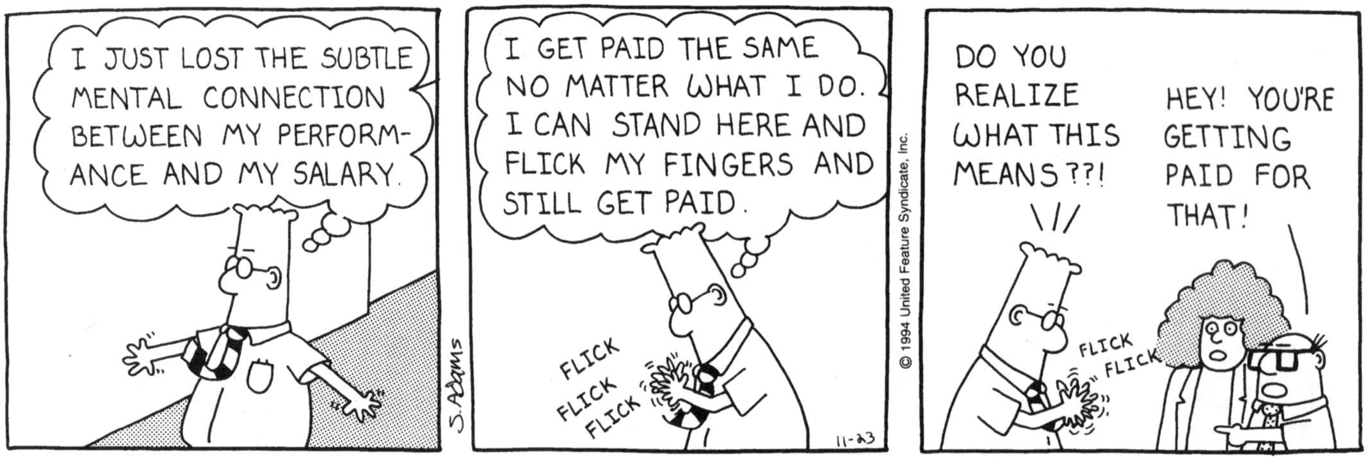
I JUST LOST THE SUBTLE MENTAL CONNECTION BETWEEN MY PERFORMANCE AND MY SALARY.
S. Adams
I GET PAID THE SAME NO MATTER WHAT I DO. I CAN STAND HERE AND FLICK MY FINGERS AND STILL GET PAID.
FLICK FLICK FLICK
11-23
© 1994 United Feature Syndicate, Inc.
DO YOU REALIZE WHAT THIS MEANS??!
HEY! YOU'RE GETTING PAID FOR THAT!
FLICK FLICK

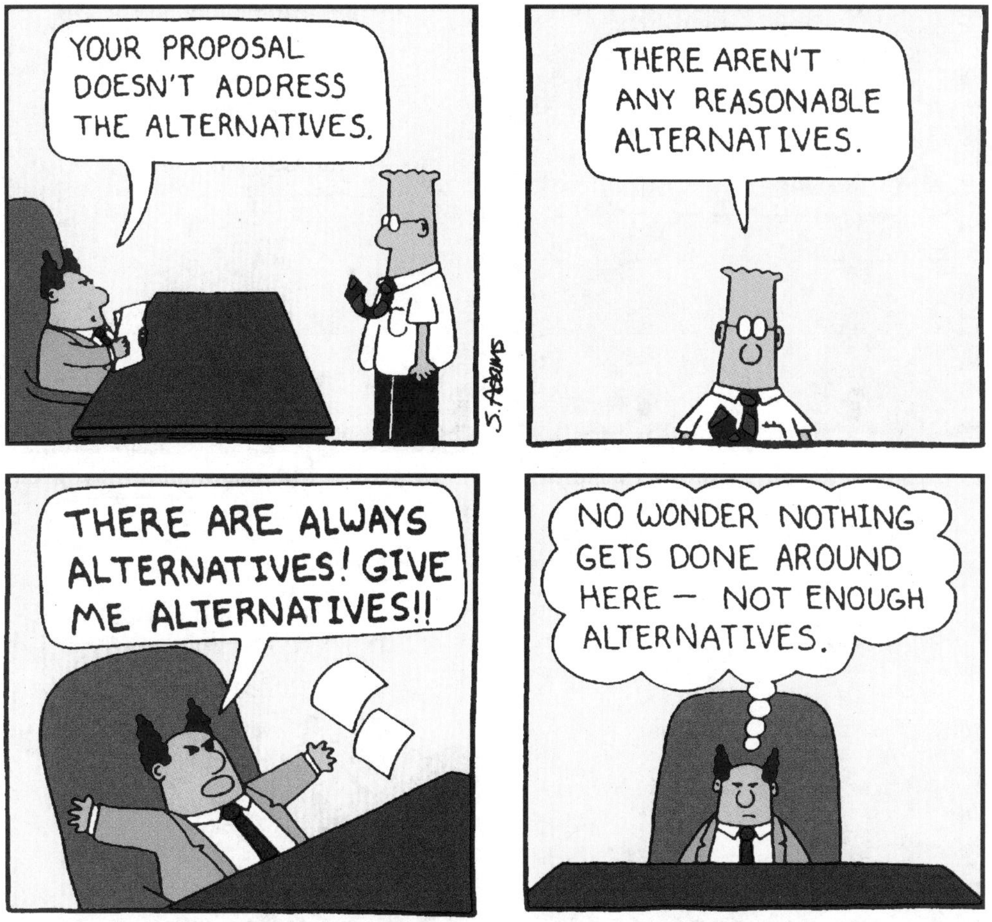
YOUR PROPOSAL DOESN'T ADDRESS THE ALTERNATIVES.
S. Adams
THERE AREN'T ANY REASONABLE ALTERNATIVES.
THERE ARE ALWAYS ALTERNATIVES! GIVE ME ALTERNATIVES!!
NO WONDER NOTHING GETS DONE AROUND HERE — NOT ENOUGH ALTERNATIVES.

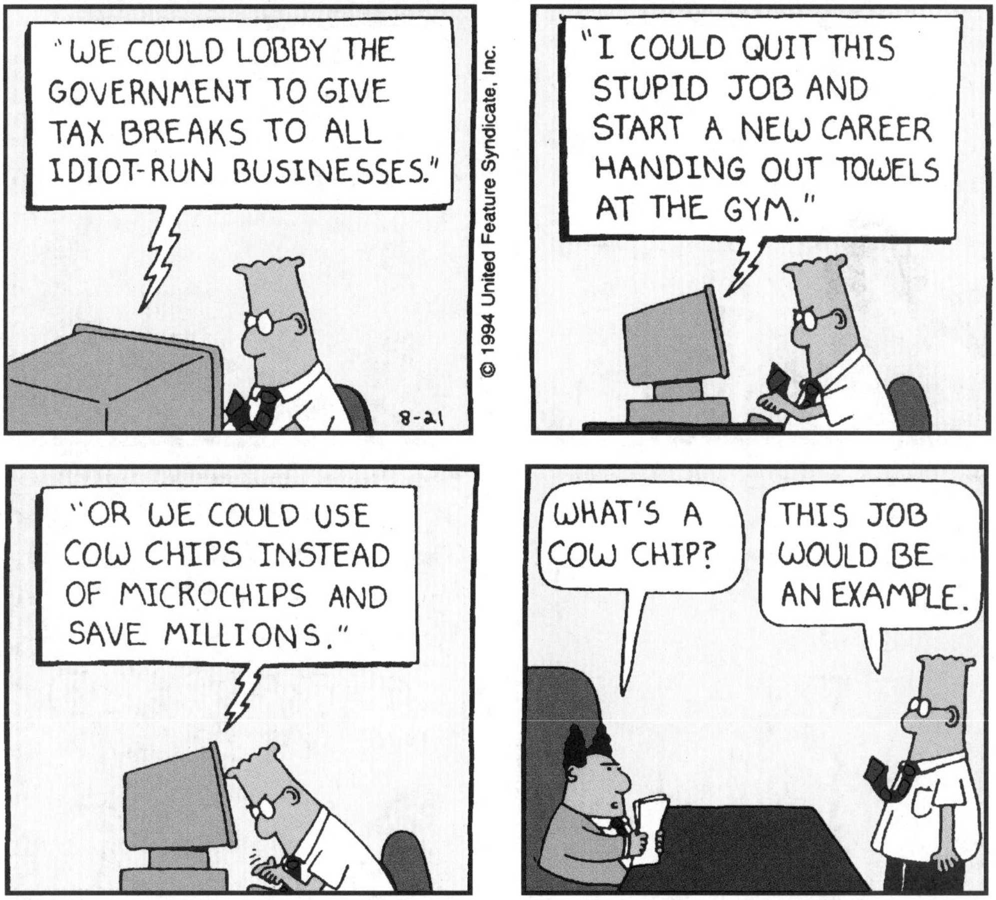
"WE COULD LOBBY THE GOVERNMENT TO GIVE TAX BREAKS TO ALL IDIOT-RUN BUSINESSES."
8-21
© 1994 United Feature Syndicate, Inc.
"I COULD QUIT THIS STUPID JOB AND START A NEW CAREER HANDING OUT TOWELS AT THE GYM."
"OR WE COULD USE COW CHIPS INSTEAD OF MICROCHIPS AND SAVE MILLIONS."
WHAT'S A COW CHIP?
THIS JOB WOULD BE AN EXAMPLE.

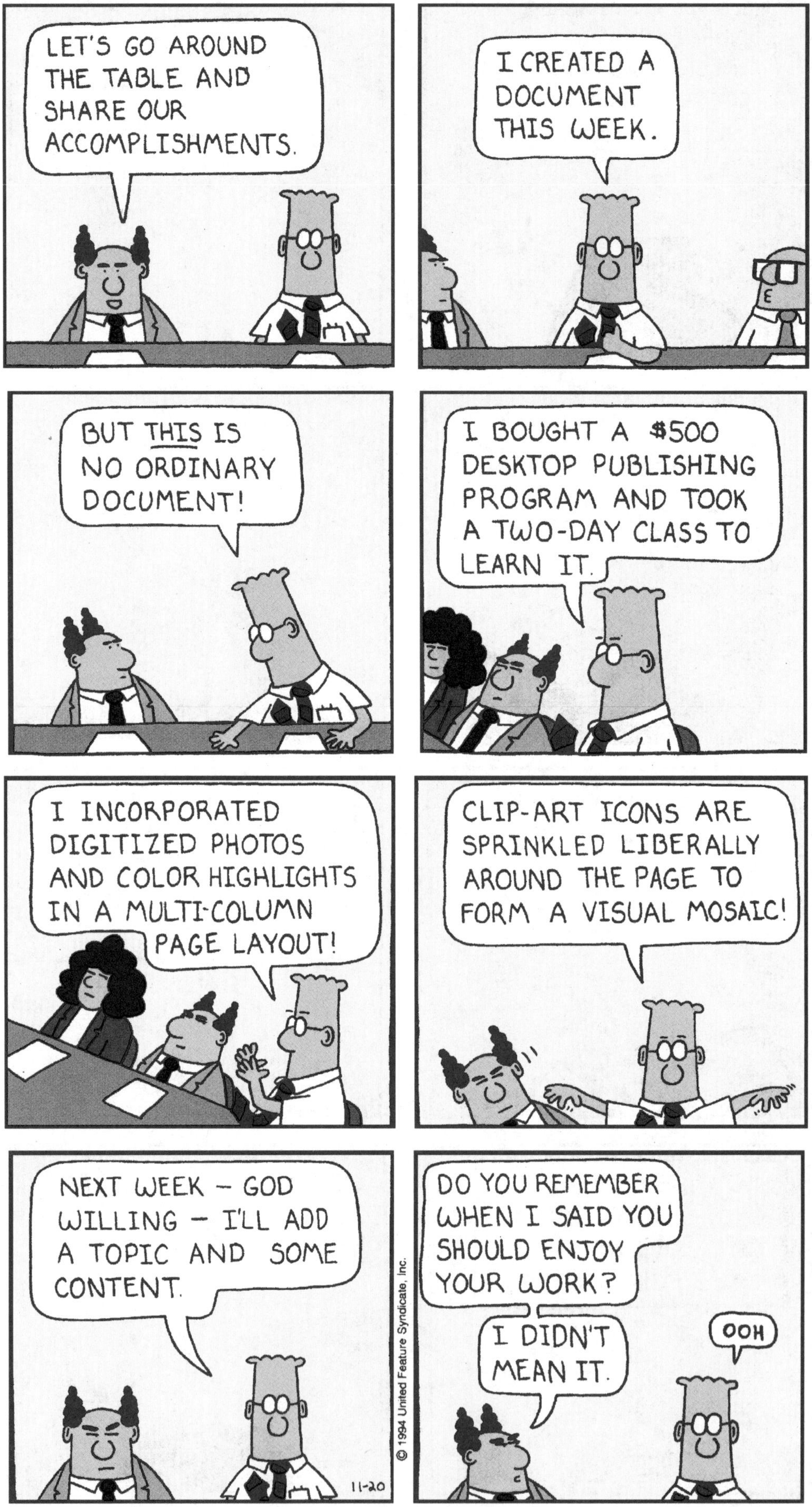
LET'S GO AROUND THE TABLE AND SHARE OUR ACCOMPLISHMENTS.
I CREATED A DOCUMENT THIS WEEK.
BUT THIS IS NO ORDINARY DOCUMENT!
I BOUGHT A $500 DESKTOP PUBLISHING PROGRAM AND TOOK A TWO-DAY CLASS TO LEARN IT.
I INCORPORATED DIGITIZED PHOTOS AND COLOR HIGHLIGHTS IN A MULTI-COLUMN PAGE LAYOUT!
CLIP-ART ICONS ARE SPRINKLED LIBERALLY AROUND THE PAGE TO FORM A VISUAL MOSAIC!
NEXT WEEK – GOD WILLING – I'LL ADD A TOPIC AND SOME CONTENT.
11-20
© 1994 United Feature Syndicate, Inc.
DO YOU REMEMBER WHEN I SAID YOU SHOULD ENJOY YOUR WORK?
I DIDN'T MEAN IT.
OOH

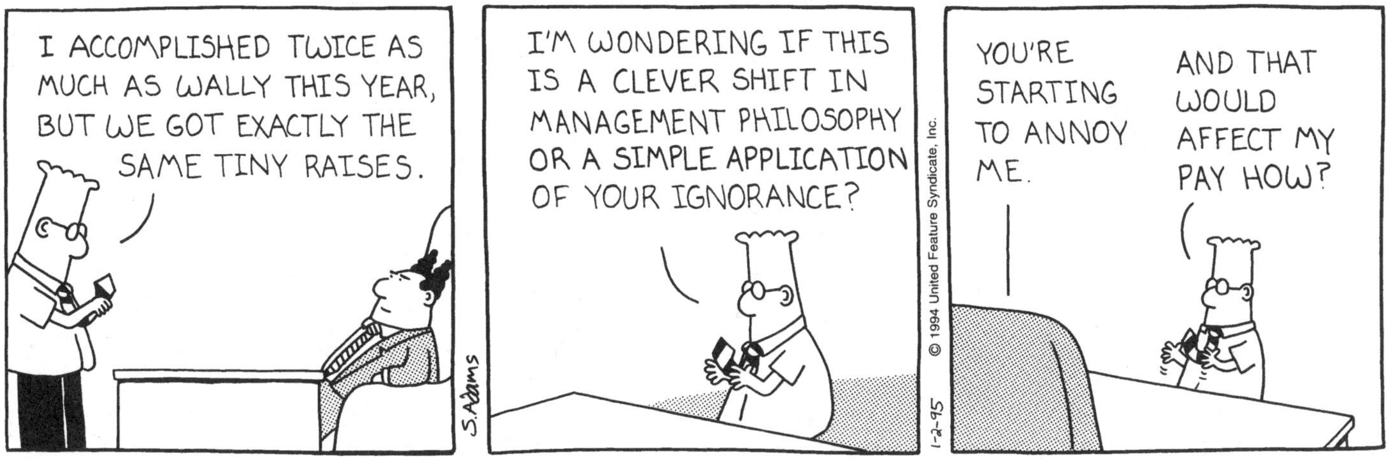
I ACCOMPLISHED TWICE AS MUCH AS WALLY THIS YEAR, BUT WE GOT EXACTLY THE SAME TINY RAISES.
S. Adams
I'M WONDERING IF THIS IS A CLEVER SHIFT IN MANAGEMENT PHILOSOPHY OR A SIMPLE APPLICATION OF YOUR IGNORANCE?
1-2-95
© 1994 United Feature Syndicate, Inc.
YOU'RE STARTING TO ANNOY ME.
AND THAT WOULD AFFECT MY PAY HOW?

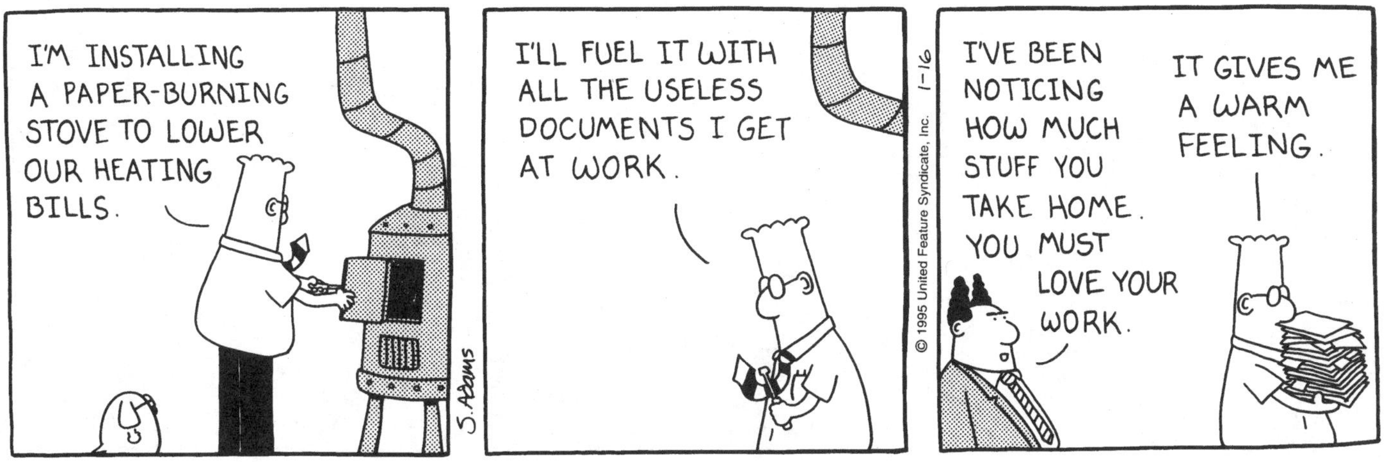
I'M INSTALLING A PAPER-BURNING STOVE TO LOWER OUR HEATING BILLS.
S. Adams
I'LL FUEL IT WITH ALL THE USELESS DOCUMENTS I GET AT WORK.
1-16
© 1995 United Feature Syndicate, Inc.
I'VE BEEN NOTICING HOW MUCH STUFF YOU TAKE HOME. YOU MUST LOVE YOUR WORK.
IT GIVES ME A WARM FEELING.

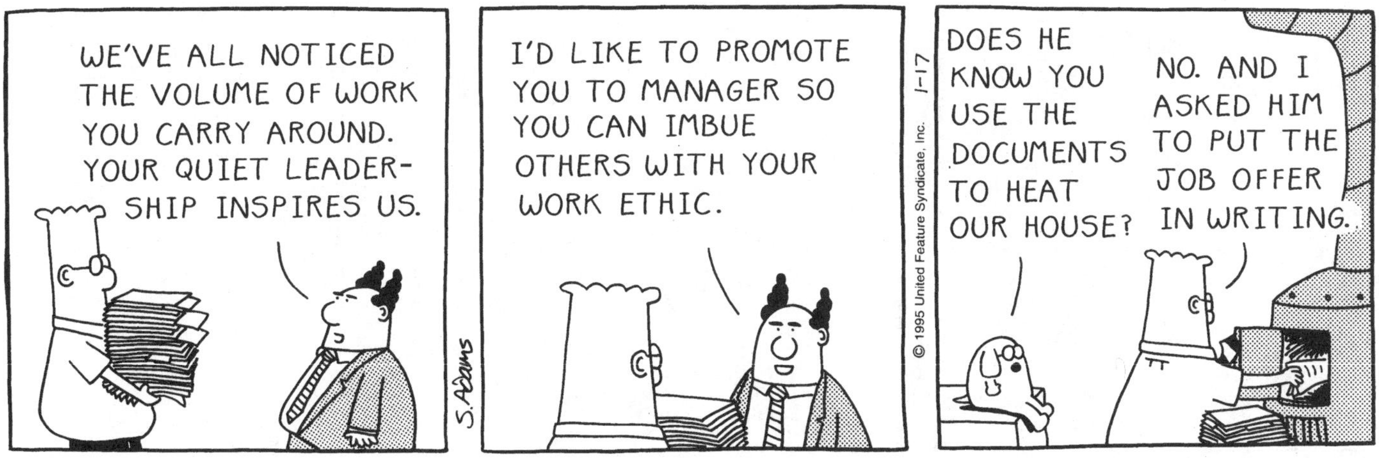
WE'VE ALL NOTICED THE VOLUME OF WORK YOU CARRY AROUND. YOUR QUIET LEADERSHIP INSPIRES US.
S. Adams
I'D LIKE TO PROMOTE YOU TO MANAGER SO YOU CAN IMBUE OTHERS WITH YOUR WORK ETHIC.
1-17
© 1995 United Feature Syndicate, Inc.
DOES HE KNOW YOU USE THE DOCUMENTS TO HEAT OUR HOUSE?
NO. AND I ASKED HIM TO PUT THE JOB OFFER IN WRITING.

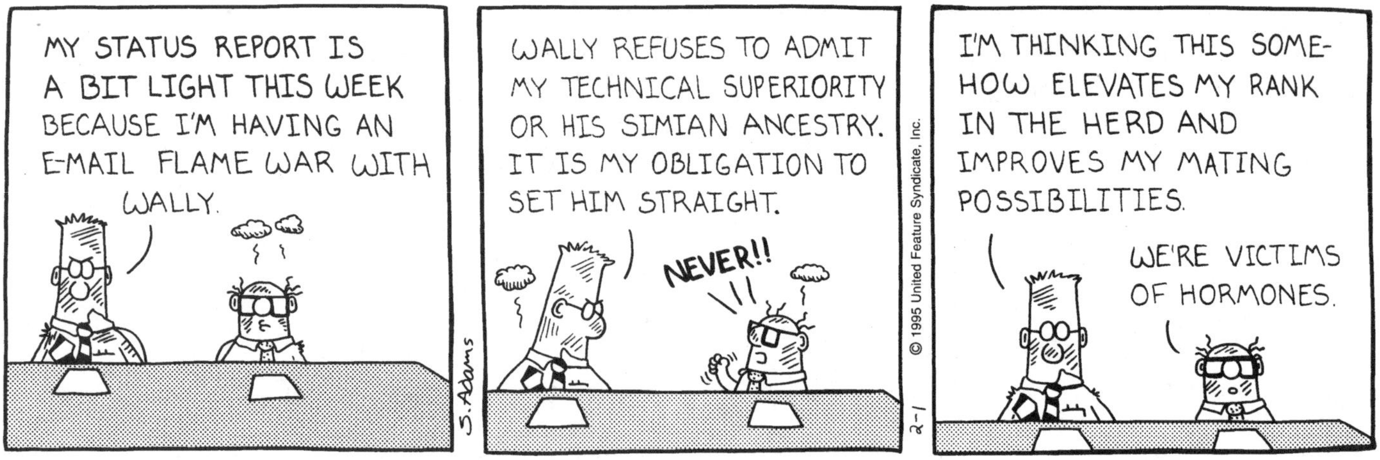
MY STATUS REPORT IS A BIT LIGHT THIS WEEK BECAUSE I'M HAVING AN E-MAIL FLAME WAR WITH WALLY.
WALLY REFUSES TO ADMIT MY TECHNICAL SUPERIORITY OR HIS SIMIAN ANCESTRY. IT IS MY OBLIGATION TO SET HIM STRAIGHT.
NEVER!!
I'M THINKING THIS SOMEHOW ELEVATES MY RANK IN THE HERD AND IMPROVES MY MATING POSSIBILITIES.
WE'RE VICTIMS OF HORMONES.
S. Adams
2-1
© 1995 United Feature Syndicate, Inc.

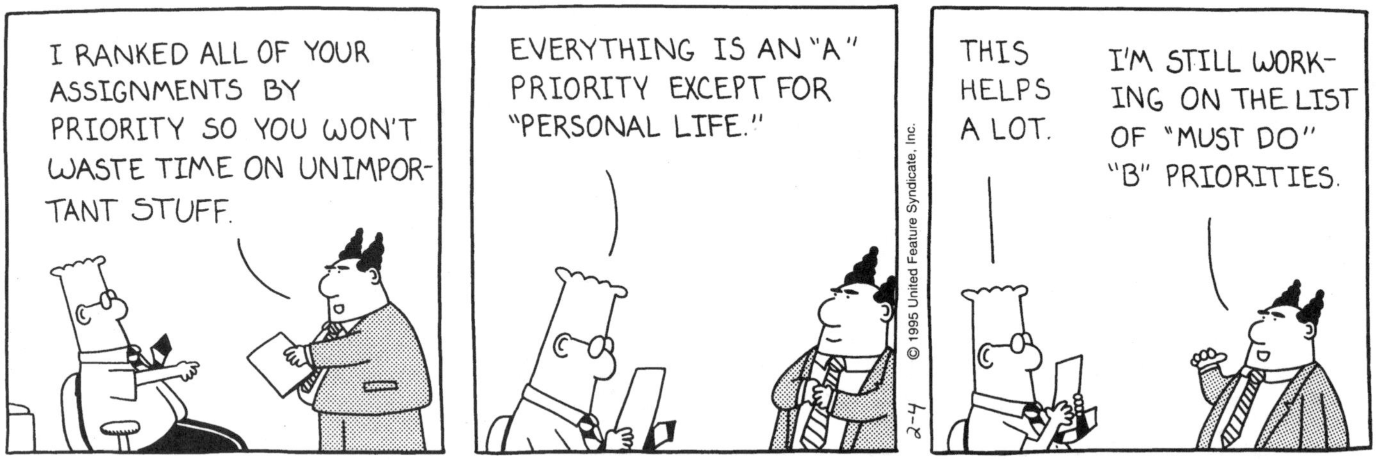
I RANKED ALL OF YOUR ASSIGNMENTS BY PRIORITY SO YOU WON'T WASTE TIME ON UNIMPORTANT STUFF.
EVERYTHING IS AN "A" PRIORITY EXCEPT FOR "PERSONAL LIFE."
THIS HELPS A LOT.
I'M STILL WORKING ON THE LIST OF "MUST DO" "B" PRIORITIES.
2-4
© 1995 United Feature Syndicate, Inc.

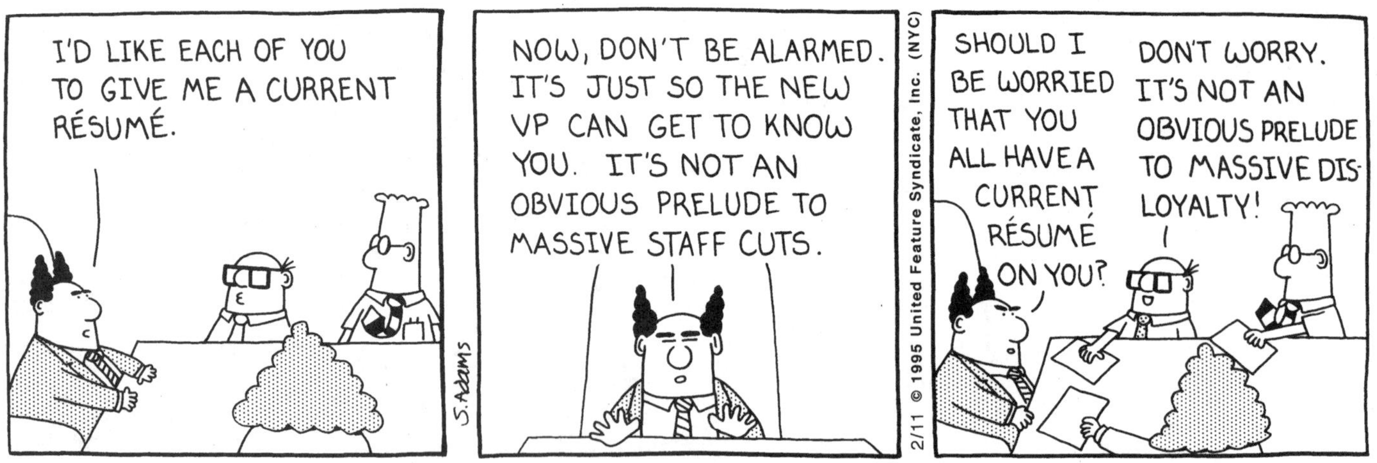
I'D LIKE EACH OF YOU TO GIVE ME A CURRENT RÉSUMÉ.
NOW, DON'T BE ALARMED. IT'S JUST SO THE NEW VP CAN GET TO KNOW YOU. IT'S NOT AN OBVIOUS PRELUDE TO MASSIVE STAFF CUTS.
SHOULD I BE WORRIED THAT YOU ALL HAVE A CURRENT RÉSUMÉ ON YOU?
DON'T WORRY. IT'S NOT AN OBVIOUS PRELUDE TO MASSIVE DISLOYALTY!
S. Adams
2/11 © 1995 United Feature Syndicate, Inc. (NYC)

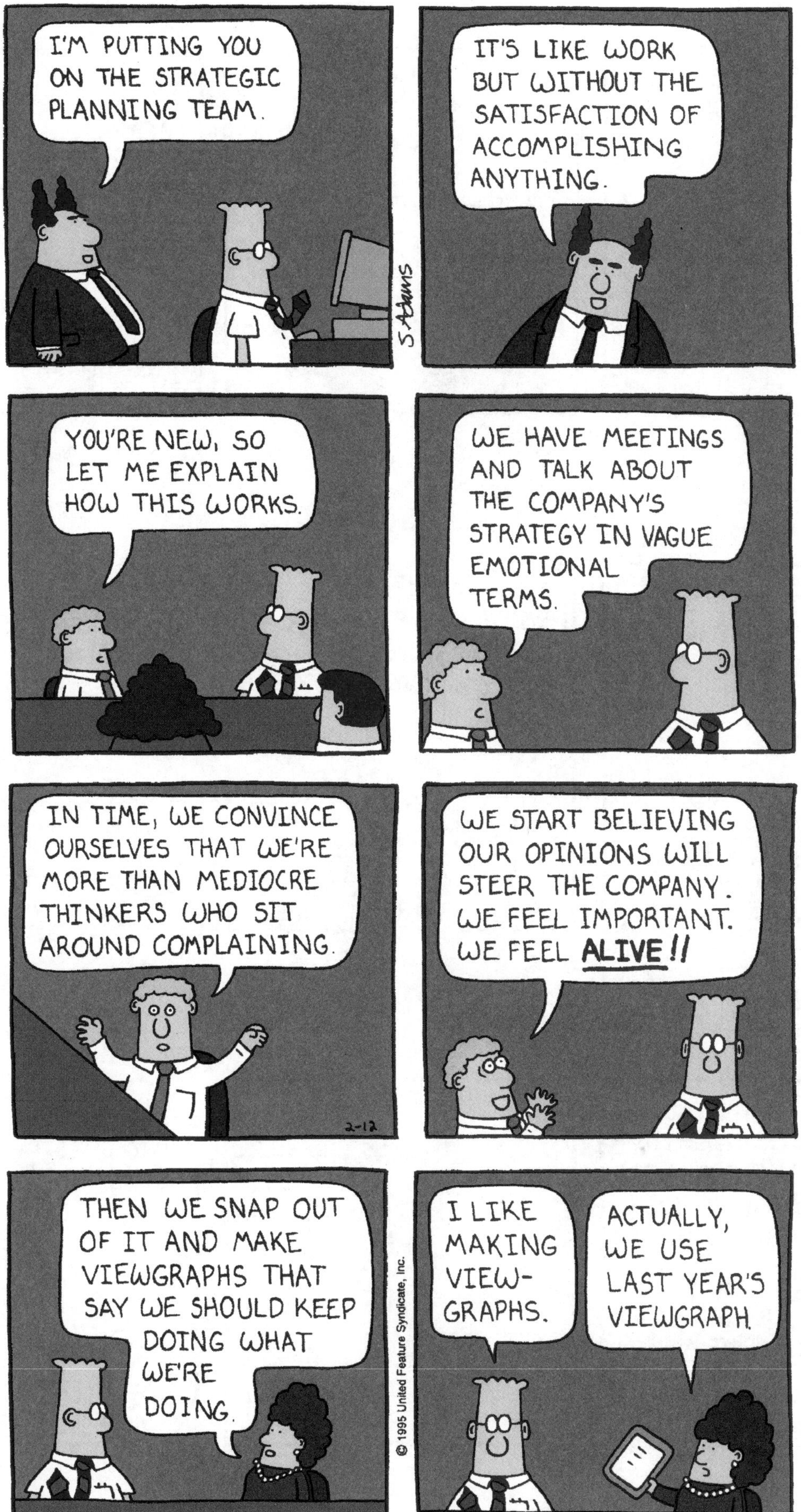
I'M PUTTING YOU ON THE STRATEGIC PLANNING TEAM.
S Adams
IT'S LIKE WORK BUT WITHOUT THE SATISFACTION OF ACCOMPLISHING ANYTHING.
YOU'RE NEW, SO LET ME EXPLAIN HOW THIS WORKS.
WE HAVE MEETINGS AND TALK ABOUT THE COMPANY'S STRATEGY IN VAGUE EMOTIONAL TERMS.
IN TIME, WE CONVINCE OURSELVES THAT WE'RE MORE THAN MEDIOCRE THINKERS WHO SIT AROUND COMPLAINING.
2-12
WE START BELIEVING OUR OPINIONS WILL STEER THE COMPANY. WE FEEL IMPORTANT. WE FEEL ALIVE!!
THEN WE SNAP OUT OF IT AND MAKE VIEWGRAPHS THAT SAY WE SHOULD KEEP DOING WHAT WE'RE DOING.
© 1995 United Feature Syndicate, Inc.
I LIKE MAKING VIEW-GRAPHS.
ACTUALLY, WE USE LAST YEAR'S VIEWGRAPH.

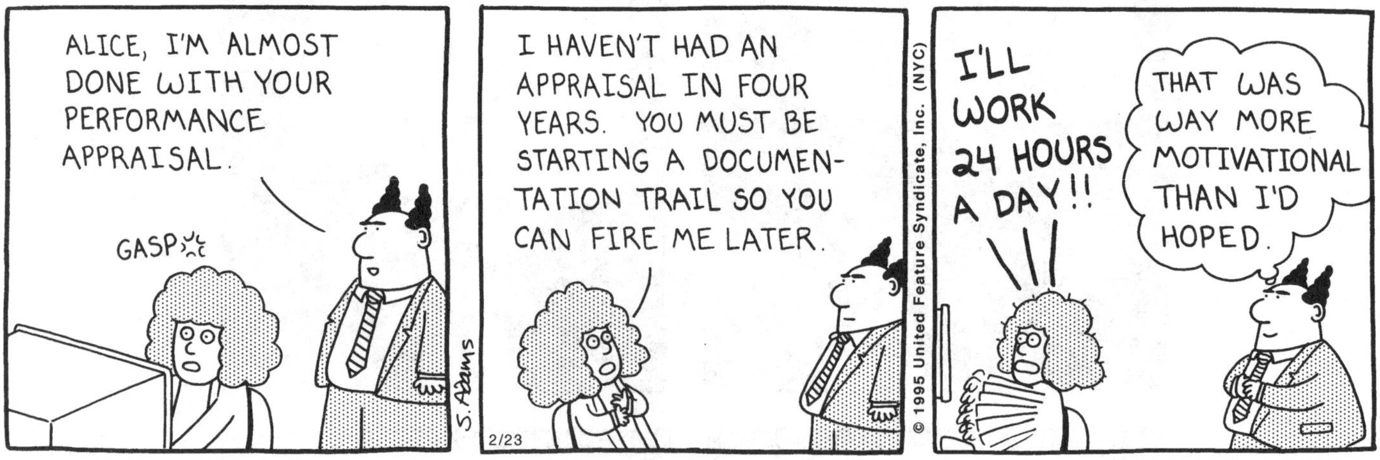
ALICE, I'M ALMOST DONE WITH YOUR PERFORMANCE APPRAISAL.
GASP
S. Adams
I HAVEN'T HAD AN APPRAISAL IN FOUR YEARS. YOU MUST BE STARTING A DOCUMENTATION TRAIL SO YOU CAN FIRE ME LATER.
2/23
© 1995 United Feature Syndicate, Inc. (NYC)
I'LL WORK 24 HOURS A DAY!!
THAT WAS WAY MORE MOTIVATIONAL THAN I'D HOPED.

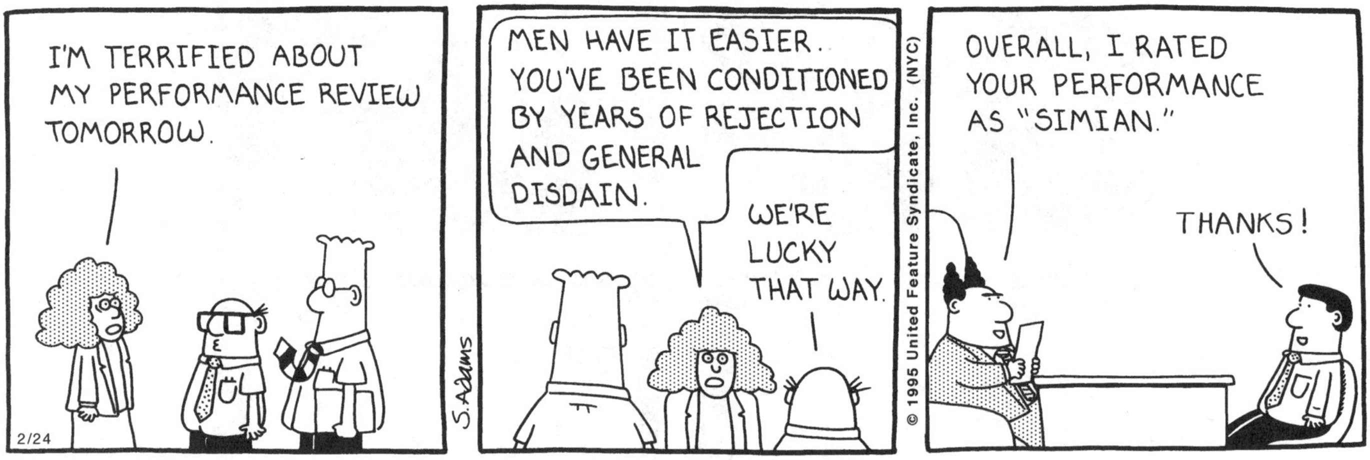
I'M TERRIFIED ABOUT MY PERFORMANCE REVIEW TOMORROW.
2/24
S. Adams
MEN HAVE IT EASIER. YOU'VE BEEN CONDITIONED BY YEARS OF REJECTION AND GENERAL DISDAIN.
WE'RE LUCKY THAT WAY.
© 1995 United Feature Syndicate, Inc. (NYC)
OVERALL, I RATED YOUR PERFORMANCE AS "SIMIAN."
THANKS!

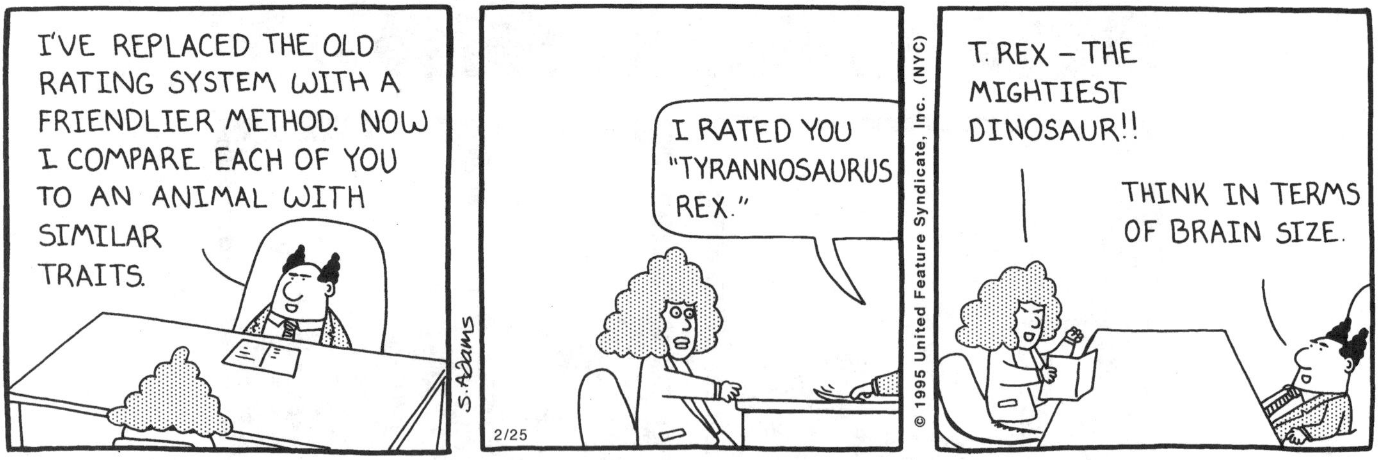
I'VE REPLACED THE OLD RATING SYSTEM WITH A FRIENDLIER METHOD. NOW I COMPARE EACH OF YOU TO AN ANIMAL WITH SIMILAR TRAITS.
S. Adams
I RATED YOU "TYRANNOSAURUS REX."
2/25
© 1995 United Feature Syndicate, Inc. (NYC)
T. REX – THE MIGHTIEST DINOSAUR!!
THINK IN TERMS OF BRAIN SIZE.

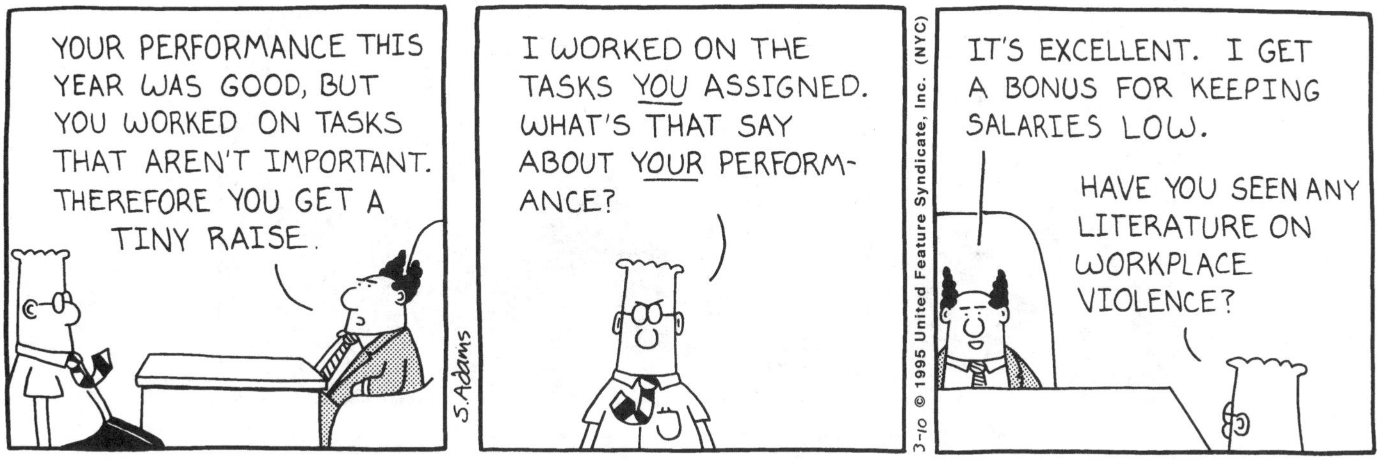
YOUR PERFORMANCE THIS YEAR WAS GOOD, BUT YOU WORKED ON TASKS THAT AREN'T IMPORTANT. THEREFORE YOU GET A TINY RAISE.
I WORKED ON THE TASKS YOU ASSIGNED. WHAT'S THAT SAY ABOUT YOUR PERFORMANCE?
IT'S EXCELLENT. I GET A BONUS FOR KEEPING SALARIES LOW.
HAVE YOU SEEN ANY LITERATURE ON WORKPLACE VIOLENCE?
S. Adams
3-10 © 1995 United Feature Syndicate, Inc. (NYC)

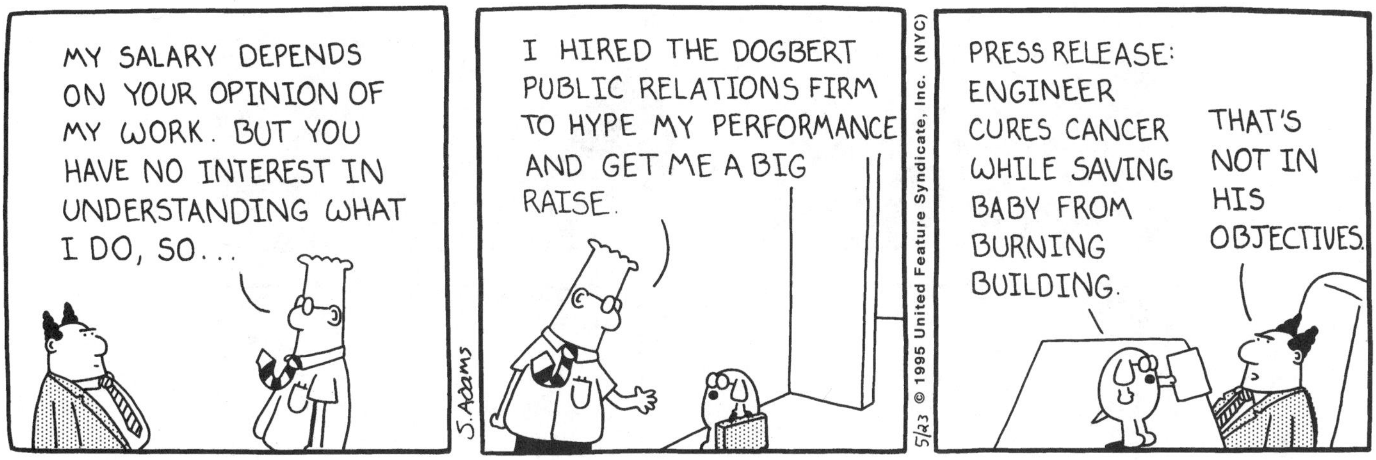
MY SALARY DEPENDS ON YOUR OPINION OF MY WORK. BUT YOU HAVE NO INTEREST IN UNDERSTANDING WHAT I DO, SO...
I HIRED THE DOGBERT PUBLIC RELATIONS FIRM TO HYPE MY PERFORMANCE AND GET ME A BIG RAISE.
PRESS RELEASE: ENGINEER CURES CANCER WHILE SAVING BABY FROM BURNING BUILDING.
THAT'S NOT IN HIS OBJECTIVES.
S. Adams
5/23 © 1995 United Feature Syndicate, Inc. (NYC)

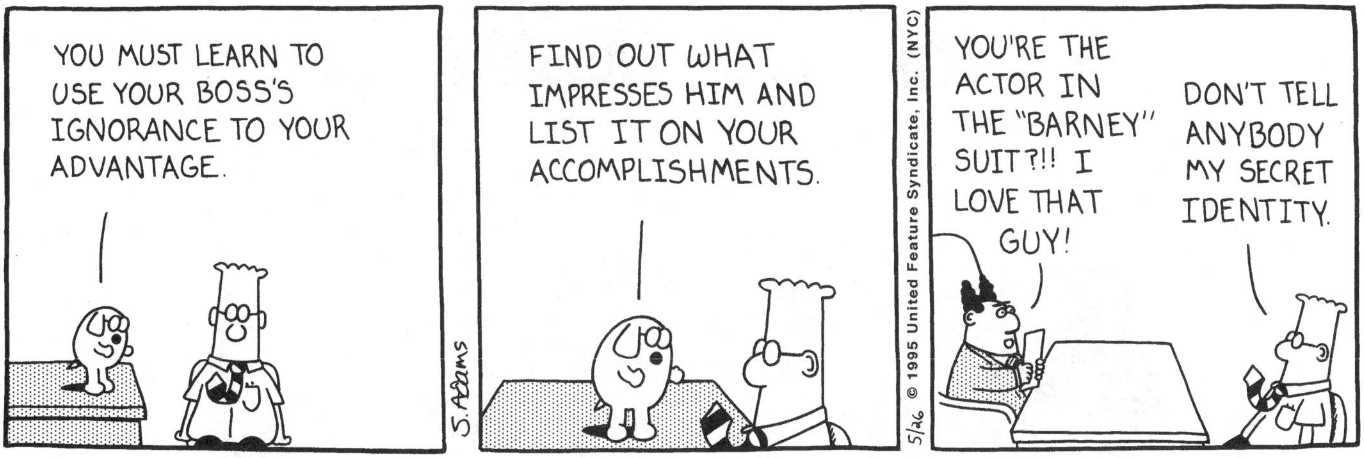
YOU MUST LEARN TO USE YOUR BOSS'S IGNORANCE TO YOUR ADVANTAGE.
FIND OUT WHAT IMPRESSES HIM AND LIST IT ON YOUR ACCOMPLISHMENTS.
YOU'RE THE ACTOR IN THE "BARNEY" SUIT?!! I LOVE THAT GUY!
DON'T TELL ANYBODY MY SECRET IDENTITY.
S. Adams
5/26 © 1995 United Feature Syndicate, Inc. (NYC)

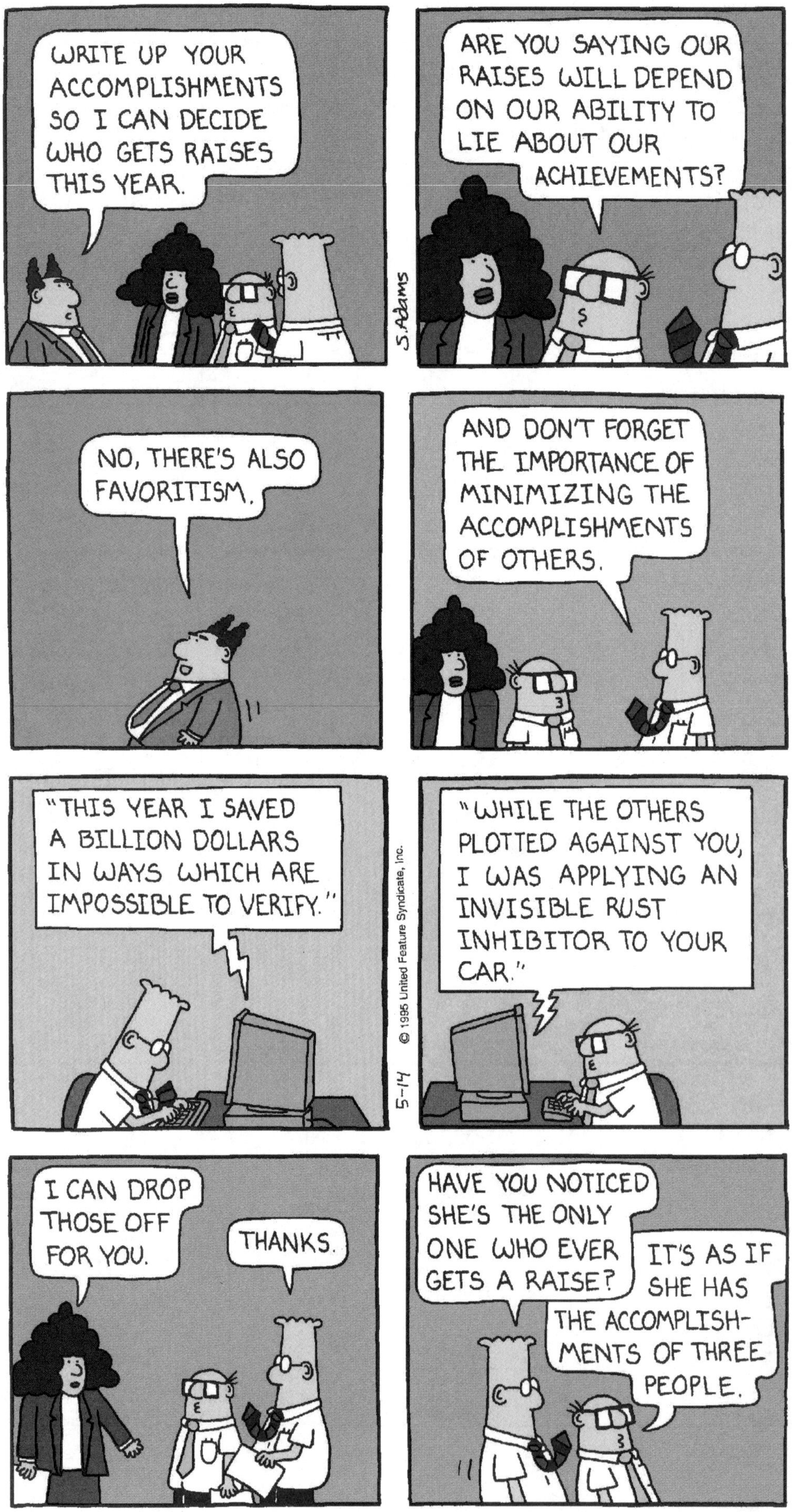
WRITE UP YOUR ACCOMPLISHMENTS SO I CAN DECIDE WHO GETS RAISES THIS YEAR.
ARE YOU SAYING OUR RAISES WILL DEPEND ON OUR ABILITY TO LIE ABOUT OUR ACHIEVEMENTS?
S. Adams
NO, THERE'S ALSO FAVORITISM.
AND DON'T FORGET THE IMPORTANCE OF MINIMIZING THE ACCOMPLISHMENTS OF OTHERS.
"THIS YEAR I SAVED A BILLION DOLLARS IN WAYS WHICH ARE IMPOSSIBLE TO VERIFY."
"WHILE THE OTHERS PLOTTED AGAINST YOU, I WAS APPLYING AN INVISIBLE RUST INHIBITOR TO YOUR CAR."
5-14
I CAN DROP THOSE OFF FOR YOU.
THANKS.
HAVE YOU NOTICED SHE'S THE ONLY ONE WHO EVER GETS A RAISE?
IT'S AS IF SHE HAS THE ACCOMPLISHMENTS OF THREE PEOPLE.

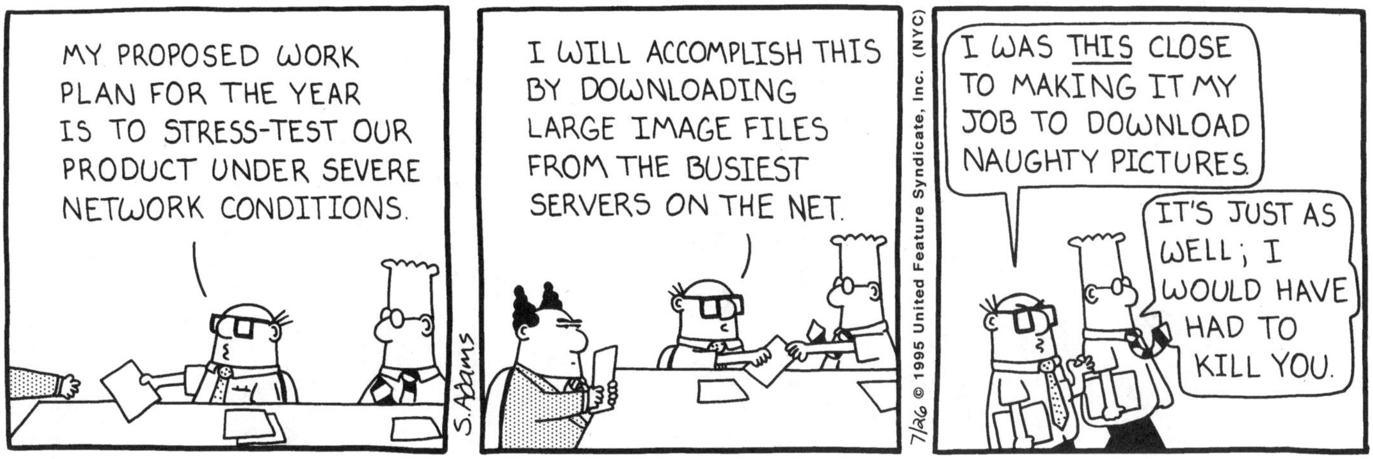
MY PROPOSED WORK PLAN FOR THE YEAR IS TO STRESS-TEST OUR PRODUCT UNDER SEVERE NETWORK CONDITIONS.
I WILL ACCOMPLISH THIS BY DOWNLOADING LARGE IMAGE FILES FROM THE BUSIEST SERVERS ON THE NET.
I WAS THIS CLOSE TO MAKING IT MY JOB TO DOWNLOAD NAUGHTY PICTURES.
IT'S JUST AS WELL; I WOULD HAVE HAD TO KILL YOU.
S. Adams
7/26 © 1995 United Feature Syndicate, Inc. (NYC)

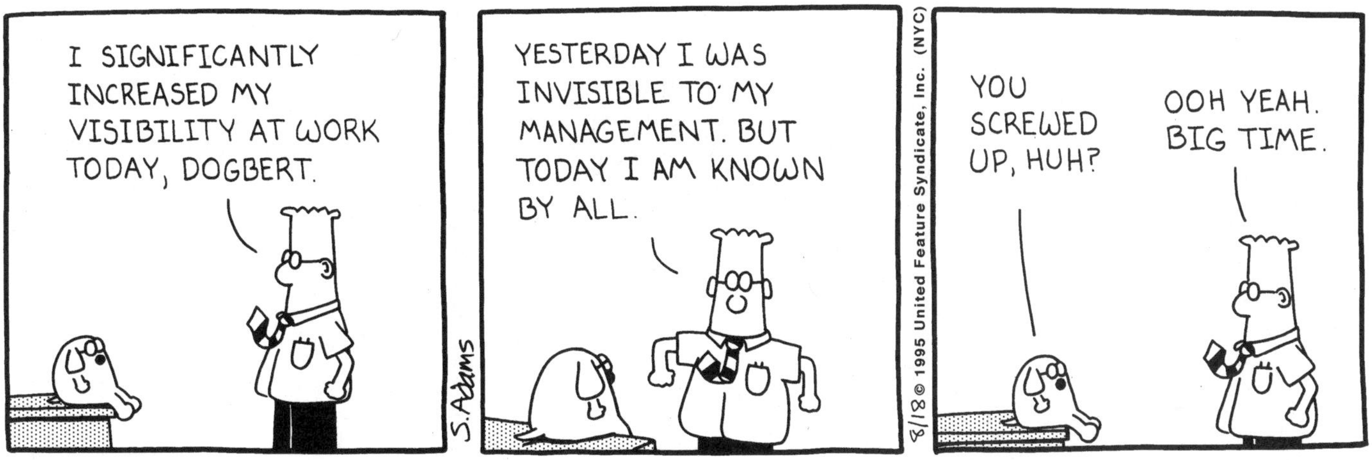
I SIGNIFICANTLY INCREASED MY VISIBILITY AT WORK TODAY, DOGBERT.
YESTERDAY I WAS INVISIBLE TO MY MANAGEMENT. BUT TODAY I AM KNOWN BY ALL.
YOU SCREWED UP, HUH?
OOH YEAH. BIG TIME.
S. Adams
8/18 © 1995 United Feature Syndicate, Inc. (NYC)

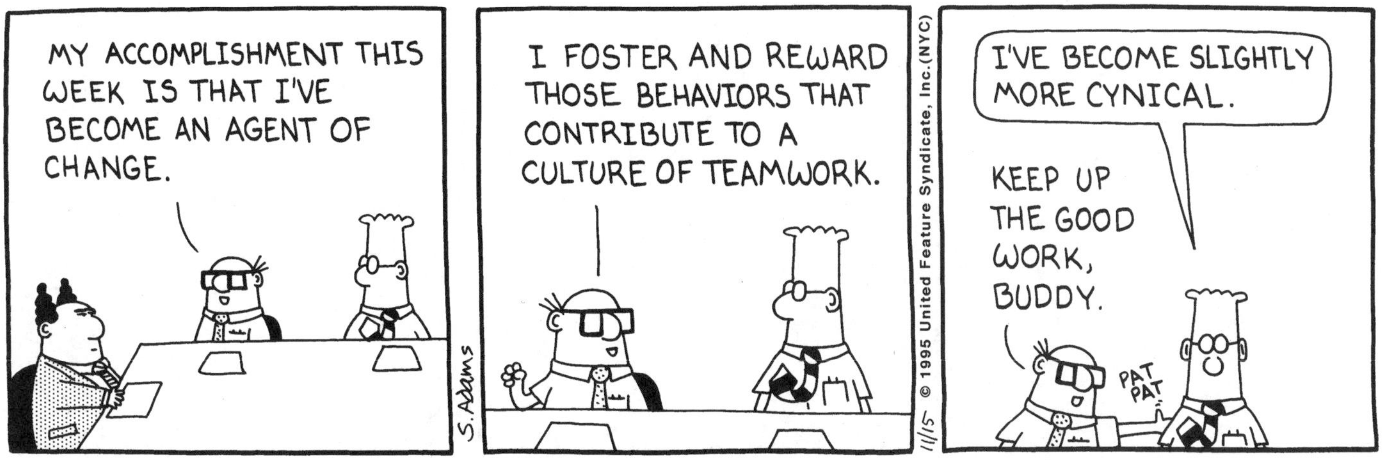
MY ACCOMPLISHMENT THIS WEEK IS THAT I'VE BECOME AN AGENT OF CHANGE.
I FOSTER AND REWARD THOSE BEHAVIORS THAT CONTRIBUTE TO A CULTURE OF TEAMWORK.
I'VE BECOME SLIGHTLY MORE CYNICAL.
KEEP UP THE GOOD WORK, BUDDY.
PAT PAT
S. Adams
11/15 © 1995 United Feature Syndicate, Inc. (NYC)

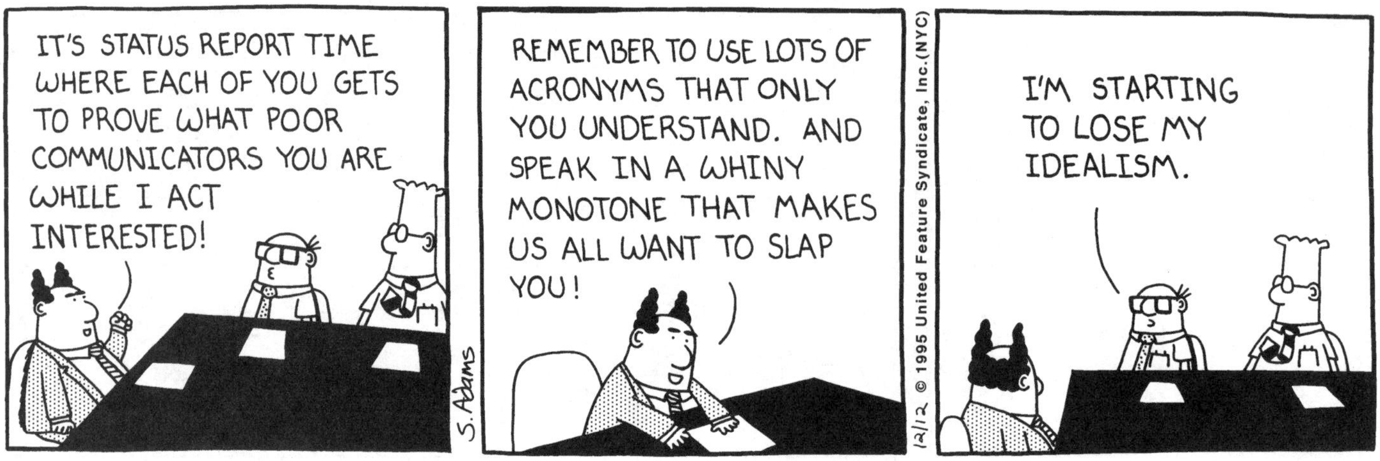
IT'S STATUS REPORT TIME WHERE EACH OF YOU GETS TO PROVE WHAT POOR COMMUNICATORS YOU ARE WHILE I ACT INTERESTED!
S. Adams
REMEMBER TO USE LOTS OF ACRONYMS THAT ONLY YOU UNDERSTAND. AND SPEAK IN A WHINY MONOTONE THAT MAKES US ALL WANT TO SLAP YOU!
12/12 © 1995 United Feature Syndicate, Inc.(NYC)
I'M STARTING TO LOSE MY IDEALISM.

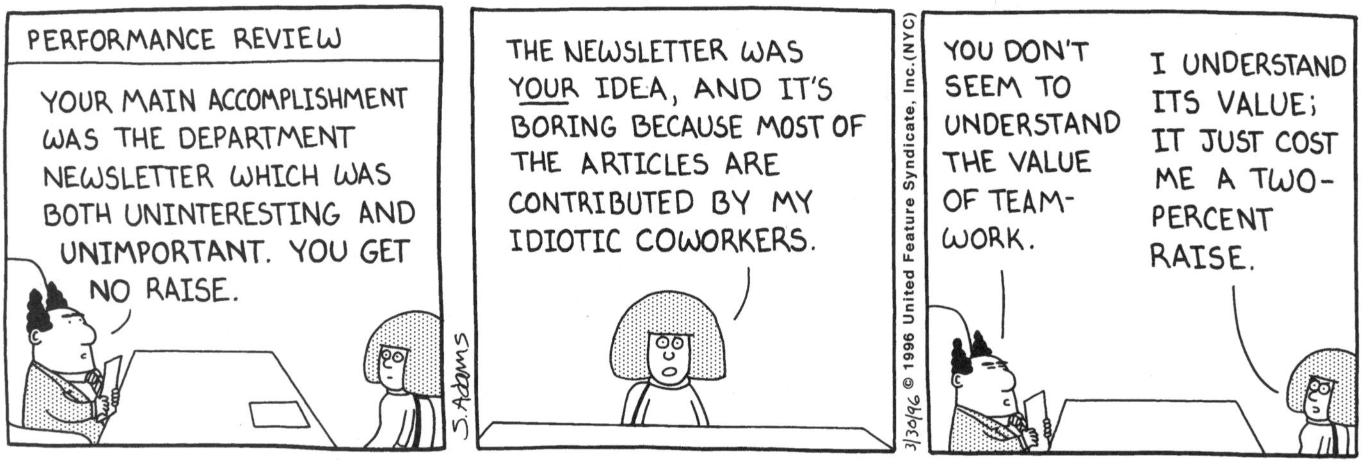
PERFORMANCE REVIEW
YOUR MAIN ACCOMPLISHMENT WAS THE DEPARTMENT NEWSLETTER WHICH WAS BOTH UNINTERESTING AND UNIMPORTANT. YOU GET NO RAISE.
S. Adams
THE NEWSLETTER WAS YOUR IDEA, AND IT'S BORING BECAUSE MOST OF THE ARTICLES ARE CONTRIBUTED BY MY IDIOTIC COWORKERS.
3/30/96 © 1996 United Feature Syndicate, Inc.(NYC)
YOU DON'T SEEM TO UNDERSTAND THE VALUE OF TEAM-WORK.
I UNDERSTAND ITS VALUE; IT JUST COST ME A TWO-PERCENT RAISE.

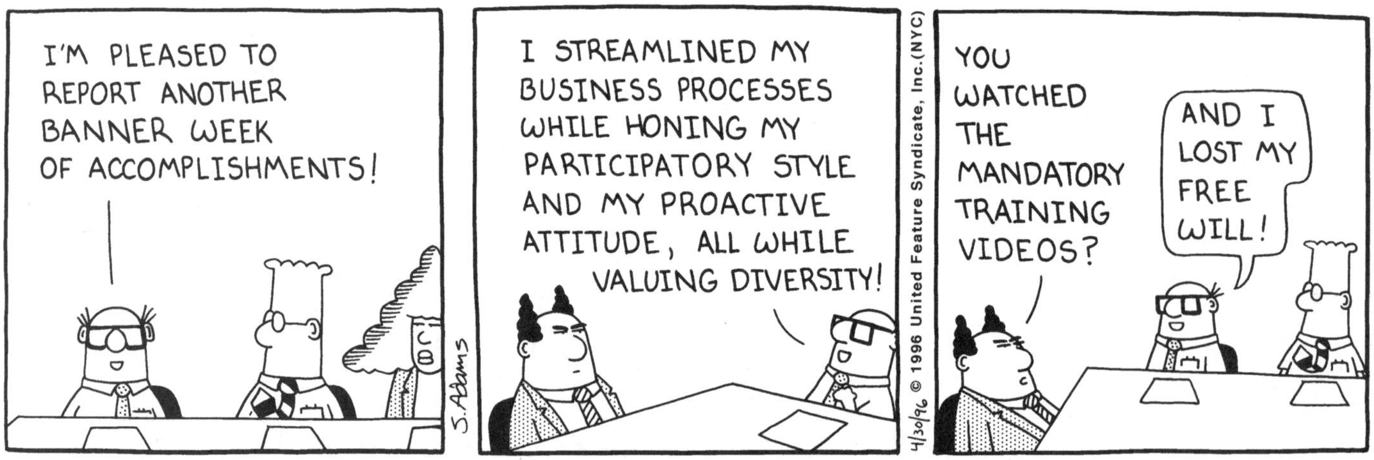
I'M PLEASED TO REPORT ANOTHER BANNER WEEK OF ACCOMPLISHMENTS!
S. Adams
I STREAMLINED MY BUSINESS PROCESSES WHILE HONING MY PARTICIPATORY STYLE AND MY PROACTIVE ATTITUDE, ALL WHILE VALUING DIVERSITY!
4/30/96 © 1996 United Feature Syndicate, Inc.(NYC)
YOU WATCHED THE MANDATORY TRAINING VIDEOS?
AND I LOST MY FREE WILL!

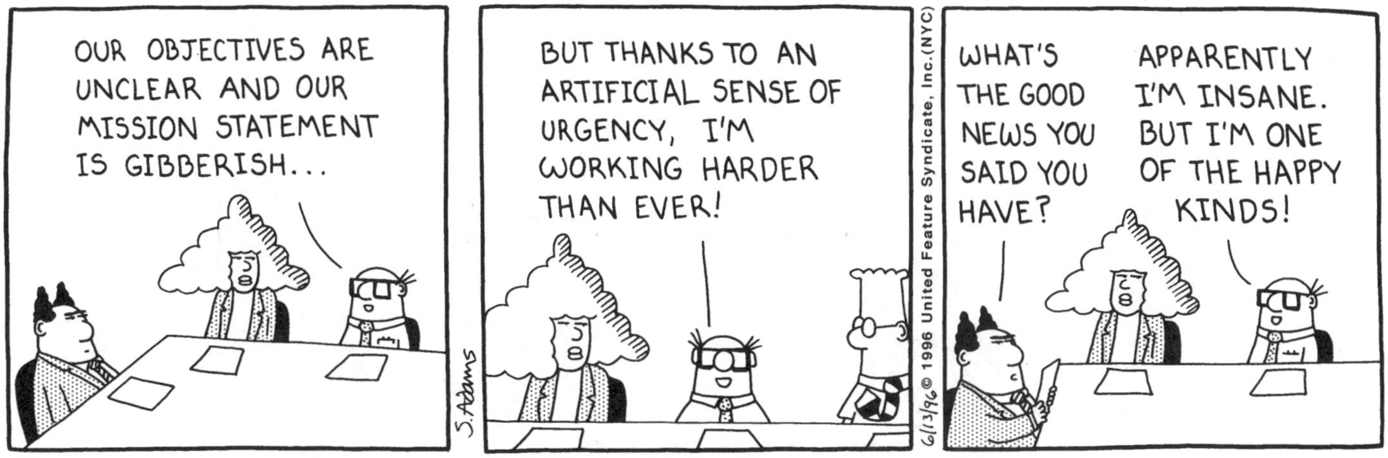
OUR OBJECTIVES ARE UNCLEAR AND OUR MISSION STATEMENT IS GIBBERISH...
S. Adams
BUT THANKS TO AN ARTIFICIAL SENSE OF URGENCY, I'M WORKING HARDER THAN EVER!
6/3/96 © 1996 United Feature Syndicate, Inc.(NYC)
WHAT'S THE GOOD NEWS YOU SAID YOU HAVE?
APPARENTLY I'M INSANE. BUT I'M ONE OF THE HAPPY KINDS!

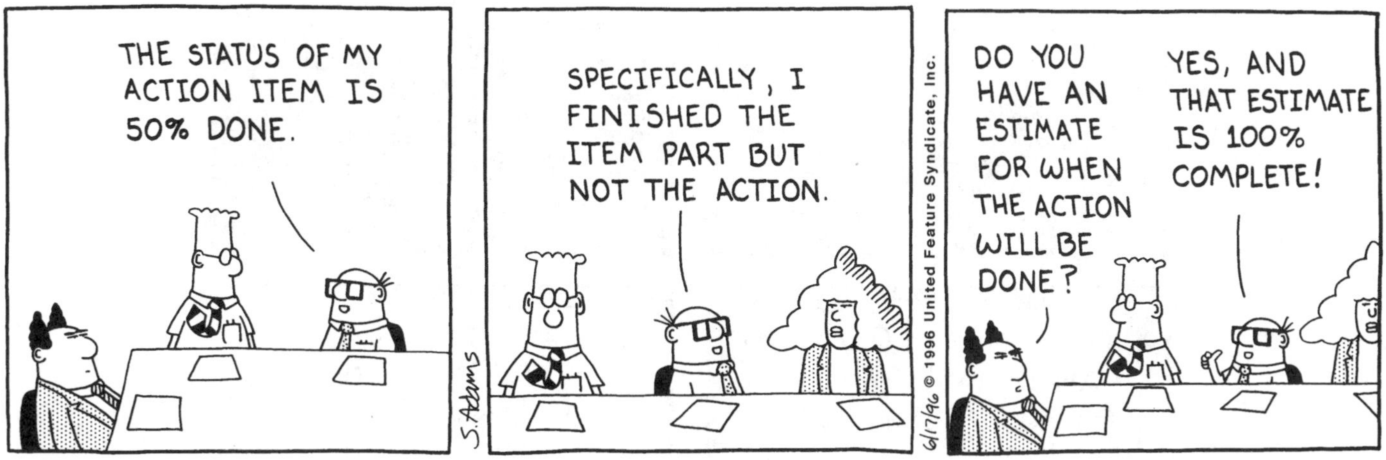
THE STATUS OF MY ACTION ITEM IS 50% DONE.
S. Adams
SPECIFICALLY, I FINISHED THE ITEM PART BUT NOT THE ACTION.
6/17/96 © 1996 United Feature Syndicate, Inc.
DO YOU HAVE AN ESTIMATE FOR WHEN THE ACTION WILL BE DONE?
YES, AND THAT ESTIMATE IS 100% COMPLETE!

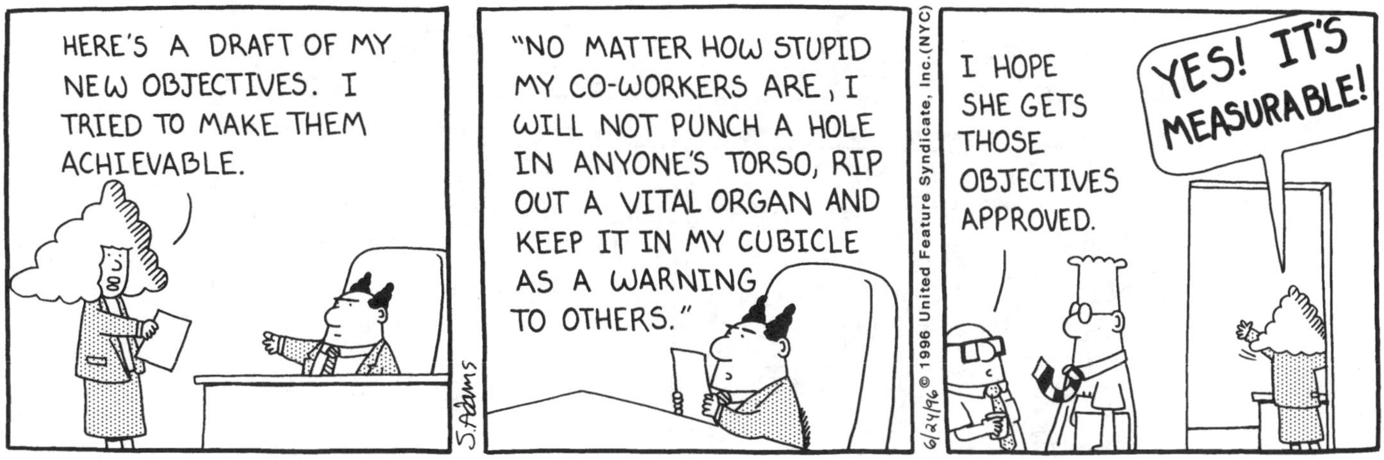
HERE'S A DRAFT OF MY NEW OBJECTIVES. I TRIED TO MAKE THEM ACHIEVABLE.
S. Adams
"NO MATTER HOW STUPID MY CO-WORKERS ARE, I WILL NOT PUNCH A HOLE IN ANYONE'S TORSO, RIP OUT A VITAL ORGAN AND KEEP IT IN MY CUBICLE AS A WARNING TO OTHERS."
6/24/96 © 1996 United Feature Syndicate, Inc.(NYC)
I HOPE SHE GETS THOSE OBJECTIVES APPROVED.
YES! IT'S MEASURABLE!

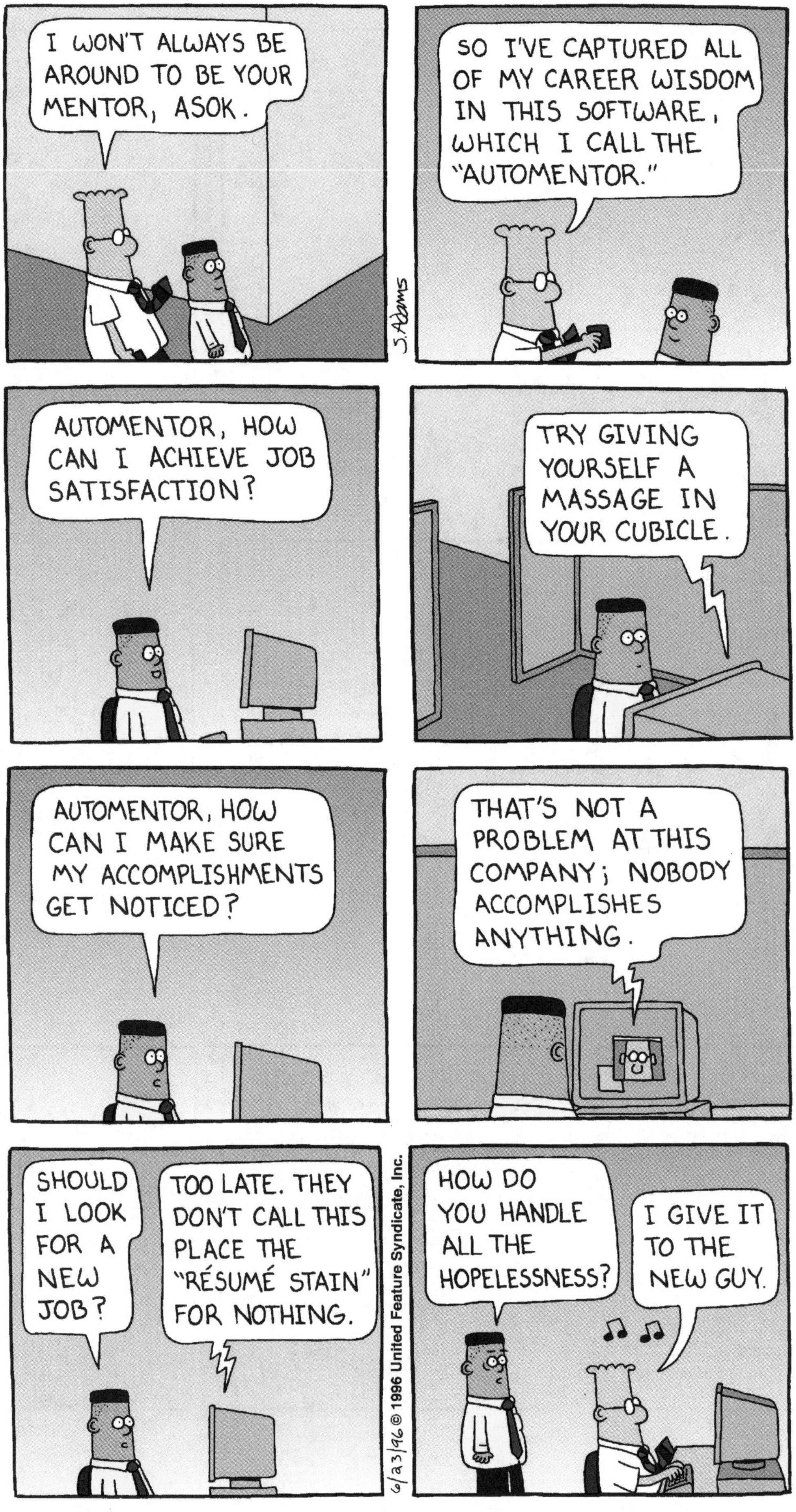
I WON'T ALWAYS BE AROUND TO BE YOUR MENTOR, ASOK.
SO I'VE CAPTURED ALL OF MY CAREER WISDOM IN THIS SOFTWARE, WHICH I CALL THE "AUTOMENTOR."
S. Adams
AUTOMENTOR, HOW CAN I ACHIEVE JOB SATISFACTION?
TRY GIVING YOURSELF A MASSAGE IN YOUR CUBICLE.
AUTOMENTOR, HOW CAN I MAKE SURE MY ACCOMPLISHMENTS GET NOTICED?
THAT'S NOT A PROBLEM AT THIS COMPANY; NOBODY ACCOMPLISHES ANYTHING.
SHOULD I LOOK FOR A NEW JOB?
TOO LATE. THEY DON'T CALL THIS PLACE THE "RÉSUMÉ STAIN" FOR NOTHING.
6/23/96 © 1996 United Feature Syndicate, Inc.
HOW DO YOU HANDLE ALL THE HOPELESSNESS?
I GIVE IT TO THE NEW GUY.

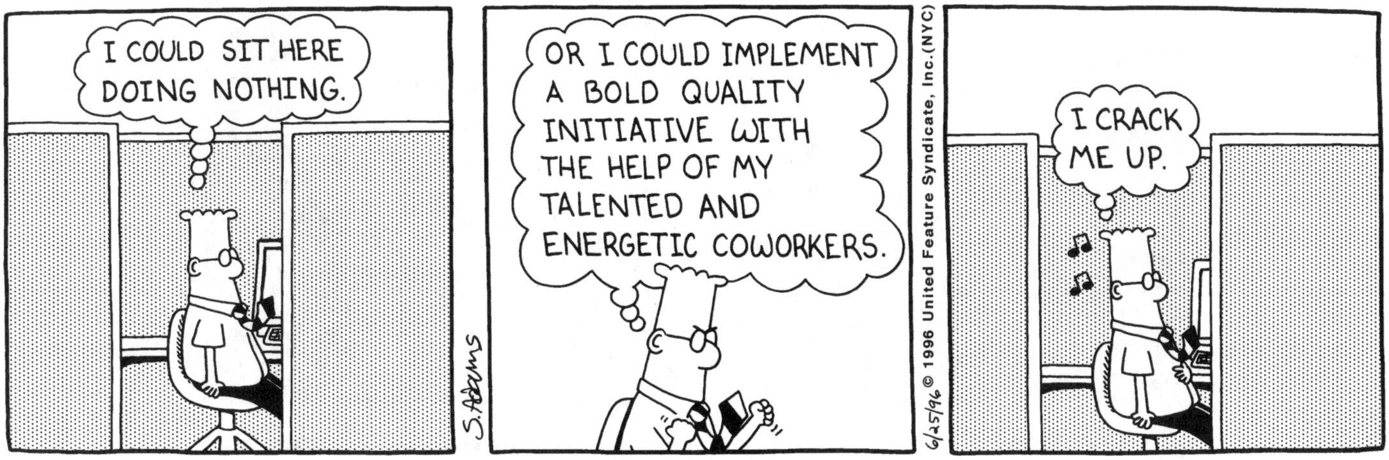
I COULD SIT HERE DOING NOTHING.
OR I COULD IMPLEMENT A BOLD QUALITY INITIATIVE WITH THE HELP OF MY TALENTED AND ENERGETIC COWORKERS.
I CRACK ME UP.
6/25/96 © 1996 United Feature Syndicate, Inc.(NYC)

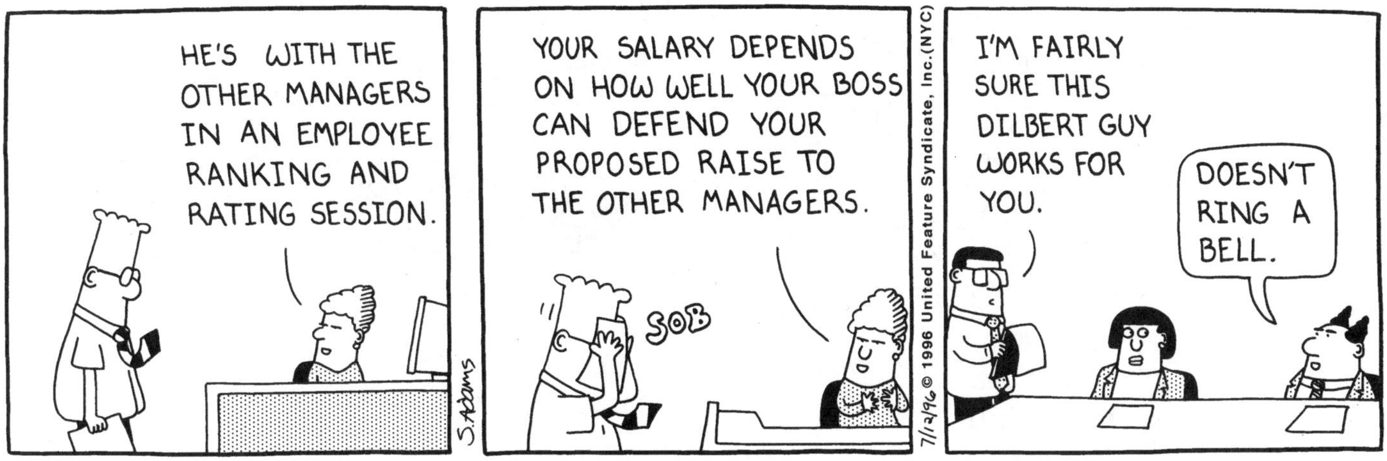
HE'S WITH THE OTHER MANAGERS IN AN EMPLOYEE RANKING AND RATING SESSION.
YOUR SALARY DEPENDS ON HOW WELL YOUR BOSS CAN DEFEND YOUR PROPOSED RAISE TO THE OTHER MANAGERS.
SOB
I'M FAIRLY SURE THIS DILBERT GUY WORKS FOR YOU.
DOESN'T RING A BELL.
7/1/96 © 1996 United Feature Syndicate, Inc.(NYC)

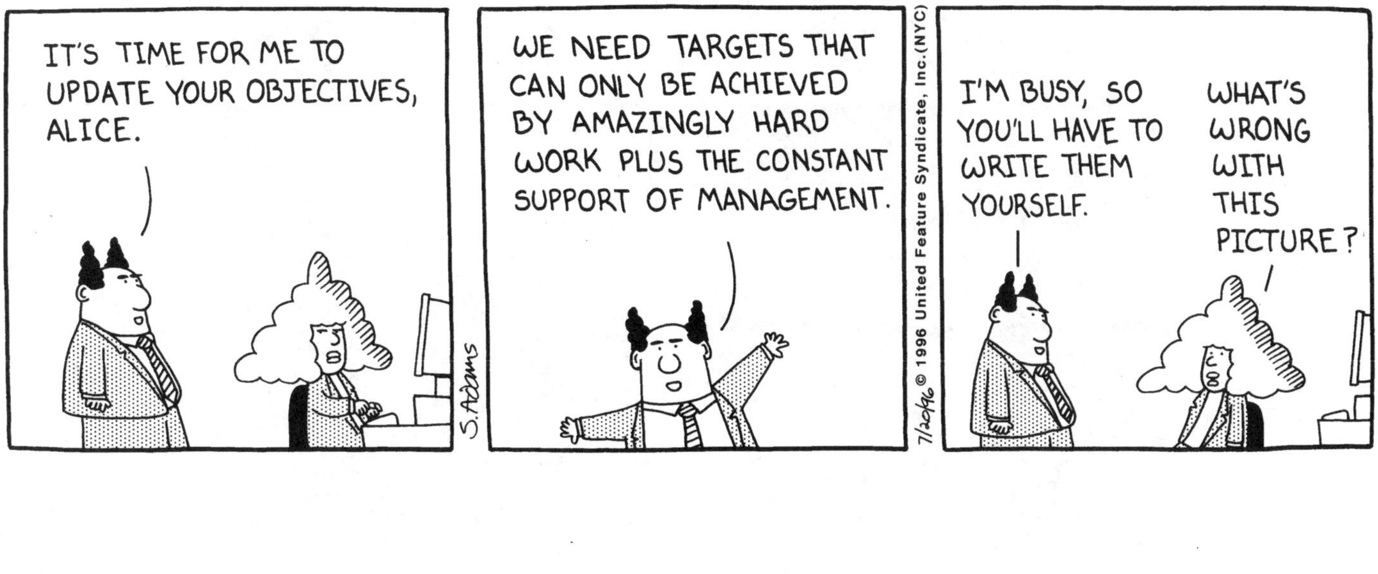
IT'S TIME FOR ME TO UPDATE YOUR OBJECTIVES, ALICE.
WE NEED TARGETS THAT CAN ONLY BE ACHIEVED BY AMAZINGLY HARD WORK PLUS THE CONSTANT SUPPORT OF MANAGEMENT.
I'M BUSY, SO YOU'LL HAVE TO WRITE THEM YOURSELF.
WHAT'S WRONG WITH THIS PICTURE?
7/20/96 © 1996 United Feature Syndicate, Inc.(NYC)

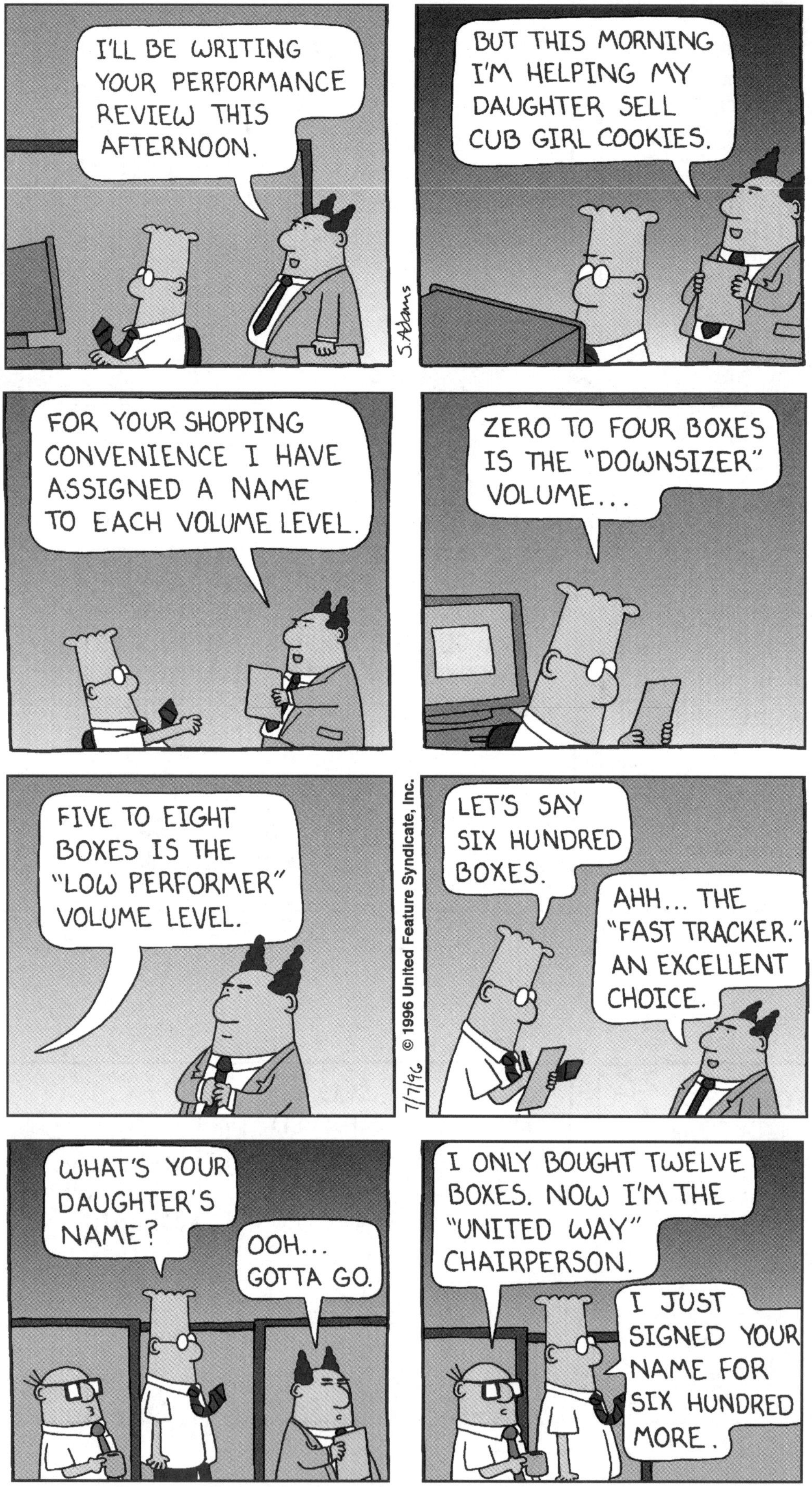
I'LL BE WRITING YOUR PERFORMANCE REVIEW THIS AFTERNOON.
S. Adams
BUT THIS MORNING I'M HELPING MY DAUGHTER SELL CUB GIRL COOKIES.
FOR YOUR SHOPPING CONVENIENCE I HAVE ASSIGNED A NAME TO EACH VOLUME LEVEL.
ZERO TO FOUR BOXES IS THE "DOWNSIZER" VOLUME...
FIVE TO EIGHT BOXES IS THE "LOW PERFORMER" VOLUME LEVEL.
7/7/96
© 1996 United Feature Syndicate, Inc.
LET'S SAY SIX HUNDRED BOXES.
AHH... THE "FAST TRACKER." AN EXCELLENT CHOICE.
WHAT'S YOUR DAUGHTER'S NAME?
OOH... GOTTA GO.
I ONLY BOUGHT TWELVE BOXES. NOW I'M THE "UNITED WAY" CHAIRPERSON.
I JUST SIGNED YOUR NAME FOR SIX HUNDRED MORE.

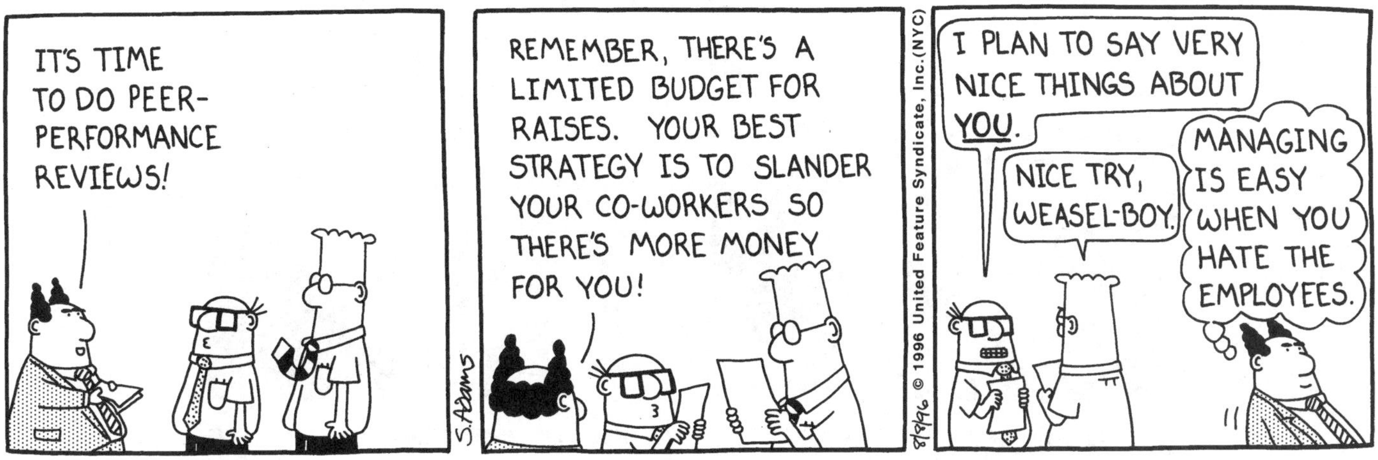
IT'S TIME TO DO PEER-PERFORMANCE REVIEWS!
REMEMBER, THERE'S A LIMITED BUDGET FOR RAISES. YOUR BEST STRATEGY IS TO SLANDER YOUR CO-WORKERS SO THERE'S MORE MONEY FOR YOU!
S. Adams
8/9/96 © 1996 United Feature Syndicate, Inc.(NYC)
I PLAN TO SAY VERY NICE THINGS ABOUT YOU.
NICE TRY, WEASEL-BOY.
MANAGING IS EASY WHEN YOU HATE THE EMPLOYEES.

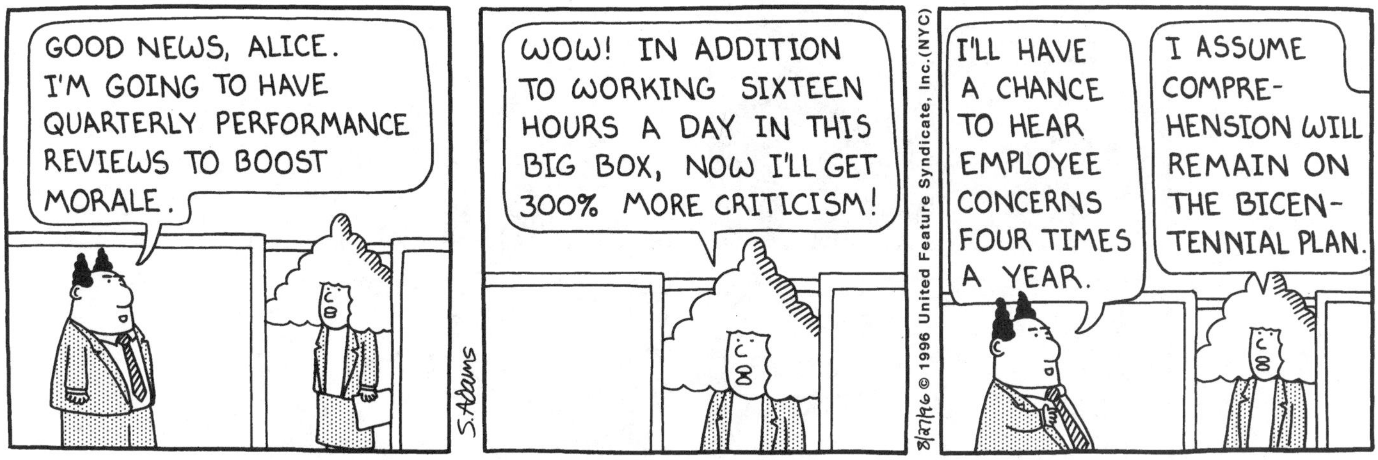
GOOD NEWS, ALICE. I'M GOING TO HAVE QUARTERLY PERFORMANCE REVIEWS TO BOOST MORALE.
S. Adams
WOW! IN ADDITION TO WORKING SIXTEEN HOURS A DAY IN THIS BIG BOX, NOW I'LL GET 300% MORE CRITICISM!
8/27/96 © 1996 United Feature Syndicate, Inc.(NYC)
I'LL HAVE A CHANCE TO HEAR EMPLOYEE CONCERNS FOUR TIMES A YEAR.
I ASSUME COMPRE-HENSION WILL REMAIN ON THE BICEN-TENNIAL PLAN.

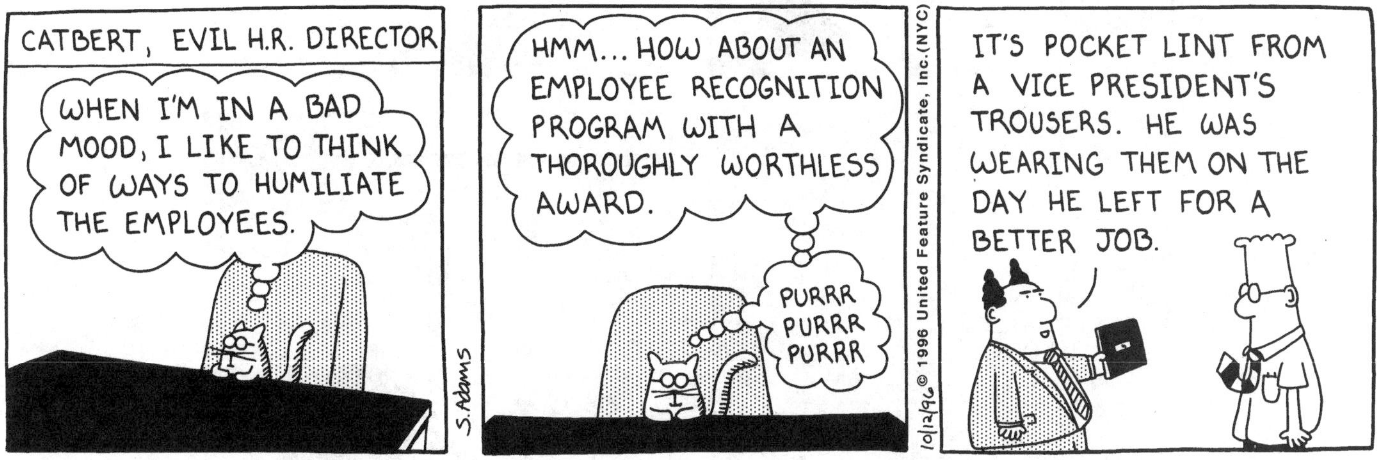
CATBERT, EVIL H.R. DIRECTOR
WHEN I'M IN A BAD MOOD, I LIKE TO THINK OF WAYS TO HUMILIATE THE EMPLOYEES.
S. Adams
HMM... HOW ABOUT AN EMPLOYEE RECOGNITION PROGRAM WITH A THOROUGHLY WORTHLESS AWARD.
PURRR PURRR PURRR
10/12/96 © 1996 United Feature Syndicate, Inc.(NYC)
IT'S POCKET LINT FROM A VICE PRESIDENT'S TROUSERS. HE WAS WEARING THEM ON THE DAY HE LEFT FOR A BETTER JOB.

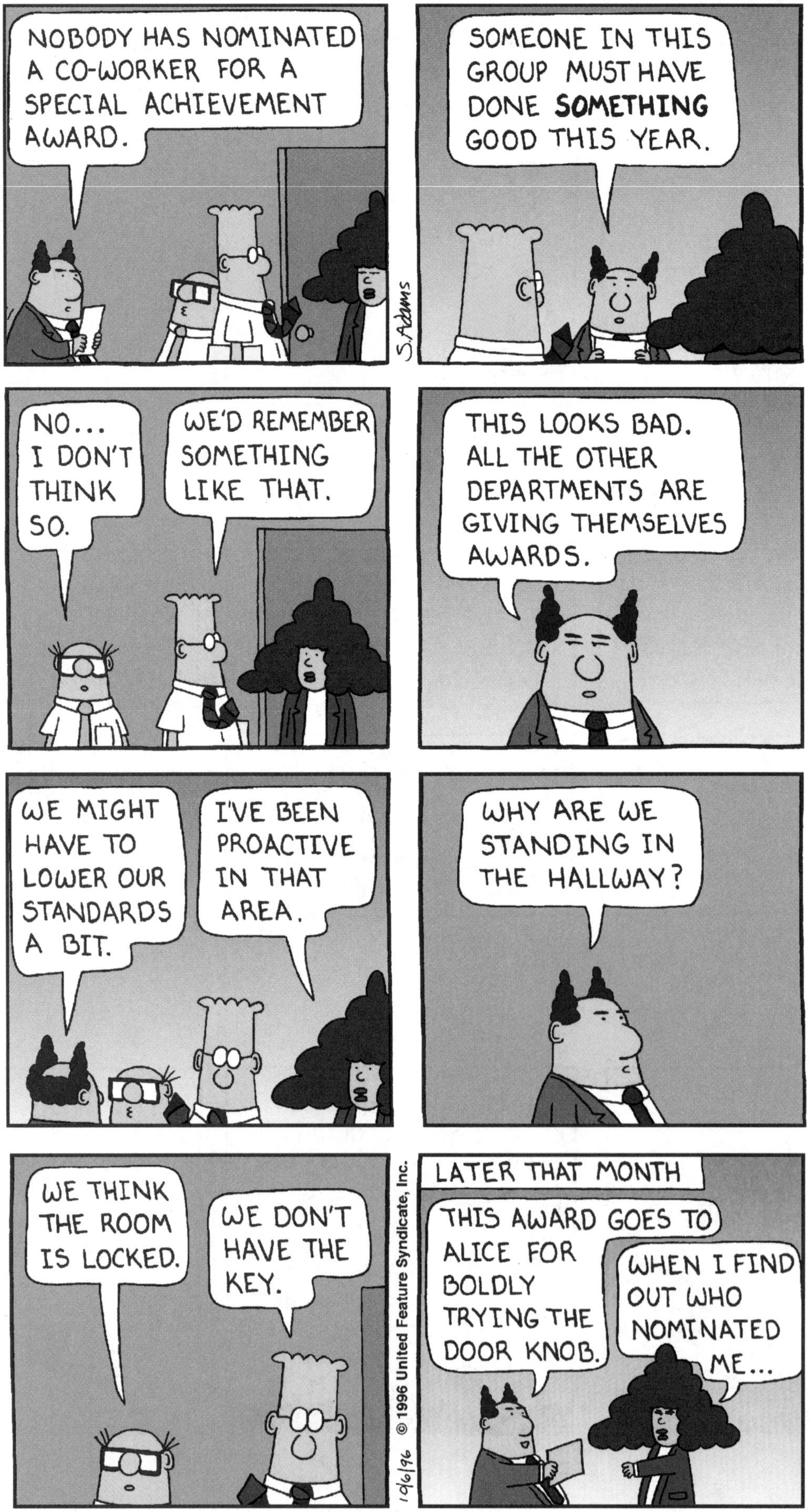
NOBODY HAS NOMINATED A CO-WORKER FOR A SPECIAL ACHIEVEMENT AWARD.
S. Adams
SOMEONE IN THIS GROUP MUST HAVE DONE **SOMETHING** GOOD THIS YEAR.
NO... I DON'T THINK SO.
WE'D REMEMBER SOMETHING LIKE THAT.
THIS LOOKS BAD. ALL THE OTHER DEPARTMENTS ARE GIVING THEMSELVES AWARDS.
WE MIGHT HAVE TO LOWER OUR STANDARDS A BIT.
I'VE BEEN PROACTIVE IN THAT AREA.
WHY ARE WE STANDING IN THE HALLWAY?
WE THINK THE ROOM IS LOCKED.
WE DON'T HAVE THE KEY.
© 1996 United Feature Syndicate, Inc.
10/6/96
LATER THAT MONTH
THIS AWARD GOES TO ALICE FOR BOLDLY TRYING THE DOOR KNOB.
WHEN I FIND OUT WHO NOMINATED ME...

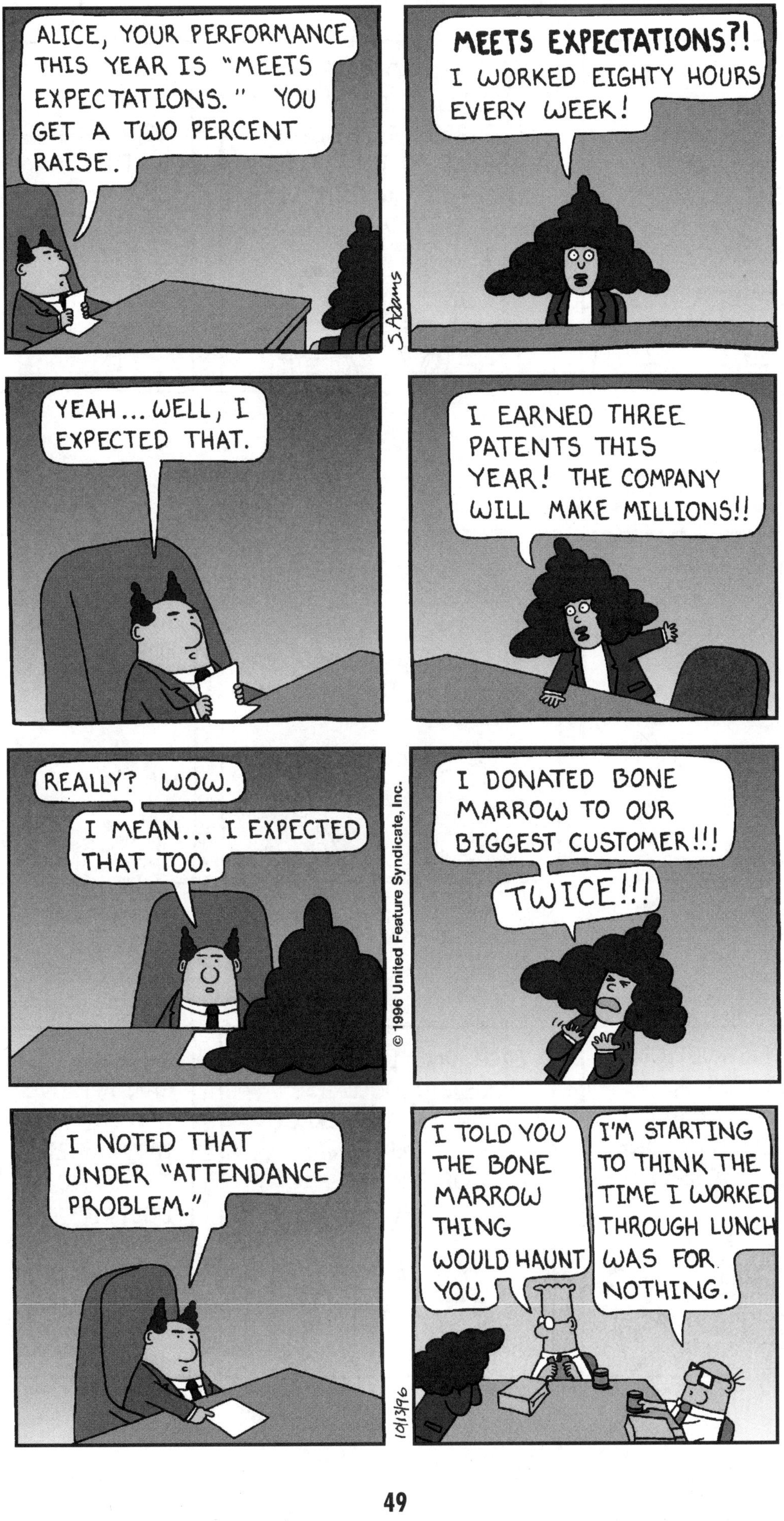
ALICE, YOUR PERFORMANCE THIS YEAR IS "MEETS EXPECTATIONS." YOU GET A TWO PERCENT RAISE.
S. Adams
MEETS EXPECTATIONS?! I WORKED EIGHTY HOURS EVERY WEEK!
YEAH... WELL, I EXPECTED THAT.
I EARNED THREE PATENTS THIS YEAR! THE COMPANY WILL MAKE MILLIONS!!
REALLY? WOW.
I MEAN... I EXPECTED THAT TOO.
© 1996 United Feature Syndicate, Inc.
I DONATED BONE MARROW TO OUR BIGGEST CUSTOMER!!!
TWICE!!!
I NOTED THAT UNDER "ATTENDANCE PROBLEM."
10/13/96
I TOLD YOU THE BONE MARROW THING WOULD HAUNT YOU.
I'M STARTING TO THINK THE TIME I WORKED THROUGH LUNCH WAS FOR NOTHING.

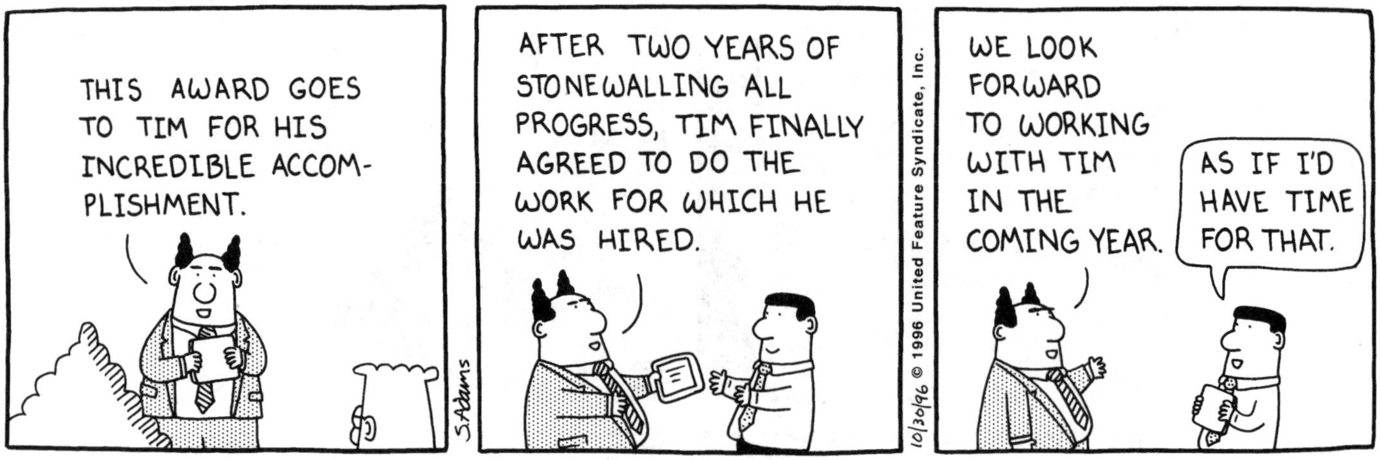
THIS AWARD GOES TO TIM FOR HIS INCREDIBLE ACCOM-PLISHMENT.
S.Adams
AFTER TWO YEARS OF STONEWALLING ALL PROGRESS, TIM FINALLY AGREED TO DO THE WORK FOR WHICH HE WAS HIRED.
10/30/96 © 1996 United Feature Syndicate, Inc.
WE LOOK FORWARD TO WORKING WITH TIM IN THE COMING YEAR.
AS IF I'D HAVE TIME FOR THAT.

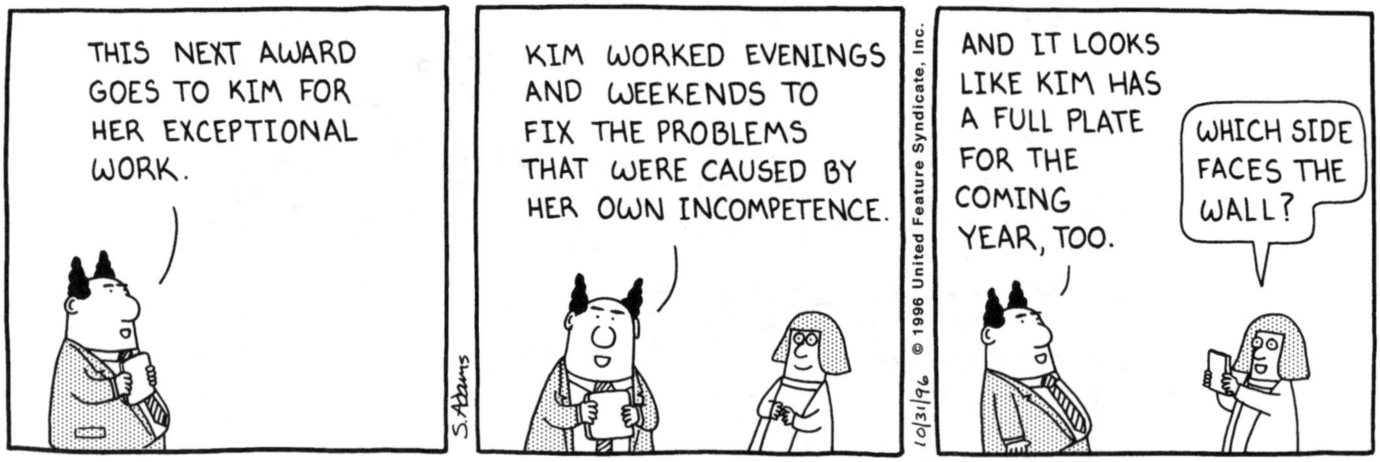
THIS NEXT AWARD GOES TO KIM FOR HER EXCEPTIONAL WORK.
S.Adams
KIM WORKED EVENINGS AND WEEKENDS TO FIX THE PROBLEMS THAT WERE CAUSED BY HER OWN INCOMPETENCE.
10/31/96 © 1996 United Feature Syndicate, Inc.
AND IT LOOKS LIKE KIM HAS A FULL PLATE FOR THE COMING YEAR, TOO.
WHICH SIDE FACES THE WALL?

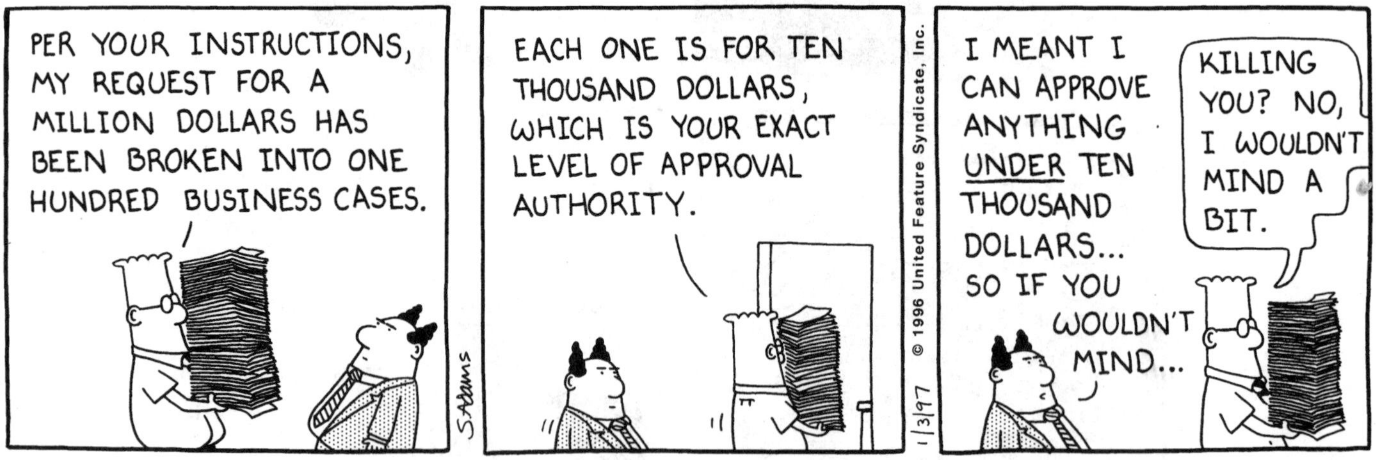
PER YOUR INSTRUCTIONS, MY REQUEST FOR A MILLION DOLLARS HAS BEEN BROKEN INTO ONE HUNDRED BUSINESS CASES.
S.Adams
EACH ONE IS FOR TEN THOUSAND DOLLARS, WHICH IS YOUR EXACT LEVEL OF APPROVAL AUTHORITY.
1/3/97 © 1996 United Feature Syndicate, Inc.
I MEANT I CAN APPROVE ANYTHING UNDER TEN THOUSAND DOLLARS... SO IF YOU WOULDN'T MIND...
KILLING YOU? NO, I WOULDN'T MIND A BIT.

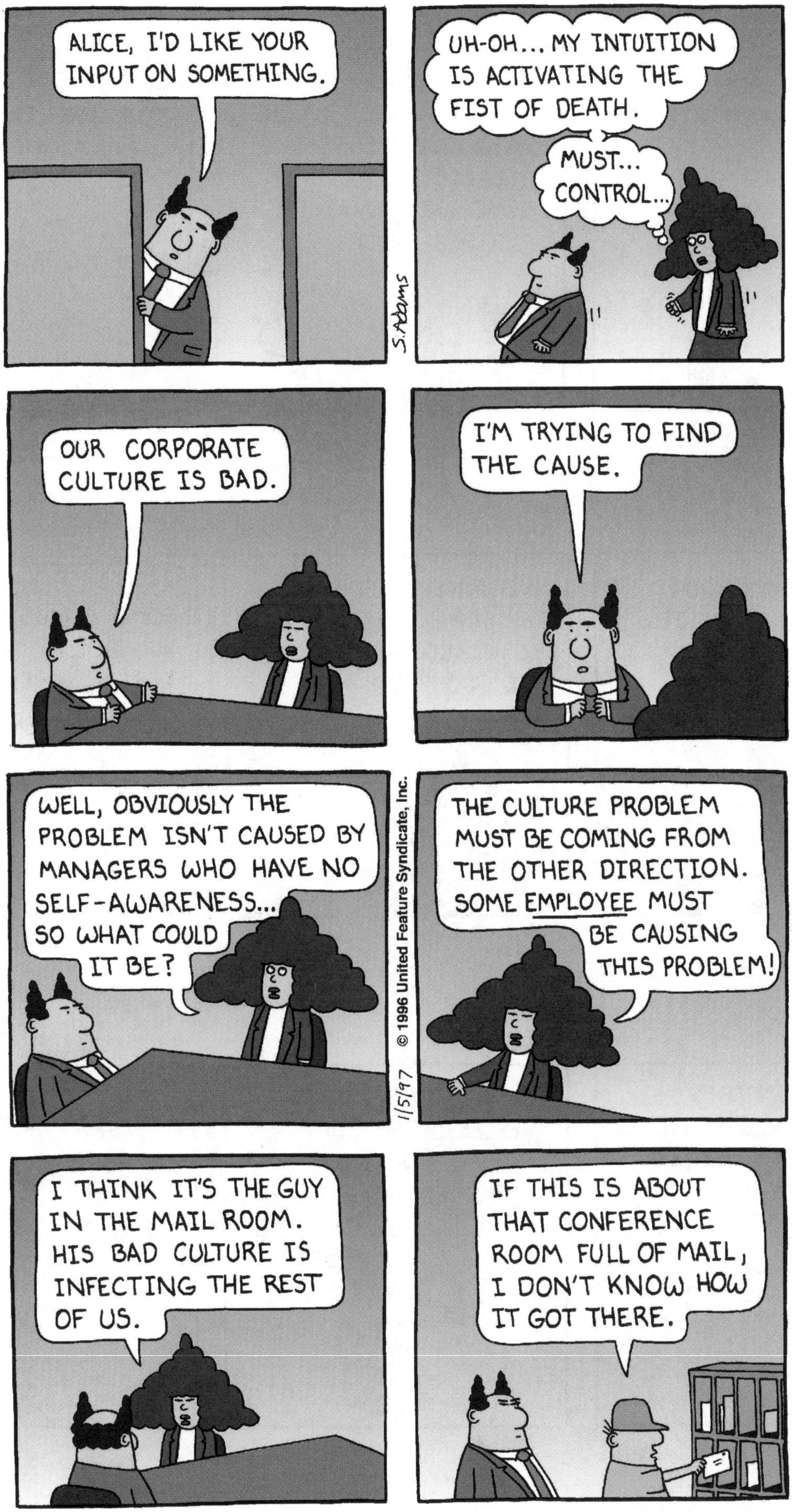
ALICE, I'D LIKE YOUR INPUT ON SOMETHING.
UH-OH... MY INTUITION IS ACTIVATING THE FIST OF DEATH.
MUST... CONTROL...
S. Adams
OUR CORPORATE CULTURE IS BAD.
I'M TRYING TO FIND THE CAUSE.
WELL, OBVIOUSLY THE PROBLEM ISN'T CAUSED BY MANAGERS WHO HAVE NO SELF-AWARENESS... SO WHAT COULD IT BE?
© 1996 United Feature Syndicate, Inc.
1/5/97
THE CULTURE PROBLEM MUST BE COMING FROM THE OTHER DIRECTION. SOME EMPLOYEE MUST BE CAUSING THIS PROBLEM!
I THINK IT'S THE GUY IN THE MAIL ROOM. HIS BAD CULTURE IS INFECTING THE REST OF US.
IF THIS IS ABOUT THAT CONFERENCE ROOM FULL OF MAIL, I DON'T KNOW HOW IT GOT THERE.

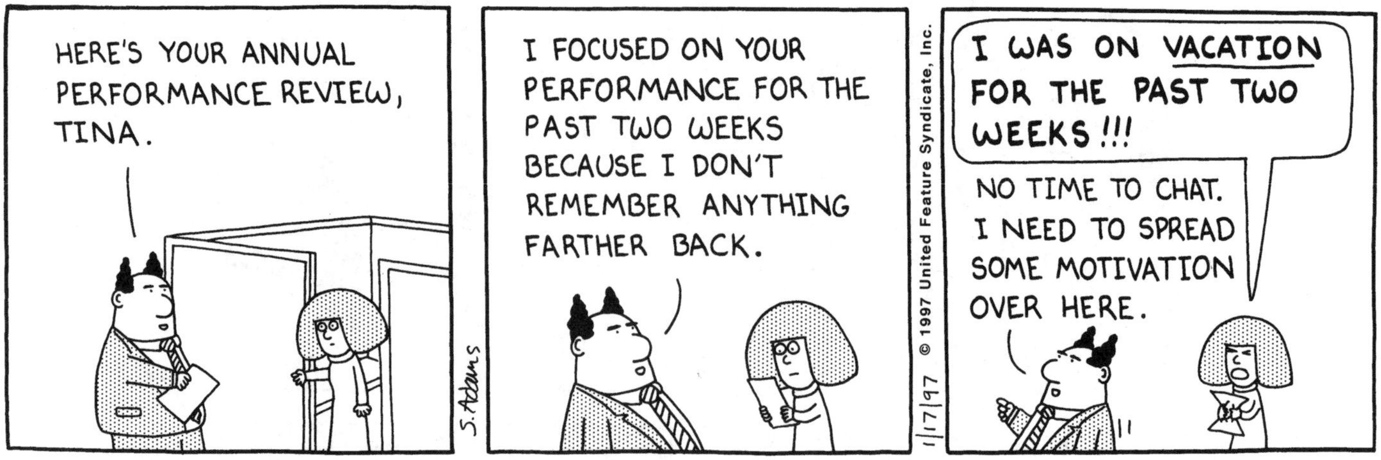
HERE'S YOUR ANNUAL PERFORMANCE REVIEW, TINA.
S. Adams
I FOCUSED ON YOUR PERFORMANCE FOR THE PAST TWO WEEKS BECAUSE I DON'T REMEMBER ANYTHING FARTHER BACK.
1/17/97 © 1997 United Feature Syndicate, Inc.
I WAS ON VACATION FOR THE PAST TWO WEEKS!!!
NO TIME TO CHAT. I NEED TO SPREAD SOME MOTIVATION OVER HERE.

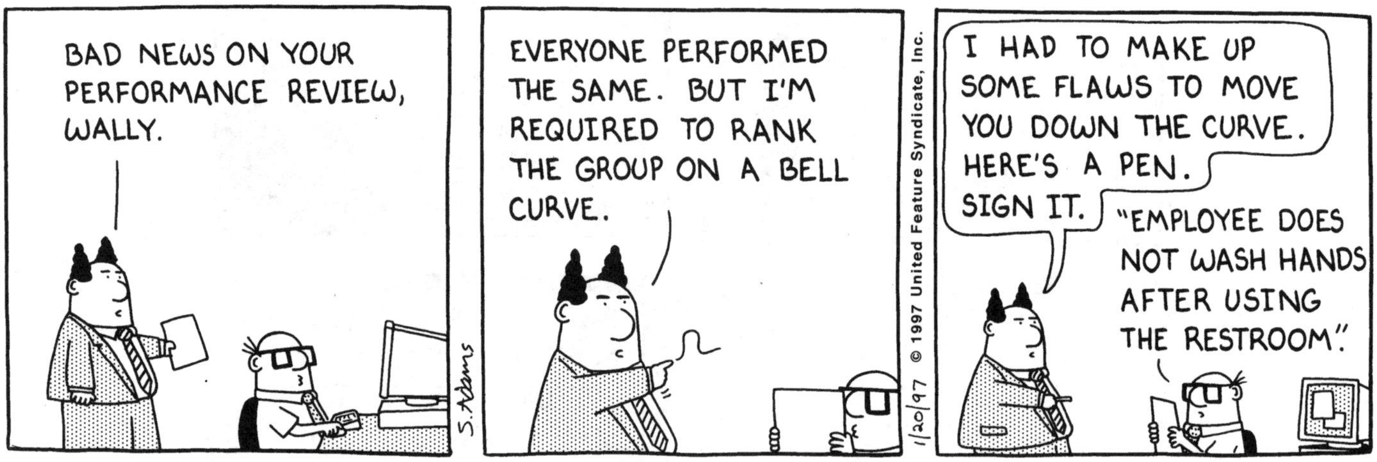
BAD NEWS ON YOUR PERFORMANCE REVIEW, WALLY.
S. Adams
EVERYONE PERFORMED THE SAME. BUT I'M REQUIRED TO RANK THE GROUP ON A BELL CURVE.
1/20/97 © 1997 United Feature Syndicate, Inc.
I HAD TO MAKE UP SOME FLAWS TO MOVE YOU DOWN THE CURVE. HERE'S A PEN. SIGN IT.
"EMPLOYEE DOES NOT WASH HANDS AFTER USING THE RESTROOM."

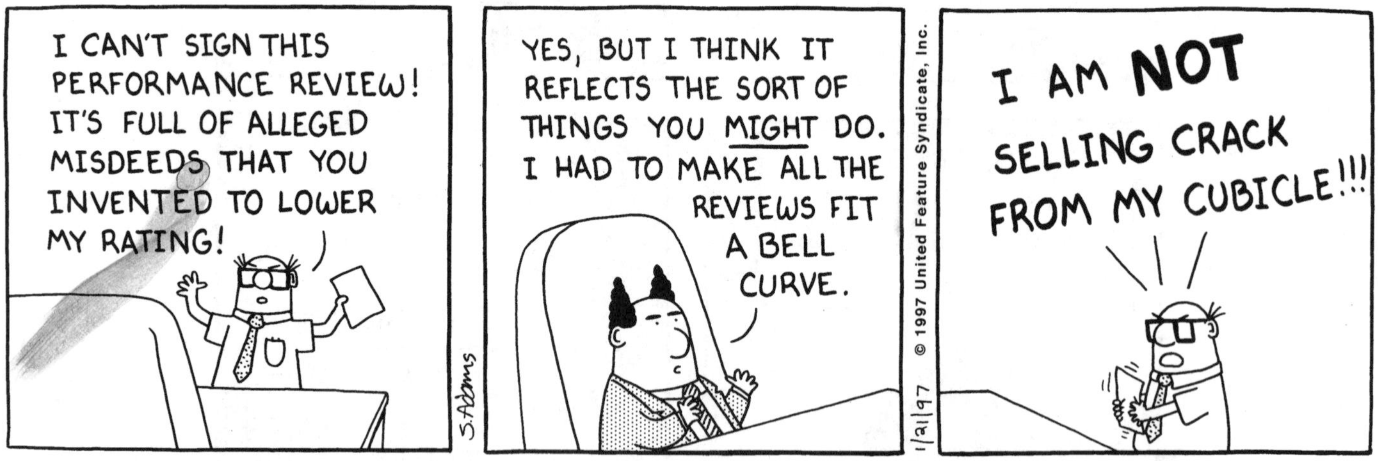
I CAN'T SIGN THIS PERFORMANCE REVIEW! IT'S FULL OF ALLEGED MISDEEDS THAT YOU INVENTED TO LOWER MY RATING!
S. Adams
YES, BUT I THINK IT REFLECTS THE SORT OF THINGS YOU MIGHT DO. I HAD TO MAKE ALL THE REVIEWS FIT A BELL CURVE.
1/21/97 © 1997 United Feature Syndicate, Inc.
I AM NOT SELLING CRACK FROM MY CUBICLE!!!

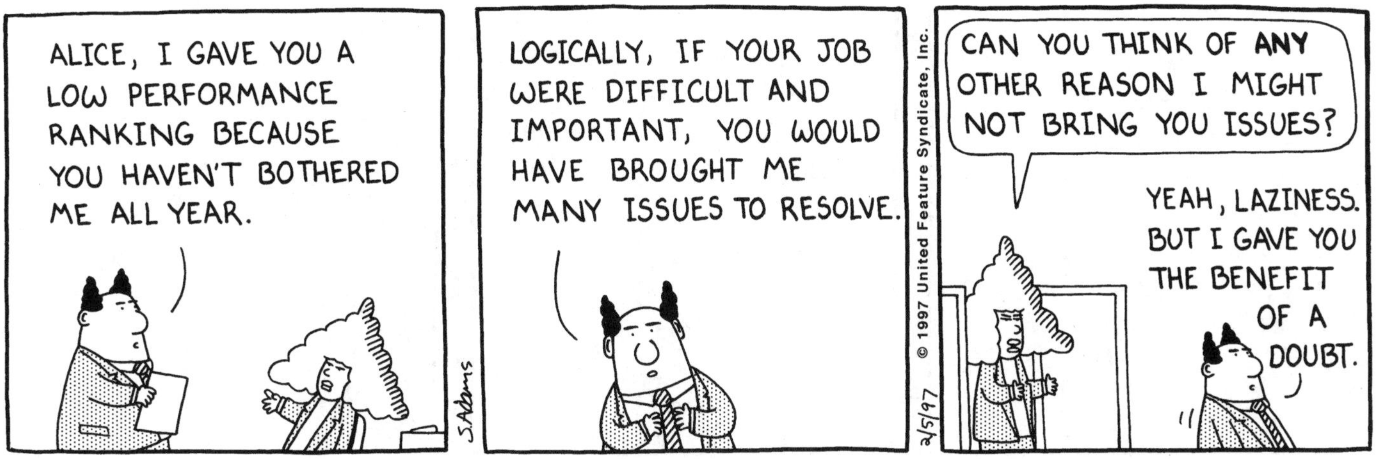
ALICE, I GAVE YOU A LOW PERFORMANCE RANKING BECAUSE YOU HAVEN'T BOTHERED ME ALL YEAR.
S. Adams
LOGICALLY, IF YOUR JOB WERE DIFFICULT AND IMPORTANT, YOU WOULD HAVE BROUGHT ME MANY ISSUES TO RESOLVE.
2/5/97
© 1997 United Feature Syndicate, Inc.
CAN YOU THINK OF **ANY** OTHER REASON I MIGHT NOT BRING YOU ISSUES?
YEAH, LAZINESS. BUT I GAVE YOU THE BENEFIT OF A DOUBT.

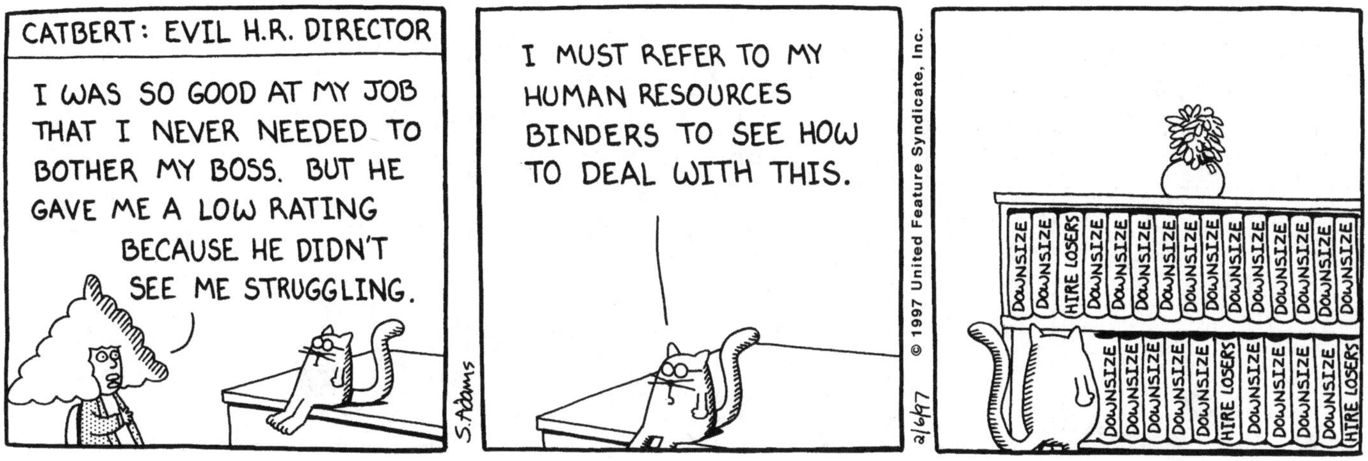
CATBERT: EVIL H.R. DIRECTOR
I WAS SO GOOD AT MY JOB THAT I NEVER NEEDED TO BOTHER MY BOSS. BUT HE GAVE ME A LOW RATING BECAUSE HE DIDN'T SEE ME STRUGGLING.
S. Adams
I MUST REFER TO MY HUMAN RESOURCES BINDERS TO SEE HOW TO DEAL WITH THIS.
2/6/97
© 1997 United Feature Syndicate, Inc.
DOWNSIZE
HIRE LOSERS

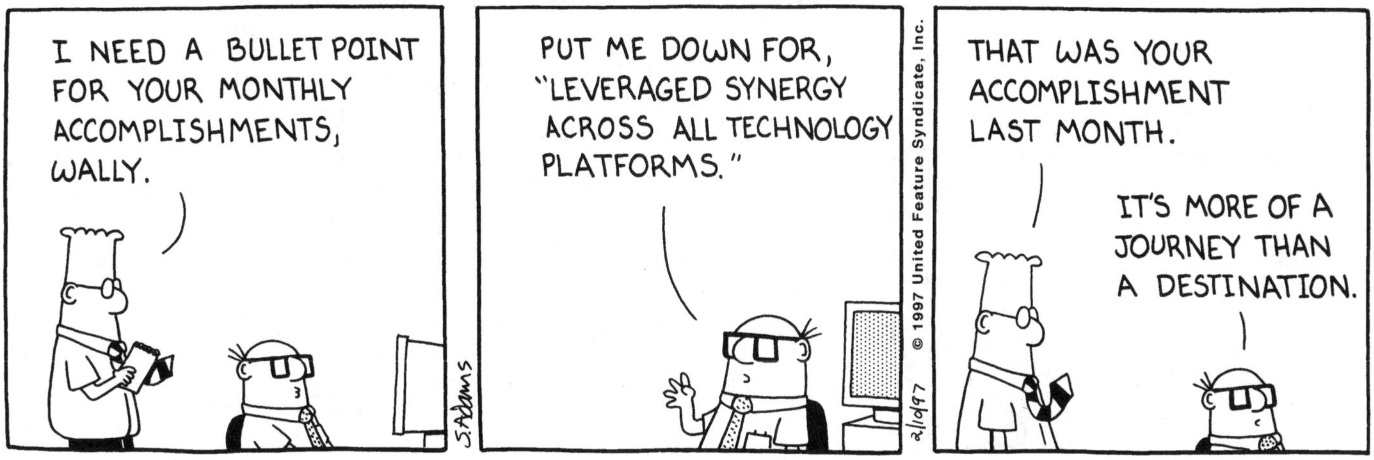
I NEED A BULLET POINT FOR YOUR MONTHLY ACCOMPLISHMENTS, WALLY.
S. Adams
PUT ME DOWN FOR, "LEVERAGED SYNERGY ACROSS ALL TECHNOLOGY PLATFORMS."
2/10/97
© 1997 United Feature Syndicate, Inc.
THAT WAS YOUR ACCOMPLISHMENT LAST MONTH.
IT'S MORE OF A JOURNEY THAN A DESTINATION.

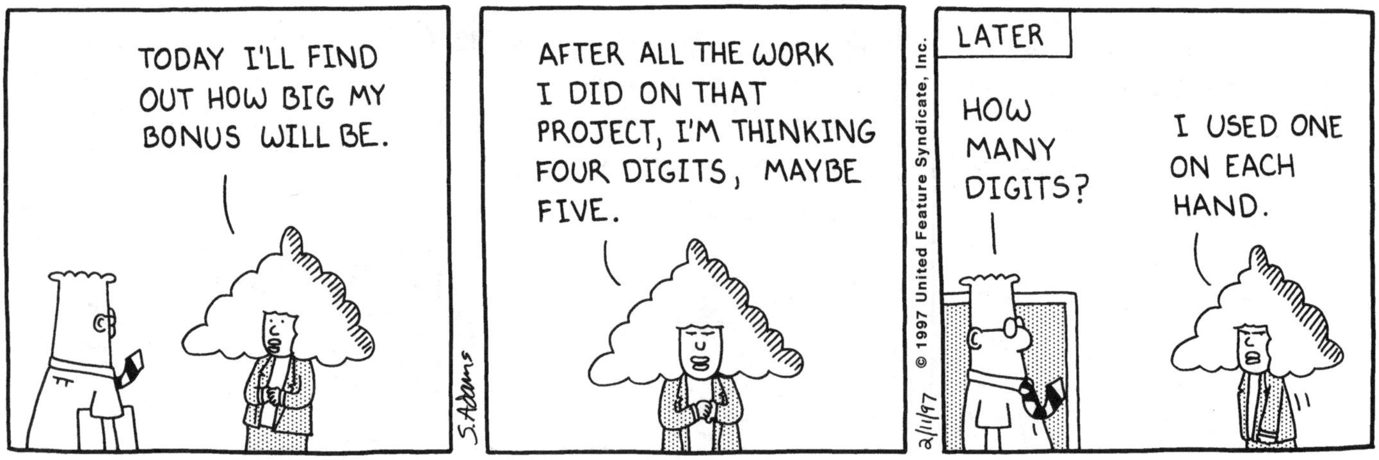
TODAY I'LL FIND OUT HOW BIG MY BONUS WILL BE.
AFTER ALL THE WORK I DID ON THAT PROJECT, I'M THINKING FOUR DIGITS, MAYBE FIVE.
LATER
HOW MANY DIGITS?
I USED ONE ON EACH HAND.
S. Adams
2/1/97
© 1997 United Feature Syndicate, Inc.

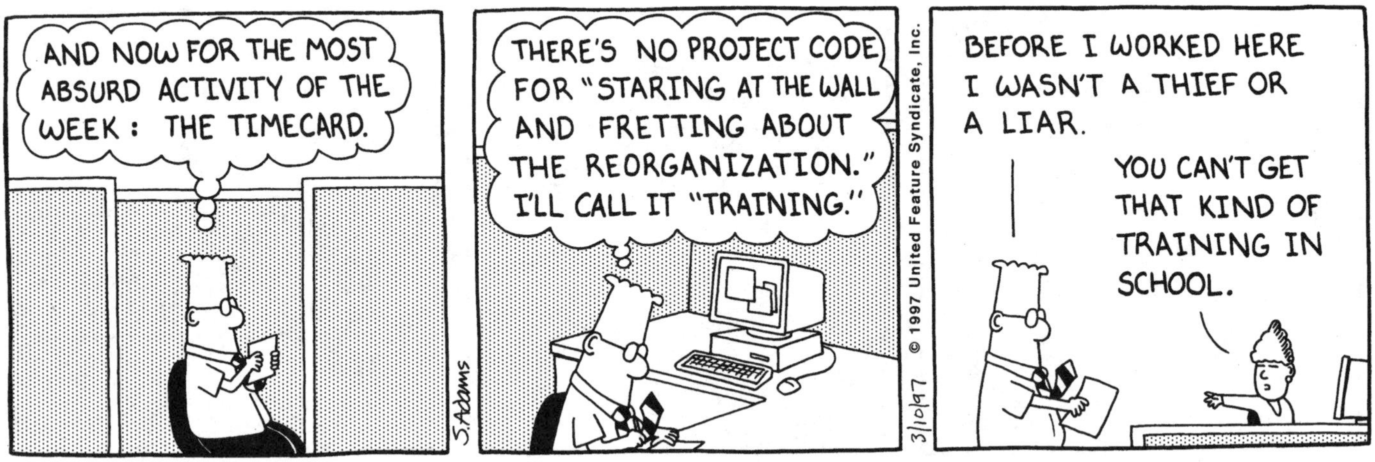
AND NOW FOR THE MOST ABSURD ACTIVITY OF THE WEEK: THE TIMECARD.
THERE'S NO PROJECT CODE FOR "STARING AT THE WALL AND FRETTING ABOUT THE REORGANIZATION." I'LL CALL IT "TRAINING."
BEFORE I WORKED HERE I WASN'T A THIEF OR A LIAR.
YOU CAN'T GET THAT KIND OF TRAINING IN SCHOOL.
S. Adams
3/10/97
© 1997 United Feature Syndicate, Inc.

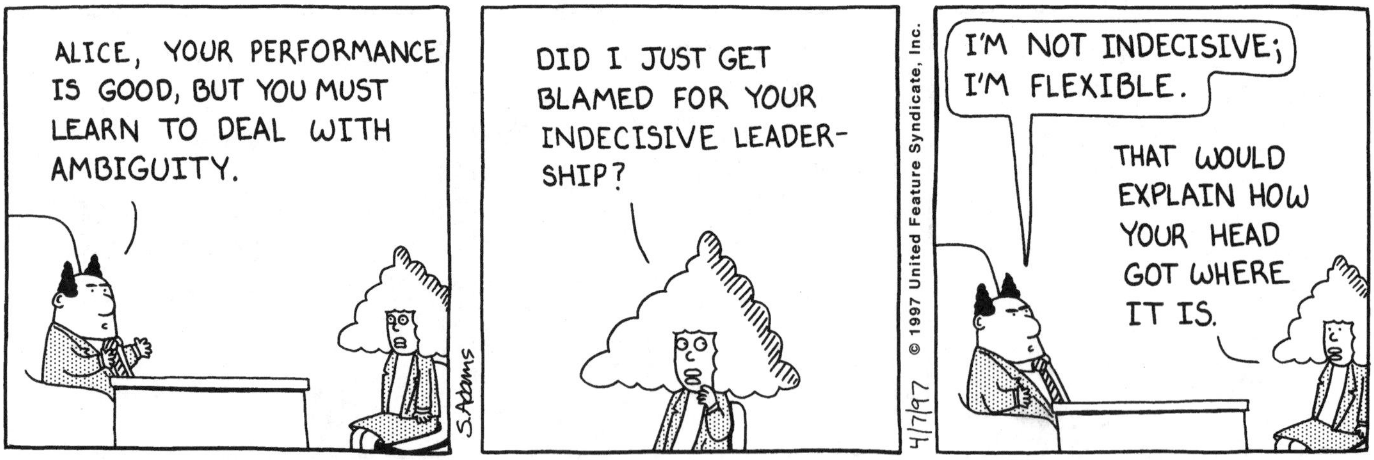
ALICE, YOUR PERFORMANCE IS GOOD, BUT YOU MUST LEARN TO DEAL WITH AMBIGUITY.
DID I JUST GET BLAMED FOR YOUR INDECISIVE LEADERSHIP?
I'M NOT INDECISIVE; I'M FLEXIBLE.
THAT WOULD EXPLAIN HOW YOUR HEAD GOT WHERE IT IS.
S. Adams
4/7/97
© 1997 United Feature Syndicate, Inc.

I DREAD THIS PART OF THE STAFF MEETING.

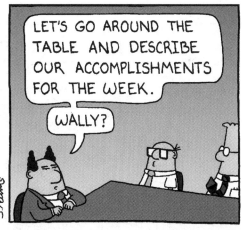
LET'S GO AROUND THE TABLE AND DESCRIBE OUR ACCOMPLISHMENTS FOR THE WEEK.

WALLY?

IT WAS ANOTHER WEEK OF AMAZING SUCCESS IN WALLYVILLE.

ON MONDAY I REALIZED MY LEFT BUN HAD FALLEN ASLEEP.

I WAS SHOCKED. THE "BOYS" HAD ALWAYS WORKED AS A TEAM BEFORE.

THINKING QUICKLY, I SHIFTED MY WEIGHT TO MY RIGHT BUN AND HOPED FOR THE BEST.

THAT'S YOUR LEFT SIDE, NOT YOUR RIGHT.

THAT'S THE OTHER THING; APPARENTLY THE BOYS SWITCHED SIDES SOMETIME DURING THE NIGHT.

2/23/97 © 1997 United Feature Syndicate, Inc.

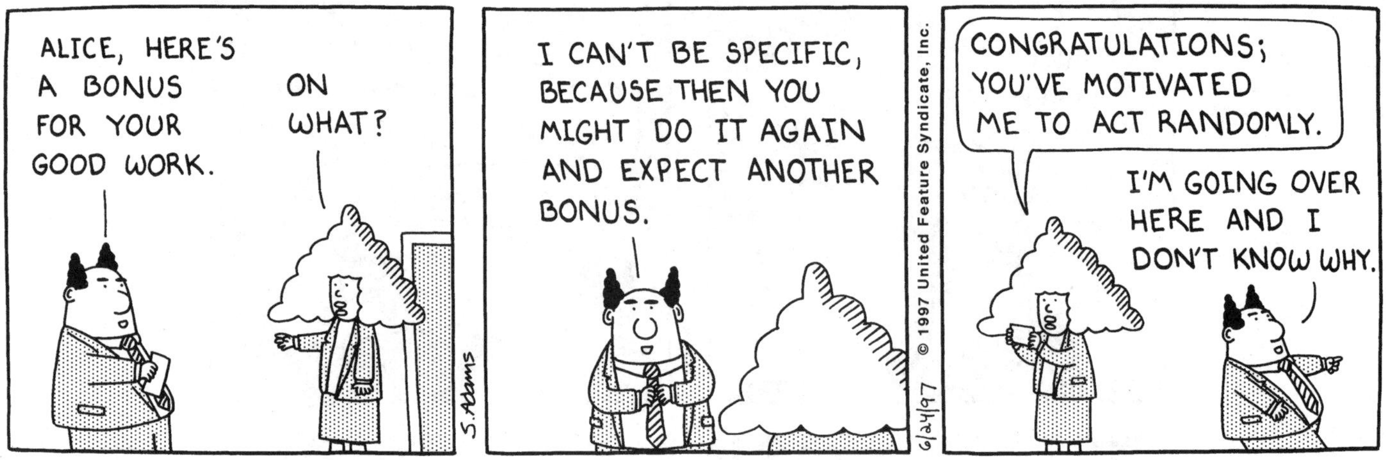
ALICE, HERE'S A BONUS FOR YOUR GOOD WORK.
ON WHAT?
S. Adams
I CAN'T BE SPECIFIC, BECAUSE THEN YOU MIGHT DO IT AGAIN AND EXPECT ANOTHER BONUS.
6/24/97 © 1997 United Feature Syndicate, Inc.
CONGRATULATIONS; YOU'VE MOTIVATED ME TO ACT RANDOMLY.
I'M GOING OVER HERE AND I DON'T KNOW WHY.

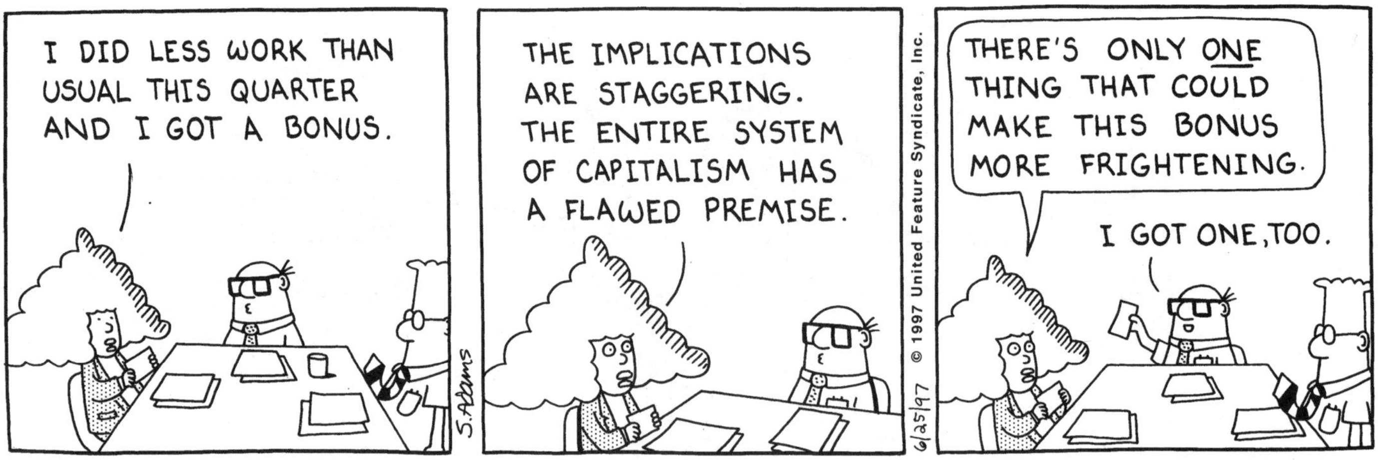
I DID LESS WORK THAN USUAL THIS QUARTER AND I GOT A BONUS.
S. Adams
THE IMPLICATIONS ARE STAGGERING. THE ENTIRE SYSTEM OF CAPITALISM HAS A FLAWED PREMISE.
6/25/97 © 1997 United Feature Syndicate, Inc.
THERE'S ONLY ONE THING THAT COULD MAKE THIS BONUS MORE FRIGHTENING.
I GOT ONE, TOO.

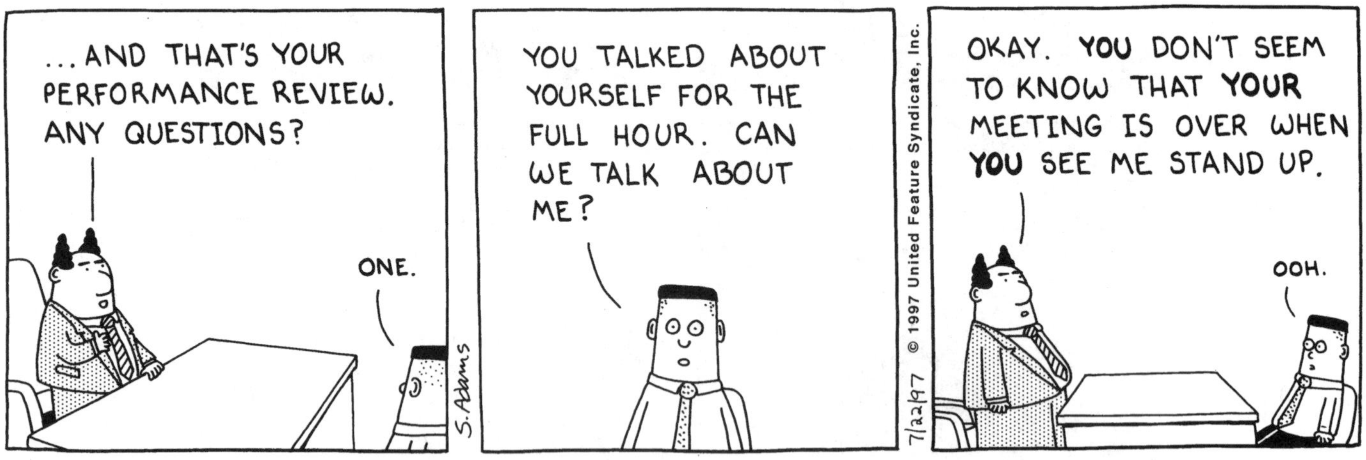
...AND THAT'S YOUR PERFORMANCE REVIEW. ANY QUESTIONS?
ONE.
S. Adams
YOU TALKED ABOUT YOURSELF FOR THE FULL HOUR. CAN WE TALK ABOUT ME?
7/22/97 © 1997 United Feature Syndicate, Inc.
OKAY. YOU DON'T SEEM TO KNOW THAT YOUR MEETING IS OVER WHEN YOU SEE ME STAND UP.
OOH.

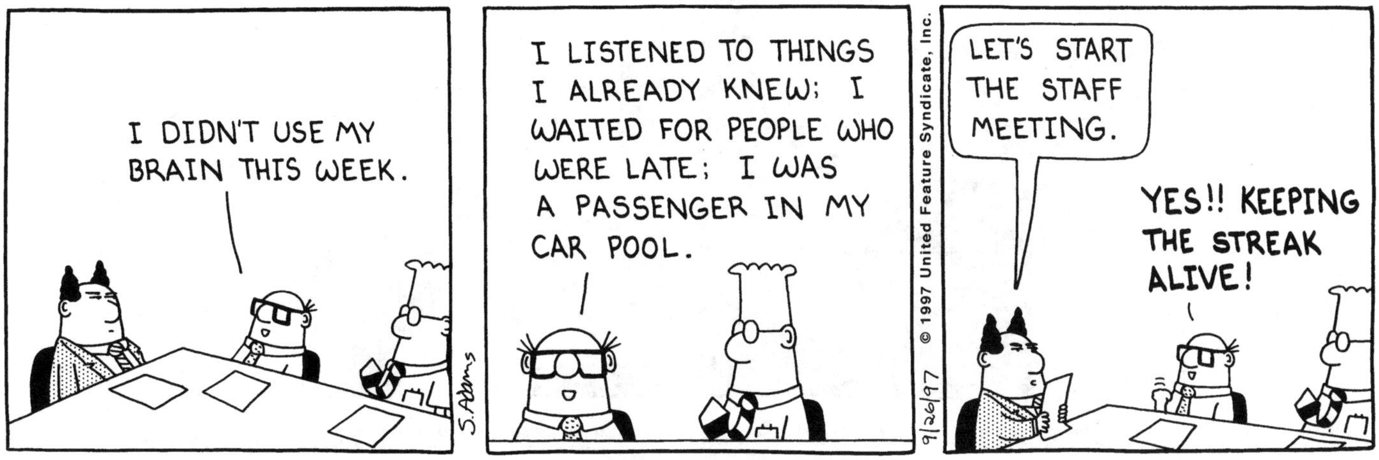
I DIDN'T USE MY BRAIN THIS WEEK.
I LISTENED TO THINGS I ALREADY KNEW; I WAITED FOR PEOPLE WHO WERE LATE; I WAS A PASSENGER IN MY CAR POOL.
LET'S START THE STAFF MEETING.
YES!! KEEPING THE STREAK ALIVE!
S. Adams
9/26/97 © 1997 United Feature Syndicate, Inc.

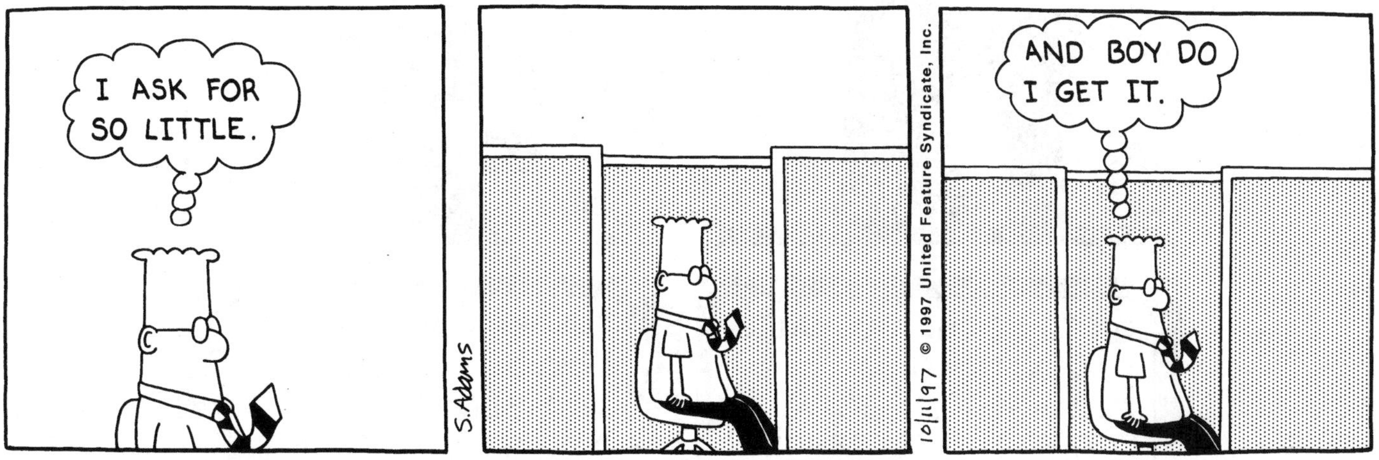
I ASK FOR SO LITTLE.
AND BOY DO I GET IT.
S. Adams
10/11/97 © 1997 United Feature Syndicate, Inc.

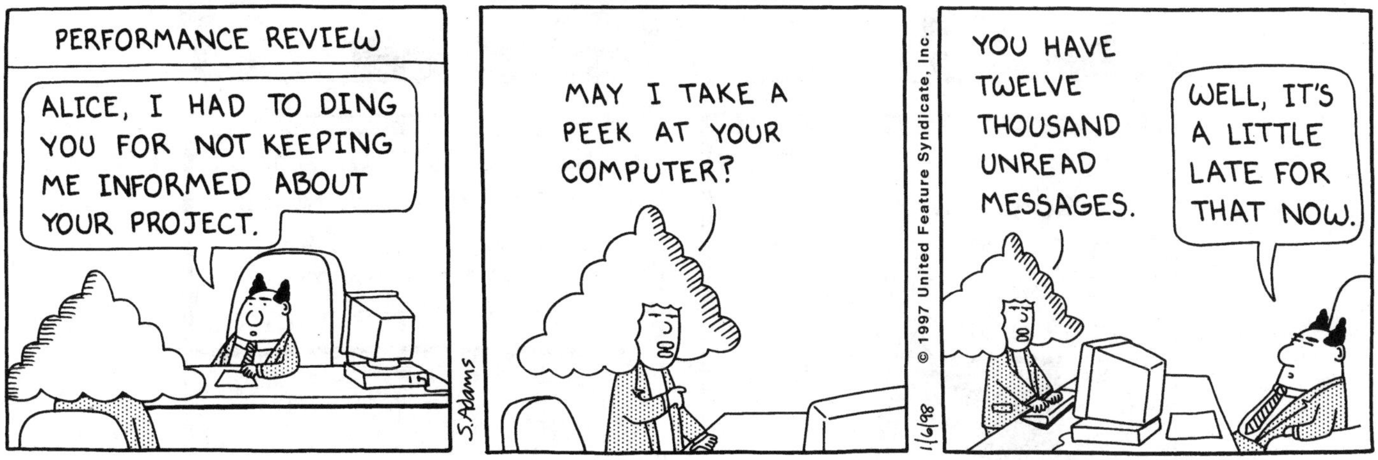
PERFORMANCE REVIEW
ALICE, I HAD TO DING YOU FOR NOT KEEPING ME INFORMED ABOUT YOUR PROJECT.
MAY I TAKE A PEEK AT YOUR COMPUTER?
YOU HAVE TWELVE THOUSAND UNREAD MESSAGES.
WELL, IT'S A LITTLE LATE FOR THAT NOW.
S. Adams
1/6/98 © 1997 United Feature Syndicate, Inc.

TINA, WE NEED TO SET MEASURABLE OBJECTIVES FOR YOU.
I'M A TECHNICAL WRITER. HOW CAN YOU MEASURE GOOD WRITING?
EVERYTHING IS MEASURABLE IF YOU TRY HARD ENOUGH.
IS THAT YOUR WELL-REASONED OPINION?
OR IS IT THE DOGMATIC BABBLING OF A MANAGER IN TOTAL COGNITIVE SURRENDER?
FOR EXAMPLE, WE COULD MEASURE THE NUMBER OF WORDS YOU TYPE.
WE'LL HAVE TO SUBTRACT WORDS YOU DELETE. THAT WAY WE WON'T MOTIVATE THE WRONG BEHAVIOR.
IN THIS EDITION OF TINA'S HOURLY NEWS-LETTER, I COMPARE OUR PROJECTS TO VARIOUS TYPES OF WOOD.
S.Adams
© 1998 United Feature Syndicate, Inc.
3/8/98

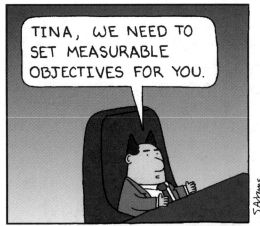

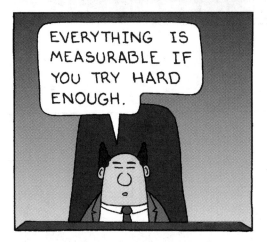

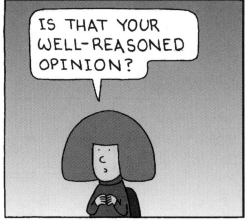

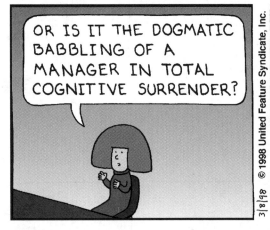

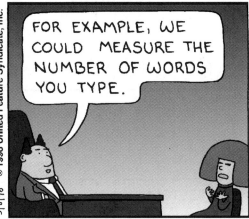

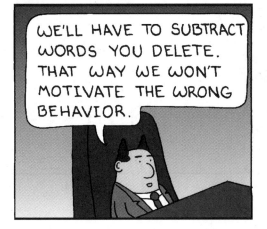

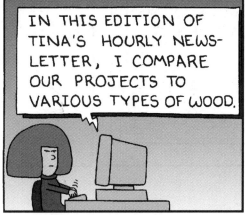

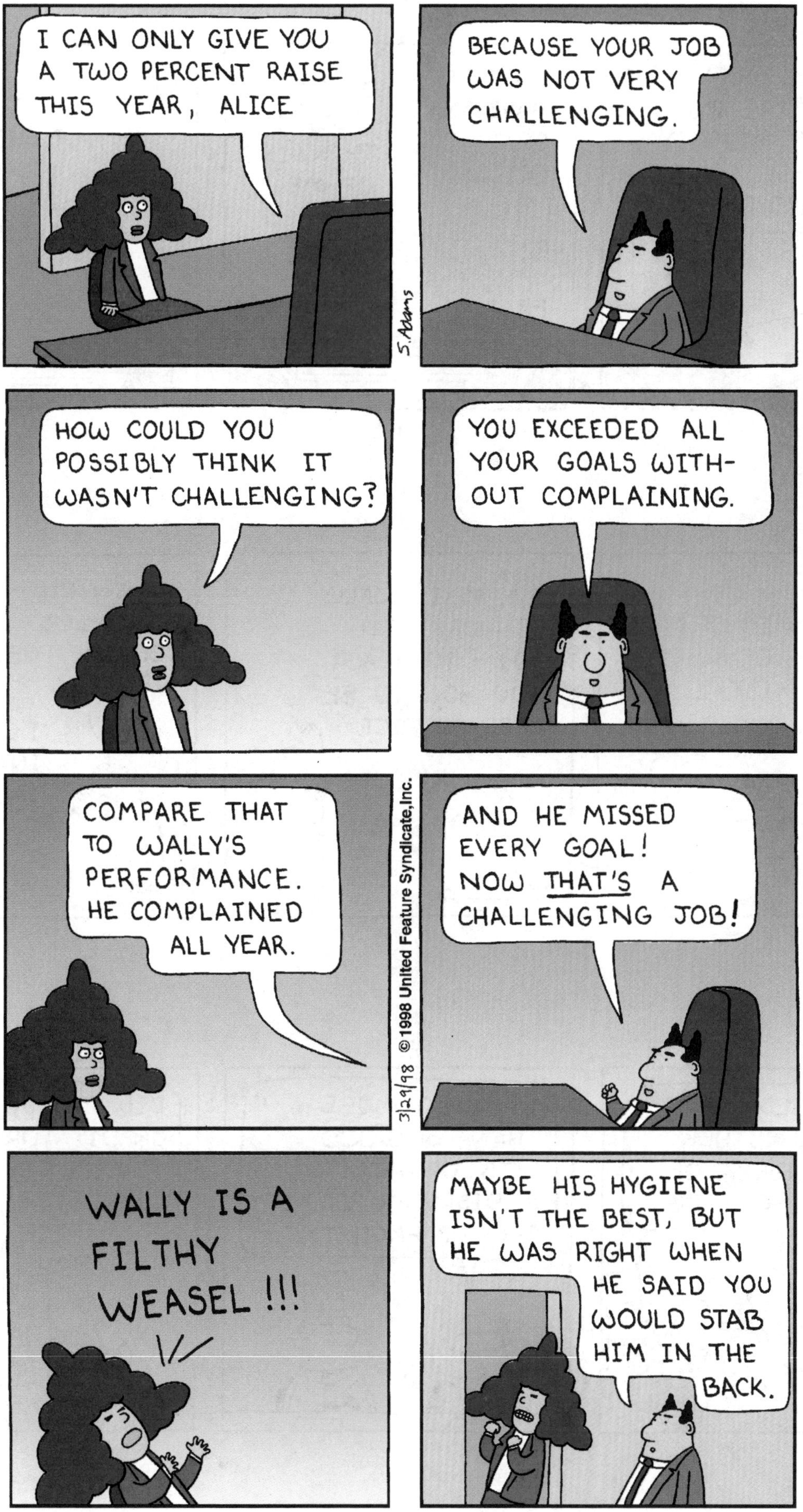
I CAN ONLY GIVE YOU A TWO PERCENT RAISE THIS YEAR, ALICE
BECAUSE YOUR JOB WAS NOT VERY CHALLENGING.
S. Adams
HOW COULD YOU POSSIBLY THINK IT WASN'T CHALLENGING?
YOU EXCEEDED ALL YOUR GOALS WITHOUT COMPLAINING.
COMPARE THAT TO WALLY'S PERFORMANCE. HE COMPLAINED ALL YEAR.
3/29/98 © 1998 United Feature Syndicate, Inc.
AND HE MISSED EVERY GOAL! NOW THAT'S A CHALLENGING JOB!
WALLY IS A FILTHY WEASEL!!!
MAYBE HIS HYGIENE ISN'T THE BEST, BUT HE WAS RIGHT WHEN HE SAID YOU WOULD STAB HIM IN THE BACK.

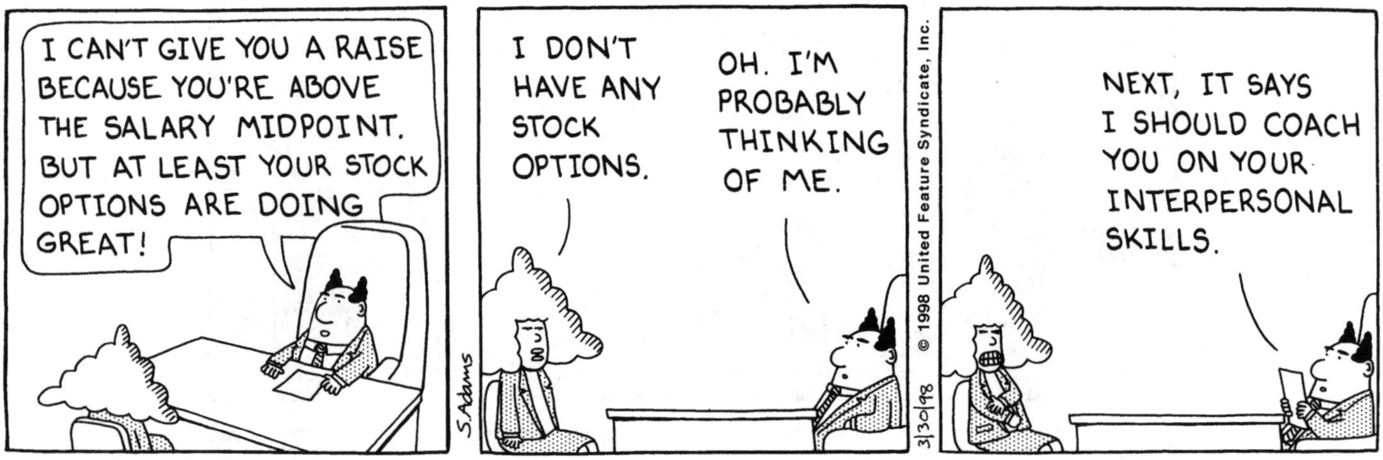
I CAN'T GIVE YOU A RAISE BECAUSE YOU'RE ABOVE THE SALARY MIDPOINT. BUT AT LEAST YOUR STOCK OPTIONS ARE DOING GREAT!
S.Adams
I DON'T HAVE ANY STOCK OPTIONS.
OH. I'M PROBABLY THINKING OF ME.
3/30/98 © 1998 United Feature Syndicate, Inc.
NEXT, IT SAYS I SHOULD COACH YOU ON YOUR INTERPERSONAL SKILLS.

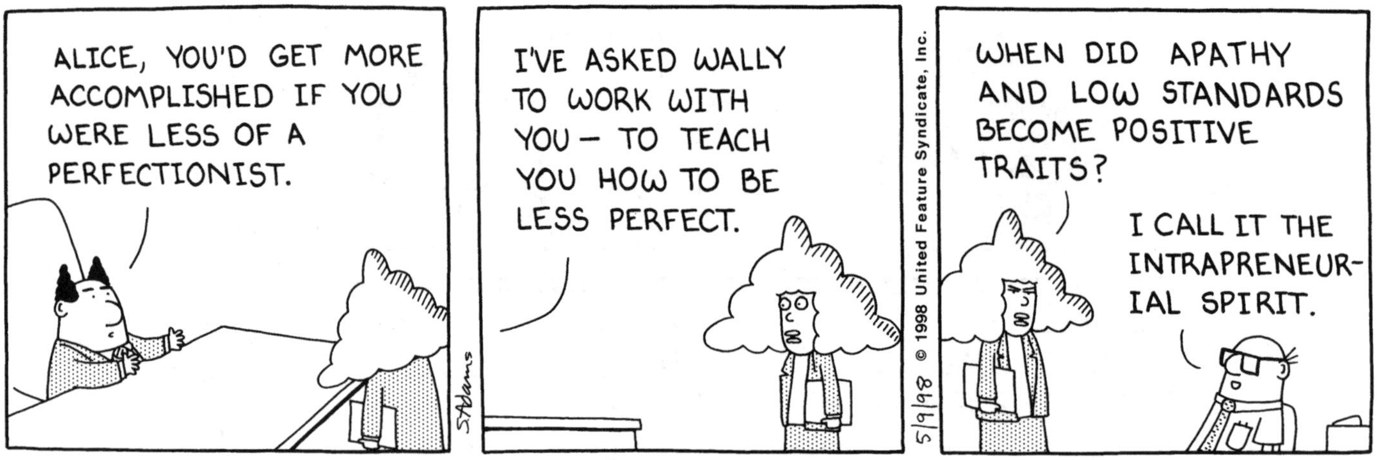
ALICE, YOU'D GET MORE ACCOMPLISHED IF YOU WERE LESS OF A PERFECTIONIST.
S.Adams
I'VE ASKED WALLY TO WORK WITH YOU – TO TEACH YOU HOW TO BE LESS PERFECT.
5/9/98 © 1998 United Feature Syndicate, Inc.
WHEN DID APATHY AND LOW STANDARDS BECOME POSITIVE TRAITS?
I CALL IT THE INTRAPRENEUR-IAL SPIRIT.

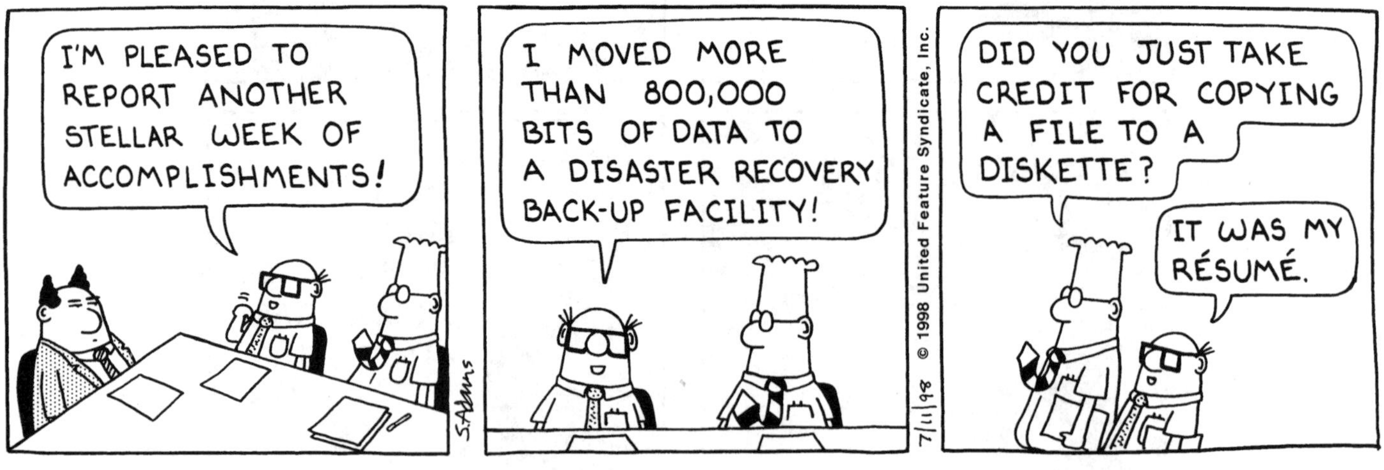
I'M PLEASED TO REPORT ANOTHER STELLAR WEEK OF ACCOMPLISHMENTS!
S.Adams
I MOVED MORE THAN 800,000 BITS OF DATA TO A DISASTER RECOVERY BACK-UP FACILITY!
7/11/98 © 1998 United Feature Syndicate, Inc.
DID YOU JUST TAKE CREDIT FOR COPYING A FILE TO A DISKETTE?
IT WAS MY RÉSUMÉ.

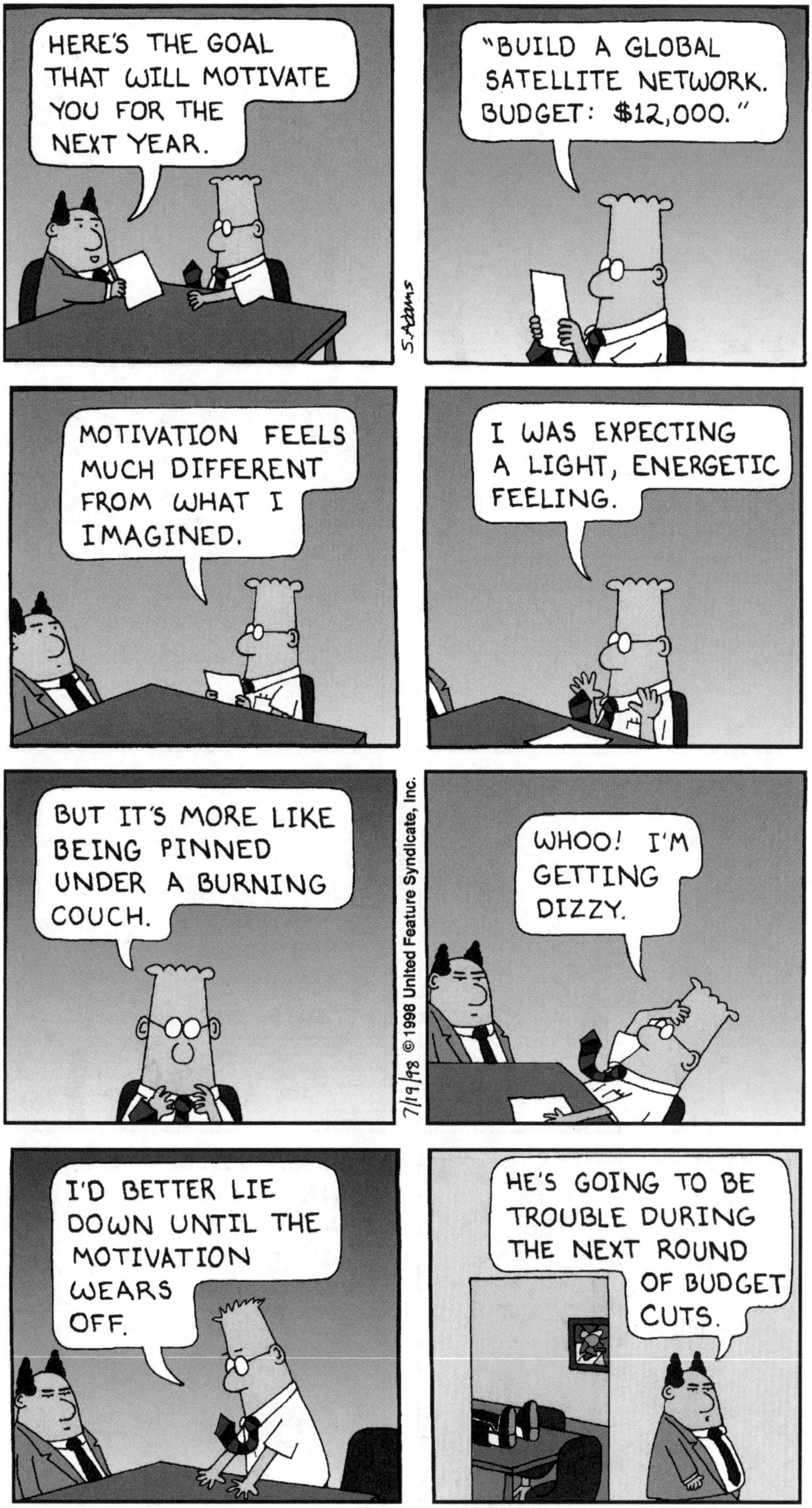
HERE'S THE GOAL THAT WILL MOTIVATE YOU FOR THE NEXT YEAR.
"BUILD A GLOBAL SATELLITE NETWORK. BUDGET: $12,000."
MOTIVATION FEELS MUCH DIFFERENT FROM WHAT I IMAGINED.
I WAS EXPECTING A LIGHT, ENERGETIC FEELING.
BUT IT'S MORE LIKE BEING PINNED UNDER A BURNING COUCH.
WHOO! I'M GETTING DIZZY.
I'D BETTER LIE DOWN UNTIL THE MOTIVATION WEARS OFF.
HE'S GOING TO BE TROUBLE DURING THE NEXT ROUND OF BUDGET CUTS.
S. Adams
7/19/98 © 1998 United Feature Syndicate, Inc.

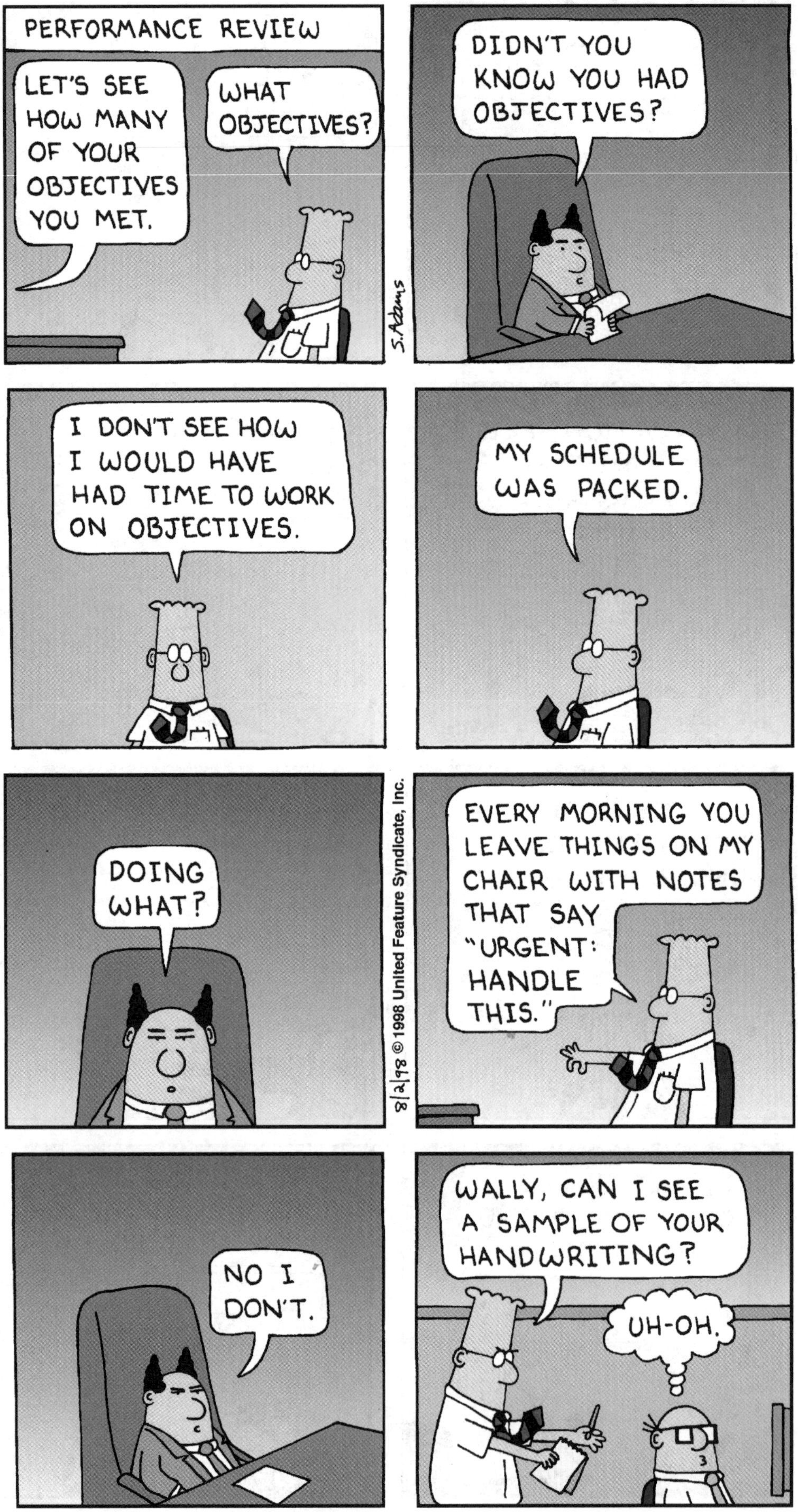
PERFORMANCE REVIEW
LET'S SEE HOW MANY OF YOUR OBJECTIVES YOU MET.
WHAT OBJECTIVES?
S. Adams
DIDN'T YOU KNOW YOU HAD OBJECTIVES?
I DON'T SEE HOW I WOULD HAVE HAD TIME TO WORK ON OBJECTIVES.
MY SCHEDULE WAS PACKED.
DOING WHAT?
8/2/98 © 1998 United Feature Syndicate, Inc.
EVERY MORNING YOU LEAVE THINGS ON MY CHAIR WITH NOTES THAT SAY "URGENT: HANDLE THIS."
NO I DON'T.
WALLY, CAN I SEE A SAMPLE OF YOUR HANDWRITING?
UH-OH.

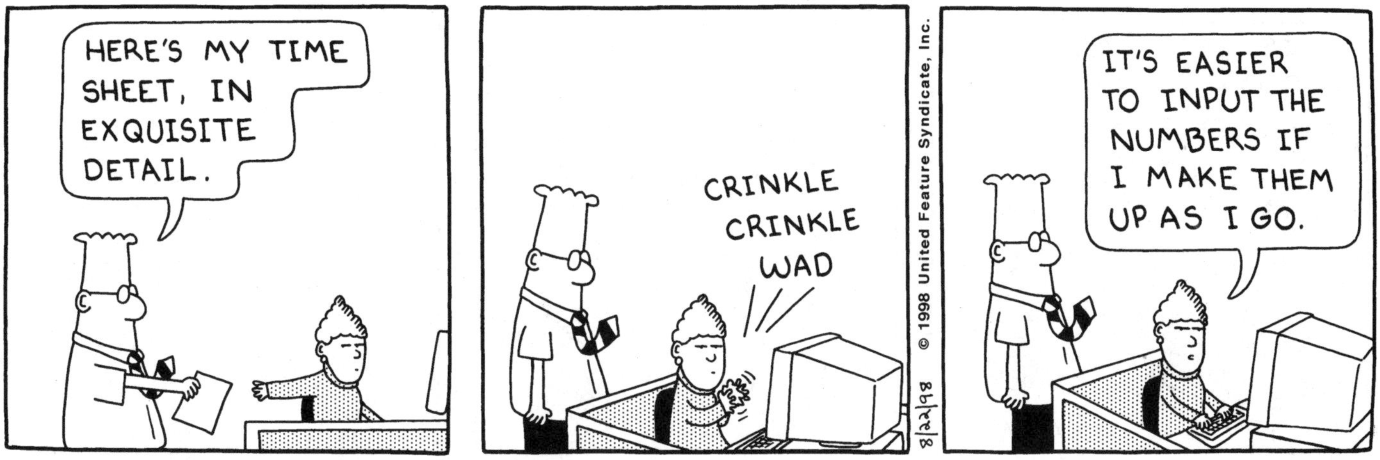
HERE'S MY TIME SHEET, IN EXQUISITE DETAIL.
CRINKLE CRINKLE WAD
IT'S EASIER TO INPUT THE NUMBERS IF I MAKE THEM UP AS I GO.
8/22/98 © 1998 United Feature Syndicate, Inc.

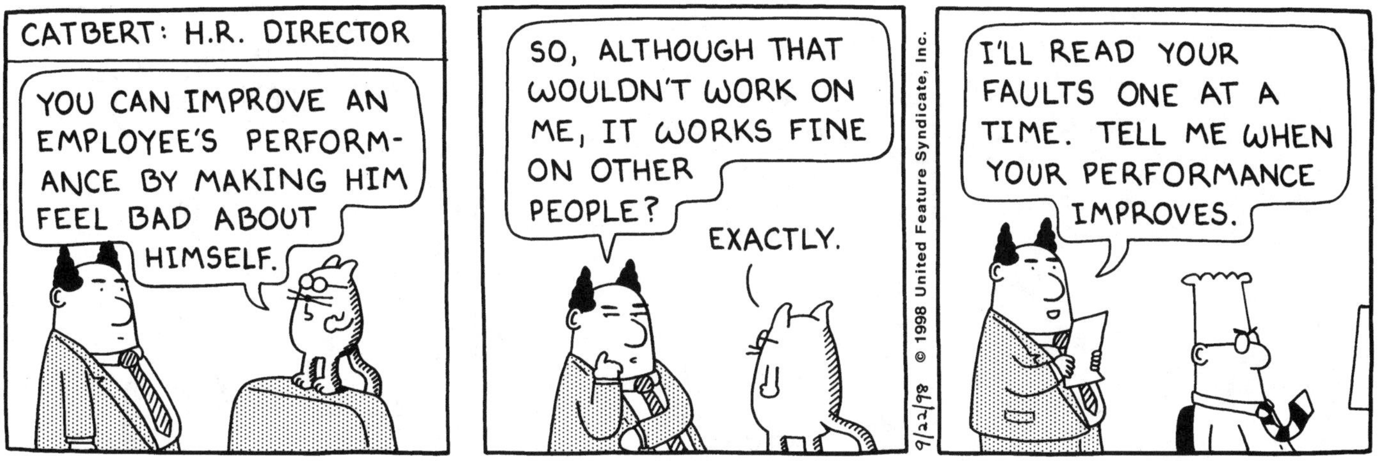
CATBERT: H.R. DIRECTOR
YOU CAN IMPROVE AN EMPLOYEE'S PERFORMANCE BY MAKING HIM FEEL BAD ABOUT HIMSELF.
SO, ALTHOUGH THAT WOULDN'T WORK ON ME, IT WORKS FINE ON OTHER PEOPLE?
EXACTLY.
I'LL READ YOUR FAULTS ONE AT A TIME. TELL ME WHEN YOUR PERFORMANCE IMPROVES.
9/22/98 © 1998 United Feature Syndicate, Inc.

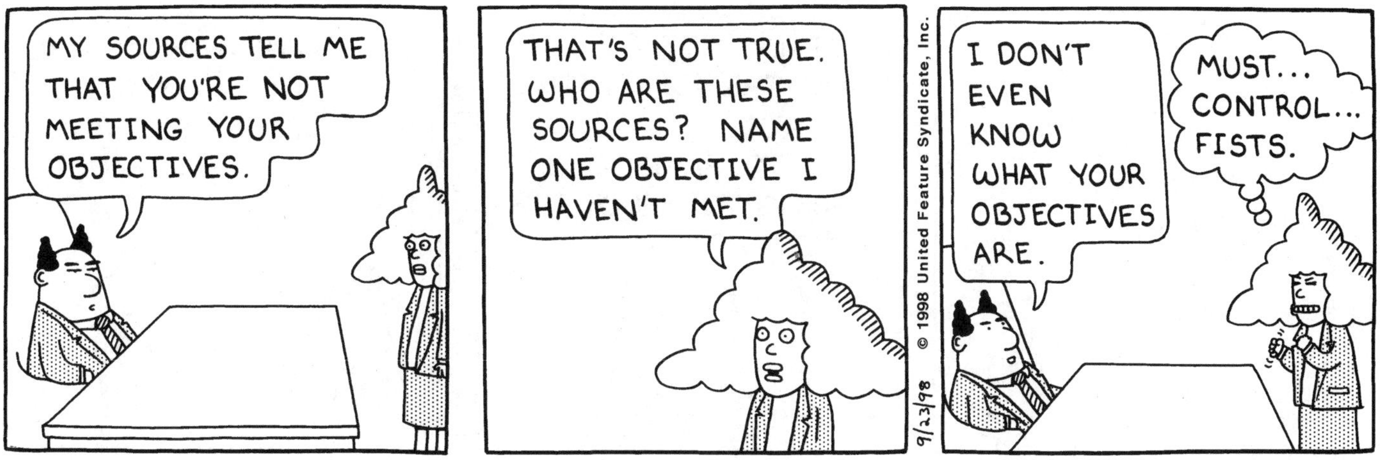
MY SOURCES TELL ME THAT YOU'RE NOT MEETING YOUR OBJECTIVES.
THAT'S NOT TRUE. WHO ARE THESE SOURCES? NAME ONE OBJECTIVE I HAVEN'T MET.
I DON'T EVEN KNOW WHAT YOUR OBJECTIVES ARE.
MUST... CONTROL... FISTS.
9/23/98 © 1998 United Feature Syndicate, Inc.

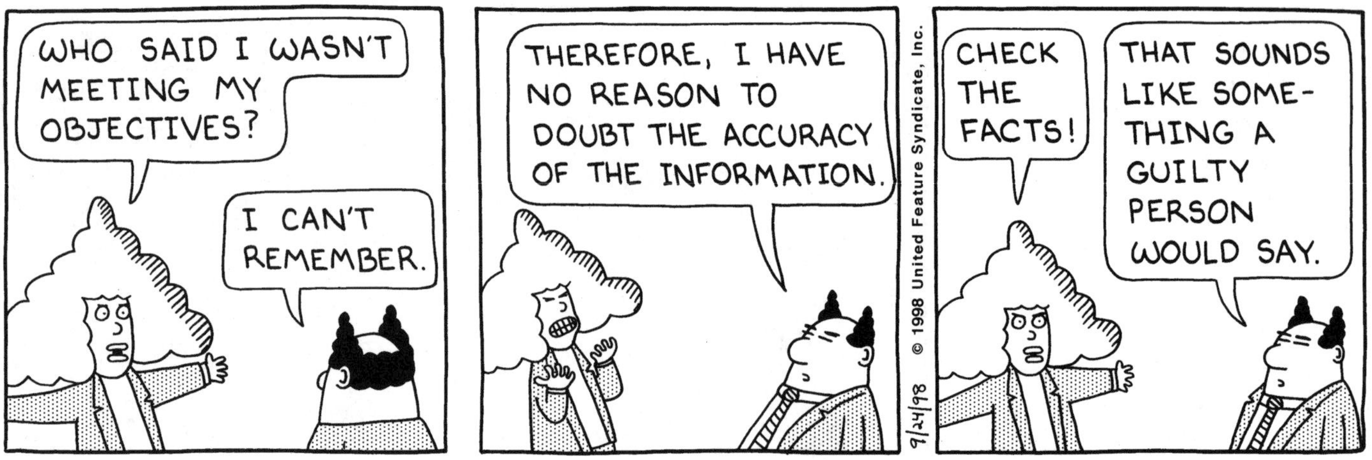
WHO SAID I WASN'T MEETING MY OBJECTIVES?
I CAN'T REMEMBER.
THEREFORE, I HAVE NO REASON TO DOUBT THE ACCURACY OF THE INFORMATION.
CHECK THE FACTS!
THAT SOUNDS LIKE SOMETHING A GUILTY PERSON WOULD SAY.
9/24/98
© 1998 United Feature Syndicate, Inc.

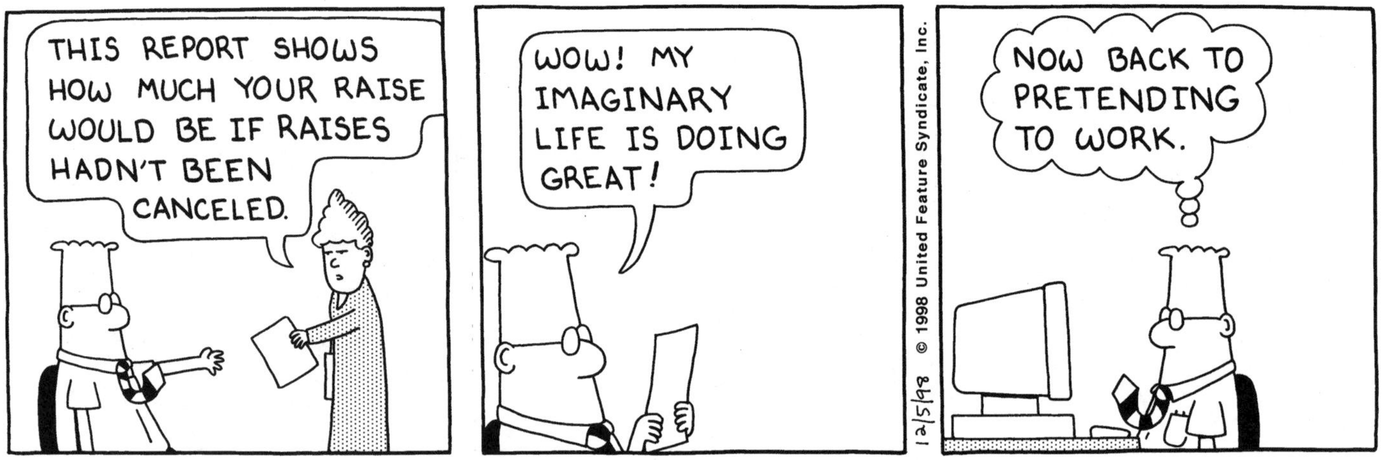
THIS REPORT SHOWS HOW MUCH YOUR RAISE WOULD BE IF RAISES HADN'T BEEN CANCELED.
WOW! MY IMAGINARY LIFE IS DOING GREAT!
NOW BACK TO PRETENDING TO WORK.
12/5/98
© 1998 United Feature Syndicate, Inc.

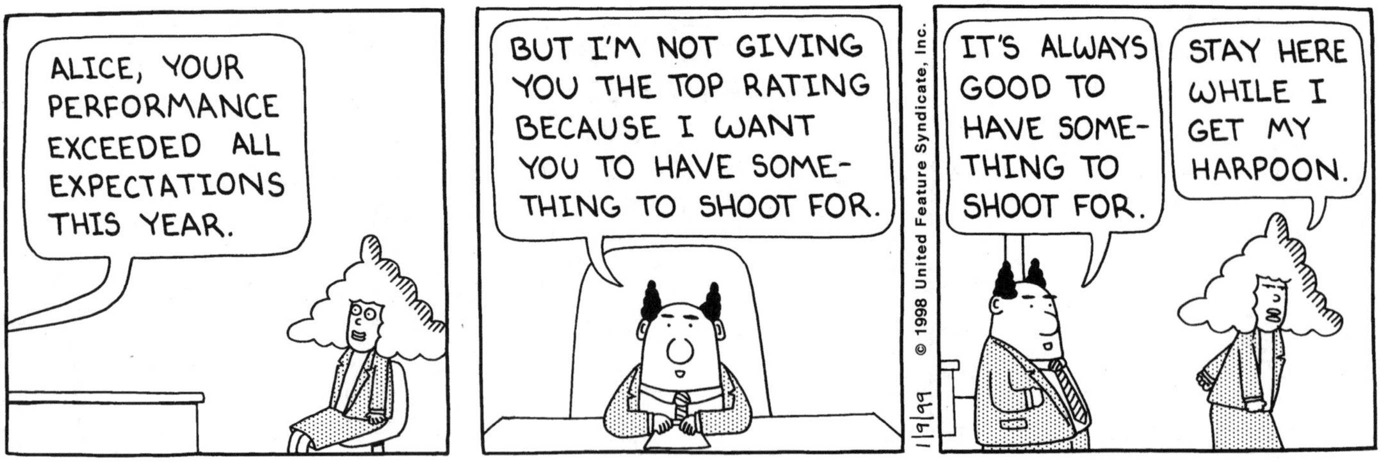
ALICE, YOUR PERFORMANCE EXCEEDED ALL EXPECTATIONS THIS YEAR.
BUT I'M NOT GIVING YOU THE TOP RATING BECAUSE I WANT YOU TO HAVE SOMETHING TO SHOOT FOR.
IT'S ALWAYS GOOD TO HAVE SOMETHING TO SHOOT FOR.
STAY HERE WHILE I GET MY HARPOON.
1/9/99
© 1998 United Feature Syndicate, Inc.

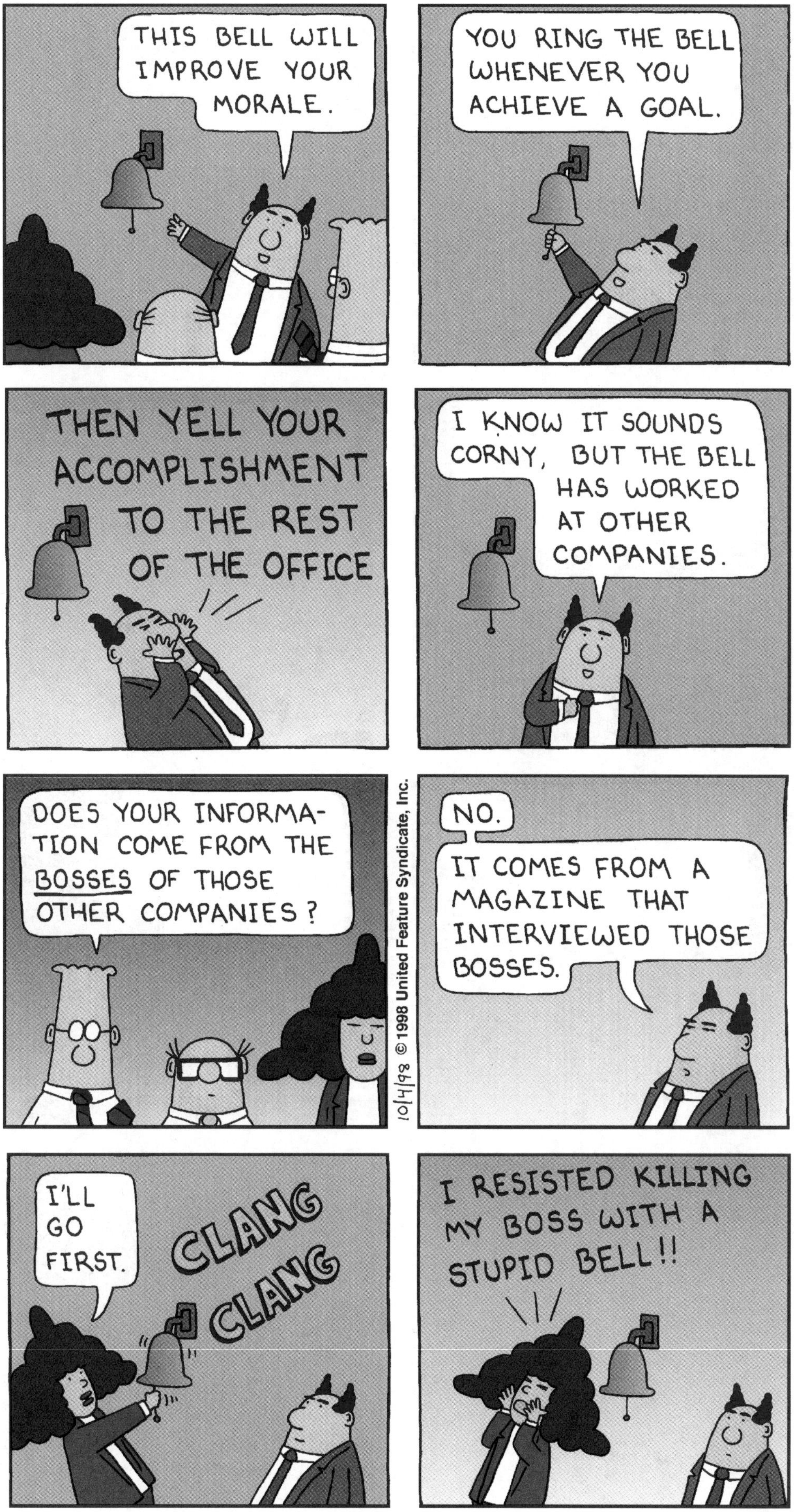
THIS BELL WILL IMPROVE YOUR MORALE.
YOU RING THE BELL WHENEVER YOU ACHIEVE A GOAL.
THEN YELL YOUR ACCOMPLISHMENT TO THE REST OF THE OFFICE
I KNOW IT SOUNDS CORNY, BUT THE BELL HAS WORKED AT OTHER COMPANIES.
DOES YOUR INFORMATION COME FROM THE BOSSES OF THOSE OTHER COMPANIES?
10/4/98 © 1998 United Feature Syndicate, Inc.
NO.
IT COMES FROM A MAGAZINE THAT INTERVIEWED THOSE BOSSES.
I'LL GO FIRST.
CLANG CLANG
I RESISTED KILLING MY BOSS WITH A STUPID BELL!!

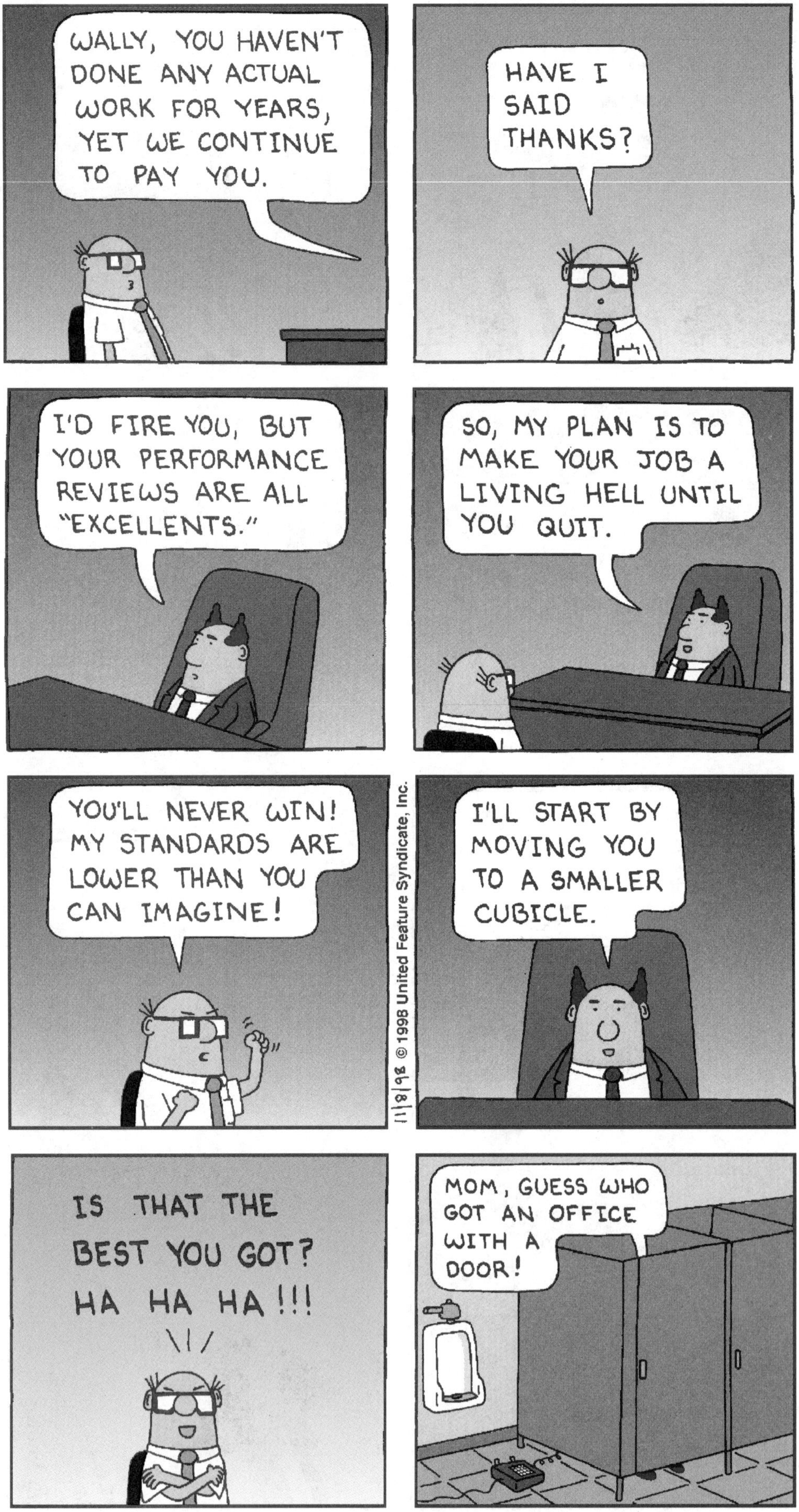
WALLY, YOU HAVEN'T DONE ANY ACTUAL WORK FOR YEARS, YET WE CONTINUE TO PAY YOU.
HAVE I SAID THANKS?
I'D FIRE YOU, BUT YOUR PERFORMANCE REVIEWS ARE ALL "EXCELLENTS."
SO, MY PLAN IS TO MAKE YOUR JOB A LIVING HELL UNTIL YOU QUIT.
YOU'LL NEVER WIN! MY STANDARDS ARE LOWER THAN YOU CAN IMAGINE!
I'LL START BY MOVING YOU TO A SMALLER CUBICLE.
IS THAT THE BEST YOU GOT? HA HA HA!!!
MOM, GUESS WHO GOT AN OFFICE WITH A DOOR!
11/8/98 © 1998 United Feature Syndicate, Inc.

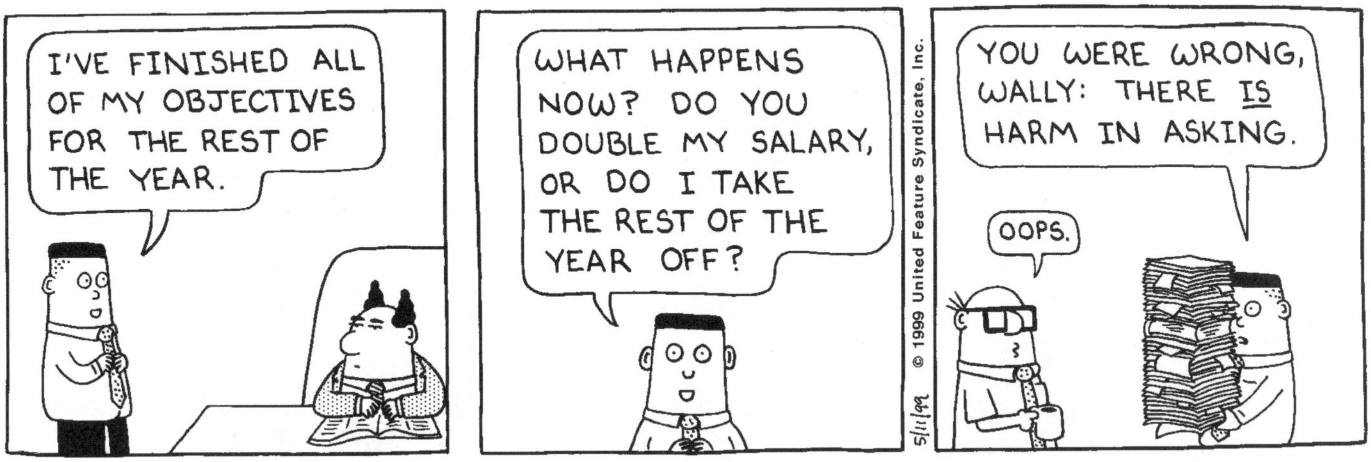
I'VE FINISHED ALL OF MY OBJECTIVES FOR THE REST OF THE YEAR.
WHAT HAPPENS NOW? DO YOU DOUBLE MY SALARY, OR DO I TAKE THE REST OF THE YEAR OFF?
© 1999 United Feature Syndicate, Inc.
YOU WERE WRONG, WALLY: THERE IS HARM IN ASKING.
OOPS.

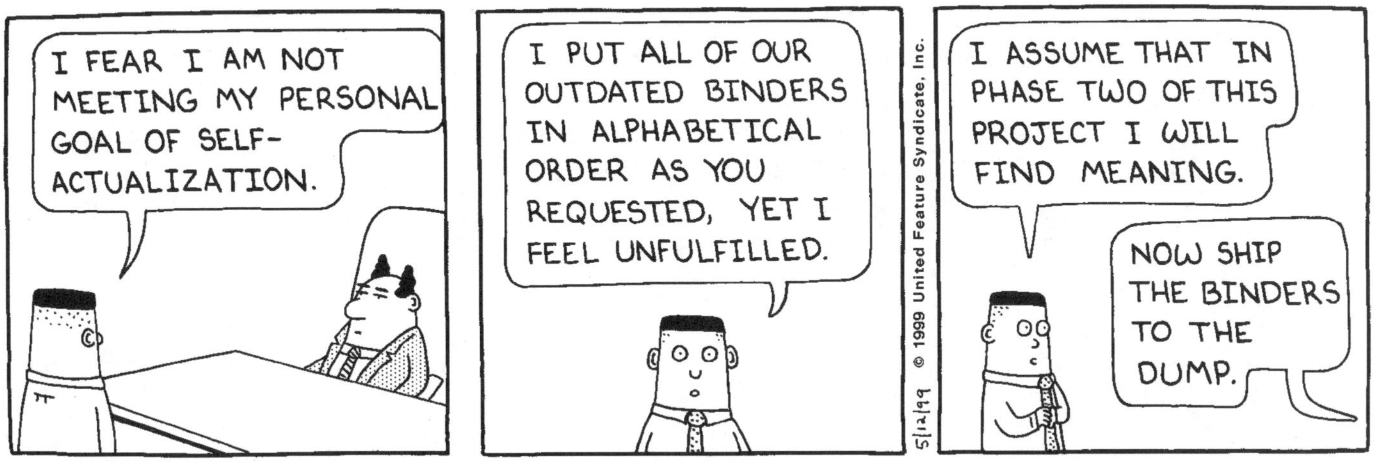
I FEAR I AM NOT MEETING MY PERSONAL GOAL OF SELF-ACTUALIZATION.
I PUT ALL OF OUR OUTDATED BINDERS IN ALPHABETICAL ORDER AS YOU REQUESTED, YET I FEEL UNFULFILLED.
© 1999 United Feature Syndicate, Inc.
I ASSUME THAT IN PHASE TWO OF THIS PROJECT I WILL FIND MEANING.
NOW SHIP THE BINDERS TO THE DUMP.

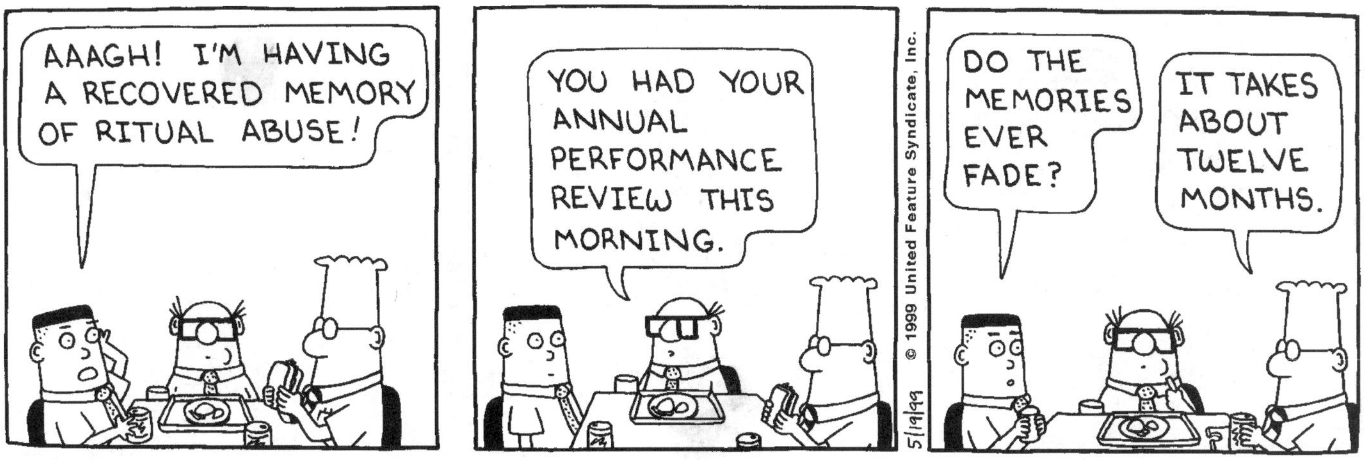
AAAGH! I'M HAVING A RECOVERED MEMORY OF RITUAL ABUSE!
YOU HAD YOUR ANNUAL PERFORMANCE REVIEW THIS MORNING.
© 1999 United Feature Syndicate, Inc.
DO THE MEMORIES EVER FADE?
IT TAKES ABOUT TWELVE MONTHS.

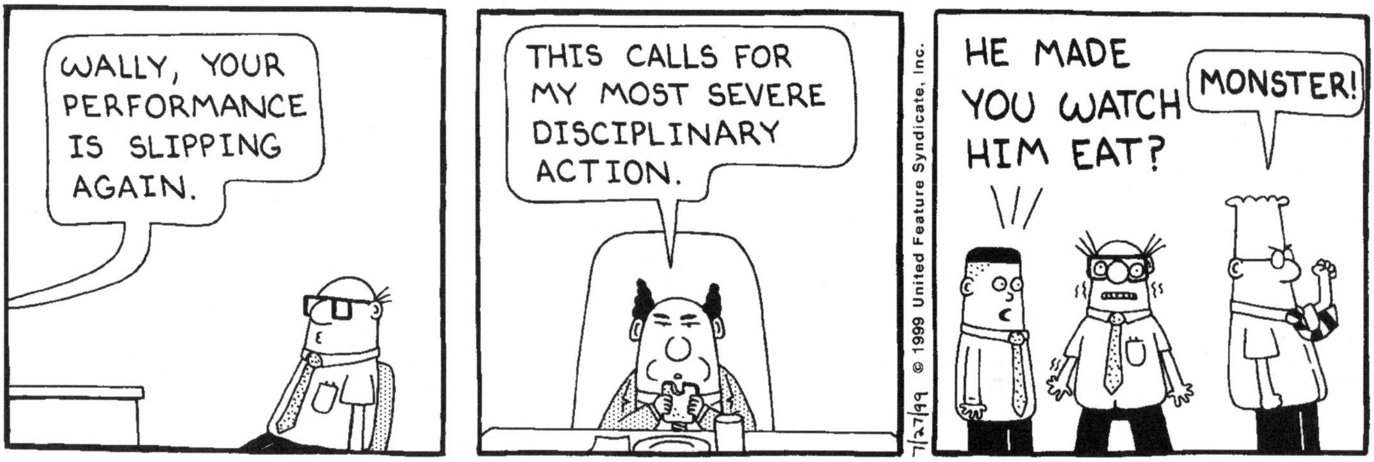
WALLY, YOUR PERFORMANCE IS SLIPPING AGAIN.
THIS CALLS FOR MY MOST SEVERE DISCIPLINARY ACTION.
7/27/99 © 1999 United Feature Syndicate, Inc.
HE MADE YOU WATCH HIM EAT?
MONSTER!

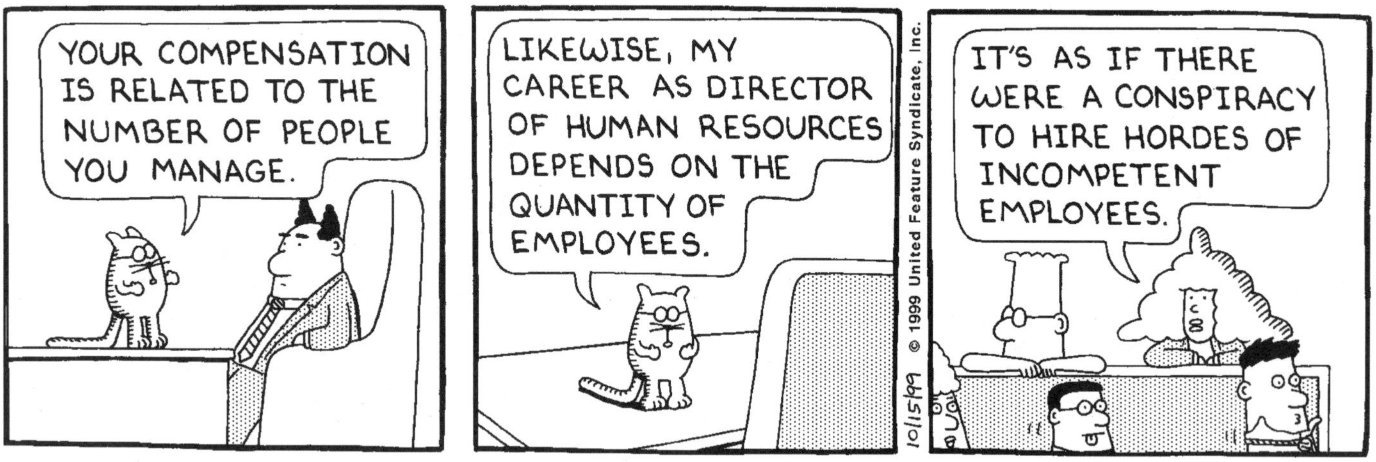
YOUR COMPENSATION IS RELATED TO THE NUMBER OF PEOPLE YOU MANAGE.
LIKEWISE, MY CAREER AS DIRECTOR OF HUMAN RESOURCES DEPENDS ON THE QUANTITY OF EMPLOYEES.
10/15/99 © 1999 United Feature Syndicate, Inc.
IT'S AS IF THERE WERE A CONSPIRACY TO HIRE HORDES OF INCOMPETENT EMPLOYEES.

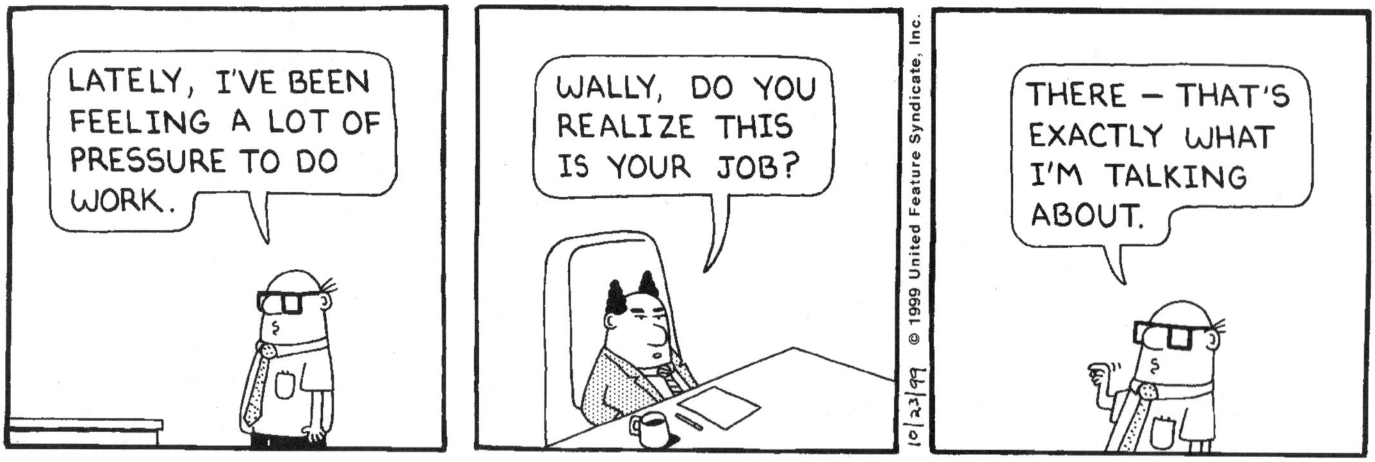
LATELY, I'VE BEEN FEELING A LOT OF PRESSURE TO DO WORK.
WALLY, DO YOU REALIZE THIS IS YOUR JOB?
10/23/99 © 1999 United Feature Syndicate, Inc.
THERE – THAT'S EXACTLY WHAT I'M TALKING ABOUT.

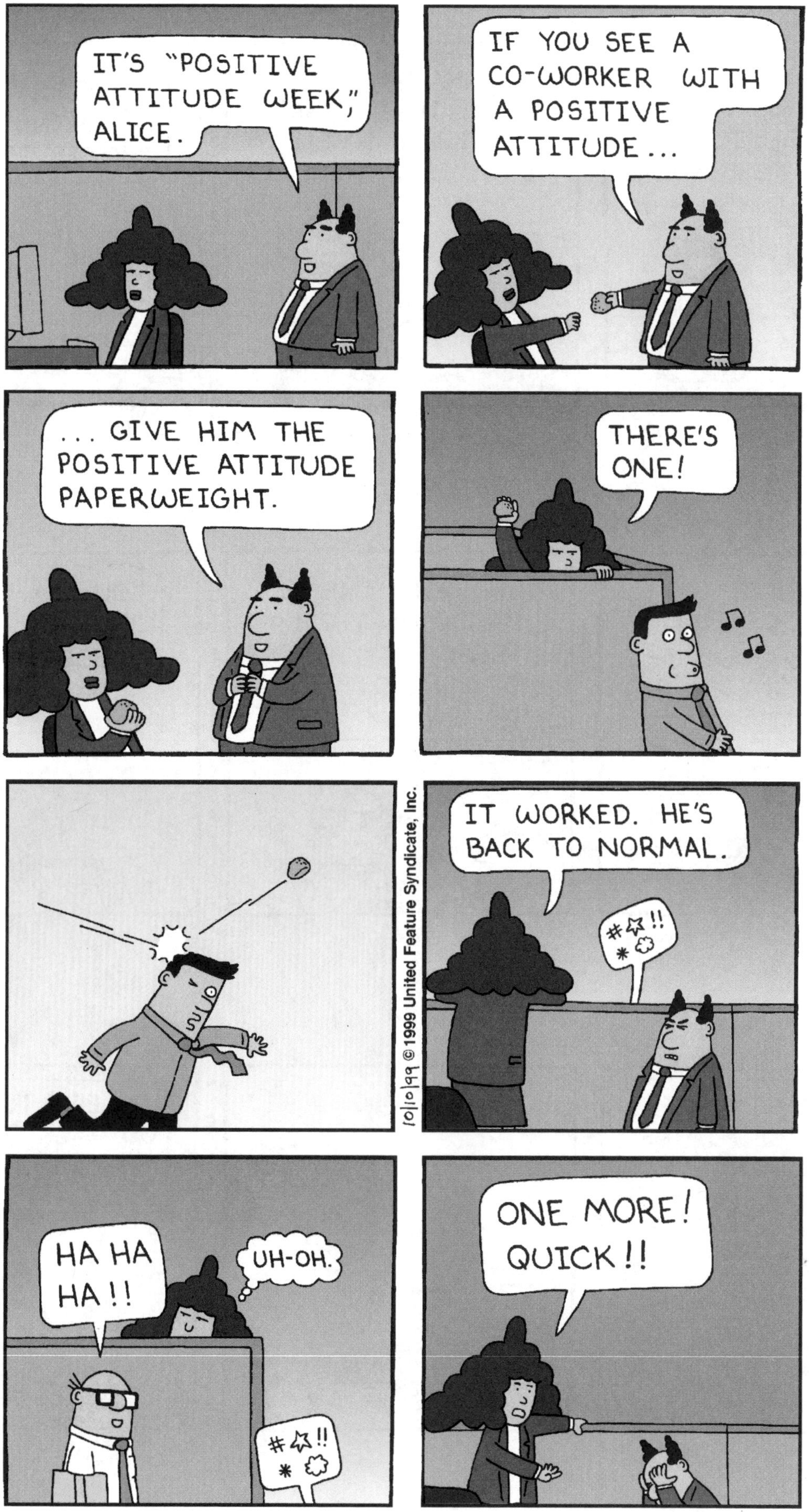
IT'S "POSITIVE ATTITUDE WEEK," ALICE.
IF YOU SEE A CO-WORKER WITH A POSITIVE ATTITUDE...
... GIVE HIM THE POSITIVE ATTITUDE PAPERWEIGHT.
THERE'S ONE!
10/10/99 © 1999 United Feature Syndicate, Inc.
IT WORKED. HE'S BACK TO NORMAL.
HA HA HA!!
UH-OH.
ONE MORE! QUICK!!

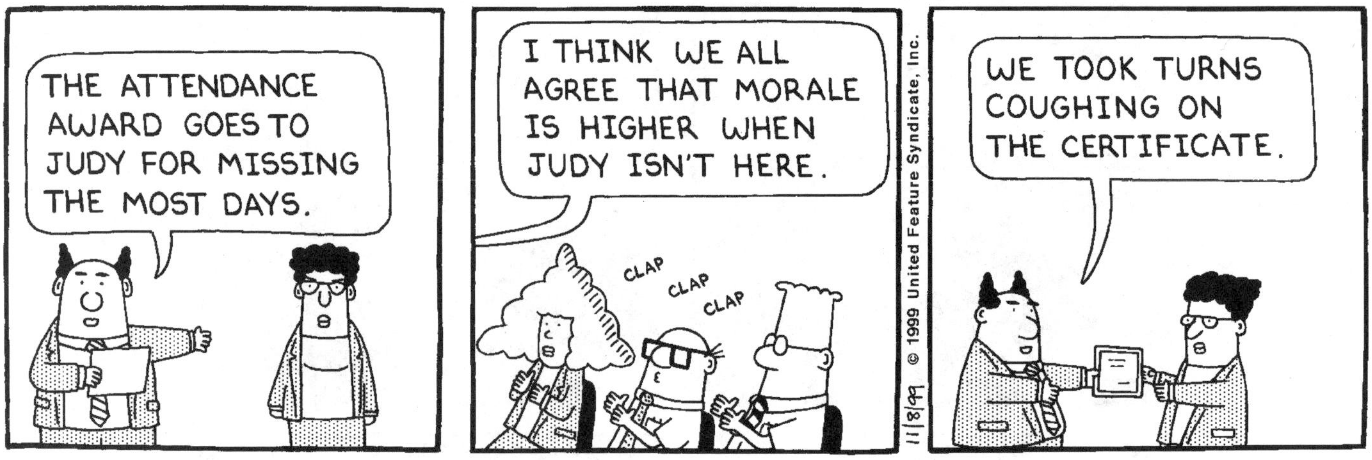
THE ATTENDANCE AWARD GOES TO JUDY FOR MISSING THE MOST DAYS.
I THINK WE ALL AGREE THAT MORALE IS HIGHER WHEN JUDY ISN'T HERE.
CLAP
CLAP
CLAP
11/8/99
© 1999 United Feature Syndicate, Inc.
WE TOOK TURNS COUGHING ON THE CERTIFICATE.

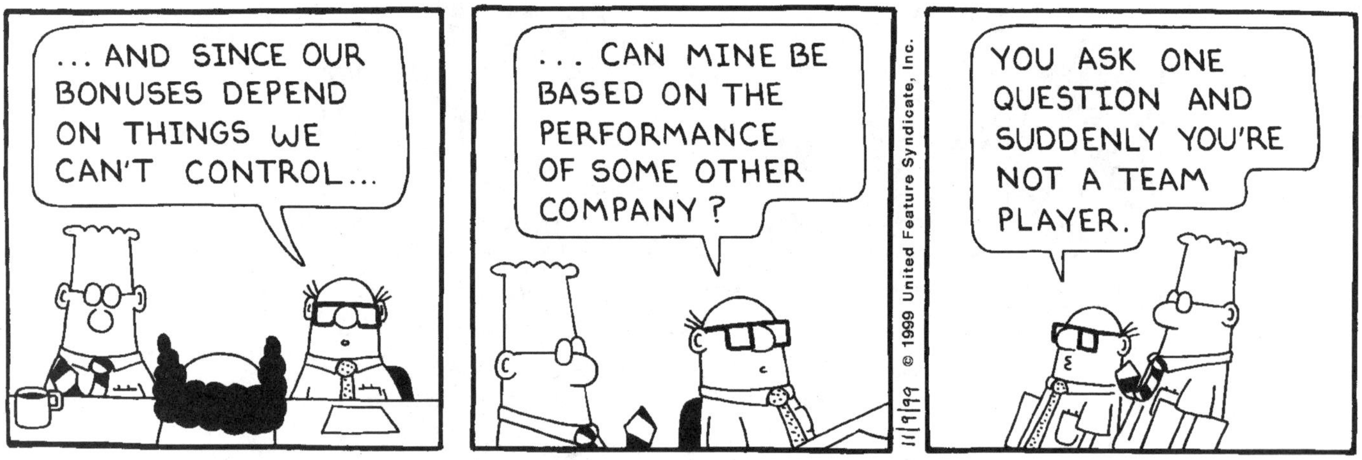
... AND SINCE OUR BONUSES DEPEND ON THINGS WE CAN'T CONTROL...
... CAN MINE BE BASED ON THE PERFORMANCE OF SOME OTHER COMPANY?
11/9/99
© 1999 United Feature Syndicate, Inc.
YOU ASK ONE QUESTION AND SUDDENLY YOU'RE NOT A TEAM PLAYER.

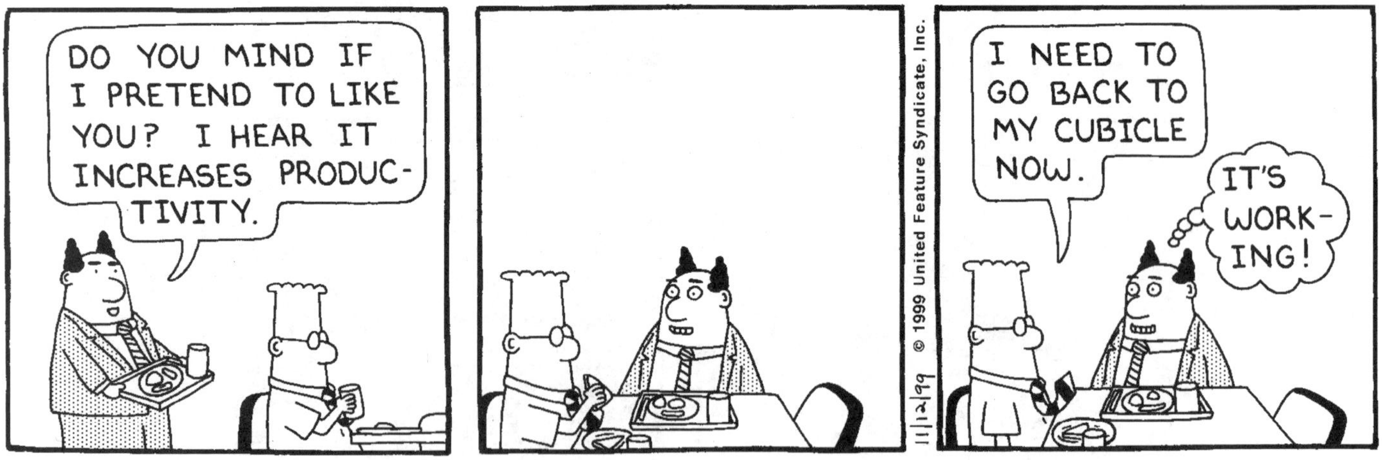
DO YOU MIND IF I PRETEND TO LIKE YOU? I HEAR IT INCREASES PRODUC-TIVITY.
11/12/99
© 1999 United Feature Syndicate, Inc.
I NEED TO GO BACK TO MY CUBICLE NOW.
IT'S WORK-ING!

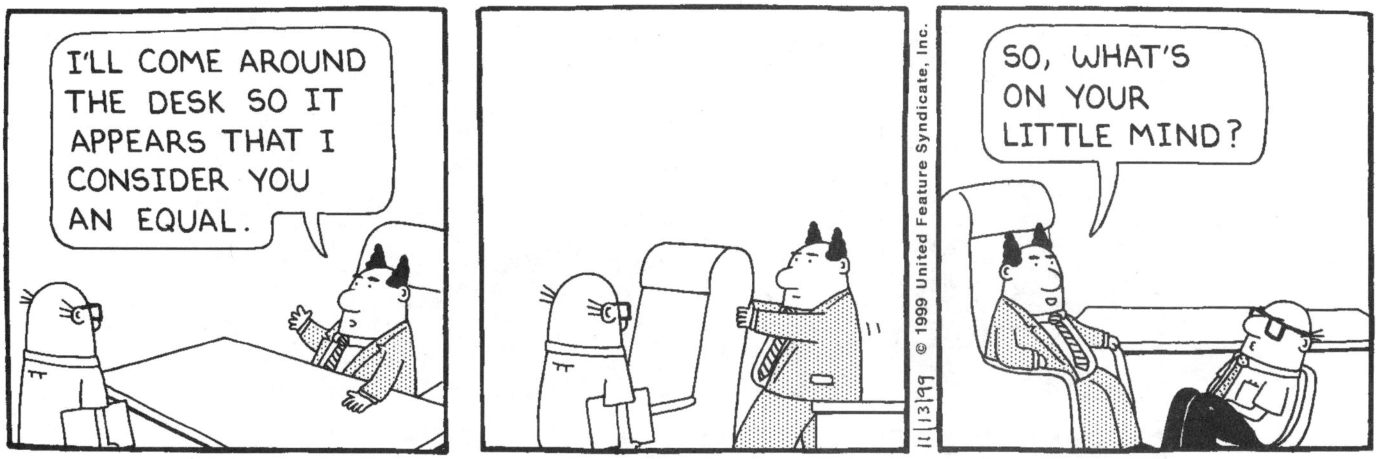
I'LL COME AROUND THE DESK SO IT APPEARS THAT I CONSIDER YOU AN EQUAL.
SO, WHAT'S ON YOUR LITTLE MIND?
11/13/99 © 1999 United Feature Syndicate, Inc.

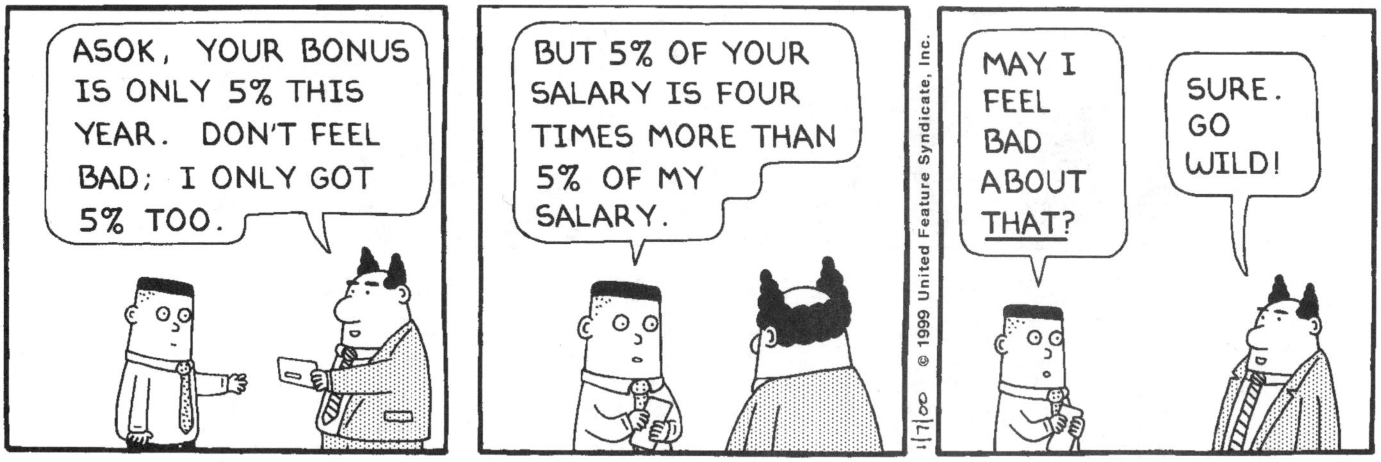
ASOK, YOUR BONUS IS ONLY 5% THIS YEAR. DON'T FEEL BAD; I ONLY GOT 5% TOO.
BUT 5% OF YOUR SALARY IS FOUR TIMES MORE THAN 5% OF MY SALARY.
MAY I FEEL BAD ABOUT THAT?
SURE. GO WILD!
1/7/00 © 1999 United Feature Syndicate, Inc.

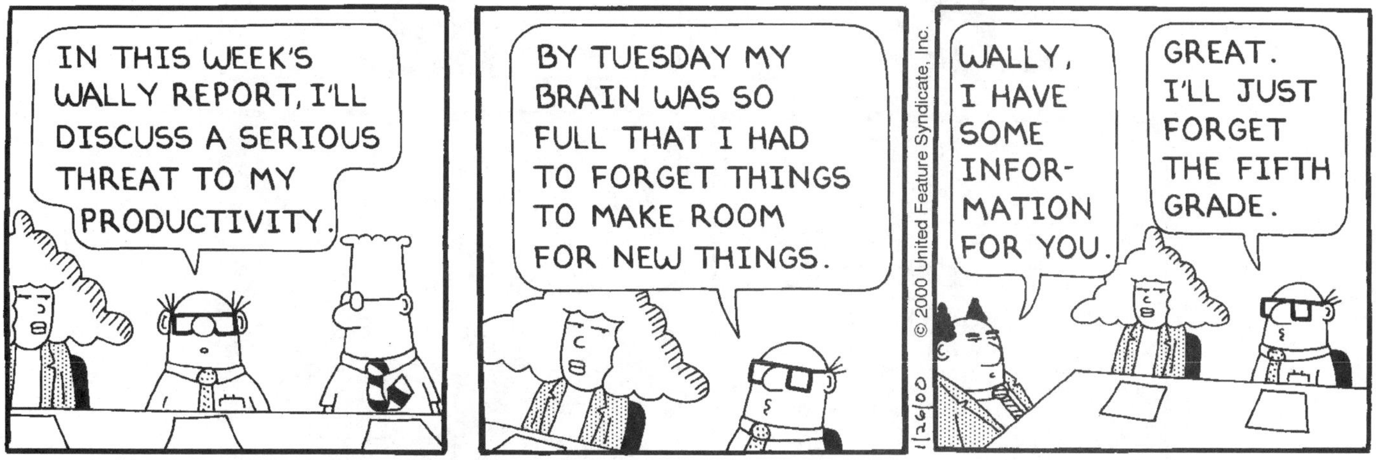
IN THIS WEEK'S WALLY REPORT, I'LL DISCUSS A SERIOUS THREAT TO MY PRODUCTIVITY.
BY TUESDAY MY BRAIN WAS SO FULL THAT I HAD TO FORGET THINGS TO MAKE ROOM FOR NEW THINGS.
WALLY, I HAVE SOME INFORMATION FOR YOU.
GREAT. I'LL JUST FORGET THE FIFTH GRADE.
1/26/00 © 2000 United Feature Syndicate, Inc.

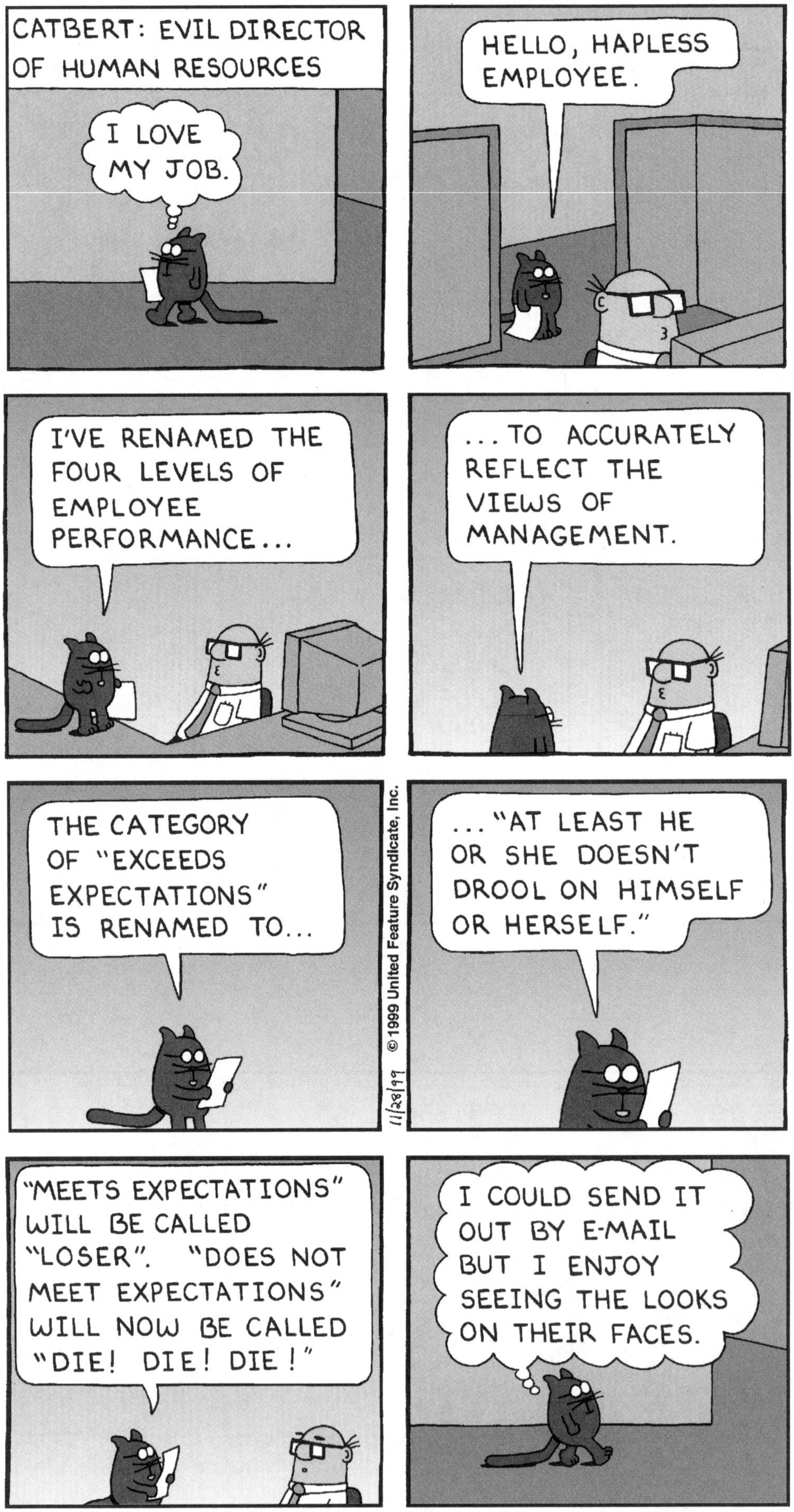
CATBERT: EVIL DIRECTOR OF HUMAN RESOURCES
I LOVE MY JOB.
HELLO, HAPLESS EMPLOYEE.
I'VE RENAMED THE FOUR LEVELS OF EMPLOYEE PERFORMANCE...
...TO ACCURATELY REFLECT THE VIEWS OF MANAGEMENT.
THE CATEGORY OF "EXCEEDS EXPECTATIONS" IS RENAMED TO...
..."AT LEAST HE OR SHE DOESN'T DROOL ON HIMSELF OR HERSELF."
"MEETS EXPECTATIONS" WILL BE CALLED "LOSER". "DOES NOT MEET EXPECTATIONS" WILL NOW BE CALLED "DIE! DIE! DIE!"
I COULD SEND IT OUT BY E-MAIL BUT I ENJOY SEEING THE LOOKS ON THEIR FACES.
© 1999 United Feature Syndicate, Inc.
11/28/99

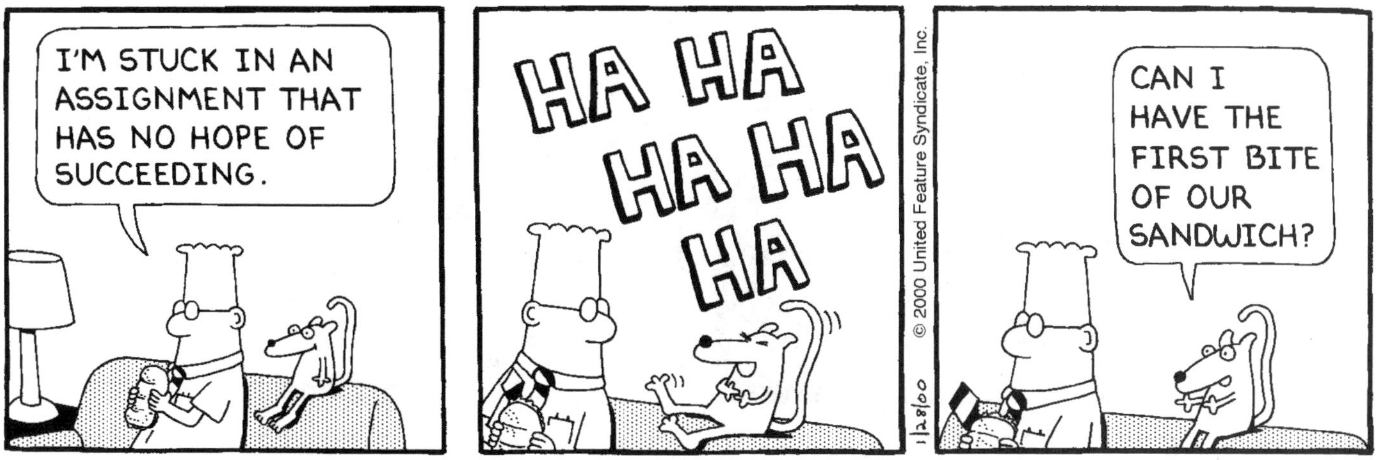
I'M STUCK IN AN ASSIGNMENT THAT HAS NO HOPE OF SUCCEEDING.
HA HA HA HA HA
© 2000 United Feature Syndicate, Inc.
1/28/00
CAN I HAVE THE FIRST BITE OF OUR SANDWICH?

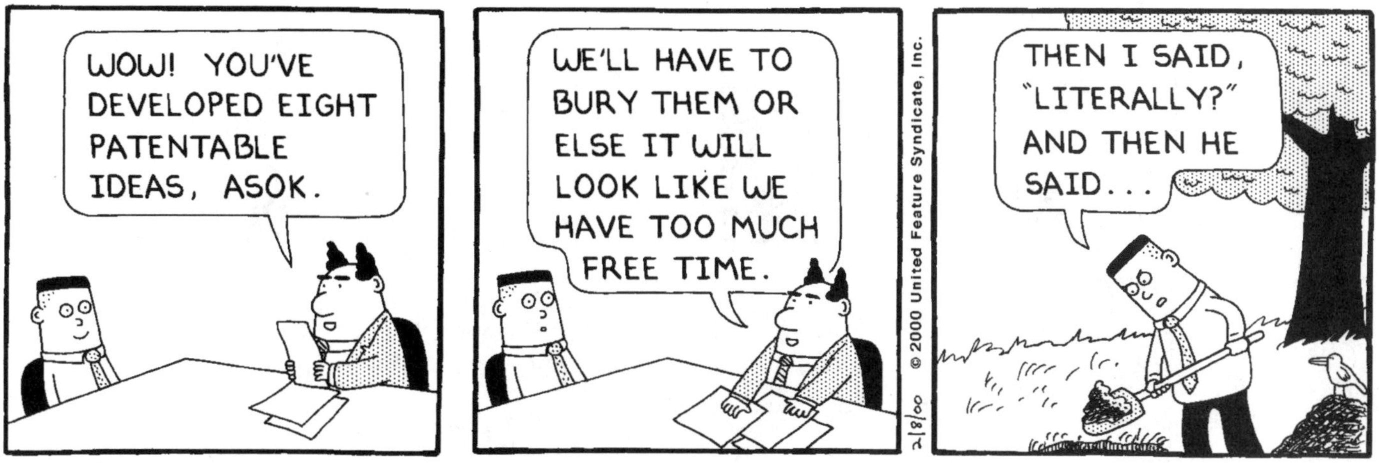
WOW! YOU'VE DEVELOPED EIGHT PATENTABLE IDEAS, ASOK.
WE'LL HAVE TO BURY THEM OR ELSE IT WILL LOOK LIKE WE HAVE TOO MUCH FREE TIME.
© 2000 United Feature Syndicate, Inc.
2/8/00
THEN I SAID, "LITERALLY?" AND THEN HE SAID...

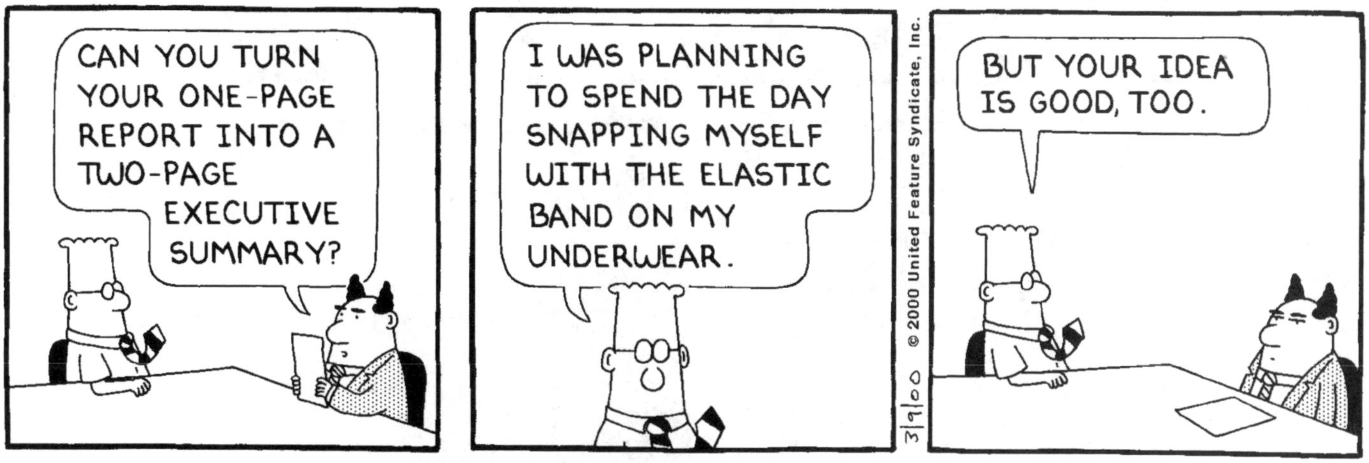
CAN YOU TURN YOUR ONE-PAGE REPORT INTO A TWO-PAGE EXECUTIVE SUMMARY?
I WAS PLANNING TO SPEND THE DAY SNAPPING MYSELF WITH THE ELASTIC BAND ON MY UNDERWEAR.
© 2000 United Feature Syndicate, Inc.
3/9/00
BUT YOUR IDEA IS GOOD, TOO.

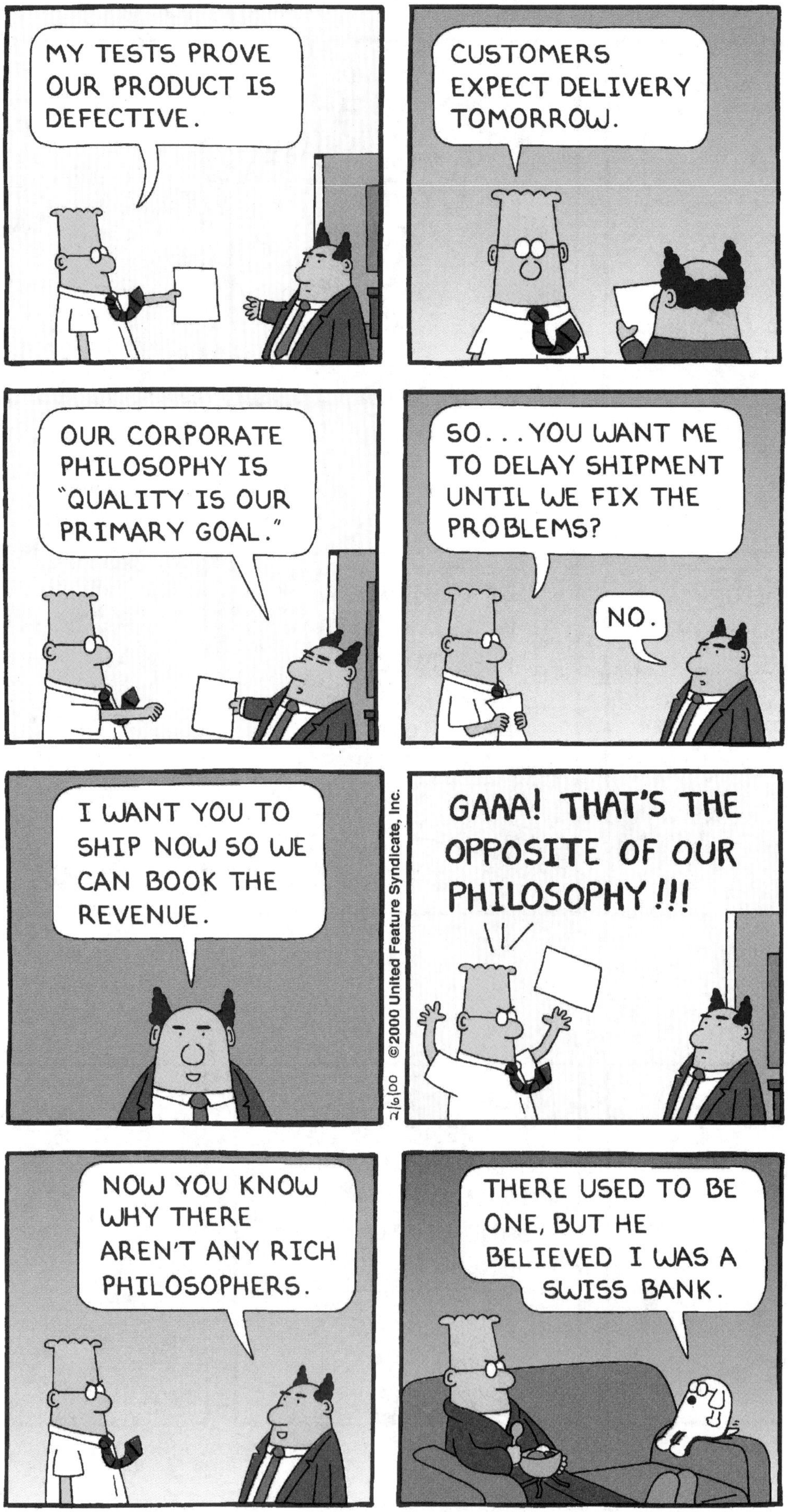
MY TESTS PROVE OUR PRODUCT IS DEFECTIVE.
CUSTOMERS EXPECT DELIVERY TOMORROW.
OUR CORPORATE PHILOSOPHY IS "QUALITY IS OUR PRIMARY GOAL."
SO . . . YOU WANT ME TO DELAY SHIPMENT UNTIL WE FIX THE PROBLEMS?
NO.
I WANT YOU TO SHIP NOW SO WE CAN BOOK THE REVENUE.
GAAA! THAT'S THE OPPOSITE OF OUR PHILOSOPHY!!!
NOW YOU KNOW WHY THERE AREN'T ANY RICH PHILOSOPHERS.
THERE USED TO BE ONE, BUT HE BELIEVED I WAS A SWISS BANK.
2/6/00 ©2000 United Feature Syndicate, Inc.

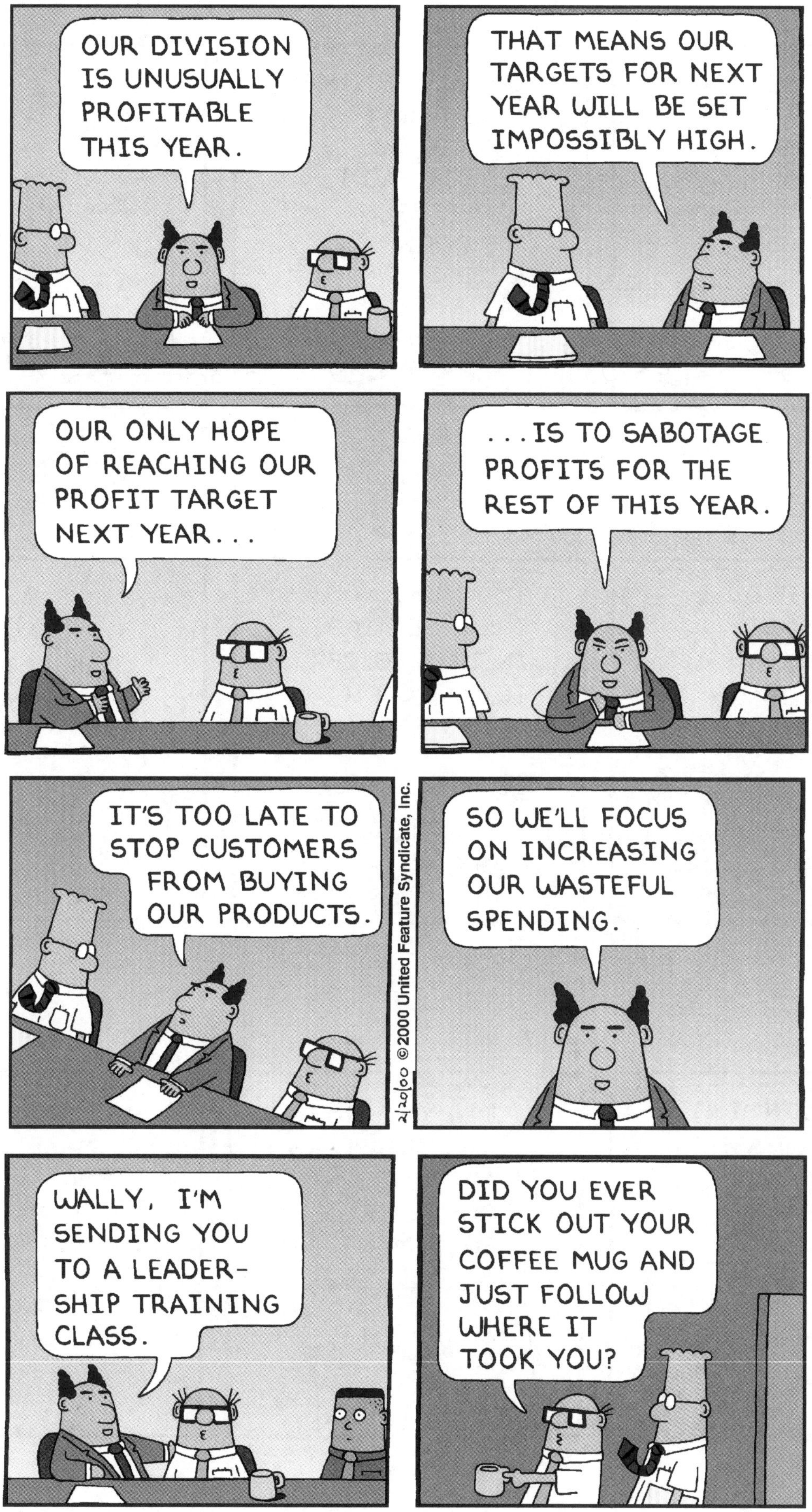
OUR DIVISION IS UNUSUALLY PROFITABLE THIS YEAR.
THAT MEANS OUR TARGETS FOR NEXT YEAR WILL BE SET IMPOSSIBLY HIGH.
OUR ONLY HOPE OF REACHING OUR PROFIT TARGET NEXT YEAR . . .
. . . IS TO SABOTAGE PROFITS FOR THE REST OF THIS YEAR.
IT'S TOO LATE TO STOP CUSTOMERS FROM BUYING OUR PRODUCTS.
2/20/00 © 2000 United Feature Syndicate, Inc.
SO WE'LL FOCUS ON INCREASING OUR WASTEFUL SPENDING.
WALLY, I'M SENDING YOU TO A LEADER-SHIP TRAINING CLASS.
DID YOU EVER STICK OUT YOUR COFFEE MUG AND JUST FOLLOW WHERE IT TOOK YOU?

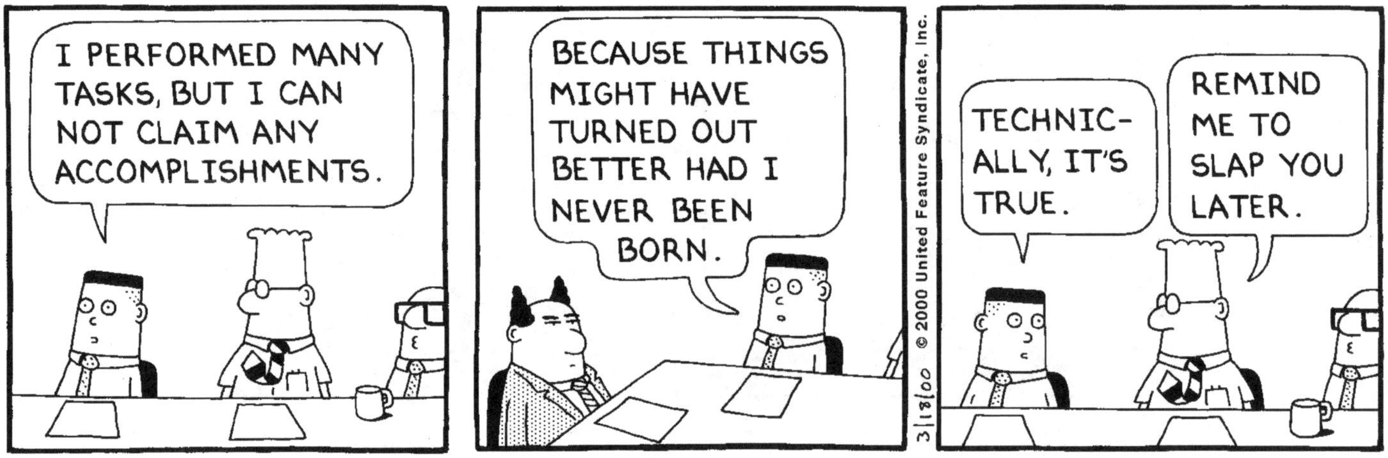
I PERFORMED MANY TASKS, BUT I CAN NOT CLAIM ANY ACCOMPLISHMENTS.
BECAUSE THINGS MIGHT HAVE TURNED OUT BETTER HAD I NEVER BEEN BORN.
3/18/00 © 2000 United Feature Syndicate, Inc.
TECHNIC-ALLY, IT'S TRUE.
REMIND ME TO SLAP YOU LATER.

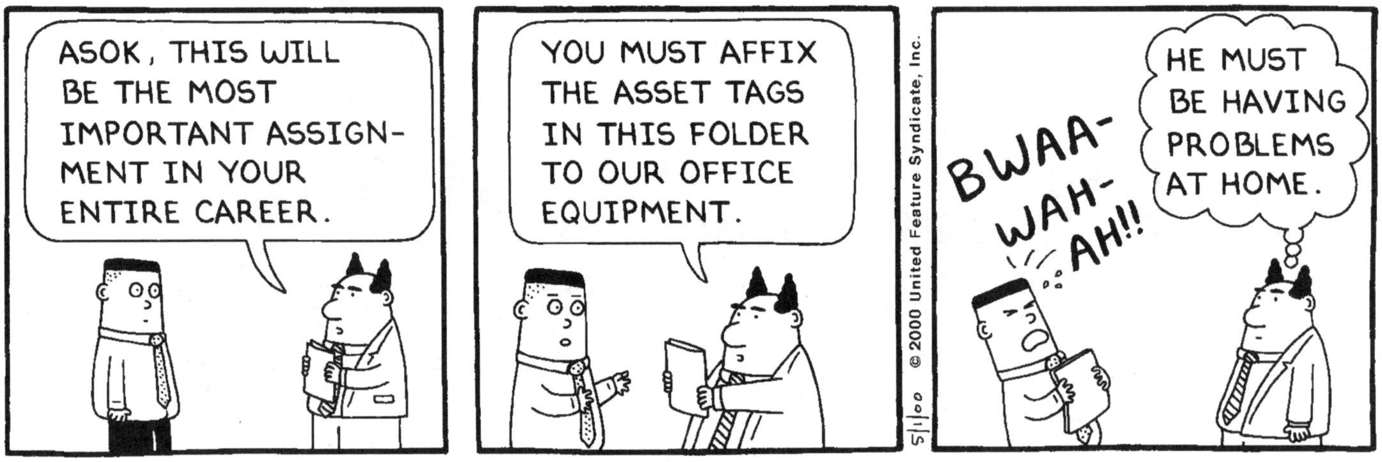
ASOK, THIS WILL BE THE MOST IMPORTANT ASSIGN-MENT IN YOUR ENTIRE CAREER.
YOU MUST AFFIX THE ASSET TAGS IN THIS FOLDER TO OUR OFFICE EQUIPMENT.
5/1/00 © 2000 United Feature Syndicate, Inc.
BWAA-WAH-AH!!
HE MUST BE HAVING PROBLEMS AT HOME.

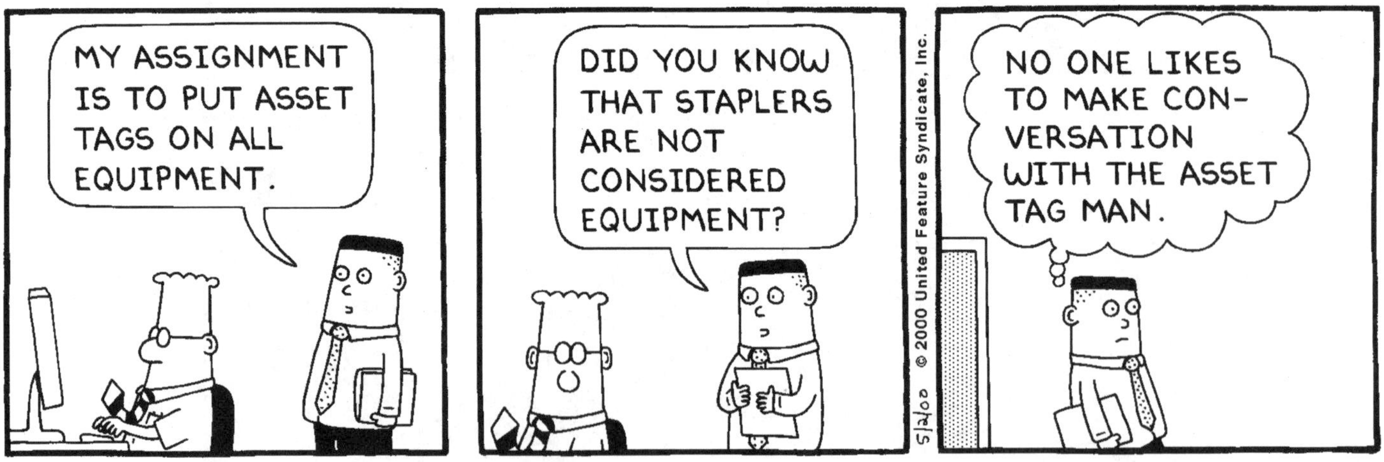
MY ASSIGNMENT IS TO PUT ASSET TAGS ON ALL EQUIPMENT.
DID YOU KNOW THAT STAPLERS ARE NOT CONSIDERED EQUIPMENT?
5/2/00 © 2000 United Feature Syndicate, Inc.
NO ONE LIKES TO MAKE CON-VERSATION WITH THE ASSET TAG MAN.

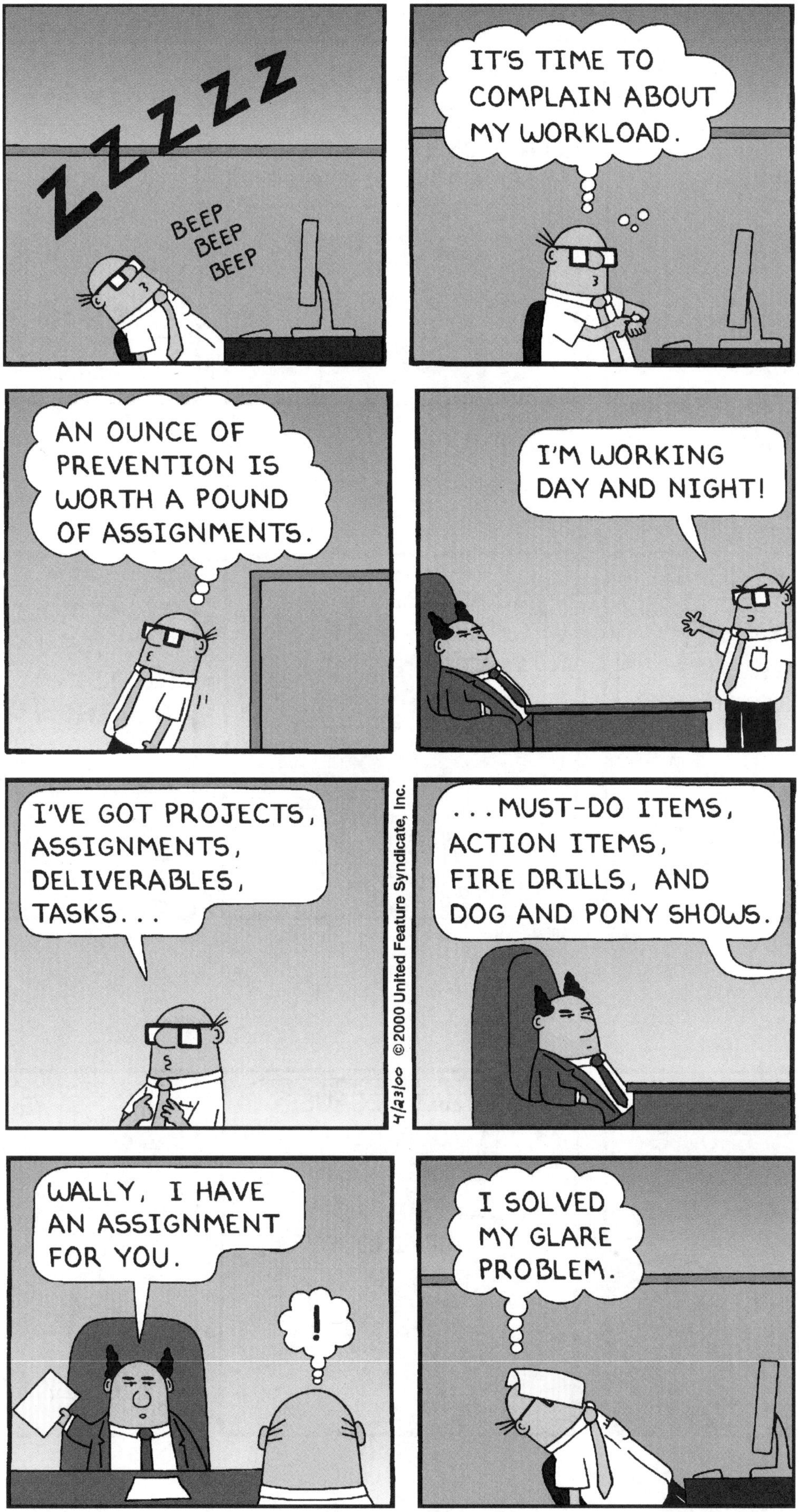
ZZZZZ
BEEP BEEP BEEP
IT'S TIME TO COMPLAIN ABOUT MY WORKLOAD.
AN OUNCE OF PREVENTION IS WORTH A POUND OF ASSIGNMENTS.
I'M WORKING DAY AND NIGHT!
I'VE GOT PROJECTS, ASSIGNMENTS, DELIVERABLES, TASKS...
...MUST-DO ITEMS, ACTION ITEMS, FIRE DRILLS, AND DOG AND PONY SHOWS.
WALLY, I HAVE AN ASSIGNMENT FOR YOU.
!
I SOLVED MY GLARE PROBLEM.
4/23/00 ©2000 United Feature Syndicate, Inc.

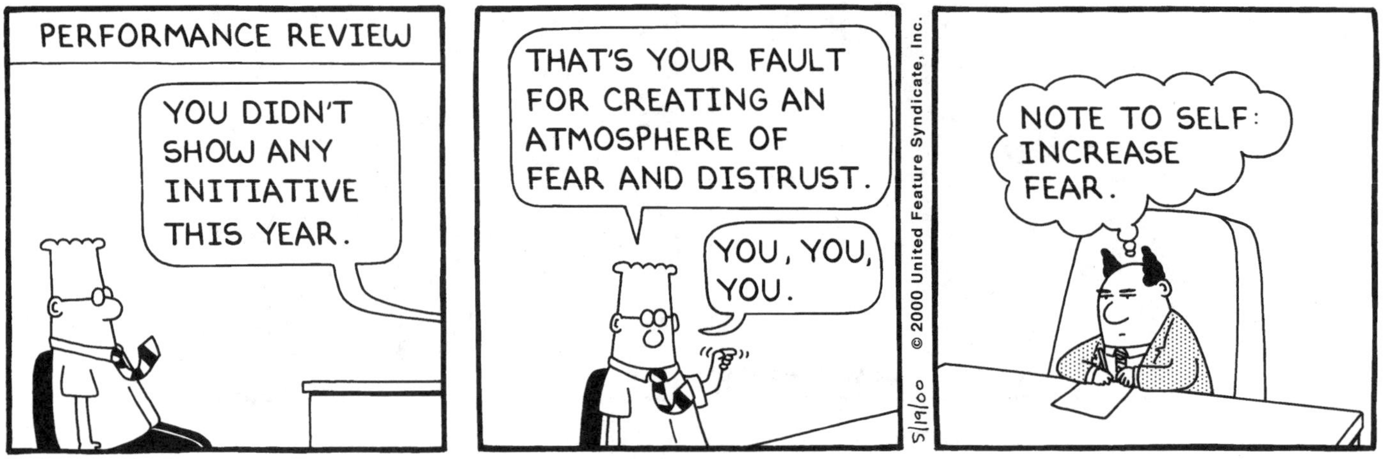
PERFORMANCE REVIEW
YOU DIDN'T SHOW ANY INITIATIVE THIS YEAR.
THAT'S YOUR FAULT FOR CREATING AN ATMOSPHERE OF FEAR AND DISTRUST.
YOU, YOU, YOU.
5/19/00 © 2000 United Feature Syndicate, Inc.
NOTE TO SELF: INCREASE FEAR.

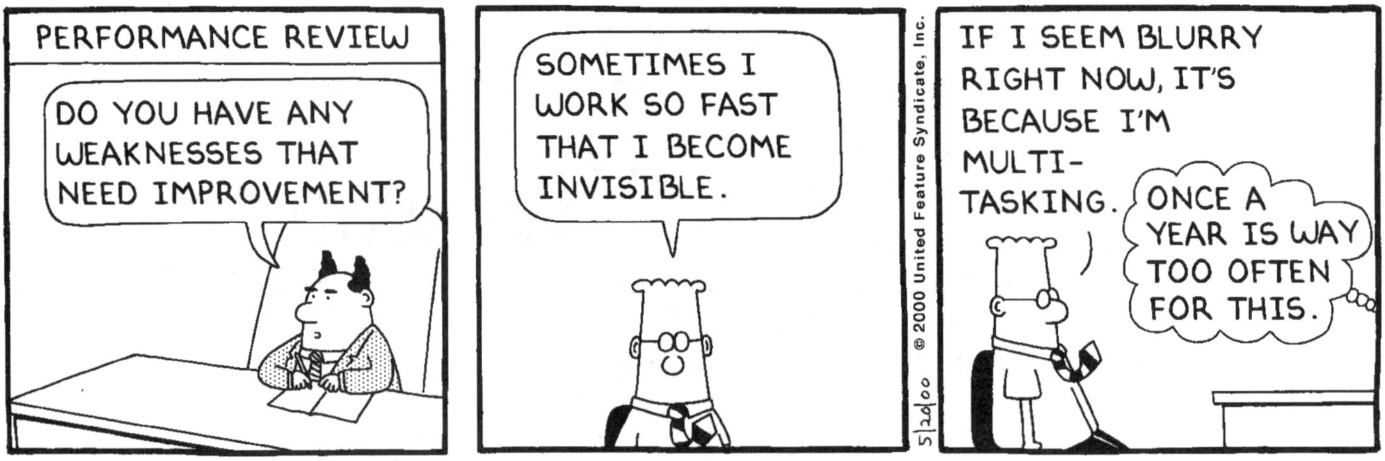
PERFORMANCE REVIEW
DO YOU HAVE ANY WEAKNESSES THAT NEED IMPROVEMENT?
SOMETIMES I WORK SO FAST THAT I BECOME INVISIBLE.
5/20/00 © 2000 United Feature Syndicate, Inc.
IF I SEEM BLURRY RIGHT NOW, IT'S BECAUSE I'M MULTI-TASKING.
ONCE A YEAR IS WAY TOO OFTEN FOR THIS.

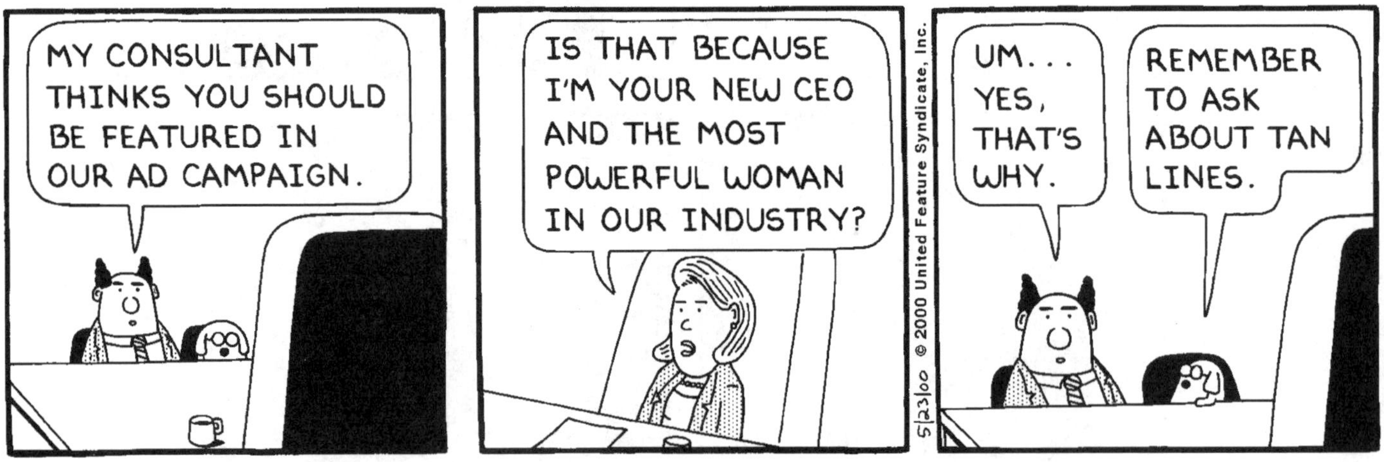
MY CONSULTANT THINKS YOU SHOULD BE FEATURED IN OUR AD CAMPAIGN.
IS THAT BECAUSE I'M YOUR NEW CEO AND THE MOST POWERFUL WOMAN IN OUR INDUSTRY?
5/23/00 © 2000 United Feature Syndicate, Inc.
UM... YES, THAT'S WHY.
REMEMBER TO ASK ABOUT TAN LINES.

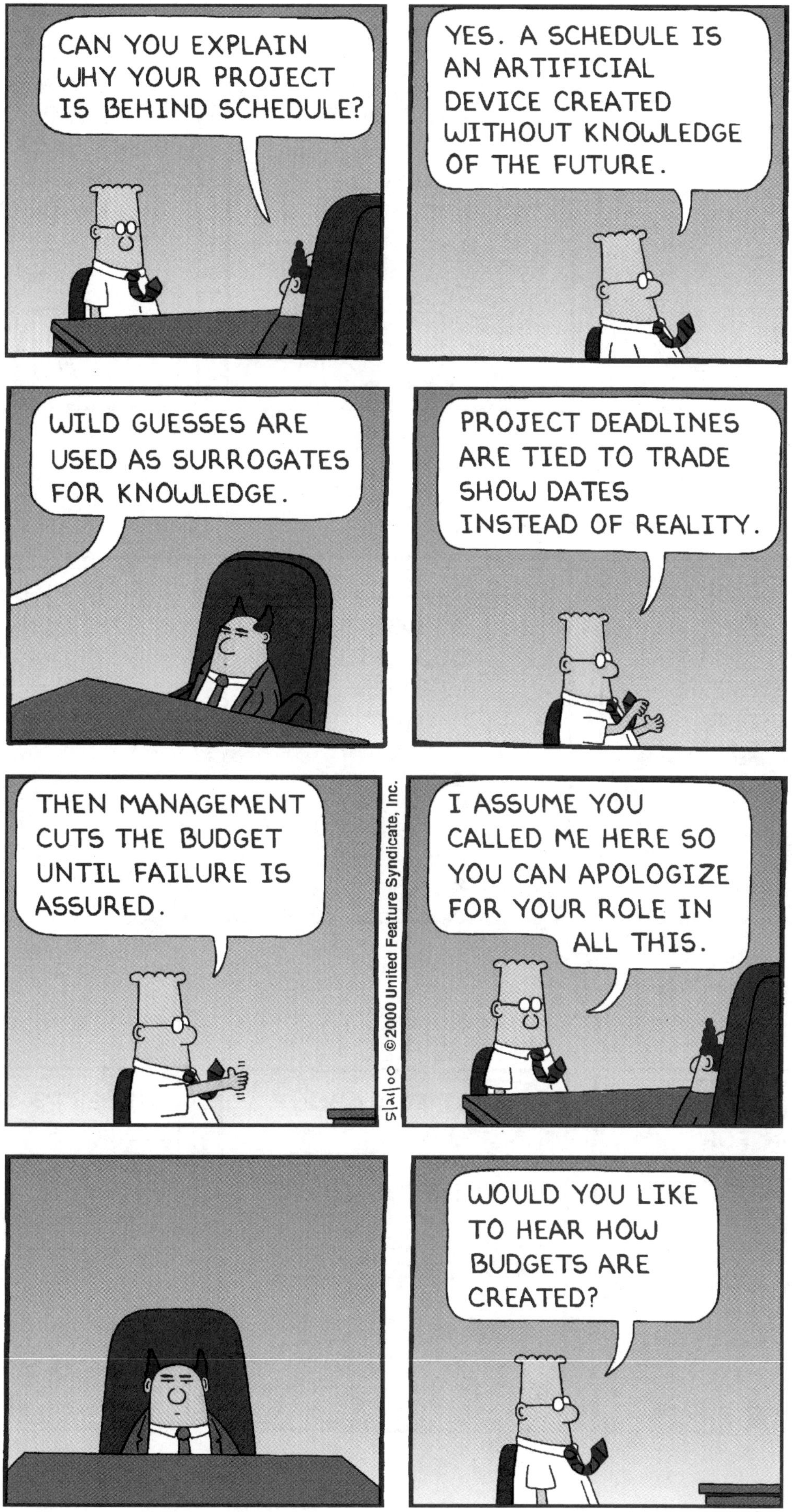
CAN YOU EXPLAIN WHY YOUR PROJECT IS BEHIND SCHEDULE?
YES. A SCHEDULE IS AN ARTIFICIAL DEVICE CREATED WITHOUT KNOWLEDGE OF THE FUTURE.
WILD GUESSES ARE USED AS SURROGATES FOR KNOWLEDGE.
PROJECT DEADLINES ARE TIED TO TRADE SHOW DATES INSTEAD OF REALITY.
THEN MANAGEMENT CUTS THE BUDGET UNTIL FAILURE IS ASSURED.
5/21/00 © 2000 United Feature Syndicate, Inc.
I ASSUME YOU CALLED ME HERE SO YOU CAN APOLOGIZE FOR YOUR ROLE IN ALL THIS.
WOULD YOU LIKE TO HEAR HOW BUDGETS ARE CREATED?

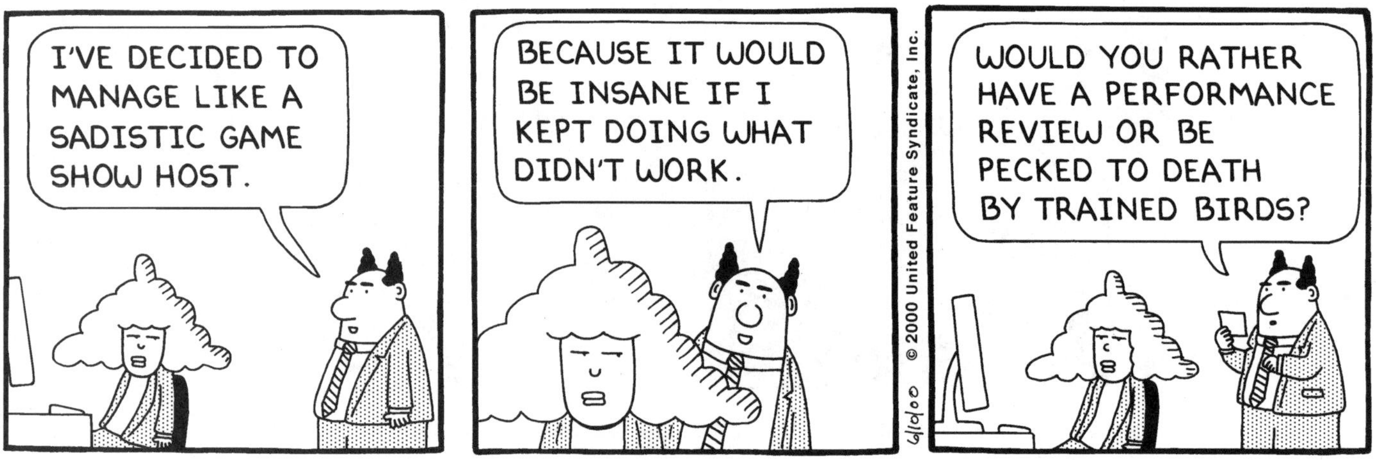
I'VE DECIDED TO MANAGE LIKE A SADISTIC GAME SHOW HOST.
BECAUSE IT WOULD BE INSANE IF I KEPT DOING WHAT DIDN'T WORK.
© 2000 United Feature Syndicate, Inc.
6/10/00
WOULD YOU RATHER HAVE A PERFORMANCE REVIEW OR BE PECKED TO DEATH BY TRAINED BIRDS?

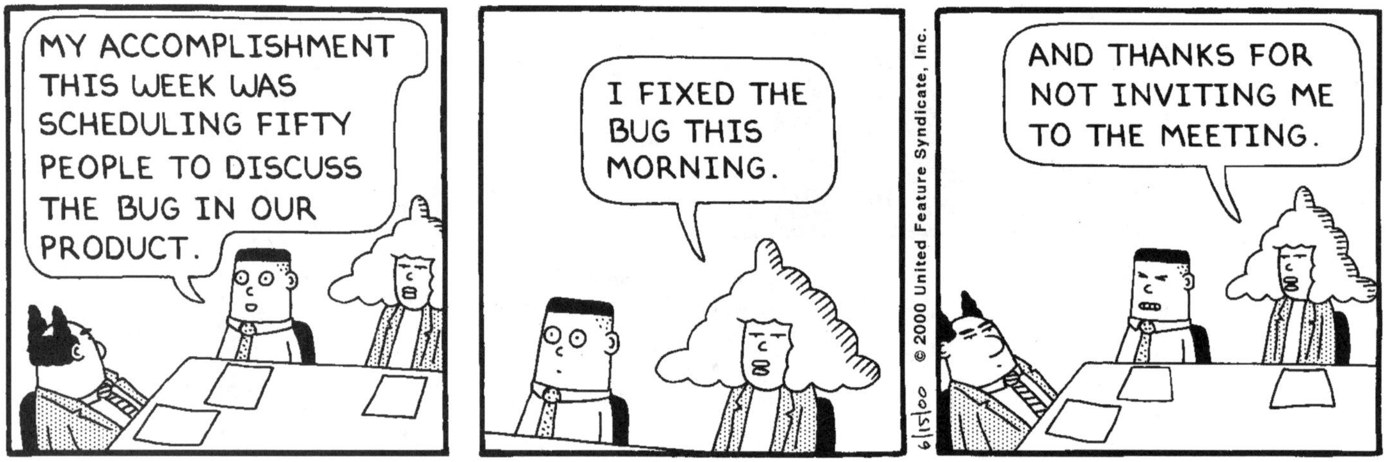
MY ACCOMPLISHMENT THIS WEEK WAS SCHEDULING FIFTY PEOPLE TO DISCUSS THE BUG IN OUR PRODUCT.
I FIXED THE BUG THIS MORNING.
© 2000 United Feature Syndicate, Inc.
6/15/00
AND THANKS FOR NOT INVITING ME TO THE MEETING.

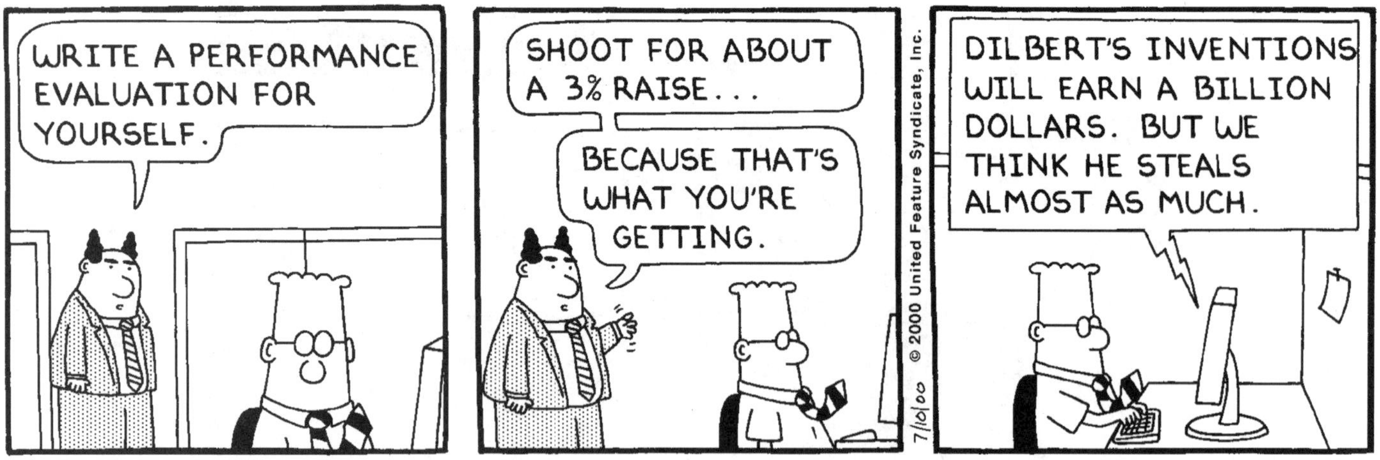
WRITE A PERFORMANCE EVALUATION FOR YOURSELF.
SHOOT FOR ABOUT A 3% RAISE...
BECAUSE THAT'S WHAT YOU'RE GETTING.
© 2000 United Feature Syndicate, Inc.
7/10/00
DILBERT'S INVENTIONS WILL EARN A BILLION DOLLARS. BUT WE THINK HE STEALS ALMOST AS MUCH.

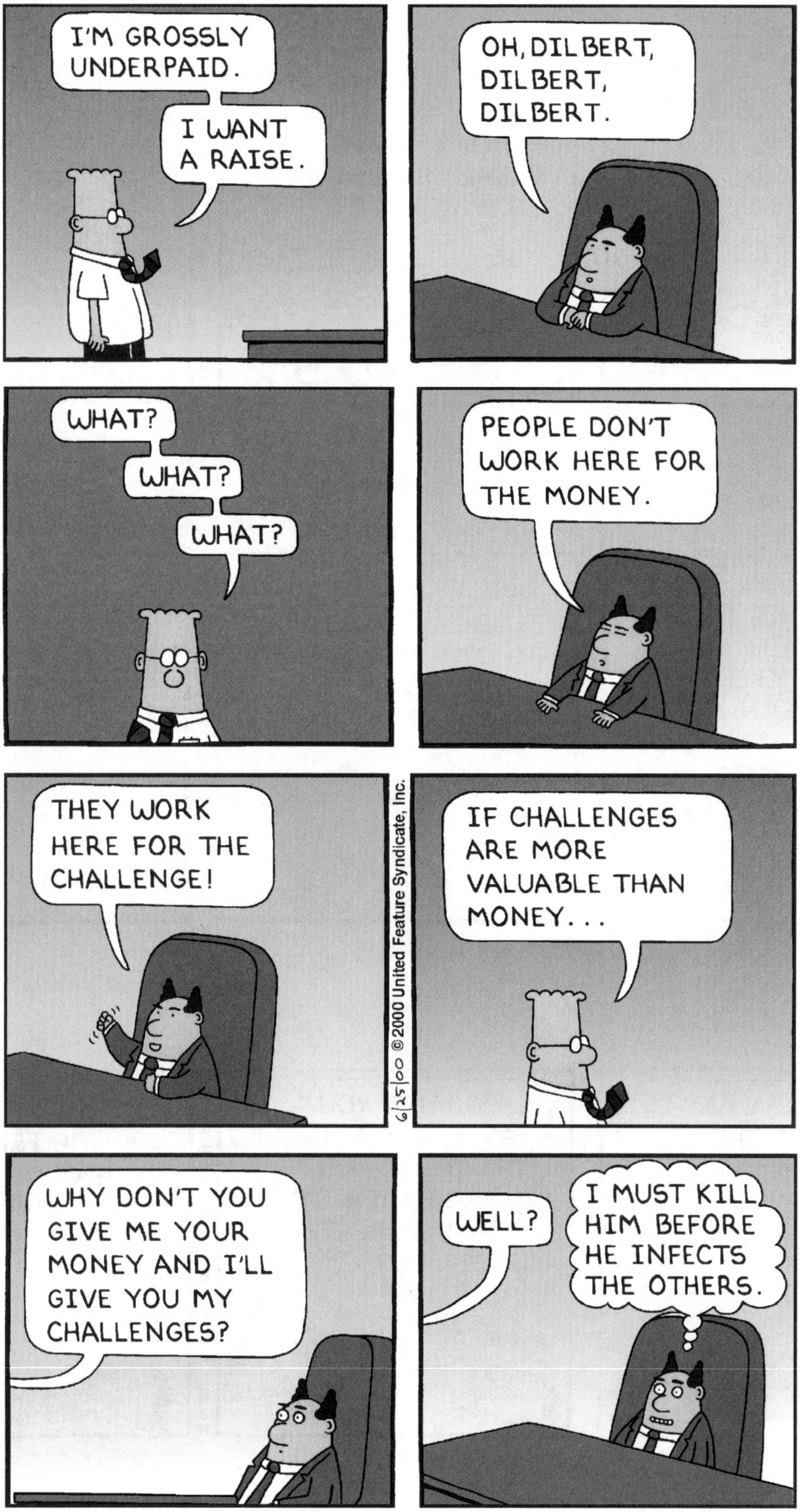

I'M GROSSLY UNDERPAID.
I WANT A RAISE.
OH, DILBERT, DILBERT, DILBERT.
WHAT?
WHAT?
WHAT?
PEOPLE DON'T WORK HERE FOR THE MONEY.
THEY WORK HERE FOR THE CHALLENGE!
IF CHALLENGES ARE MORE VALUABLE THAN MONEY...
WHY DON'T YOU GIVE ME YOUR MONEY AND I'LL GIVE YOU MY CHALLENGES?
WELL?
I MUST KILL HIM BEFORE HE INFECTS THE OTHERS.
6/25/00 © 2000 United Feature Syndicate, Inc.

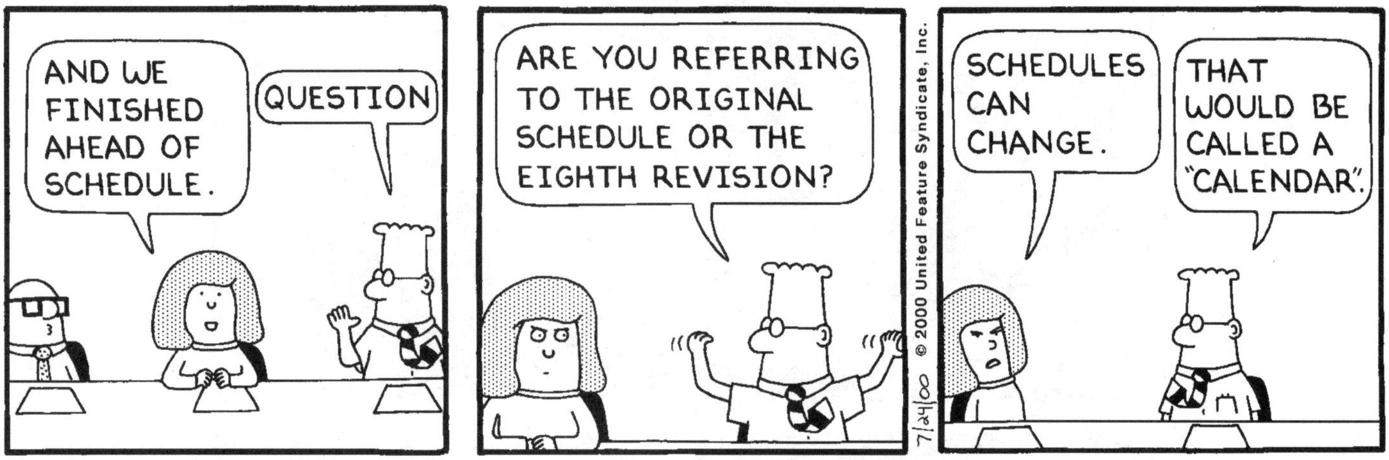
AND WE FINISHED AHEAD OF SCHEDULE.
QUESTION
ARE YOU REFERRING TO THE ORIGINAL SCHEDULE OR THE EIGHTH REVISION?
SCHEDULES CAN CHANGE.
THAT WOULD BE CALLED A "CALENDAR".
7/24/00 © 2000 United Feature Syndicate, Inc.

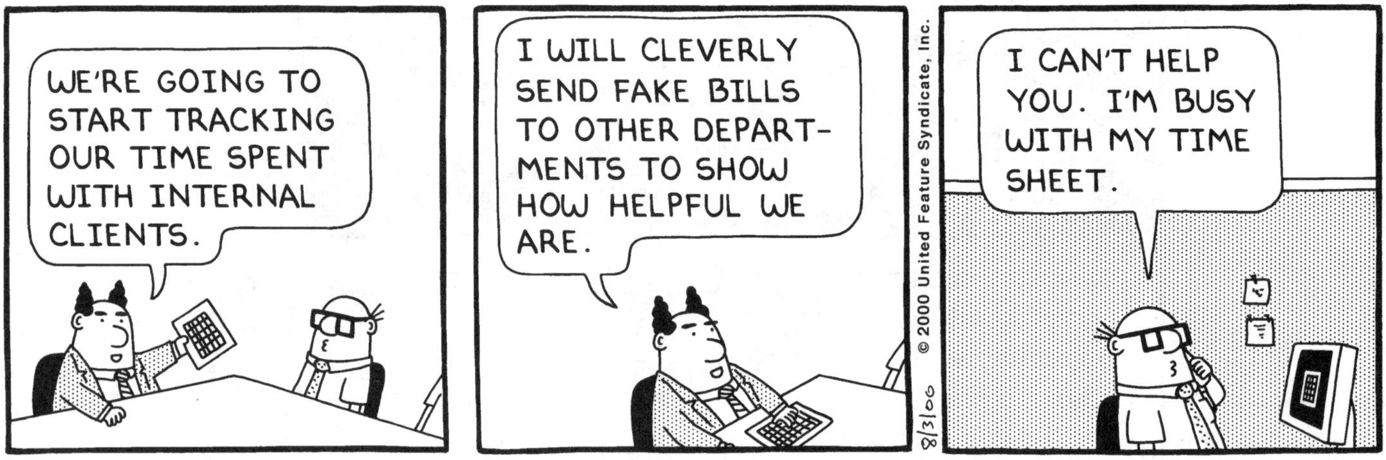
WE'RE GOING TO START TRACKING OUR TIME SPENT WITH INTERNAL CLIENTS.
I WILL CLEVERLY SEND FAKE BILLS TO OTHER DEPART-MENTS TO SHOW HOW HELPFUL WE ARE.
I CAN'T HELP YOU. I'M BUSY WITH MY TIME SHEET.
8/3/00 © 2000 United Feature Syndicate, Inc.

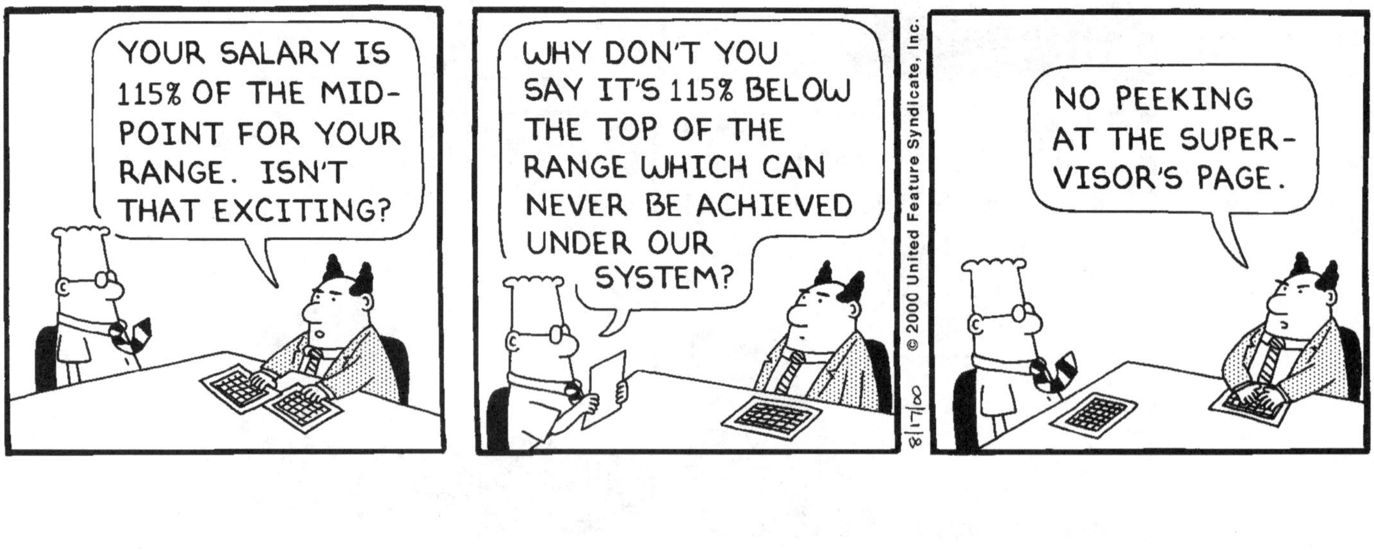
YOUR SALARY IS 115% OF THE MID-POINT FOR YOUR RANGE. ISN'T THAT EXCITING?
WHY DON'T YOU SAY IT'S 115% BELOW THE TOP OF THE RANGE WHICH CAN NEVER BE ACHIEVED UNDER OUR SYSTEM?
NO PEEKING AT THE SUPER-VISOR'S PAGE.
8/17/00 © 2000 United Feature Syndicate, Inc.

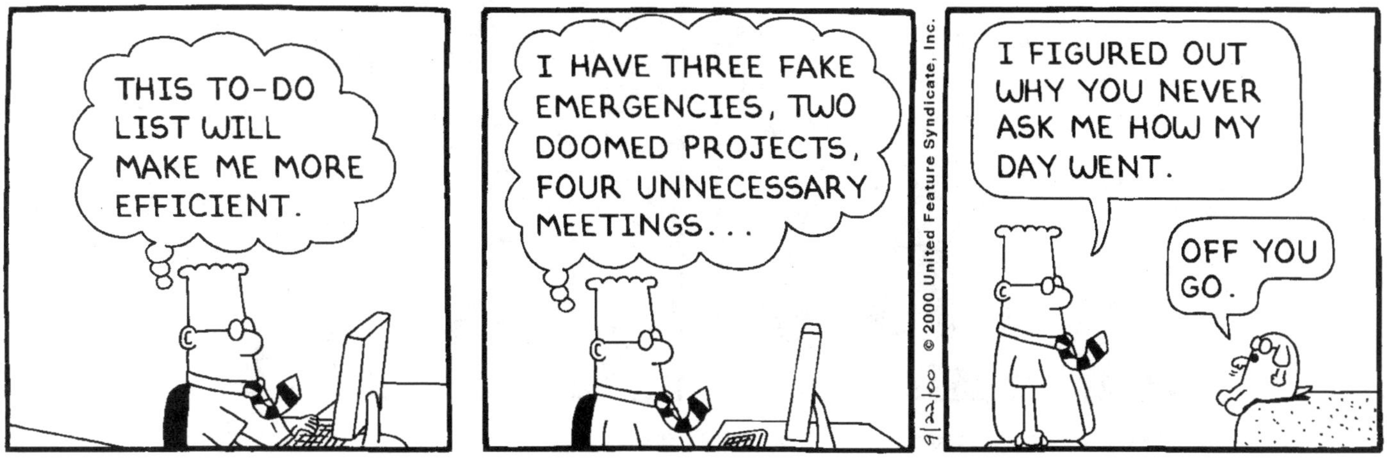
THIS TO-DO LIST WILL MAKE ME MORE EFFICIENT.
I HAVE THREE FAKE EMERGENCIES, TWO DOOMED PROJECTS, FOUR UNNECESSARY MEETINGS...
9/22/00 © 2000 United Feature Syndicate, Inc.
I FIGURED OUT WHY YOU NEVER ASK ME HOW MY DAY WENT.
OFF YOU GO.

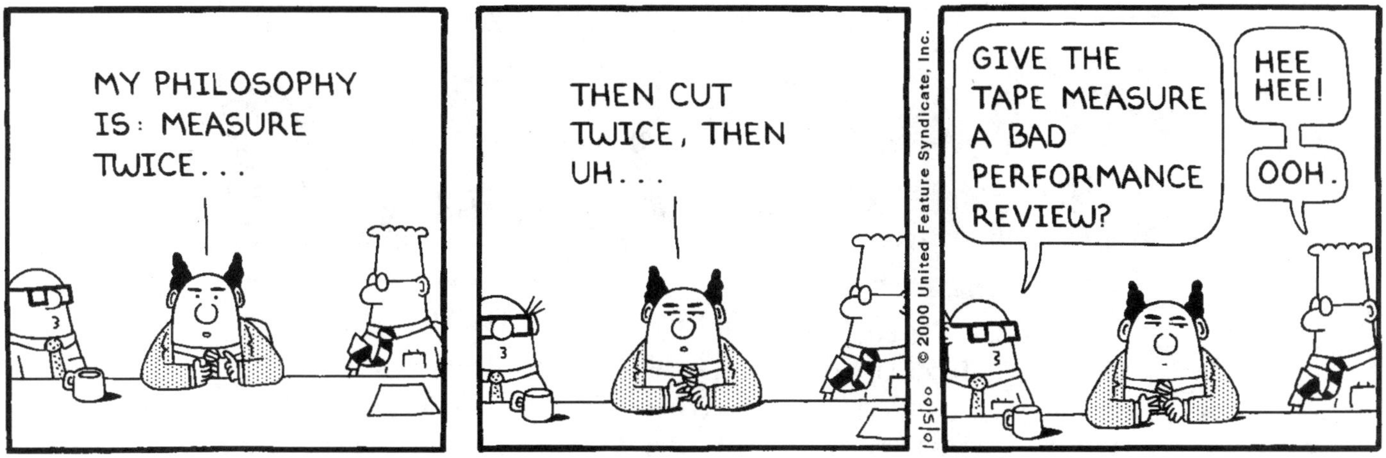
MY PHILOSOPHY IS: MEASURE TWICE...
THEN CUT TWICE, THEN UH...
10/5/00 © 2000 United Feature Syndicate, Inc.
GIVE THE TAPE MEASURE A BAD PERFORMANCE REVIEW?
HEE HEE!
OOH.

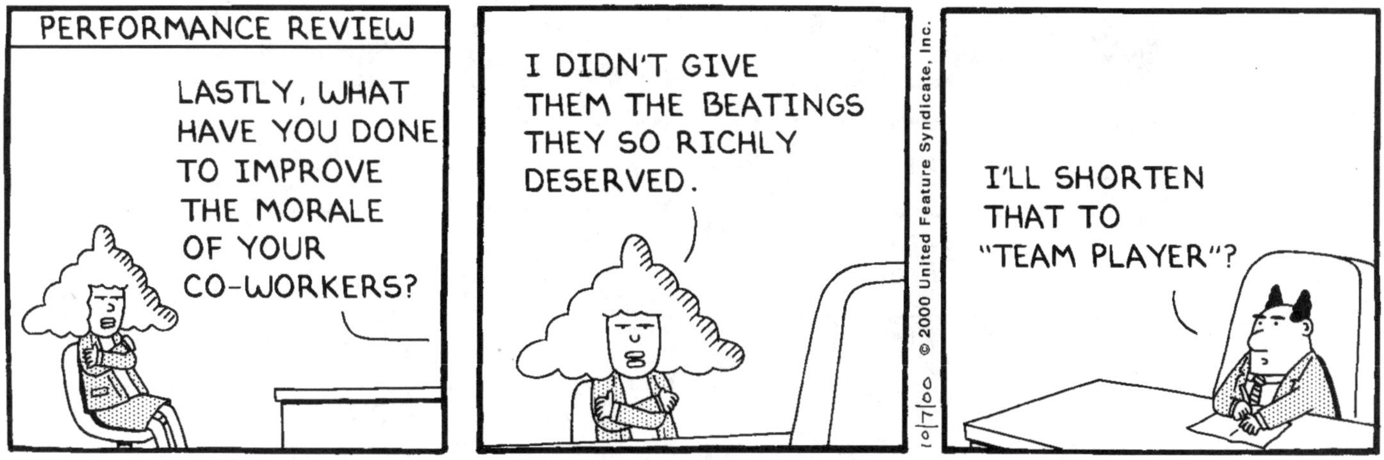
PERFORMANCE REVIEW
LASTLY, WHAT HAVE YOU DONE TO IMPROVE THE MORALE OF YOUR CO-WORKERS?
I DIDN'T GIVE THEM THE BEATINGS THEY SO RICHLY DESERVED.
10/7/00 © 2000 United Feature Syndicate, Inc.
I'LL SHORTEN THAT TO "TEAM PLAYER"?

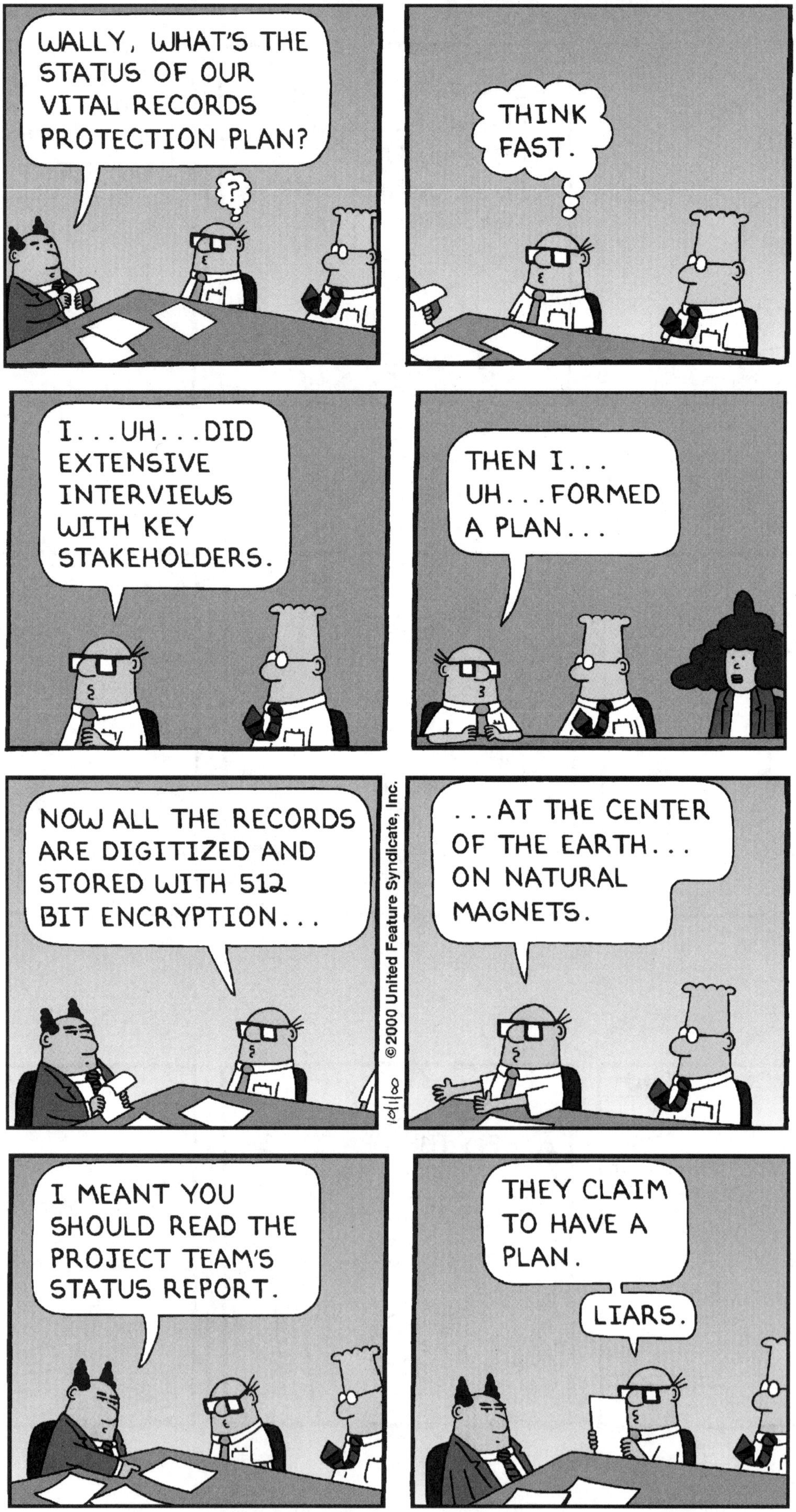
WALLY, WHAT'S THE STATUS OF OUR VITAL RECORDS PROTECTION PLAN?
?
THINK FAST.
I...UH...DID EXTENSIVE INTERVIEWS WITH KEY STAKEHOLDERS.
THEN I... UH...FORMED A PLAN...
NOW ALL THE RECORDS ARE DIGITIZED AND STORED WITH 512 BIT ENCRYPTION...
...AT THE CENTER OF THE EARTH... ON NATURAL MAGNETS.
I MEANT YOU SHOULD READ THE PROJECT TEAM'S STATUS REPORT.
THEY CLAIM TO HAVE A PLAN.
LIARS.
©2000 United Feature Syndicate, Inc.
10/1/00

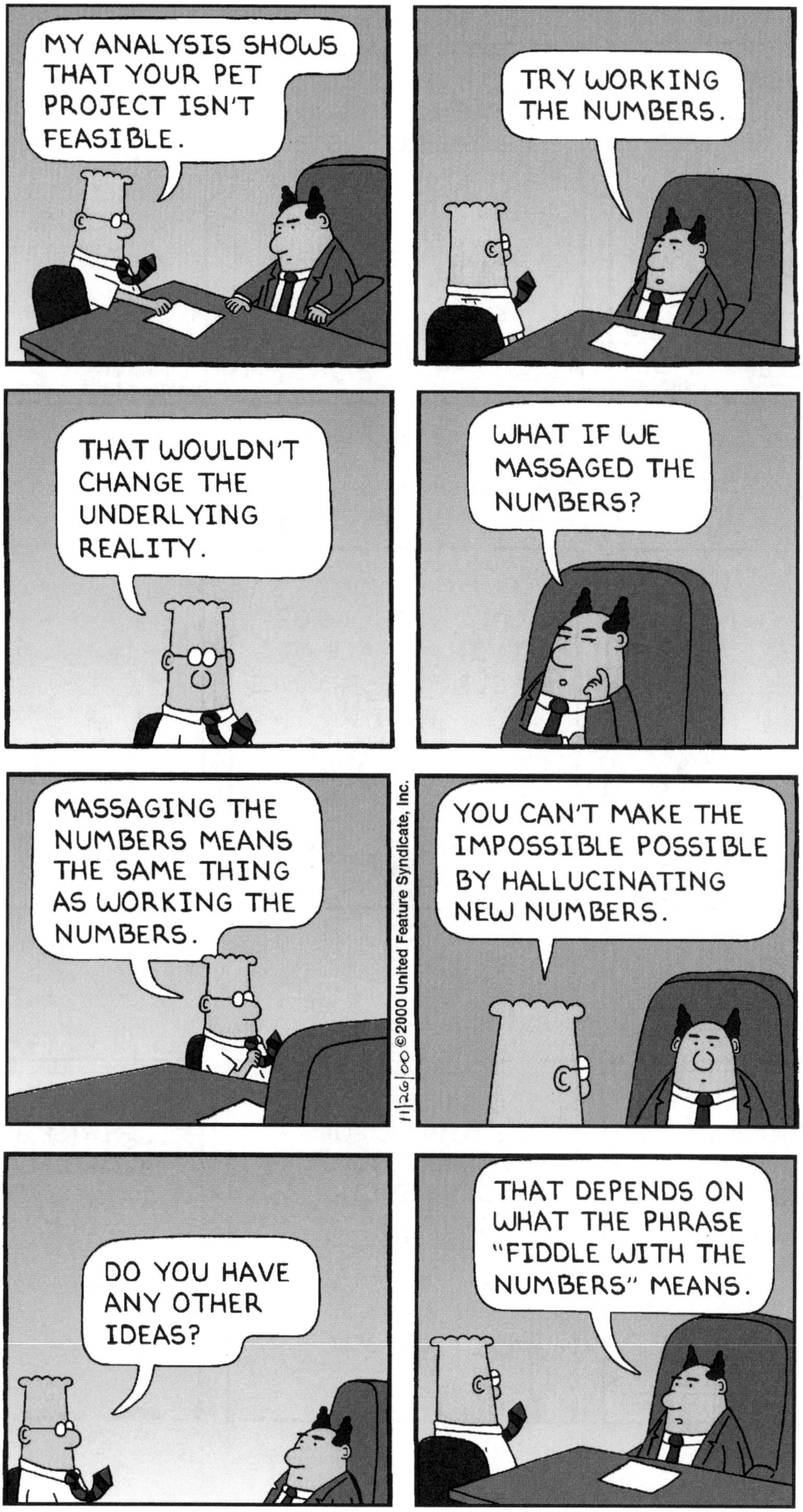
MY ANALYSIS SHOWS THAT YOUR PET PROJECT ISN'T FEASIBLE.
TRY WORKING THE NUMBERS.
THAT WOULDN'T CHANGE THE UNDERLYING REALITY.
WHAT IF WE MASSAGED THE NUMBERS?
MASSAGING THE NUMBERS MEANS THE SAME THING AS WORKING THE NUMBERS.
YOU CAN'T MAKE THE IMPOSSIBLE POSSIBLE BY HALLUCINATING NEW NUMBERS.
DO YOU HAVE ANY OTHER IDEAS?
THAT DEPENDS ON WHAT THE PHRASE "FIDDLE WITH THE NUMBERS" MEANS.
11/26/00 ©2000 United Feature Syndicate, Inc.

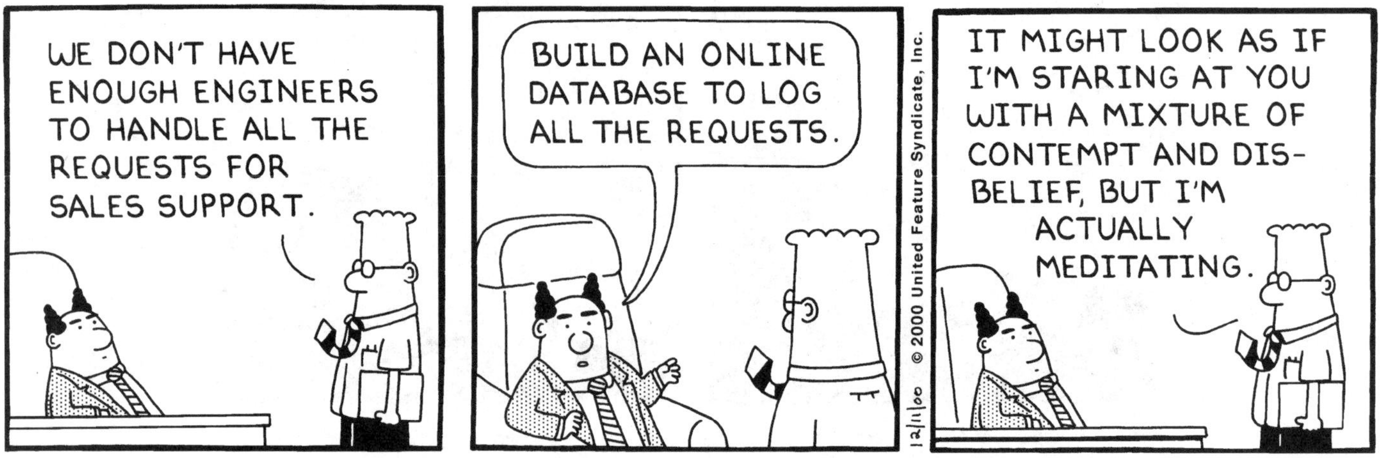
WE DON'T HAVE ENOUGH ENGINEERS TO HANDLE ALL THE REQUESTS FOR SALES SUPPORT.
BUILD AN ONLINE DATABASE TO LOG ALL THE REQUESTS.
12/11/00 © 2000 United Feature Syndicate, Inc.
IT MIGHT LOOK AS IF I'M STARING AT YOU WITH A MIXTURE OF CONTEMPT AND DIS-BELIEF, BUT I'M ACTUALLY MEDITATING.

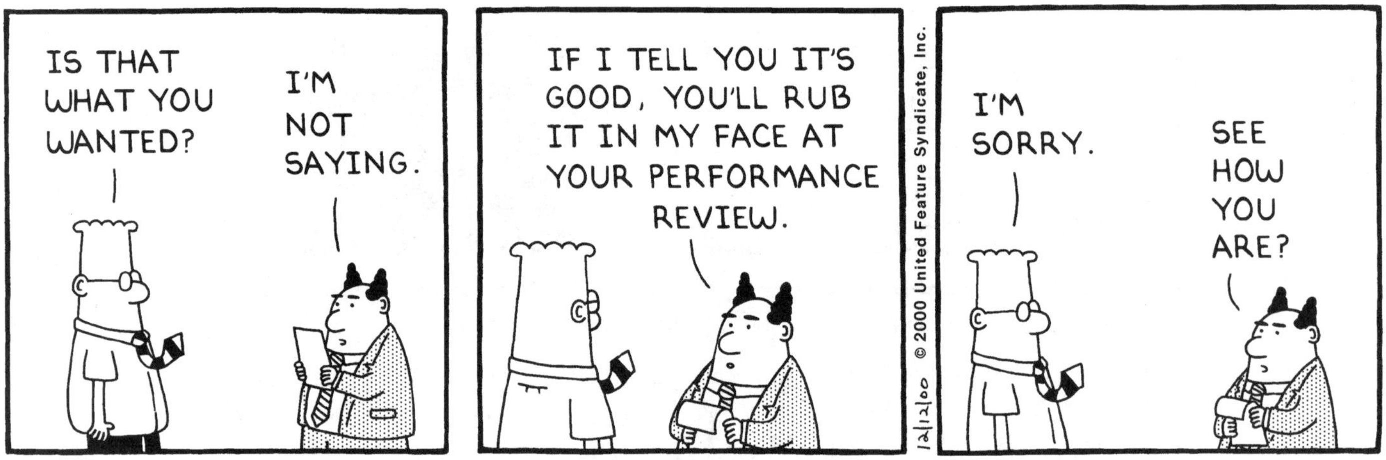
IS THAT WHAT YOU WANTED?
I'M NOT SAYING.
IF I TELL YOU IT'S GOOD, YOU'LL RUB IT IN MY FACE AT YOUR PERFORMANCE REVIEW.
12/12/00 © 2000 United Feature Syndicate, Inc.
I'M SORRY.
SEE HOW YOU ARE?

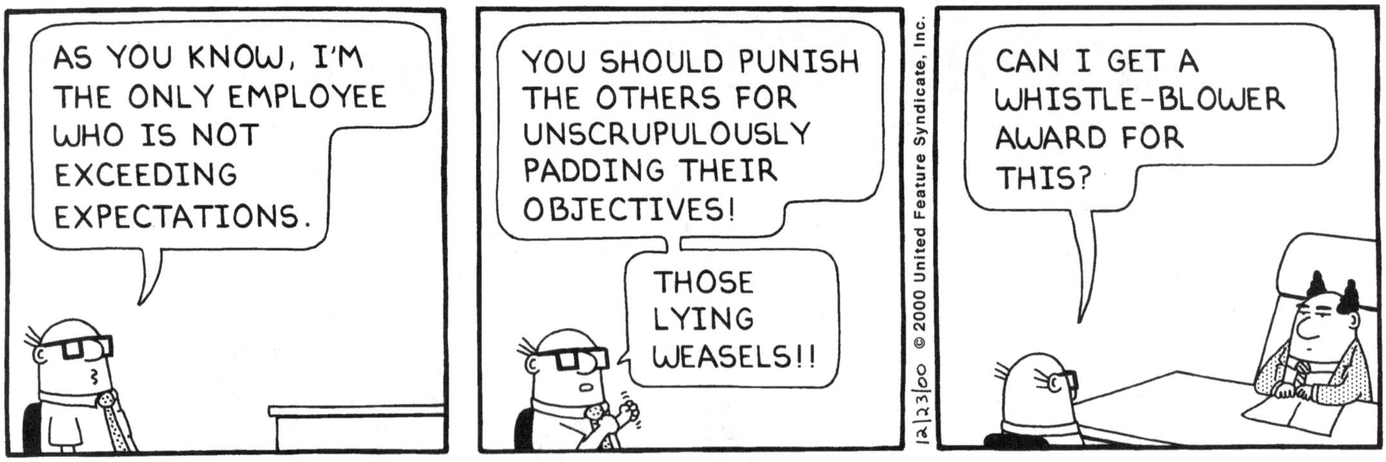
AS YOU KNOW, I'M THE ONLY EMPLOYEE WHO IS NOT EXCEEDING EXPECTATIONS.
YOU SHOULD PUNISH THE OTHERS FOR UNSCRUPULOUSLY PADDING THEIR OBJECTIVES!
THOSE LYING WEASELS!!
12/23/00 © 2000 United Feature Syndicate, Inc.
CAN I GET A WHISTLE-BLOWER AWARD FOR THIS?

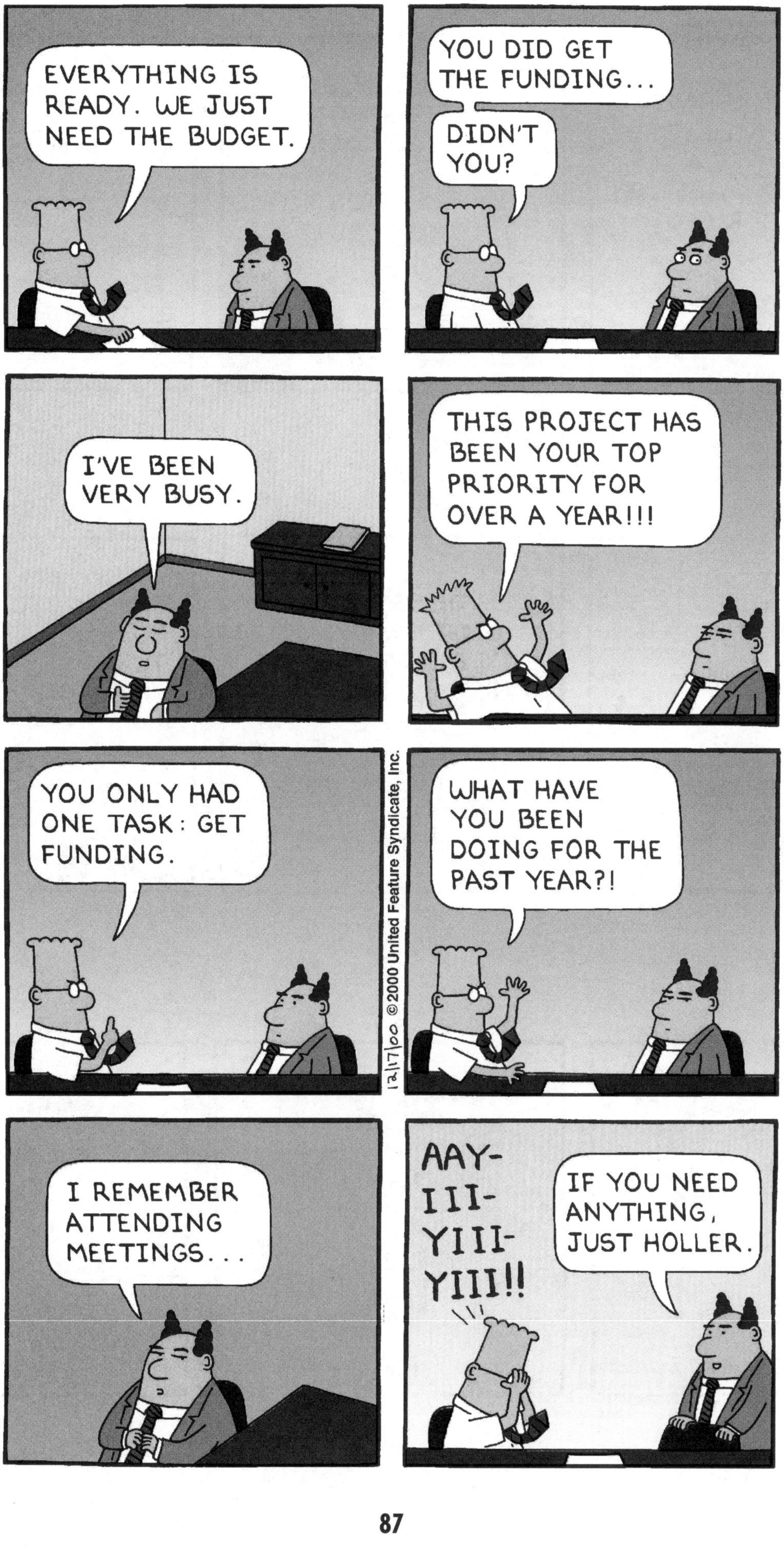
EVERYTHING IS READY. WE JUST NEED THE BUDGET.
YOU DID GET THE FUNDING...
DIDN'T YOU?
I'VE BEEN VERY BUSY.
THIS PROJECT HAS BEEN YOUR TOP PRIORITY FOR OVER A YEAR!!!
YOU ONLY HAD ONE TASK: GET FUNDING.
WHAT HAVE YOU BEEN DOING FOR THE PAST YEAR?!
I REMEMBER ATTENDING MEETINGS...
AAY-III-YIII-YIII!!
IF YOU NEED ANYTHING, JUST HOLLER.
12/17/00 © 2000 United Feature Syndicate, Inc.

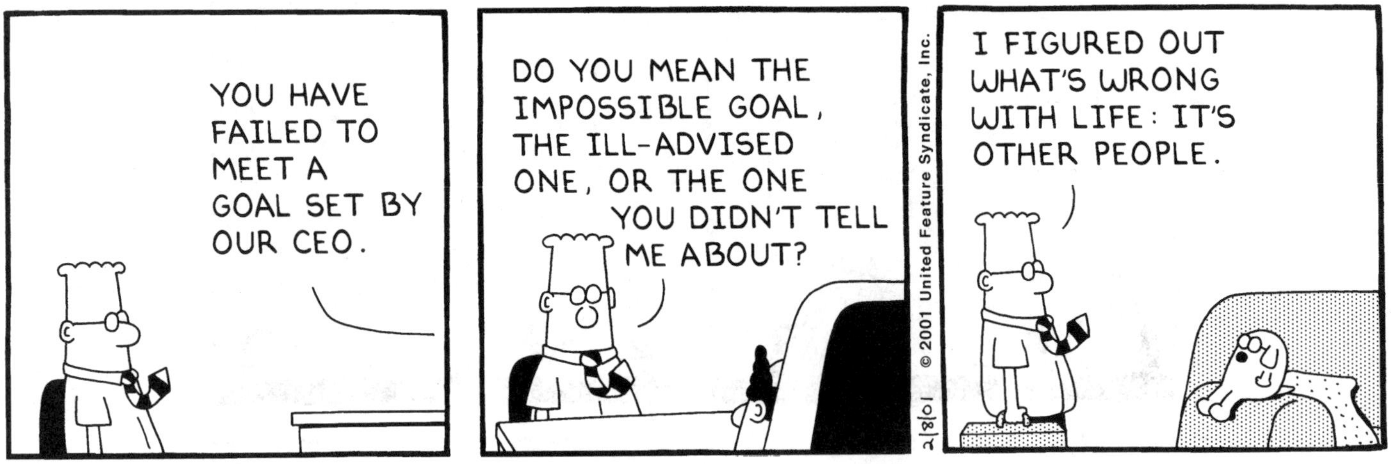
YOU HAVE FAILED TO MEET A GOAL SET BY OUR CEO.
DO YOU MEAN THE IMPOSSIBLE GOAL, THE ILL-ADVISED ONE, OR THE ONE YOU DIDN'T TELL ME ABOUT?
2/8/01 © 2001 United Feature Syndicate, Inc.
I FIGURED OUT WHAT'S WRONG WITH LIFE: IT'S OTHER PEOPLE.

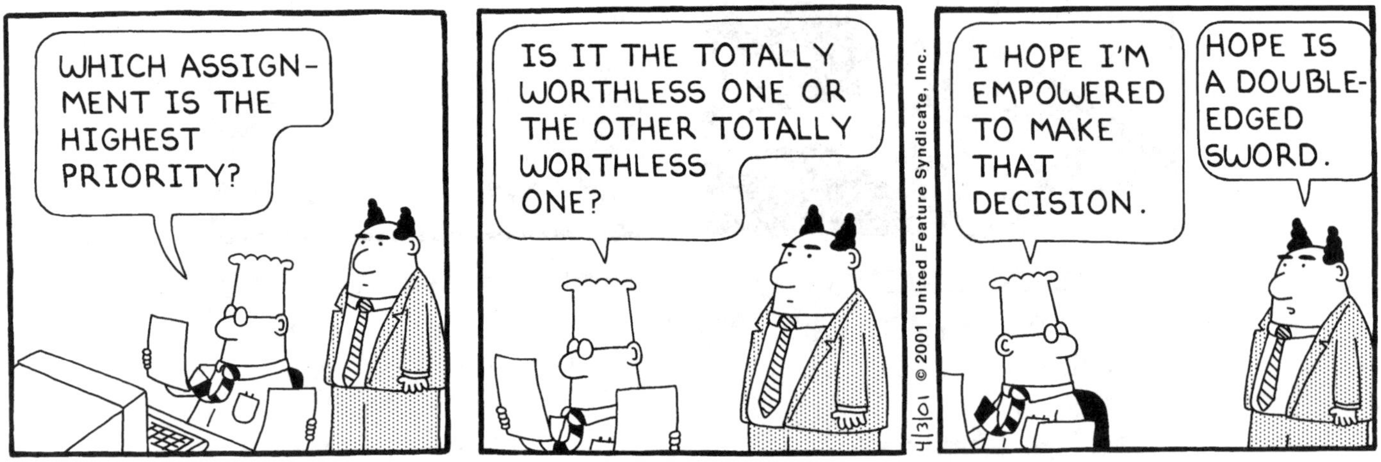
WHICH ASSIGN-MENT IS THE HIGHEST PRIORITY?
IS IT THE TOTALLY WORTHLESS ONE OR THE OTHER TOTALLY WORTHLESS ONE?
4/3/01 © 2001 United Feature Syndicate, Inc.
I HOPE I'M EMPOWERED TO MAKE THAT DECISION.
HOPE IS A DOUBLE-EDGED SWORD.

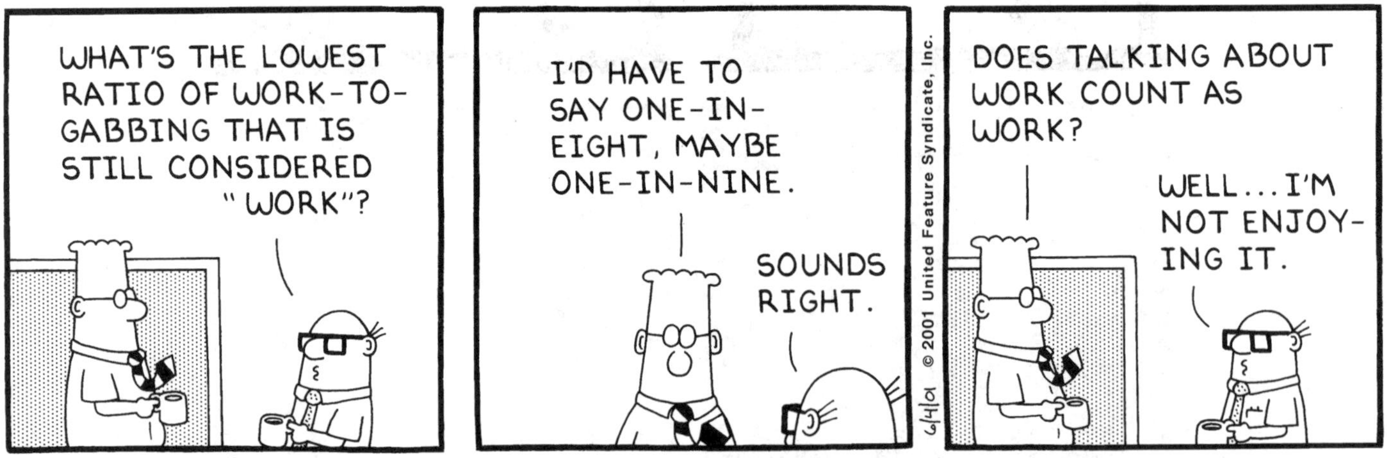
WHAT'S THE LOWEST RATIO OF WORK-TO-GABBING THAT IS STILL CONSIDERED "WORK"?
I'D HAVE TO SAY ONE-IN-EIGHT, MAYBE ONE-IN-NINE.
SOUNDS RIGHT.
6/4/01 © 2001 United Feature Syndicate, Inc.
DOES TALKING ABOUT WORK COUNT AS WORK?
WELL... I'M NOT ENJOY-ING IT.

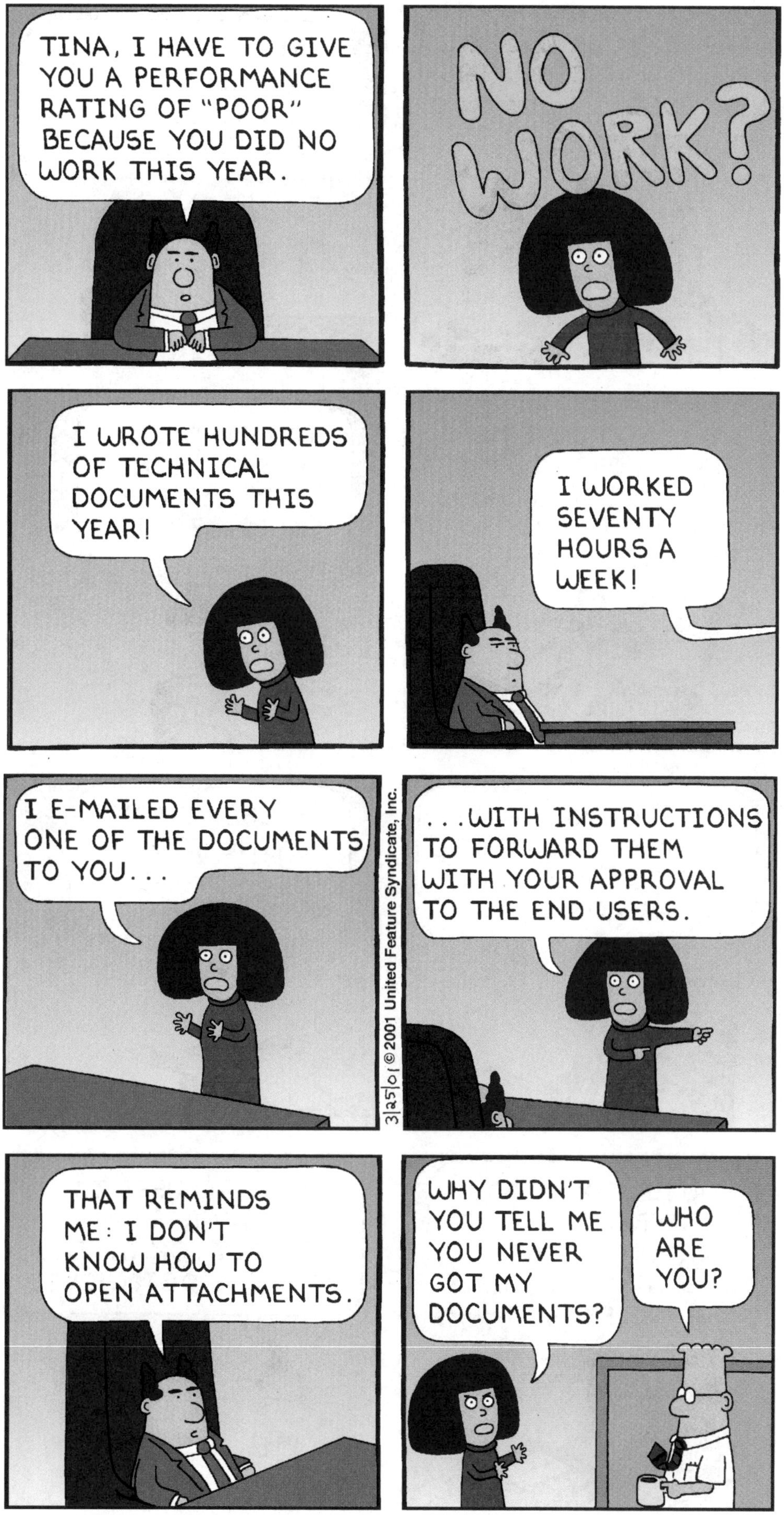
TINA, I HAVE TO GIVE YOU A PERFORMANCE RATING OF "POOR" BECAUSE YOU DID NO WORK THIS YEAR.
NO WORK?
I WROTE HUNDREDS OF TECHNICAL DOCUMENTS THIS YEAR!
I WORKED SEVENTY HOURS A WEEK!
I E-MAILED EVERY ONE OF THE DOCUMENTS TO YOU...
...WITH INSTRUCTIONS TO FORWARD THEM WITH YOUR APPROVAL TO THE END USERS.
3/25/01 © 2001 United Feature Syndicate, Inc.
THAT REMINDS ME: I DON'T KNOW HOW TO OPEN ATTACHMENTS.
WHY DIDN'T YOU TELL ME YOU NEVER GOT MY DOCUMENTS?
WHO ARE YOU?

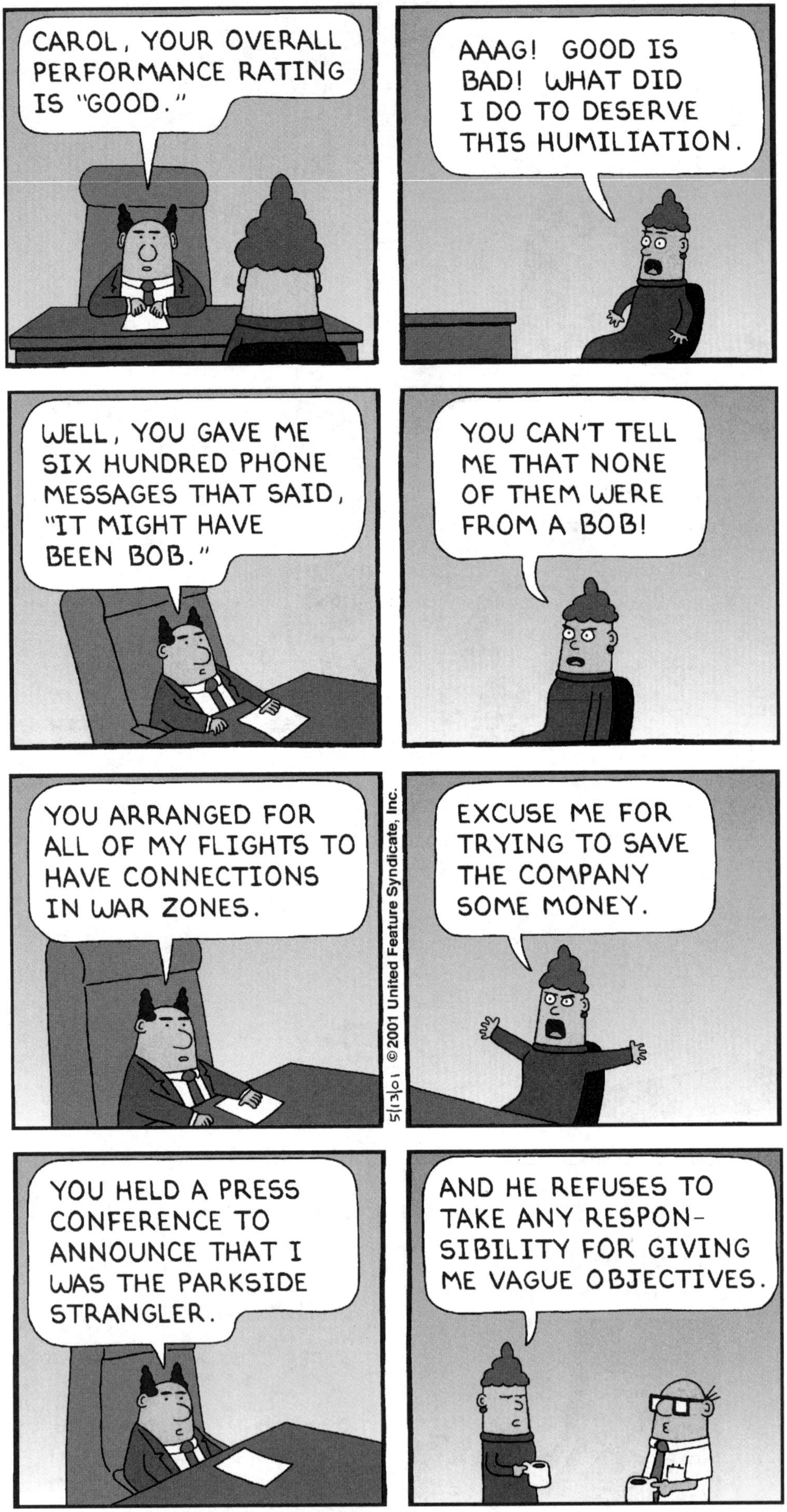
CAROL, YOUR OVERALL PERFORMANCE RATING IS "GOOD."
AAAG! GOOD IS BAD! WHAT DID I DO TO DESERVE THIS HUMILIATION.
WELL, YOU GAVE ME SIX HUNDRED PHONE MESSAGES THAT SAID, "IT MIGHT HAVE BEEN BOB."
YOU CAN'T TELL ME THAT NONE OF THEM WERE FROM A BOB!
YOU ARRANGED FOR ALL OF MY FLIGHTS TO HAVE CONNECTIONS IN WAR ZONES.
EXCUSE ME FOR TRYING TO SAVE THE COMPANY SOME MONEY.
YOU HELD A PRESS CONFERENCE TO ANNOUNCE THAT I WAS THE PARKSIDE STRANGLER.
AND HE REFUSES TO TAKE ANY RESPON-SIBILITY FOR GIVING ME VAGUE OBJECTIVES.

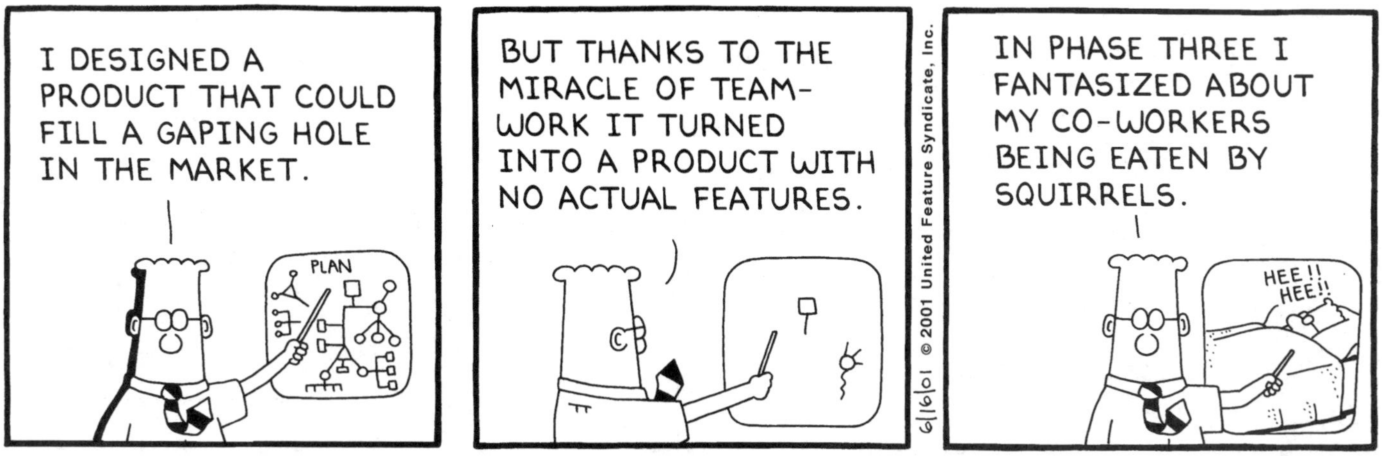
I DESIGNED A PRODUCT THAT COULD FILL A GAPING HOLE IN THE MARKET.
PLAN
BUT THANKS TO THE MIRACLE OF TEAM-WORK IT TURNED INTO A PRODUCT WITH NO ACTUAL FEATURES.
6/16/01 © 2001 United Feature Syndicate, Inc.
IN PHASE THREE I FANTASIZED ABOUT MY CO-WORKERS BEING EATEN BY SQUIRRELS.
HEE!! HEE!!

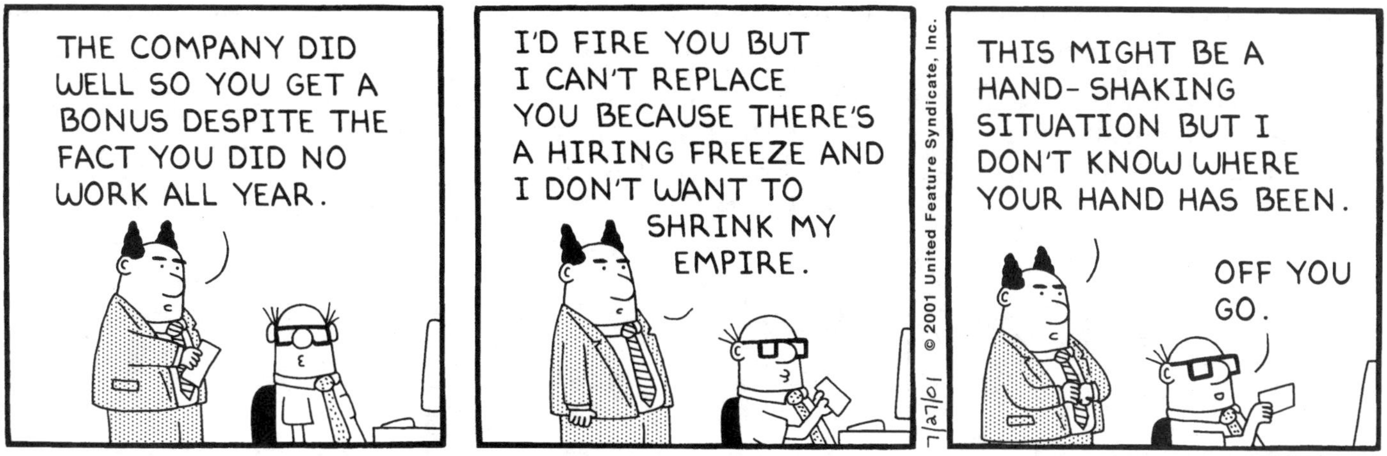
THE COMPANY DID WELL SO YOU GET A BONUS DESPITE THE FACT YOU DID NO WORK ALL YEAR.
I'D FIRE YOU BUT I CAN'T REPLACE YOU BECAUSE THERE'S A HIRING FREEZE AND I DON'T WANT TO SHRINK MY EMPIRE.
7/27/01 © 2001 United Feature Syndicate, Inc.
THIS MIGHT BE A HAND-SHAKING SITUATION BUT I DON'T KNOW WHERE YOUR HAND HAS BEEN.
OFF YOU GO.

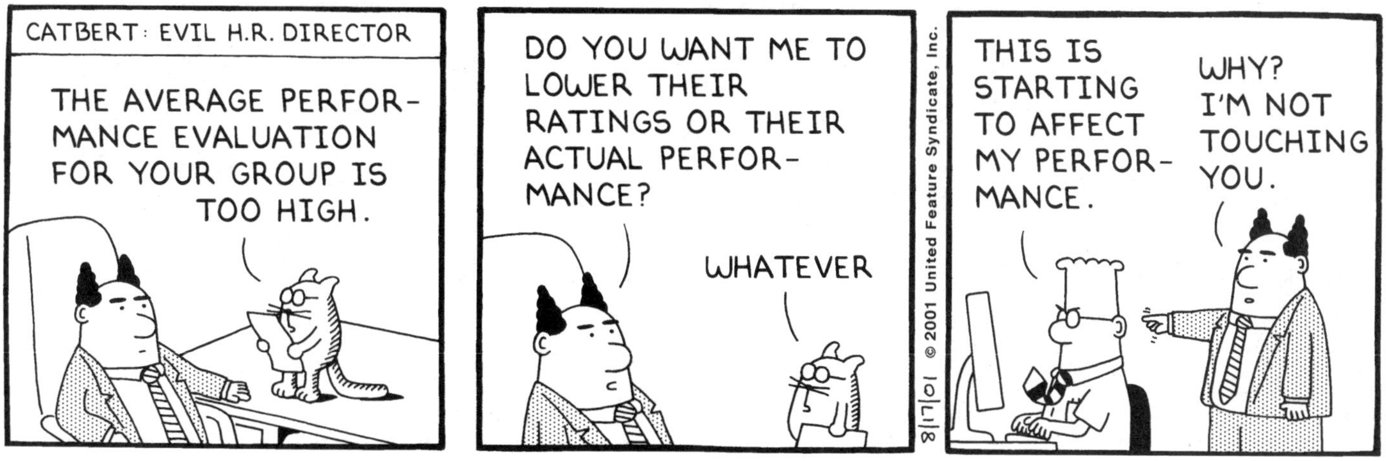
CATBERT: EVIL H.R. DIRECTOR
THE AVERAGE PERFORMANCE EVALUATION FOR YOUR GROUP IS TOO HIGH.
DO YOU WANT ME TO LOWER THEIR RATINGS OR THEIR ACTUAL PERFORMANCE?
WHATEVER
8/17/01 © 2001 United Feature Syndicate, Inc.
THIS IS STARTING TO AFFECT MY PERFORMANCE.
WHY? I'M NOT TOUCHING YOU.

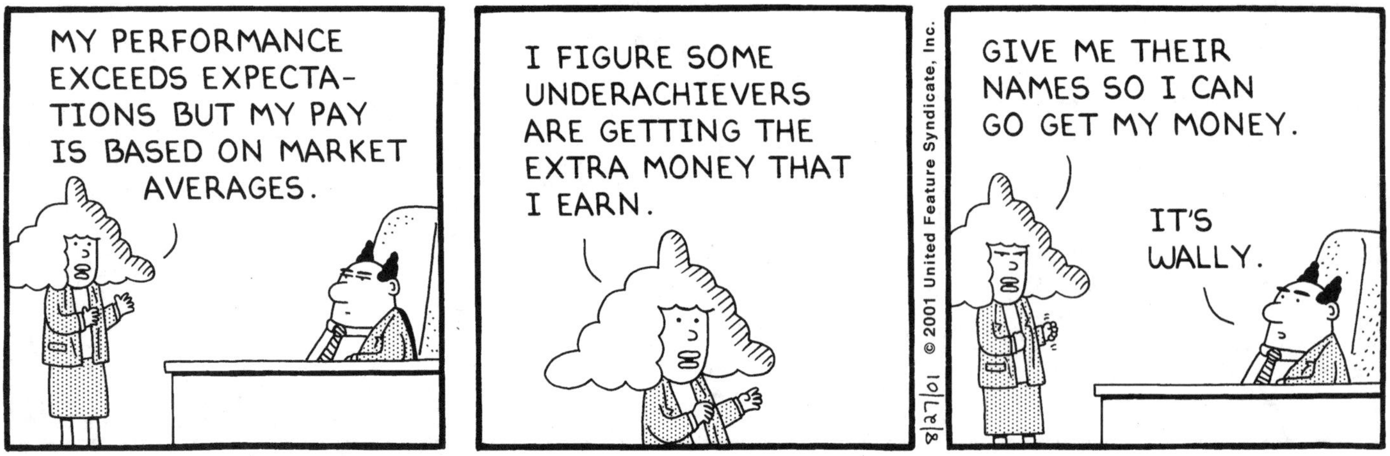
MY PERFORMANCE EXCEEDS EXPECTA-TIONS BUT MY PAY IS BASED ON MARKET AVERAGES.
I FIGURE SOME UNDERACHIEVERS ARE GETTING THE EXTRA MONEY THAT I EARN.
8/27/01 © 2001 United Feature Syndicate, Inc.
GIVE ME THEIR NAMES SO I CAN GO GET MY MONEY.
IT'S WALLY.

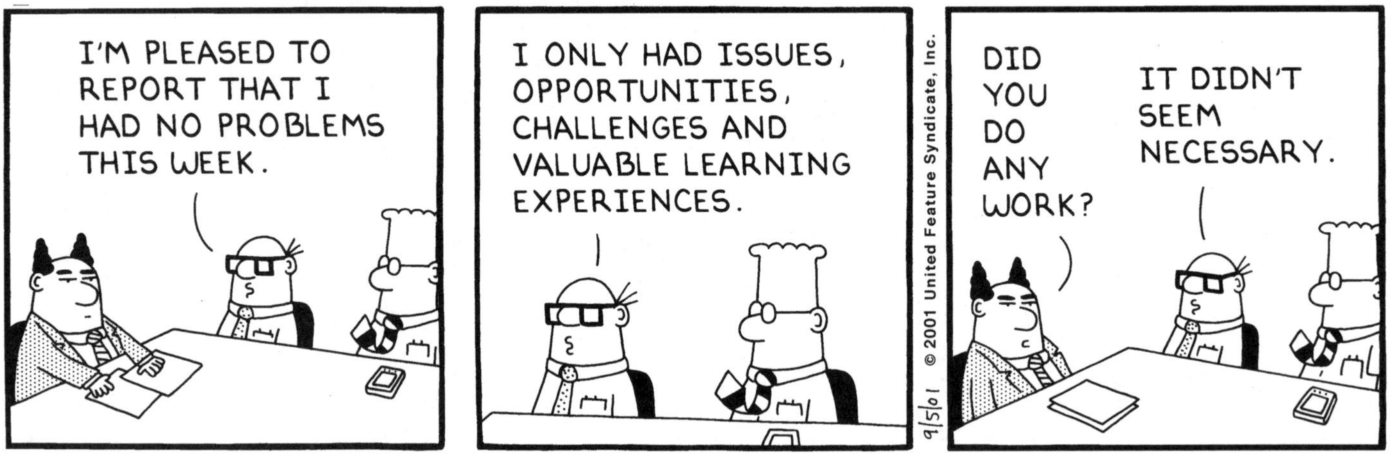
I'M PLEASED TO REPORT THAT I HAD NO PROBLEMS THIS WEEK.
I ONLY HAD ISSUES, OPPORTUNITIES, CHALLENGES AND VALUABLE LEARNING EXPERIENCES.
9/5/01 © 2001 United Feature Syndicate, Inc.
DID YOU DO ANY WORK?
IT DIDN'T SEEM NECESSARY.

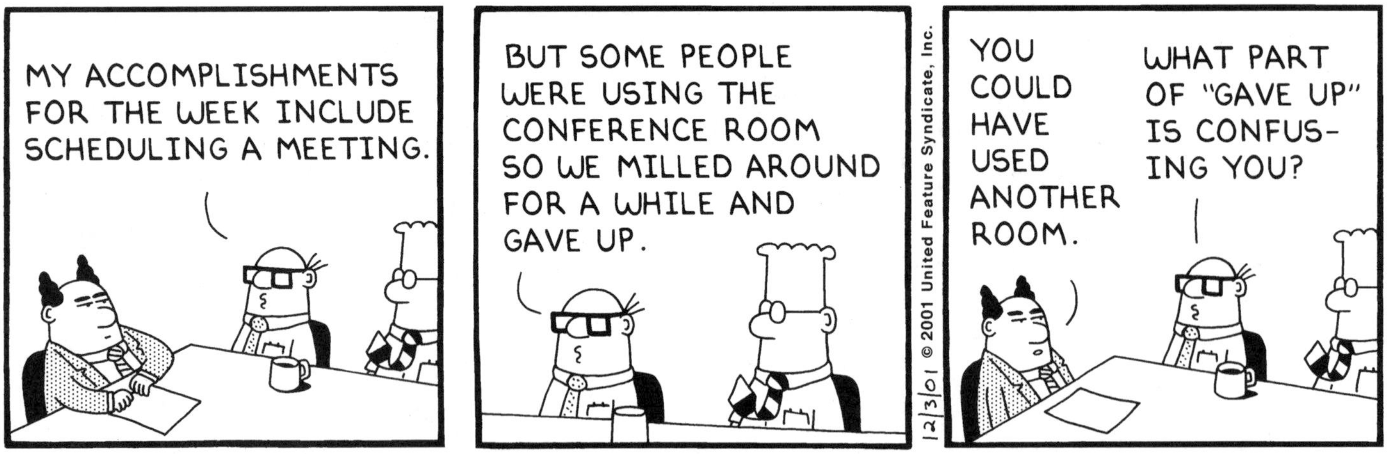
MY ACCOMPLISHMENTS FOR THE WEEK INCLUDE SCHEDULING A MEETING.
BUT SOME PEOPLE WERE USING THE CONFERENCE ROOM SO WE MILLED AROUND FOR A WHILE AND GAVE UP.
12/3/01 © 2001 United Feature Syndicate, Inc.
YOU COULD HAVE USED ANOTHER ROOM.
WHAT PART OF "GAVE UP" IS CONFUS-ING YOU?

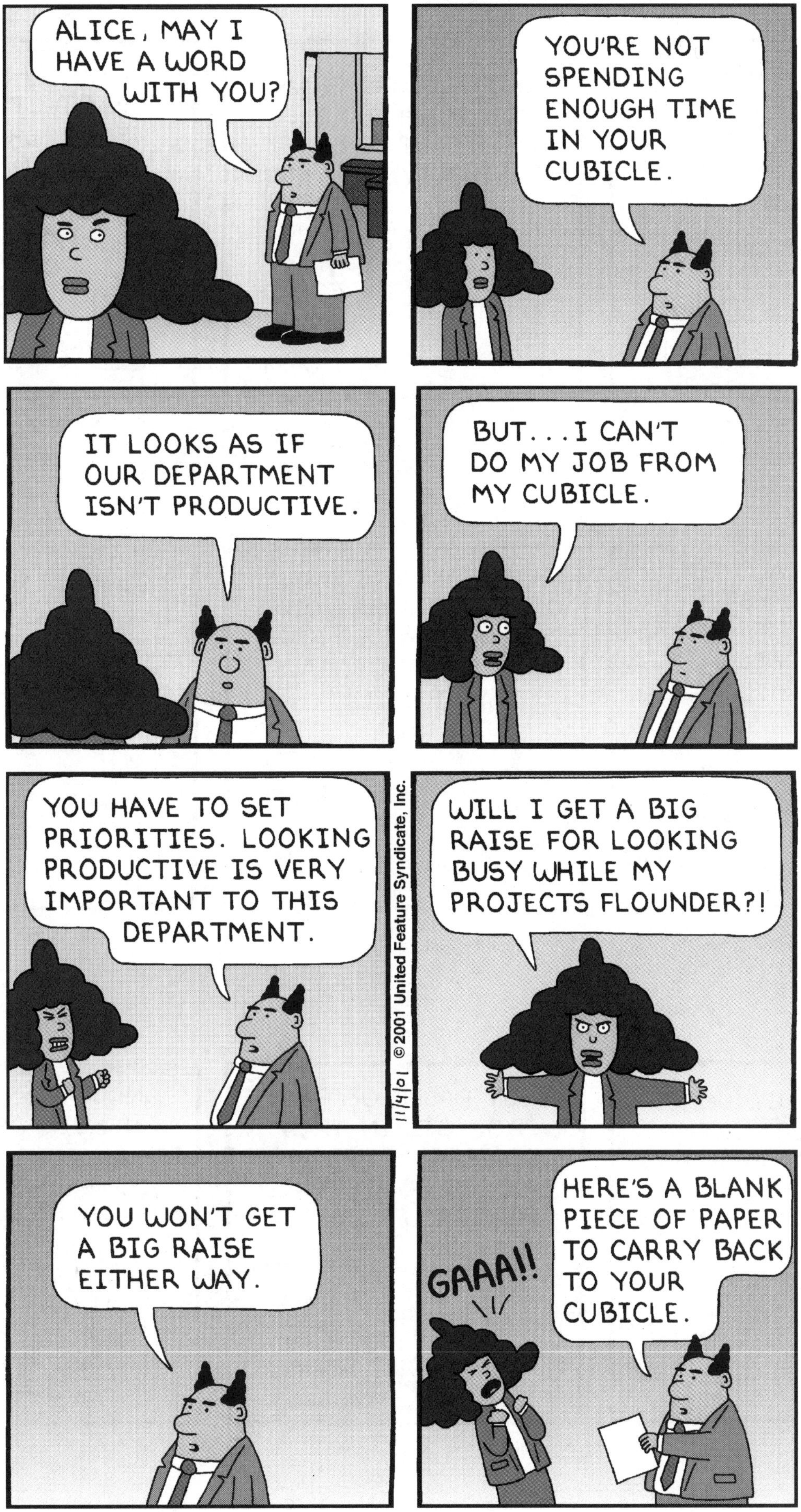
ALICE, MAY I HAVE A WORD WITH YOU?
YOU'RE NOT SPENDING ENOUGH TIME IN YOUR CUBICLE.
IT LOOKS AS IF OUR DEPARTMENT ISN'T PRODUCTIVE.
BUT. . . I CAN'T DO MY JOB FROM MY CUBICLE.
YOU HAVE TO SET PRIORITIES. LOOKING PRODUCTIVE IS VERY IMPORTANT TO THIS DEPARTMENT.
11/4/01 © 2001 United Feature Syndicate, Inc.
WILL I GET A BIG RAISE FOR LOOKING BUSY WHILE MY PROJECTS FLOUNDER?!
YOU WON'T GET A BIG RAISE EITHER WAY.
GAAA!!
HERE'S A BLANK PIECE OF PAPER TO CARRY BACK TO YOUR CUBICLE.

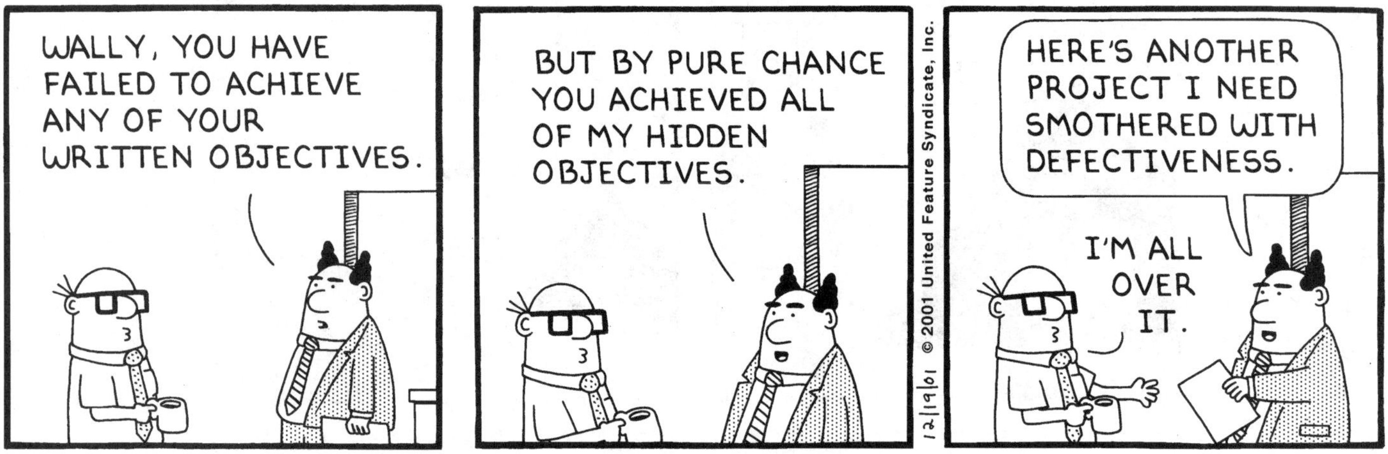
WALLY, YOU HAVE FAILED TO ACHIEVE ANY OF YOUR WRITTEN OBJECTIVES.
BUT BY PURE CHANCE YOU ACHIEVED ALL OF MY HIDDEN OBJECTIVES.
12/19/01 © 2001 United Feature Syndicate, Inc.
HERE'S ANOTHER PROJECT I NEED SMOTHERED WITH DEFECTIVENESS.
I'M ALL OVER IT.

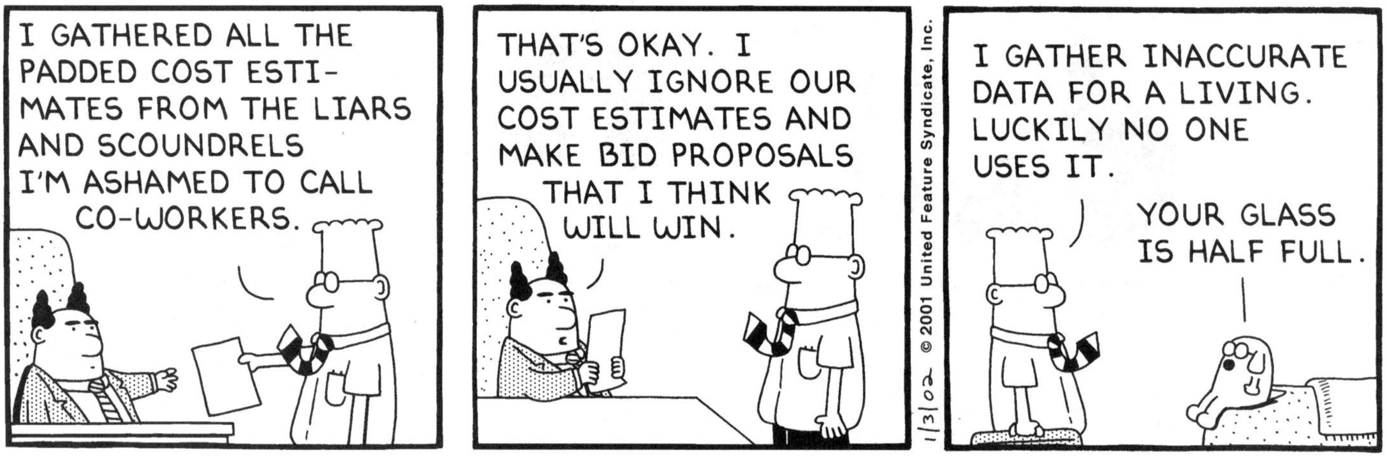
I GATHERED ALL THE PADDED COST ESTIMATES FROM THE LIARS AND SCOUNDRELS I'M ASHAMED TO CALL CO-WORKERS.
THAT'S OKAY. I USUALLY IGNORE OUR COST ESTIMATES AND MAKE BID PROPOSALS THAT I THINK WILL WIN.
1/3/02 © 2001 United Feature Syndicate, Inc.
I GATHER INACCURATE DATA FOR A LIVING. LUCKILY NO ONE USES IT.
YOUR GLASS IS HALF FULL.

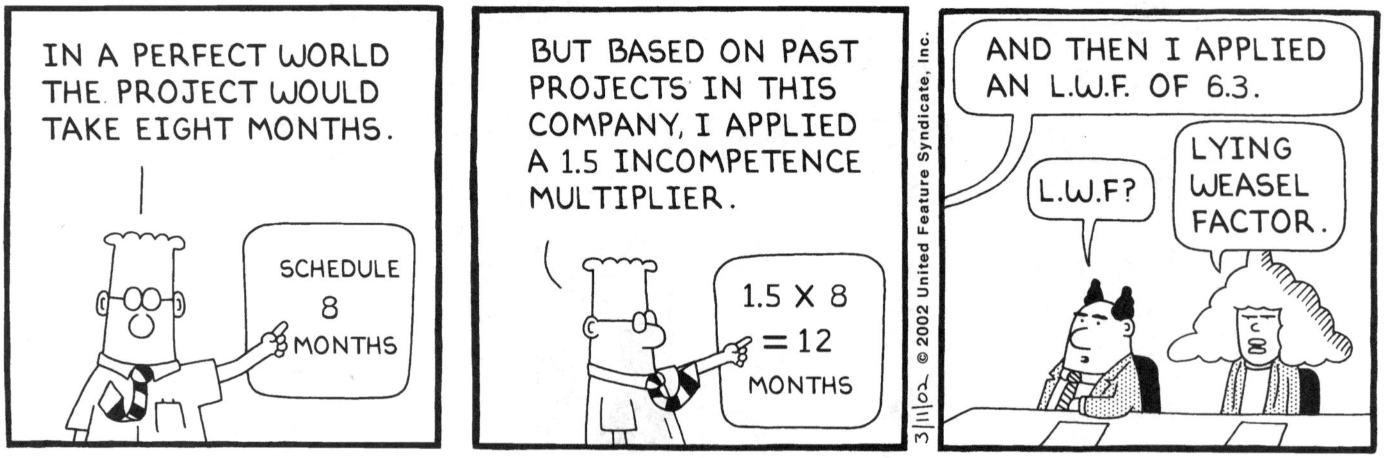
IN A PERFECT WORLD THE PROJECT WOULD TAKE EIGHT MONTHS.
SCHEDULE 8 MONTHS
BUT BASED ON PAST PROJECTS IN THIS COMPANY, I APPLIED A 1.5 INCOMPETENCE MULTIPLIER.
1.5 X 8 = 12 MONTHS
3/11/02 © 2002 United Feature Syndicate, Inc.
AND THEN I APPLIED AN L.W.F. OF 6.3.
L.W.F?
LYING WEASEL FACTOR.

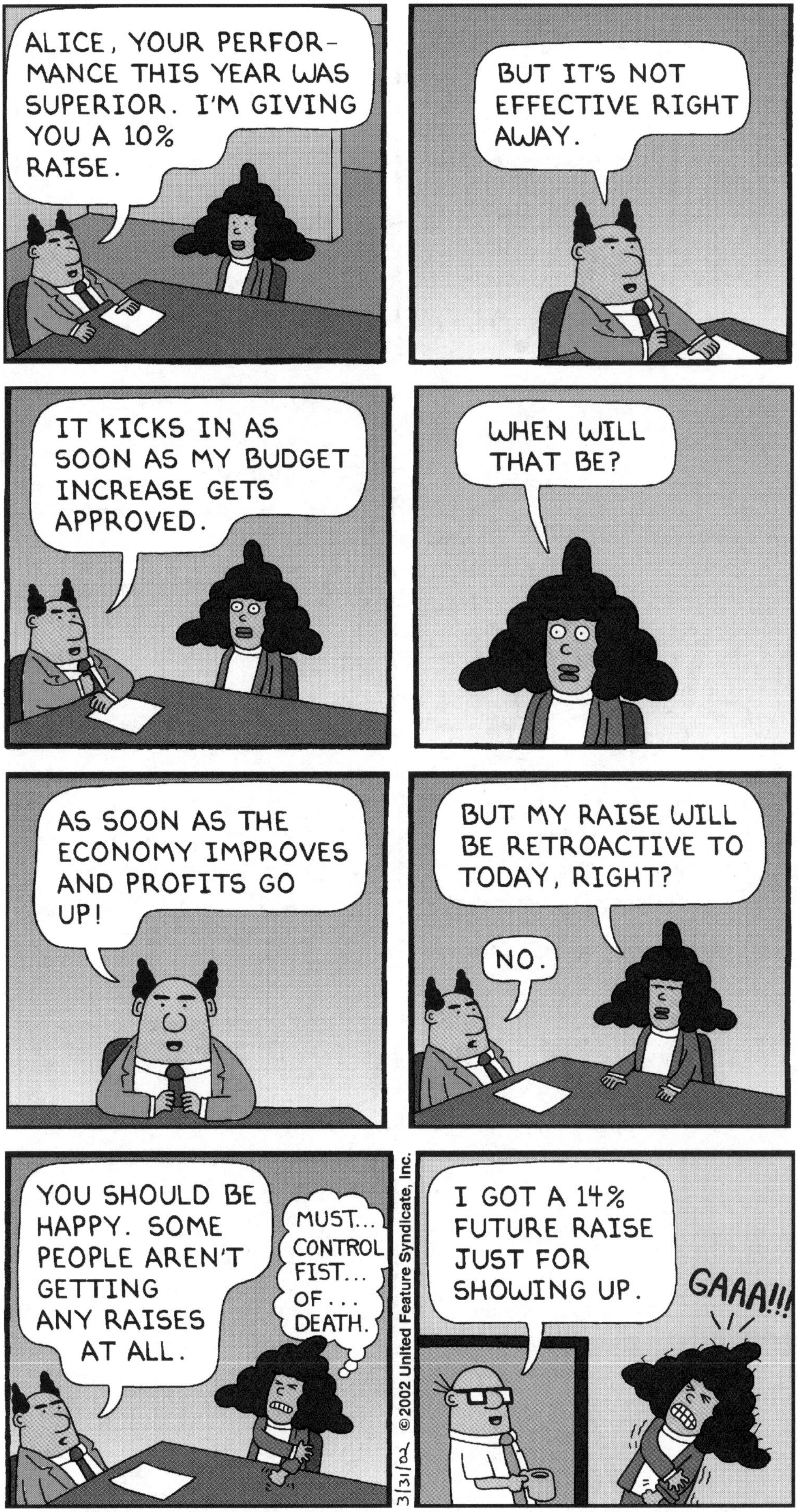
ALICE, YOUR PERFORMANCE THIS YEAR WAS SUPERIOR. I'M GIVING YOU A 10% RAISE.
BUT IT'S NOT EFFECTIVE RIGHT AWAY.
IT KICKS IN AS SOON AS MY BUDGET INCREASE GETS APPROVED.
WHEN WILL THAT BE?
AS SOON AS THE ECONOMY IMPROVES AND PROFITS GO UP!
BUT MY RAISE WILL BE RETROACTIVE TO TODAY, RIGHT?
NO.
YOU SHOULD BE HAPPY. SOME PEOPLE AREN'T GETTING ANY RAISES AT ALL.
MUST... CONTROL FIST... OF... DEATH.
3/31/02 ©2002 United Feature Syndicate, Inc.
I GOT A 14% FUTURE RAISE JUST FOR SHOWING UP.
GAAA!!!

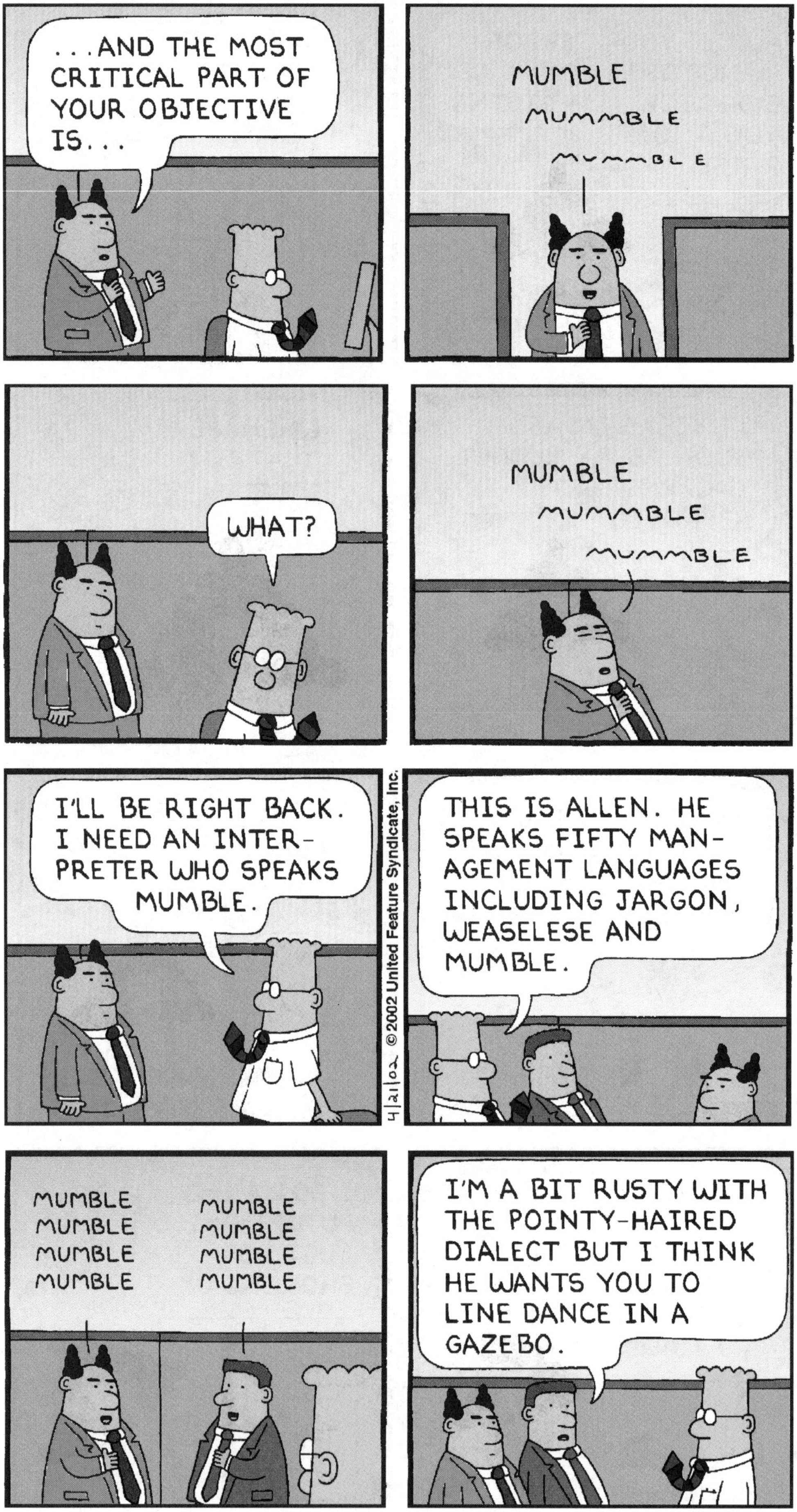
...AND THE MOST CRITICAL PART OF YOUR OBJECTIVE IS...
MUMBLE
MUMMBLE
MUMMBLE
WHAT?
MUMBLE
MUMMBLE
MUMMBLE
I'LL BE RIGHT BACK. I NEED AN INTER-PRETER WHO SPEAKS MUMBLE.
©2002 United Feature Syndicate, Inc.
4/21/02
THIS IS ALLEN. HE SPEAKS FIFTY MAN-AGEMENT LANGUAGES INCLUDING JARGON, WEASELESE AND MUMBLE.
MUMBLE MUMBLE MUMBLE MUMBLE
MUMBLE MUMBLE MUMBLE MUMBLE
I'M A BIT RUSTY WITH THE POINTY-HAIRED DIALECT BUT I THINK HE WANTS YOU TO LINE DANCE IN A GAZEBO.

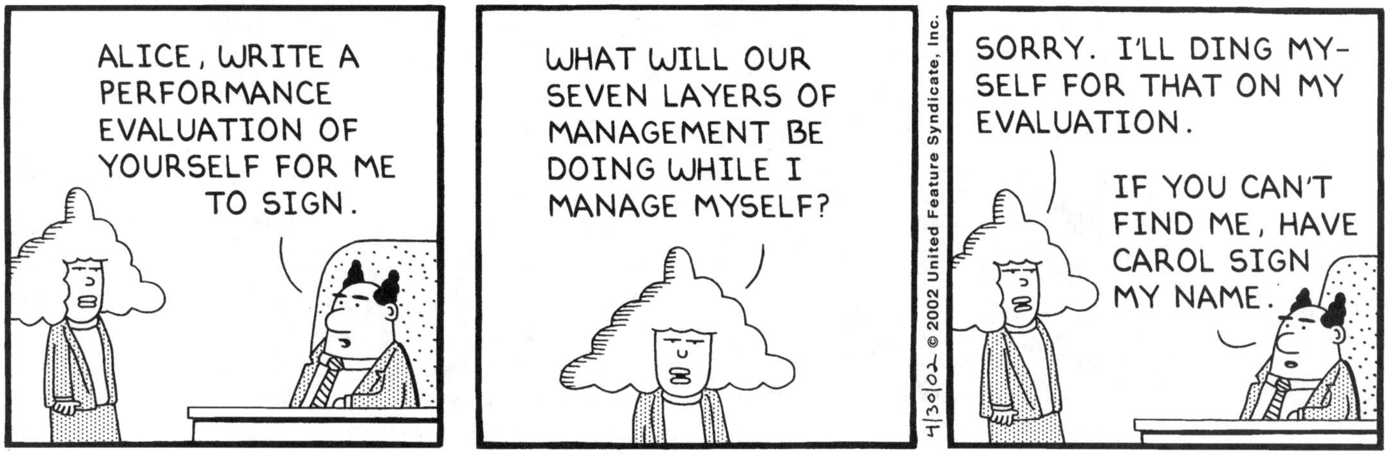
ALICE, WRITE A PERFORMANCE EVALUATION OF YOURSELF FOR ME TO SIGN.
WHAT WILL OUR SEVEN LAYERS OF MANAGEMENT BE DOING WHILE I MANAGE MYSELF?
4/30/02 © 2002 United Feature Syndicate, Inc.
SORRY. I'LL DING MY-SELF FOR THAT ON MY EVALUATION.
IF YOU CAN'T FIND ME, HAVE CAROL SIGN MY NAME.

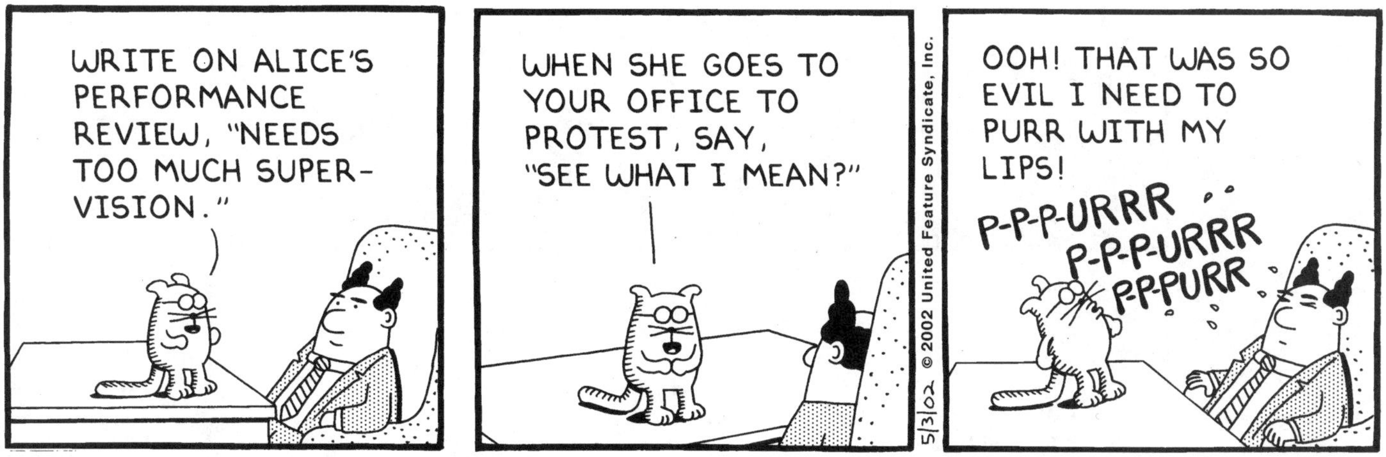
WRITE ON ALICE'S PERFORMANCE REVIEW, "NEEDS TOO MUCH SUPER-VISION."
WHEN SHE GOES TO YOUR OFFICE TO PROTEST, SAY, "SEE WHAT I MEAN?"
5/3/02 © 2002 United Feature Syndicate, Inc.
OOH! THAT WAS SO EVIL I NEED TO PURR WITH MY LIPS!
P-P-P-URRR
P-P-P-URRR
P-P-PURR

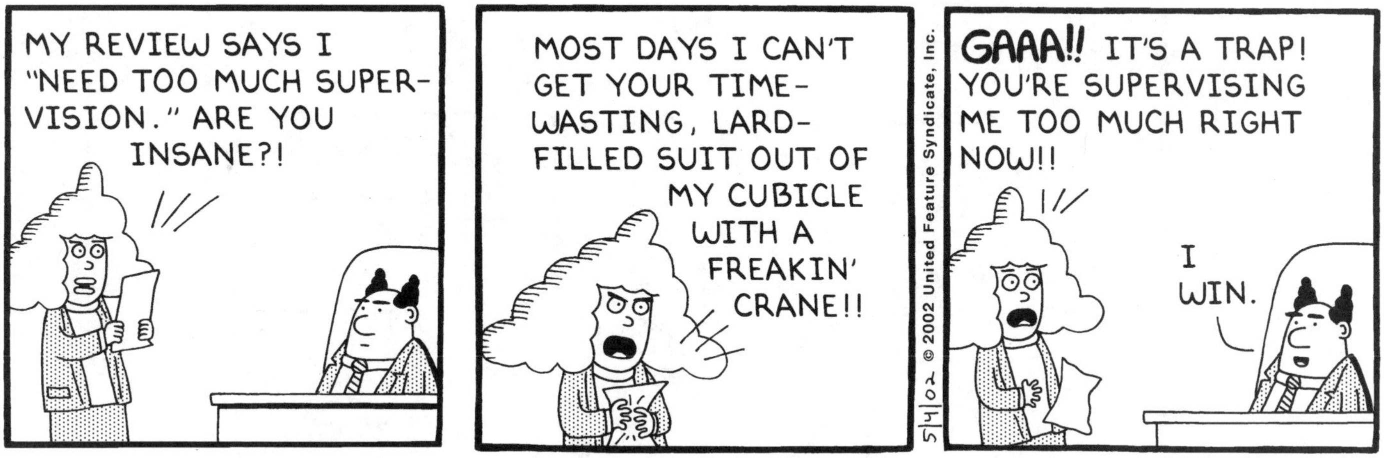
MY REVIEW SAYS I "NEED TOO MUCH SUPER-VISION." ARE YOU INSANE?!
MOST DAYS I CAN'T GET YOUR TIME-WASTING, LARD-FILLED SUIT OUT OF MY CUBICLE WITH A FREAKIN' CRANE!!
5/4/02 © 2002 United Feature Syndicate, Inc.
GAAA!! IT'S A TRAP! YOU'RE SUPERVISING ME TOO MUCH RIGHT NOW!!
I WIN.

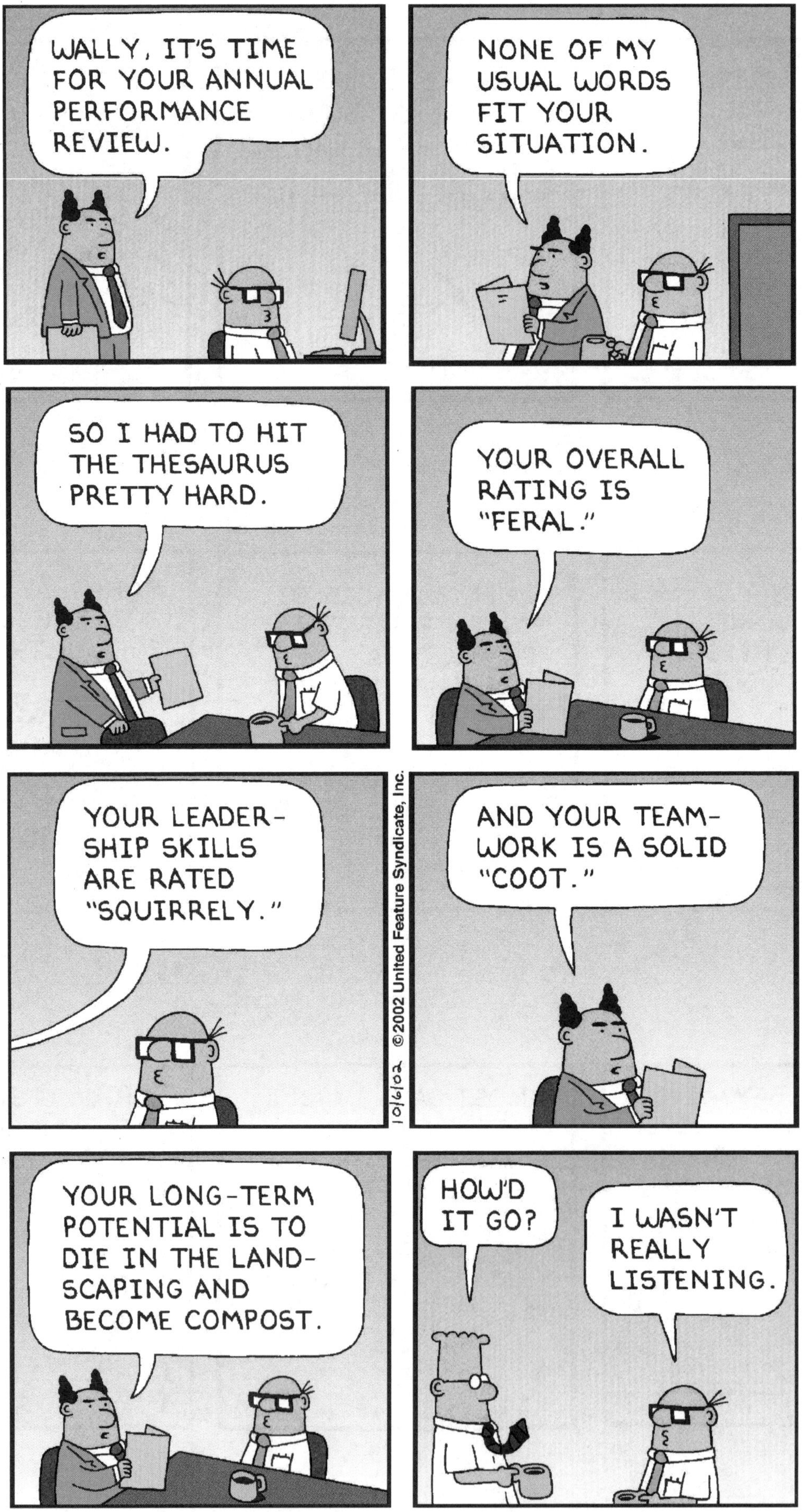
WALLY, IT'S TIME FOR YOUR ANNUAL PERFORMANCE REVIEW.
NONE OF MY USUAL WORDS FIT YOUR SITUATION.
SO I HAD TO HIT THE THESAURUS PRETTY HARD.
YOUR OVERALL RATING IS "FERAL."
YOUR LEADER-SHIP SKILLS ARE RATED "SQUIRRELY."
10/6/02 ©2002 United Feature Syndicate, Inc.
AND YOUR TEAM-WORK IS A SOLID "COOT."
YOUR LONG-TERM POTENTIAL IS TO DIE IN THE LAND-SCAPING AND BECOME COMPOST.
HOW'D IT GO?
I WASN'T REALLY LISTENING.

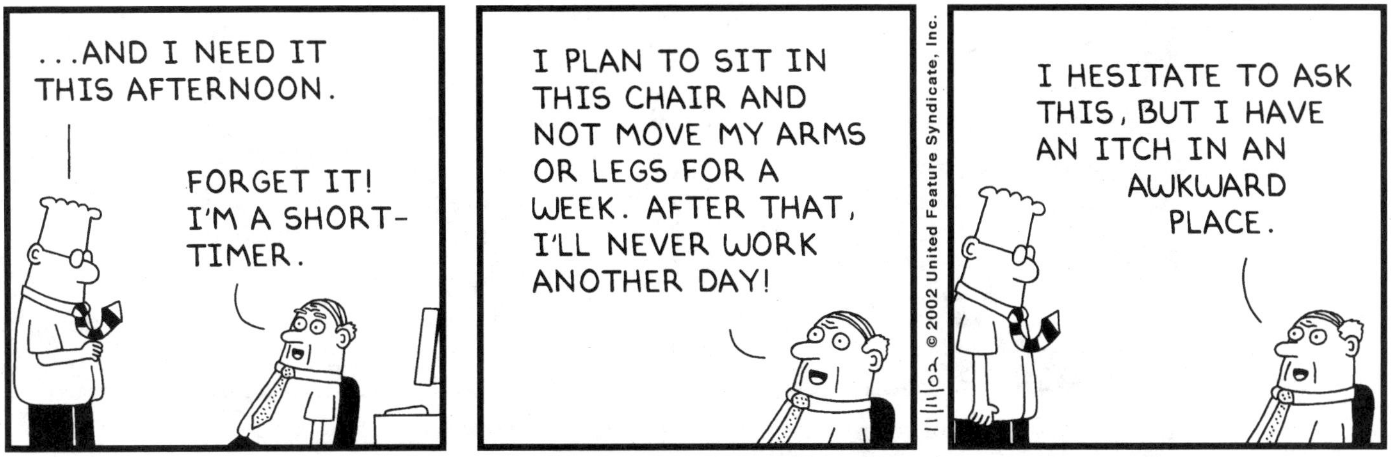
...AND I NEED IT THIS AFTERNOON.
FORGET IT! I'M A SHORT-TIMER.
I PLAN TO SIT IN THIS CHAIR AND NOT MOVE MY ARMS OR LEGS FOR A WEEK. AFTER THAT, I'LL NEVER WORK ANOTHER DAY!
11/11/02 © 2002 United Feature Syndicate, Inc.
I HESITATE TO ASK THIS, BUT I HAVE AN ITCH IN AN AWKWARD PLACE.

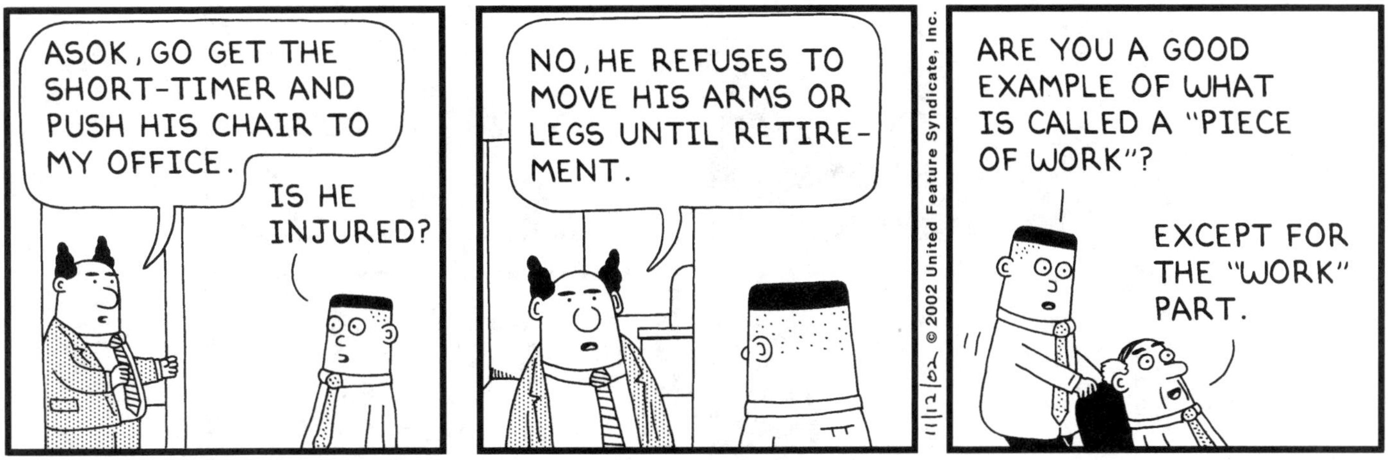
ASOK, GO GET THE SHORT-TIMER AND PUSH HIS CHAIR TO MY OFFICE.
IS HE INJURED?
NO, HE REFUSES TO MOVE HIS ARMS OR LEGS UNTIL RETIRE-MENT.
11/12/02 © 2002 United Feature Syndicate, Inc.
ARE YOU A GOOD EXAMPLE OF WHAT IS CALLED A "PIECE OF WORK"?
EXCEPT FOR THE "WORK" PART.

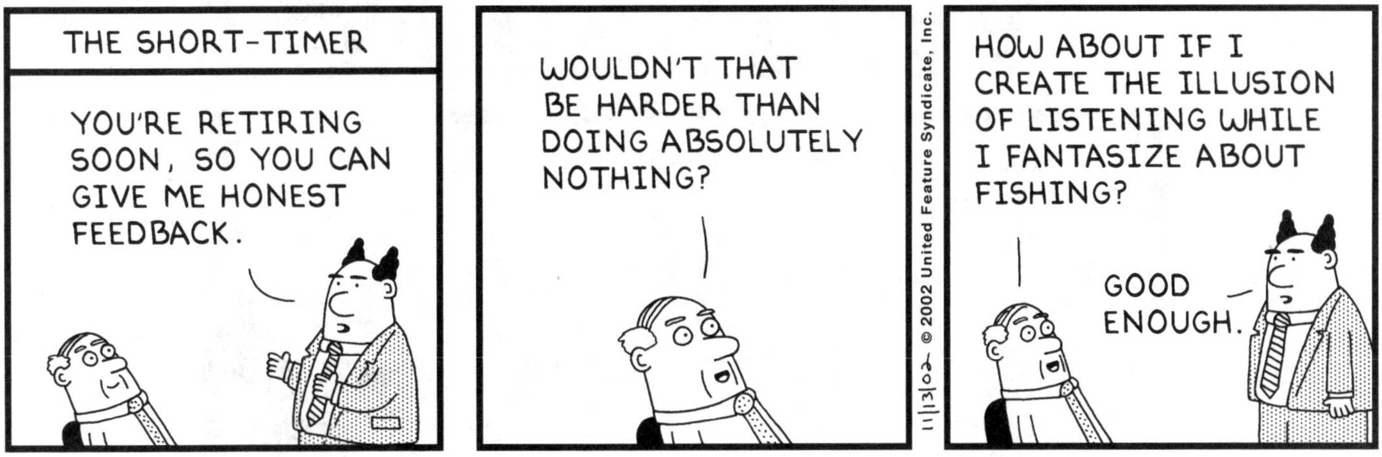
THE SHORT-TIMER
YOU'RE RETIRING SOON, SO YOU CAN GIVE ME HONEST FEEDBACK.
WOULDN'T THAT BE HARDER THAN DOING ABSOLUTELY NOTHING?
11/13/02 © 2002 United Feature Syndicate, Inc.
HOW ABOUT IF I CREATE THE ILLUSION OF LISTENING WHILE I FANTASIZE ABOUT FISHING?
GOOD ENOUGH.

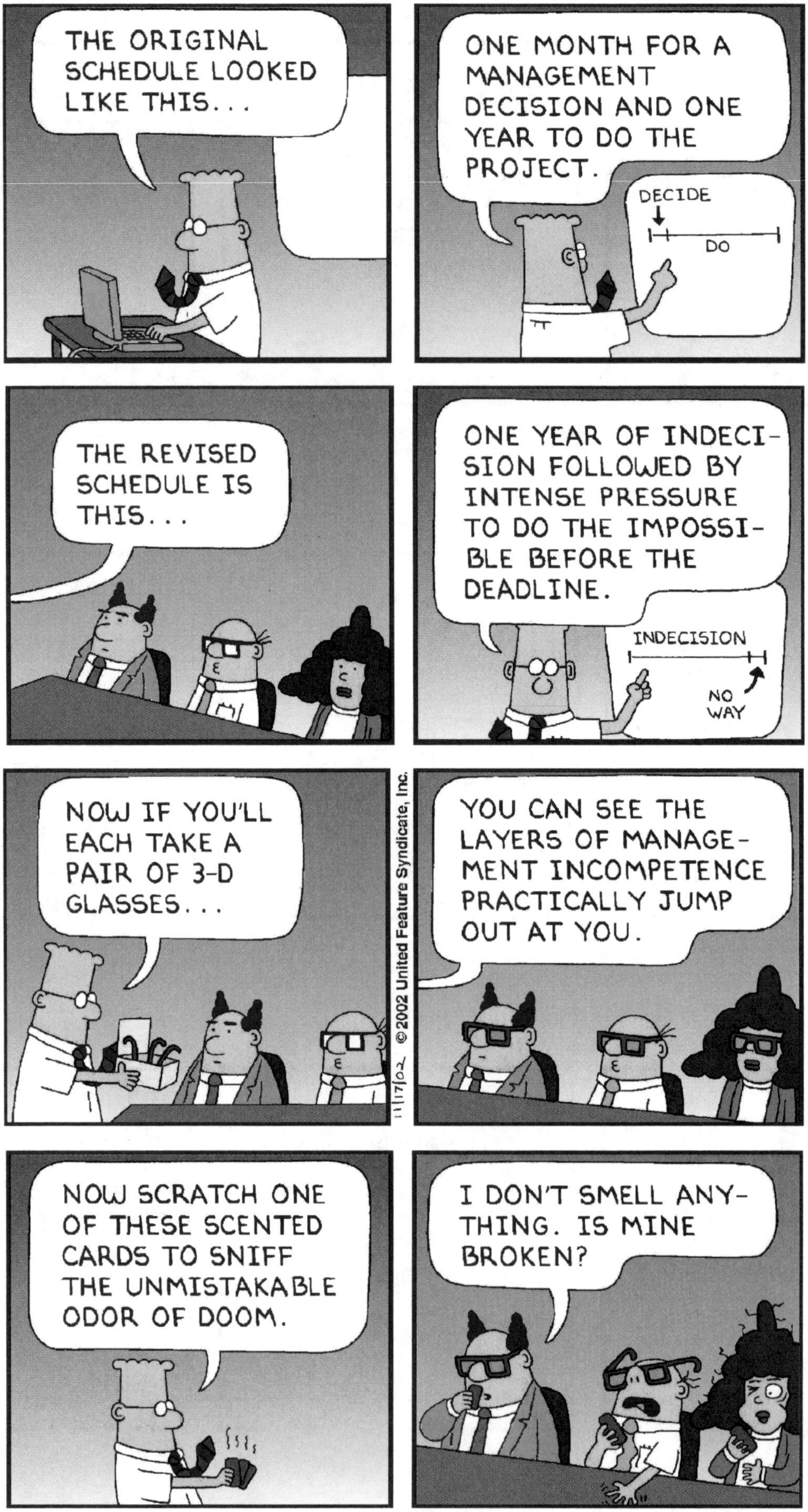
THE ORIGINAL SCHEDULE LOOKED LIKE THIS...
ONE MONTH FOR A MANAGEMENT DECISION AND ONE YEAR TO DO THE PROJECT.
DECIDE
DO
THE REVISED SCHEDULE IS THIS...
ONE YEAR OF INDECISION FOLLOWED BY INTENSE PRESSURE TO DO THE IMPOSSIBLE BEFORE THE DEADLINE.
INDECISION
NO WAY
NOW IF YOU'LL EACH TAKE A PAIR OF 3-D GLASSES...
YOU CAN SEE THE LAYERS OF MANAGEMENT INCOMPETENCE PRACTICALLY JUMP OUT AT YOU.
© 2002 United Feature Syndicate, Inc.
11/17/02
NOW SCRATCH ONE OF THESE SCENTED CARDS TO SNIFF THE UNMISTAKABLE ODOR OF DOOM.
I DON'T SMELL ANYTHING. IS MINE BROKEN?

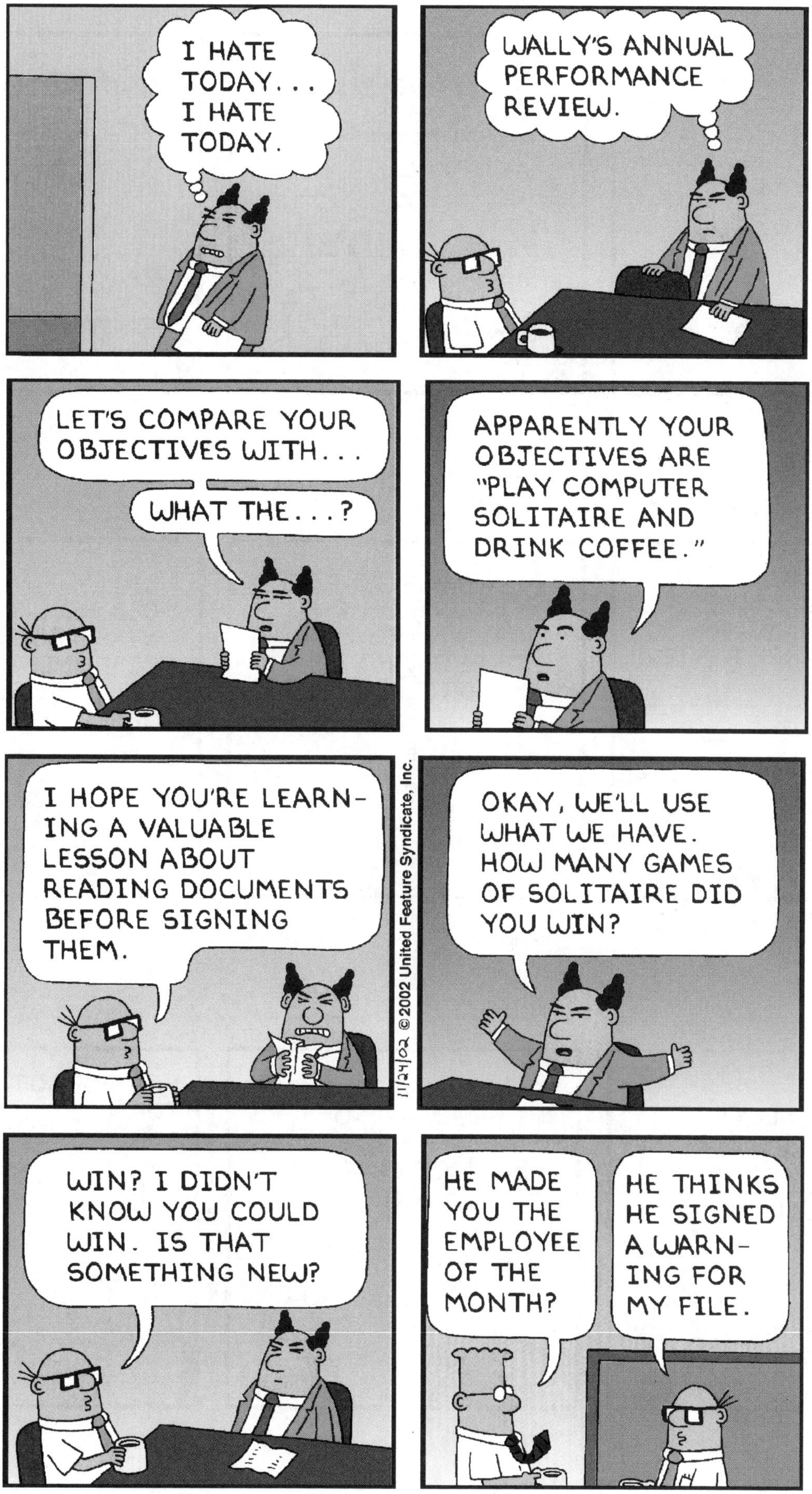
I HATE TODAY... I HATE TODAY.
WALLY'S ANNUAL PERFORMANCE REVIEW.
LET'S COMPARE YOUR OBJECTIVES WITH...
WHAT THE...?
APPARENTLY YOUR OBJECTIVES ARE "PLAY COMPUTER SOLITAIRE AND DRINK COFFEE."
I HOPE YOU'RE LEARNING A VALUABLE LESSON ABOUT READING DOCUMENTS BEFORE SIGNING THEM.
OKAY, WE'LL USE WHAT WE HAVE. HOW MANY GAMES OF SOLITAIRE DID YOU WIN?
11/24/02 ©2002 United Feature Syndicate, Inc.
WIN? I DIDN'T KNOW YOU COULD WIN. IS THAT SOMETHING NEW?
HE MADE YOU THE EMPLOYEE OF THE MONTH?
HE THINKS HE SIGNED A WARNING FOR MY FILE.

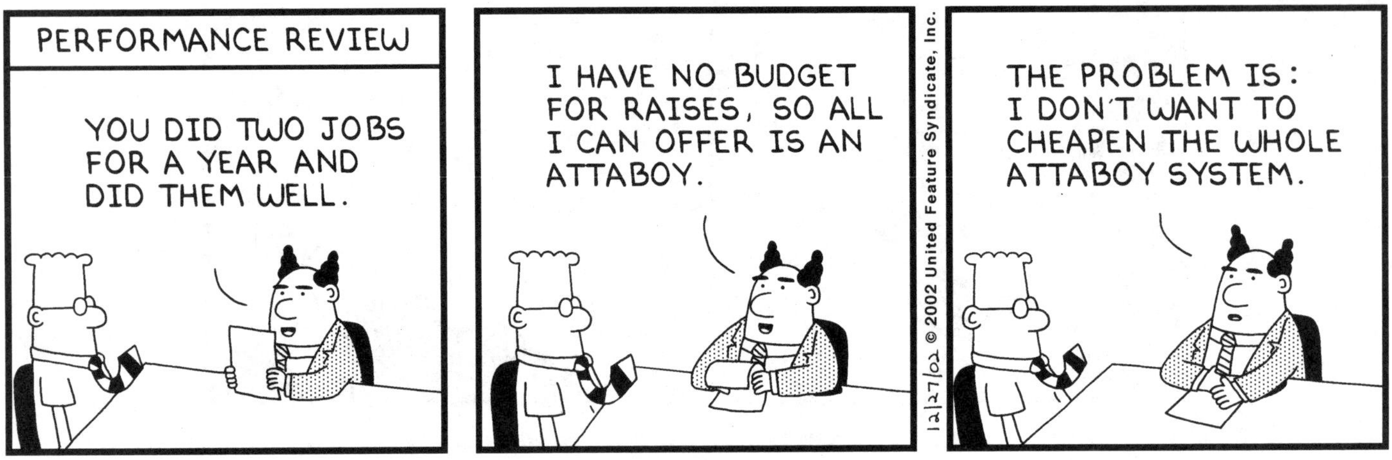
PERFORMANCE REVIEW
YOU DID TWO JOBS FOR A YEAR AND DID THEM WELL.
I HAVE NO BUDGET FOR RAISES, SO ALL I CAN OFFER IS AN ATTABOY.
12/27/02 © 2002 United Feature Syndicate, Inc.
THE PROBLEM IS: I DON'T WANT TO CHEAPEN THE WHOLE ATTABOY SYSTEM.

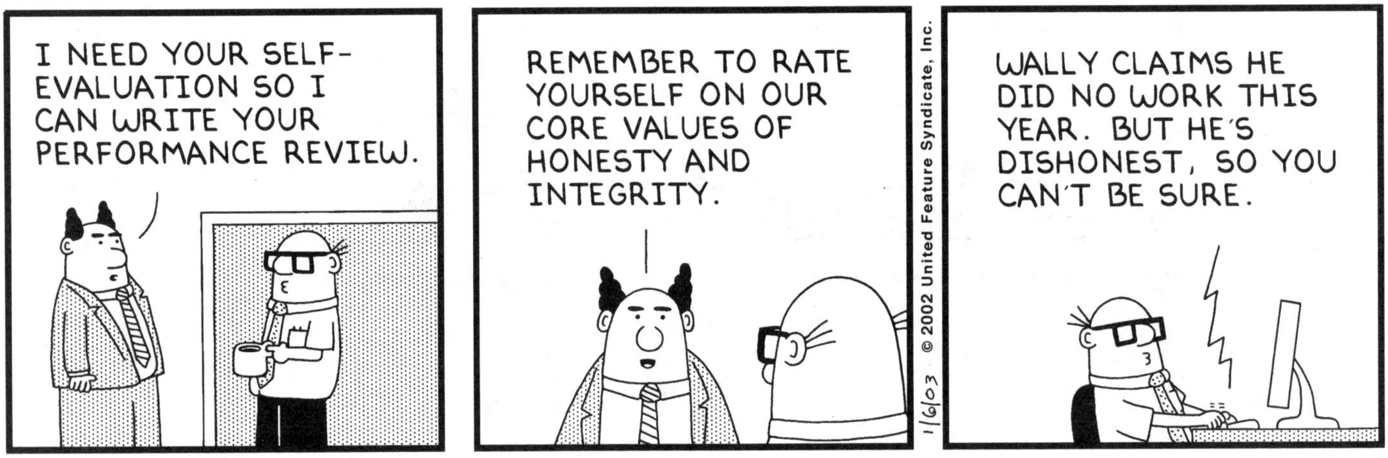
I NEED YOUR SELF-EVALUATION SO I CAN WRITE YOUR PERFORMANCE REVIEW.
REMEMBER TO RATE YOURSELF ON OUR CORE VALUES OF HONESTY AND INTEGRITY.
1/6/03 © 2002 United Feature Syndicate, Inc.
WALLY CLAIMS HE DID NO WORK THIS YEAR. BUT HE'S DISHONEST, SO YOU CAN'T BE SURE.

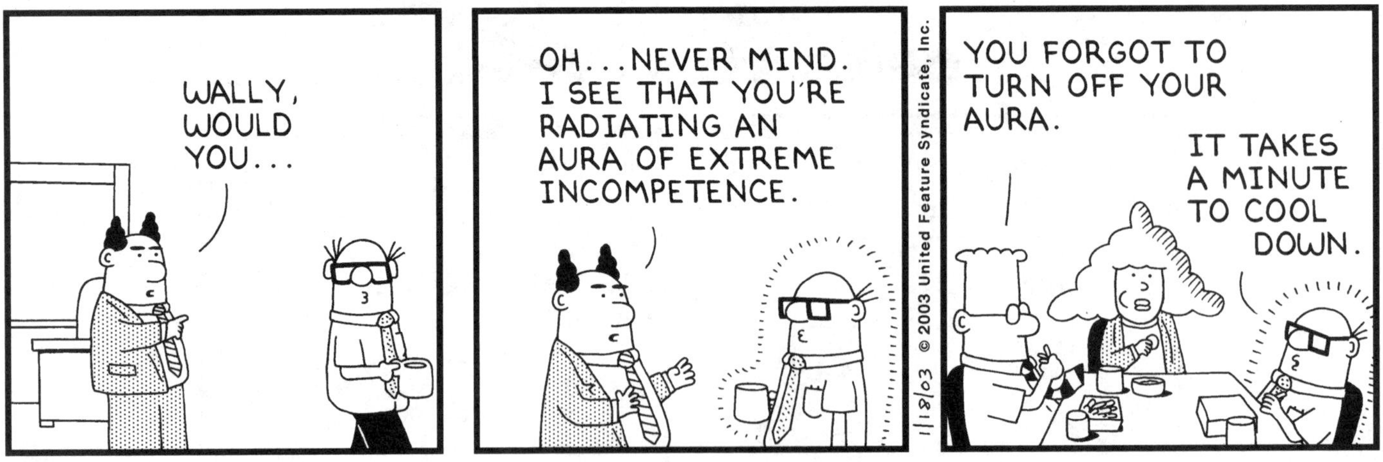
WALLY, WOULD YOU...
OH...NEVER MIND. I SEE THAT YOU'RE RADIATING AN AURA OF EXTREME INCOMPETENCE.
1/18/03 © 2003 United Feature Syndicate, Inc.
YOU FORGOT TO TURN OFF YOUR AURA.
IT TAKES A MINUTE TO COOL DOWN.

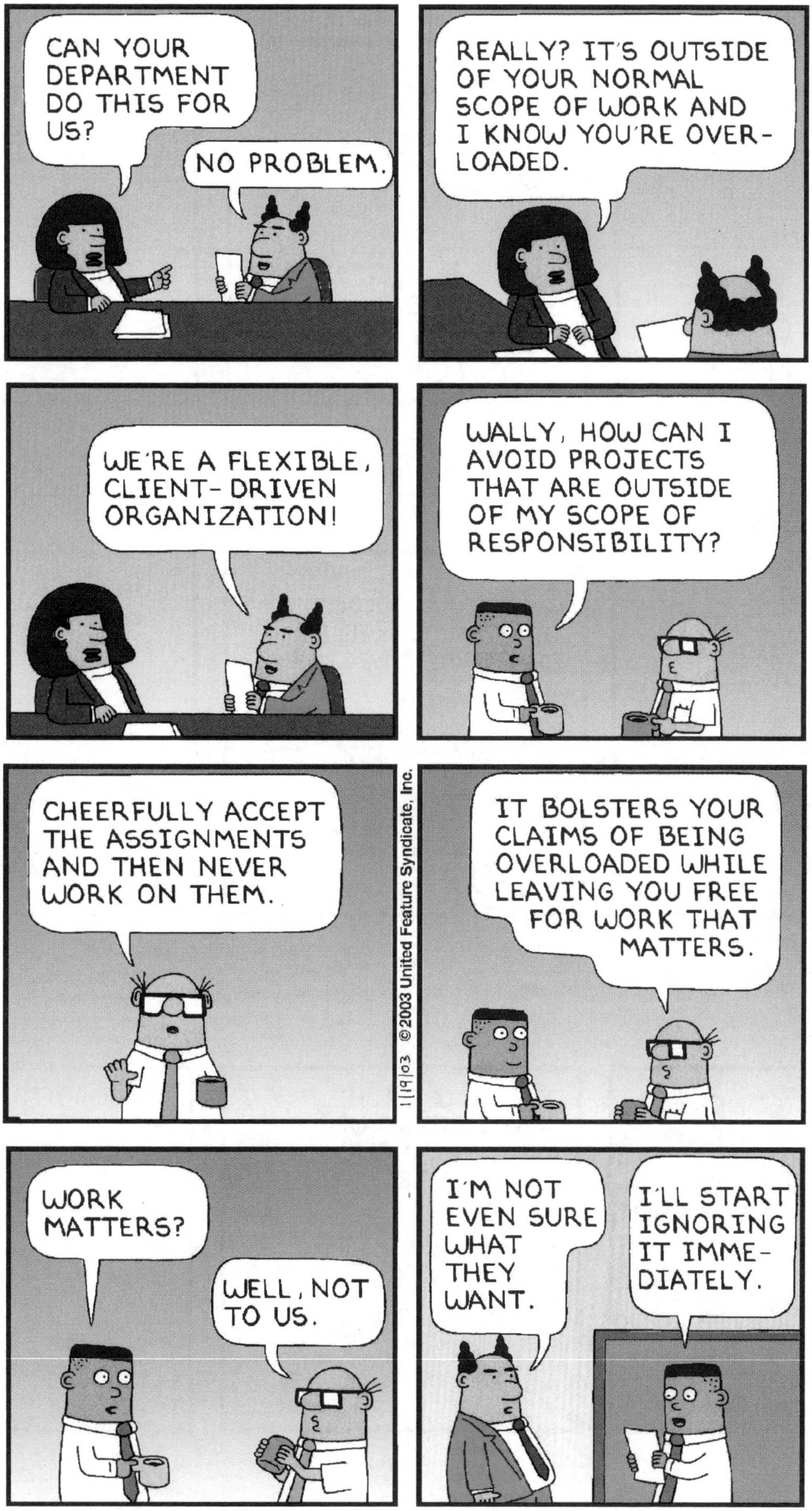
CAN YOUR DEPARTMENT DO THIS FOR US?
NO PROBLEM.
REALLY? IT'S OUTSIDE OF YOUR NORMAL SCOPE OF WORK AND I KNOW YOU'RE OVER-LOADED.
WE'RE A FLEXIBLE, CLIENT-DRIVEN ORGANIZATION!
WALLY, HOW CAN I AVOID PROJECTS THAT ARE OUTSIDE OF MY SCOPE OF RESPONSIBILITY?
CHEERFULLY ACCEPT THE ASSIGNMENTS AND THEN NEVER WORK ON THEM.
1/19/03 ©2003 United Feature Syndicate, Inc.
IT BOLSTERS YOUR CLAIMS OF BEING OVERLOADED WHILE LEAVING YOU FREE FOR WORK THAT MATTERS.
WORK MATTERS?
WELL, NOT TO US.
I'M NOT EVEN SURE WHAT THEY WANT.
I'LL START IGNORING IT IMME-DIATELY.

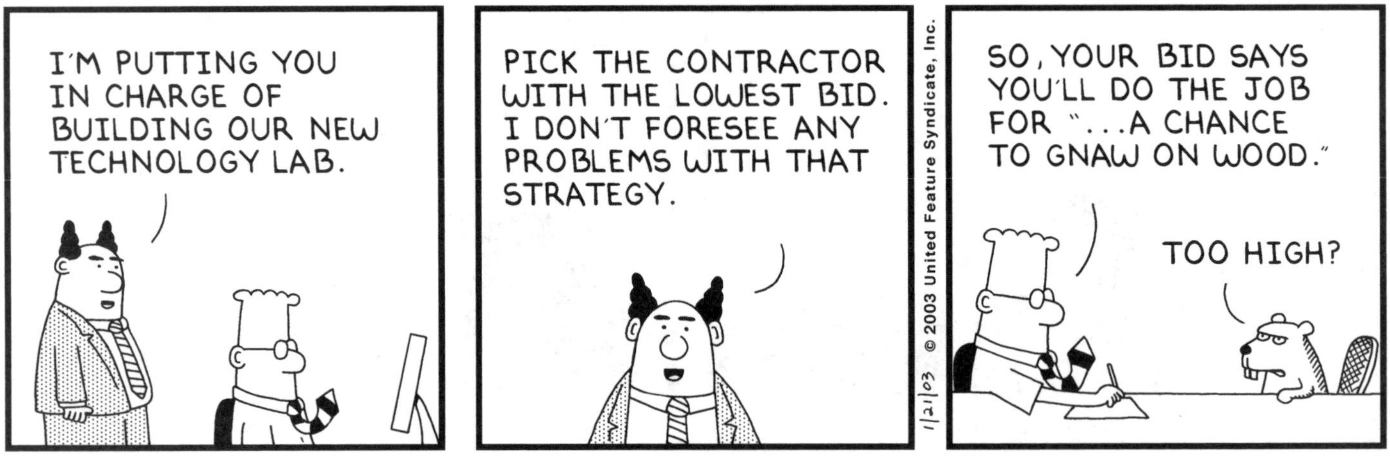
I'M PUTTING YOU IN CHARGE OF BUILDING OUR NEW TECHNOLOGY LAB.
PICK THE CONTRACTOR WITH THE LOWEST BID. I DON'T FORESEE ANY PROBLEMS WITH THAT STRATEGY.
1/21/03 © 2003 United Feature Syndicate, Inc.
SO, YOUR BID SAYS YOU'LL DO THE JOB FOR "...A CHANCE TO GNAW ON WOOD."
TOO HIGH?

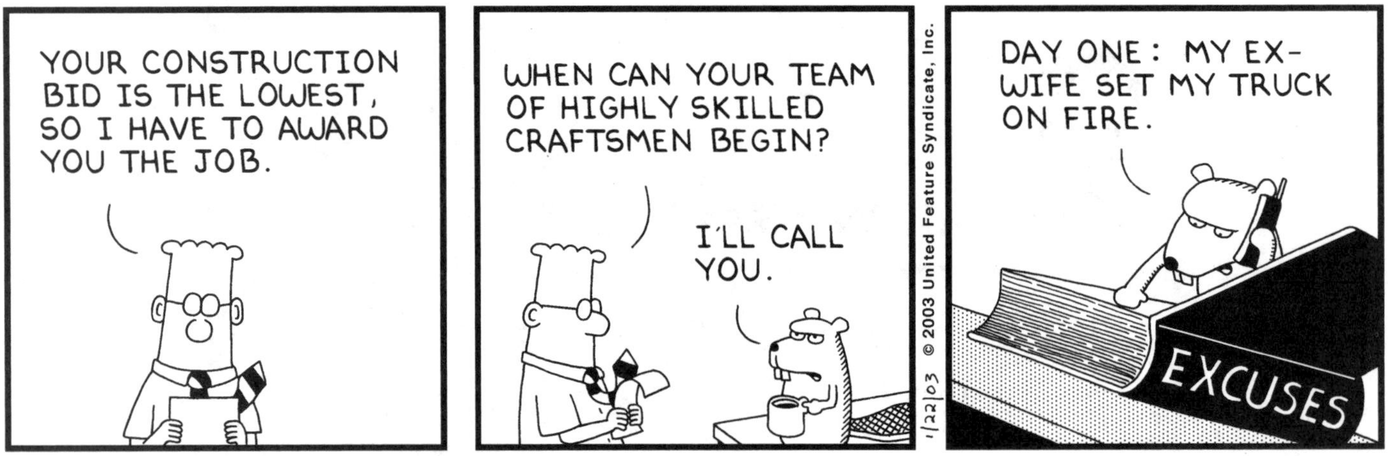
YOUR CONSTRUCTION BID IS THE LOWEST, SO I HAVE TO AWARD YOU THE JOB.
WHEN CAN YOUR TEAM OF HIGHLY SKILLED CRAFTSMEN BEGIN?
I'LL CALL YOU.
1/22/03 © 2003 United Feature Syndicate, Inc.
DAY ONE: MY EX-WIFE SET MY TRUCK ON FIRE.
EXCUSES

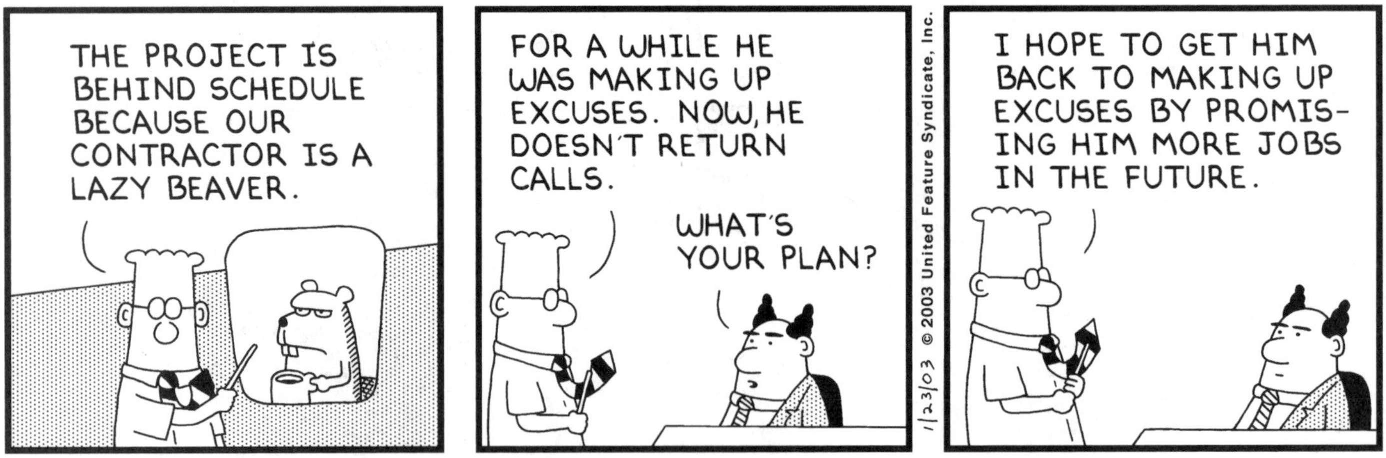
THE PROJECT IS BEHIND SCHEDULE BECAUSE OUR CONTRACTOR IS A LAZY BEAVER.
FOR A WHILE HE WAS MAKING UP EXCUSES. NOW, HE DOESN'T RETURN CALLS.
WHAT'S YOUR PLAN?
1/23/03 © 2003 United Feature Syndicate, Inc.
I HOPE TO GET HIM BACK TO MAKING UP EXCUSES BY PROMISING HIM MORE JOBS IN THE FUTURE.

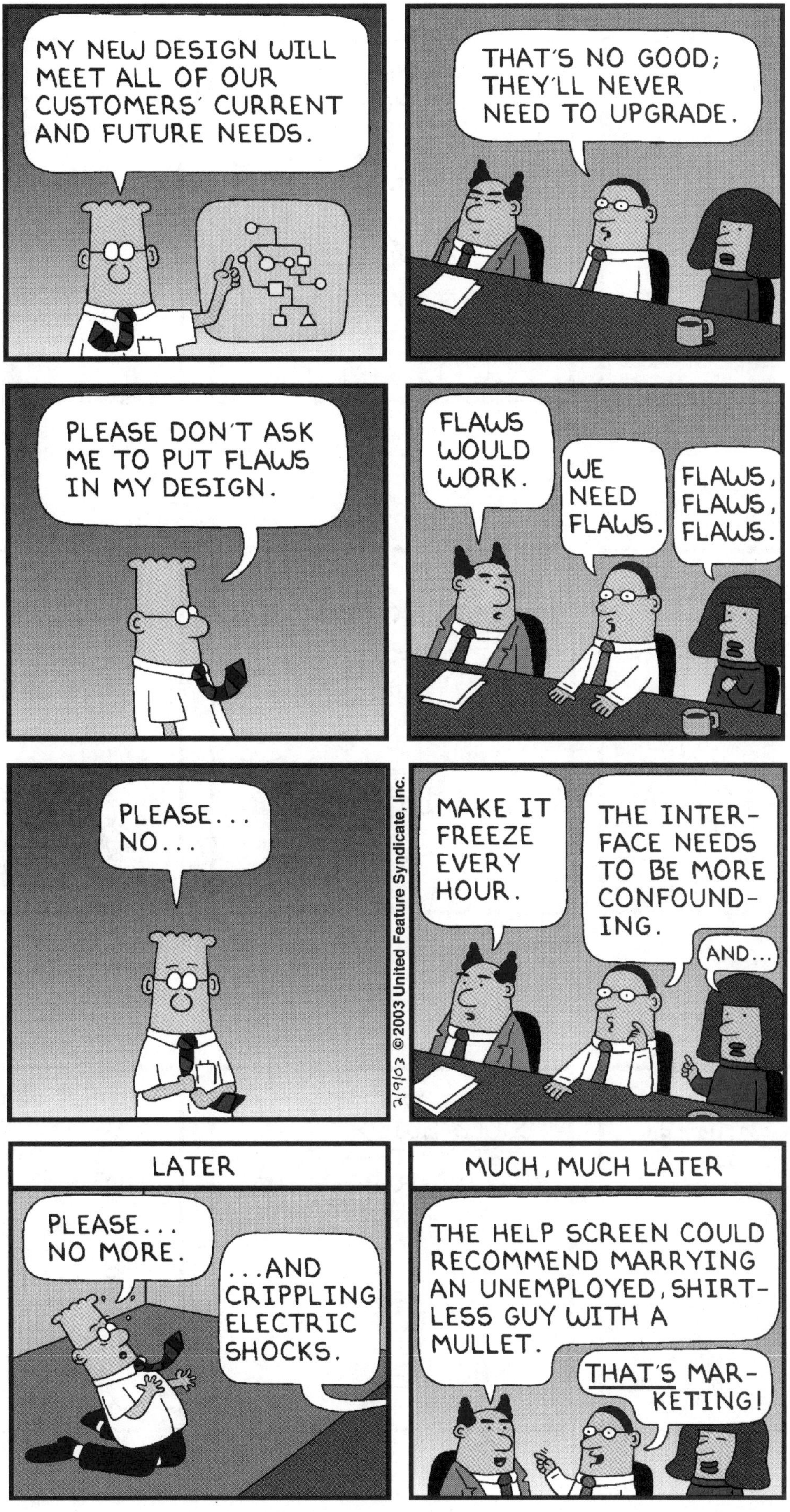
MY NEW DESIGN WILL MEET ALL OF OUR CUSTOMERS' CURRENT AND FUTURE NEEDS.
THAT'S NO GOOD; THEY'LL NEVER NEED TO UPGRADE.
PLEASE DON'T ASK ME TO PUT FLAWS IN MY DESIGN.
FLAWS WOULD WORK.
WE NEED FLAWS.
FLAWS, FLAWS, FLAWS.
PLEASE... NO...
©2003 United Feature Syndicate, Inc.
2/9/03
MAKE IT FREEZE EVERY HOUR.
THE INTER-FACE NEEDS TO BE MORE CONFOUND-ING.
AND...
LATER
PLEASE... NO MORE.
...AND CRIPPLING ELECTRIC SHOCKS.
MUCH, MUCH LATER
THE HELP SCREEN COULD RECOMMEND MARRYING AN UNEMPLOYED, SHIRT-LESS GUY WITH A MULLET.
THAT'S MAR-KETING!

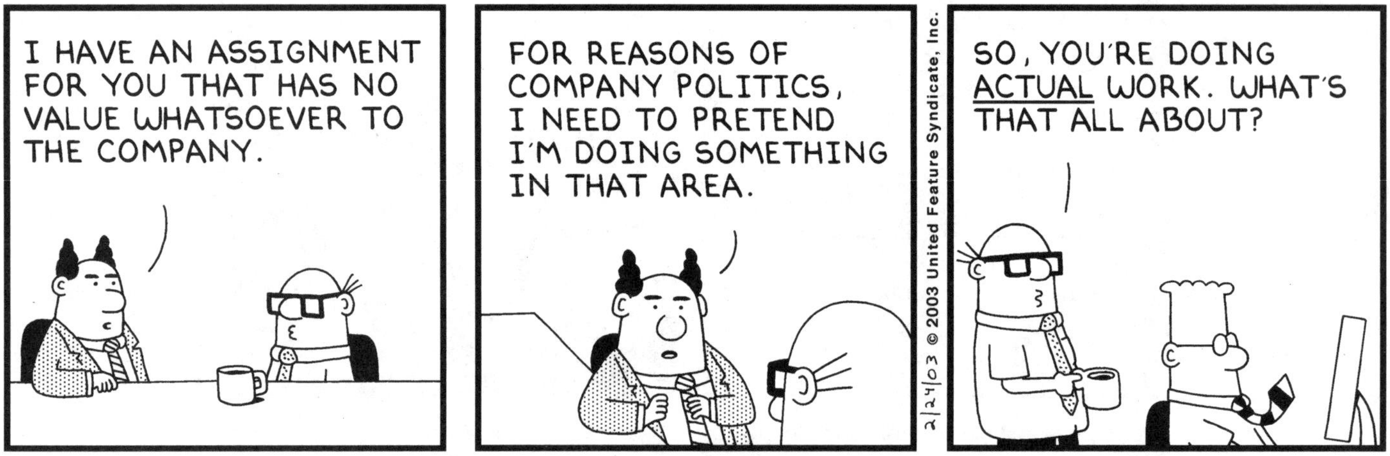
I HAVE AN ASSIGNMENT FOR YOU THAT HAS NO VALUE WHATSOEVER TO THE COMPANY.
FOR REASONS OF COMPANY POLITICS, I NEED TO PRETEND I'M DOING SOMETHING IN THAT AREA.
2/24/03 © 2003 United Feature Syndicate, Inc.
SO, YOU'RE DOING ACTUAL WORK. WHAT'S THAT ALL ABOUT?

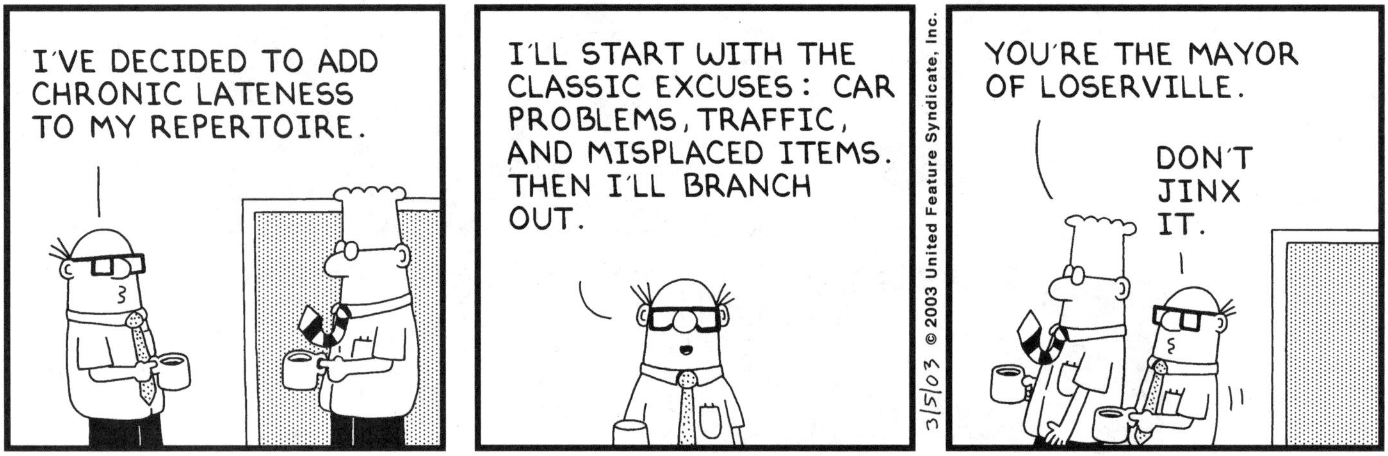
I'VE DECIDED TO ADD CHRONIC LATENESS TO MY REPERTOIRE.
I'LL START WITH THE CLASSIC EXCUSES: CAR PROBLEMS, TRAFFIC, AND MISPLACED ITEMS. THEN I'LL BRANCH OUT.
3/5/03 © 2003 United Feature Syndicate, Inc.
YOU'RE THE MAYOR OF LOSERVILLE.
DON'T JINX IT.

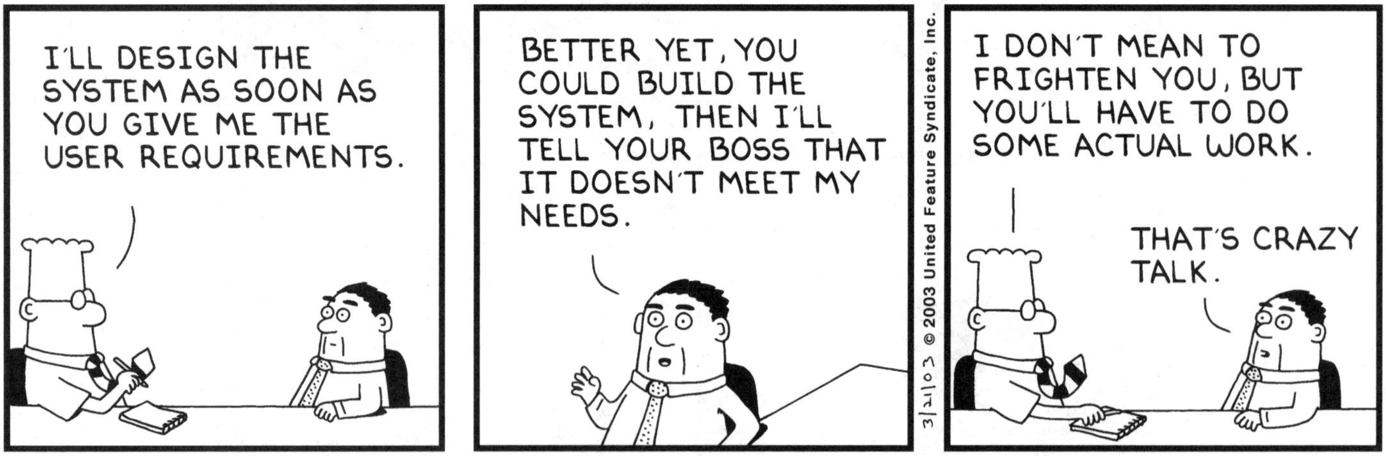
I'LL DESIGN THE SYSTEM AS SOON AS YOU GIVE ME THE USER REQUIREMENTS.
BETTER YET, YOU COULD BUILD THE SYSTEM, THEN I'LL TELL YOUR BOSS THAT IT DOESN'T MEET MY NEEDS.
3/21/03 © 2003 United Feature Syndicate, Inc.
I DON'T MEAN TO FRIGHTEN YOU, BUT YOU'LL HAVE TO DO SOME ACTUAL WORK.
THAT'S CRAZY TALK.

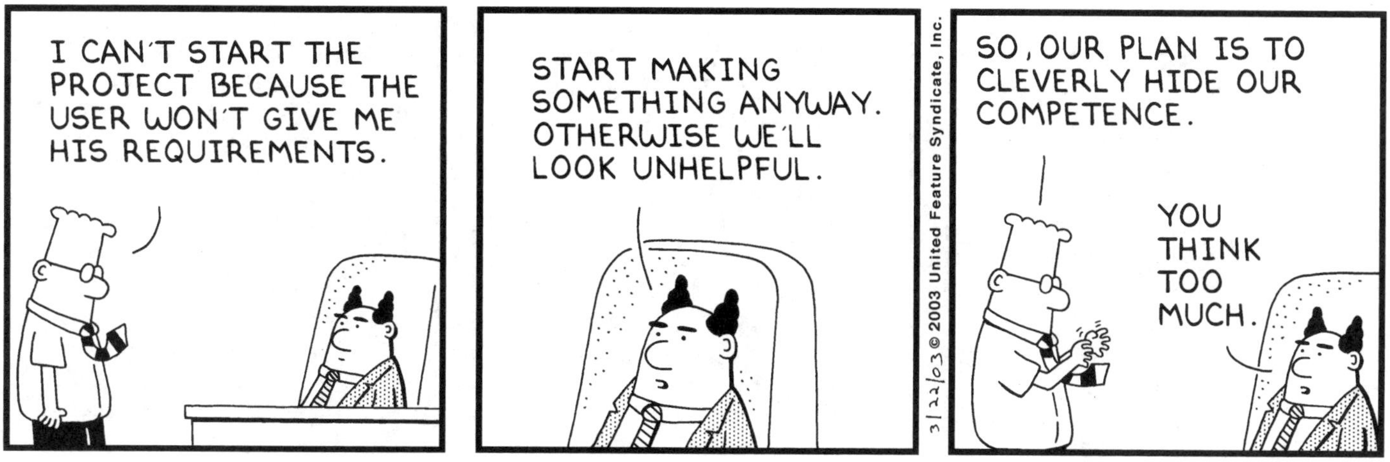
I CAN'T START THE PROJECT BECAUSE THE USER WON'T GIVE ME HIS REQUIREMENTS.
START MAKING SOMETHING ANYWAY. OTHERWISE WE'LL LOOK UNHELPFUL.
3/22/03 © 2003 United Feature Syndicate, Inc.
SO, OUR PLAN IS TO CLEVERLY HIDE OUR COMPETENCE.
YOU THINK TOO MUCH.

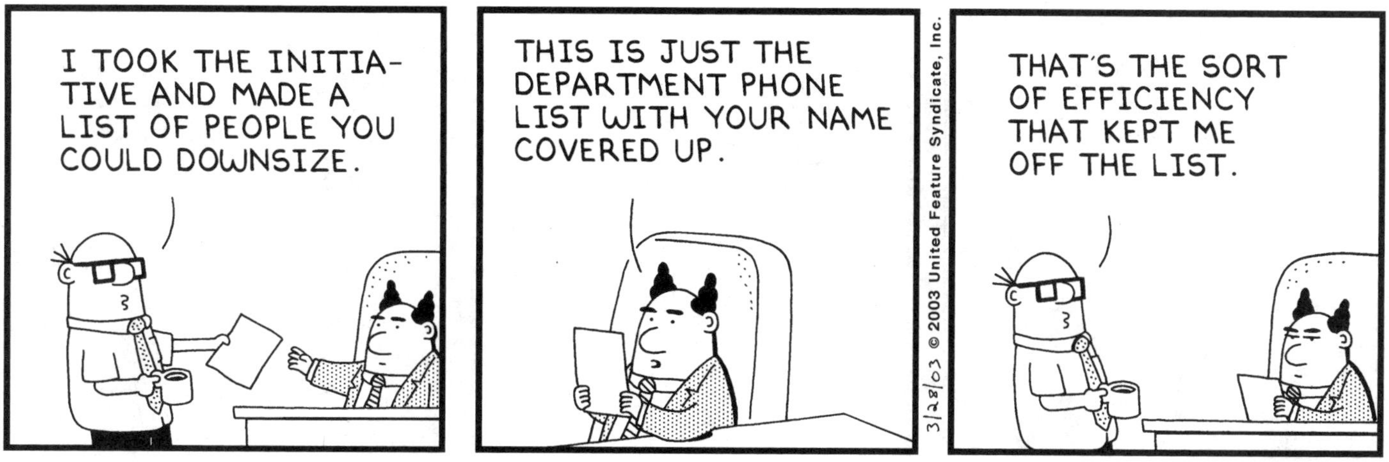
I TOOK THE INITIATIVE AND MADE A LIST OF PEOPLE YOU COULD DOWNSIZE.
THIS IS JUST THE DEPARTMENT PHONE LIST WITH YOUR NAME COVERED UP.
3/28/03 © 2003 United Feature Syndicate, Inc.
THAT'S THE SORT OF EFFICIENCY THAT KEPT ME OFF THE LIST.

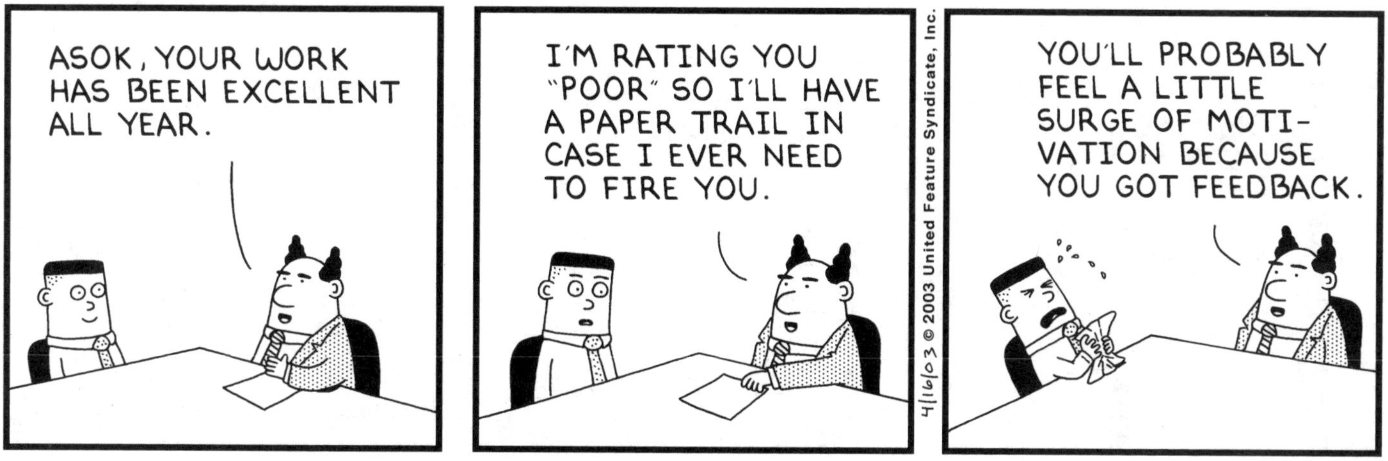
ASOK, YOUR WORK HAS BEEN EXCELLENT ALL YEAR.
I'M RATING YOU "POOR" SO I'LL HAVE A PAPER TRAIL IN CASE I EVER NEED TO FIRE YOU.
4/16/03 © 2003 United Feature Syndicate, Inc.
YOU'LL PROBABLY FEEL A LITTLE SURGE OF MOTIVATION BECAUSE YOU GOT FEEDBACK.

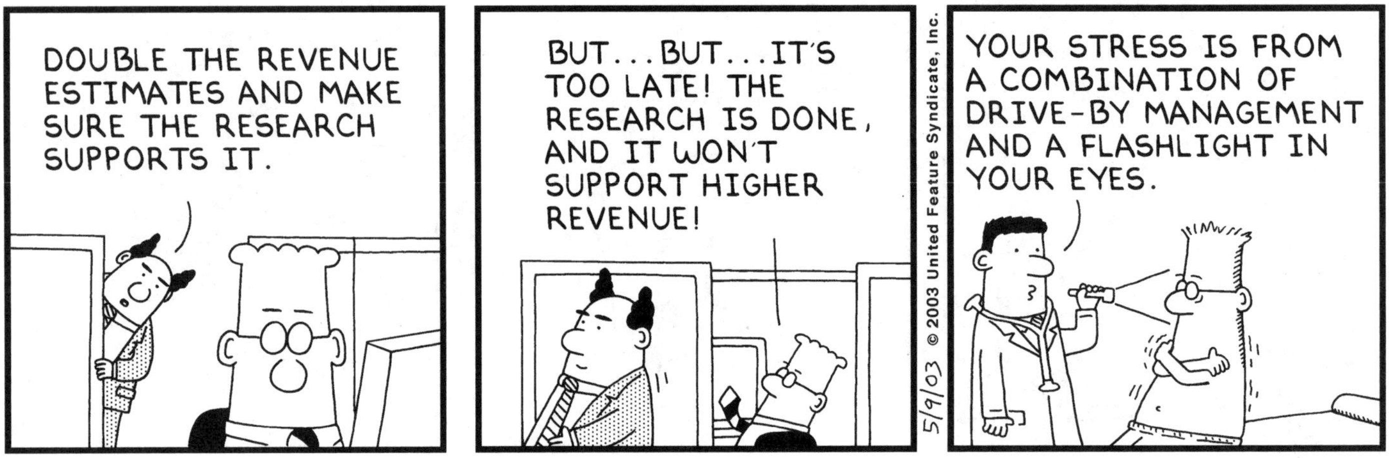
DOUBLE THE REVENUE ESTIMATES AND MAKE SURE THE RESEARCH SUPPORTS IT.
BUT...BUT...IT'S TOO LATE! THE RESEARCH IS DONE, AND IT WON'T SUPPORT HIGHER REVENUE!
5/9/03 © 2003 United Feature Syndicate, Inc.
YOUR STRESS IS FROM A COMBINATION OF DRIVE-BY MANAGEMENT AND A FLASHLIGHT IN YOUR EYES.

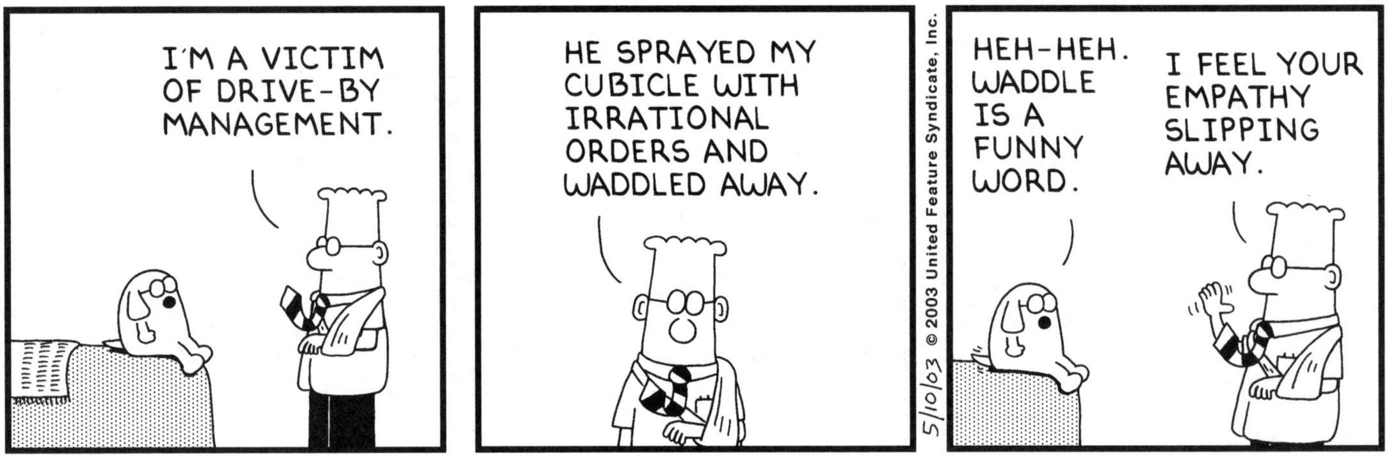
I'M A VICTIM OF DRIVE-BY MANAGEMENT.
HE SPRAYED MY CUBICLE WITH IRRATIONAL ORDERS AND WADDLED AWAY.
5/10/03 © 2003 United Feature Syndicate, Inc.
HEH-HEH. WADDLE IS A FUNNY WORD.
I FEEL YOUR EMPATHY SLIPPING AWAY.

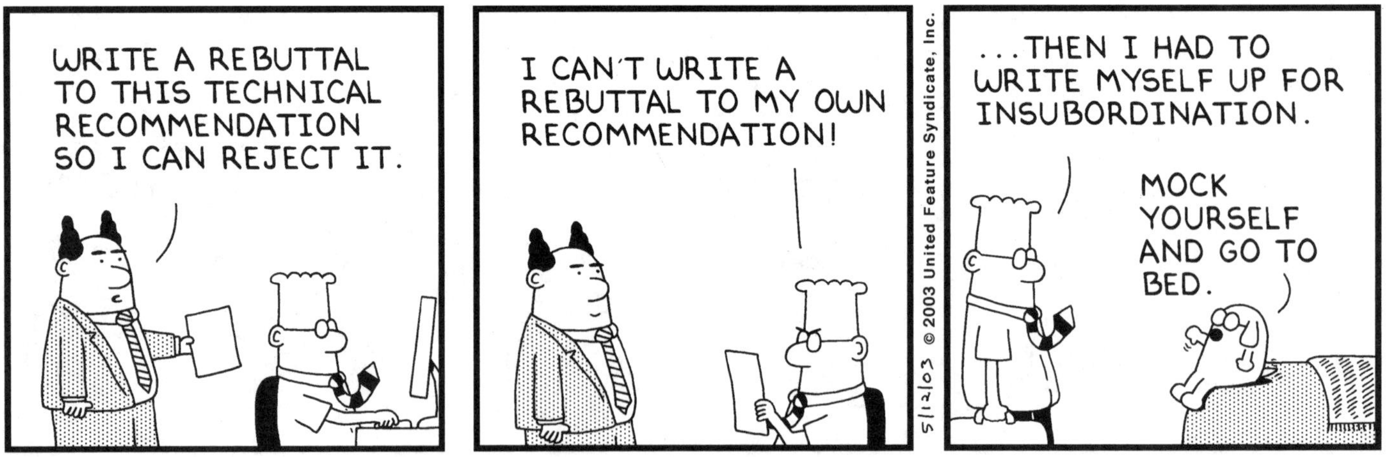
WRITE A REBUTTAL TO THIS TECHNICAL RECOMMENDATION SO I CAN REJECT IT.
I CAN'T WRITE A REBUTTAL TO MY OWN RECOMMENDATION!
5/12/03 © 2003 United Feature Syndicate, Inc.
...THEN I HAD TO WRITE MYSELF UP FOR INSUBORDINATION.
MOCK YOURSELF AND GO TO BED.

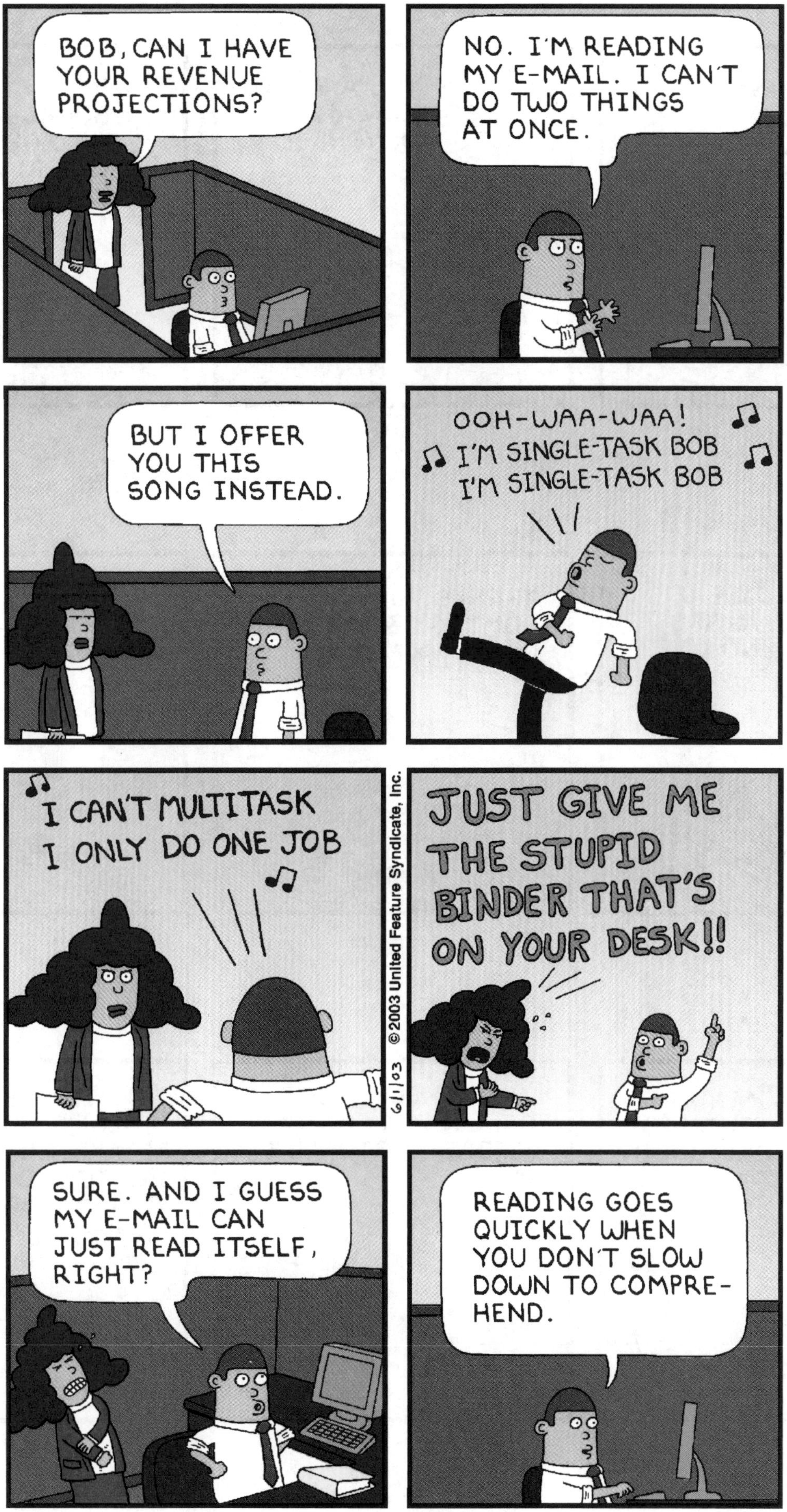
BOB, CAN I HAVE YOUR REVENUE PROJECTIONS?
NO. I'M READING MY E-MAIL. I CAN'T DO TWO THINGS AT ONCE.
BUT I OFFER YOU THIS SONG INSTEAD.
OOH-WAA-WAA!
I'M SINGLE-TASK BOB
I'M SINGLE-TASK BOB
I CAN'T MULTITASK
I ONLY DO ONE JOB
©2003 United Feature Syndicate, Inc.
6/1/03
JUST GIVE ME THE STUPID BINDER THAT'S ON YOUR DESK!!
SURE. AND I GUESS MY E-MAIL CAN JUST READ ITSELF, RIGHT?
READING GOES QUICKLY WHEN YOU DON'T SLOW DOWN TO COMPRE-HEND.

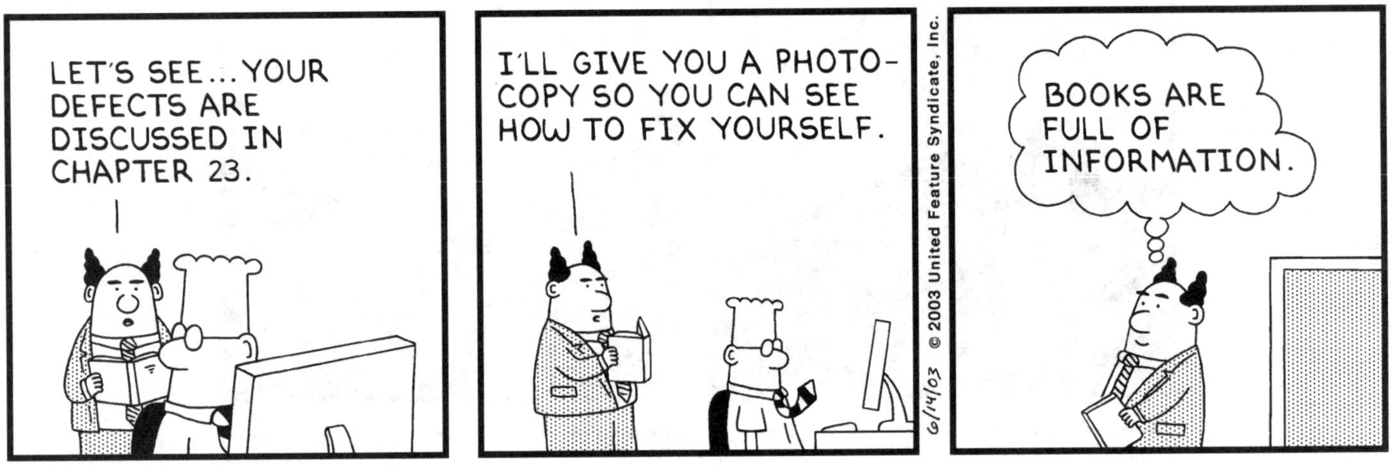
LET'S SEE... YOUR DEFECTS ARE DISCUSSED IN CHAPTER 23.
I'LL GIVE YOU A PHOTOCOPY SO YOU CAN SEE HOW TO FIX YOURSELF.
BOOKS ARE FULL OF INFORMATION.
6/14/03 © 2003 United Feature Syndicate, Inc.

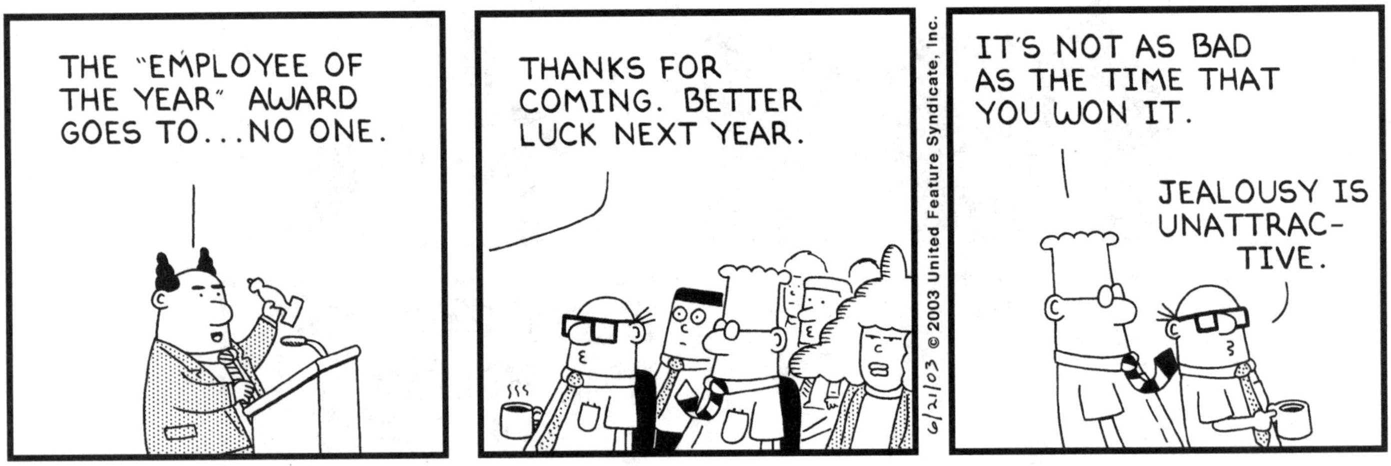
THE "EMPLOYEE OF THE YEAR" AWARD GOES TO... NO ONE.
THANKS FOR COMING. BETTER LUCK NEXT YEAR.
IT'S NOT AS BAD AS THE TIME THAT YOU WON IT.
JEALOUSY IS UNATTRACTIVE.
6/21/03 © 2003 United Feature Syndicate, Inc.

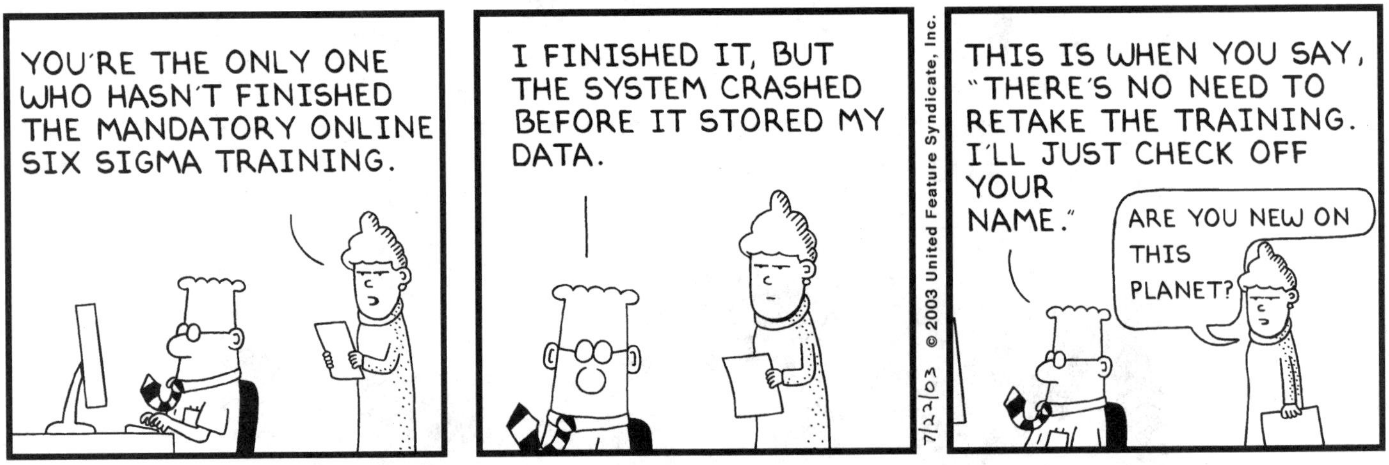
YOU'RE THE ONLY ONE WHO HASN'T FINISHED THE MANDATORY ONLINE SIX SIGMA TRAINING.
I FINISHED IT, BUT THE SYSTEM CRASHED BEFORE IT STORED MY DATA.
THIS IS WHEN YOU SAY, "THERE'S NO NEED TO RETAKE THE TRAINING. I'LL JUST CHECK OFF YOUR NAME."
ARE YOU NEW ON THIS PLANET?
7/22/03 © 2003 United Feature Syndicate, Inc.

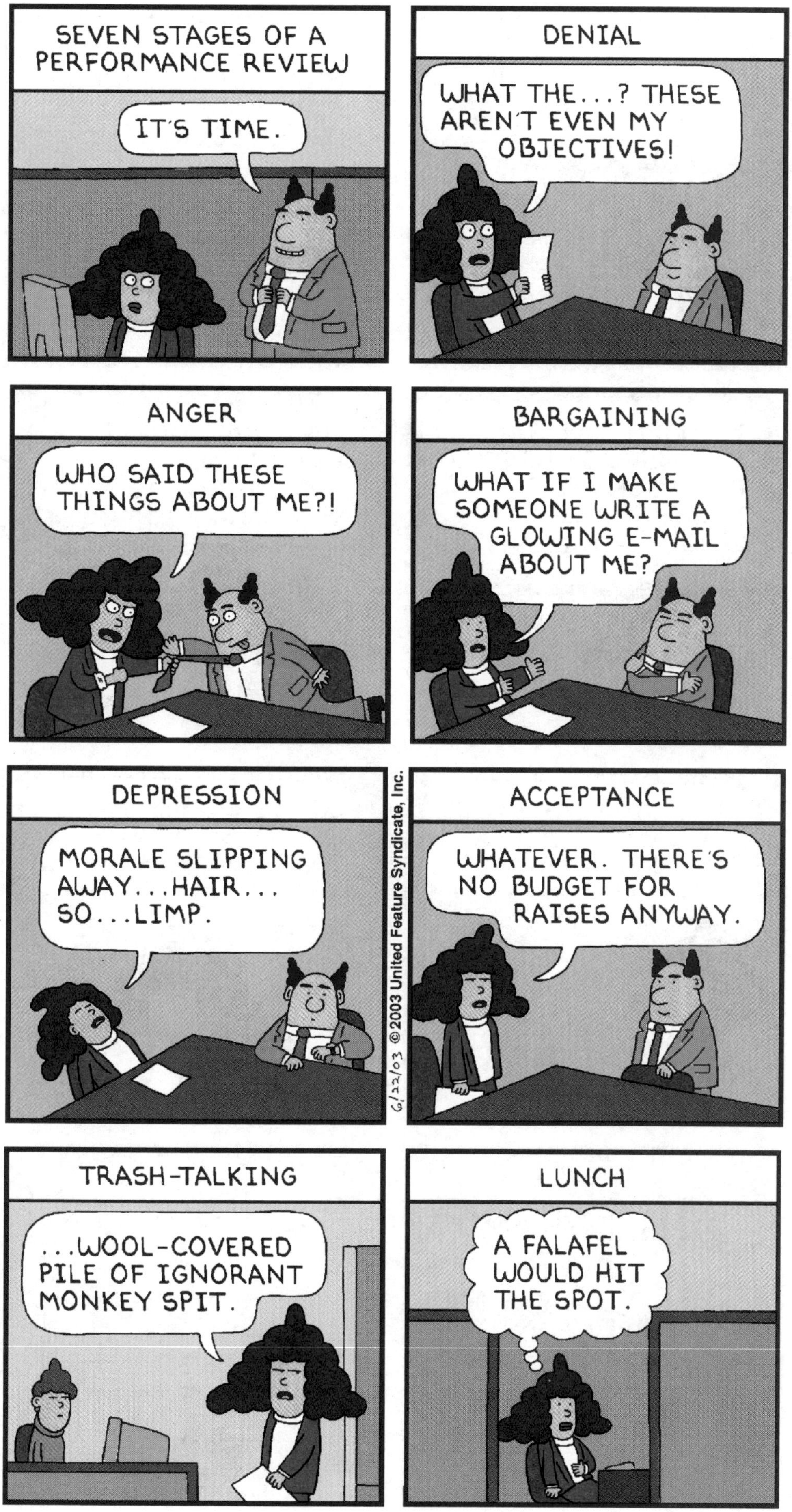
SEVEN STAGES OF A PERFORMANCE REVIEW
IT'S TIME.
DENIAL
WHAT THE...? THESE AREN'T EVEN MY OBJECTIVES!
ANGER
WHO SAID THESE THINGS ABOUT ME?!
BARGAINING
WHAT IF I MAKE SOMEONE WRITE A GLOWING E-MAIL ABOUT ME?
DEPRESSION
MORALE SLIPPING AWAY...HAIR... SO...LIMP.
ACCEPTANCE
WHATEVER. THERE'S NO BUDGET FOR RAISES ANYWAY.
TRASH-TALKING
...WOOL-COVERED PILE OF IGNORANT MONKEY SPIT.
LUNCH
A FALAFEL WOULD HIT THE SPOT.
6/22/03 ©2003 United Feature Syndicate, Inc.

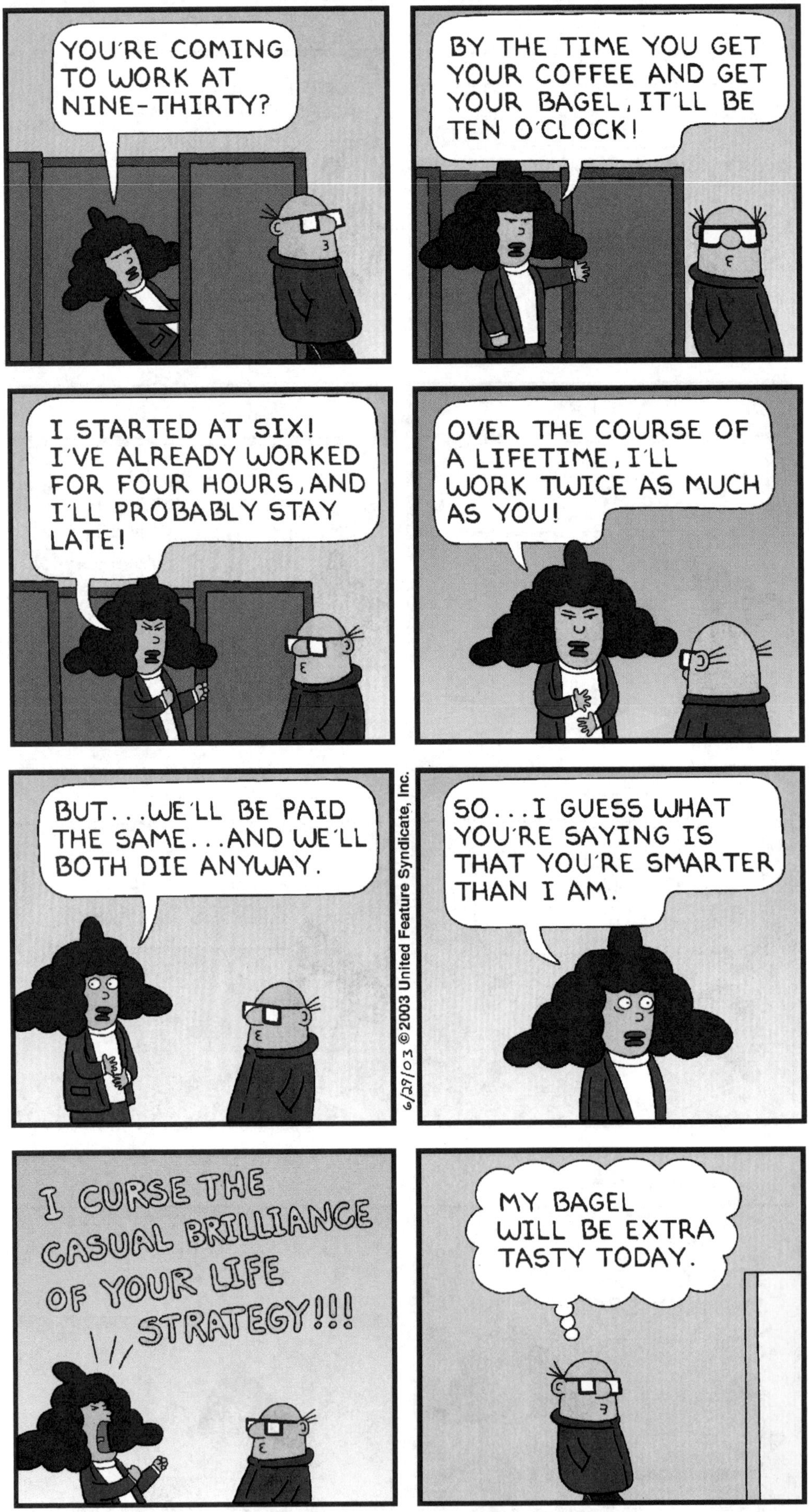
YOU'RE COMING TO WORK AT NINE-THIRTY?
BY THE TIME YOU GET YOUR COFFEE AND GET YOUR BAGEL, IT'LL BE TEN O'CLOCK!
I STARTED AT SIX! I'VE ALREADY WORKED FOR FOUR HOURS, AND I'LL PROBABLY STAY LATE!
OVER THE COURSE OF A LIFETIME, I'LL WORK TWICE AS MUCH AS YOU!
BUT...WE'LL BE PAID THE SAME...AND WE'LL BOTH DIE ANYWAY.
SO...I GUESS WHAT YOU'RE SAYING IS THAT YOU'RE SMARTER THAN I AM.
I CURSE THE CASUAL BRILLIANCE OF YOUR LIFE STRATEGY!!!
MY BAGEL WILL BE EXTRA TASTY TODAY.
6/29/03 ©2003 United Feature Syndicate, Inc.

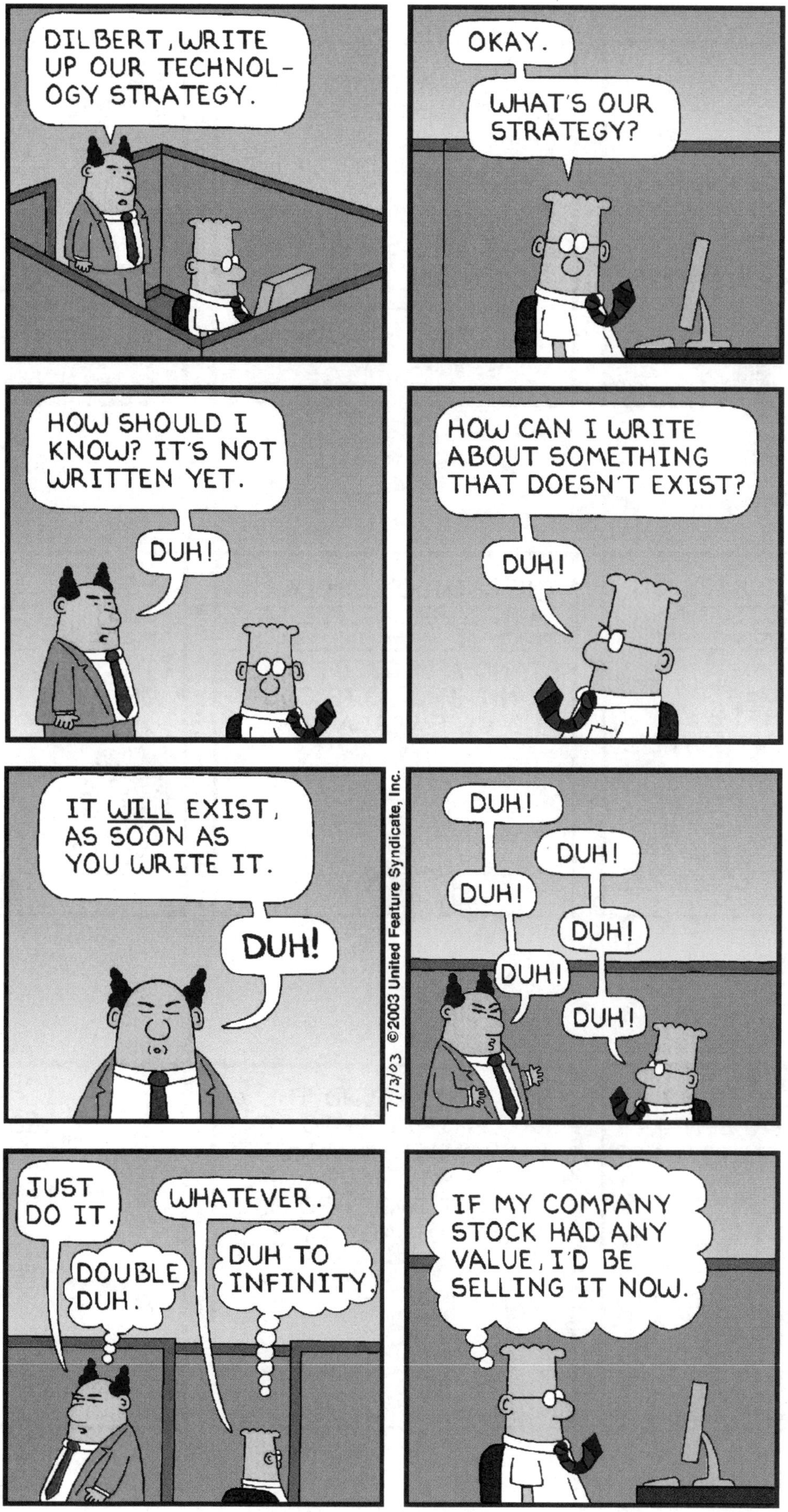
DILBERT, WRITE UP OUR TECHNOLOGY STRATEGY.
OKAY.
WHAT'S OUR STRATEGY?
HOW SHOULD I KNOW? IT'S NOT WRITTEN YET.
DUH!
HOW CAN I WRITE ABOUT SOMETHING THAT DOESN'T EXIST?
DUH!
IT WILL EXIST, AS SOON AS YOU WRITE IT.
DUH!
7/13/03 ©2003 United Feature Syndicate, Inc.
DUH!
DUH!
DUH!
DUH!
DUH!
DUH!
JUST DO IT.
DOUBLE DUH.
WHATEVER.
DUH TO INFINITY.
IF MY COMPANY STOCK HAD ANY VALUE, I'D BE SELLING IT NOW.

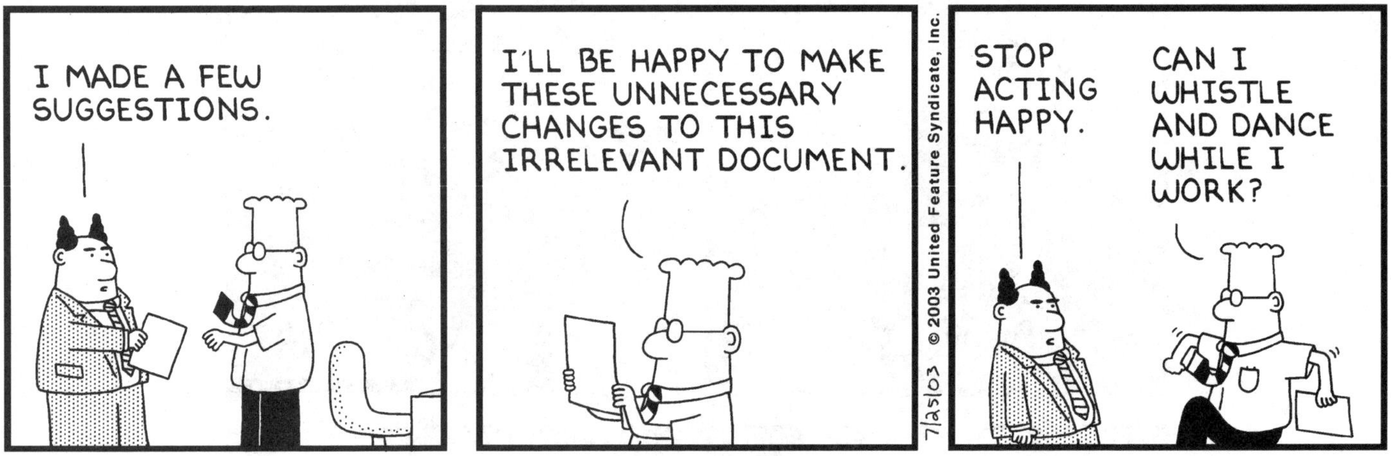
I MADE A FEW SUGGESTIONS.
I'LL BE HAPPY TO MAKE THESE UNNECESSARY CHANGES TO THIS IRRELEVANT DOCUMENT.
7/25/03 © 2003 United Feature Syndicate, Inc.
STOP ACTING HAPPY.
CAN I WHISTLE AND DANCE WHILE I WORK?

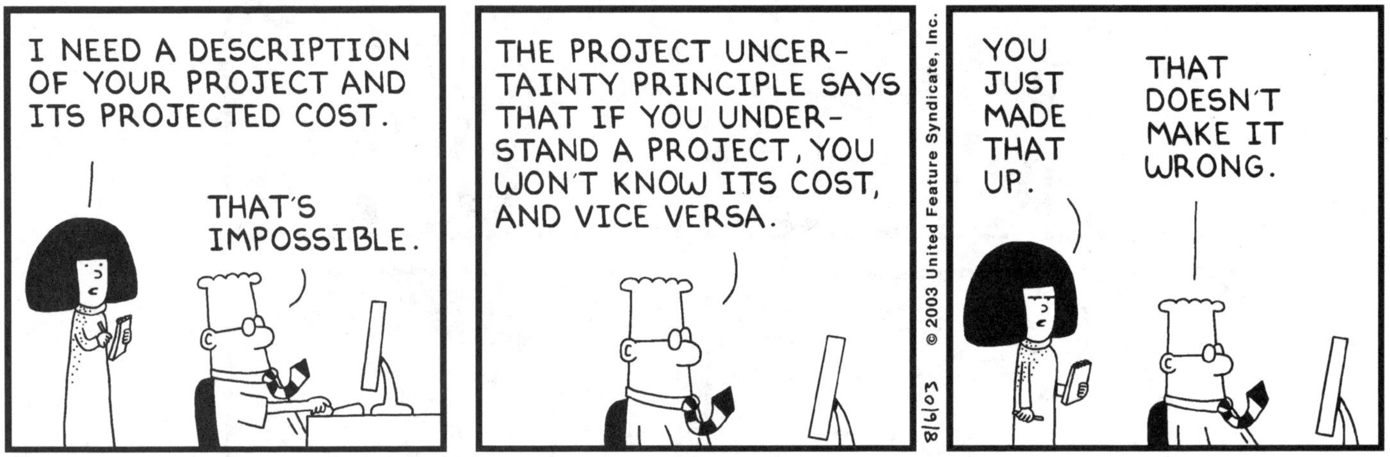
I NEED A DESCRIPTION OF YOUR PROJECT AND ITS PROJECTED COST.
THAT'S IMPOSSIBLE.
THE PROJECT UNCERTAINTY PRINCIPLE SAYS THAT IF YOU UNDERSTAND A PROJECT, YOU WON'T KNOW ITS COST, AND VICE VERSA.
8/6/03 © 2003 United Feature Syndicate, Inc.
YOU JUST MADE THAT UP.
THAT DOESN'T MAKE IT WRONG.

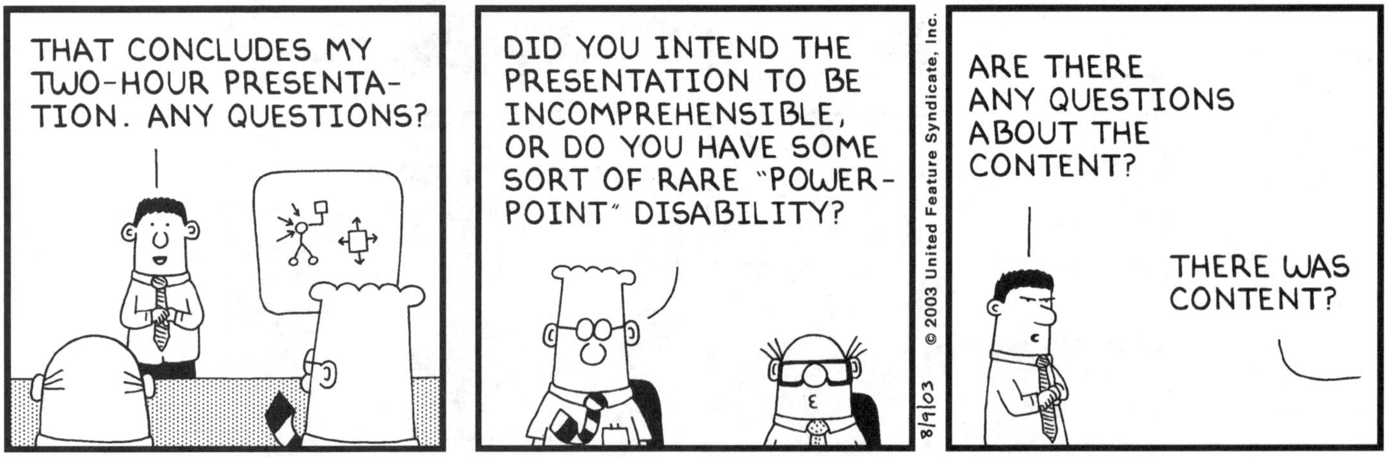
THAT CONCLUDES MY TWO-HOUR PRESENTATION. ANY QUESTIONS?
DID YOU INTEND THE PRESENTATION TO BE INCOMPREHENSIBLE, OR DO YOU HAVE SOME SORT OF RARE "POWERPOINT" DISABILITY?
8/9/03 © 2003 United Feature Syndicate, Inc.
ARE THERE ANY QUESTIONS ABOUT THE CONTENT?
THERE WAS CONTENT?

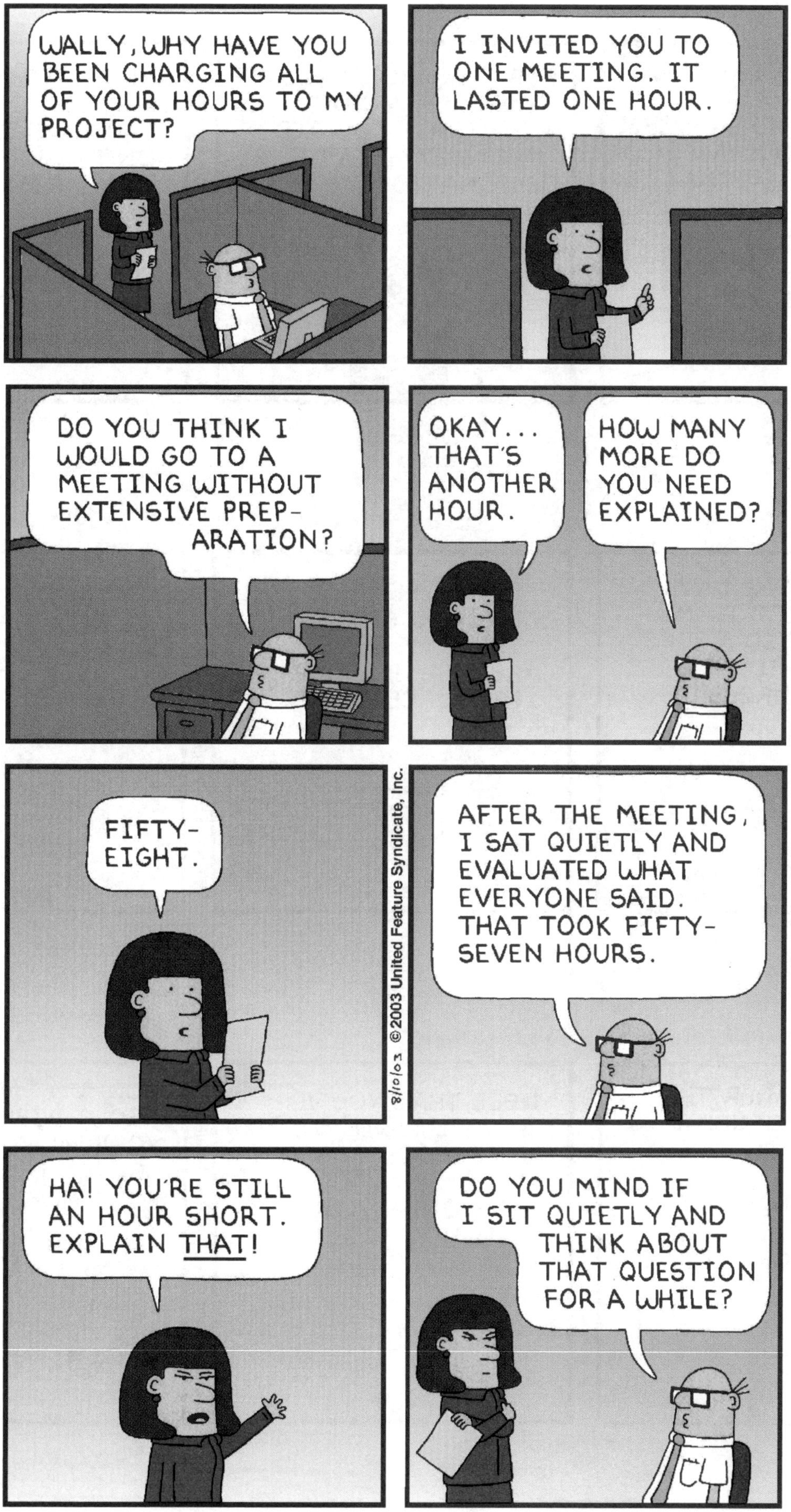
WALLY, WHY HAVE YOU BEEN CHARGING ALL OF YOUR HOURS TO MY PROJECT?
I INVITED YOU TO ONE MEETING. IT LASTED ONE HOUR.
DO YOU THINK I WOULD GO TO A MEETING WITHOUT EXTENSIVE PREP-ARATION?
OKAY... THAT'S ANOTHER HOUR.
HOW MANY MORE DO YOU NEED EXPLAINED?
FIFTY-EIGHT.
AFTER THE MEETING, I SAT QUIETLY AND EVALUATED WHAT EVERYONE SAID. THAT TOOK FIFTY-SEVEN HOURS.
HA! YOU'RE STILL AN HOUR SHORT. EXPLAIN THAT!
DO YOU MIND IF I SIT QUIETLY AND THINK ABOUT THAT QUESTION FOR A WHILE?
8/10/03 ©2003 United Feature Syndicate, Inc.

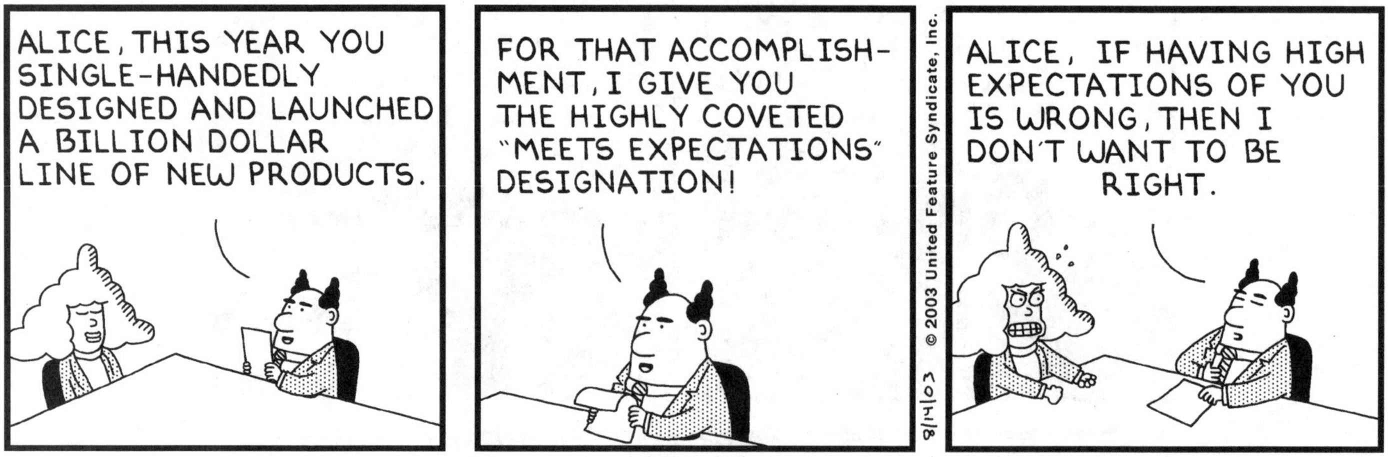
ALICE, THIS YEAR YOU SINGLE-HANDEDLY DESIGNED AND LAUNCHED A BILLION DOLLAR LINE OF NEW PRODUCTS.
FOR THAT ACCOMPLISHMENT, I GIVE YOU THE HIGHLY COVETED "MEETS EXPECTATIONS" DESIGNATION!
8/14/03
© 2003 United Feature Syndicate, Inc.
ALICE, IF HAVING HIGH EXPECTATIONS OF YOU IS WRONG, THEN I DON'T WANT TO BE RIGHT.

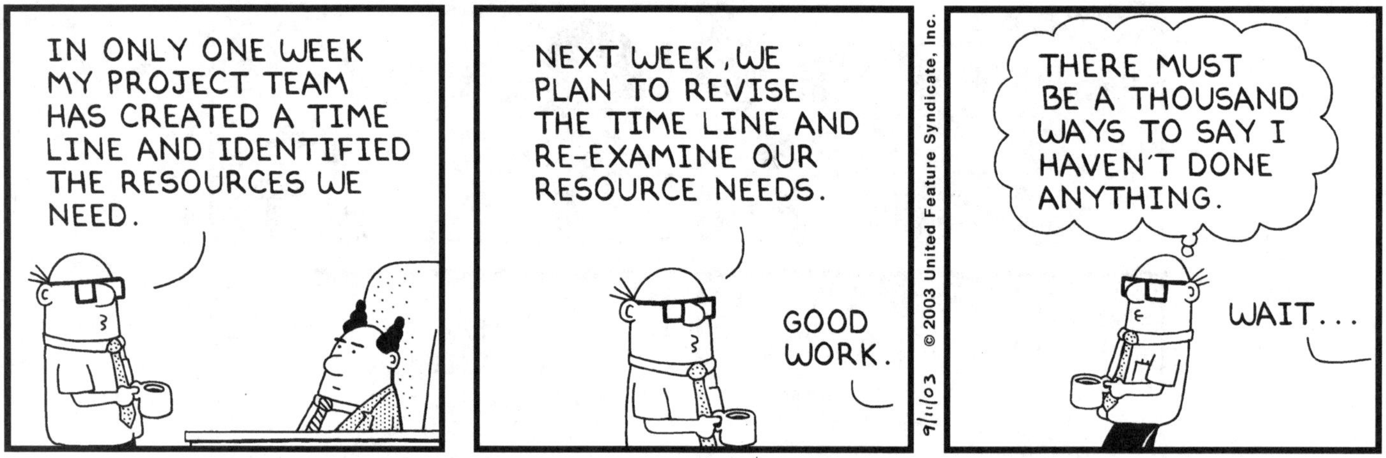
IN ONLY ONE WEEK MY PROJECT TEAM HAS CREATED A TIME LINE AND IDENTIFIED THE RESOURCES WE NEED.
NEXT WEEK, WE PLAN TO REVISE THE TIME LINE AND RE-EXAMINE OUR RESOURCE NEEDS.
GOOD WORK.
9/11/03
© 2003 United Feature Syndicate, Inc.
THERE MUST BE A THOUSAND WAYS TO SAY I HAVEN'T DONE ANYTHING.
WAIT...

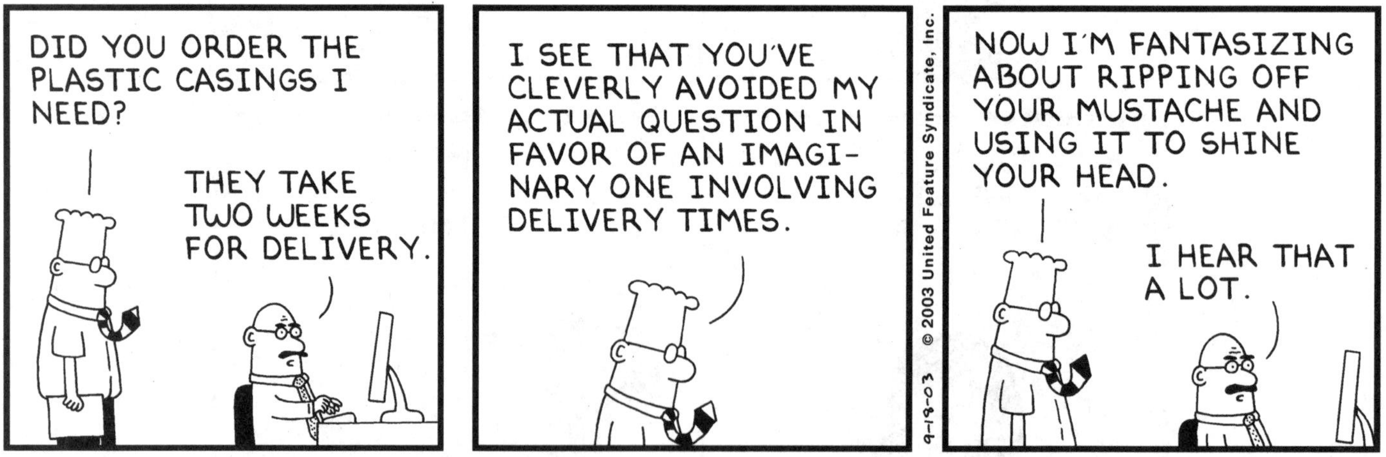
DID YOU ORDER THE PLASTIC CASINGS I NEED?
THEY TAKE TWO WEEKS FOR DELIVERY.
I SEE THAT YOU'VE CLEVERLY AVOIDED MY ACTUAL QUESTION IN FAVOR OF AN IMAGINARY ONE INVOLVING DELIVERY TIMES.
9-19-03
© 2003 United Feature Syndicate, Inc.
NOW I'M FANTASIZING ABOUT RIPPING OFF YOUR MUSTACHE AND USING IT TO SHINE YOUR HEAD.
I HEAR THAT A LOT.

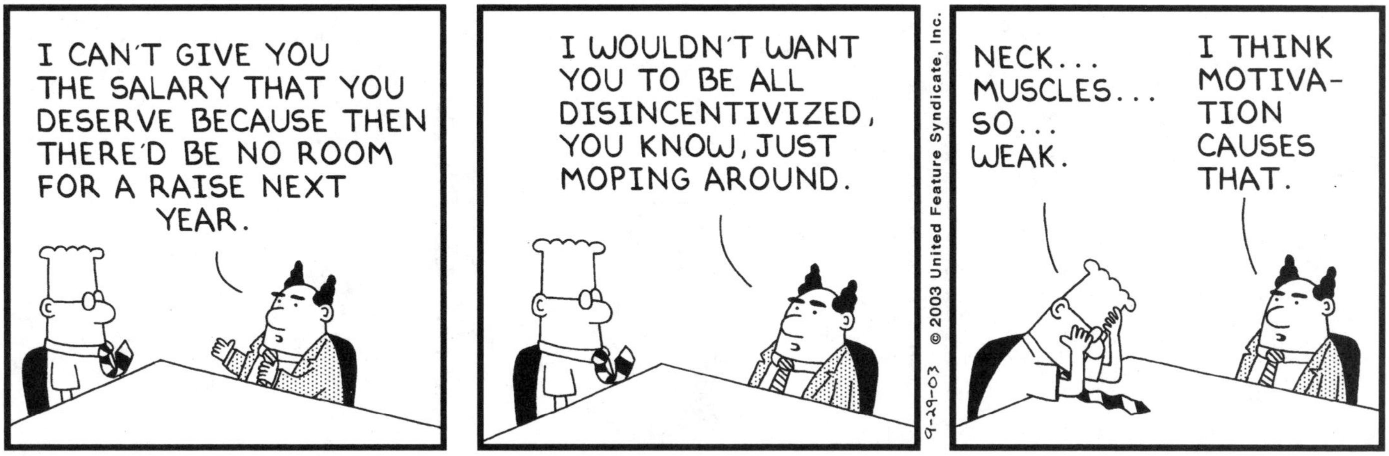
I CAN'T GIVE YOU THE SALARY THAT YOU DESERVE BECAUSE THEN THERE'D BE NO ROOM FOR A RAISE NEXT YEAR.
I WOULDN'T WANT YOU TO BE ALL DISINCENTIVIZED, YOU KNOW, JUST MOPING AROUND.
9-29-03 © 2003 United Feature Syndicate, Inc.
NECK... MUSCLES... SO... WEAK.
I THINK MOTIVATION CAUSES THAT.

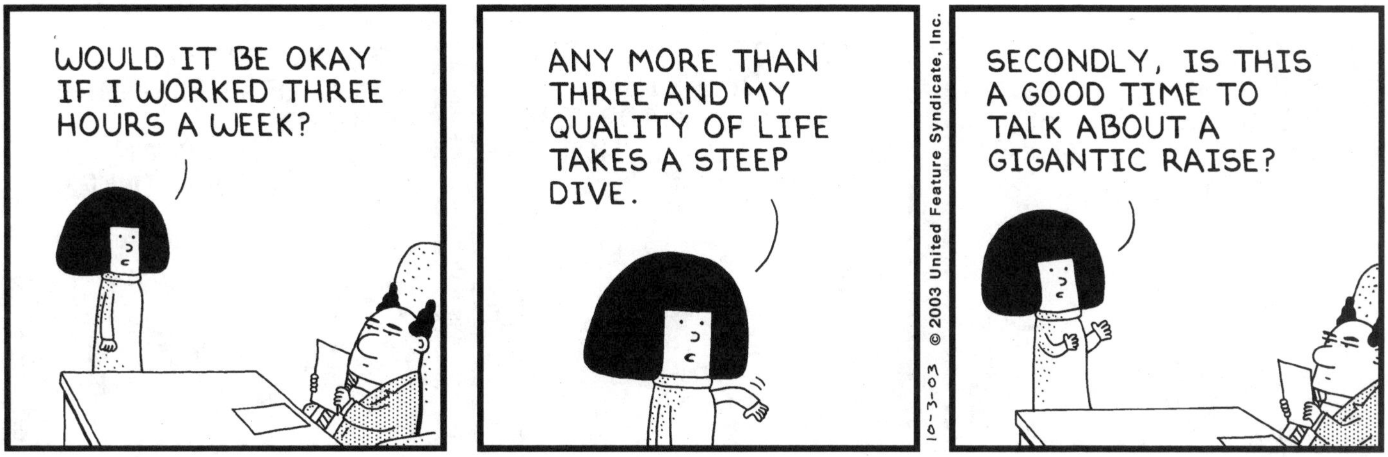
WOULD IT BE OKAY IF I WORKED THREE HOURS A WEEK?
ANY MORE THAN THREE AND MY QUALITY OF LIFE TAKES A STEEP DIVE.
10-3-03 © 2003 United Feature Syndicate, Inc.
SECONDLY, IS THIS A GOOD TIME TO TALK ABOUT A GIGANTIC RAISE?

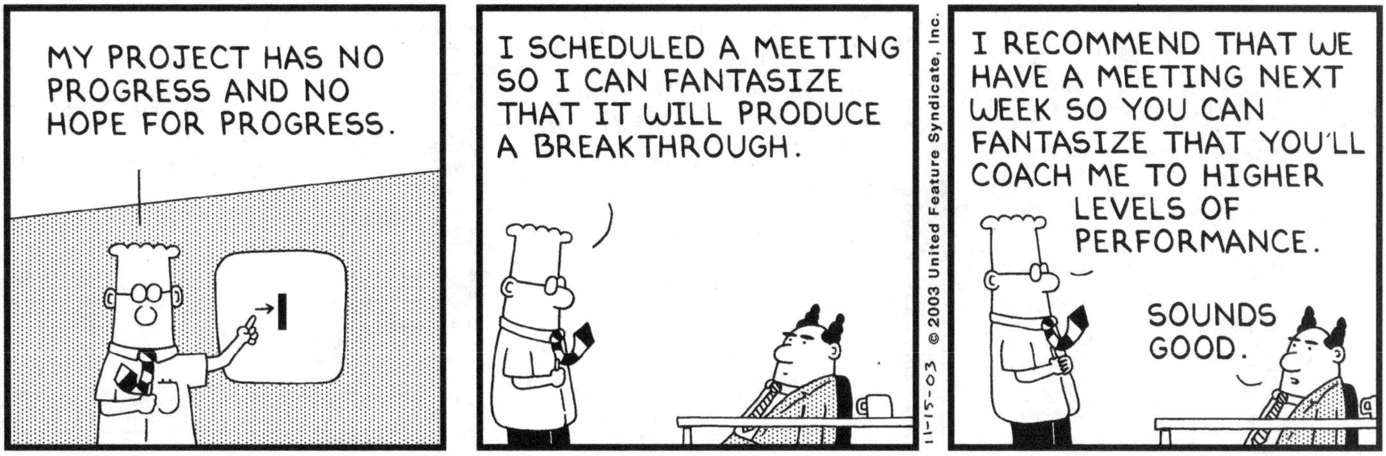
MY PROJECT HAS NO PROGRESS AND NO HOPE FOR PROGRESS.
I SCHEDULED A MEETING SO I CAN FANTASIZE THAT IT WILL PRODUCE A BREAKTHROUGH.
11-15-03 © 2003 United Feature Syndicate, Inc.
I RECOMMEND THAT WE HAVE A MEETING NEXT WEEK SO YOU CAN FANTASIZE THAT YOU'LL COACH ME TO HIGHER LEVELS OF PERFORMANCE.
SOUNDS GOOD.

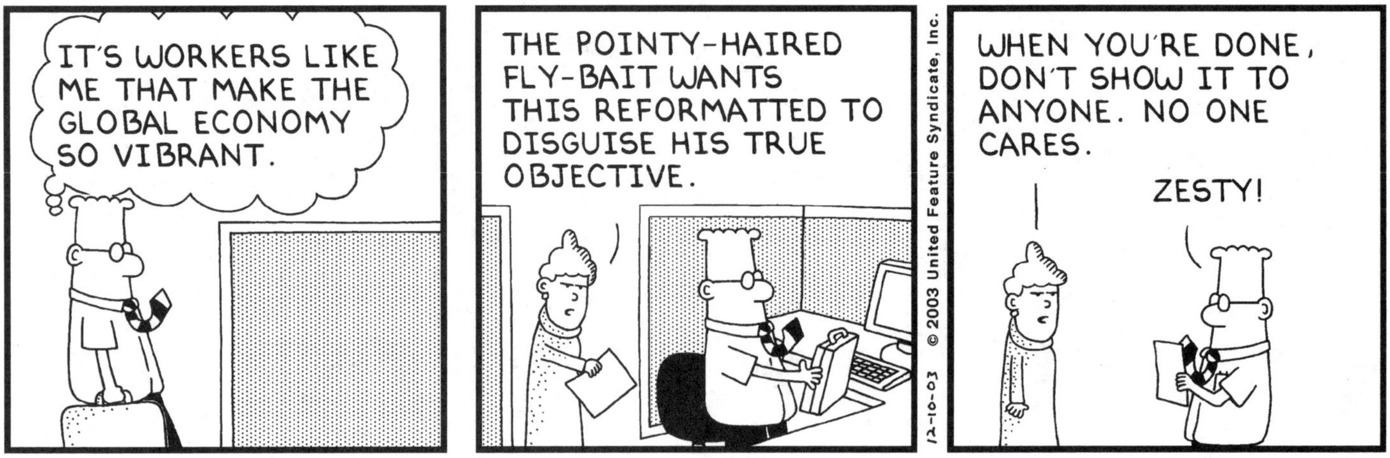
IT'S WORKERS LIKE ME THAT MAKE THE GLOBAL ECONOMY SO VIBRANT.
THE POINTY-HAIRED FLY-BAIT WANTS THIS REFORMATTED TO DISGUISE HIS TRUE OBJECTIVE.
12-10-03 © 2003 United Feature Syndicate, Inc.
WHEN YOU'RE DONE, DON'T SHOW IT TO ANYONE. NO ONE CARES.
ZESTY!

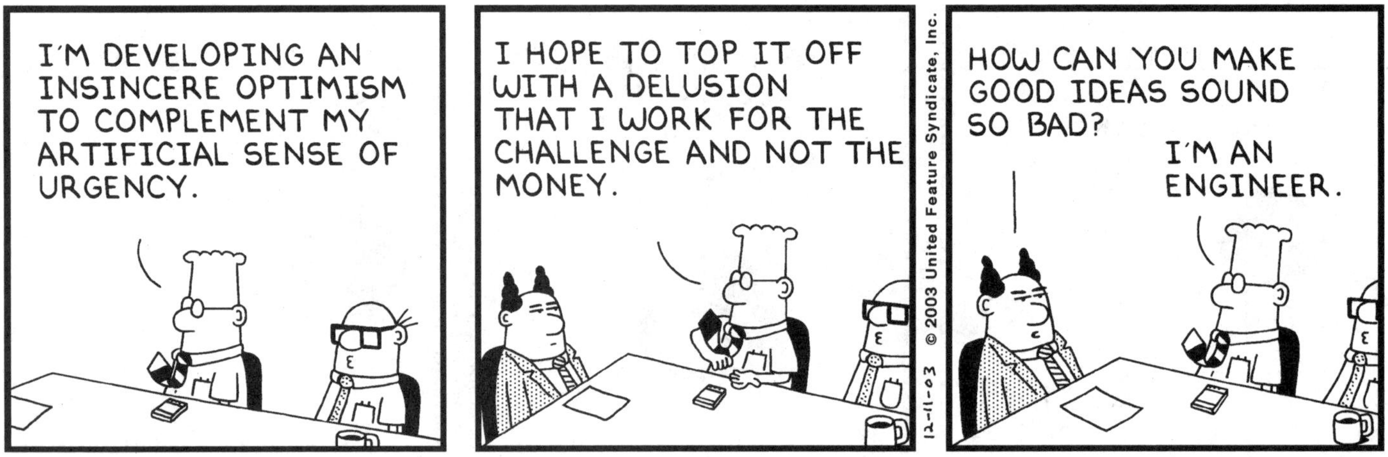
I'M DEVELOPING AN INSINCERE OPTIMISM TO COMPLEMENT MY ARTIFICIAL SENSE OF URGENCY.
I HOPE TO TOP IT OFF WITH A DELUSION THAT I WORK FOR THE CHALLENGE AND NOT THE MONEY.
12-11-03 © 2003 United Feature Syndicate, Inc.
HOW CAN YOU MAKE GOOD IDEAS SOUND SO BAD?
I'M AN ENGINEER.

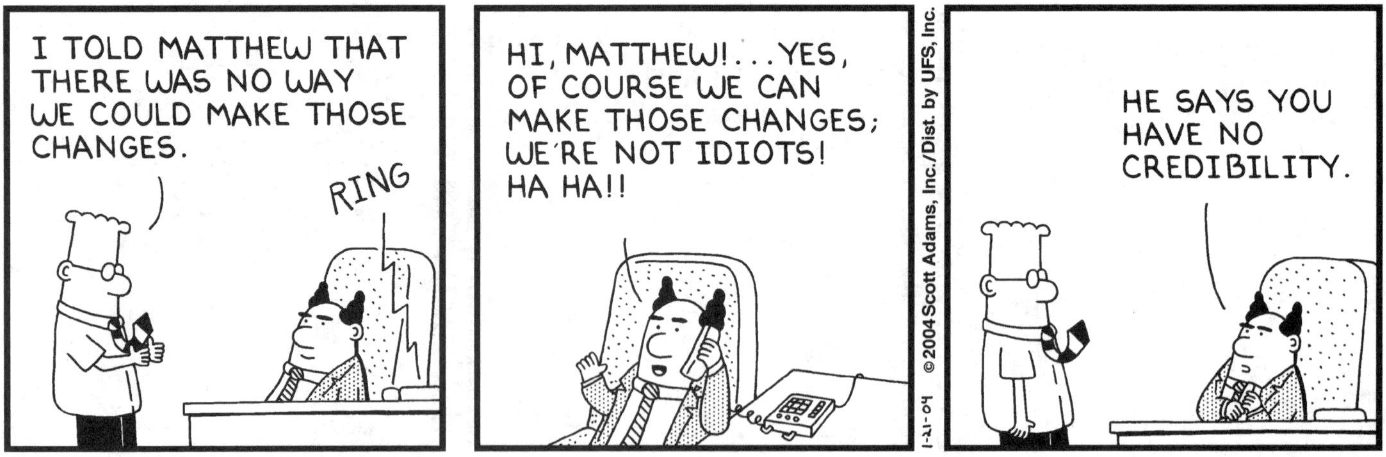
I TOLD MATTHEW THAT THERE WAS NO WAY WE COULD MAKE THOSE CHANGES.
RING
HI, MATTHEW! ... YES, OF COURSE WE CAN MAKE THOSE CHANGES; WE'RE NOT IDIOTS! HA HA!!
1-21-04 © 2004 Scott Adams, Inc./Dist. by UFS, Inc.
HE SAYS YOU HAVE NO CREDIBILITY.

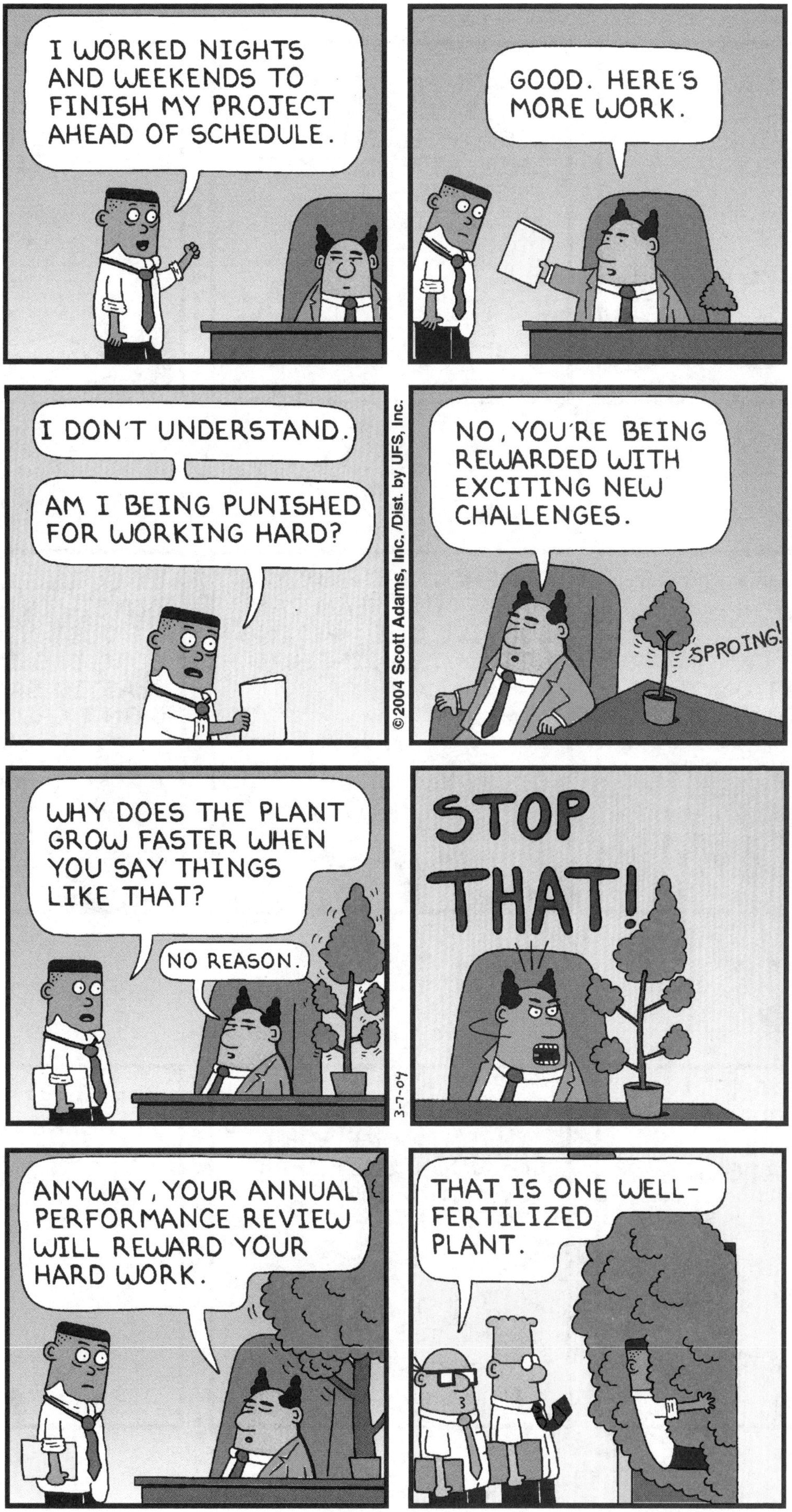
I WORKED NIGHTS AND WEEKENDS TO FINISH MY PROJECT AHEAD OF SCHEDULE.
GOOD. HERE'S MORE WORK.
I DON'T UNDERSTAND.
AM I BEING PUNISHED FOR WORKING HARD?
©2004 Scott Adams, Inc./Dist. by UFS, Inc.
NO, YOU'RE BEING REWARDED WITH EXCITING NEW CHALLENGES.
SPROING!
WHY DOES THE PLANT GROW FASTER WHEN YOU SAY THINGS LIKE THAT?
NO REASON.
3-7-04
STOP THAT!
ANYWAY, YOUR ANNUAL PERFORMANCE REVIEW WILL REWARD YOUR HARD WORK.
THAT IS ONE WELL-FERTILIZED PLANT.

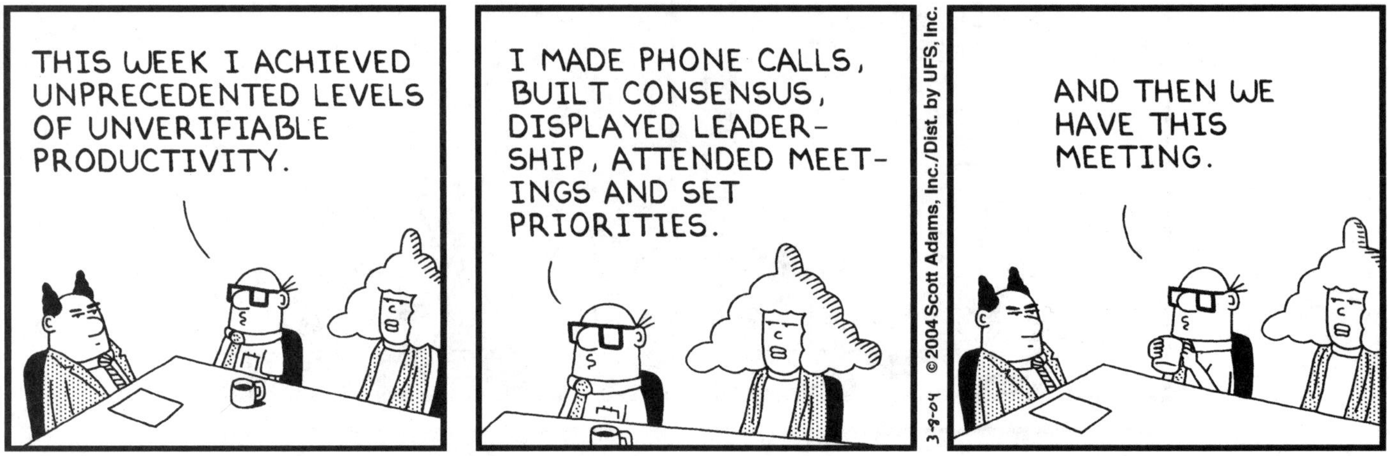
THIS WEEK I ACHIEVED UNPRECEDENTED LEVELS OF UNVERIFIABLE PRODUCTIVITY.
I MADE PHONE CALLS, BUILT CONSENSUS, DISPLAYED LEADER-SHIP, ATTENDED MEET-INGS AND SET PRIORITIES.
AND THEN WE HAVE THIS MEETING.
3-8-04 © 2004 Scott Adams, Inc./Dist. by UFS, Inc.

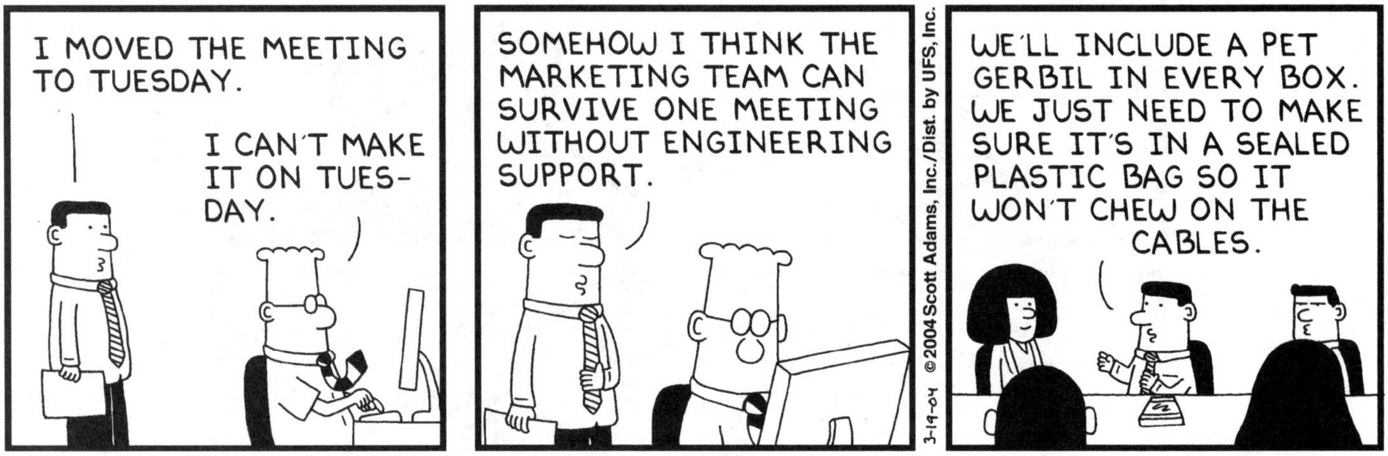
I MOVED THE MEETING TO TUESDAY.
I CAN'T MAKE IT ON TUES-DAY.
SOMEHOW I THINK THE MARKETING TEAM CAN SURVIVE ONE MEETING WITHOUT ENGINEERING SUPPORT.
WE'LL INCLUDE A PET GERBIL IN EVERY BOX. WE JUST NEED TO MAKE SURE IT'S IN A SEALED PLASTIC BAG SO IT WON'T CHEW ON THE CABLES.
3-19-04 © 2004 Scott Adams, Inc./Dist. by UFS, Inc.

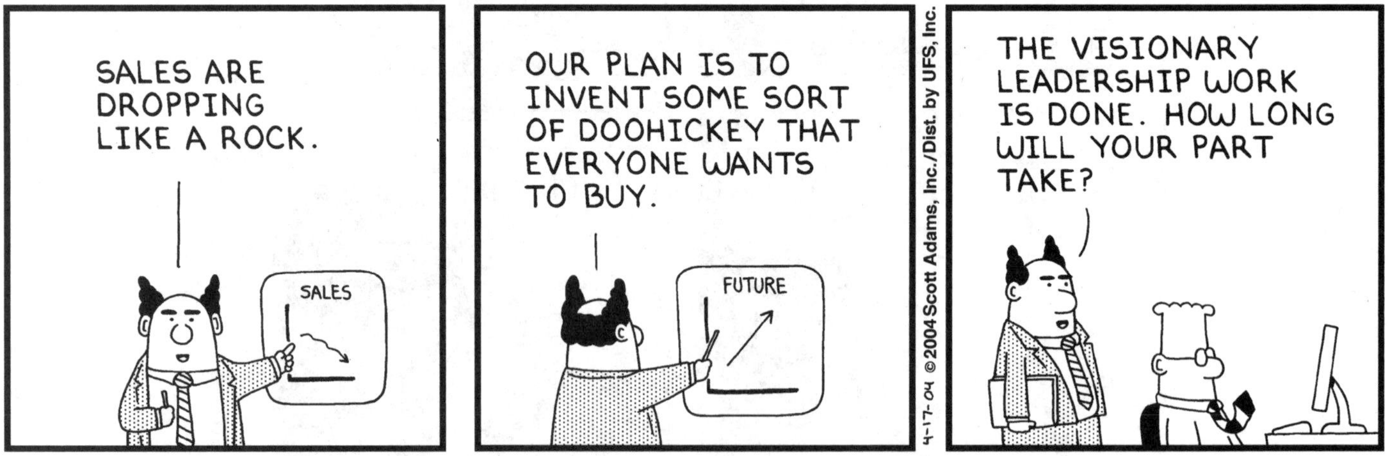
SALES ARE DROPPING LIKE A ROCK.
SALES
OUR PLAN IS TO INVENT SOME SORT OF DOOHICKEY THAT EVERYONE WANTS TO BUY.
FUTURE
THE VISIONARY LEADERSHIP WORK IS DONE. HOW LONG WILL YOUR PART TAKE?
4-17-04 © 2004 Scott Adams, Inc./Dist. by UFS, Inc.

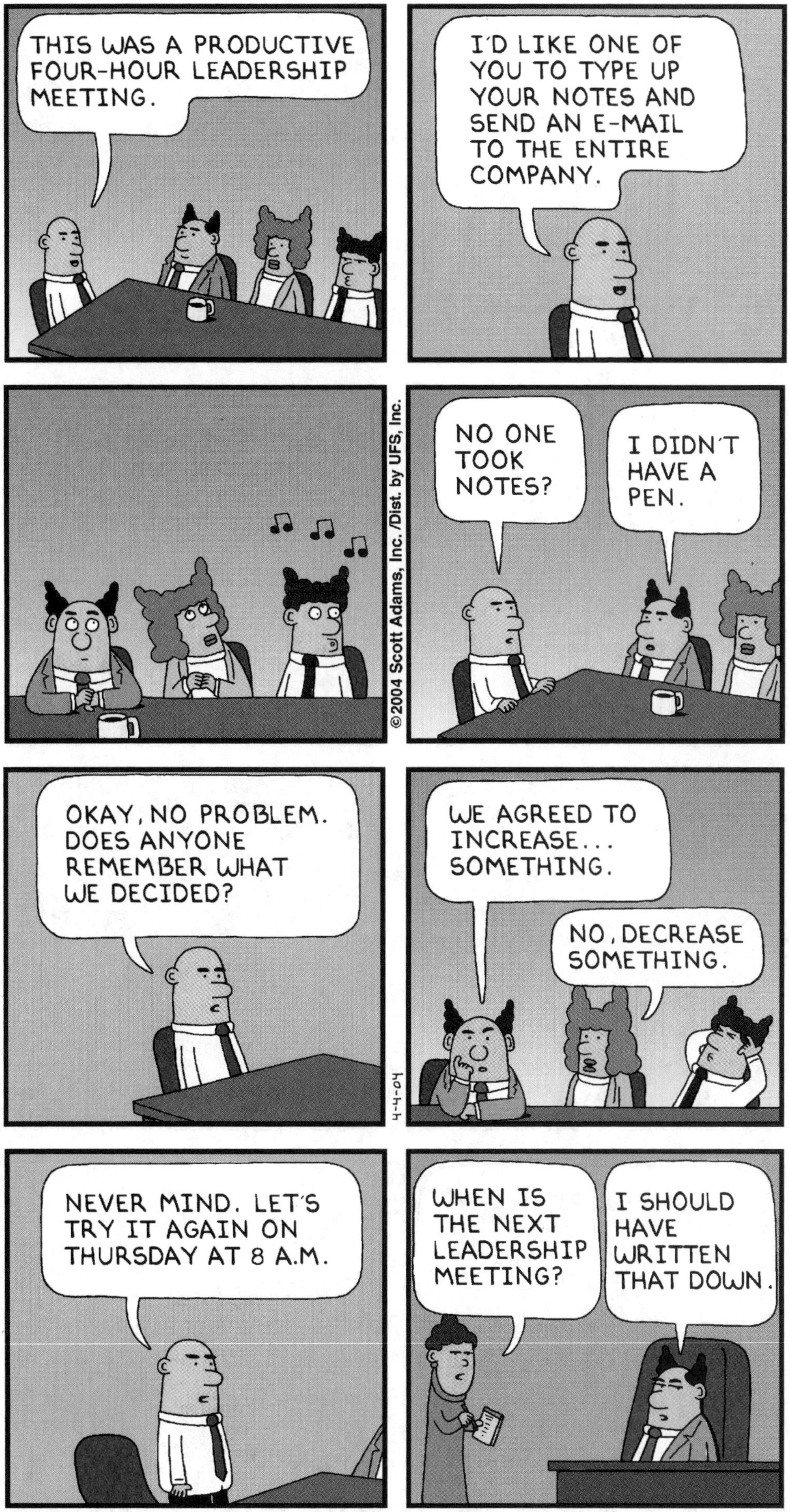
THIS WAS A PRODUCTIVE FOUR-HOUR LEADERSHIP MEETING.
I'D LIKE ONE OF YOU TO TYPE UP YOUR NOTES AND SEND AN E-MAIL TO THE ENTIRE COMPANY.
NO ONE TOOK NOTES?
I DIDN'T HAVE A PEN.
OKAY, NO PROBLEM. DOES ANYONE REMEMBER WHAT WE DECIDED?
WE AGREED TO INCREASE... SOMETHING.
NO, DECREASE SOMETHING.
4-4-04
NEVER MIND. LET'S TRY IT AGAIN ON THURSDAY AT 8 A.M.
WHEN IS THE NEXT LEADERSHIP MEETING?
I SHOULD HAVE WRITTEN THAT DOWN.

PERFORMANCE REVIEW

PEOPLE SAY YOU'RE TOO NEGATIVE IN MEETINGS.

NEGATIVE?

WHEN?

ACCORDING TO THE MARKETING DEPARTMENT. YOU POO-POOED A NUMBER OF THEIR IDEAS...

...THE COLD FUSION SCOOTER, PERPETUAL MOTION CLOTHES DRYER, ANTIGRAVITY PANTS, MRI VENDING MACHINE, AND THE LIST GOES ON.

THOSE ARE TERRIBLE IDEAS!

NEGATIVE ATTITUDE!!! GOTTCHA!!!

OKAY, YOU'RE RIGHT. FROM NOW ON, I WILL SUPPORT ALL TERRIBLE IDEAS.

GOOD.

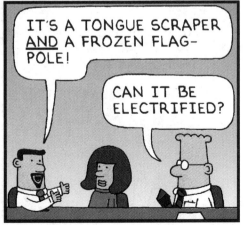

IT'S A TONGUE SCRAPER AND A FROZEN FLAG-POLE!

CAN IT BE ELECTRIFIED?

© 2004 Scott Adams, Inc. /Dist. by UFS, Inc.

5-23-04

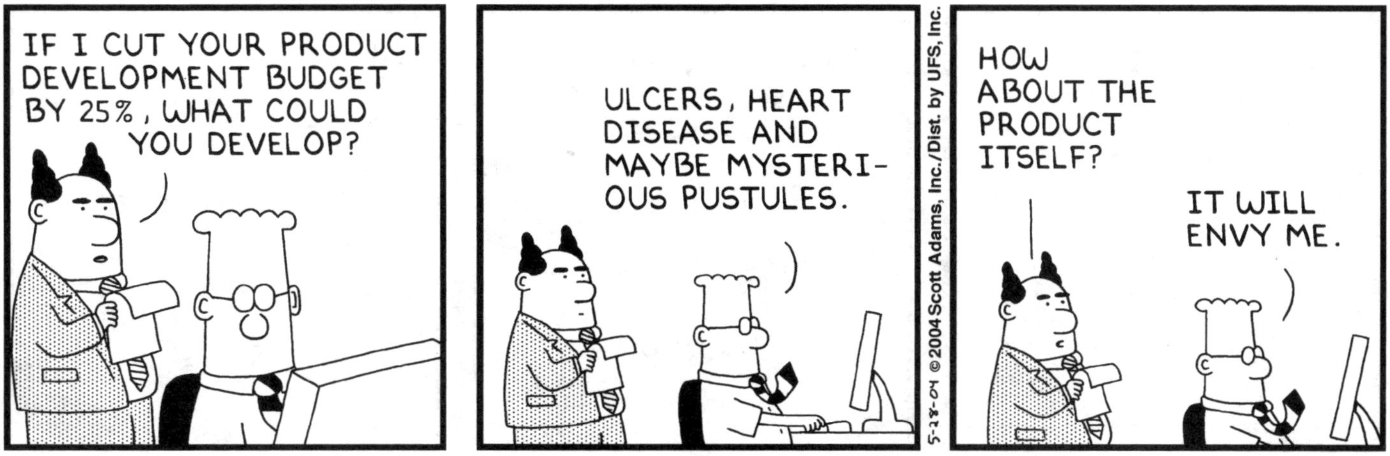
IF I CUT YOUR PRODUCT DEVELOPMENT BUDGET BY 25%, WHAT COULD YOU DEVELOP?
ULCERS, HEART DISEASE AND MAYBE MYSTERIOUS PUSTULES.
5-28-04 ©2004 Scott Adams, Inc./Dist. by UFS, Inc.
HOW ABOUT THE PRODUCT ITSELF?
IT WILL ENVY ME.

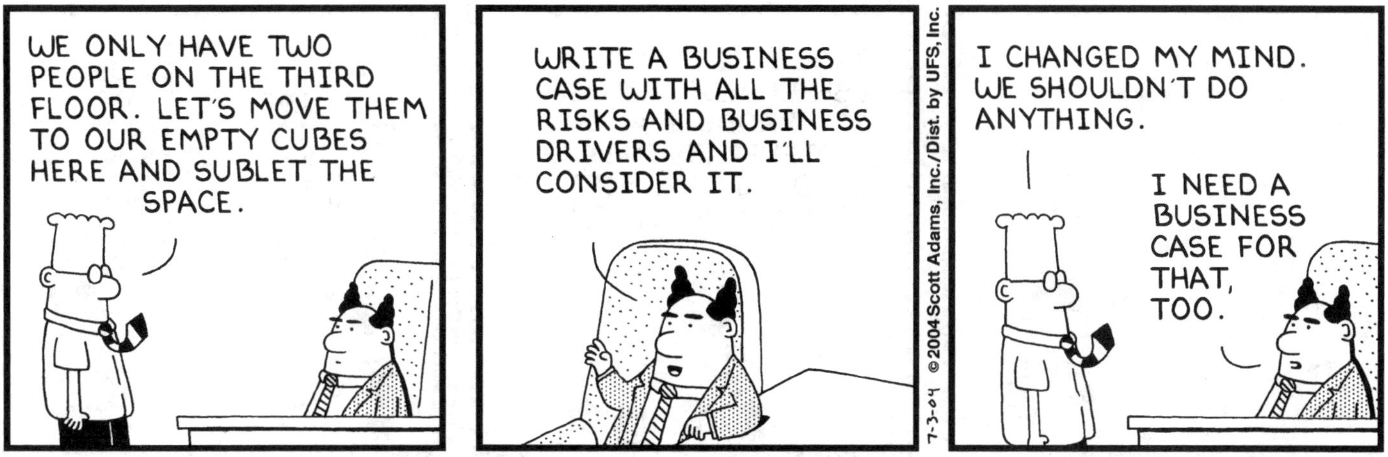
WE ONLY HAVE TWO PEOPLE ON THE THIRD FLOOR. LET'S MOVE THEM TO OUR EMPTY CUBES HERE AND SUBLET THE SPACE.
WRITE A BUSINESS CASE WITH ALL THE RISKS AND BUSINESS DRIVERS AND I'LL CONSIDER IT.
7-3-04 ©2004 Scott Adams, Inc./Dist. by UFS, Inc.
I CHANGED MY MIND. WE SHOULDN'T DO ANYTHING.
I NEED A BUSINESS CASE FOR THAT, TOO.

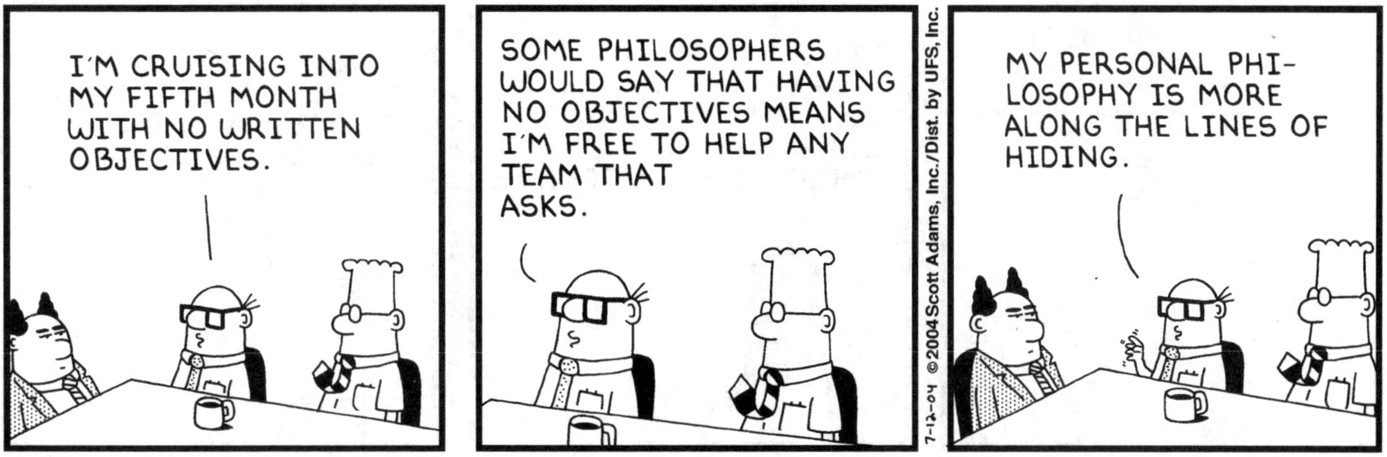
I'M CRUISING INTO MY FIFTH MONTH WITH NO WRITTEN OBJECTIVES.
SOME PHILOSOPHERS WOULD SAY THAT HAVING NO OBJECTIVES MEANS I'M FREE TO HELP ANY TEAM THAT ASKS.
7-12-04 ©2004 Scott Adams, Inc./Dist. by UFS, Inc.
MY PERSONAL PHILOSOPHY IS MORE ALONG THE LINES OF HIDING.

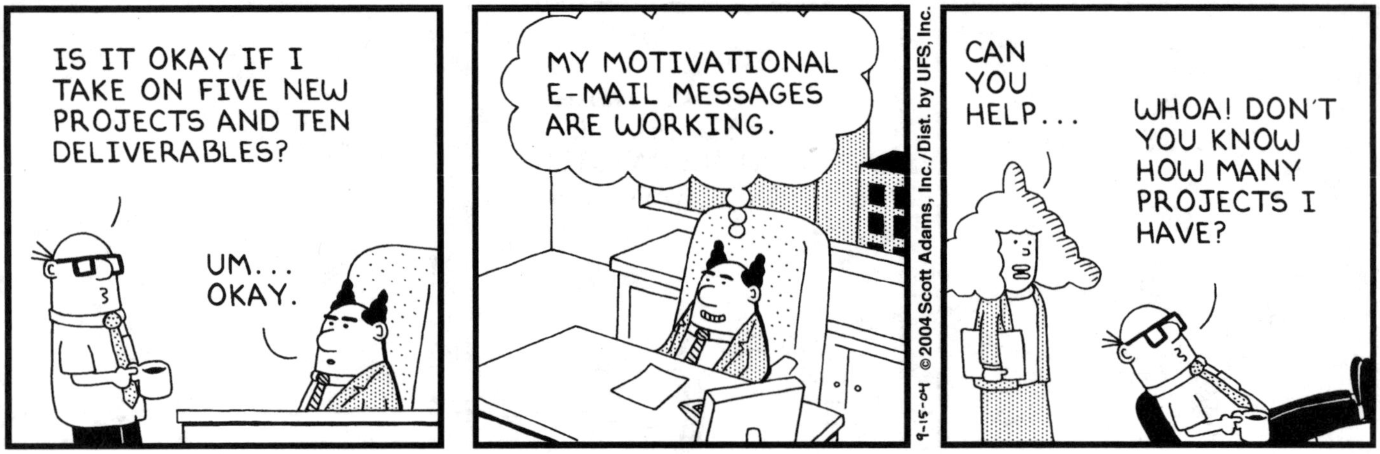
IS IT OKAY IF I TAKE ON FIVE NEW PROJECTS AND TEN DELIVERABLES?
UM... OKAY.
MY MOTIVATIONAL E-MAIL MESSAGES ARE WORKING.
9-15-04 © 2004 Scott Adams, Inc./Dist. by UFS, Inc.
CAN YOU HELP...
WHOA! DON'T YOU KNOW HOW MANY PROJECTS I HAVE?

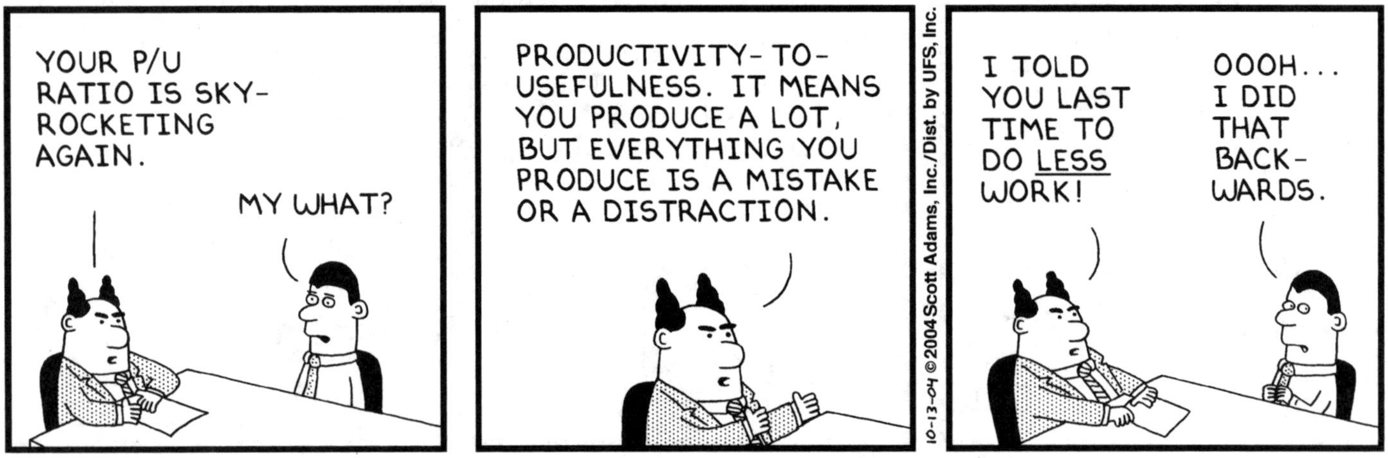
YOUR P/U RATIO IS SKY-ROCKETING AGAIN.
MY WHAT?
PRODUCTIVITY-TO-USEFULNESS. IT MEANS YOU PRODUCE A LOT, BUT EVERYTHING YOU PRODUCE IS A MISTAKE OR A DISTRACTION.
10-13-04 © 2004 Scott Adams, Inc./Dist. by UFS, Inc.
I TOLD YOU LAST TIME TO DO LESS WORK!
OOOH... I DID THAT BACK-WARDS.

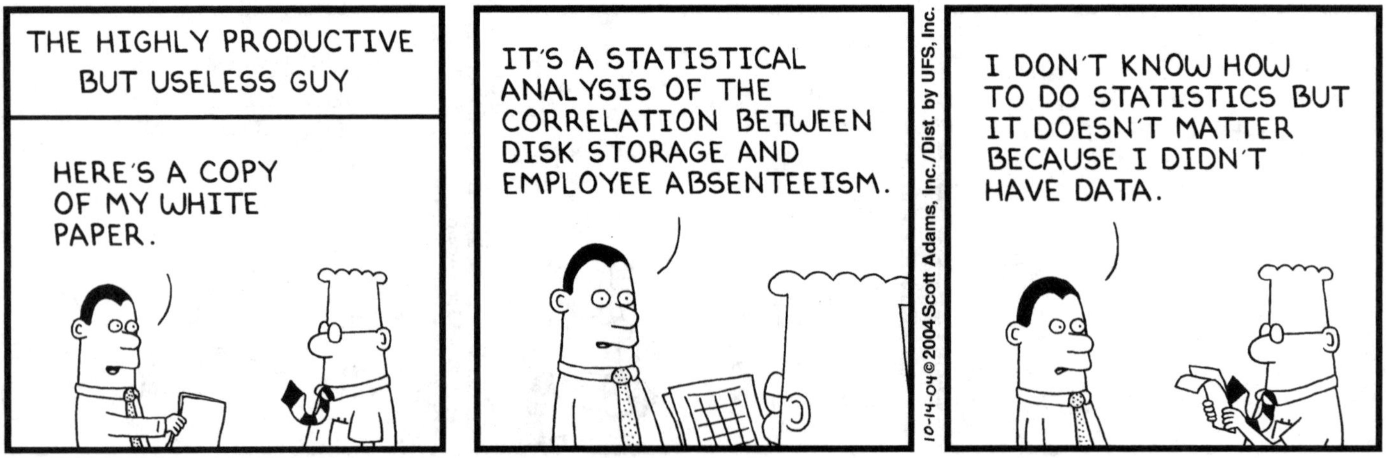
THE HIGHLY PRODUCTIVE BUT USELESS GUY
HERE'S A COPY OF MY WHITE PAPER.
IT'S A STATISTICAL ANALYSIS OF THE CORRELATION BETWEEN DISK STORAGE AND EMPLOYEE ABSENTEEISM.
10-14-04 © 2004 Scott Adams, Inc./Dist. by UFS, Inc.
I DON'T KNOW HOW TO DO STATISTICS BUT IT DOESN'T MATTER BECAUSE I DIDN'T HAVE DATA.

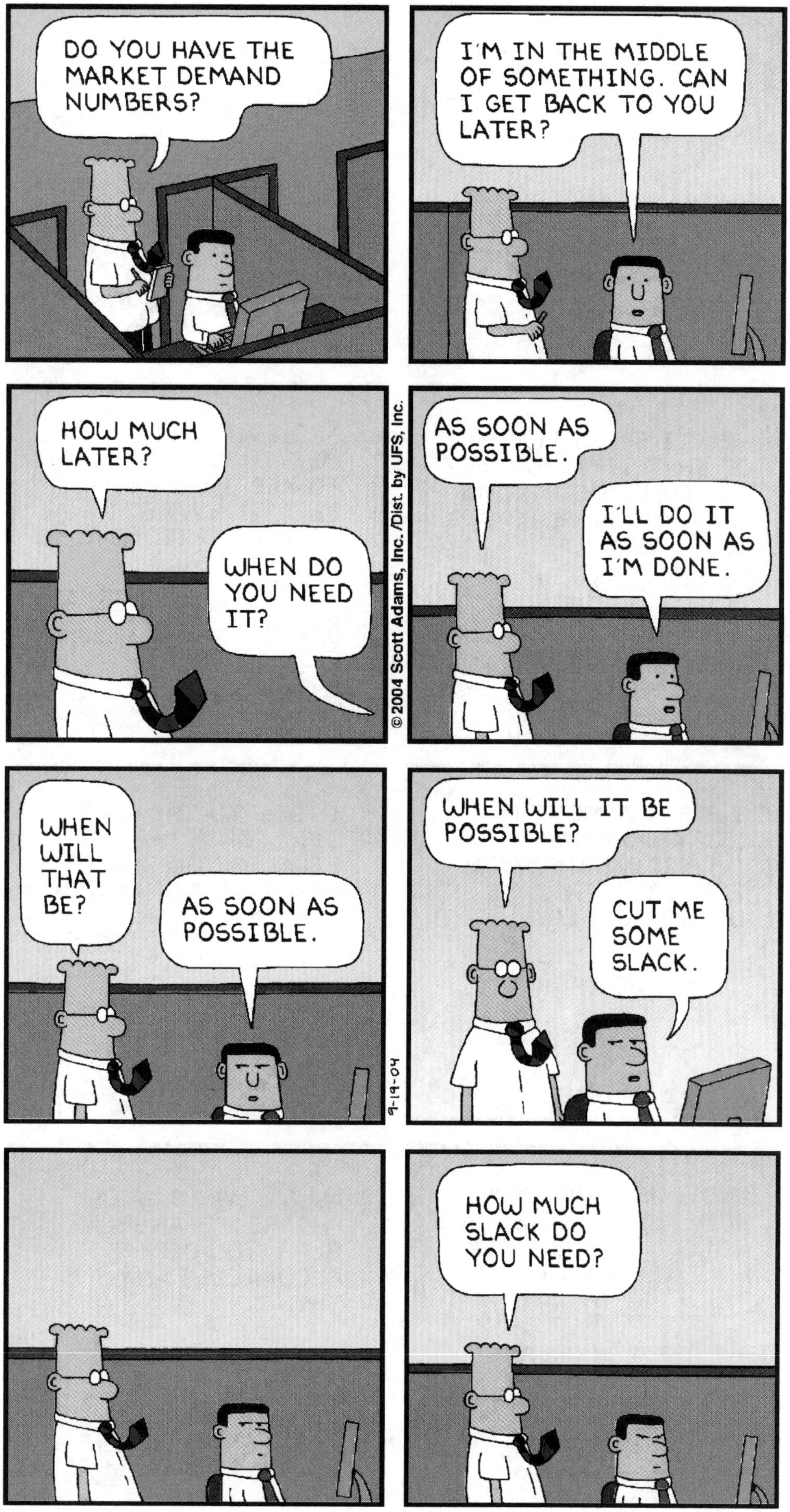
DO YOU HAVE THE MARKET DEMAND NUMBERS?
I'M IN THE MIDDLE OF SOMETHING. CAN I GET BACK TO YOU LATER?
HOW MUCH LATER?
WHEN DO YOU NEED IT?
AS SOON AS POSSIBLE.
I'LL DO IT AS SOON AS I'M DONE.
WHEN WILL THAT BE?
AS SOON AS POSSIBLE.
WHEN WILL IT BE POSSIBLE?
CUT ME SOME SLACK.
HOW MUCH SLACK DO YOU NEED?
©2004 Scott Adams, Inc./Dist. by UFS, Inc.
9-19-04

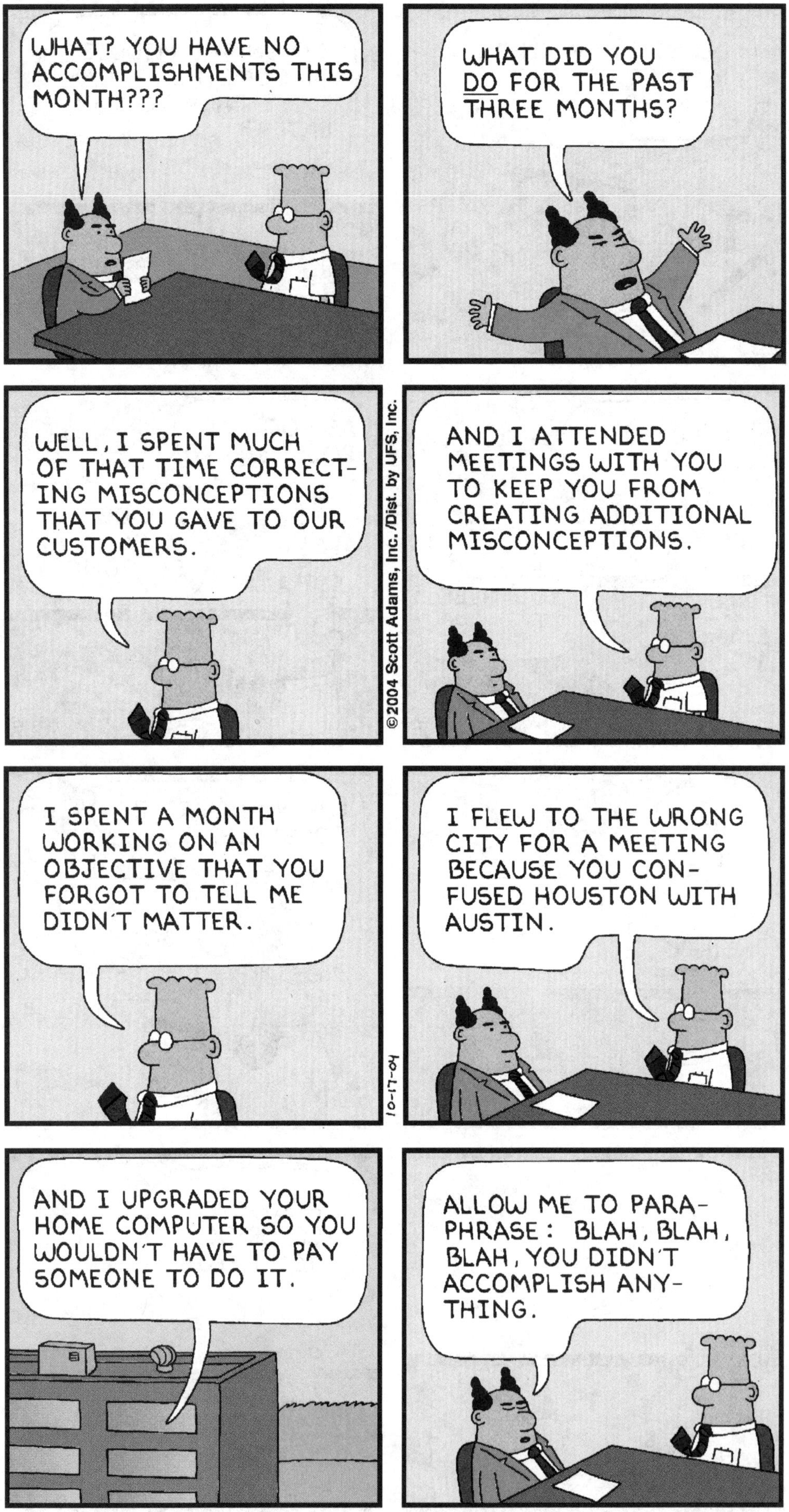
WHAT? YOU HAVE NO ACCOMPLISHMENTS THIS MONTH???
WHAT DID YOU DO FOR THE PAST THREE MONTHS?
WELL, I SPENT MUCH OF THAT TIME CORRECTING MISCONCEPTIONS THAT YOU GAVE TO OUR CUSTOMERS.
AND I ATTENDED MEETINGS WITH YOU TO KEEP YOU FROM CREATING ADDITIONAL MISCONCEPTIONS.
I SPENT A MONTH WORKING ON AN OBJECTIVE THAT YOU FORGOT TO TELL ME DIDN'T MATTER.
I FLEW TO THE WRONG CITY FOR A MEETING BECAUSE YOU CONFUSED HOUSTON WITH AUSTIN.
AND I UPGRADED YOUR HOME COMPUTER SO YOU WOULDN'T HAVE TO PAY SOMEONE TO DO IT.
ALLOW ME TO PARAPHRASE: BLAH, BLAH, BLAH, YOU DIDN'T ACCOMPLISH ANYTHING.
©2004 Scott Adams, Inc./Dist. by UFS, Inc.
10-17-04

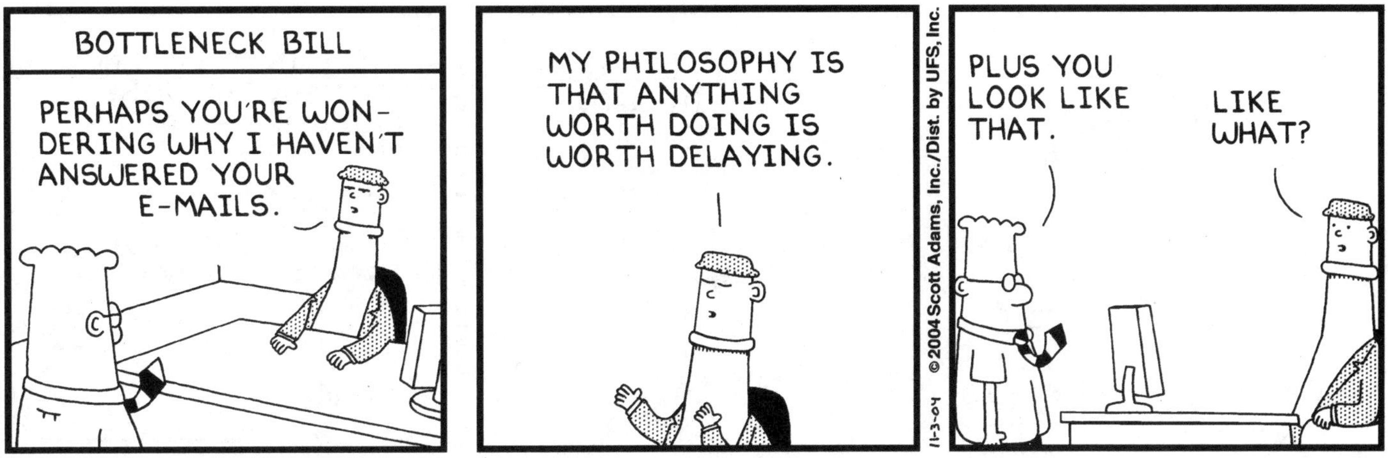
BOTTLENECK BILL
PERHAPS YOU'RE WONDERING WHY I HAVEN'T ANSWERED YOUR E-MAILS.
MY PHILOSOPHY IS THAT ANYTHING WORTH DOING IS WORTH DELAYING.
11-3-04 ©2004 Scott Adams, Inc./Dist. by UFS, Inc.
PLUS YOU LOOK LIKE THAT.
LIKE WHAT?

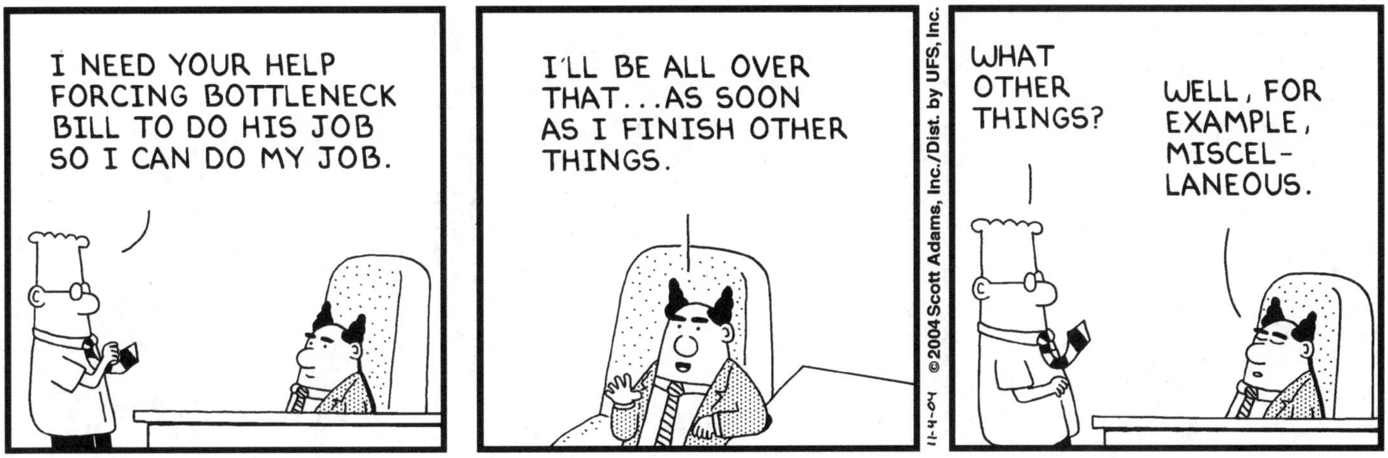
I NEED YOUR HELP FORCING BOTTLENECK BILL TO DO HIS JOB SO I CAN DO MY JOB.
I'LL BE ALL OVER THAT...AS SOON AS I FINISH OTHER THINGS.
11-4-04 ©2004 Scott Adams, Inc./Dist. by UFS, Inc.
WHAT OTHER THINGS?
WELL, FOR EXAMPLE, MISCELLANEOUS.

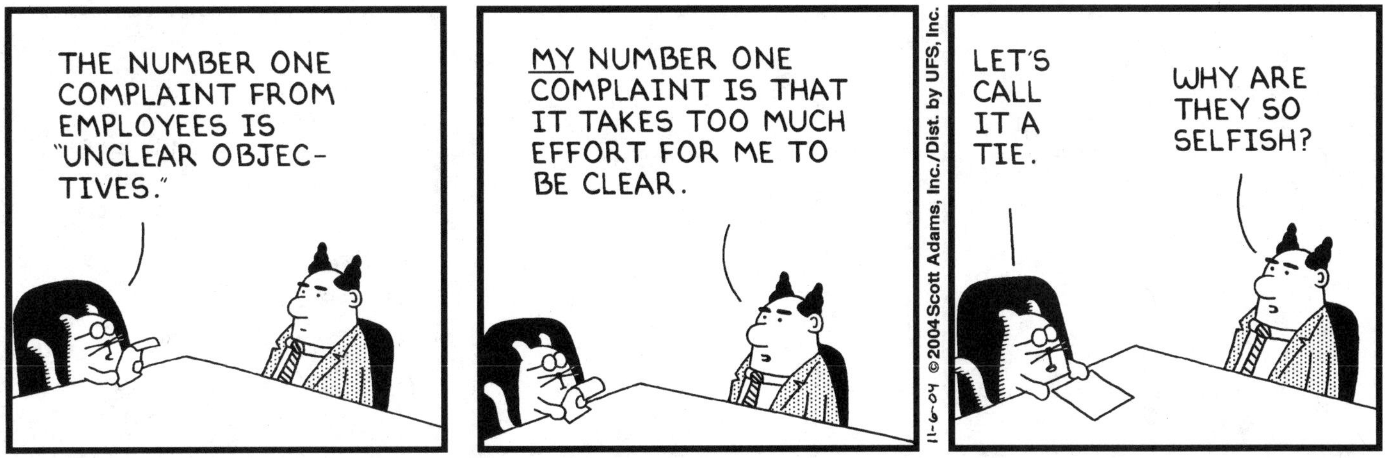
THE NUMBER ONE COMPLAINT FROM EMPLOYEES IS "UNCLEAR OBJECTIVES."
MY NUMBER ONE COMPLAINT IS THAT IT TAKES TOO MUCH EFFORT FOR ME TO BE CLEAR.
11-6-04 ©2004 Scott Adams, Inc./Dist. by UFS, Inc.
LET'S CALL IT A TIE.
WHY ARE THEY SO SELFISH?

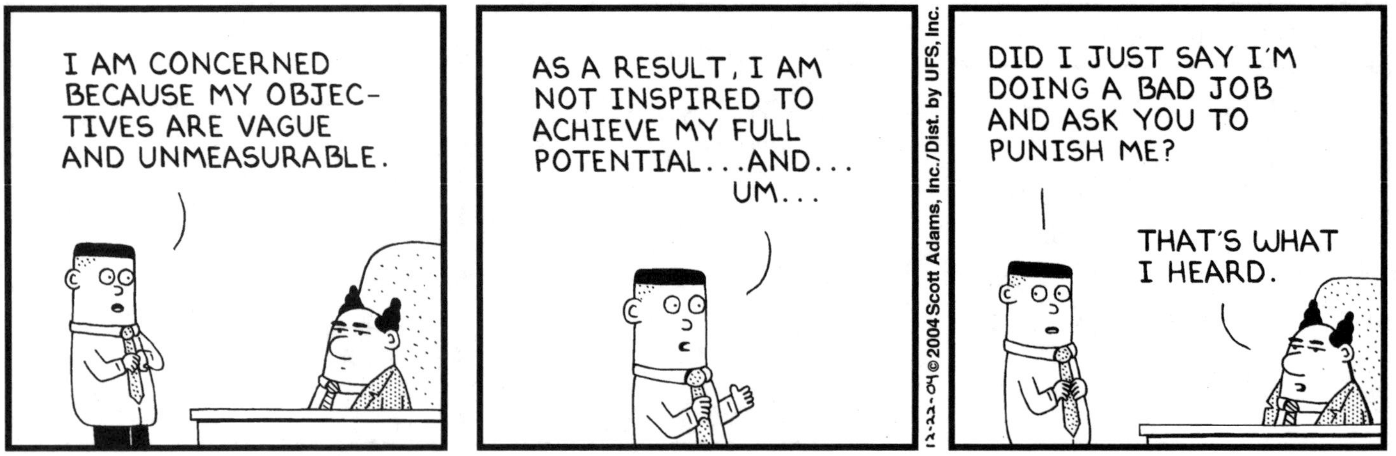
I AM CONCERNED BECAUSE MY OBJECTIVES ARE VAGUE AND UNMEASURABLE.
AS A RESULT, I AM NOT INSPIRED TO ACHIEVE MY FULL POTENTIAL...AND... UM...
12-22-04 © 2004 Scott Adams, Inc./Dist. by UFS, Inc.
DID I JUST SAY I'M DOING A BAD JOB AND ASK YOU TO PUNISH ME?
THAT'S WHAT I HEARD.

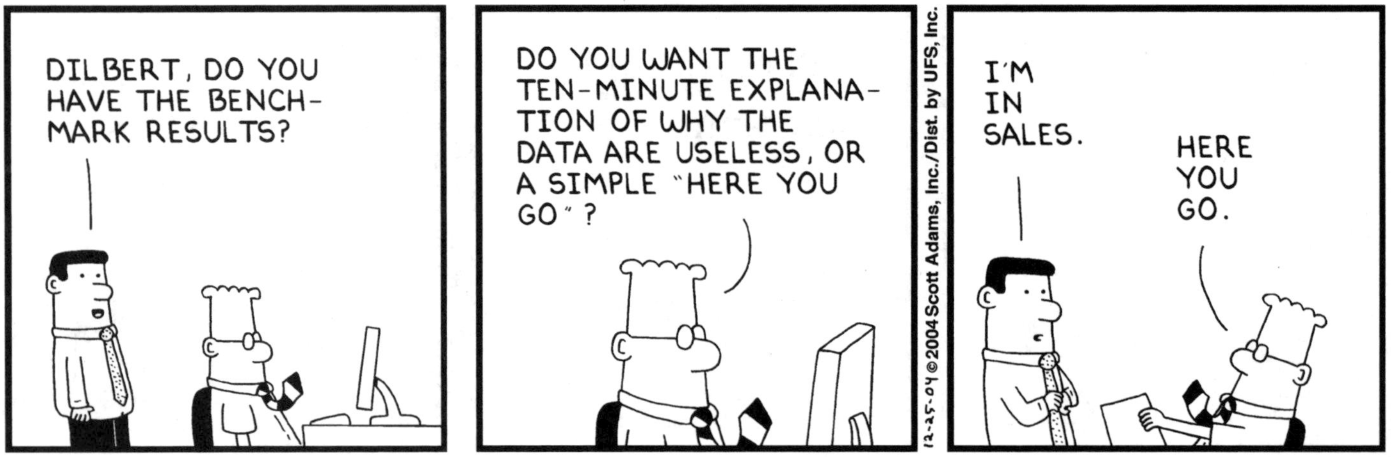
DILBERT, DO YOU HAVE THE BENCHMARK RESULTS?
DO YOU WANT THE TEN-MINUTE EXPLANATION OF WHY THE DATA ARE USELESS, OR A SIMPLE "HERE YOU GO"?
12-25-04 © 2004 Scott Adams, Inc./Dist. by UFS, Inc.
I'M IN SALES.
HERE YOU GO.

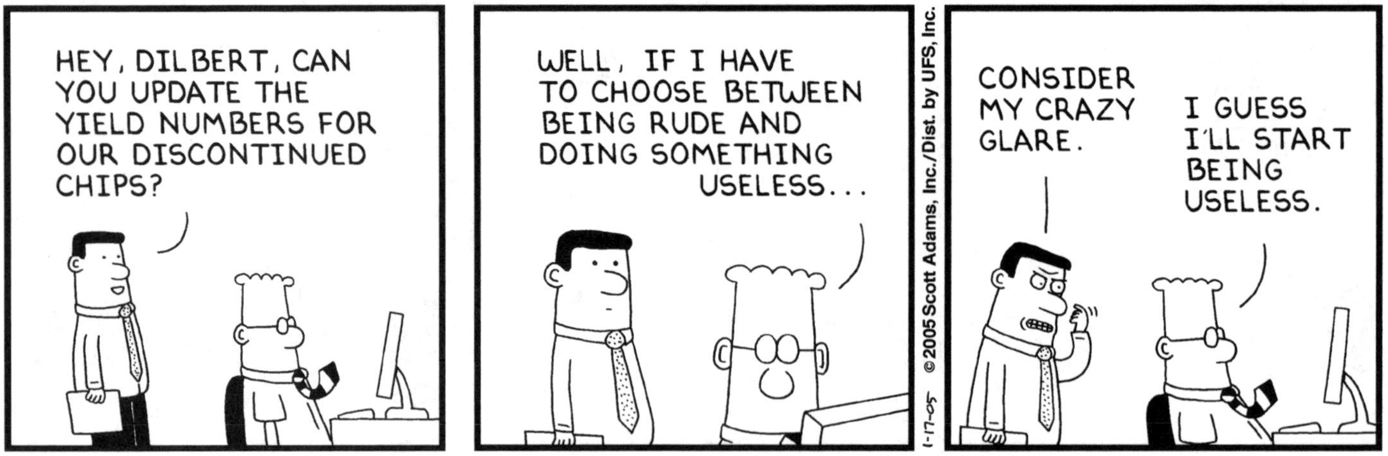
HEY, DILBERT, CAN YOU UPDATE THE YIELD NUMBERS FOR OUR DISCONTINUED CHIPS?
WELL, IF I HAVE TO CHOOSE BETWEEN BEING RUDE AND DOING SOMETHING USELESS...
1-17-05 © 2005 Scott Adams, Inc./Dist. by UFS, Inc.
CONSIDER MY CRAZY GLARE.
I GUESS I'LL START BEING USELESS.

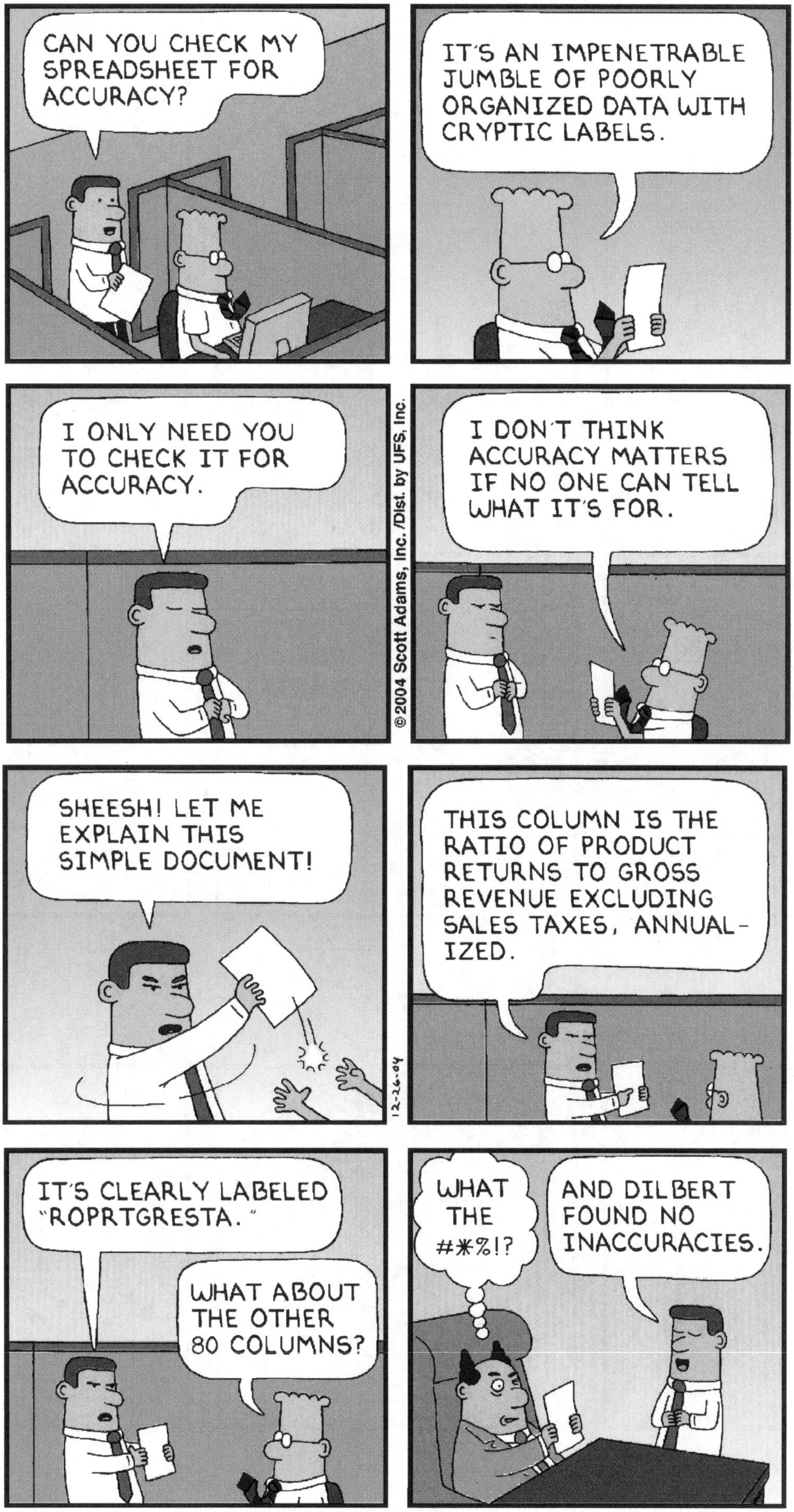
CAN YOU CHECK MY SPREADSHEET FOR ACCURACY?
IT'S AN IMPENETRABLE JUMBLE OF POORLY ORGANIZED DATA WITH CRYPTIC LABELS.
I ONLY NEED YOU TO CHECK IT FOR ACCURACY.
I DON'T THINK ACCURACY MATTERS IF NO ONE CAN TELL WHAT IT'S FOR.
©2004 Scott Adams, Inc./Dist. by UFS, Inc.
SHEESH! LET ME EXPLAIN THIS SIMPLE DOCUMENT!
12-26-04
THIS COLUMN IS THE RATIO OF PRODUCT RETURNS TO GROSS REVENUE EXCLUDING SALES TAXES, ANNUAL-IZED.
IT'S CLEARLY LABELED "ROPRTGRESTA."
WHAT ABOUT THE OTHER 80 COLUMNS?
WHAT THE #*%!?
AND DILBERT FOUND NO INACCURACIES.

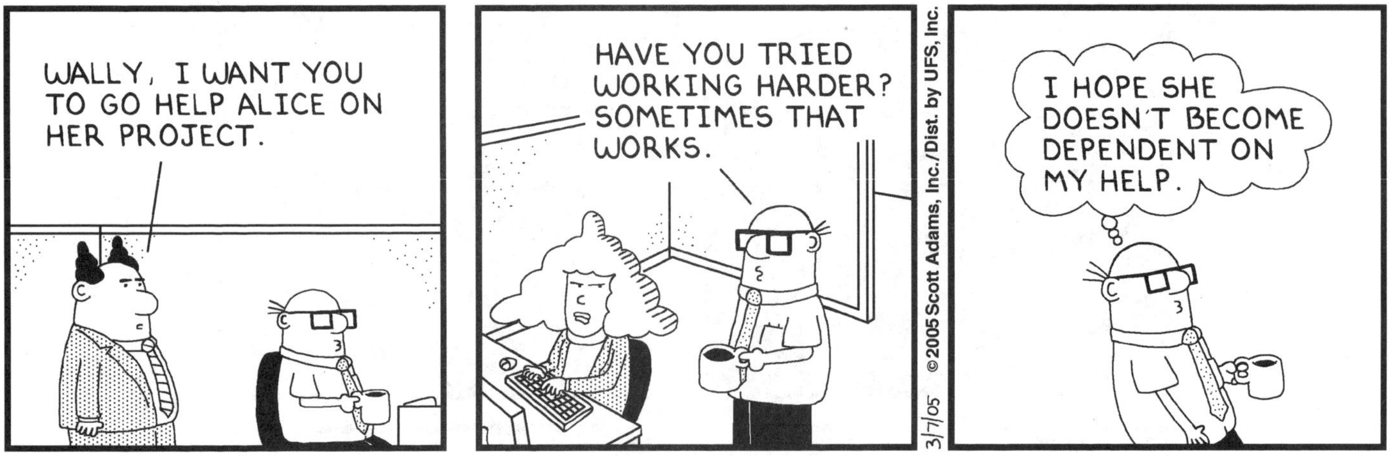
WALLY, I WANT YOU TO GO HELP ALICE ON HER PROJECT.
HAVE YOU TRIED WORKING HARDER? SOMETIMES THAT WORKS.
3/7/05 © 2005 Scott Adams, Inc./Dist. by UFS, Inc.
I HOPE SHE DOESN'T BECOME DEPENDENT ON MY HELP.

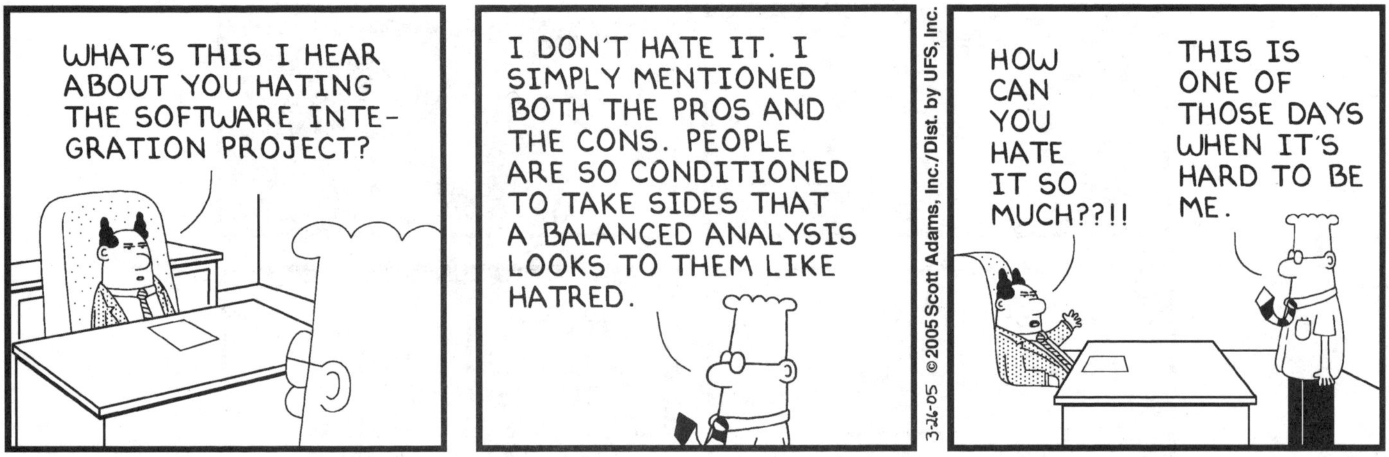
WHAT'S THIS I HEAR ABOUT YOU HATING THE SOFTWARE INTEGRATION PROJECT?
I DON'T HATE IT. I SIMPLY MENTIONED BOTH THE PROS AND THE CONS. PEOPLE ARE SO CONDITIONED TO TAKE SIDES THAT A BALANCED ANALYSIS LOOKS TO THEM LIKE HATRED.
3-26-05 © 2005 Scott Adams, Inc./Dist. by UFS, Inc.
HOW CAN YOU HATE IT SO MUCH??!!
THIS IS ONE OF THOSE DAYS WHEN IT'S HARD TO BE ME.

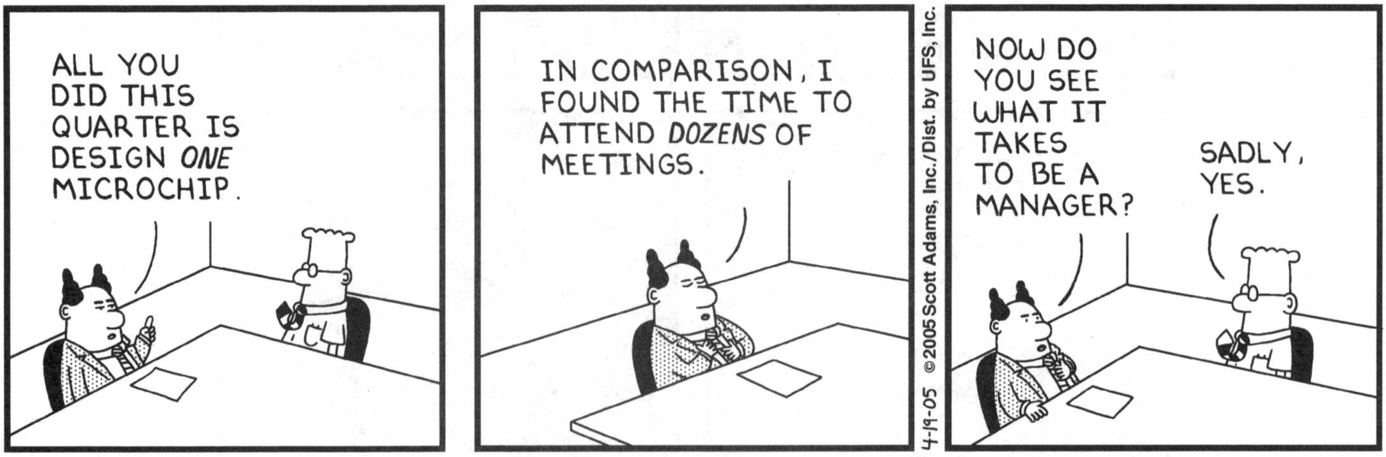
ALL YOU DID THIS QUARTER IS DESIGN *ONE* MICROCHIP.
IN COMPARISON, I FOUND THE TIME TO ATTEND *DOZENS* OF MEETINGS.
4-19-05 © 2005 Scott Adams, Inc./Dist. by UFS, Inc.
NOW DO YOU SEE WHAT IT TAKES TO BE A MANAGER?
SADLY, YES.

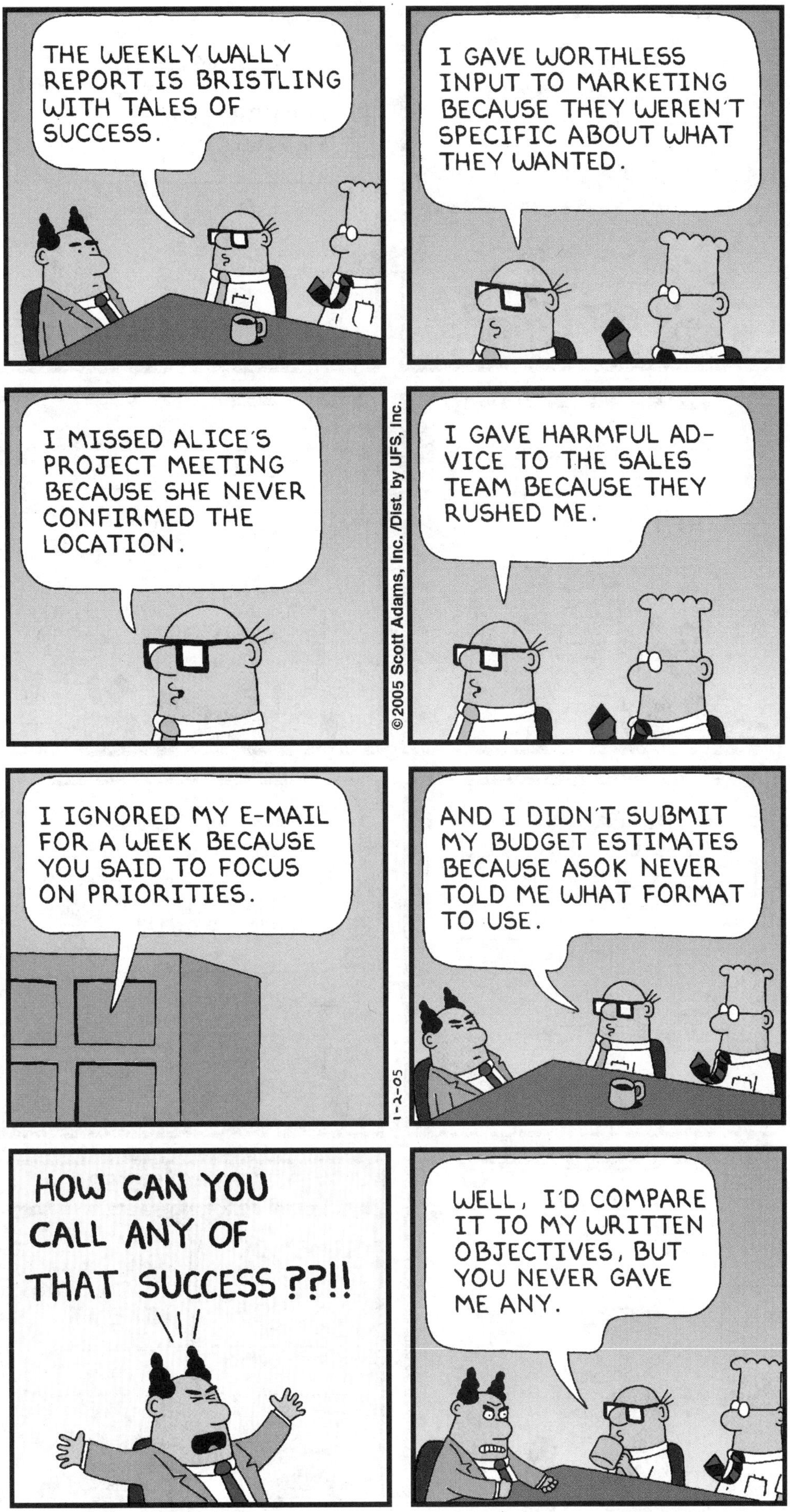
THE WEEKLY WALLY REPORT IS BRISTLING WITH TALES OF SUCCESS.
I GAVE WORTHLESS INPUT TO MARKETING BECAUSE THEY WEREN'T SPECIFIC ABOUT WHAT THEY WANTED.
I MISSED ALICE'S PROJECT MEETING BECAUSE SHE NEVER CONFIRMED THE LOCATION.
I GAVE HARMFUL AD-VICE TO THE SALES TEAM BECAUSE THEY RUSHED ME.
©2005 Scott Adams, Inc./Dist. by UFS, Inc.
I IGNORED MY E-MAIL FOR A WEEK BECAUSE YOU SAID TO FOCUS ON PRIORITIES.
1-2-05
AND I DIDN'T SUBMIT MY BUDGET ESTIMATES BECAUSE ASOK NEVER TOLD ME WHAT FORMAT TO USE.
HOW CAN YOU CALL ANY OF THAT SUCCESS ??!!
WELL, I'D COMPARE IT TO MY WRITTEN OBJECTIVES, BUT YOU NEVER GAVE ME ANY.

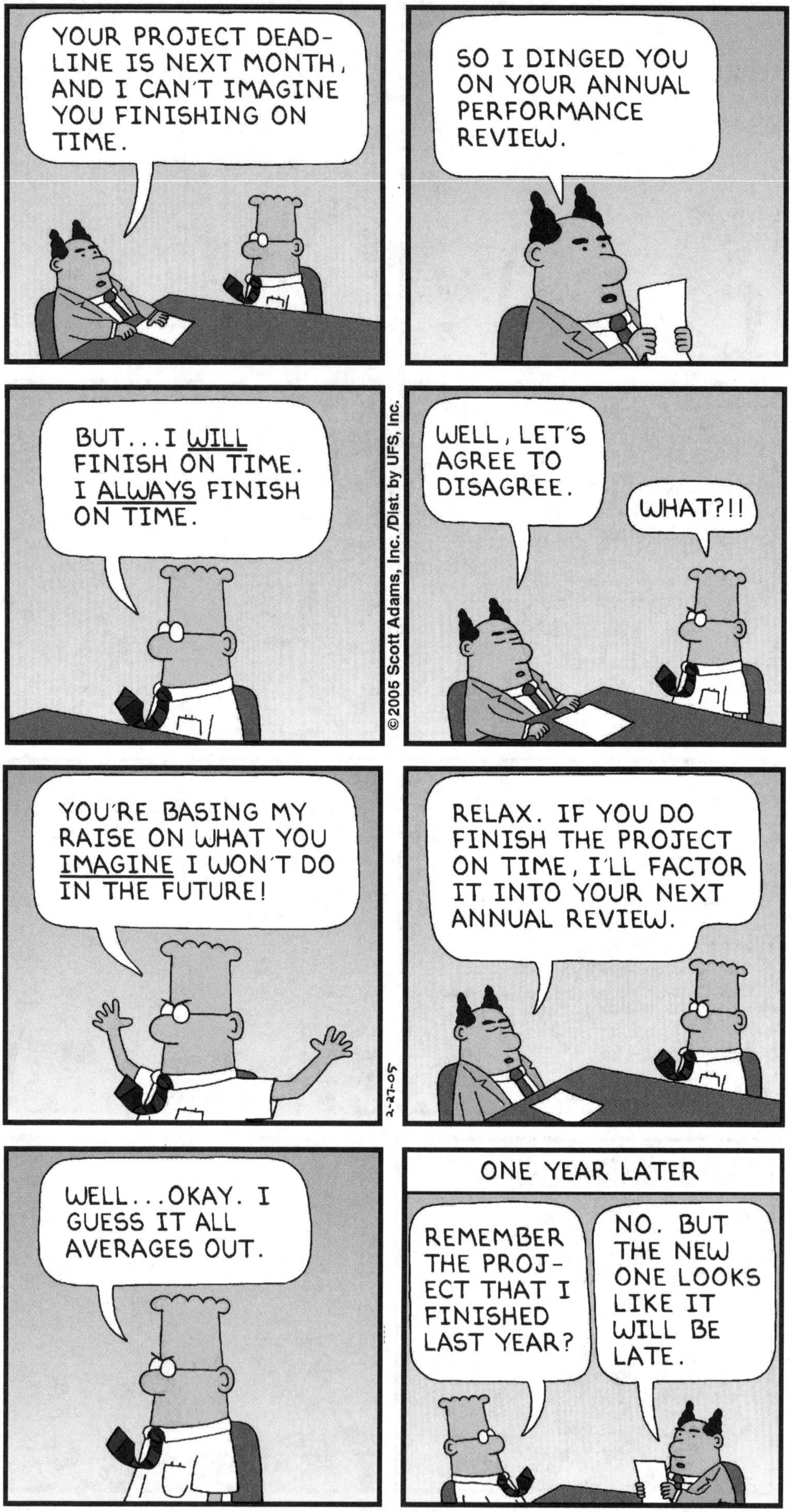
YOUR PROJECT DEAD-LINE IS NEXT MONTH, AND I CAN'T IMAGINE YOU FINISHING ON TIME.
SO I DINGED YOU ON YOUR ANNUAL PERFORMANCE REVIEW.
BUT... I WILL FINISH ON TIME. I ALWAYS FINISH ON TIME.
WELL, LET'S AGREE TO DISAGREE.
WHAT?!!
YOU'RE BASING MY RAISE ON WHAT YOU IMAGINE I WON'T DO IN THE FUTURE!
RELAX. IF YOU DO FINISH THE PROJECT ON TIME, I'LL FACTOR IT INTO YOUR NEXT ANNUAL REVIEW.
WELL... OKAY. I GUESS IT ALL AVERAGES OUT.
ONE YEAR LATER
REMEMBER THE PROJ-ECT THAT I FINISHED LAST YEAR?
NO. BUT THE NEW ONE LOOKS LIKE IT WILL BE LATE.
©2005 Scott Adams, Inc./Dist. by UFS, Inc.
2-27-05

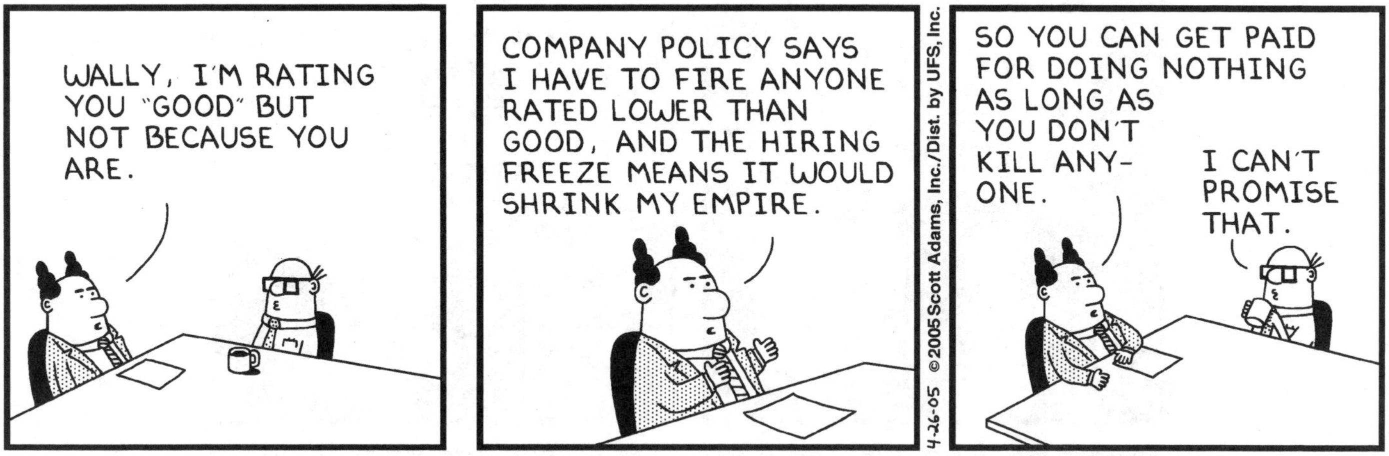
WALLY, I'M RATING YOU "GOOD" BUT NOT BECAUSE YOU ARE.
COMPANY POLICY SAYS I HAVE TO FIRE ANYONE RATED LOWER THAN GOOD, AND THE HIRING FREEZE MEANS IT WOULD SHRINK MY EMPIRE.
4-26-05 ©2005 Scott Adams, Inc./Dist. by UFS, Inc.
SO YOU CAN GET PAID FOR DOING NOTHING AS LONG AS YOU DON'T KILL ANYONE.
I CAN'T PROMISE THAT.

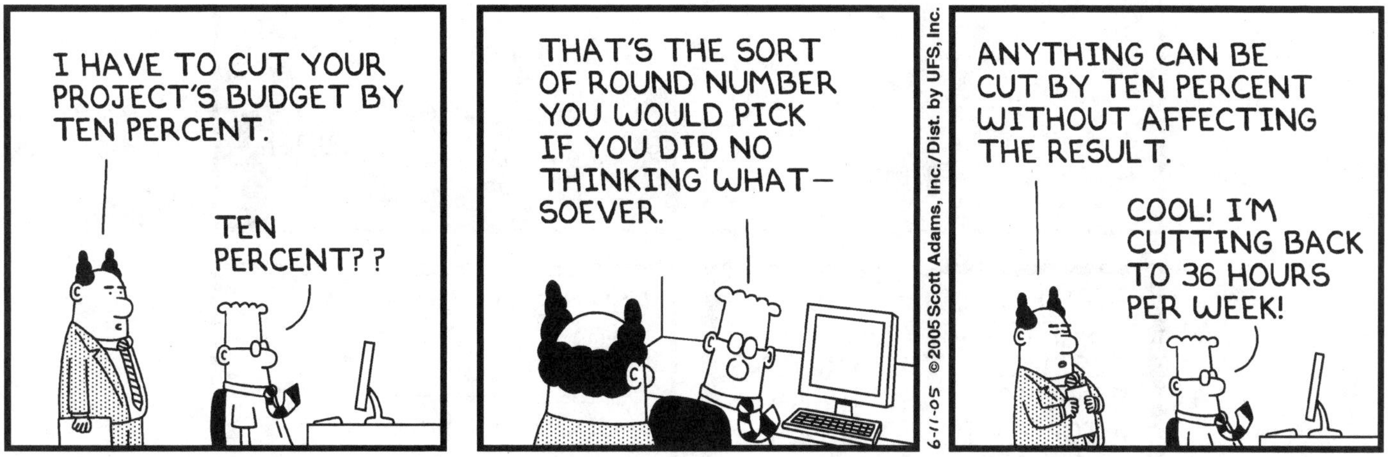
I HAVE TO CUT YOUR PROJECT'S BUDGET BY TEN PERCENT.
TEN PERCENT??
THAT'S THE SORT OF ROUND NUMBER YOU WOULD PICK IF YOU DID NO THINKING WHATSOEVER.
6-11-05 ©2005 Scott Adams, Inc./Dist. by UFS, Inc.
ANYTHING CAN BE CUT BY TEN PERCENT WITHOUT AFFECTING THE RESULT.
COOL! I'M CUTTING BACK TO 36 HOURS PER WEEK!

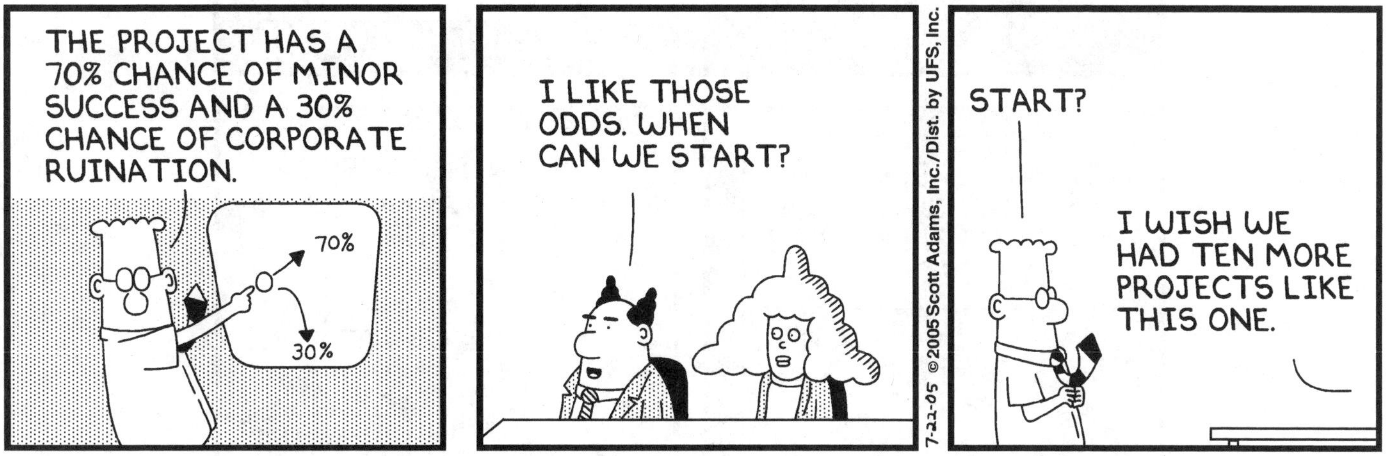
THE PROJECT HAS A 70% CHANCE OF MINOR SUCCESS AND A 30% CHANCE OF CORPORATE RUINATION.
70%
30%
I LIKE THOSE ODDS. WHEN CAN WE START?
7-21-05 ©2005 Scott Adams, Inc./Dist. by UFS, Inc.
START?
I WISH WE HAD TEN MORE PROJECTS LIKE THIS ONE.

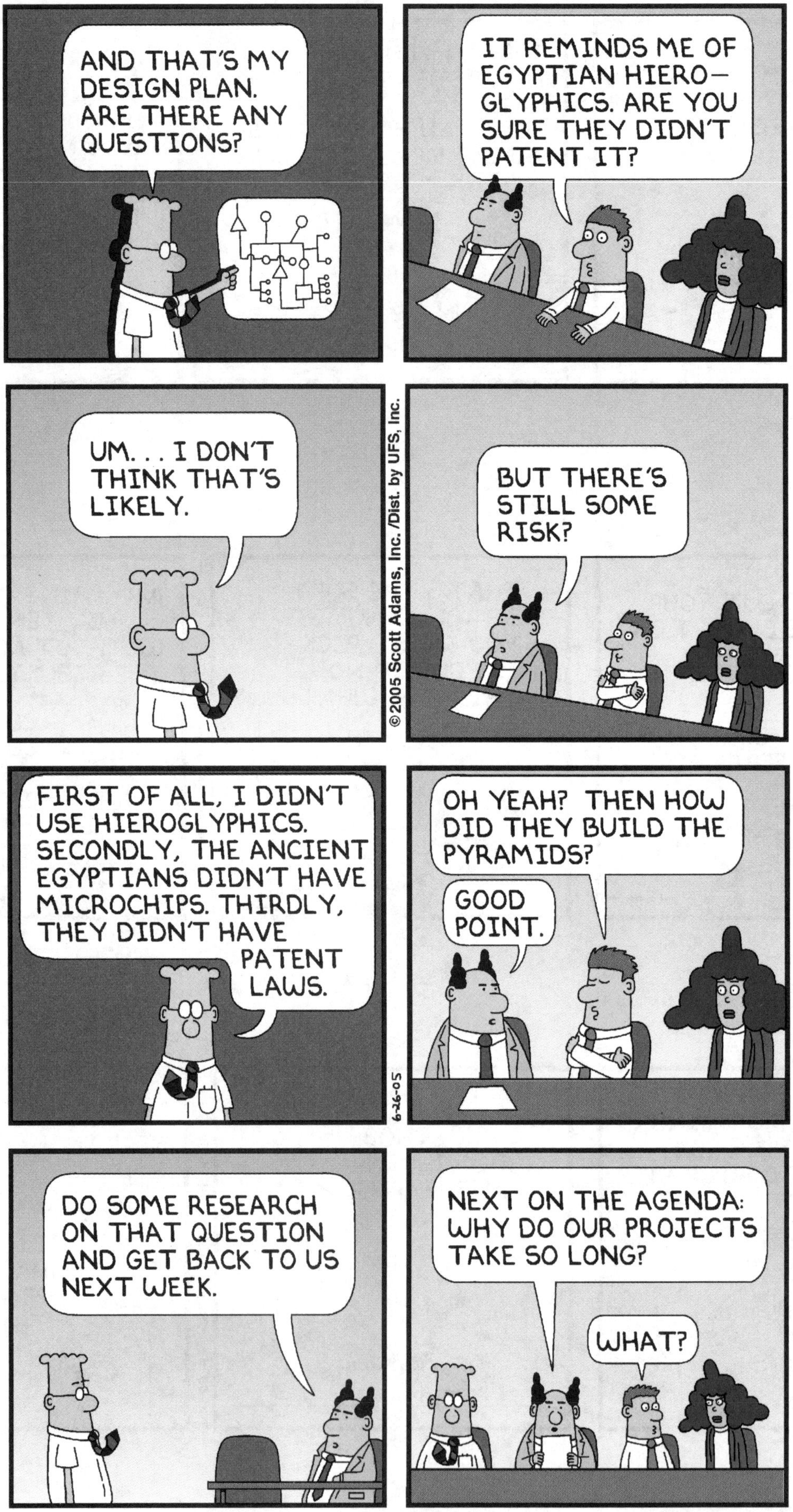
AND THAT'S MY DESIGN PLAN. ARE THERE ANY QUESTIONS?
IT REMINDS ME OF EGYPTIAN HIERO-GLYPHICS. ARE YOU SURE THEY DIDN'T PATENT IT?
UM. . . I DON'T THINK THAT'S LIKELY.
BUT THERE'S STILL SOME RISK?
©2005 Scott Adams, Inc. /Dist. by UFS, Inc.
FIRST OF ALL, I DIDN'T USE HIEROGLYPHICS. SECONDLY, THE ANCIENT EGYPTIANS DIDN'T HAVE MICROCHIPS. THIRDLY, THEY DIDN'T HAVE PATENT LAWS.
OH YEAH? THEN HOW DID THEY BUILD THE PYRAMIDS?
GOOD POINT.
6-26-05
DO SOME RESEARCH ON THAT QUESTION AND GET BACK TO US NEXT WEEK.
NEXT ON THE AGENDA: WHY DO OUR PROJECTS TAKE SO LONG?
WHAT?

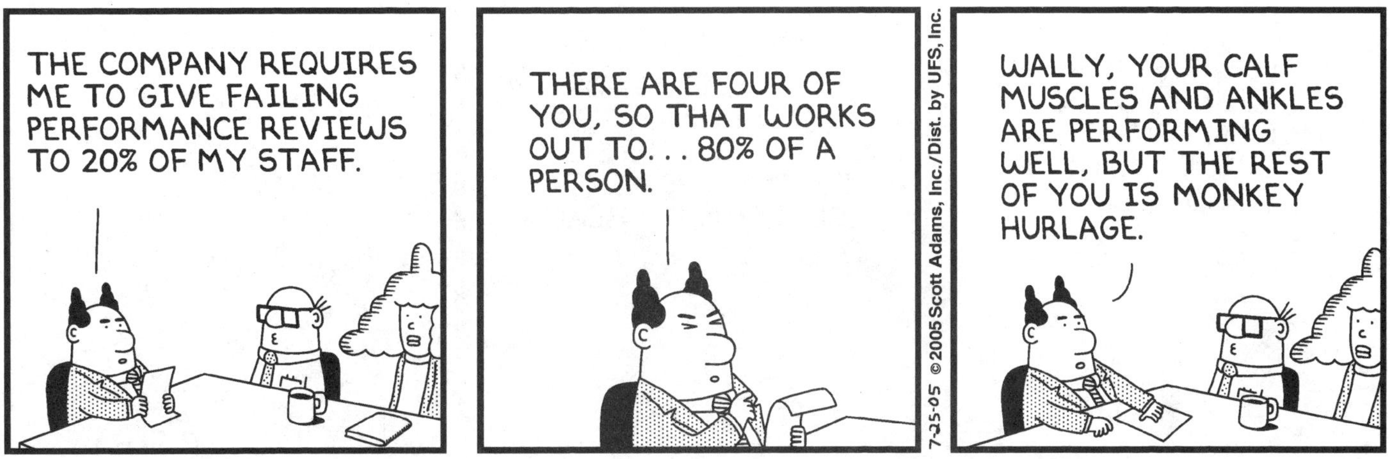
THE COMPANY REQUIRES ME TO GIVE FAILING PERFORMANCE REVIEWS TO 20% OF MY STAFF.
THERE ARE FOUR OF YOU, SO THAT WORKS OUT TO. . . 80% OF A PERSON.
WALLY, YOUR CALF MUSCLES AND ANKLES ARE PERFORMING WELL, BUT THE REST OF YOU IS MONKEY HURLAGE.
7-25-05 © 2005 Scott Adams, Inc./Dist. by UFS, Inc.

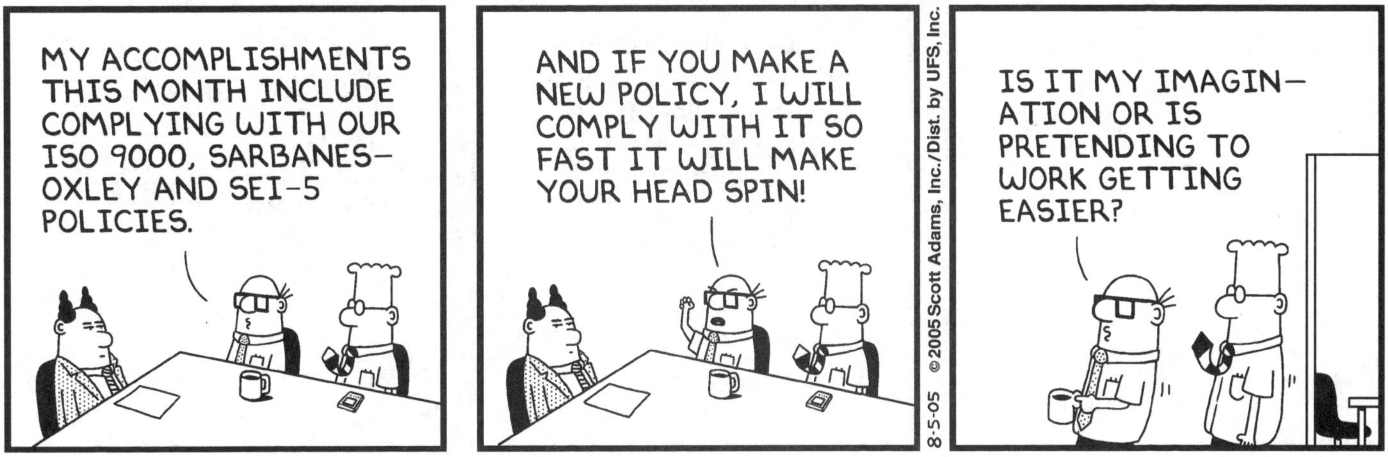
MY ACCOMPLISHMENTS THIS MONTH INCLUDE COMPLYING WITH OUR ISO 9000, SARBANES-OXLEY AND SEI-5 POLICIES.
AND IF YOU MAKE A NEW POLICY, I WILL COMPLY WITH IT SO FAST IT WILL MAKE YOUR HEAD SPIN!
IS IT MY IMAGIN-ATION OR IS PRETENDING TO WORK GETTING EASIER?
8-5-05 © 2005 Scott Adams, Inc./Dist. by UFS, Inc.

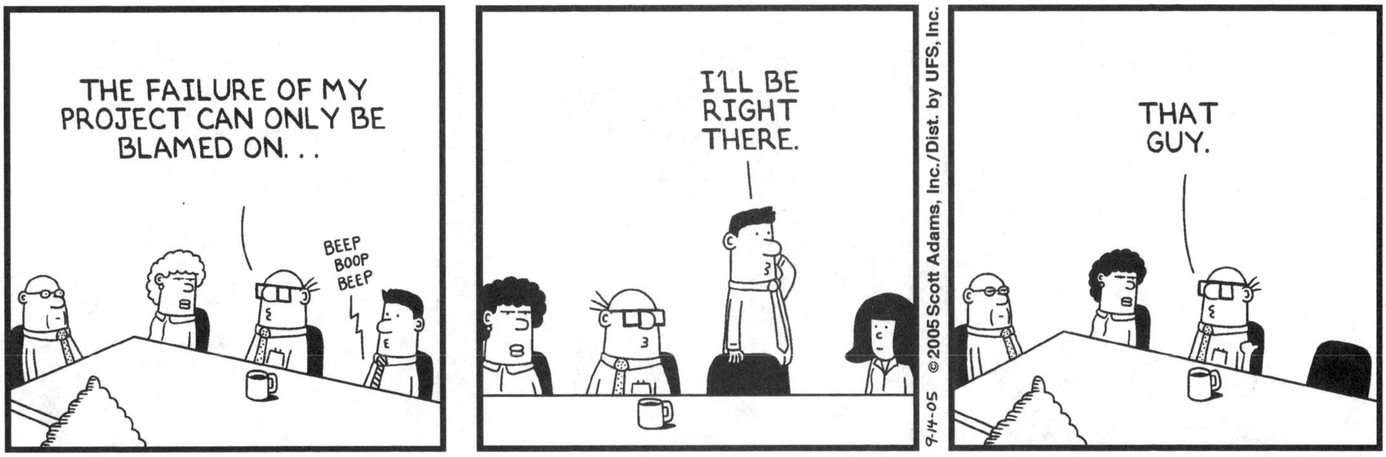
THE FAILURE OF MY PROJECT CAN ONLY BE BLAMED ON. . .
BEEP BOOP BEEP
I'LL BE RIGHT THERE.
THAT GUY.
9-14-05 © 2005 Scott Adams, Inc./Dist. by UFS, Inc.

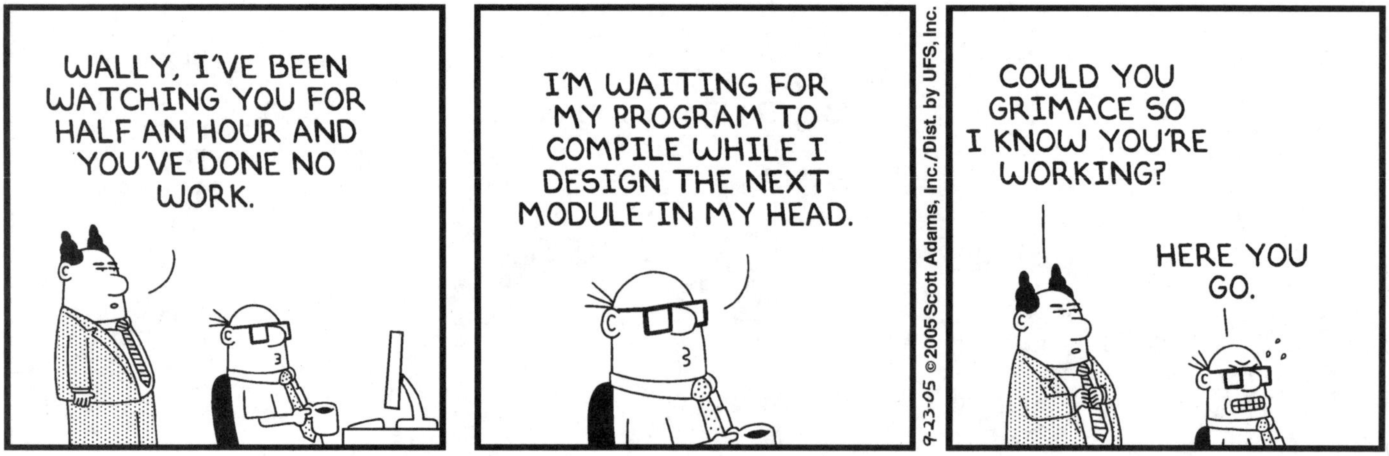
WALLY, I'VE BEEN WATCHING YOU FOR HALF AN HOUR AND YOU'VE DONE NO WORK.
I'M WAITING FOR MY PROGRAM TO COMPILE WHILE I DESIGN THE NEXT MODULE IN MY HEAD.
9-23-05 © 2005 Scott Adams, Inc./Dist. by UFS, Inc.
COULD YOU GRIMACE SO I KNOW YOU'RE WORKING?
HERE YOU GO.

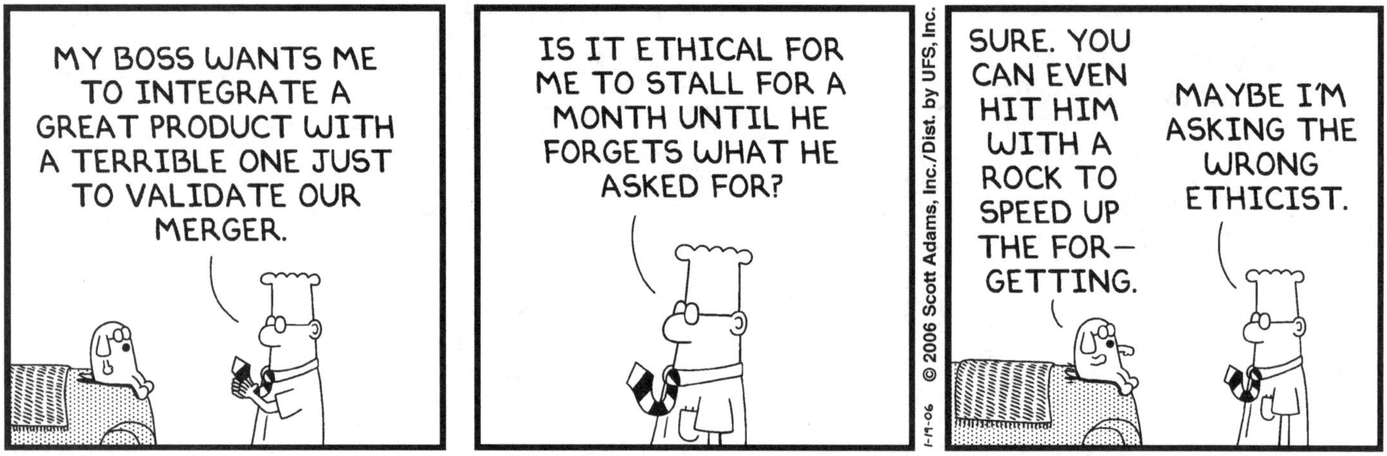
MY BOSS WANTS ME TO INTEGRATE A GREAT PRODUCT WITH A TERRIBLE ONE JUST TO VALIDATE OUR MERGER.
IS IT ETHICAL FOR ME TO STALL FOR A MONTH UNTIL HE FORGETS WHAT HE ASKED FOR?
1-19-06 © 2006 Scott Adams, Inc./Dist. by UFS, Inc.
SURE. YOU CAN EVEN HIT HIM WITH A ROCK TO SPEED UP THE FOR-GETTING.
MAYBE I'M ASKING THE WRONG ETHICIST.

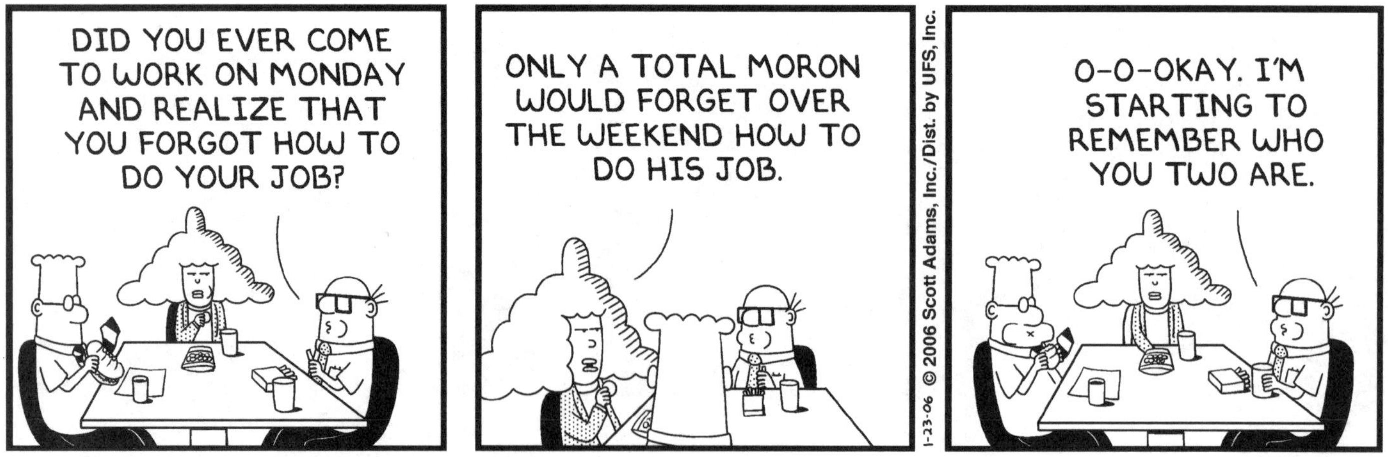
DID YOU EVER COME TO WORK ON MONDAY AND REALIZE THAT YOU FORGOT HOW TO DO YOUR JOB?
ONLY A TOTAL MORON WOULD FORGET OVER THE WEEKEND HOW TO DO HIS JOB.
1-23-06 © 2006 Scott Adams, Inc./Dist. by UFS, Inc.
O-O-OKAY. I'M STARTING TO REMEMBER WHO YOU TWO ARE.

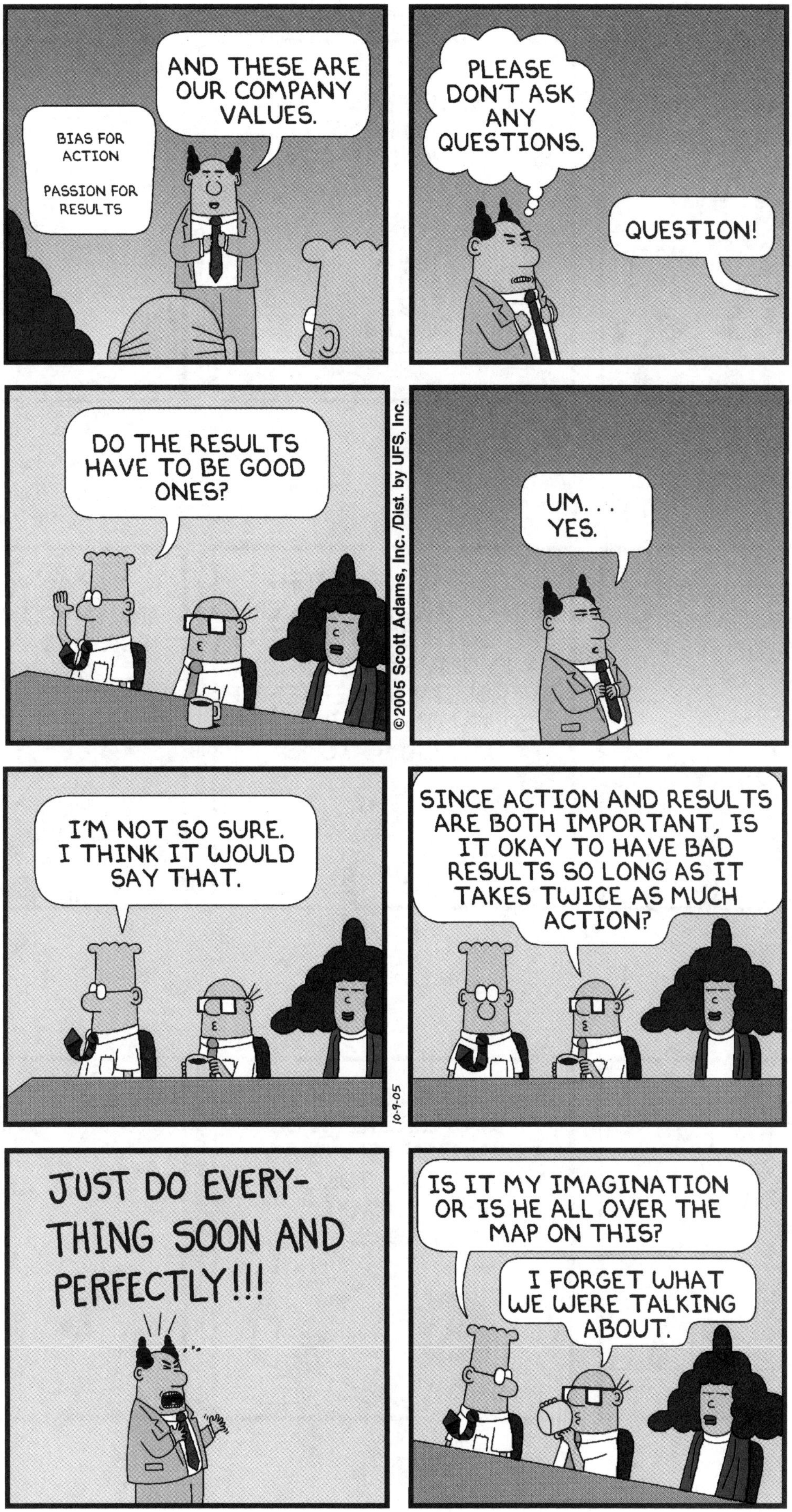
AND THESE ARE OUR COMPANY VALUES.
BIAS FOR ACTION
PASSION FOR RESULTS
PLEASE DON'T ASK ANY QUESTIONS.
QUESTION!
DO THE RESULTS HAVE TO BE GOOD ONES?
©2005 Scott Adams, Inc. /Dist. by UFS, Inc.
UM. . . YES.
I'M NOT SO SURE. I THINK IT WOULD SAY THAT.
SINCE ACTION AND RESULTS ARE BOTH IMPORTANT, IS IT OKAY TO HAVE BAD RESULTS SO LONG AS IT TAKES TWICE AS MUCH ACTION?
10-9-05
JUST DO EVERY-THING SOON AND PERFECTLY!!!
IS IT MY IMAGINATION OR IS HE ALL OVER THE MAP ON THIS?
I FORGET WHAT WE WERE TALKING ABOUT.

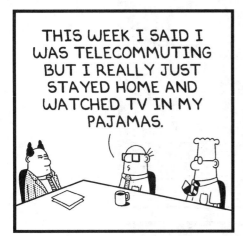

THIS WEEK I SAID I WAS TELECOMMUTING BUT I REALLY JUST STAYED HOME AND WATCHED TV IN MY PAJAMAS.
I'LL NEVER KNOW HOW THE TV GOT INTO MY PAJAMAS. HA HA!
WELL, YOU HAD TO BE THERE.
2-20-06 © 2006 Scott Adams, Inc./Dist. by UFS, Inc.

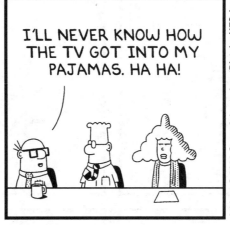

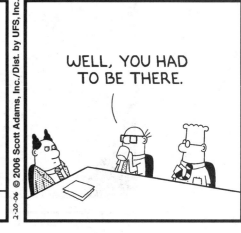

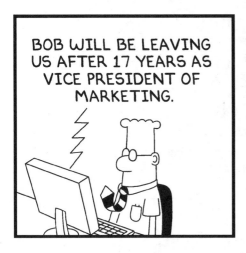

BOB WILL BE LEAVING US AFTER 17 YEARS AS VICE PRESIDENT OF MARKETING.
BOB'S ACCOMPLISHMENTS INCLUDE LOWERING BOTH OUR MARGINS AND OUR SALES WHILE OVERSEEING A SERIES OF CONFUSING MARKETING CAMPAIGNS.
I HOPE YOU'LL ALL JOIN ME IN WISHING FOR A PIANO TO FALL ON HIS HEAD.
3-3-06 © 2006 Scott Adams, Inc./Dist. by UFS, Inc.

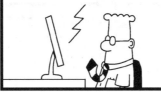

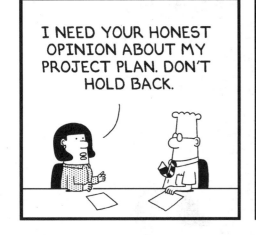

I NEED YOUR HONEST OPINION ABOUT MY PROJECT PLAN. DON'T HOLD BACK.
YOUR PLAN LOOKS LIKE IT WAS WRITTEN BY A DRUNKEN LEMUR AS A PRACTICAL JOKE ON OTHER DRUNKEN LEMURS.
TODAY I LEARNED THAT PEOPLE DON'T LIKE DRUNKEN LEMUR ANALOGIES.
4-17-06 © 2006 Scott Adams, Inc./Dist. by UFS, Inc.

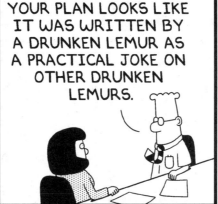

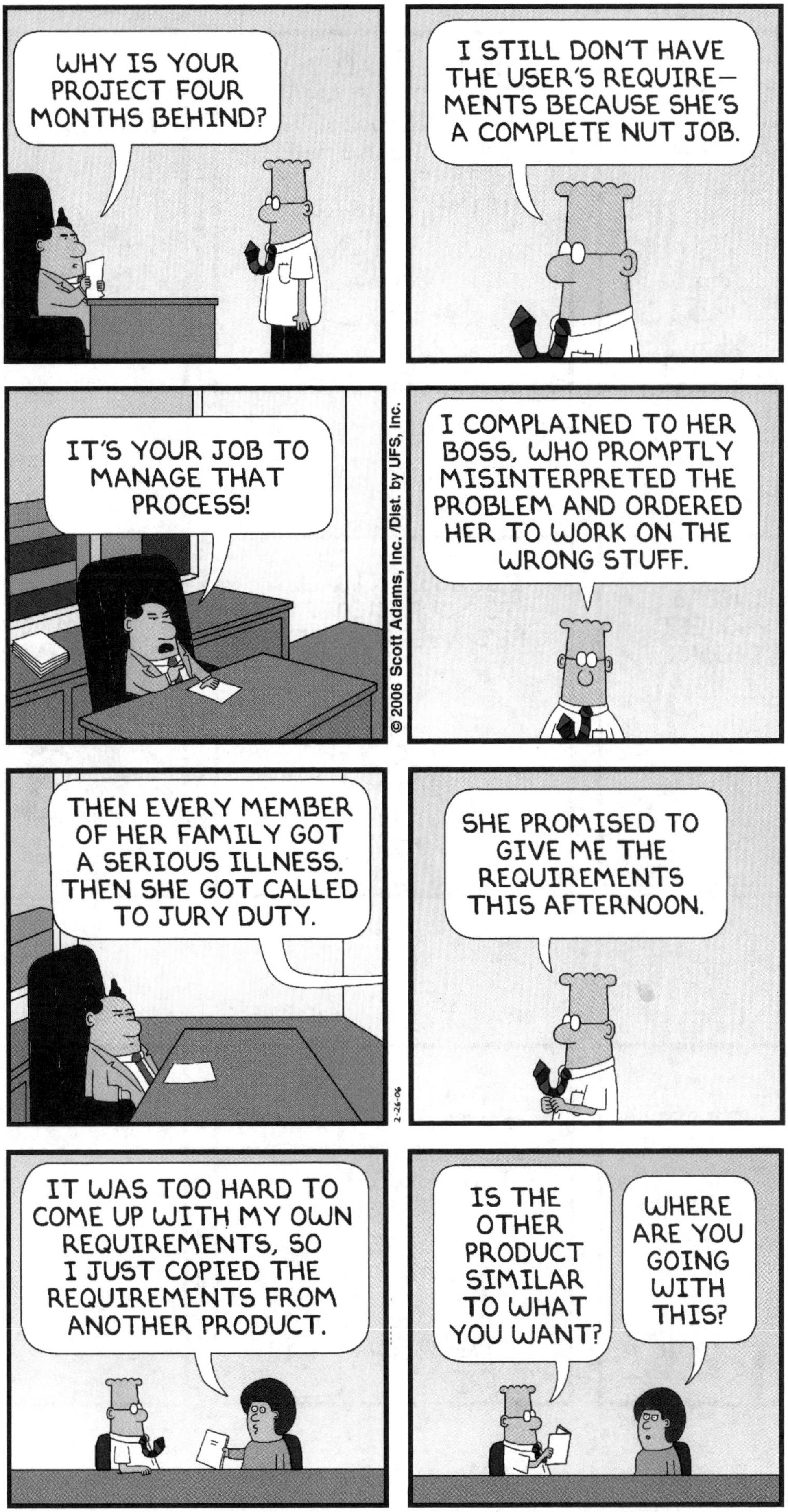
WHY IS YOUR PROJECT FOUR MONTHS BEHIND?
I STILL DON'T HAVE THE USER'S REQUIRE-MENTS BECAUSE SHE'S A COMPLETE NUT JOB.
IT'S YOUR JOB TO MANAGE THAT PROCESS!
I COMPLAINED TO HER BOSS, WHO PROMPTLY MISINTERPRETED THE PROBLEM AND ORDERED HER TO WORK ON THE WRONG STUFF.
THEN EVERY MEMBER OF HER FAMILY GOT A SERIOUS ILLNESS. THEN SHE GOT CALLED TO JURY DUTY.
SHE PROMISED TO GIVE ME THE REQUIREMENTS THIS AFTERNOON.
IT WAS TOO HARD TO COME UP WITH MY OWN REQUIREMENTS, SO I JUST COPIED THE REQUIREMENTS FROM ANOTHER PRODUCT.
IS THE OTHER PRODUCT SIMILAR TO WHAT YOU WANT?
WHERE ARE YOU GOING WITH THIS?
© 2006 Scott Adams, Inc. /Dist. by UFS, Inc.
2-26-06

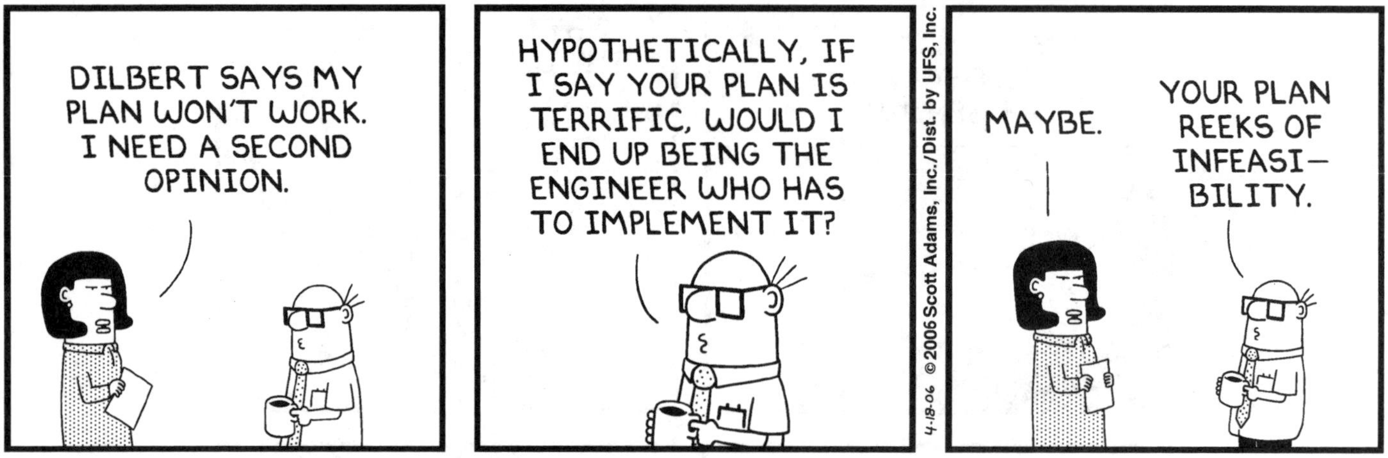
DILBERT SAYS MY PLAN WON'T WORK. I NEED A SECOND OPINION.
HYPOTHETICALLY, IF I SAY YOUR PLAN IS TERRIFIC, WOULD I END UP BEING THE ENGINEER WHO HAS TO IMPLEMENT IT?
4-18-06 © 2006 Scott Adams, Inc./Dist. by UFS, Inc.
MAYBE.
YOUR PLAN REEKS OF INFEASI-BILITY.

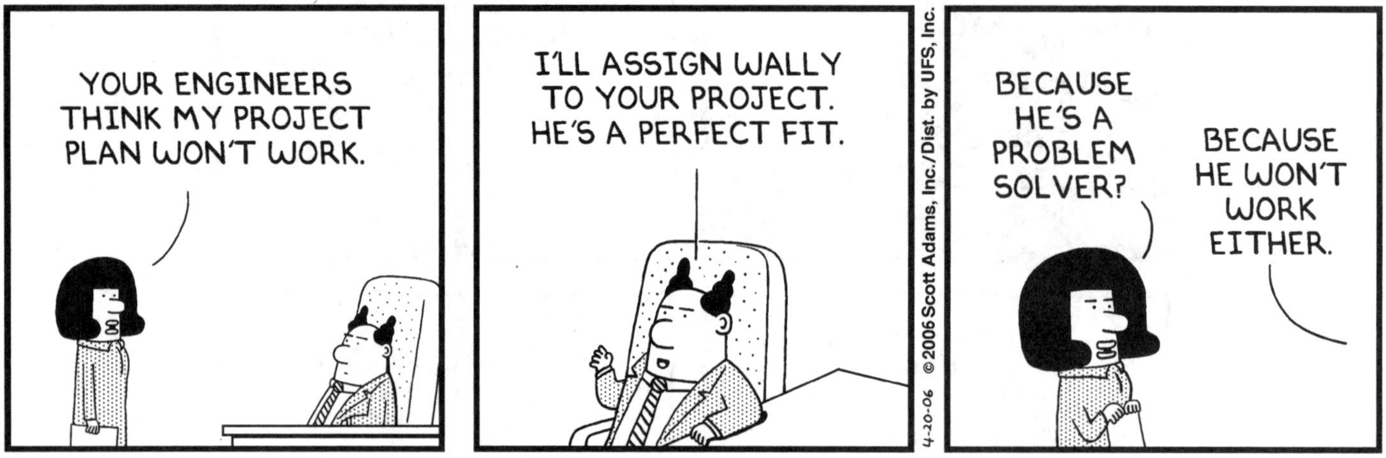
YOUR ENGINEERS THINK MY PROJECT PLAN WON'T WORK.
I'LL ASSIGN WALLY TO YOUR PROJECT. HE'S A PERFECT FIT.
4-20-06 © 2006 Scott Adams, Inc./Dist. by UFS, Inc.
BECAUSE HE'S A PROBLEM SOLVER?
BECAUSE HE WON'T WORK EITHER.

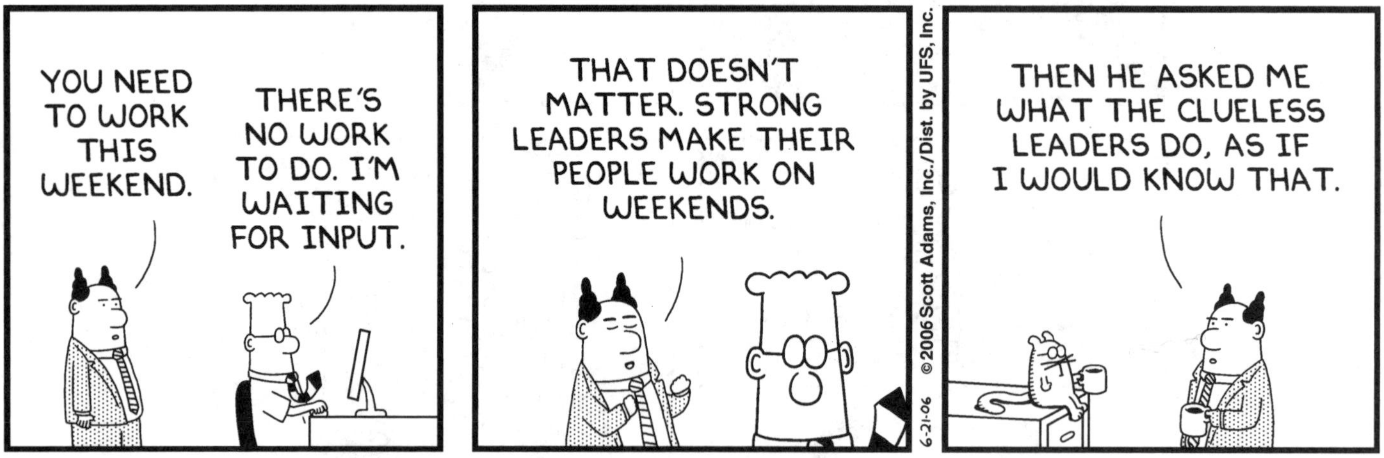
YOU NEED TO WORK THIS WEEKEND.
THERE'S NO WORK TO DO. I'M WAITING FOR INPUT.
THAT DOESN'T MATTER. STRONG LEADERS MAKE THEIR PEOPLE WORK ON WEEKENDS.
6-21-06 © 2006 Scott Adams, Inc./Dist. by UFS, Inc.
THEN HE ASKED ME WHAT THE CLUELESS LEADERS DO, AS IF I WOULD KNOW THAT.

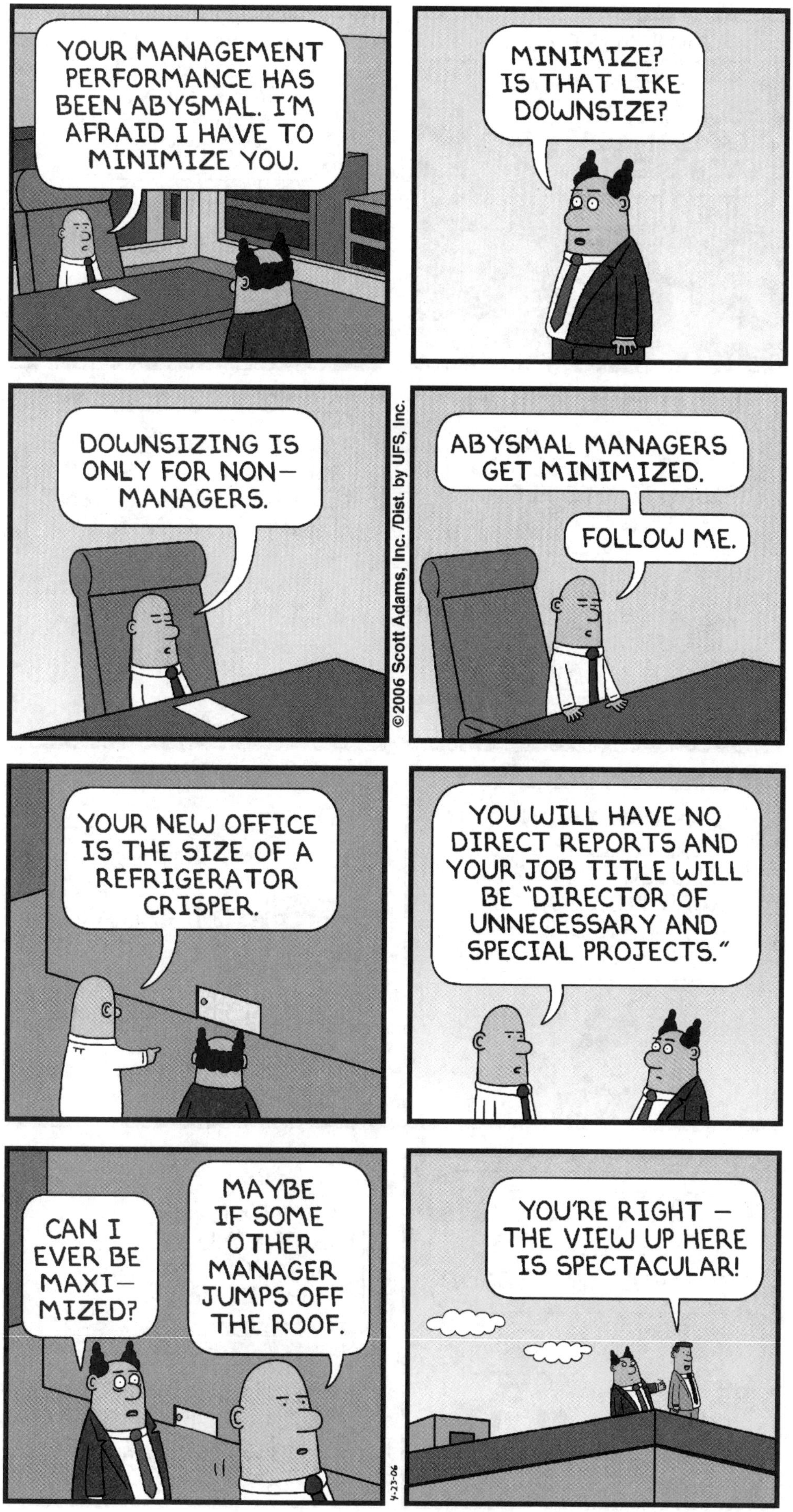
YOUR MANAGEMENT PERFORMANCE HAS BEEN ABYSMAL. I'M AFRAID I HAVE TO MINIMIZE YOU.
MINIMIZE? IS THAT LIKE DOWNSIZE?
DOWNSIZING IS ONLY FOR NON-MANAGERS.
ABYSMAL MANAGERS GET MINIMIZED.
FOLLOW ME.
©2006 Scott Adams, Inc. /Dist. by UFS, Inc.
YOUR NEW OFFICE IS THE SIZE OF A REFRIGERATOR CRISPER.
YOU WILL HAVE NO DIRECT REPORTS AND YOUR JOB TITLE WILL BE "DIRECTOR OF UNNECESSARY AND SPECIAL PROJECTS."
CAN I EVER BE MAXI-MIZED?
MAYBE IF SOME OTHER MANAGER JUMPS OFF THE ROOF.
YOU'RE RIGHT — THE VIEW UP HERE IS SPECTACULAR!
4-23-06

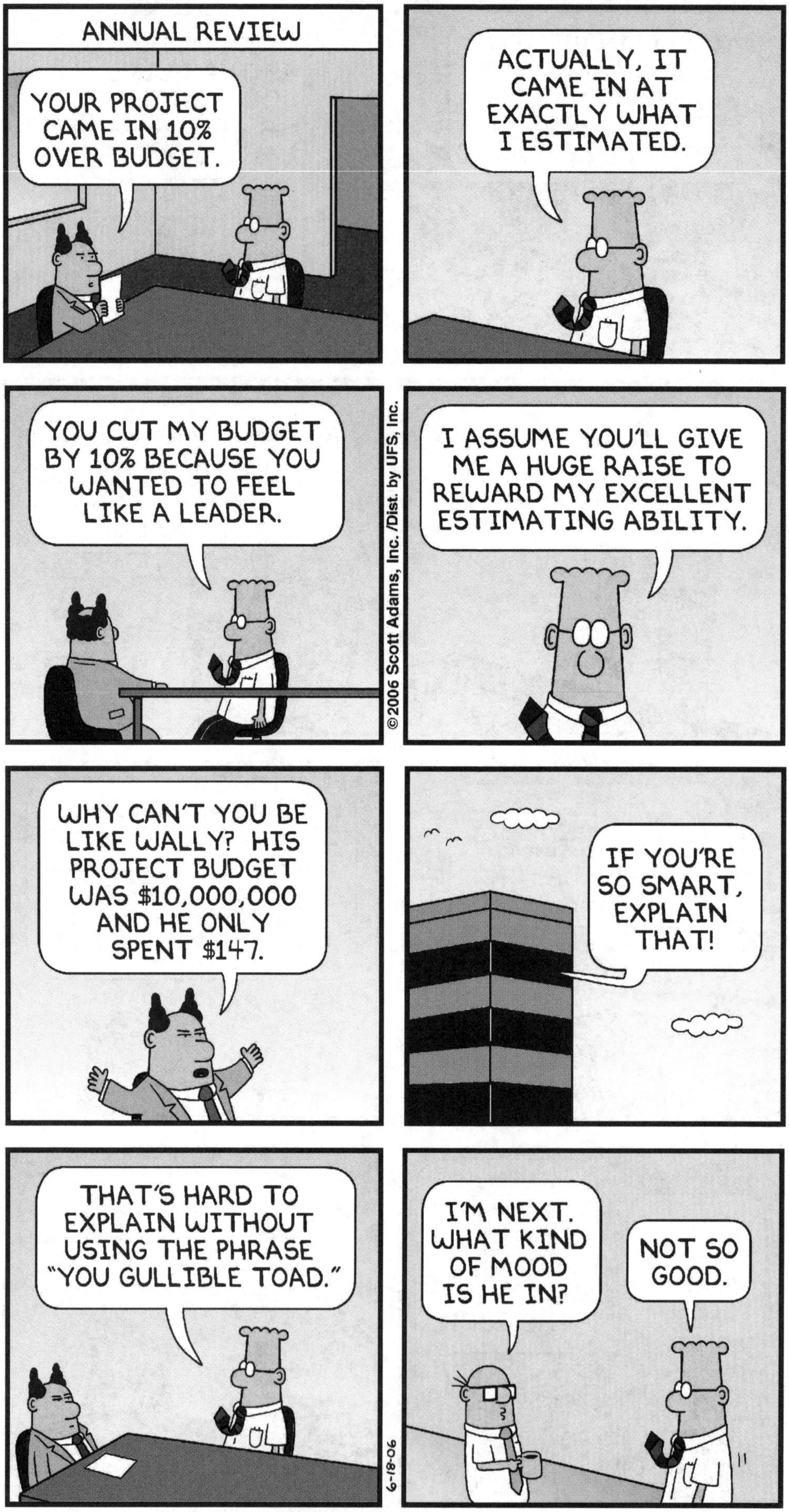
ANNUAL REVIEW
YOUR PROJECT CAME IN 10% OVER BUDGET.
ACTUALLY, IT CAME IN AT EXACTLY WHAT I ESTIMATED.
YOU CUT MY BUDGET BY 10% BECAUSE YOU WANTED TO FEEL LIKE A LEADER.
©2006 Scott Adams, Inc. /Dist. by UFS, Inc.
I ASSUME YOU'LL GIVE ME A HUGE RAISE TO REWARD MY EXCELLENT ESTIMATING ABILITY.
WHY CAN'T YOU BE LIKE WALLY? HIS PROJECT BUDGET WAS $10,000,000 AND HE ONLY SPENT $147.
IF YOU'RE SO SMART, EXPLAIN THAT!
THAT'S HARD TO EXPLAIN WITHOUT USING THE PHRASE "YOU GULLIBLE TOAD."
6-18-06
I'M NEXT. WHAT KIND OF MOOD IS HE IN?
NOT SO GOOD.

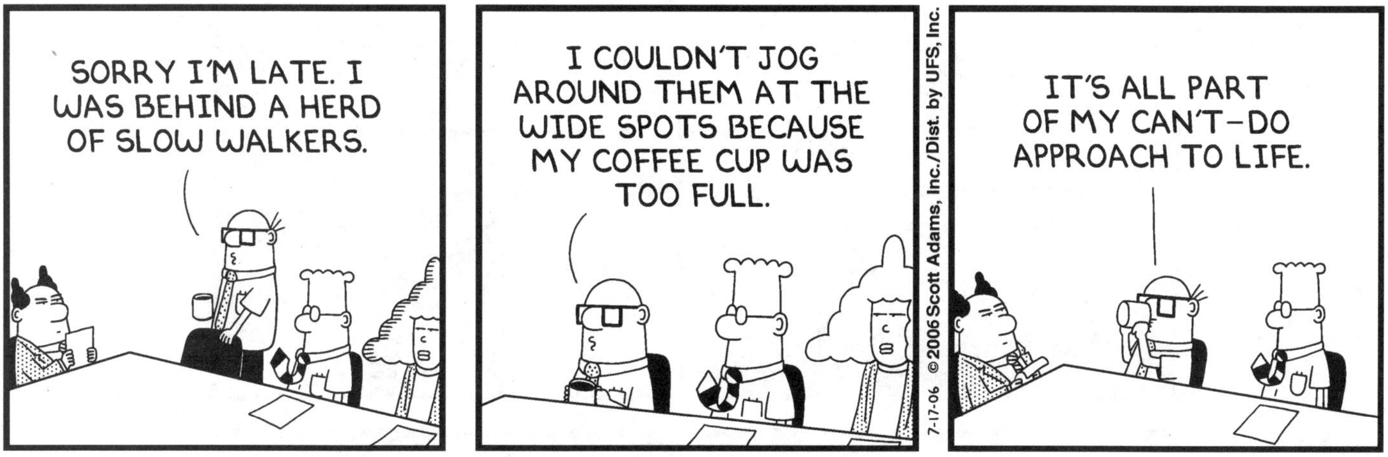
SORRY I'M LATE. I WAS BEHIND A HERD OF SLOW WALKERS.
I COULDN'T JOG AROUND THEM AT THE WIDE SPOTS BECAUSE MY COFFEE CUP WAS TOO FULL.
7-17-06 ©2006 Scott Adams, Inc./Dist. by UFS, Inc.
IT'S ALL PART OF MY CAN'T-DO APPROACH TO LIFE.

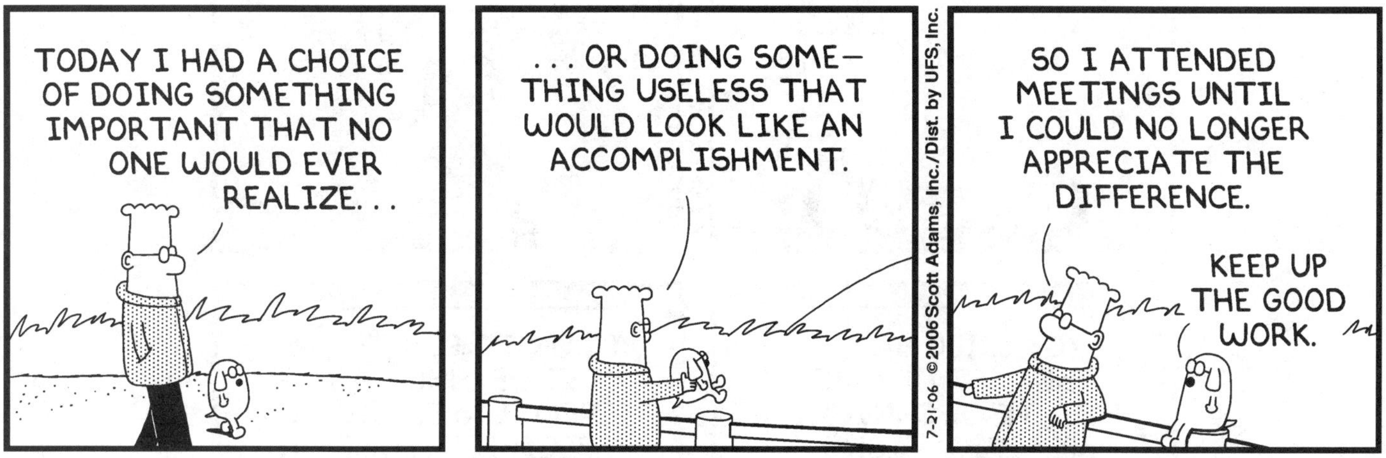
TODAY I HAD A CHOICE OF DOING SOMETHING IMPORTANT THAT NO ONE WOULD EVER REALIZE...
...OR DOING SOME-THING USELESS THAT WOULD LOOK LIKE AN ACCOMPLISHMENT.
7-21-06 ©2006 Scott Adams, Inc./Dist. by UFS, Inc.
SO I ATTENDED MEETINGS UNTIL I COULD NO LONGER APPRECIATE THE DIFFERENCE.
KEEP UP THE GOOD WORK.

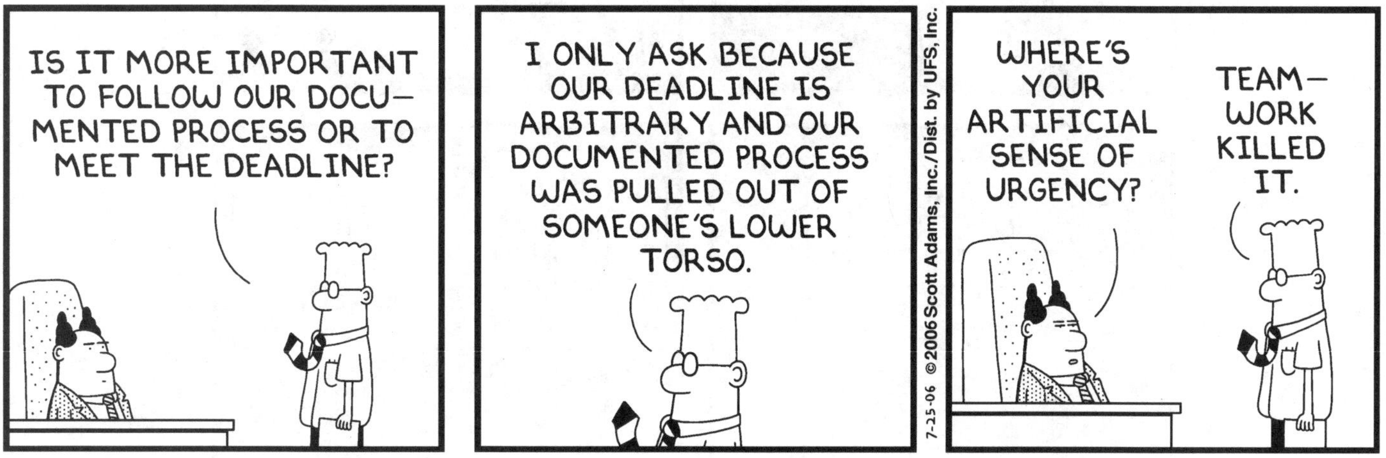
IS IT MORE IMPORTANT TO FOLLOW OUR DOCU-MENTED PROCESS OR TO MEET THE DEADLINE?
I ONLY ASK BECAUSE OUR DEADLINE IS ARBITRARY AND OUR DOCUMENTED PROCESS WAS PULLED OUT OF SOMEONE'S LOWER TORSO.
7-25-06 ©2006 Scott Adams, Inc./Dist. by UFS, Inc.
WHERE'S YOUR ARTIFICIAL SENSE OF URGENCY?
TEAM-WORK KILLED IT.

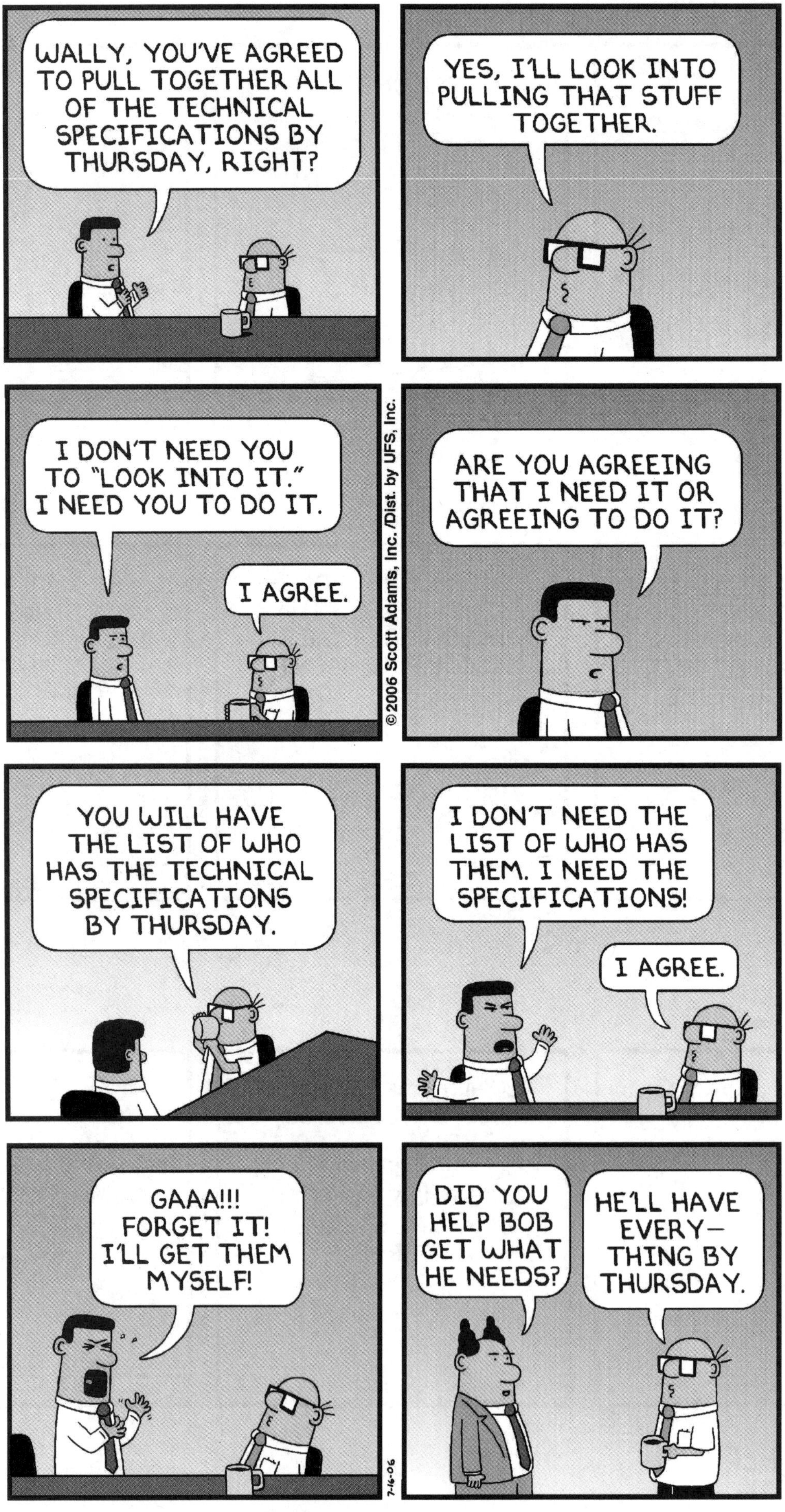
WALLY, YOU'VE AGREED TO PULL TOGETHER ALL OF THE TECHNICAL SPECIFICATIONS BY THURSDAY, RIGHT?
YES, I'LL LOOK INTO PULLING THAT STUFF TOGETHER.
I DON'T NEED YOU TO "LOOK INTO IT." I NEED YOU TO DO IT.
I AGREE.
©2006 Scott Adams, Inc. /Dist. by UFS, Inc.
ARE YOU AGREEING THAT I NEED IT OR AGREEING TO DO IT?
YOU WILL HAVE THE LIST OF WHO HAS THE TECHNICAL SPECIFICATIONS BY THURSDAY.
I DON'T NEED THE LIST OF WHO HAS THEM. I NEED THE SPECIFICATIONS!
I AGREE.
GAAA!!! FORGET IT! I'LL GET THEM MYSELF!
7-16-06
DID YOU HELP BOB GET WHAT HE NEEDS?
HE'LL HAVE EVERY-THING BY THURSDAY.

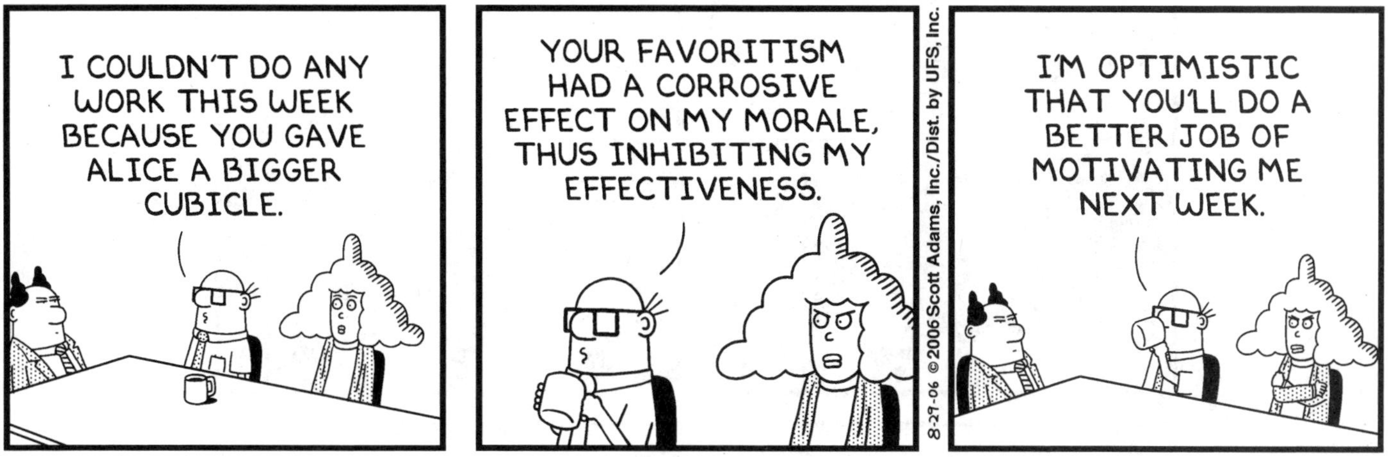
I COULDN'T DO ANY WORK THIS WEEK BECAUSE YOU GAVE ALICE A BIGGER CUBICLE.
YOUR FAVORITISM HAD A CORROSIVE EFFECT ON MY MORALE, THUS INHIBITING MY EFFECTIVENESS.
8-29-06 © 2006 Scott Adams, Inc./Dist. by UFS, Inc.
I'M OPTIMISTIC THAT YOU'LL DO A BETTER JOB OF MOTIVATING ME NEXT WEEK.

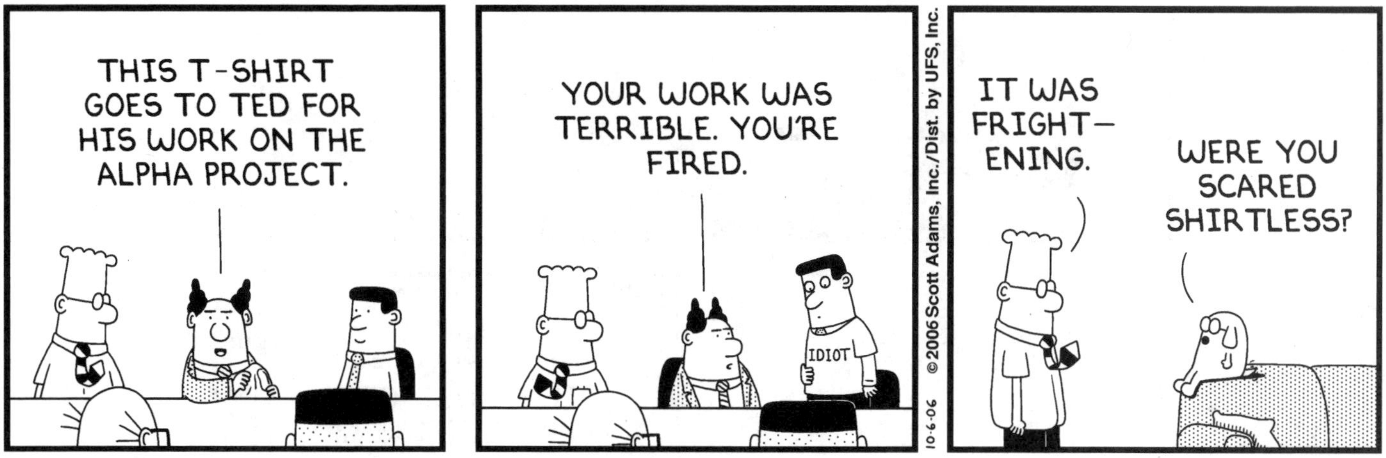
THIS T-SHIRT GOES TO TED FOR HIS WORK ON THE ALPHA PROJECT.
YOUR WORK WAS TERRIBLE. YOU'RE FIRED.
IDIOT
10-6-06 © 2006 Scott Adams, Inc./Dist. by UFS, Inc.
IT WAS FRIGHT– ENING.
WERE YOU SCARED SHIRTLESS?

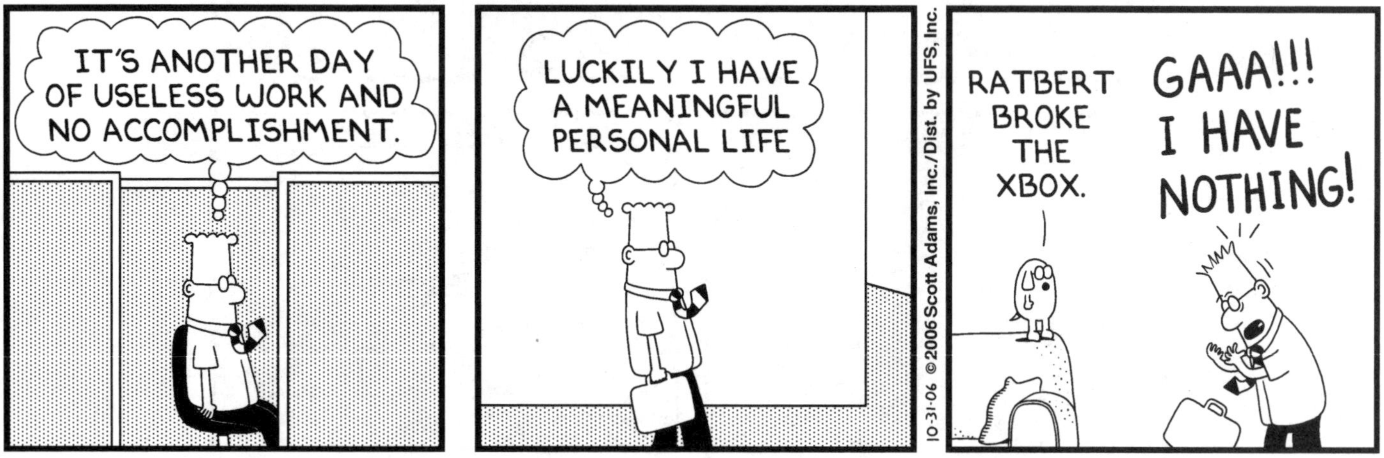
IT'S ANOTHER DAY OF USELESS WORK AND NO ACCOMPLISHMENT.
LUCKILY I HAVE A MEANINGFUL PERSONAL LIFE
10-31-06 © 2006 Scott Adams, Inc./Dist. by UFS, Inc.
RATBERT BROKE THE XBOX.
GAAA!!! I HAVE NOTHING!

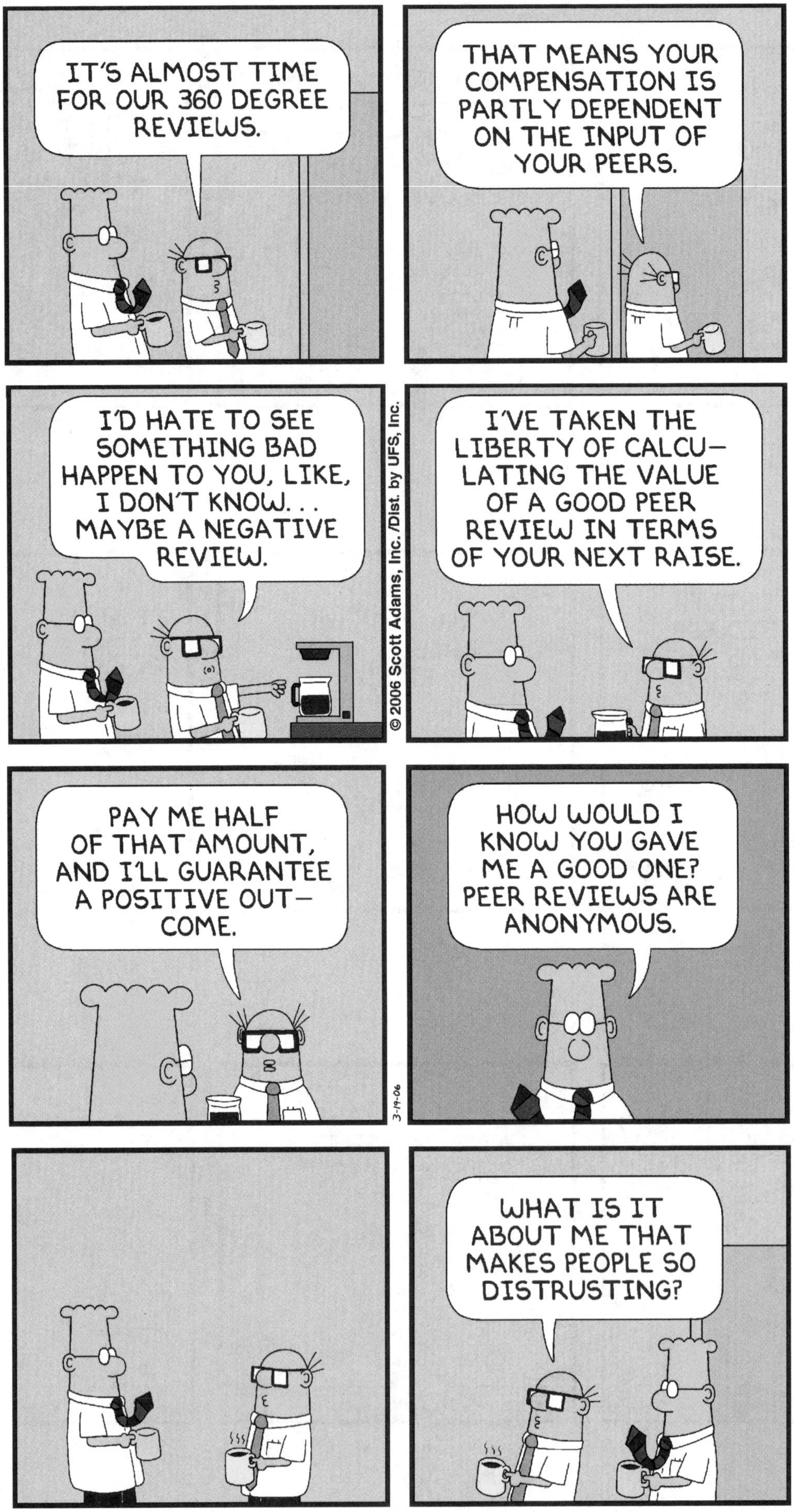
IT'S ALMOST TIME FOR OUR 360 DEGREE REVIEWS.
THAT MEANS YOUR COMPENSATION IS PARTLY DEPENDENT ON THE INPUT OF YOUR PEERS.
I'D HATE TO SEE SOMETHING BAD HAPPEN TO YOU, LIKE, I DON'T KNOW... MAYBE A NEGATIVE REVIEW.
© 2006 Scott Adams, Inc./Dist. by UFS, Inc.
I'VE TAKEN THE LIBERTY OF CALCU-LATING THE VALUE OF A GOOD PEER REVIEW IN TERMS OF YOUR NEXT RAISE.
PAY ME HALF OF THAT AMOUNT, AND I'LL GUARANTEE A POSITIVE OUT-COME.
3-19-06
HOW WOULD I KNOW YOU GAVE ME A GOOD ONE? PEER REVIEWS ARE ANONYMOUS.
WHAT IS IT ABOUT ME THAT MAKES PEOPLE SO DISTRUSTING?

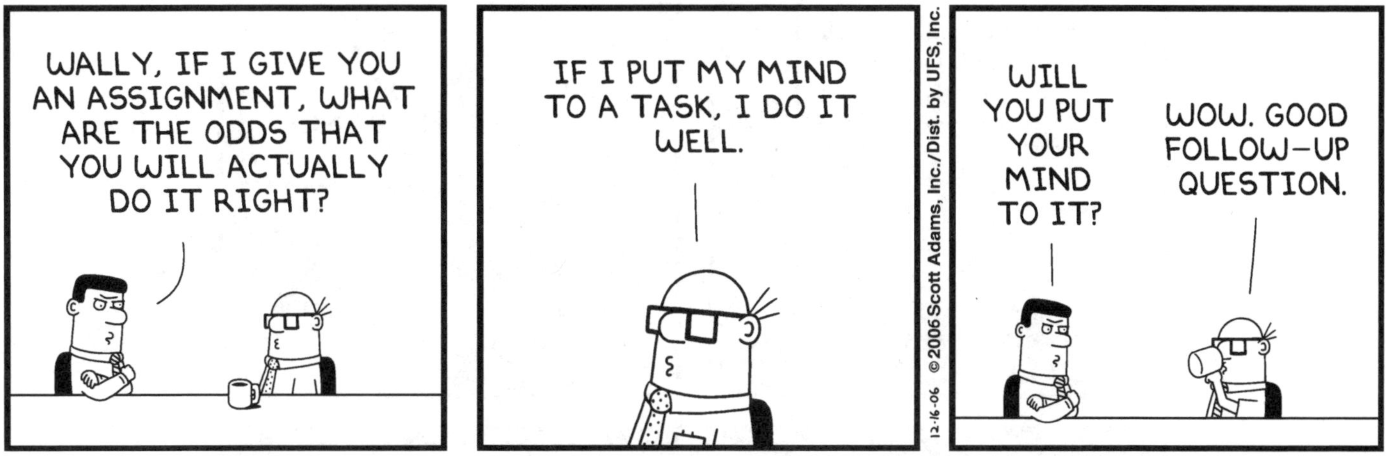
WALLY, IF I GIVE YOU AN ASSIGNMENT, WHAT ARE THE ODDS THAT YOU WILL ACTUALLY DO IT RIGHT?
IF I PUT MY MIND TO A TASK, I DO IT WELL.
12-16-06 © 2006 Scott Adams, Inc./Dist. by UFS, Inc.
WILL YOU PUT YOUR MIND TO IT?
WOW. GOOD FOLLOW-UP QUESTION.

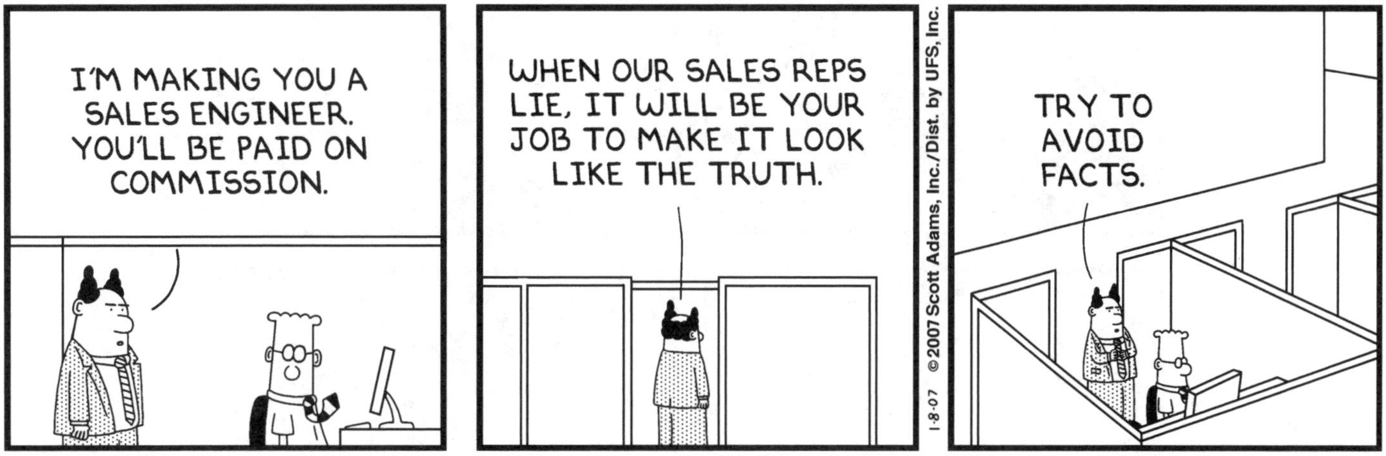
I'M MAKING YOU A SALES ENGINEER. YOU'LL BE PAID ON COMMISSION.
WHEN OUR SALES REPS LIE, IT WILL BE YOUR JOB TO MAKE IT LOOK LIKE THE TRUTH.
1-8-07 © 2007 Scott Adams, Inc./Dist. by UFS, Inc.
TRY TO AVOID FACTS.

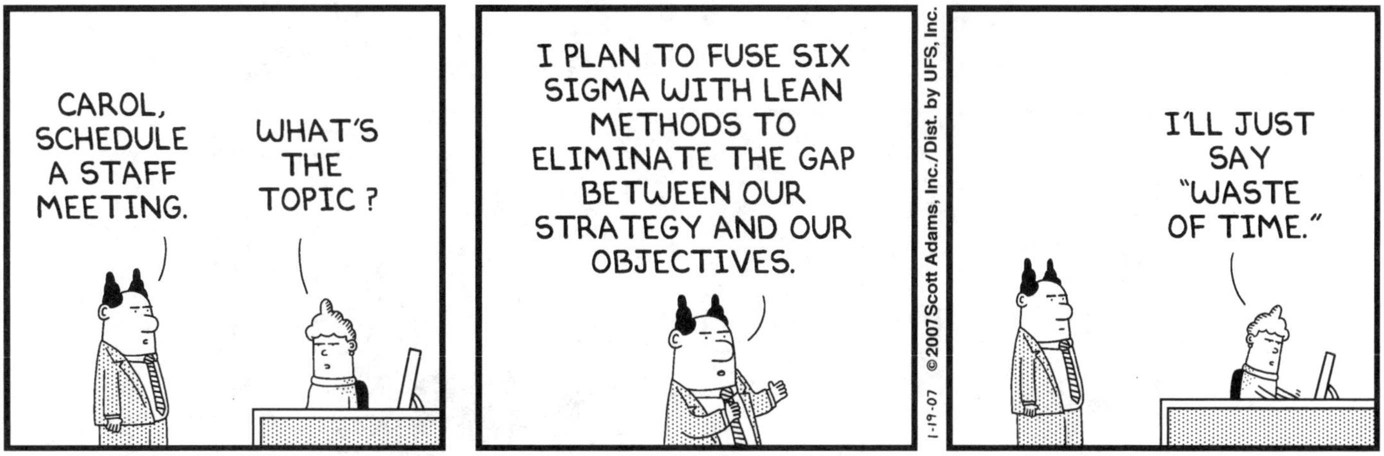
CAROL, SCHEDULE A STAFF MEETING.
WHAT'S THE TOPIC ?
I PLAN TO FUSE SIX SIGMA WITH LEAN METHODS TO ELIMINATE THE GAP BETWEEN OUR STRATEGY AND OUR OBJECTIVES.
1-19-07 © 2007 Scott Adams, Inc./Dist. by UFS, Inc.
I'LL JUST SAY "WASTE OF TIME."

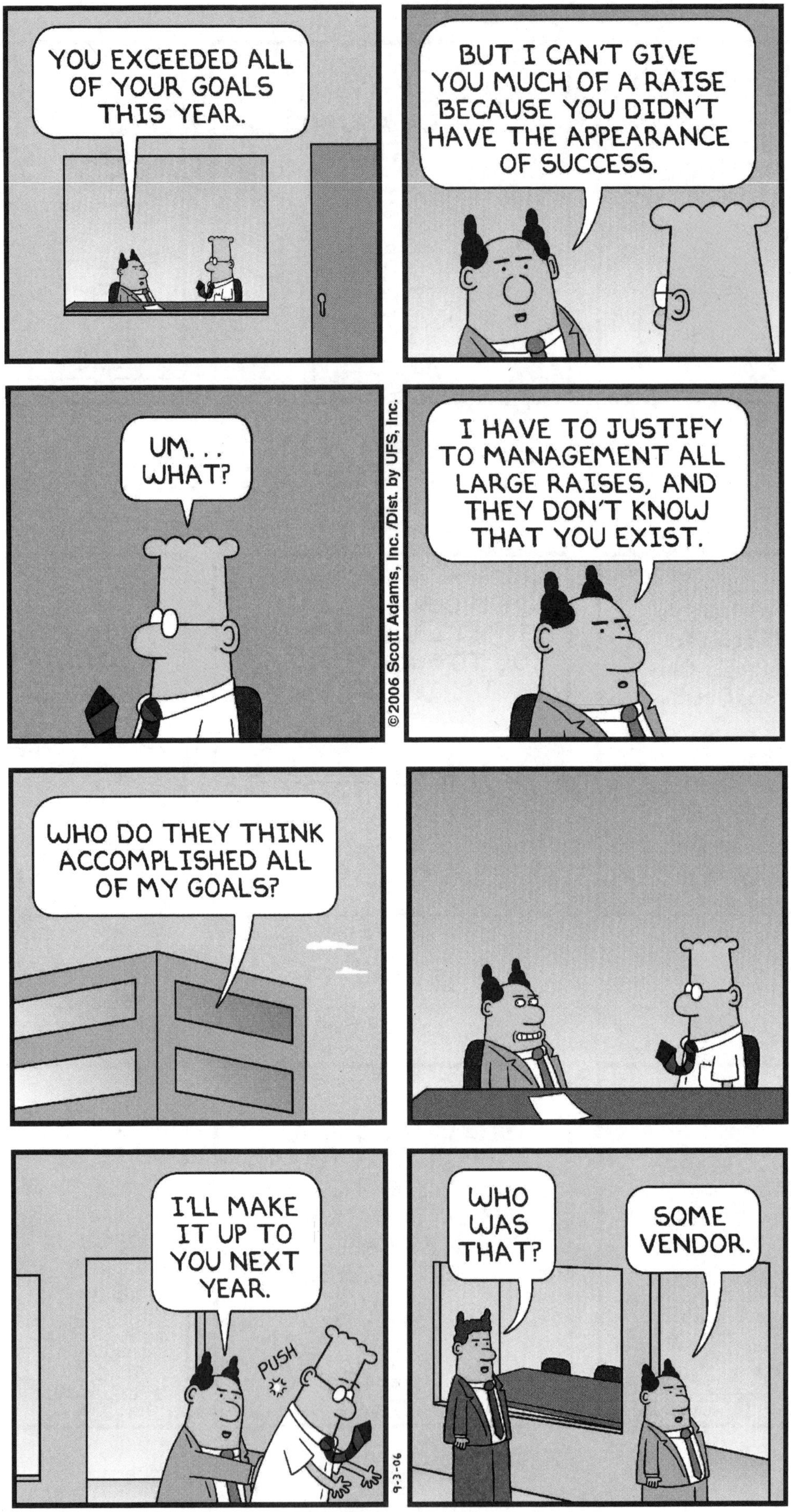
YOU EXCEEDED ALL OF YOUR GOALS THIS YEAR.
BUT I CAN'T GIVE YOU MUCH OF A RAISE BECAUSE YOU DIDN'T HAVE THE APPEARANCE OF SUCCESS.
UM... WHAT?
©2006 Scott Adams, Inc./Dist. by UFS, Inc.
I HAVE TO JUSTIFY TO MANAGEMENT ALL LARGE RAISES, AND THEY DON'T KNOW THAT YOU EXIST.
WHO DO THEY THINK ACCOMPLISHED ALL OF MY GOALS?
I'LL MAKE IT UP TO YOU NEXT YEAR.
PUSH
9-3-06
WHO WAS THAT?
SOME VENDOR.

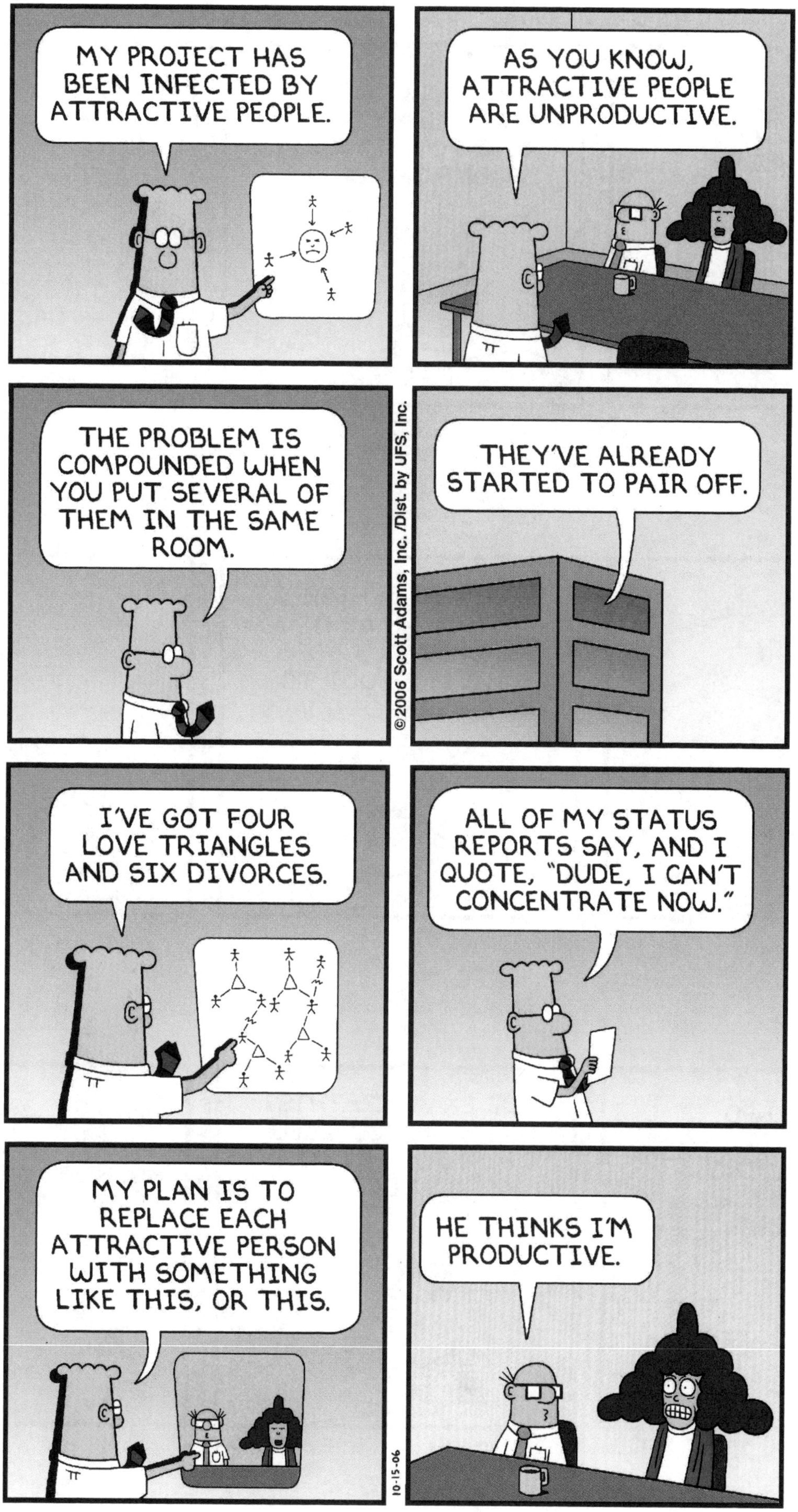
MY PROJECT HAS BEEN INFECTED BY ATTRACTIVE PEOPLE.
AS YOU KNOW, ATTRACTIVE PEOPLE ARE UNPRODUCTIVE.
THE PROBLEM IS COMPOUNDED WHEN YOU PUT SEVERAL OF THEM IN THE SAME ROOM.
©2006 Scott Adams, Inc. /Dist. by UFS, Inc.
THEY'VE ALREADY STARTED TO PAIR OFF.
I'VE GOT FOUR LOVE TRIANGLES AND SIX DIVORCES.
ALL OF MY STATUS REPORTS SAY, AND I QUOTE, "DUDE, I CAN'T CONCENTRATE NOW."
MY PLAN IS TO REPLACE EACH ATTRACTIVE PERSON WITH SOMETHING LIKE THIS, OR THIS.
10-15-06
HE THINKS I'M PRODUCTIVE.

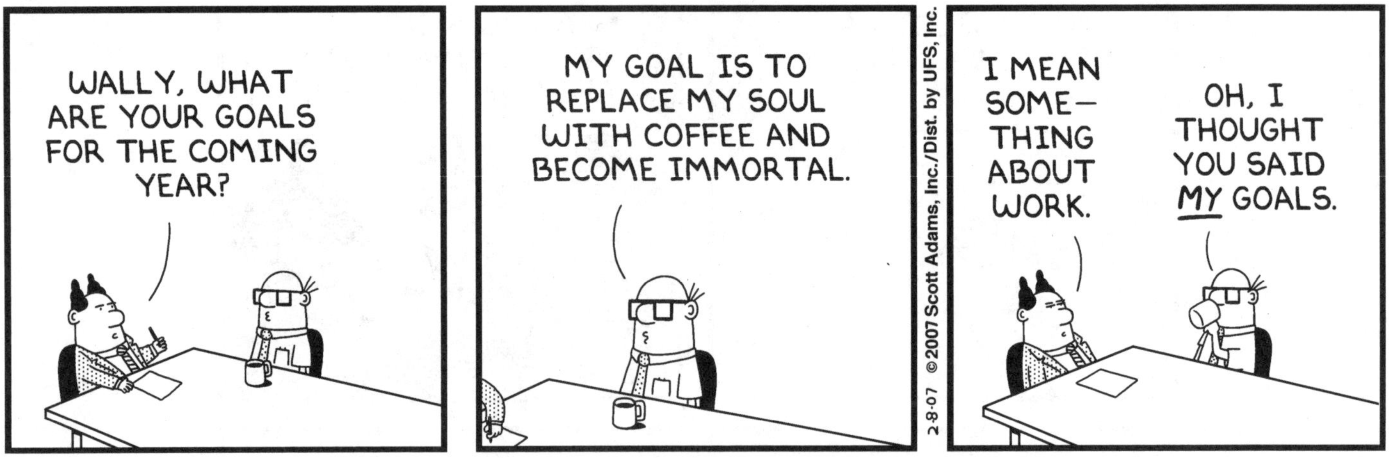
WALLY, WHAT ARE YOUR GOALS FOR THE COMING YEAR?
MY GOAL IS TO REPLACE MY SOUL WITH COFFEE AND BECOME IMMORTAL.
2-8-07 ©2007 Scott Adams, Inc./Dist. by UFS, Inc.
I MEAN SOME-THING ABOUT WORK.
OH, I THOUGHT YOU SAID MY GOALS.

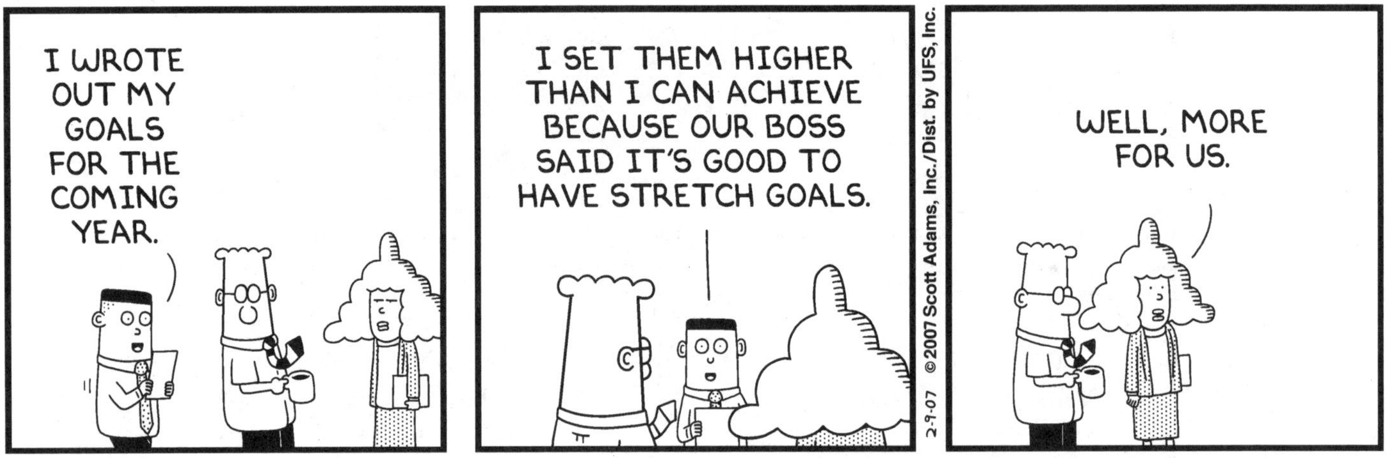
I WROTE OUT MY GOALS FOR THE COMING YEAR.
I SET THEM HIGHER THAN I CAN ACHIEVE BECAUSE OUR BOSS SAID IT'S GOOD TO HAVE STRETCH GOALS.
2-9-07 ©2007 Scott Adams, Inc./Dist. by UFS, Inc.
WELL, MORE FOR US.

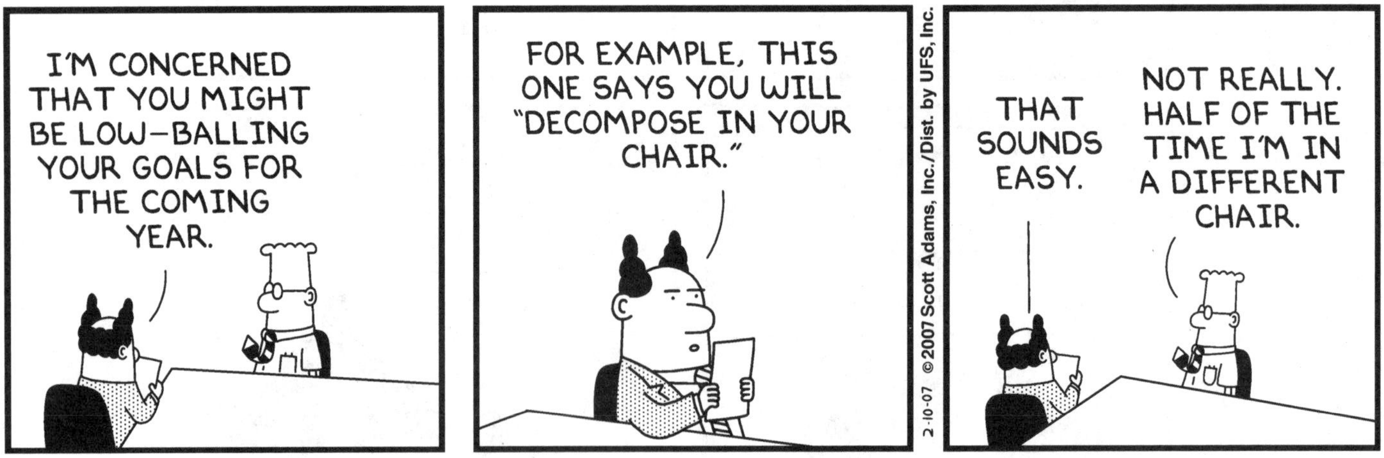
I'M CONCERNED THAT YOU MIGHT BE LOW-BALLING YOUR GOALS FOR THE COMING YEAR.
FOR EXAMPLE, THIS ONE SAYS YOU WILL "DECOMPOSE IN YOUR CHAIR."
2-10-07 ©2007 Scott Adams, Inc./Dist. by UFS, Inc.
THAT SOUNDS EASY.
NOT REALLY. HALF OF THE TIME I'M IN A DIFFERENT CHAIR.

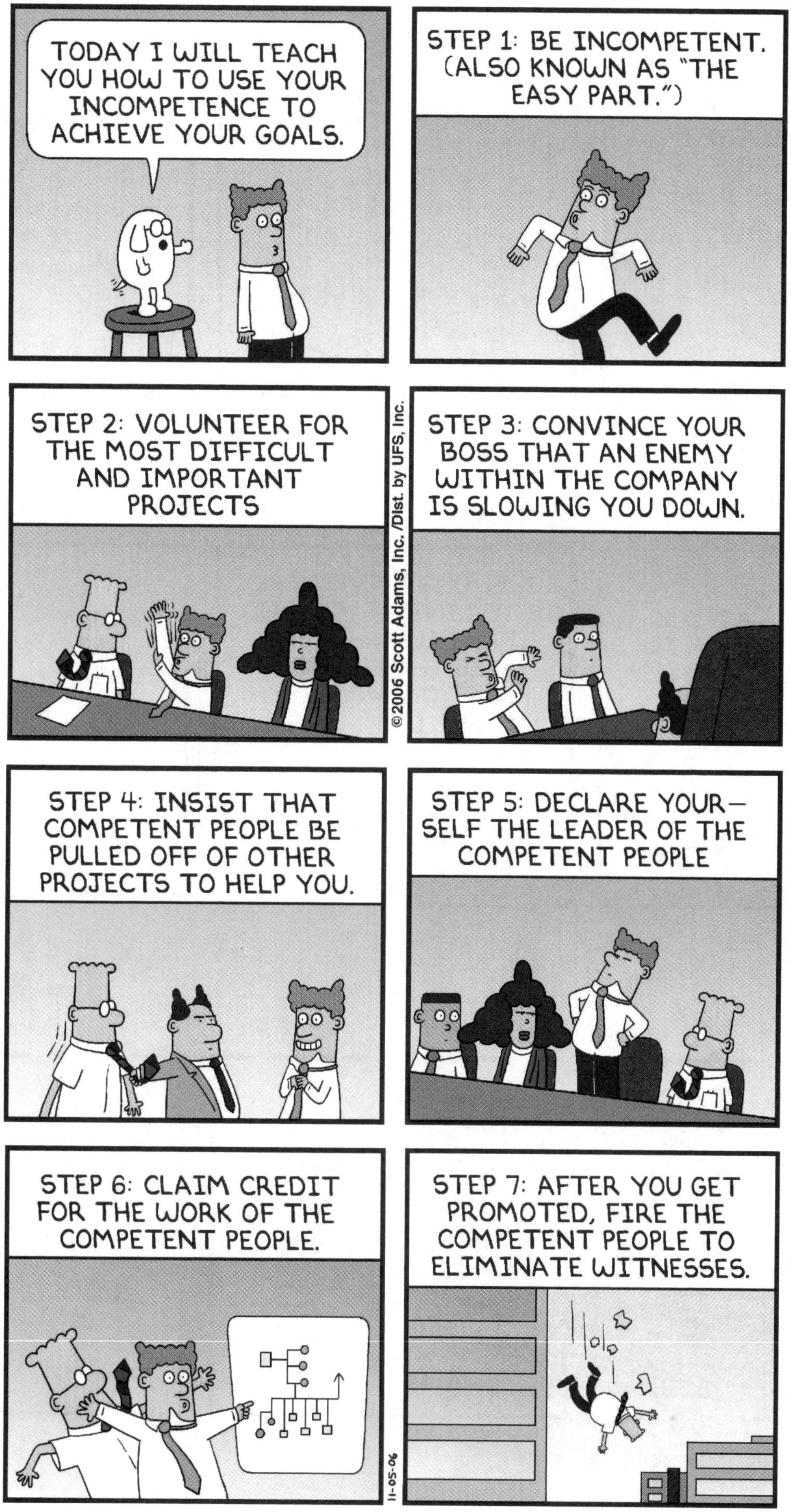
TODAY I WILL TEACH YOU HOW TO USE YOUR INCOMPETENCE TO ACHIEVE YOUR GOALS.
STEP 1: BE INCOMPETENT. (ALSO KNOWN AS "THE EASY PART.")
STEP 2: VOLUNTEER FOR THE MOST DIFFICULT AND IMPORTANT PROJECTS
STEP 3: CONVINCE YOUR BOSS THAT AN ENEMY WITHIN THE COMPANY IS SLOWING YOU DOWN.
STEP 4: INSIST THAT COMPETENT PEOPLE BE PULLED OFF OF OTHER PROJECTS TO HELP YOU.
STEP 5: DECLARE YOUR-SELF THE LEADER OF THE COMPETENT PEOPLE
STEP 6: CLAIM CREDIT FOR THE WORK OF THE COMPETENT PEOPLE.
STEP 7: AFTER YOU GET PROMOTED, FIRE THE COMPETENT PEOPLE TO ELIMINATE WITNESSES.
©2006 Scott Adams, Inc. /Dist. by UFS, Inc.
11-05-06

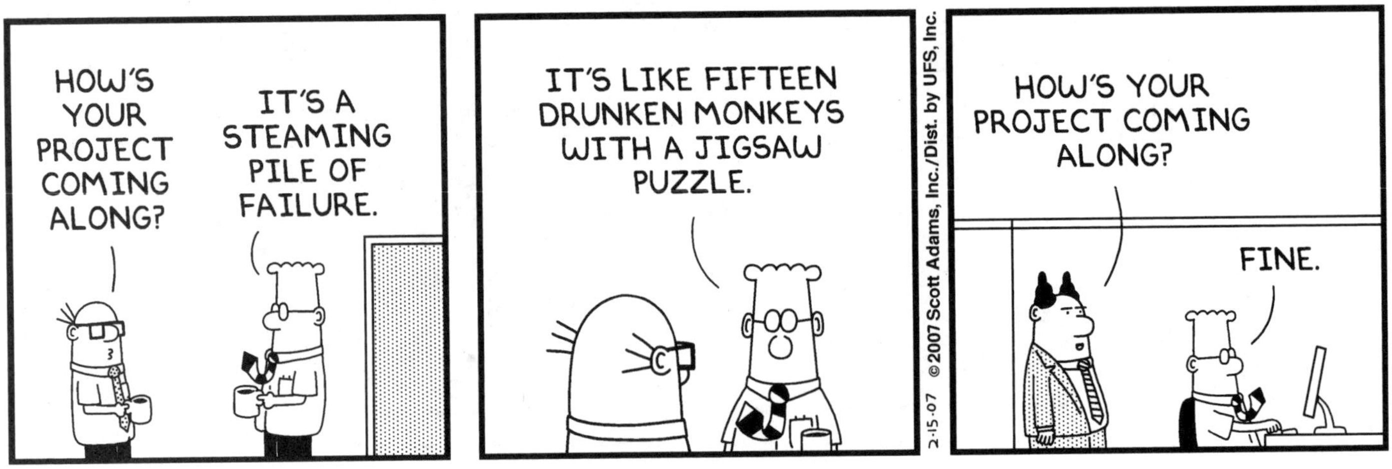
HOW'S YOUR PROJECT COMING ALONG?
IT'S A STEAMING PILE OF FAILURE.
IT'S LIKE FIFTEEN DRUNKEN MONKEYS WITH A JIGSAW PUZZLE.
2-15-07 © 2007 Scott Adams, Inc./Dist. by UFS, Inc.
HOW'S YOUR PROJECT COMING ALONG?
FINE.

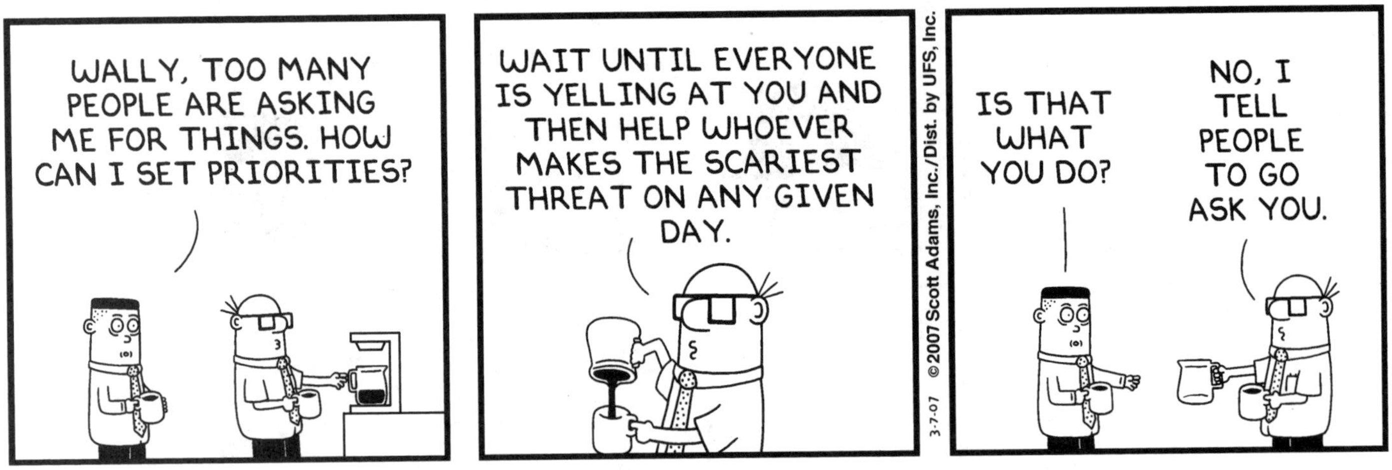
WALLY, TOO MANY PEOPLE ARE ASKING ME FOR THINGS. HOW CAN I SET PRIORITIES?
WAIT UNTIL EVERYONE IS YELLING AT YOU AND THEN HELP WHOEVER MAKES THE SCARIEST THREAT ON ANY GIVEN DAY.
3-7-07 © 2007 Scott Adams, Inc./Dist. by UFS, Inc.
IS THAT WHAT YOU DO?
NO, I TELL PEOPLE TO GO ASK YOU.

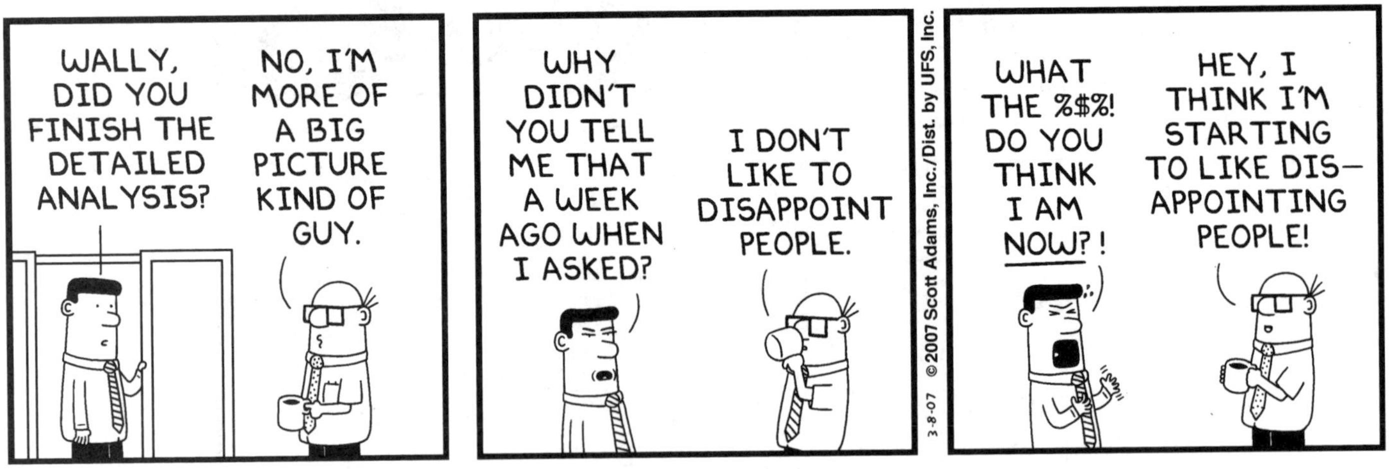
WALLY, DID YOU FINISH THE DETAILED ANALYSIS?
NO, I'M MORE OF A BIG PICTURE KIND OF GUY.
WHY DIDN'T YOU TELL ME THAT A WEEK AGO WHEN I ASKED?
I DON'T LIKE TO DISAPPOINT PEOPLE.
3-8-07 © 2007 Scott Adams, Inc./Dist. by UFS, Inc.
WHAT THE %$%! DO YOU THINK I AM NOW? !
HEY, I THINK I'M STARTING TO LIKE DIS- APPOINTING PEOPLE!

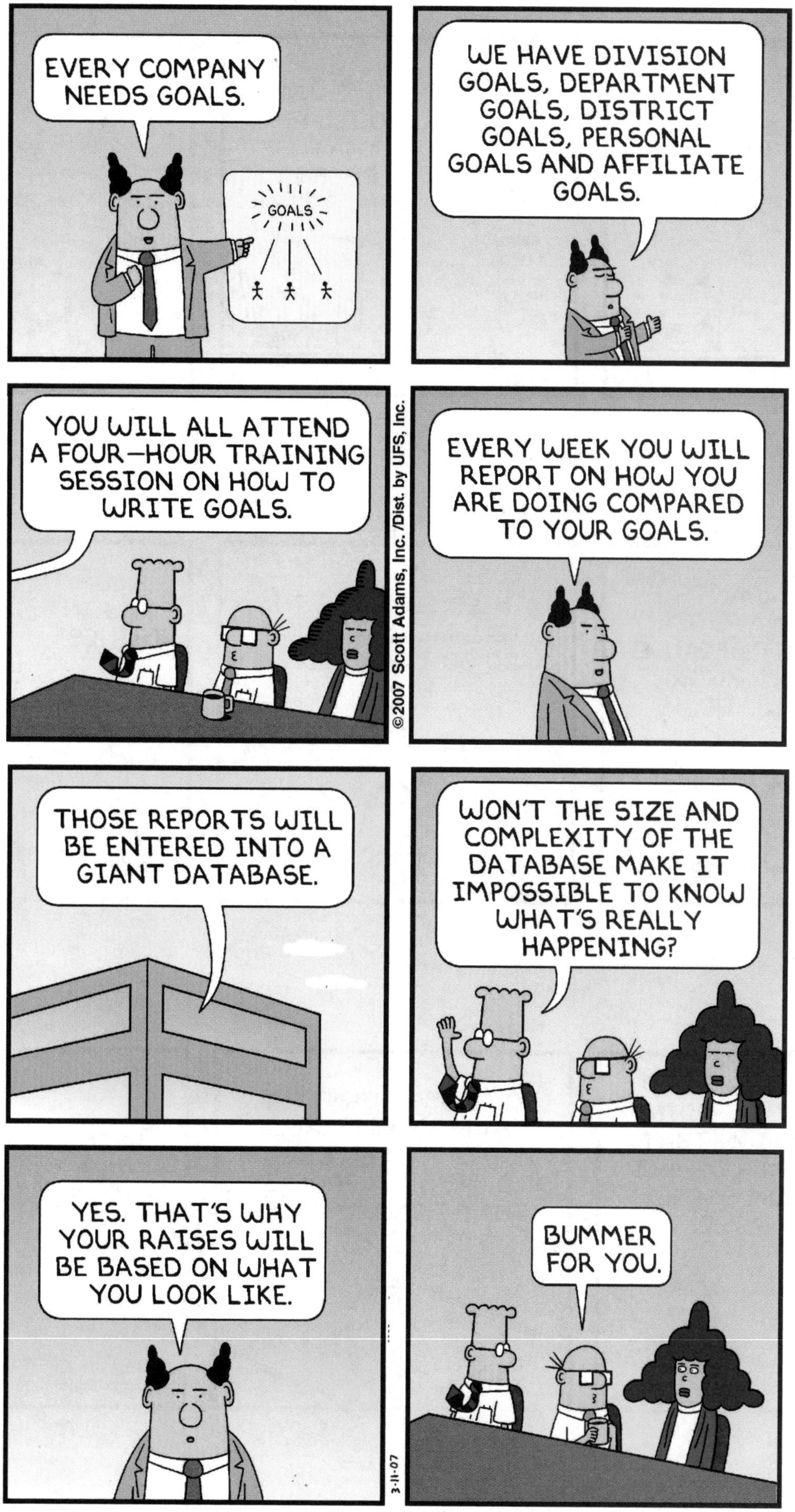
EVERY COMPANY NEEDS GOALS.
GOALS
WE HAVE DIVISION GOALS, DEPARTMENT GOALS, DISTRICT GOALS, PERSONAL GOALS AND AFFILIATE GOALS.
YOU WILL ALL ATTEND A FOUR-HOUR TRAINING SESSION ON HOW TO WRITE GOALS.
©2007 Scott Adams, Inc. /Dist. by UFS, Inc.
EVERY WEEK YOU WILL REPORT ON HOW YOU ARE DOING COMPARED TO YOUR GOALS.
THOSE REPORTS WILL BE ENTERED INTO A GIANT DATABASE.
WON'T THE SIZE AND COMPLEXITY OF THE DATABASE MAKE IT IMPOSSIBLE TO KNOW WHAT'S REALLY HAPPENING?
YES. THAT'S WHY YOUR RAISES WILL BE BASED ON WHAT YOU LOOK LIKE.
3-11-07
BUMMER FOR YOU.

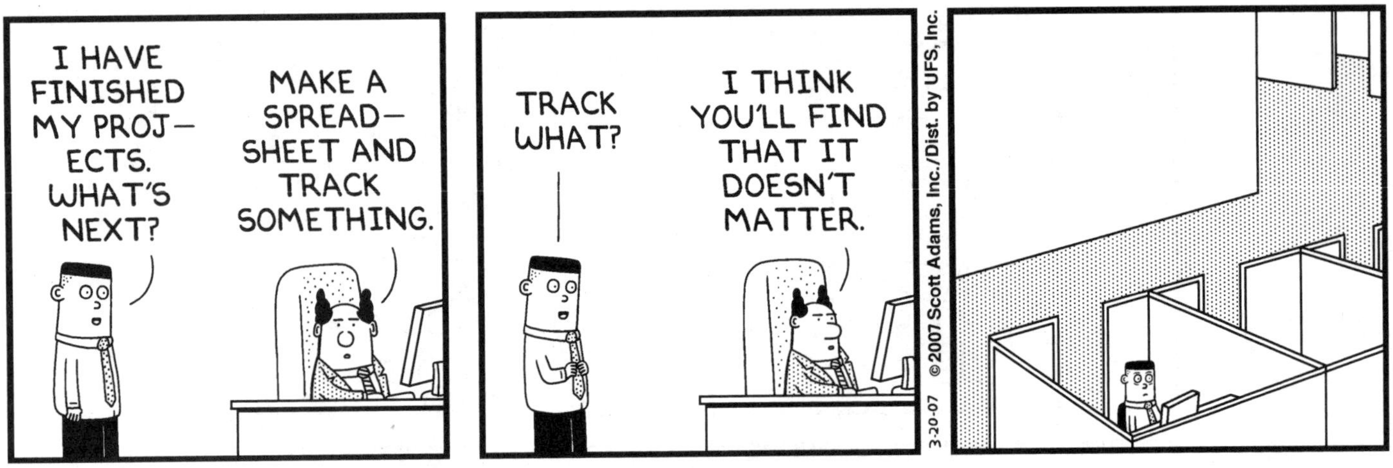
I HAVE FINISHED MY PROJ- ECTS. WHAT'S NEXT?
MAKE A SPREAD- SHEET AND TRACK SOMETHING.
TRACK WHAT?
I THINK YOU'LL FIND THAT IT DOESN'T MATTER.
3-20-07 © 2007 Scott Adams, Inc./Dist. by UFS, Inc.

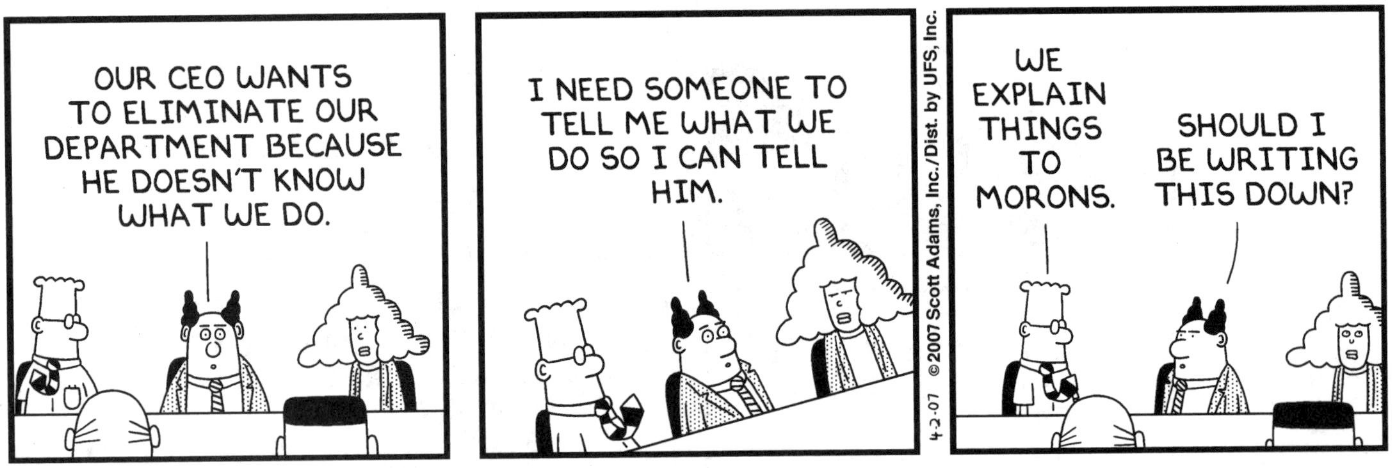
OUR CEO WANTS TO ELIMINATE OUR DEPARTMENT BECAUSE HE DOESN'T KNOW WHAT WE DO.
I NEED SOMEONE TO TELL ME WHAT WE DO SO I CAN TELL HIM.
WE EXPLAIN THINGS TO MORONS.
SHOULD I BE WRITING THIS DOWN?
4-2-07 © 2007 Scott Adams, Inc./Dist. by UFS, Inc.

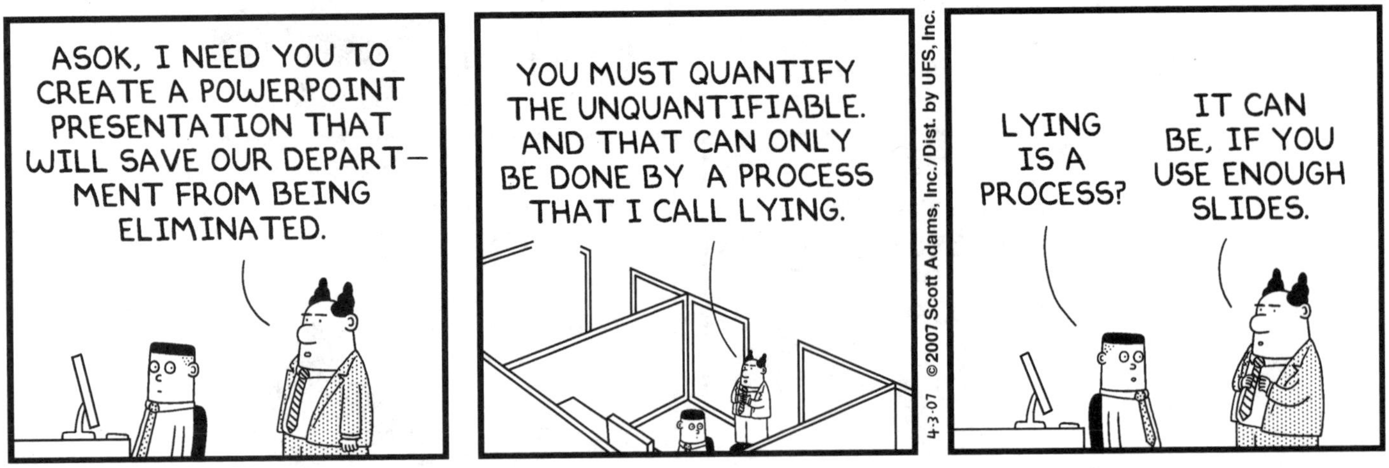
ASOK, I NEED YOU TO CREATE A POWERPOINT PRESENTATION THAT WILL SAVE OUR DEPART- MENT FROM BEING ELIMINATED.
YOU MUST QUANTIFY THE UNQUANTIFIABLE. AND THAT CAN ONLY BE DONE BY A PROCESS THAT I CALL LYING.
LYING IS A PROCESS?
IT CAN BE, IF YOU USE ENOUGH SLIDES.
4-3-07 © 2007 Scott Adams, Inc./Dist. by UFS, Inc.

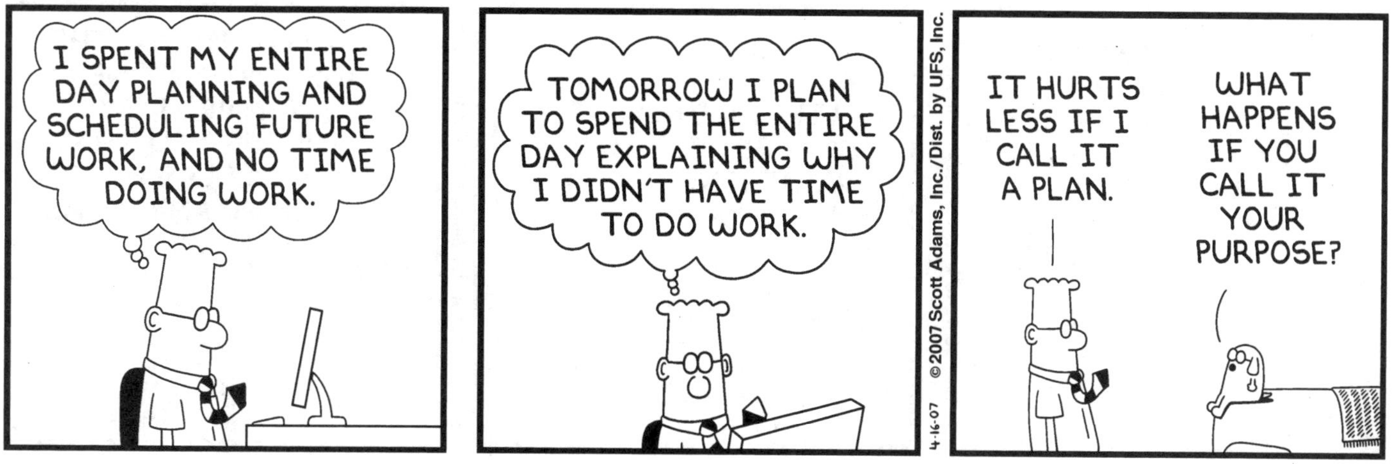
I SPENT MY ENTIRE DAY PLANNING AND SCHEDULING FUTURE WORK, AND NO TIME DOING WORK.
TOMORROW I PLAN TO SPEND THE ENTIRE DAY EXPLAINING WHY I DIDN'T HAVE TIME TO DO WORK.
4-16-07 © 2007 Scott Adams, Inc./Dist. by UFS, Inc.
IT HURTS LESS IF I CALL IT A PLAN.
WHAT HAPPENS IF YOU CALL IT YOUR PURPOSE?

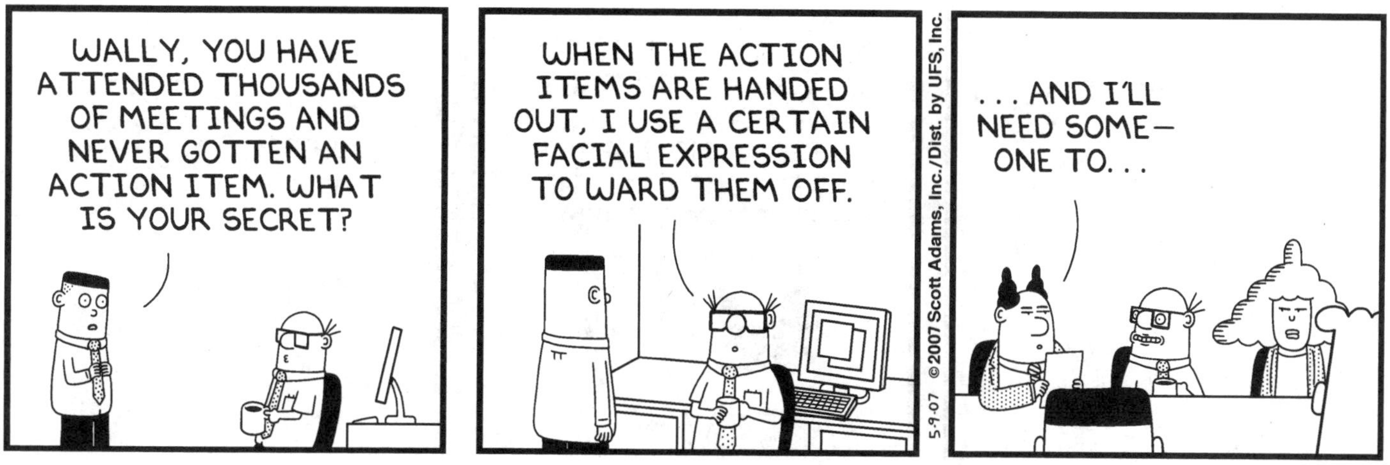
WALLY, YOU HAVE ATTENDED THOUSANDS OF MEETINGS AND NEVER GOTTEN AN ACTION ITEM. WHAT IS YOUR SECRET?
WHEN THE ACTION ITEMS ARE HANDED OUT, I USE A CERTAIN FACIAL EXPRESSION TO WARD THEM OFF.
5-9-07 © 2007 Scott Adams, Inc./Dist. by UFS, Inc.
. . . AND I'LL NEED SOME-ONE TO. . .

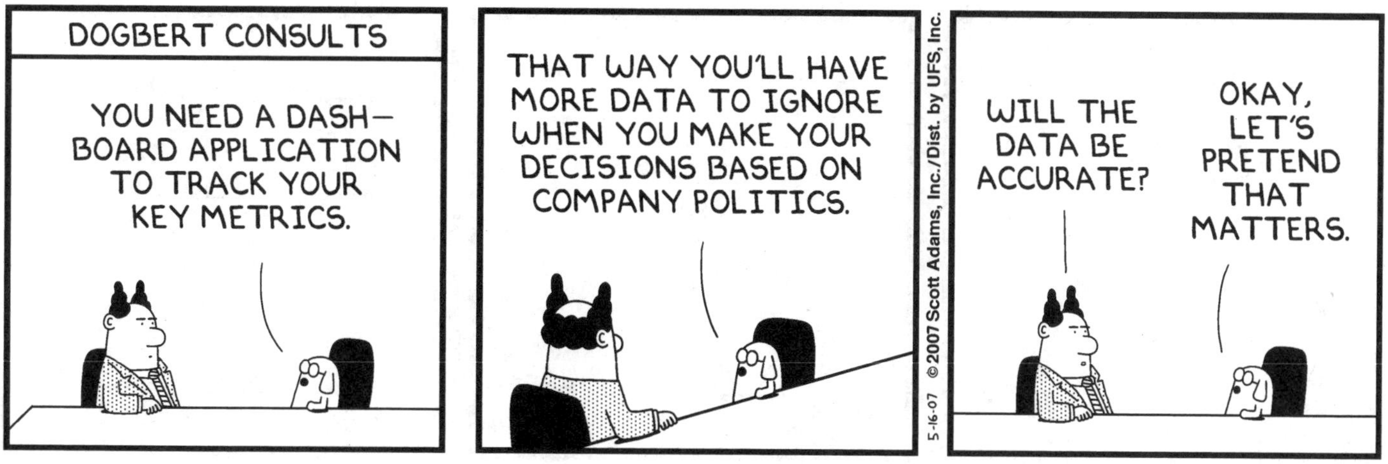
DOGBERT CONSULTS
YOU NEED A DASH-BOARD APPLICATION TO TRACK YOUR KEY METRICS.
THAT WAY YOU'LL HAVE MORE DATA TO IGNORE WHEN YOU MAKE YOUR DECISIONS BASED ON COMPANY POLITICS.
5-16-07 © 2007 Scott Adams, Inc./Dist. by UFS, Inc.
WILL THE DATA BE ACCURATE?
OKAY, LET'S PRETEND THAT MATTERS.

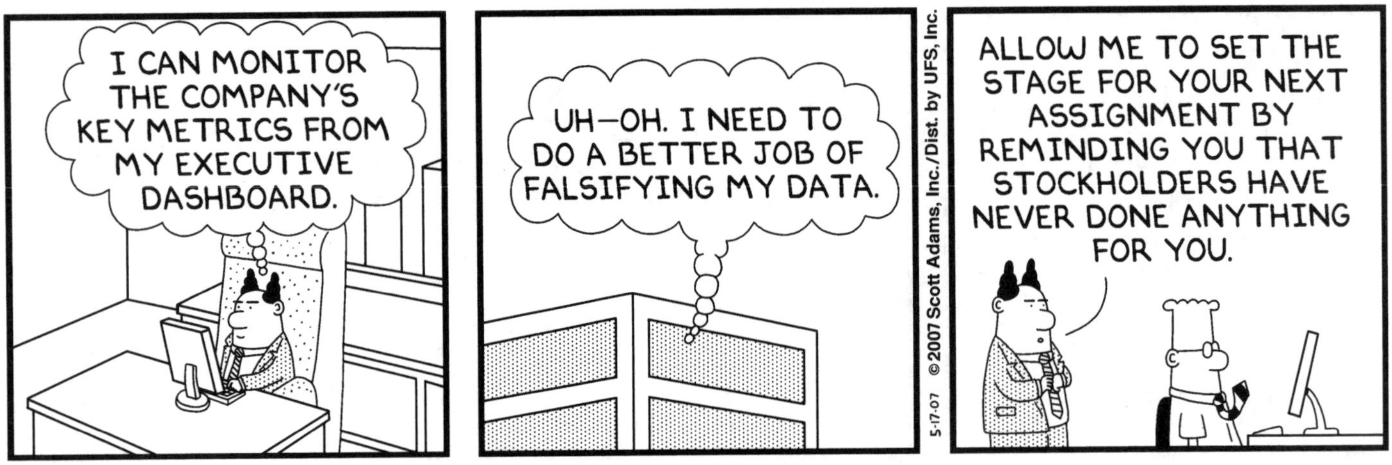
I CAN MONITOR THE COMPANY'S KEY METRICS FROM MY EXECUTIVE DASHBOARD.
UH—OH. I NEED TO DO A BETTER JOB OF FALSIFYING MY DATA.
5-17-07 © 2007 Scott Adams, Inc./Dist. by UFS, Inc.
ALLOW ME TO SET THE STAGE FOR YOUR NEXT ASSIGNMENT BY REMINDING YOU THAT STOCKHOLDERS HAVE NEVER DONE ANYTHING FOR YOU.

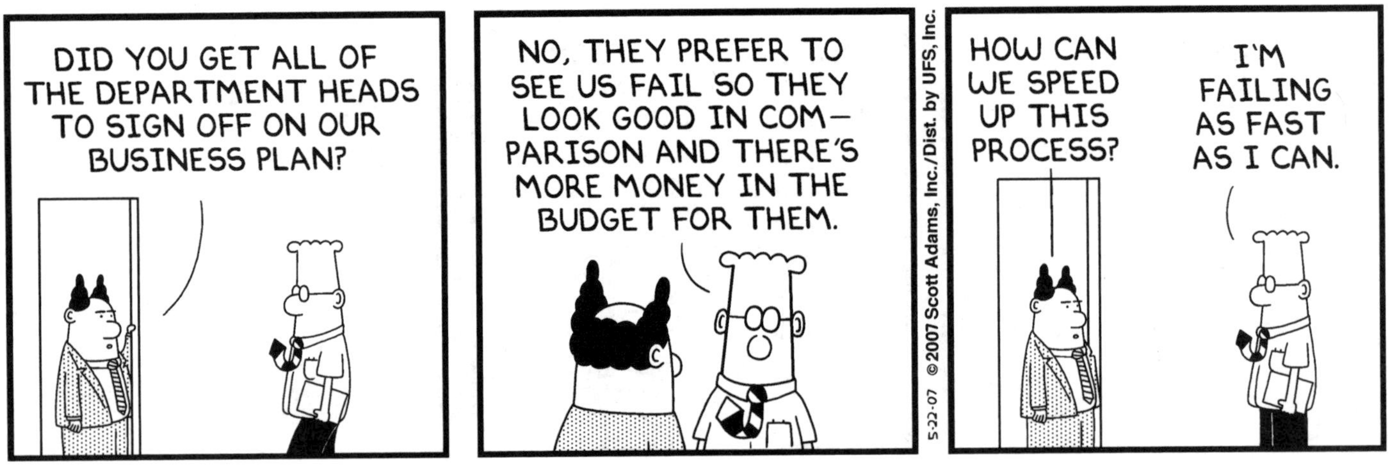
DID YOU GET ALL OF THE DEPARTMENT HEADS TO SIGN OFF ON OUR BUSINESS PLAN?
NO, THEY PREFER TO SEE US FAIL SO THEY LOOK GOOD IN COM— PARISON AND THERE'S MORE MONEY IN THE BUDGET FOR THEM.
5-22-07 © 2007 Scott Adams, Inc./Dist. by UFS, Inc.
HOW CAN WE SPEED UP THIS PROCESS?
I'M FAILING AS FAST AS I CAN.

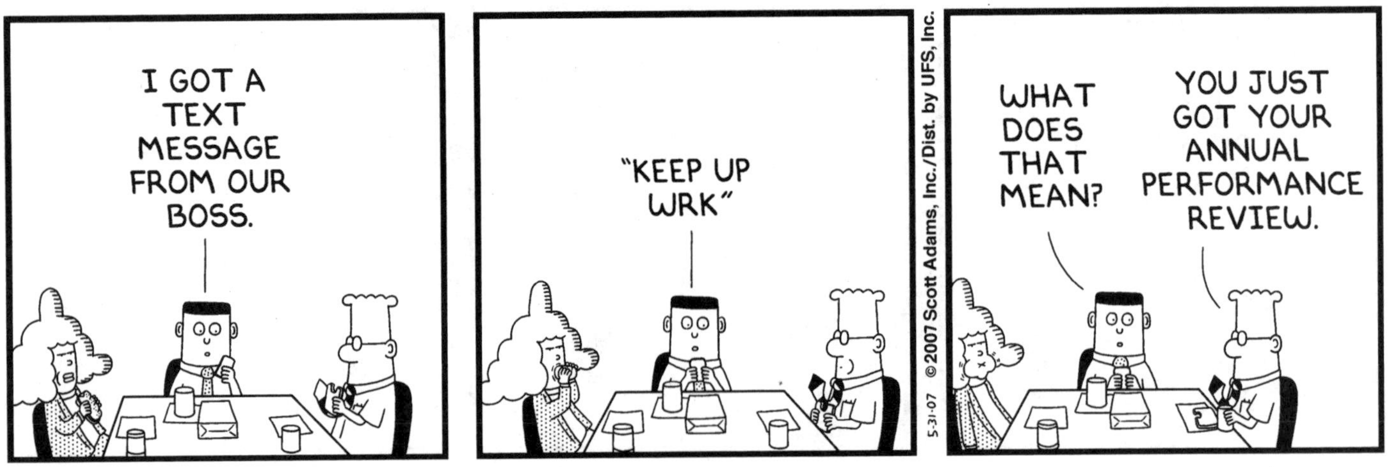
I GOT A TEXT MESSAGE FROM OUR BOSS.
"KEEP UP WRK"
5-31-07 © 2007 Scott Adams, Inc./Dist. by UFS, Inc.
WHAT DOES THAT MEAN?
YOU JUST GOT YOUR ANNUAL PERFORMANCE REVIEW.

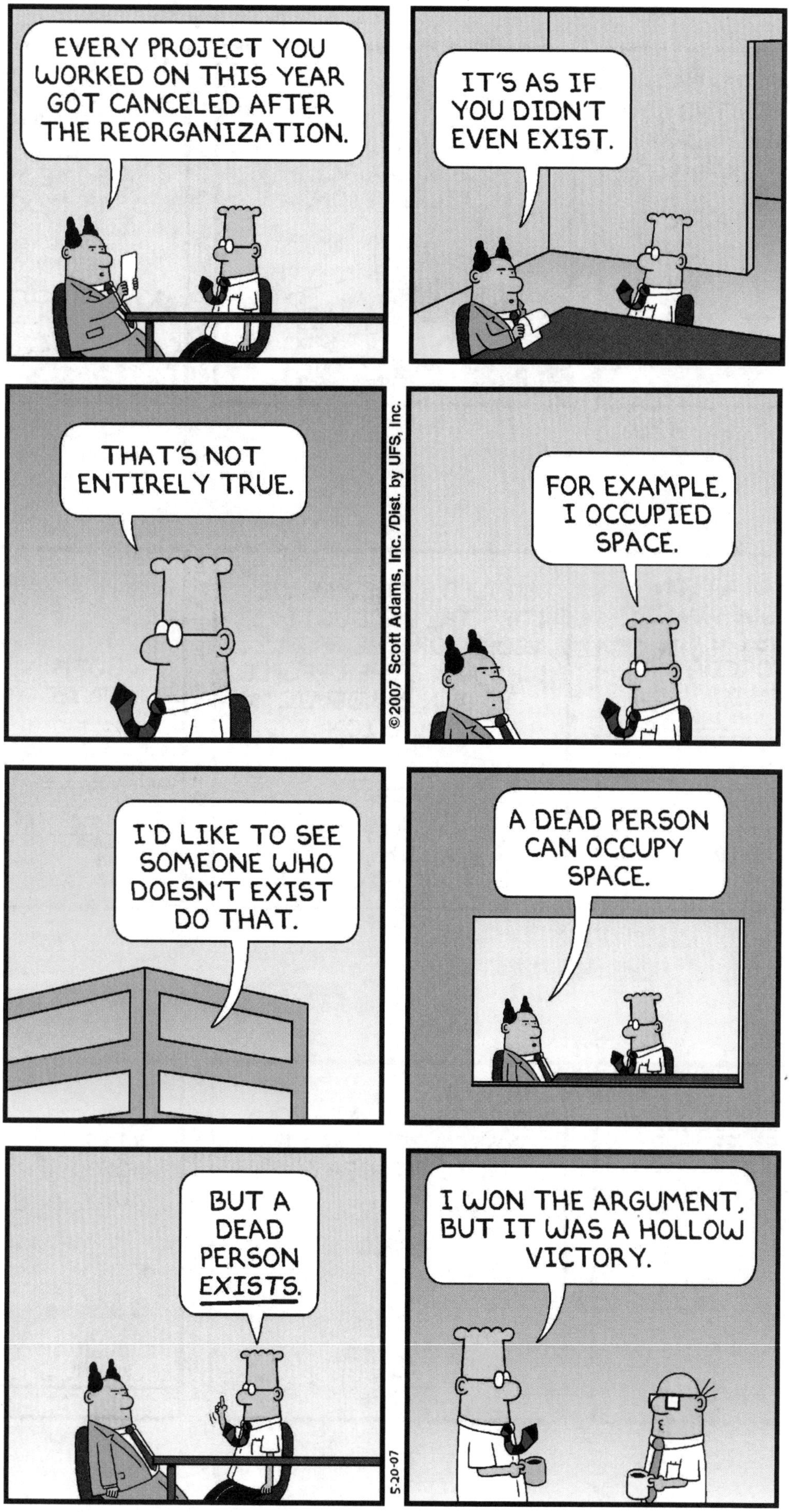
EVERY PROJECT YOU WORKED ON THIS YEAR GOT CANCELED AFTER THE REORGANIZATION.
IT'S AS IF YOU DIDN'T EVEN EXIST.
THAT'S NOT ENTIRELY TRUE.
FOR EXAMPLE, I OCCUPIED SPACE.
I'D LIKE TO SEE SOMEONE WHO DOESN'T EXIST DO THAT.
A DEAD PERSON CAN OCCUPY SPACE.
BUT A DEAD PERSON EXISTS.
I WON THE ARGUMENT, BUT IT WAS A HOLLOW VICTORY.
©2007 Scott Adams, Inc. /Dist. by UFS, Inc.
5-20-07

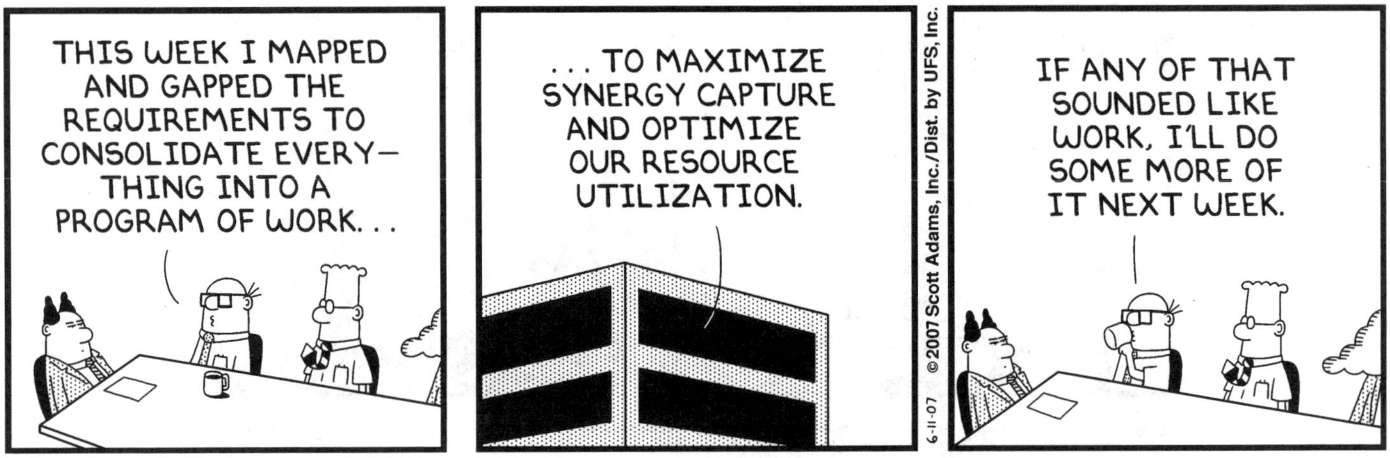
THIS WEEK I MAPPED AND GAPPED THE REQUIREMENTS TO CONSOLIDATE EVERY-THING INTO A PROGRAM OF WORK...
... TO MAXIMIZE SYNERGY CAPTURE AND OPTIMIZE OUR RESOURCE UTILIZATION.
6-11-07 ©2007 Scott Adams, Inc./Dist. by UFS, Inc.
IF ANY OF THAT SOUNDED LIKE WORK, I'LL DO SOME MORE OF IT NEXT WEEK.

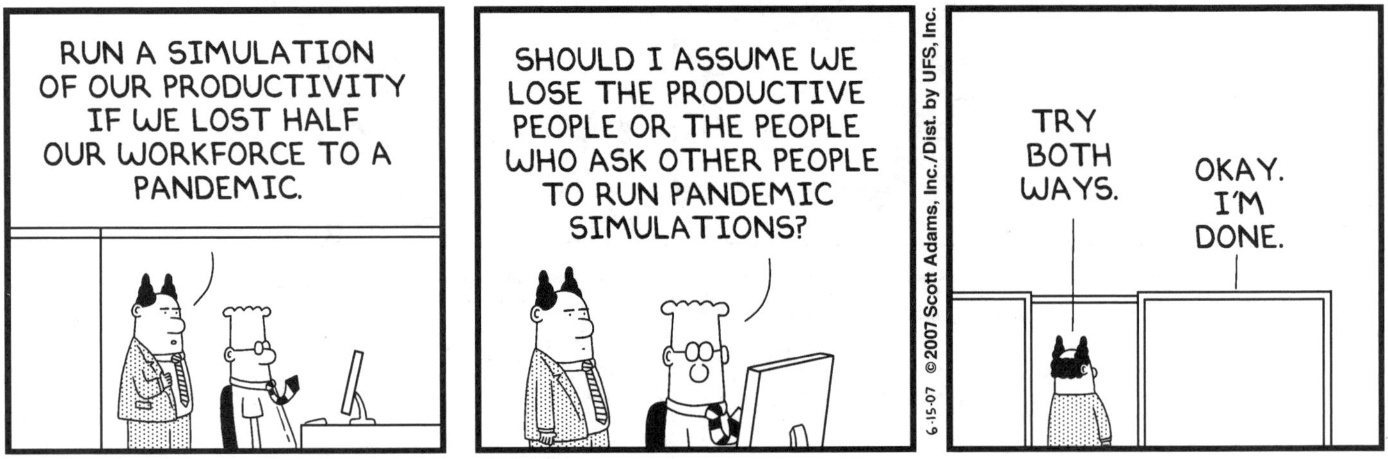
RUN A SIMULATION OF OUR PRODUCTIVITY IF WE LOST HALF OUR WORKFORCE TO A PANDEMIC.
SHOULD I ASSUME WE LOSE THE PRODUCTIVE PEOPLE OR THE PEOPLE WHO ASK OTHER PEOPLE TO RUN PANDEMIC SIMULATIONS?
6-15-07 ©2007 Scott Adams, Inc./Dist. by UFS, Inc.
TRY BOTH WAYS.
OKAY. I'M DONE.

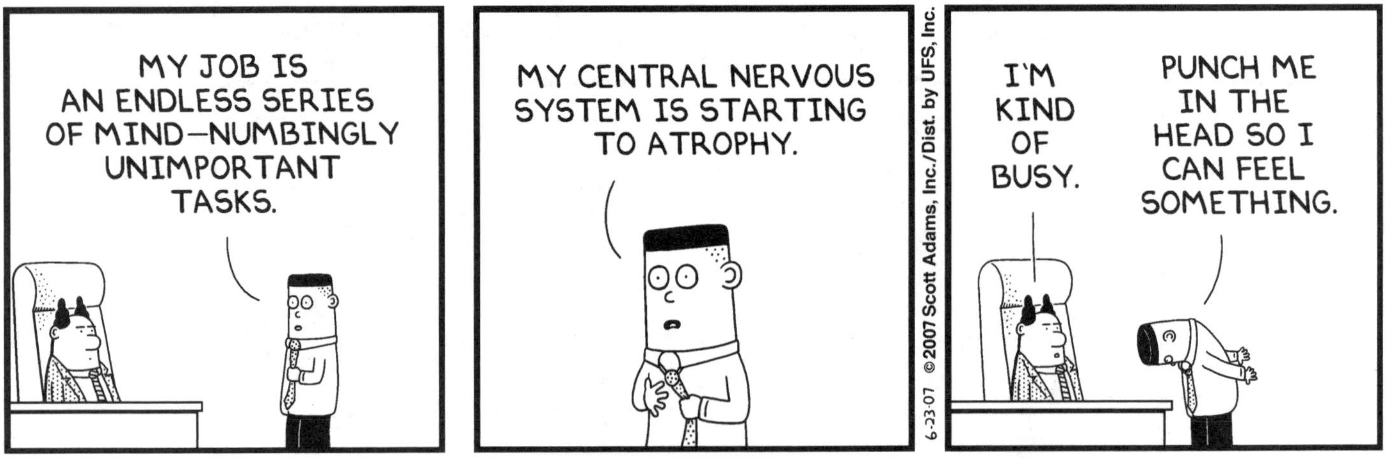
MY JOB IS AN ENDLESS SERIES OF MIND-NUMBINGLY UNIMPORTANT TASKS.
MY CENTRAL NERVOUS SYSTEM IS STARTING TO ATROPHY.
6-23-07 ©2007 Scott Adams, Inc./Dist. by UFS, Inc.
I'M KIND OF BUSY.
PUNCH ME IN THE HEAD SO I CAN FEEL SOMETHING.

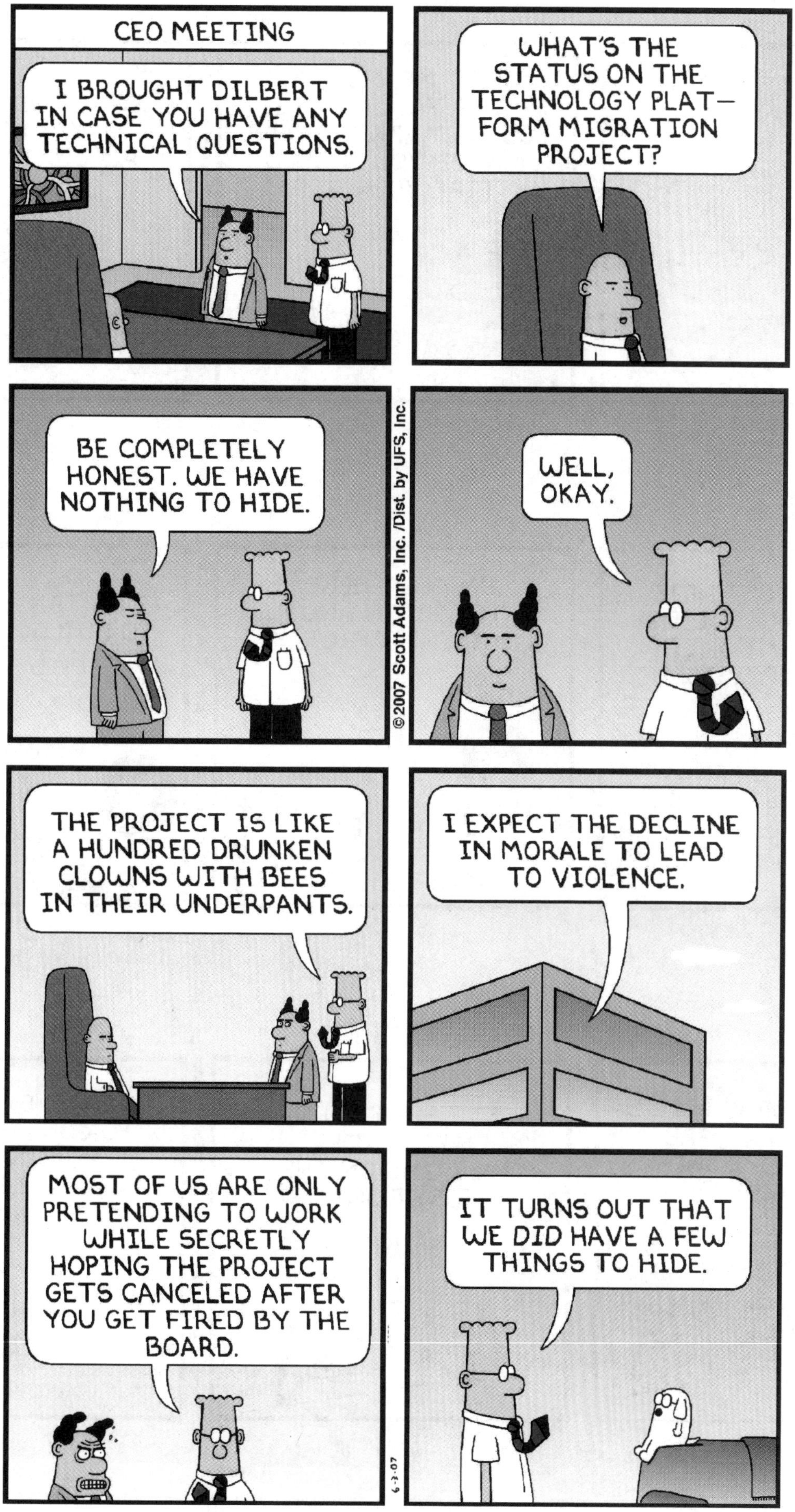
CEO MEETING
I BROUGHT DILBERT IN CASE YOU HAVE ANY TECHNICAL QUESTIONS.
WHAT'S THE STATUS ON THE TECHNOLOGY PLAT-FORM MIGRATION PROJECT?
BE COMPLETELY HONEST. WE HAVE NOTHING TO HIDE.
WELL, OKAY.
©2007 Scott Adams, Inc./Dist. by UFS, Inc.
THE PROJECT IS LIKE A HUNDRED DRUNKEN CLOWNS WITH BEES IN THEIR UNDERPANTS.
I EXPECT THE DECLINE IN MORALE TO LEAD TO VIOLENCE.
MOST OF US ARE ONLY PRETENDING TO WORK WHILE SECRETLY HOPING THE PROJECT GETS CANCELED AFTER YOU GET FIRED BY THE BOARD.
IT TURNS OUT THAT WE *DID* HAVE A FEW THINGS TO HIDE.
6-3-07

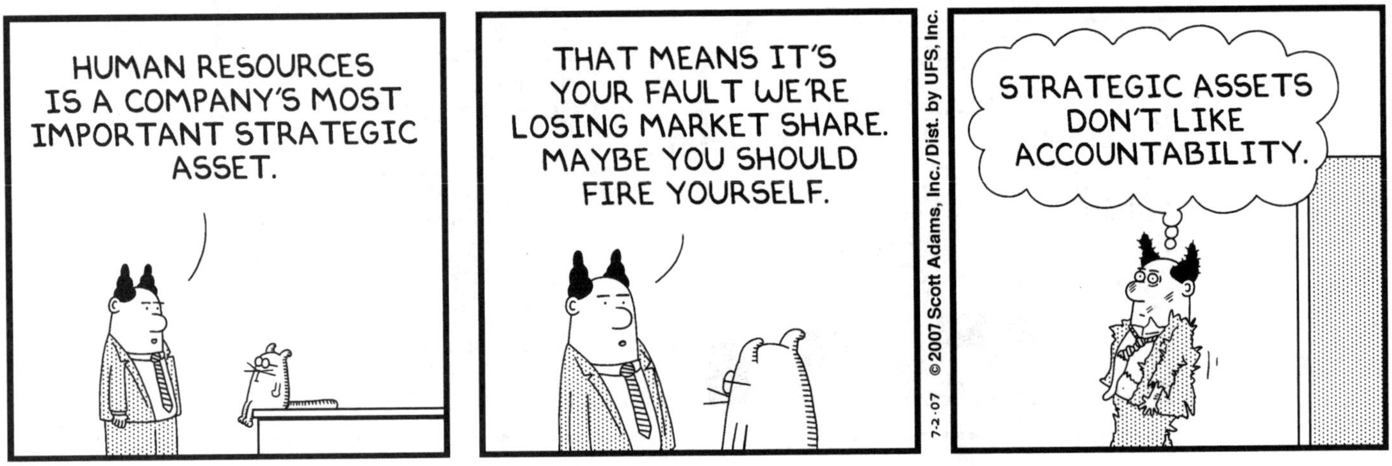
HUMAN RESOURCES IS A COMPANY'S MOST IMPORTANT STRATEGIC ASSET.
THAT MEANS IT'S YOUR FAULT WE'RE LOSING MARKET SHARE. MAYBE YOU SHOULD FIRE YOURSELF.
7-2-07 ©2007 Scott Adams, Inc./Dist. by UFS, Inc.
STRATEGIC ASSETS DON'T LIKE ACCOUNTABILITY.

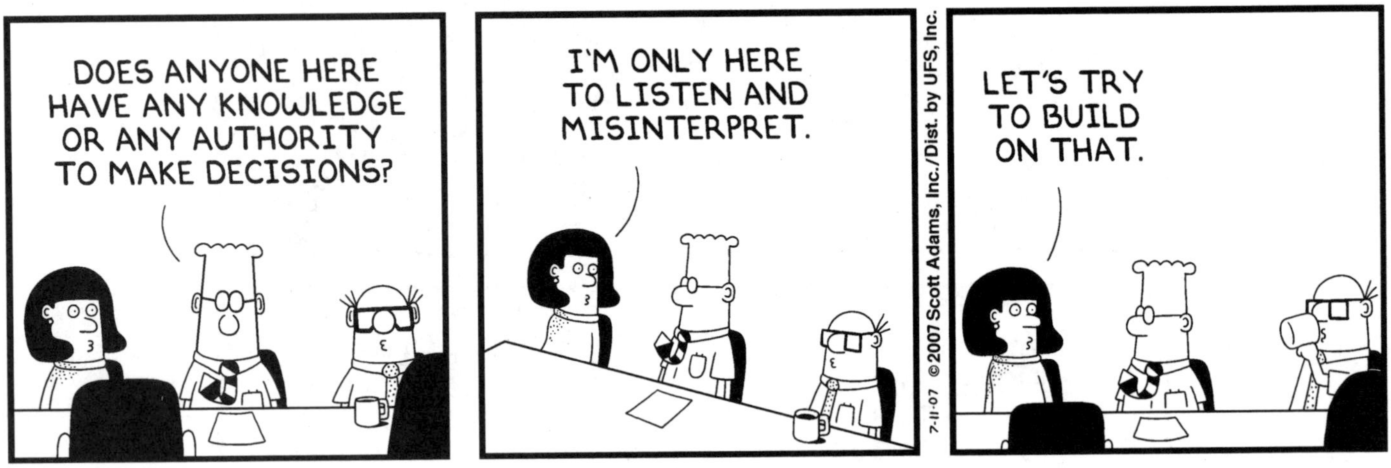
DOES ANYONE HERE HAVE ANY KNOWLEDGE OR ANY AUTHORITY TO MAKE DECISIONS?
I'M ONLY HERE TO LISTEN AND MISINTERPRET.
7-11-07 ©2007 Scott Adams, Inc./Dist. by UFS, Inc.
LET'S TRY TO BUILD ON THAT.

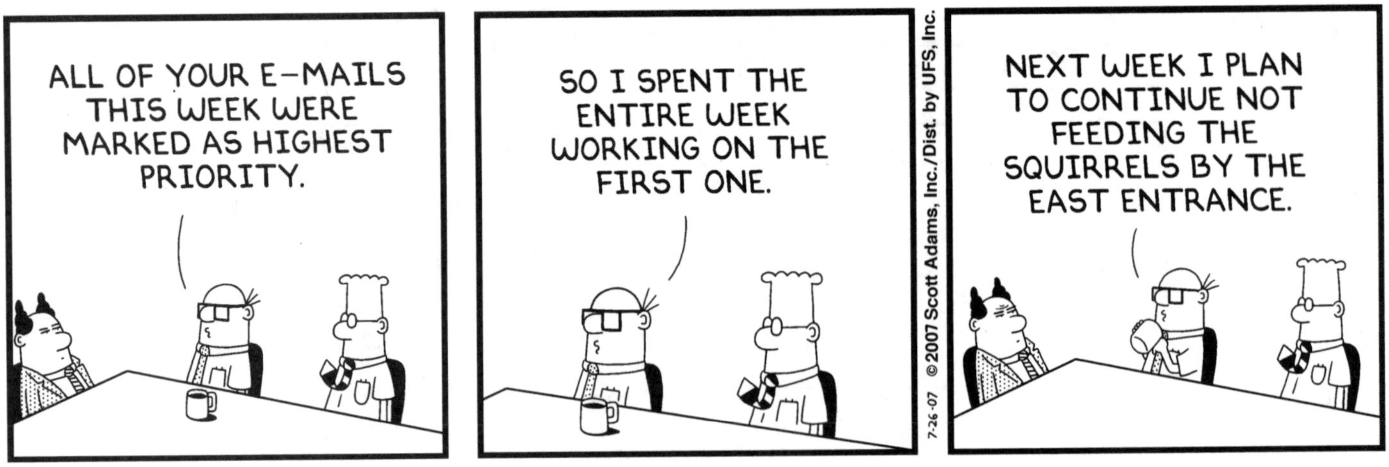
ALL OF YOUR E-MAILS THIS WEEK WERE MARKED AS HIGHEST PRIORITY.
SO I SPENT THE ENTIRE WEEK WORKING ON THE FIRST ONE.
7-26-07 ©2007 Scott Adams, Inc./Dist. by UFS, Inc.
NEXT WEEK I PLAN TO CONTINUE NOT FEEDING THE SQUIRRELS BY THE EAST ENTRANCE.

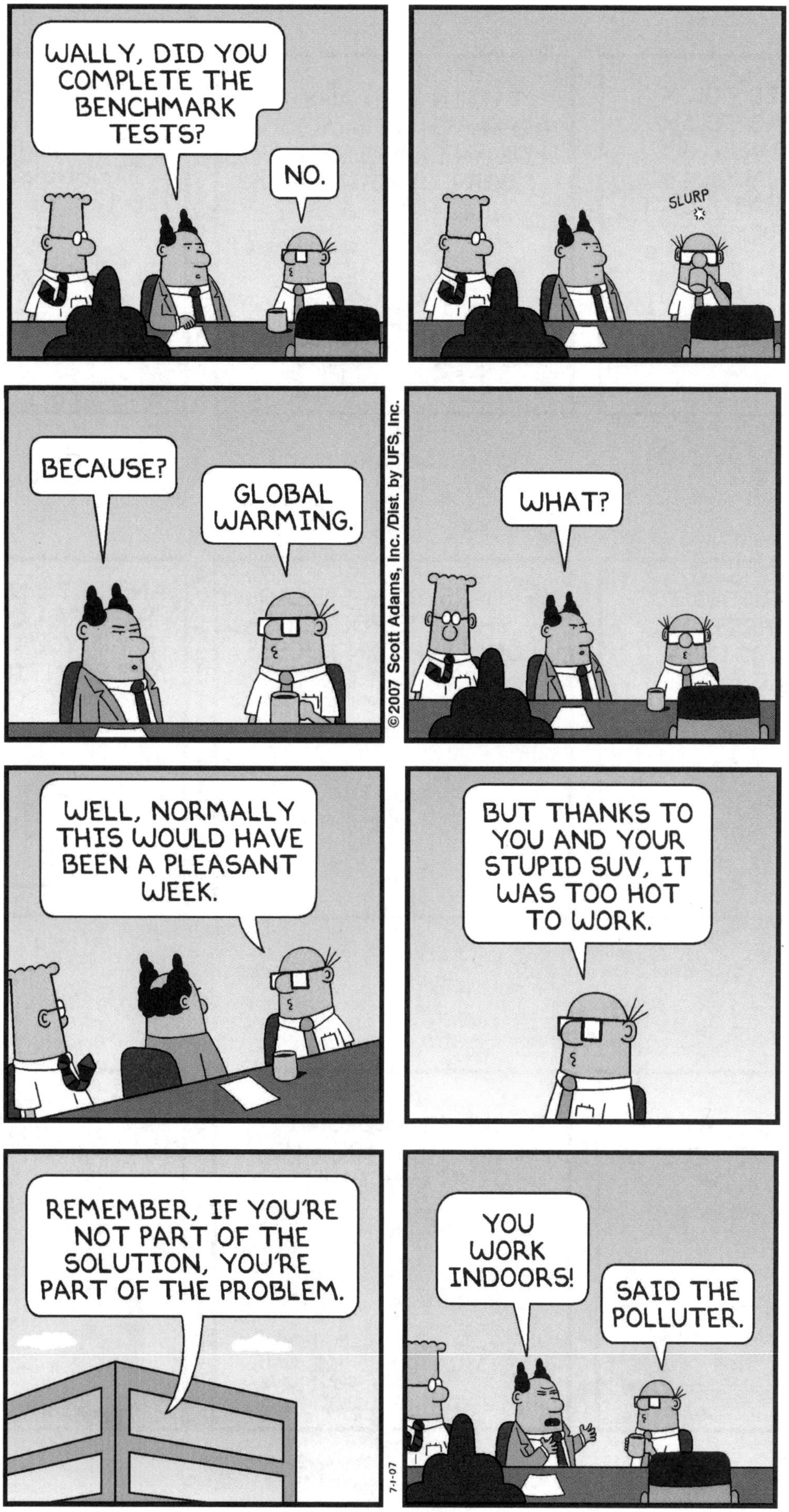
WALLY, DID YOU COMPLETE THE BENCHMARK TESTS?
NO.
SLURP
BECAUSE?
GLOBAL WARMING.
©2007 Scott Adams, Inc./Dist. by UFS, Inc.
WHAT?
WELL, NORMALLY THIS WOULD HAVE BEEN A PLEASANT WEEK.
BUT THANKS TO YOU AND YOUR STUPID SUV, IT WAS TOO HOT TO WORK.
REMEMBER, IF YOU'RE NOT PART OF THE SOLUTION, YOU'RE PART OF THE PROBLEM.
7-1-07
YOU WORK INDOORS!
SAID THE POLLUTER.

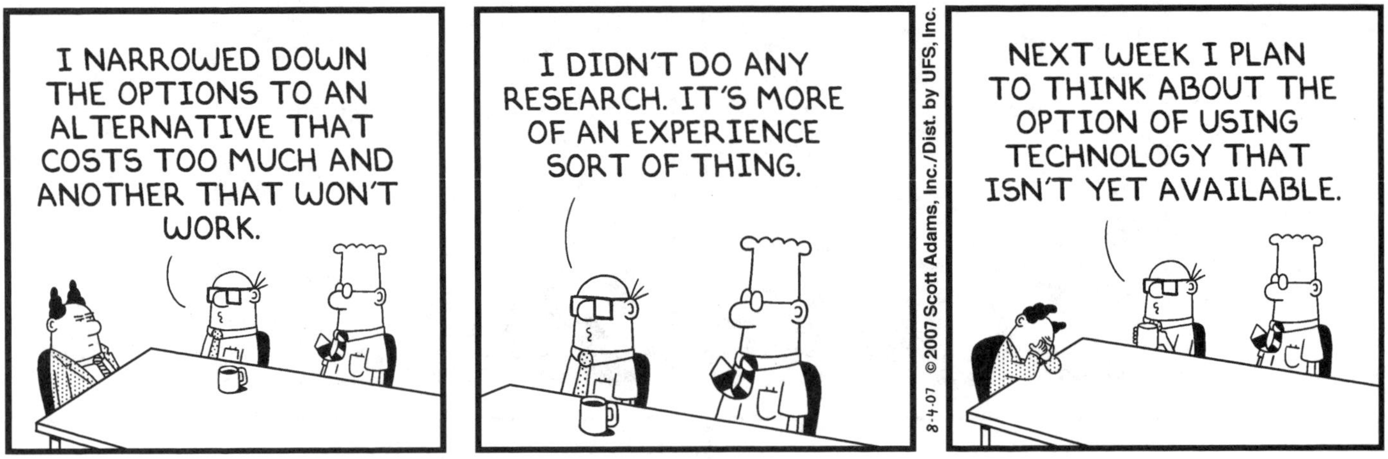
I NARROWED DOWN THE OPTIONS TO AN ALTERNATIVE THAT COSTS TOO MUCH AND ANOTHER THAT WON'T WORK.
I DIDN'T DO ANY RESEARCH. IT'S MORE OF AN EXPERIENCE SORT OF THING.
8-4-07 ©2007 Scott Adams, Inc./Dist. by UFS, Inc.
NEXT WEEK I PLAN TO THINK ABOUT THE OPTION OF USING TECHNOLOGY THAT ISN'T YET AVAILABLE.

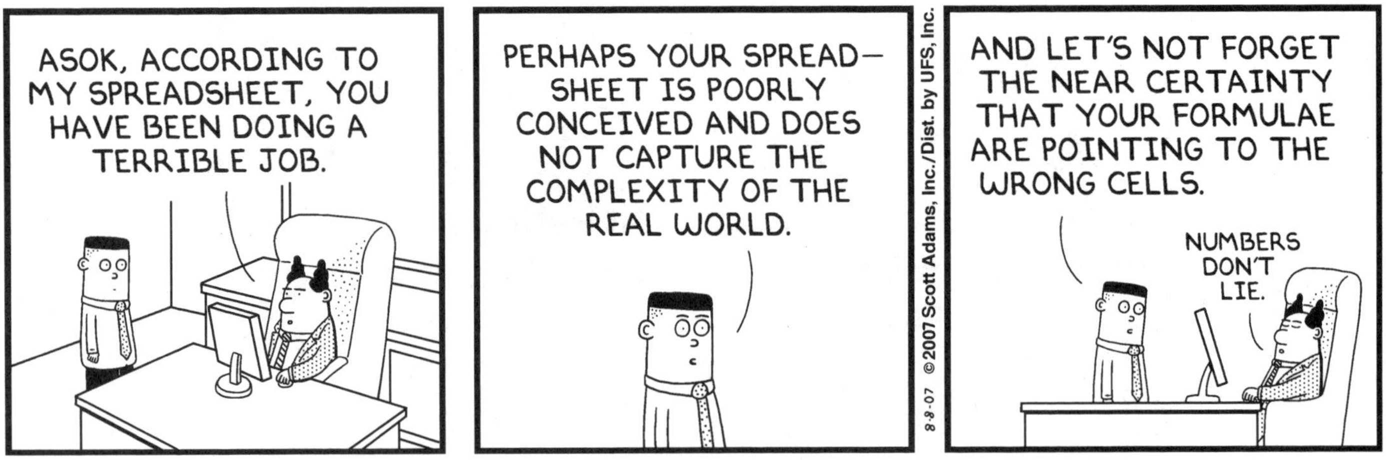
ASOK, ACCORDING TO MY SPREADSHEET, YOU HAVE BEEN DOING A TERRIBLE JOB.
PERHAPS YOUR SPREAD-SHEET IS POORLY CONCEIVED AND DOES NOT CAPTURE THE COMPLEXITY OF THE REAL WORLD.
8-8-07 ©2007 Scott Adams, Inc./Dist. by UFS, Inc.
AND LET'S NOT FORGET THE NEAR CERTAINTY THAT YOUR FORMULAE ARE POINTING TO THE WRONG CELLS.
NUMBERS DON'T LIE.

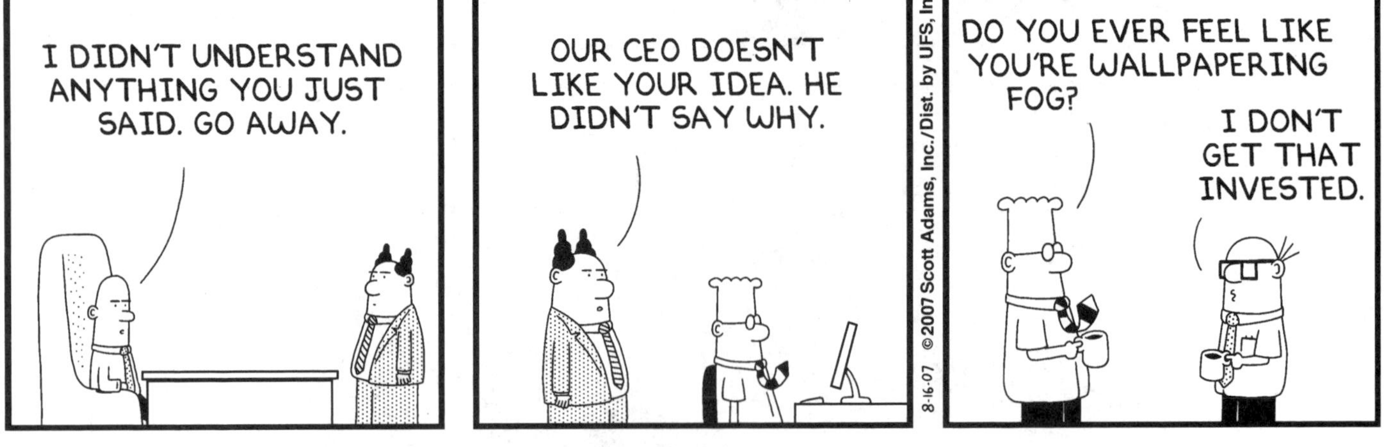
I DIDN'T UNDERSTAND ANYTHING YOU JUST SAID. GO AWAY.
OUR CEO DOESN'T LIKE YOUR IDEA. HE DIDN'T SAY WHY.
8-16-07 ©2007 Scott Adams, Inc./Dist. by UFS, Inc.
DO YOU EVER FEEL LIKE YOU'RE WALLPAPERING FOG?
I DON'T GET THAT INVESTED.

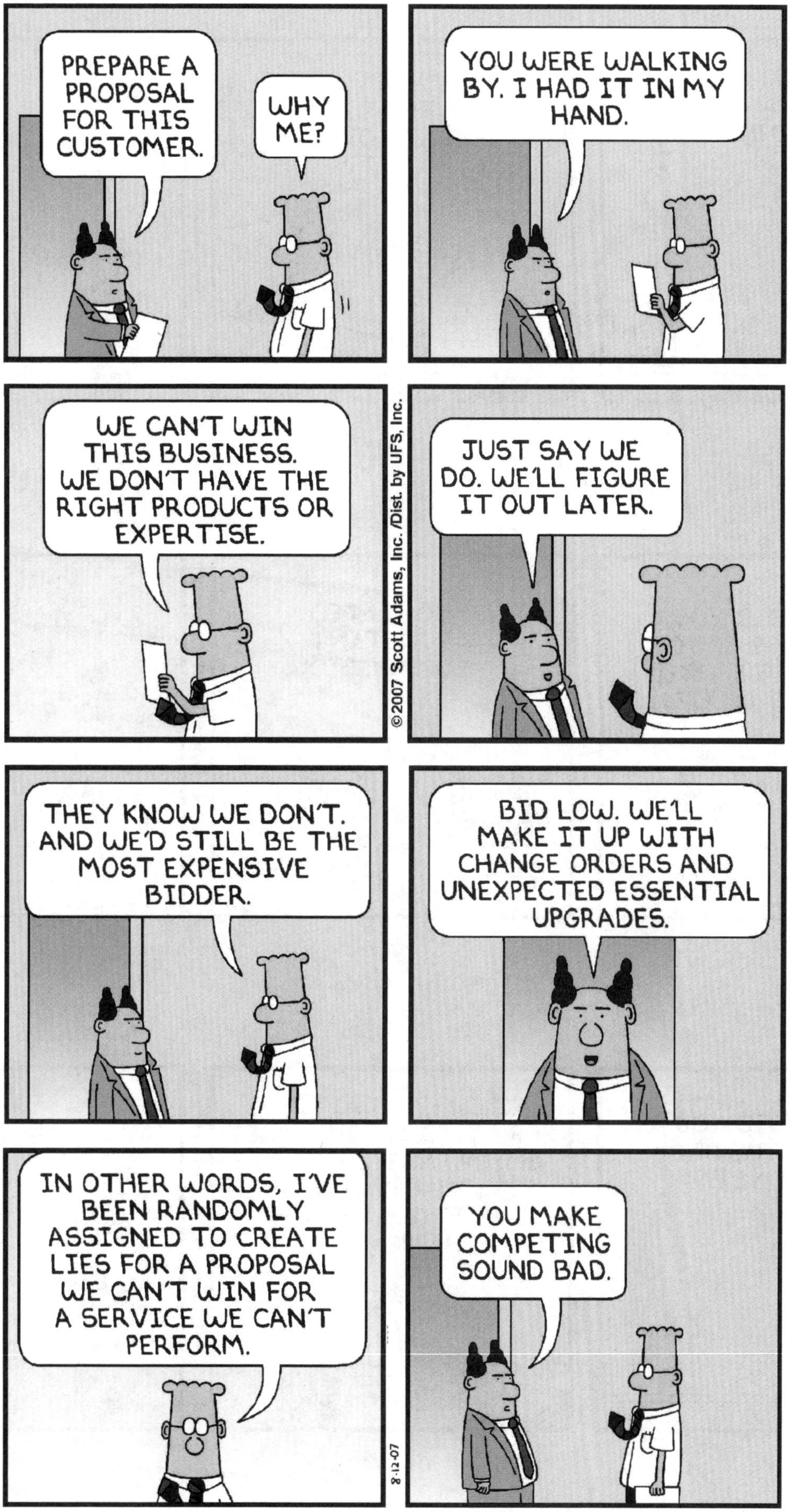
PREPARE A PROPOSAL FOR THIS CUSTOMER.
WHY ME?
YOU WERE WALKING BY. I HAD IT IN MY HAND.
WE CAN'T WIN THIS BUSINESS. WE DON'T HAVE THE RIGHT PRODUCTS OR EXPERTISE.
©2007 Scott Adams, Inc./Dist. by UFS, Inc.
JUST SAY WE DO. WE'LL FIGURE IT OUT LATER.
THEY KNOW WE DON'T. AND WE'D STILL BE THE MOST EXPENSIVE BIDDER.
BID LOW. WE'LL MAKE IT UP WITH CHANGE ORDERS AND UNEXPECTED ESSENTIAL UPGRADES.
IN OTHER WORDS, I'VE BEEN RANDOMLY ASSIGNED TO CREATE LIES FOR A PROPOSAL WE CAN'T WIN FOR A SERVICE WE CAN'T PERFORM.
8-12-07
YOU MAKE COMPETING SOUND BAD.

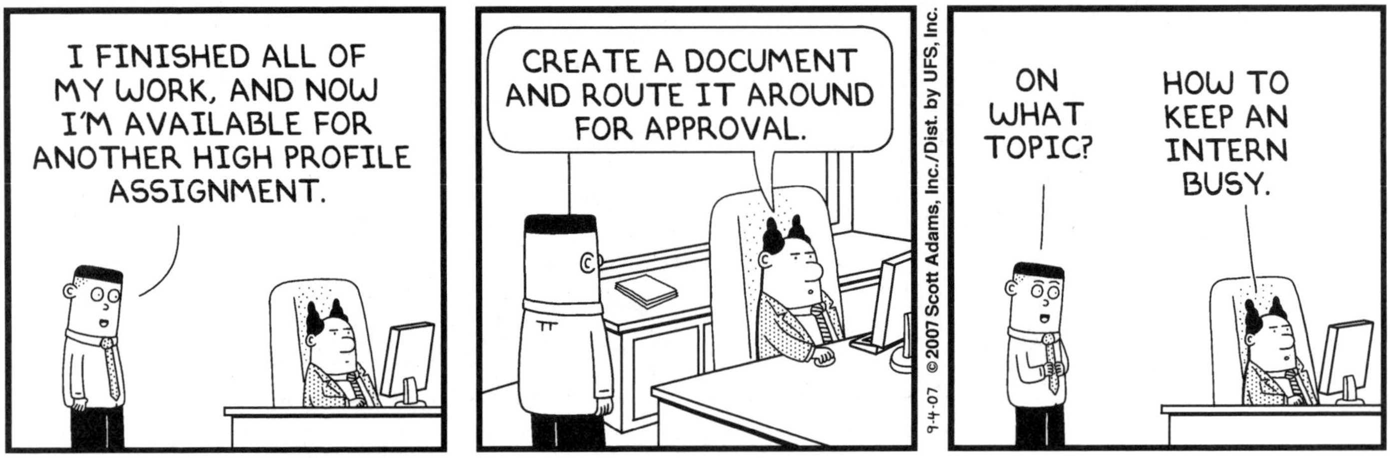
I FINISHED ALL OF MY WORK, AND NOW I'M AVAILABLE FOR ANOTHER HIGH PROFILE ASSIGNMENT.
CREATE A DOCUMENT AND ROUTE IT AROUND FOR APPROVAL.
ON WHAT TOPIC?
HOW TO KEEP AN INTERN BUSY.
9-4-07

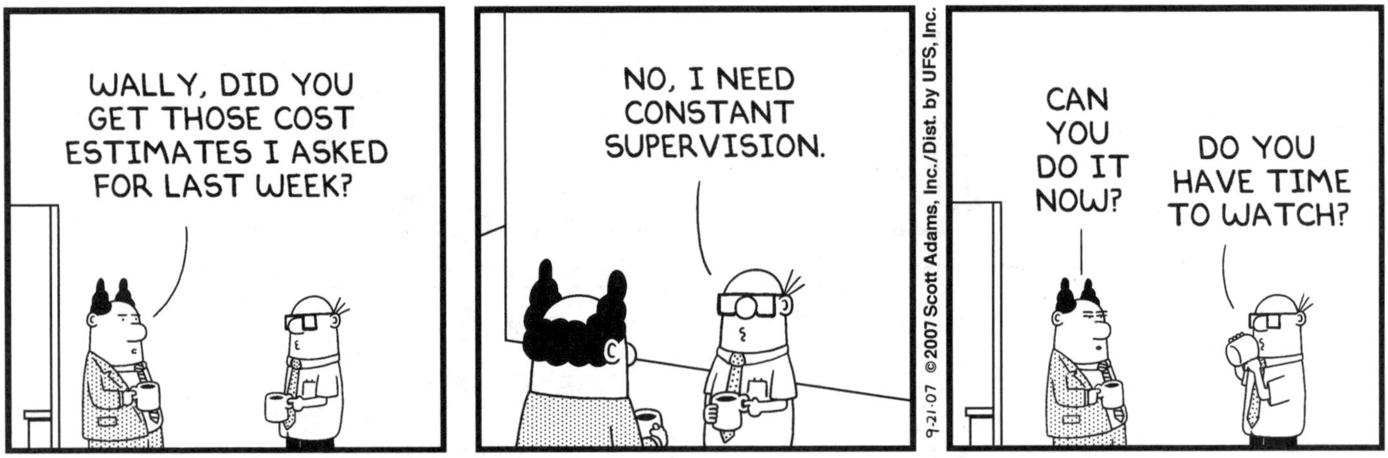
WALLY, DID YOU GET THOSE COST ESTIMATES I ASKED FOR LAST WEEK?
NO, I NEED CONSTANT SUPERVISION.
CAN YOU DO IT NOW?
DO YOU HAVE TIME TO WATCH?
9-21-07

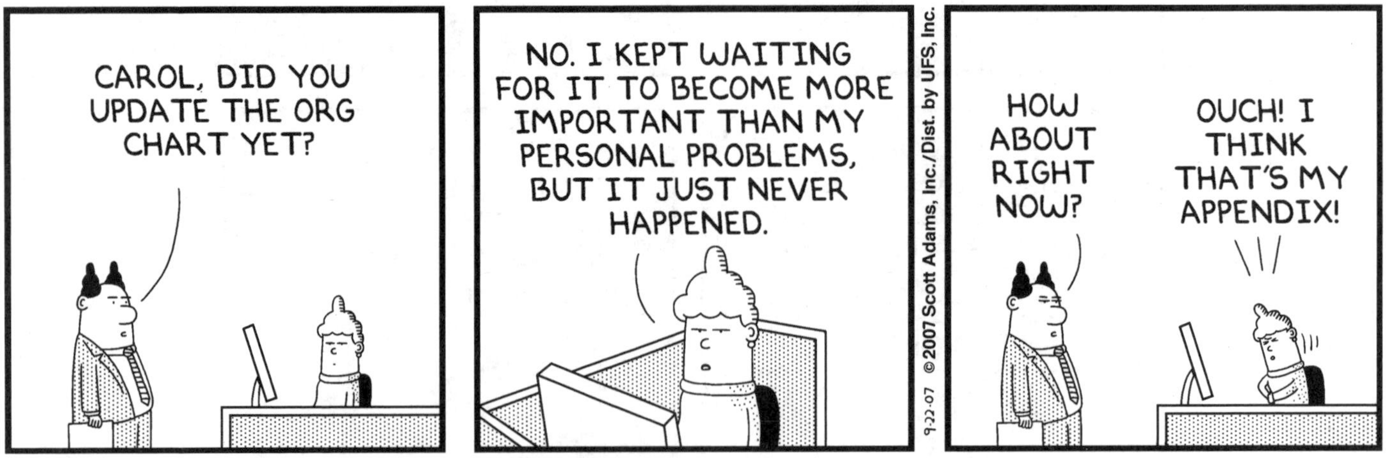
CAROL, DID YOU UPDATE THE ORG CHART YET?
NO. I KEPT WAITING FOR IT TO BECOME MORE IMPORTANT THAN MY PERSONAL PROBLEMS, BUT IT JUST NEVER HAPPENED.
HOW ABOUT RIGHT NOW?
OUCH! I THINK THAT'S MY APPENDIX!
9-22-07

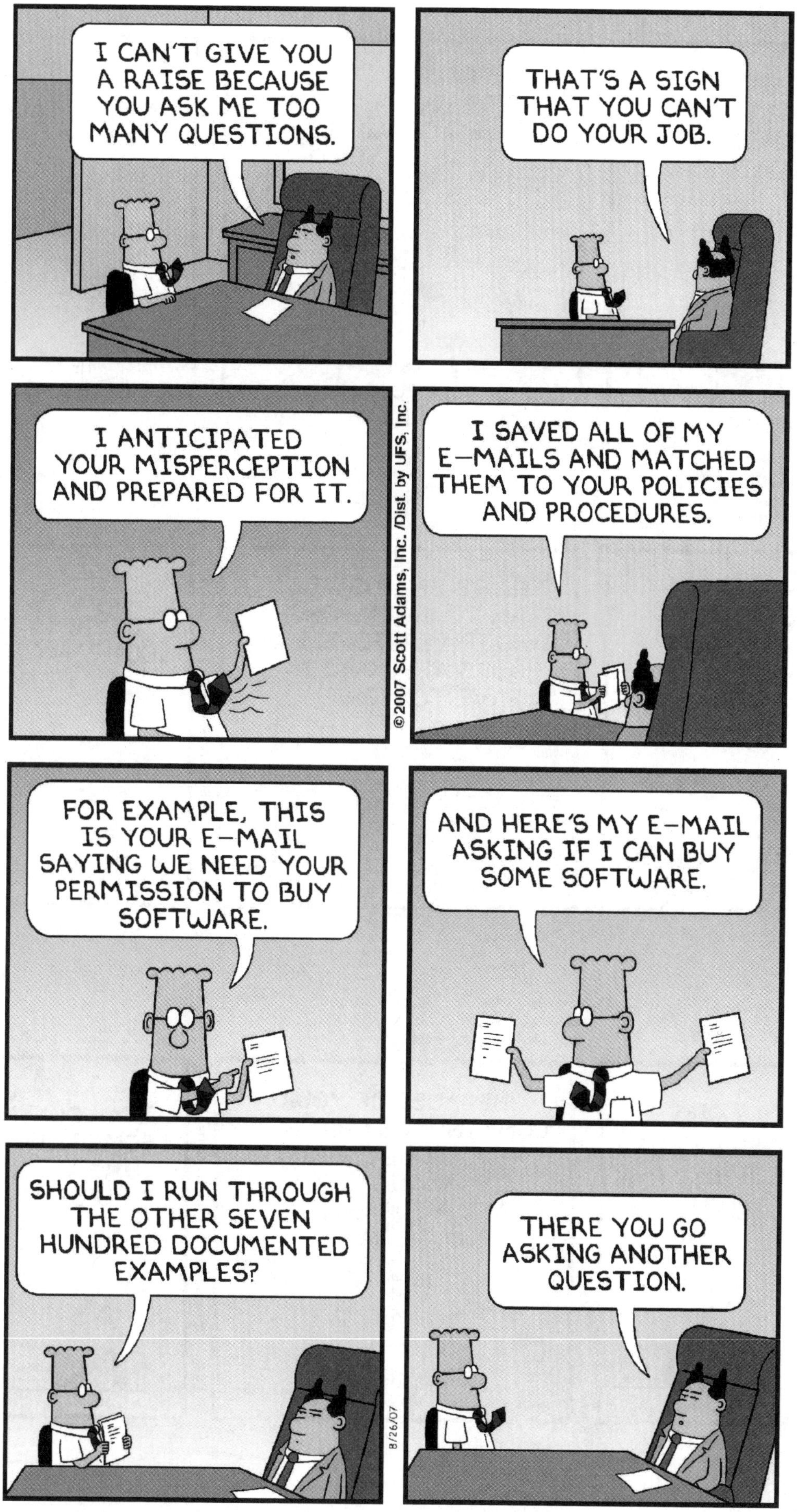
I CAN'T GIVE YOU A RAISE BECAUSE YOU ASK ME TOO MANY QUESTIONS.
THAT'S A SIGN THAT YOU CAN'T DO YOUR JOB.
I ANTICIPATED YOUR MISPERCEPTION AND PREPARED FOR IT.
©2007 Scott Adams, Inc./Dist. by UFS, Inc.
I SAVED ALL OF MY E-MAILS AND MATCHED THEM TO YOUR POLICIES AND PROCEDURES.
FOR EXAMPLE, THIS IS YOUR E-MAIL SAYING WE NEED YOUR PERMISSION TO BUY SOFTWARE.
AND HERE'S MY E-MAIL ASKING IF I CAN BUY SOME SOFTWARE.
SHOULD I RUN THROUGH THE OTHER SEVEN HUNDRED DOCUMENTED EXAMPLES?
8/26/07
THERE YOU GO ASKING ANOTHER QUESTION.

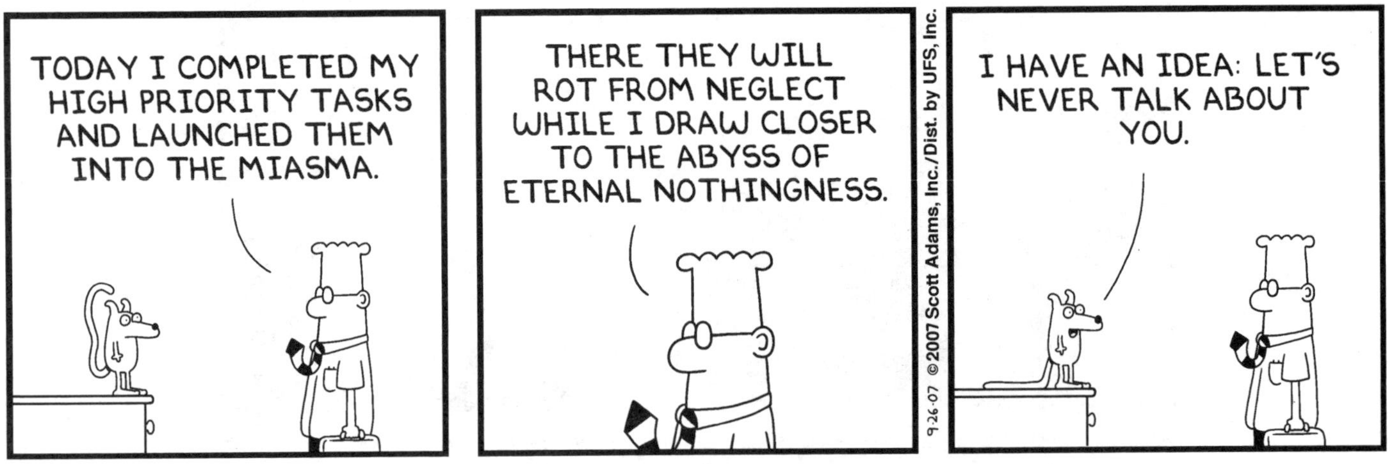
TODAY I COMPLETED MY HIGH PRIORITY TASKS AND LAUNCHED THEM INTO THE MIASMA.
THERE THEY WILL ROT FROM NEGLECT WHILE I DRAW CLOSER TO THE ABYSS OF ETERNAL NOTHINGNESS.
9-26-07 © 2007 Scott Adams, Inc./Dist. by UFS, Inc.
I HAVE AN IDEA: LET'S NEVER TALK ABOUT YOU.

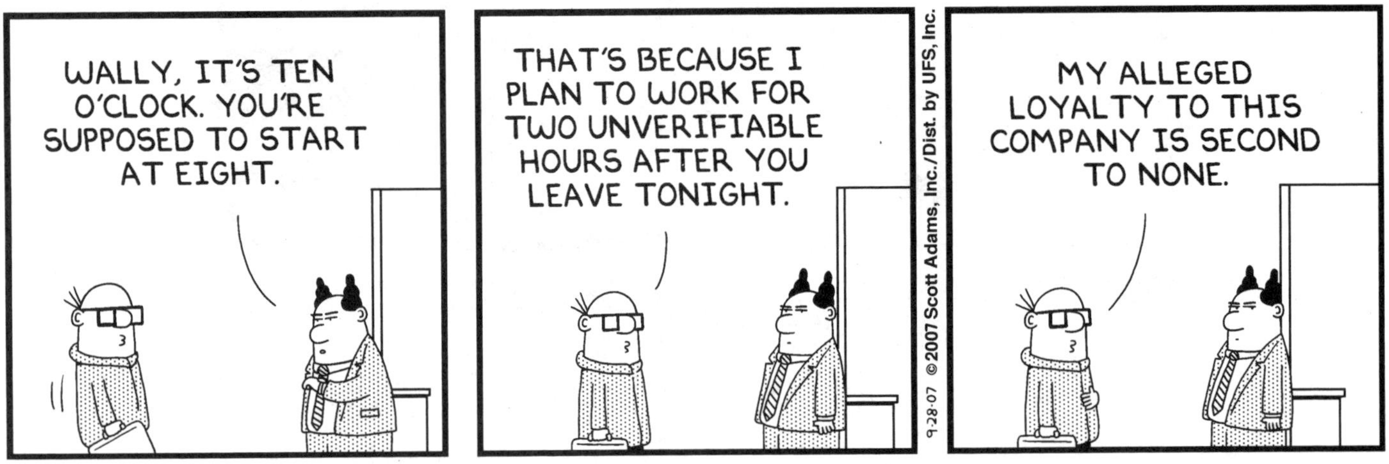
WALLY, IT'S TEN O'CLOCK. YOU'RE SUPPOSED TO START AT EIGHT.
THAT'S BECAUSE I PLAN TO WORK FOR TWO UNVERIFIABLE HOURS AFTER YOU LEAVE TONIGHT.
9-28-07 © 2007 Scott Adams, Inc./Dist. by UFS, Inc.
MY ALLEGED LOYALTY TO THIS COMPANY IS SECOND TO NONE.

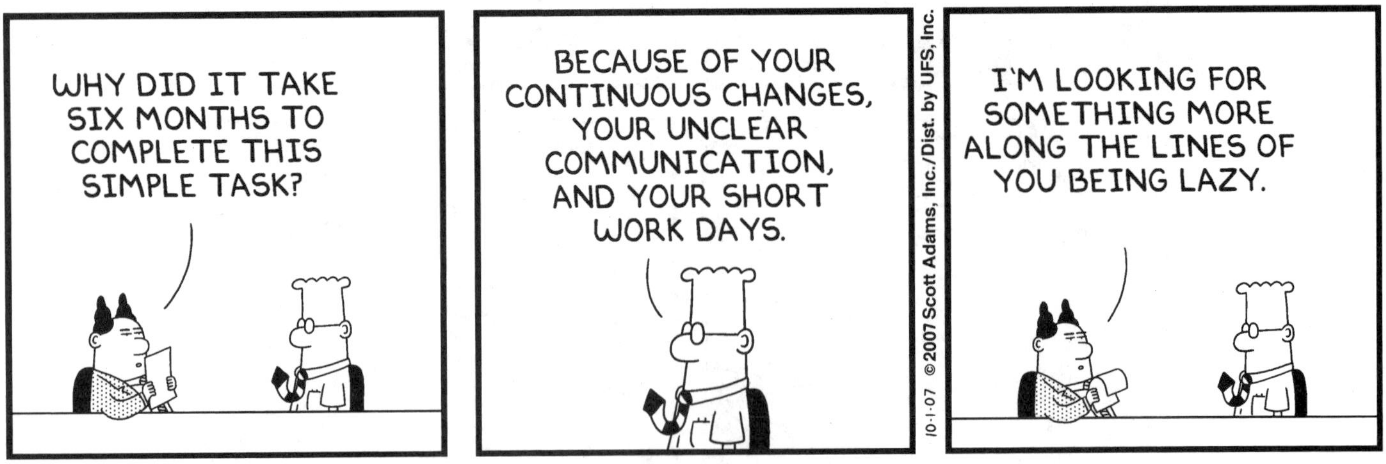
WHY DID IT TAKE SIX MONTHS TO COMPLETE THIS SIMPLE TASK?
BECAUSE OF YOUR CONTINUOUS CHANGES, YOUR UNCLEAR COMMUNICATION, AND YOUR SHORT WORK DAYS.
10-1-07 © 2007 Scott Adams, Inc./Dist. by UFS, Inc.
I'M LOOKING FOR SOMETHING MORE ALONG THE LINES OF YOU BEING LAZY.

I DIDN'T HAVE TIME TO FINISH MY TASKS FOR THIS MEETING.
NO PROBLEM.
IF YOU GET CORNERED, READ THIS POWERFUL ANTI-MEETING SPELL.
ASOK, DID YOU FINISH THE TRAFFIC ESTIMATES?
ERK
UM. . . I WAS WONDERING IF OUR NEW SERVICE IS WEB 2.0 OR WEB 1.0.
©2007 Scott Adams, Inc. /Dist. by UFS, Inc.
OBVIOUSLY IT'S A WEB 2.0 APPLICATION BECAUSE OF THE TAG-BASED FOLKSONOMIES
NO IT ISN'T. ALL OF OUR TECHNOLOGY EXISTED BEFORE THE INTERNET BUBBLE.
"WHEN" DOESN'T MATTER. IT ONLY MATTERS THAT WE USE THE WEB AS A PLATFORM!
9-9-07
EVERY-THING IS A PLAT-FORM!
FREAKY.

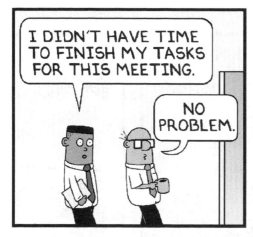

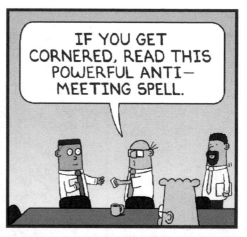

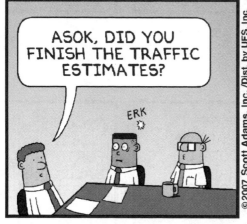

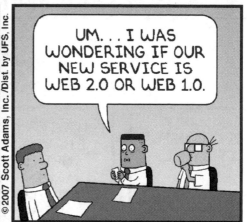

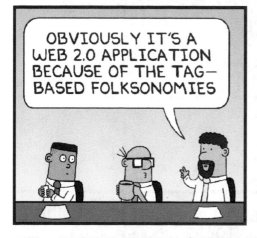

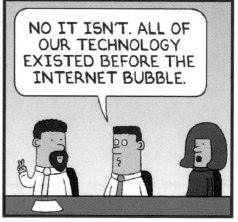

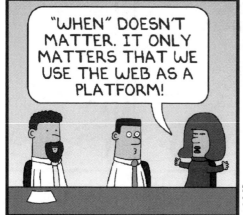

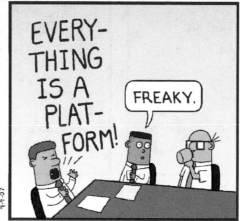

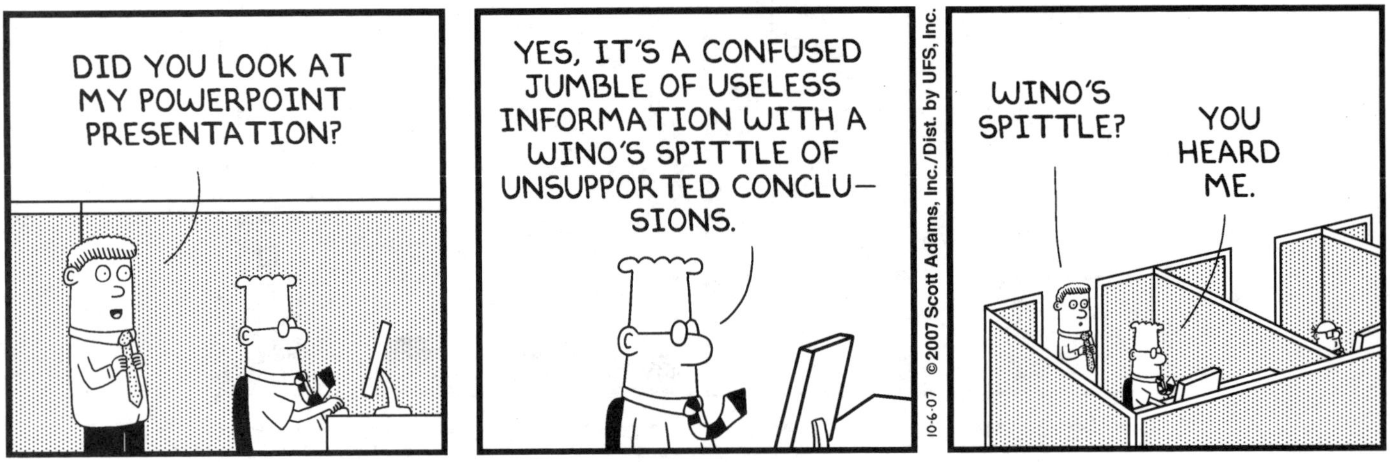
DID YOU LOOK AT MY POWERPOINT PRESENTATION?
YES, IT'S A CONFUSED JUMBLE OF USELESS INFORMATION WITH A WINO'S SPITTLE OF UNSUPPORTED CONCLU-SIONS.
WINO'S SPITTLE?
YOU HEARD ME.

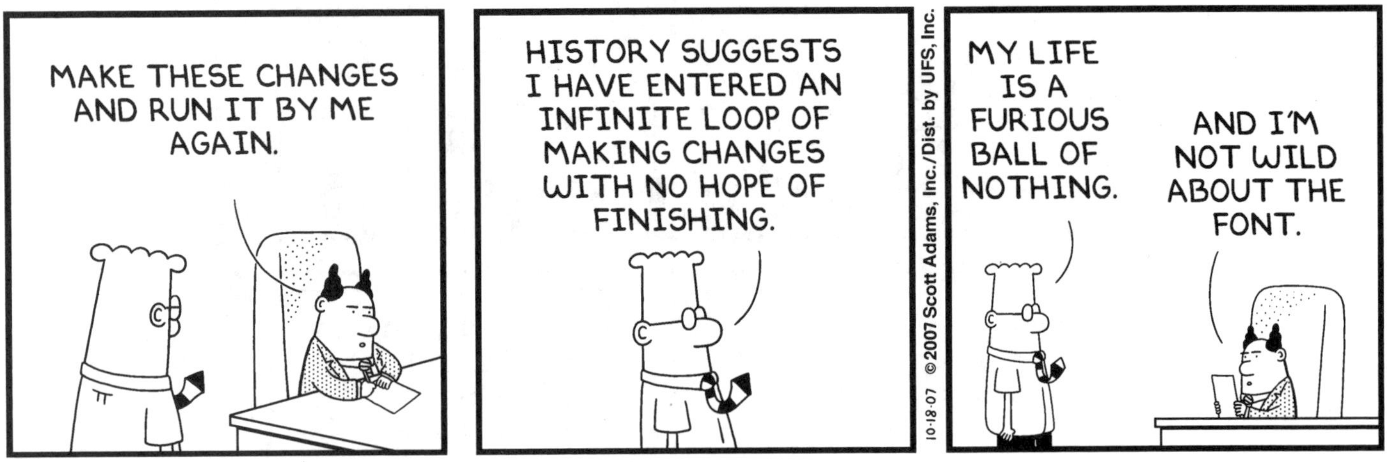
MAKE THESE CHANGES AND RUN IT BY ME AGAIN.
HISTORY SUGGESTS I HAVE ENTERED AN INFINITE LOOP OF MAKING CHANGES WITH NO HOPE OF FINISHING.
MY LIFE IS A FURIOUS BALL OF NOTHING.
AND I'M NOT WILD ABOUT THE FONT.

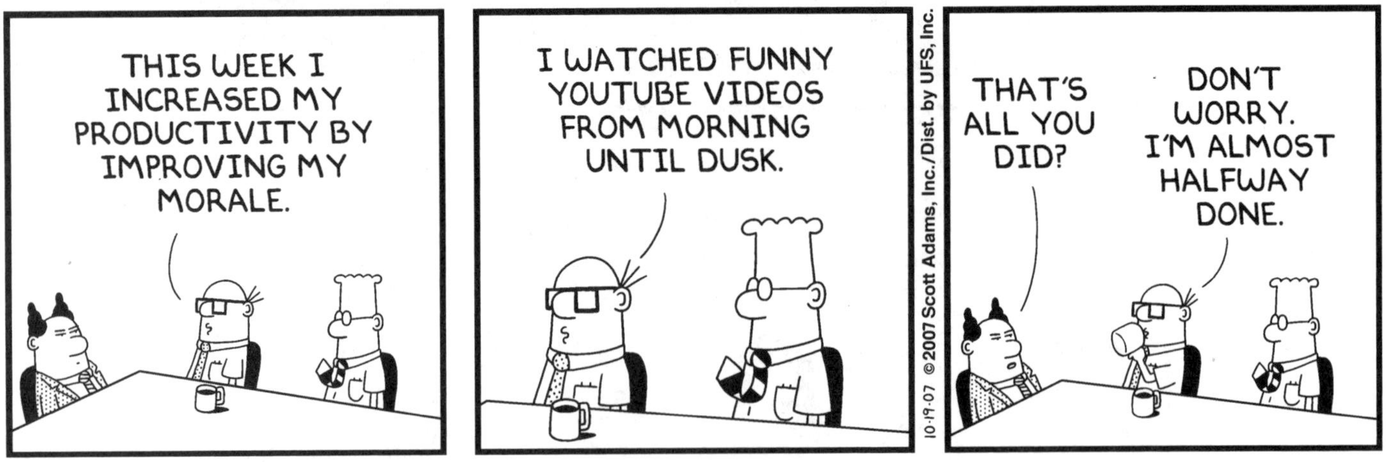
THIS WEEK I INCREASED MY PRODUCTIVITY BY IMPROVING MY MORALE.
I WATCHED FUNNY YOUTUBE VIDEOS FROM MORNING UNTIL DUSK.
THAT'S ALL YOU DID?
DON'T WORRY. I'M ALMOST HALFWAY DONE.

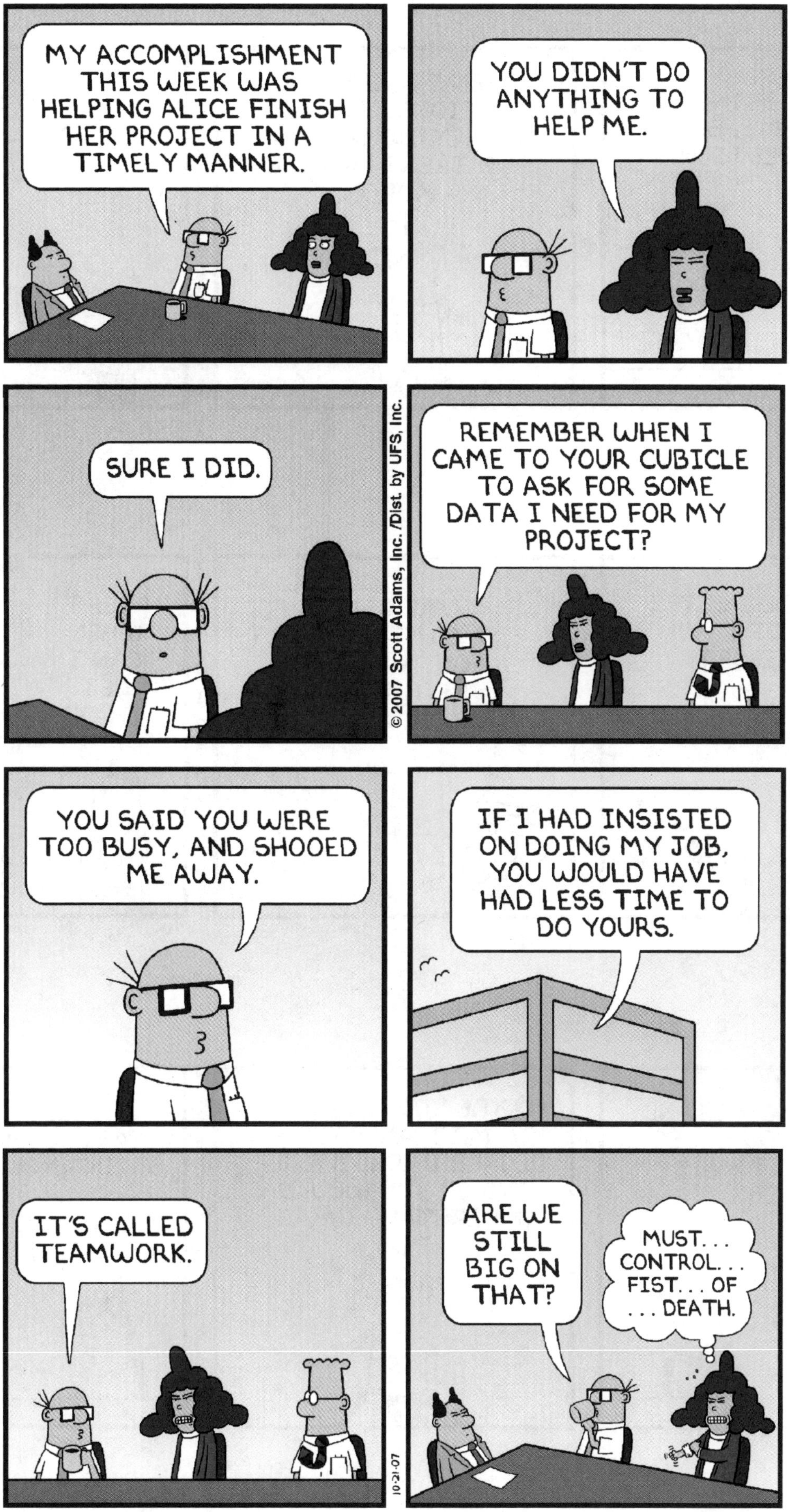
MY ACCOMPLISHMENT THIS WEEK WAS HELPING ALICE FINISH HER PROJECT IN A TIMELY MANNER.
YOU DIDN'T DO ANYTHING TO HELP ME.
SURE I DID.
REMEMBER WHEN I CAME TO YOUR CUBICLE TO ASK FOR SOME DATA I NEED FOR MY PROJECT?
©2007 Scott Adams, Inc. /Dist. by UFS, Inc.
YOU SAID YOU WERE TOO BUSY, AND SHOOED ME AWAY.
IF I HAD INSISTED ON DOING MY JOB, YOU WOULD HAVE HAD LESS TIME TO DO YOURS.
IT'S CALLED TEAMWORK.
10-21-07
ARE WE STILL BIG ON THAT?
MUST... CONTROL... FIST... OF ... DEATH.

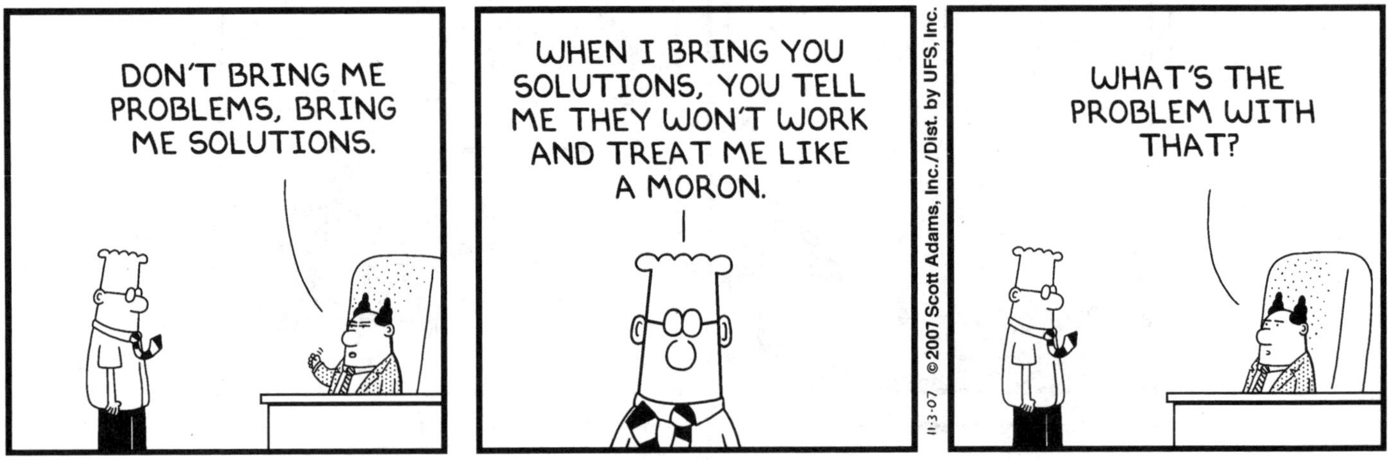
DON'T BRING ME PROBLEMS, BRING ME SOLUTIONS.
WHEN I BRING YOU SOLUTIONS, YOU TELL ME THEY WON'T WORK AND TREAT ME LIKE A MORON.
11-3-07 ©2007 Scott Adams, Inc./Dist. by UFS, Inc.
WHAT'S THE PROBLEM WITH THAT?

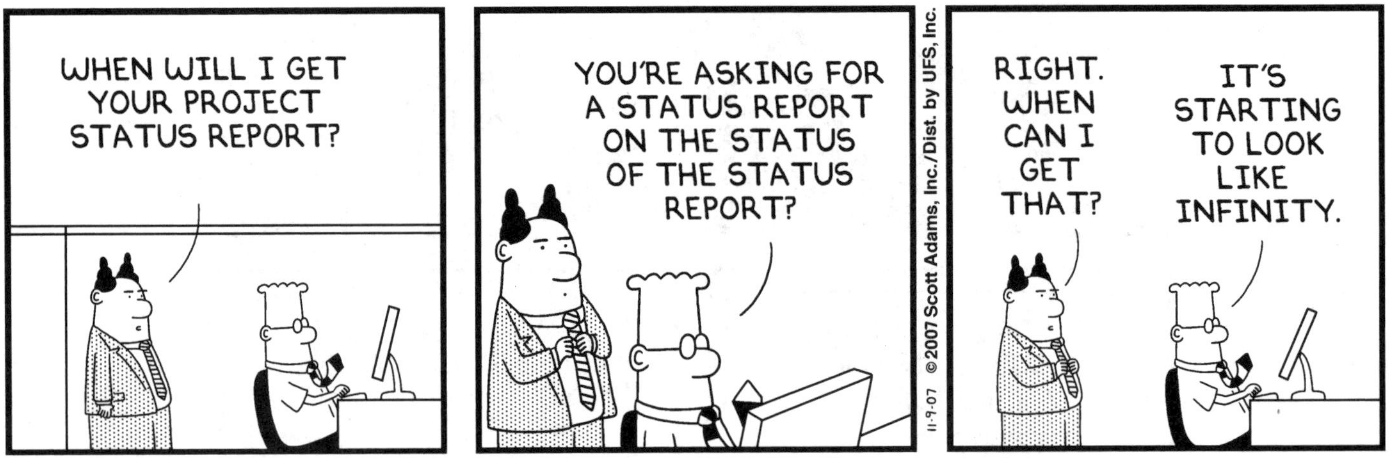
WHEN WILL I GET YOUR PROJECT STATUS REPORT?
YOU'RE ASKING FOR A STATUS REPORT ON THE STATUS OF THE STATUS REPORT?
11-9-07 ©2007 Scott Adams, Inc./Dist. by UFS, Inc.
RIGHT. WHEN CAN I GET THAT?
IT'S STARTING TO LOOK LIKE INFINITY.

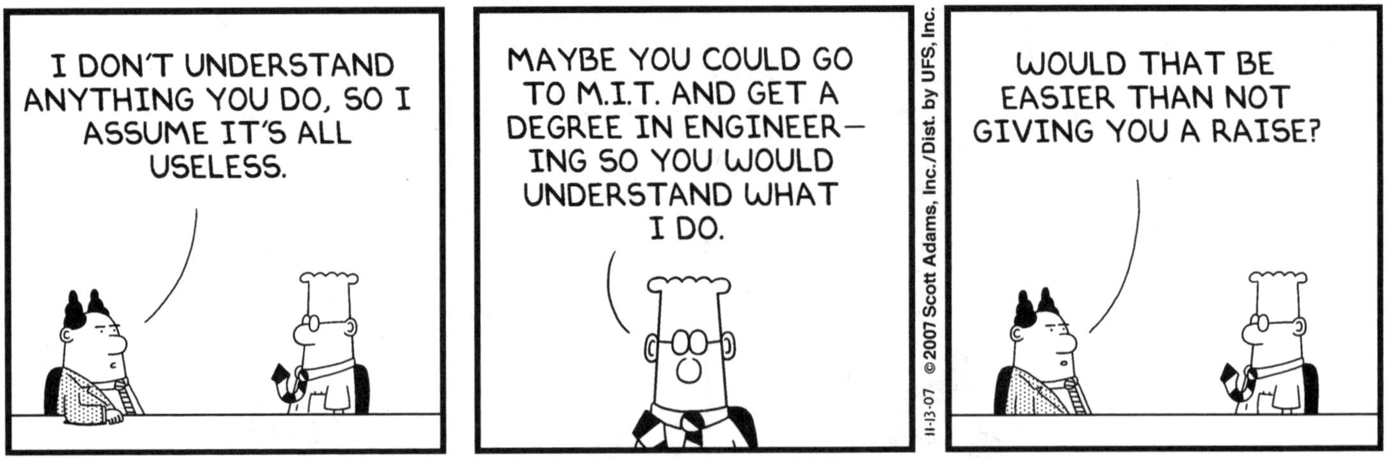
I DON'T UNDERSTAND ANYTHING YOU DO, SO I ASSUME IT'S ALL USELESS.
MAYBE YOU COULD GO TO M.I.T. AND GET A DEGREE IN ENGINEER-ING SO YOU WOULD UNDERSTAND WHAT I DO.
11-13-07 ©2007 Scott Adams, Inc./Dist. by UFS, Inc.
WOULD THAT BE EASIER THAN NOT GIVING YOU A RAISE?

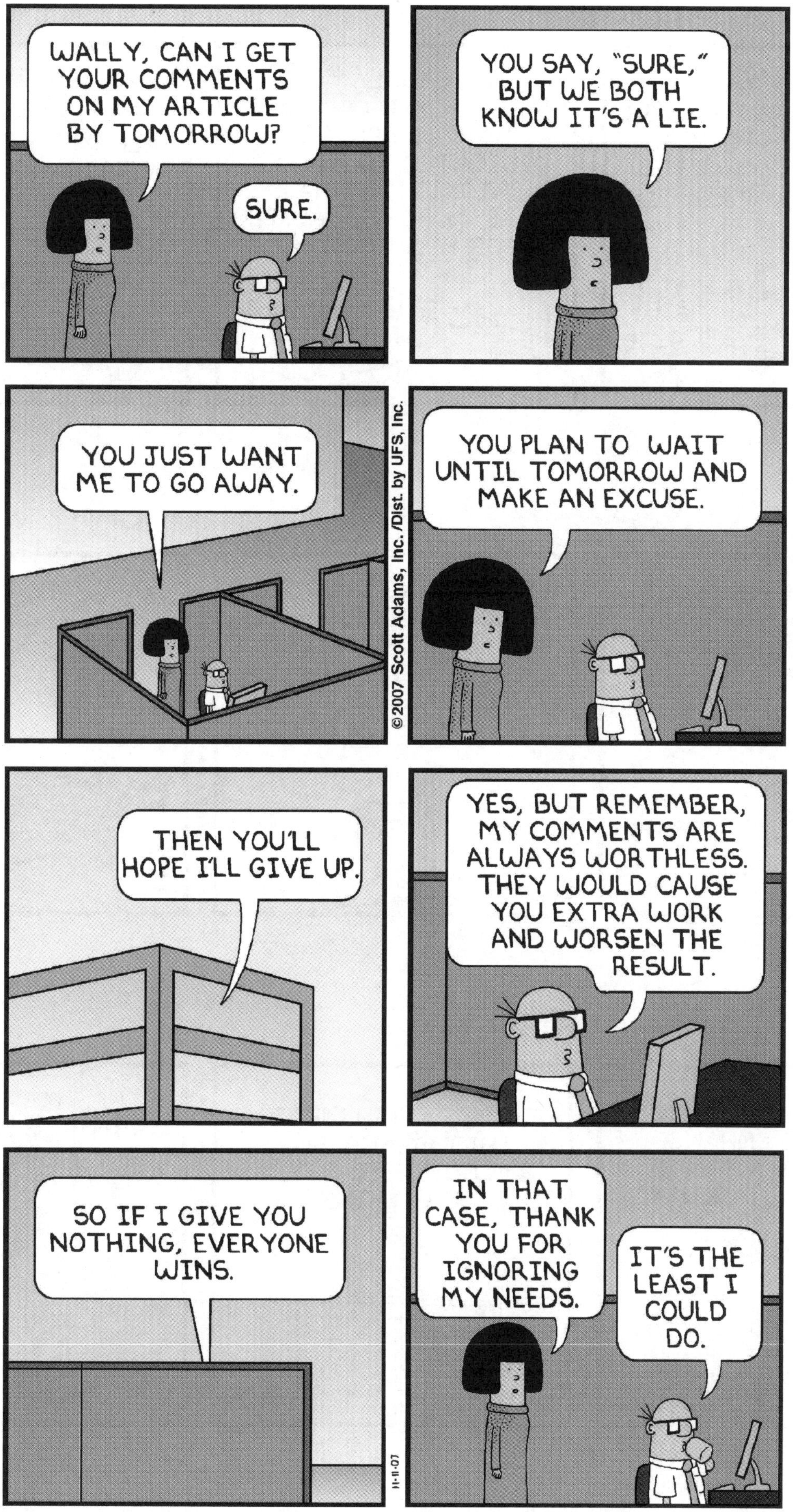
WALLY, CAN I GET YOUR COMMENTS ON MY ARTICLE BY TOMORROW?
SURE.
YOU SAY, "SURE," BUT WE BOTH KNOW IT'S A LIE.
YOU JUST WANT ME TO GO AWAY.
YOU PLAN TO WAIT UNTIL TOMORROW AND MAKE AN EXCUSE.
THEN YOU'LL HOPE I'LL GIVE UP.
YES, BUT REMEMBER, MY COMMENTS ARE ALWAYS WORTHLESS. THEY WOULD CAUSE YOU EXTRA WORK AND WORSEN THE RESULT.
SO IF I GIVE YOU NOTHING, EVERYONE WINS.
IN THAT CASE, THANK YOU FOR IGNORING MY NEEDS.
IT'S THE LEAST I COULD DO.
©2007 Scott Adams, Inc./Dist. by UFS, Inc.
11-11-07

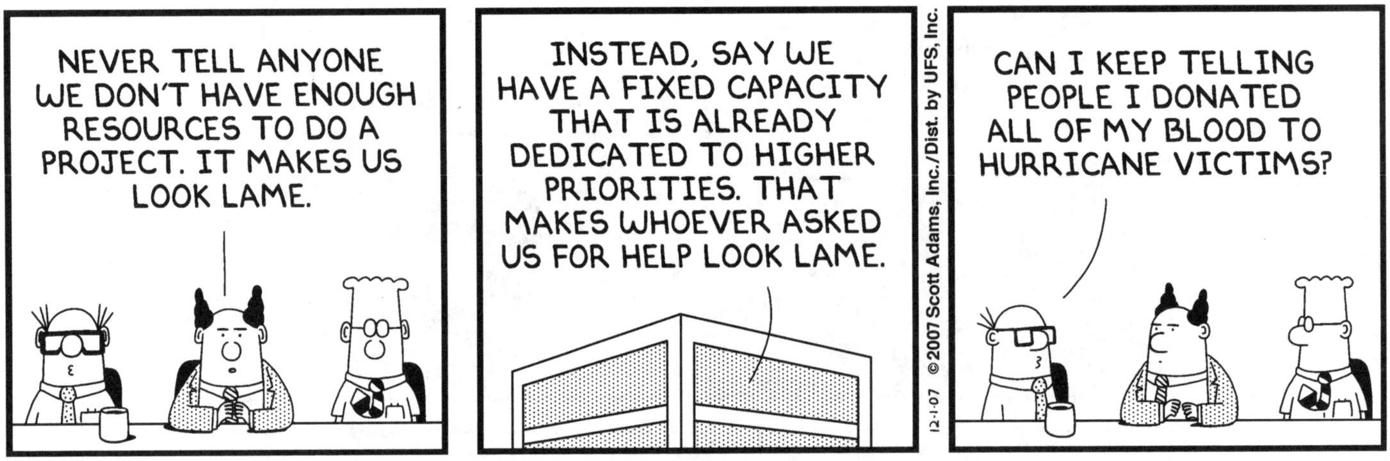
NEVER TELL ANYONE WE DON'T HAVE ENOUGH RESOURCES TO DO A PROJECT. IT MAKES US LOOK LAME.
INSTEAD, SAY WE HAVE A FIXED CAPACITY THAT IS ALREADY DEDICATED TO HIGHER PRIORITIES. THAT MAKES WHOEVER ASKED US FOR HELP LOOK LAME.
12-1-07 ©2007 Scott Adams, Inc./Dist. by UFS, Inc.
CAN I KEEP TELLING PEOPLE I DONATED ALL OF MY BLOOD TO HURRICANE VICTIMS?

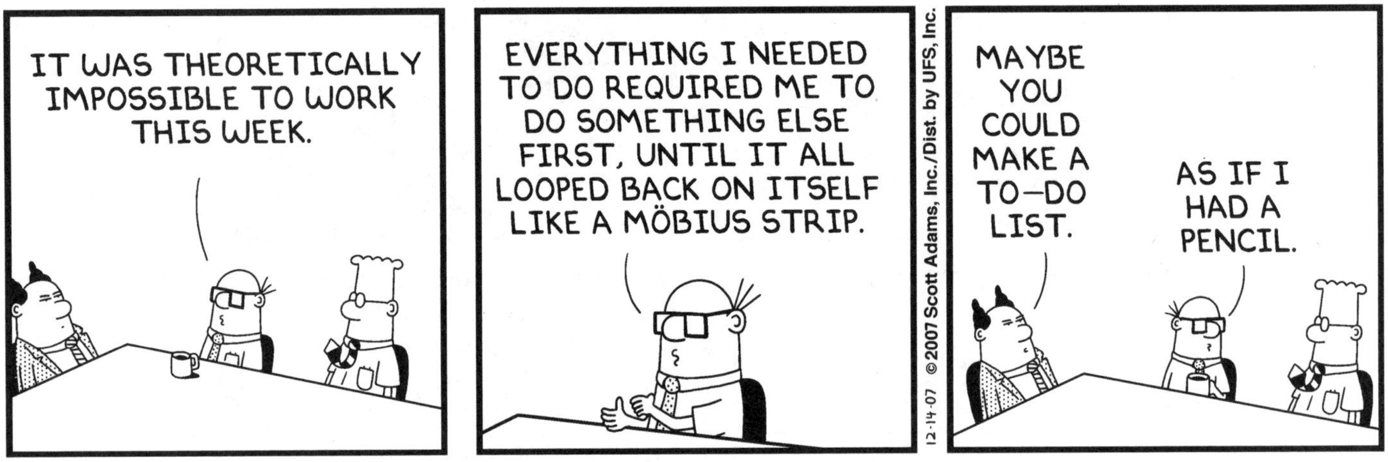
IT WAS THEORETICALLY IMPOSSIBLE TO WORK THIS WEEK.
EVERYTHING I NEEDED TO DO REQUIRED ME TO DO SOMETHING ELSE FIRST, UNTIL IT ALL LOOPED BACK ON ITSELF LIKE A MÖBIUS STRIP.
12-14-07 ©2007 Scott Adams, Inc./Dist. by UFS, Inc.
MAYBE YOU COULD MAKE A TO-DO LIST.
AS IF I HAD A PENCIL.

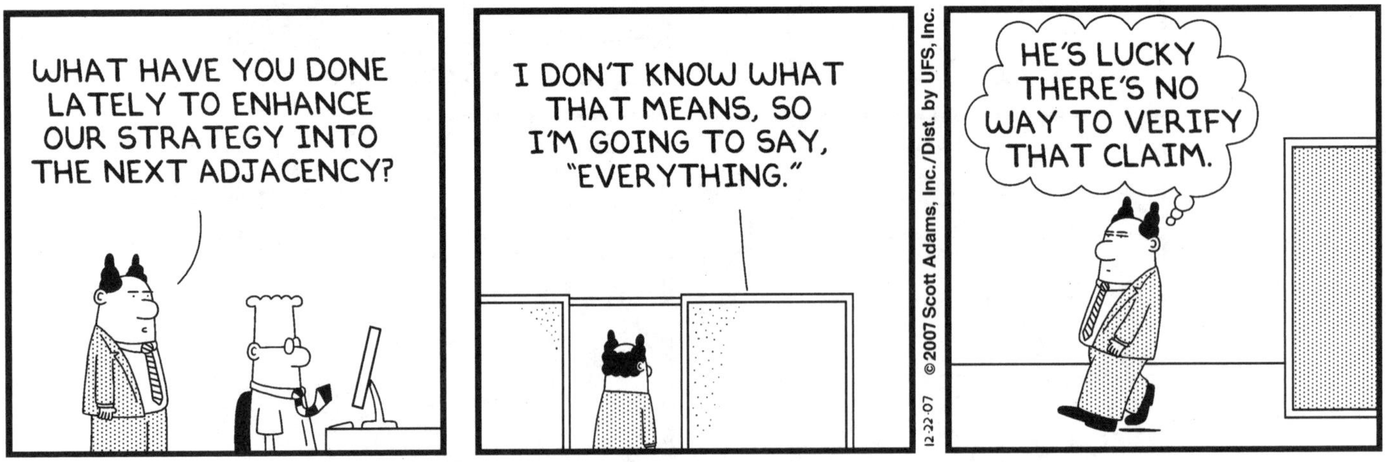
WHAT HAVE YOU DONE LATELY TO ENHANCE OUR STRATEGY INTO THE NEXT ADJACENCY?
I DON'T KNOW WHAT THAT MEANS, SO I'M GOING TO SAY, "EVERYTHING."
12-22-07 ©2007 Scott Adams, Inc./Dist. by UFS, Inc.
HE'S LUCKY THERE'S NO WAY TO VERIFY THAT CLAIM.

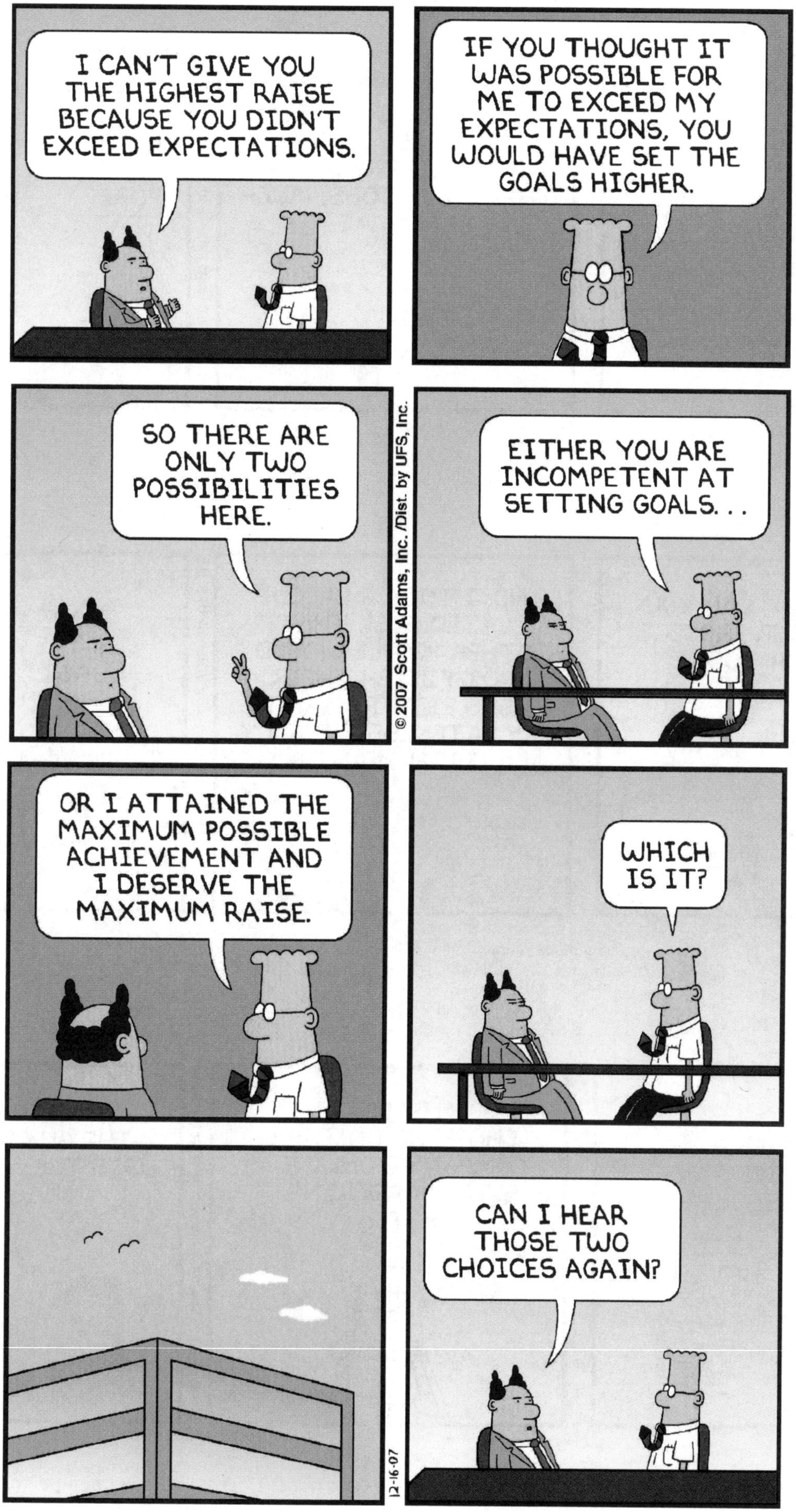
I CAN'T GIVE YOU THE HIGHEST RAISE BECAUSE YOU DIDN'T EXCEED EXPECTATIONS.
IF YOU THOUGHT IT WAS POSSIBLE FOR ME TO EXCEED MY EXPECTATIONS, YOU WOULD HAVE SET THE GOALS HIGHER.
SO THERE ARE ONLY TWO POSSIBILITIES HERE.
EITHER YOU ARE INCOMPETENT AT SETTING GOALS. . .
OR I ATTAINED THE MAXIMUM POSSIBLE ACHIEVEMENT AND I DESERVE THE MAXIMUM RAISE.
WHICH IS IT?
CAN I HEAR THOSE TWO CHOICES AGAIN?
©2007 Scott Adams, Inc./Dist. by UFS, Inc.
12-16-07

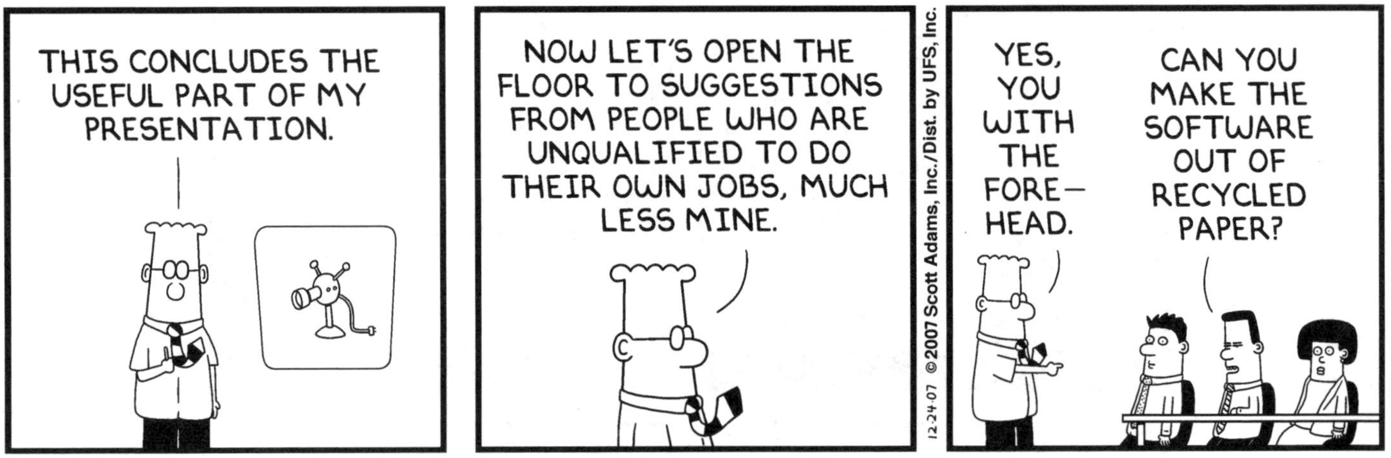
THIS CONCLUDES THE USEFUL PART OF MY PRESENTATION.
NOW LET'S OPEN THE FLOOR TO SUGGESTIONS FROM PEOPLE WHO ARE UNQUALIFIED TO DO THEIR OWN JOBS, MUCH LESS MINE.
12-24-07 © 2007 Scott Adams, Inc./Dist. by UFS, Inc.
YES, YOU WITH THE FORE-HEAD.
CAN YOU MAKE THE SOFTWARE OUT OF RECYCLED PAPER?

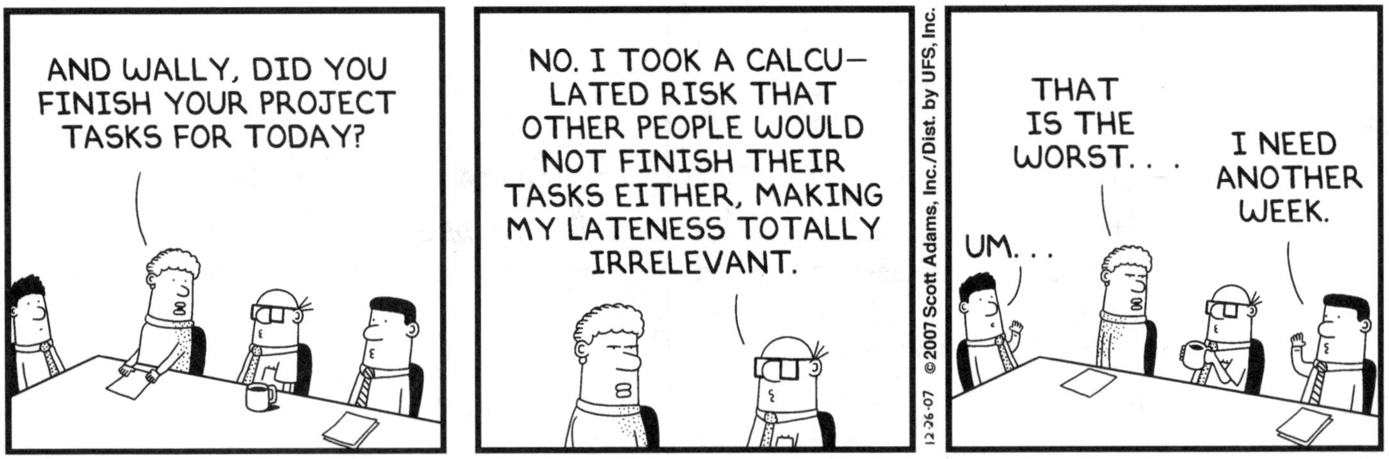
AND WALLY, DID YOU FINISH YOUR PROJECT TASKS FOR TODAY?
NO. I TOOK A CALCU-LATED RISK THAT OTHER PEOPLE WOULD NOT FINISH THEIR TASKS EITHER, MAKING MY LATENESS TOTALLY IRRELEVANT.
12-26-07 © 2007 Scott Adams, Inc./Dist. by UFS, Inc.
UM. . .
THAT IS THE WORST. . .
I NEED ANOTHER WEEK.

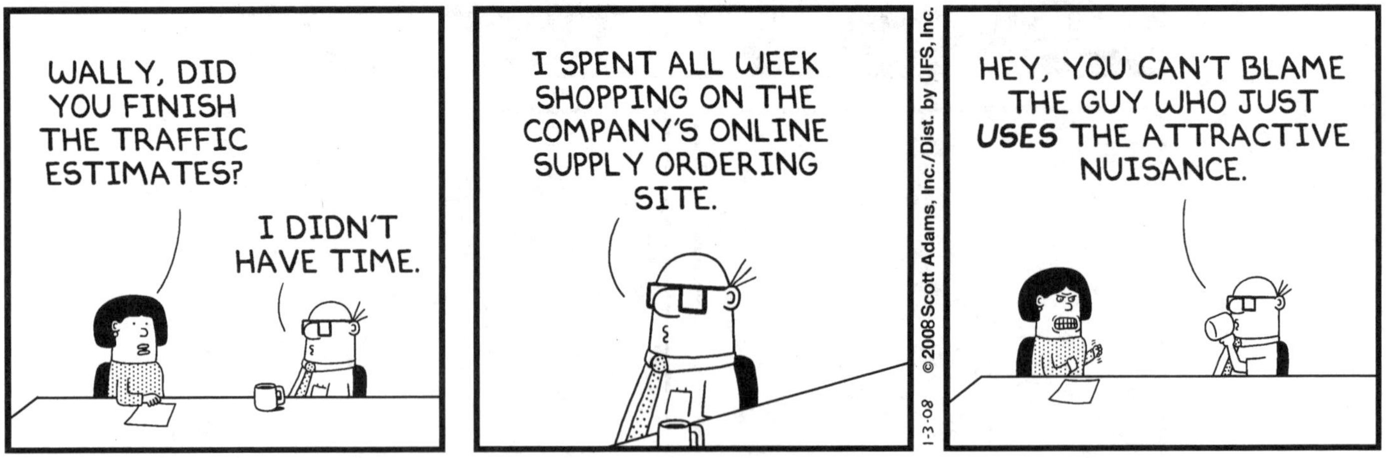
WALLY, DID YOU FINISH THE TRAFFIC ESTIMATES?
I DIDN'T HAVE TIME.
I SPENT ALL WEEK SHOPPING ON THE COMPANY'S ONLINE SUPPLY ORDERING SITE.
1-3-08 © 2008 Scott Adams, Inc./Dist. by UFS, Inc.
HEY, YOU CAN'T BLAME THE GUY WHO JUST USES THE ATTRACTIVE NUISANCE.

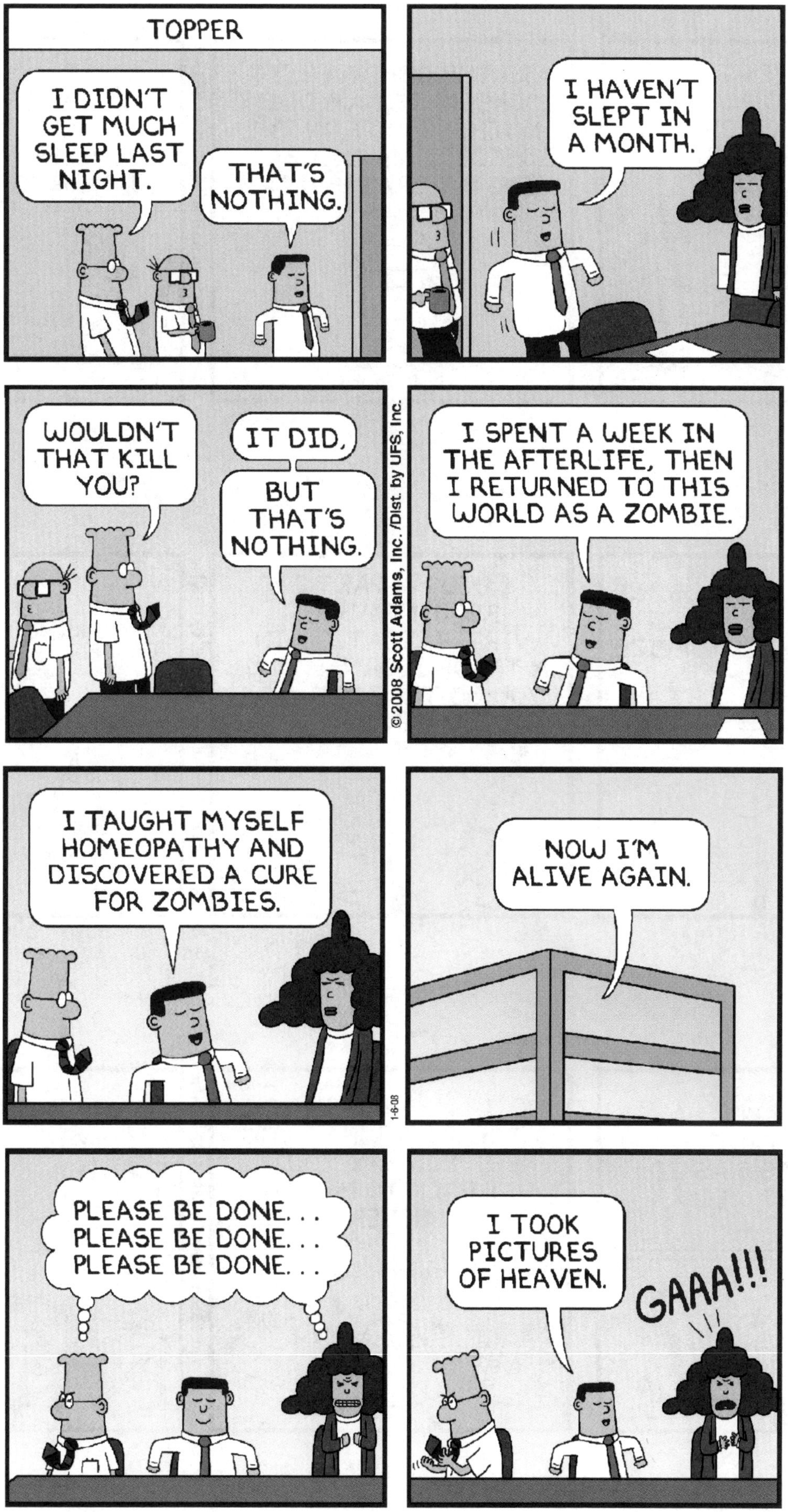
TOPPER
I DIDN'T GET MUCH SLEEP LAST NIGHT.
THAT'S NOTHING.
I HAVEN'T SLEPT IN A MONTH.
WOULDN'T THAT KILL YOU?
IT DID,
BUT THAT'S NOTHING.
©2008 Scott Adams, Inc. /Dist. by UFS, Inc.
I SPENT A WEEK IN THE AFTERLIFE, THEN I RETURNED TO THIS WORLD AS A ZOMBIE.
I TAUGHT MYSELF HOMEOPATHY AND DISCOVERED A CURE FOR ZOMBIES.
1-6-08
NOW I'M ALIVE AGAIN.
PLEASE BE DONE. . . PLEASE BE DONE. . . PLEASE BE DONE. . .
I TOOK PICTURES OF HEAVEN.
GAAA!!!

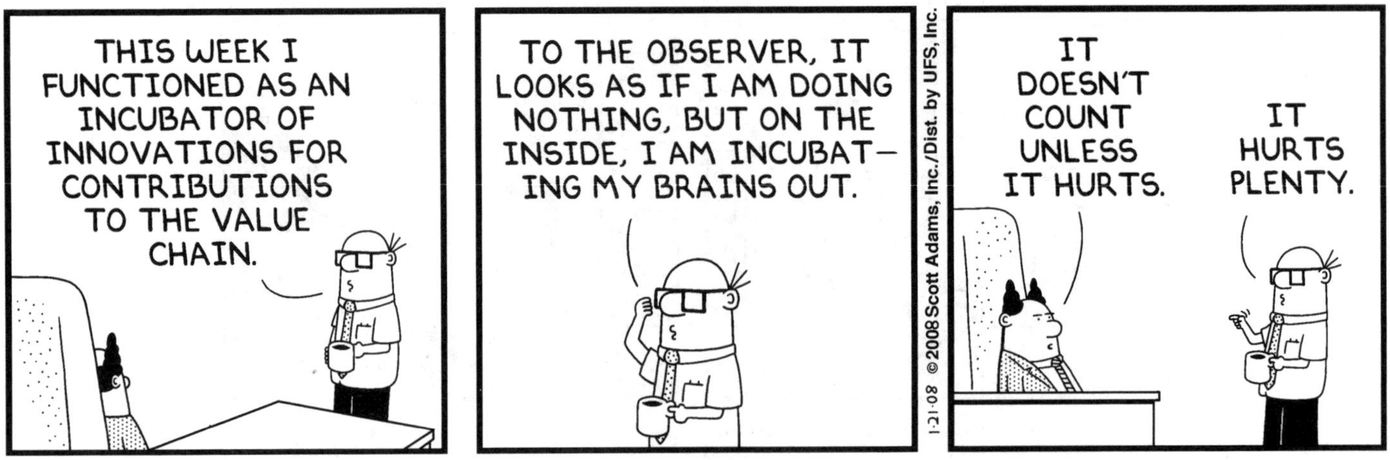
THIS WEEK I FUNCTIONED AS AN INCUBATOR OF INNOVATIONS FOR CONTRIBUTIONS TO THE VALUE CHAIN.
TO THE OBSERVER, IT LOOKS AS IF I AM DOING NOTHING, BUT ON THE INSIDE, I AM INCUBATING MY BRAINS OUT.
1-21-08 ©2008 Scott Adams, Inc./Dist. by UFS, Inc.
IT DOESN'T COUNT UNLESS IT HURTS.
IT HURTS PLENTY.

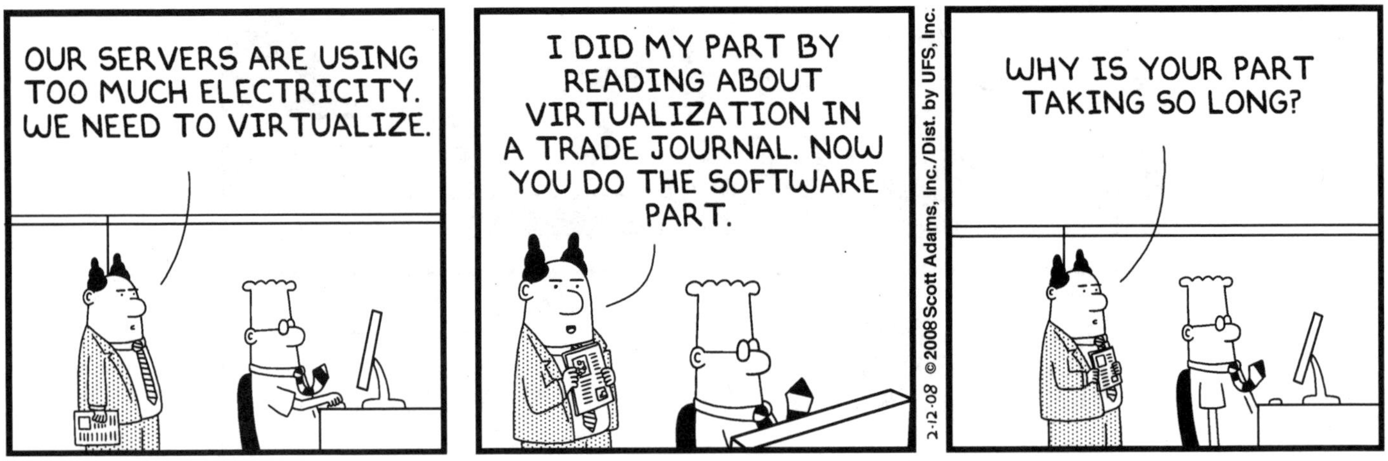
OUR SERVERS ARE USING TOO MUCH ELECTRICITY. WE NEED TO VIRTUALIZE.
I DID MY PART BY READING ABOUT VIRTUALIZATION IN A TRADE JOURNAL. NOW YOU DO THE SOFTWARE PART.
2-12-08 ©2008 Scott Adams, Inc./Dist. by UFS, Inc.
WHY IS YOUR PART TAKING SO LONG?

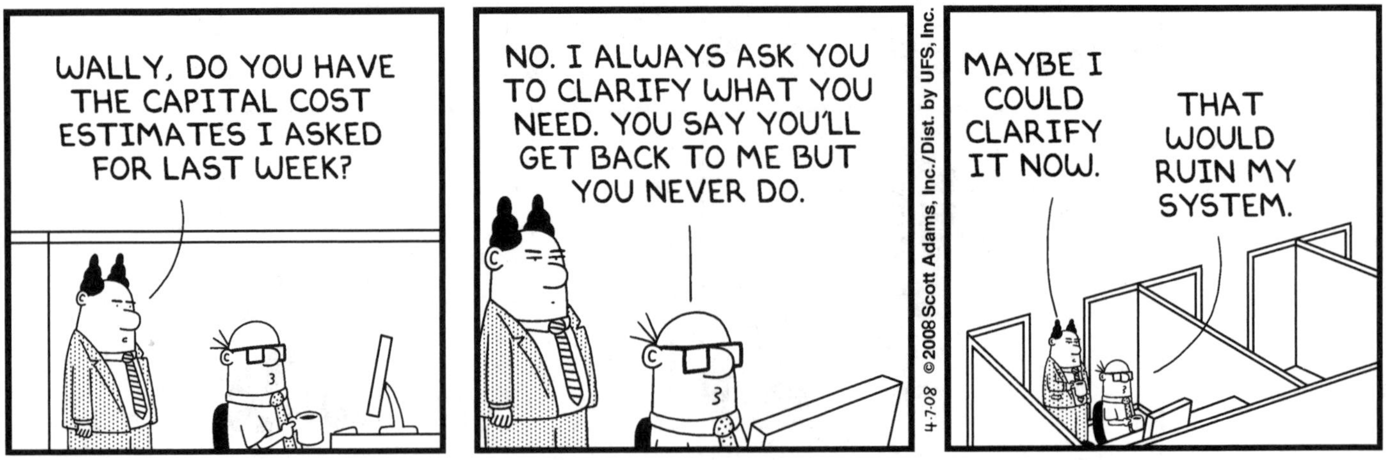
WALLY, DO YOU HAVE THE CAPITAL COST ESTIMATES I ASKED FOR LAST WEEK?
NO. I ALWAYS ASK YOU TO CLARIFY WHAT YOU NEED. YOU SAY YOU'LL GET BACK TO ME BUT YOU NEVER DO.
4-7-08 ©2008 Scott Adams, Inc./Dist. by UFS, Inc.
MAYBE I COULD CLARIFY IT NOW.
THAT WOULD RUIN MY SYSTEM.

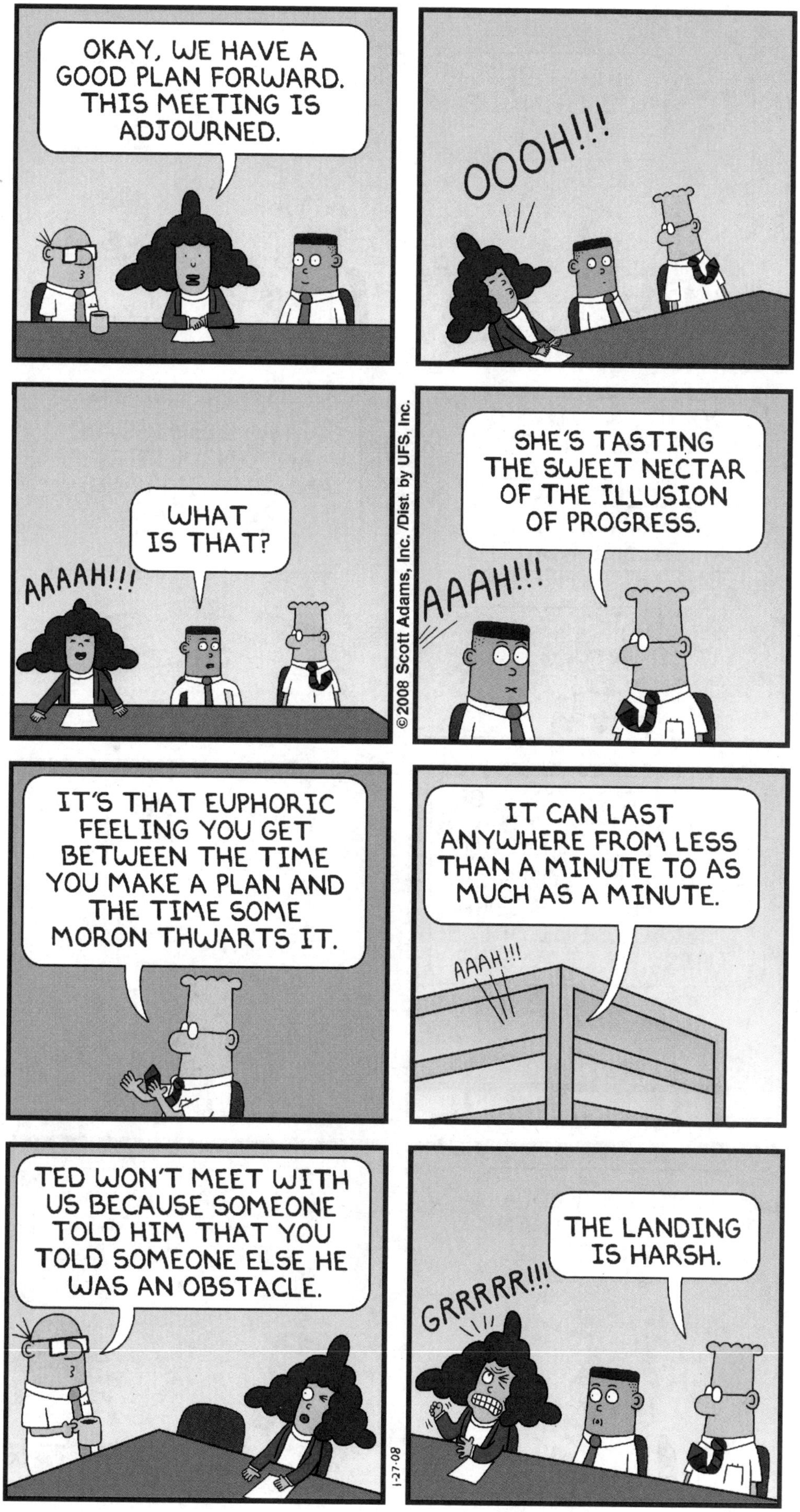

OKAY, WE HAVE A GOOD PLAN FORWARD. THIS MEETING IS ADJOURNED.
OOOH!!!
AAAAH!!!
WHAT IS THAT?
©2008 Scott Adams, Inc. /Dist. by UFS, Inc.
AAAH!!!
SHE'S TASTING THE SWEET NECTAR OF THE ILLUSION OF PROGRESS.
IT'S THAT EUPHORIC FEELING YOU GET BETWEEN THE TIME YOU MAKE A PLAN AND THE TIME SOME MORON THWARTS IT.
AAAH!!!
IT CAN LAST ANYWHERE FROM LESS THAN A MINUTE TO AS MUCH AS A MINUTE.
TED WON'T MEET WITH US BECAUSE SOMEONE TOLD HIM THAT YOU TOLD SOMEONE ELSE HE WAS AN OBSTACLE.
1-27-08
GRRRRR!!!
THE LANDING IS HARSH.

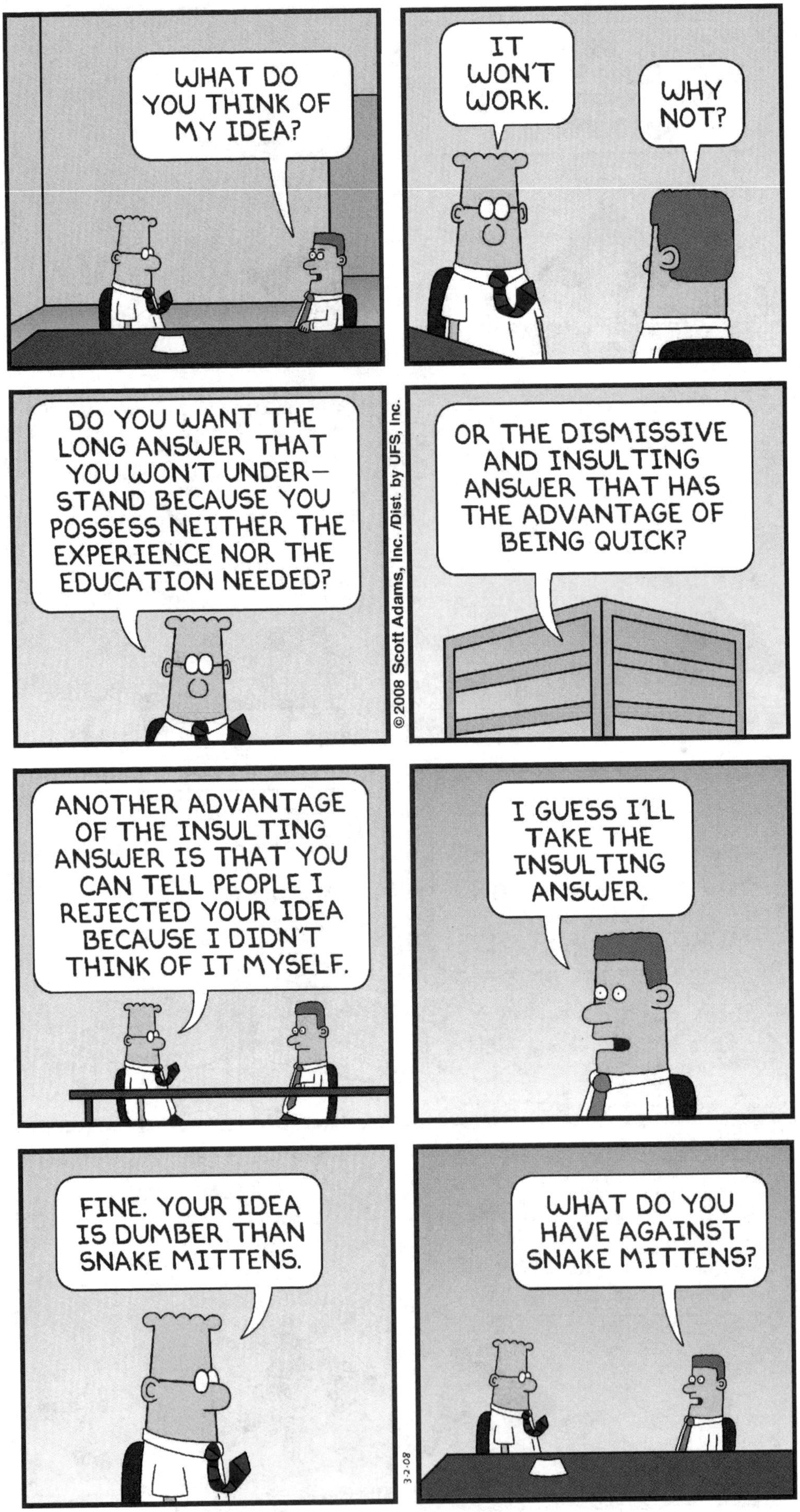
WHAT DO YOU THINK OF MY IDEA?
IT WON'T WORK.
WHY NOT?
DO YOU WANT THE LONG ANSWER THAT YOU WON'T UNDER- STAND BECAUSE YOU POSSESS NEITHER THE EXPERIENCE NOR THE EDUCATION NEEDED?
©2008 Scott Adams, Inc. /Dist. by UFS, Inc.
OR THE DISMISSIVE AND INSULTING ANSWER THAT HAS THE ADVANTAGE OF BEING QUICK?
ANOTHER ADVANTAGE OF THE INSULTING ANSWER IS THAT YOU CAN TELL PEOPLE I REJECTED YOUR IDEA BECAUSE I DIDN'T THINK OF IT MYSELF.
I GUESS I'LL TAKE THE INSULTING ANSWER.
FINE. YOUR IDEA IS DUMBER THAN SNAKE MITTENS.
3-2-08
WHAT DO YOU HAVE AGAINST SNAKE MITTENS?

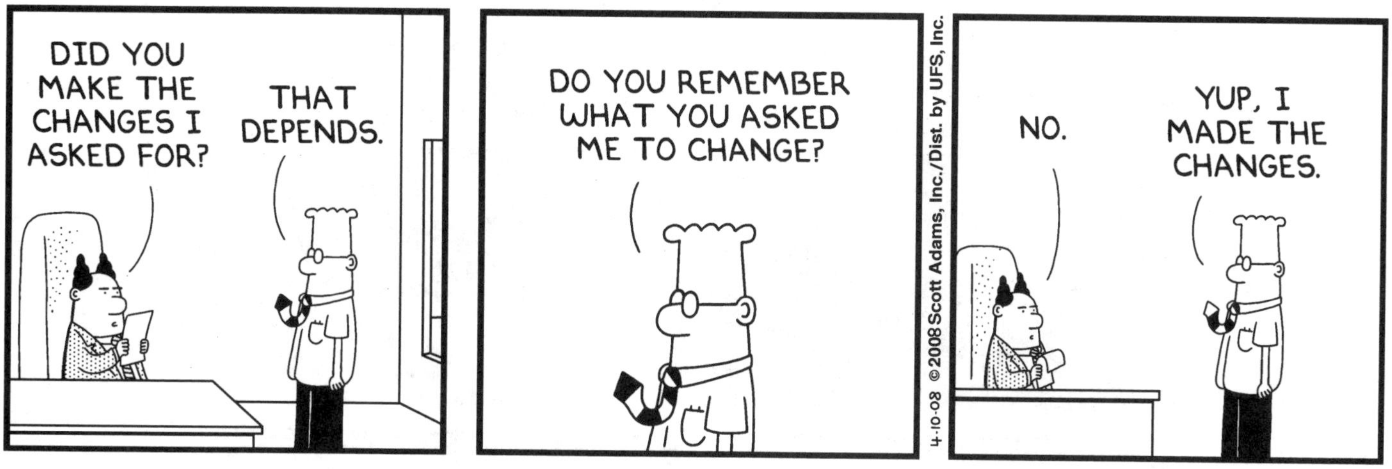
DID YOU MAKE THE CHANGES I ASKED FOR?
THAT DEPENDS.
DO YOU REMEMBER WHAT YOU ASKED ME TO CHANGE?
4-10-08 © 2008 Scott Adams, Inc./Dist. by UFS, Inc.
NO.
YUP, I MADE THE CHANGES.

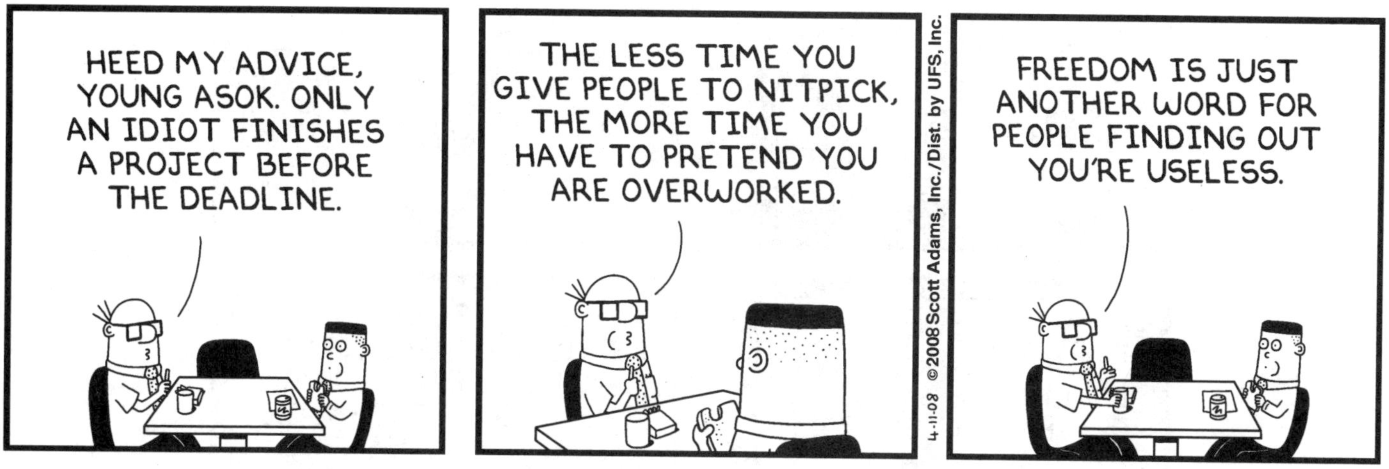
HEED MY ADVICE, YOUNG ASOK. ONLY AN IDIOT FINISHES A PROJECT BEFORE THE DEADLINE.
THE LESS TIME YOU GIVE PEOPLE TO NITPICK, THE MORE TIME YOU HAVE TO PRETEND YOU ARE OVERWORKED.
4-11-08 © 2008 Scott Adams, Inc./Dist. by UFS, Inc.
FREEDOM IS JUST ANOTHER WORD FOR PEOPLE FINDING OUT YOU'RE USELESS.

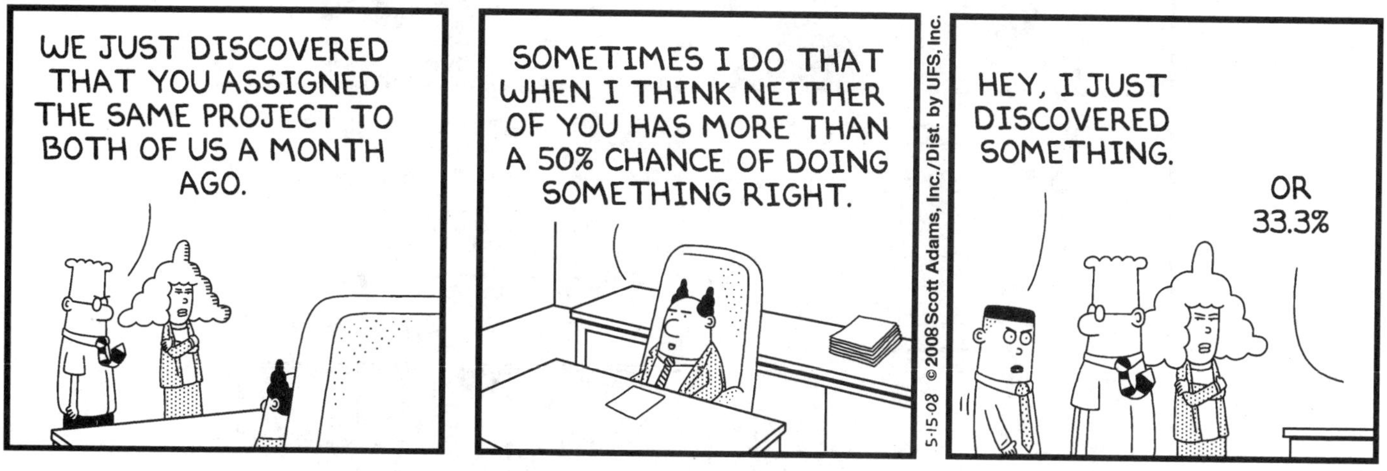
WE JUST DISCOVERED THAT YOU ASSIGNED THE SAME PROJECT TO BOTH OF US A MONTH AGO.
SOMETIMES I DO THAT WHEN I THINK NEITHER OF YOU HAS MORE THAN A 50% CHANCE OF DOING SOMETHING RIGHT.
5-15-08 © 2008 Scott Adams, Inc./Dist. by UFS, Inc.
HEY, I JUST DISCOVERED SOMETHING.
OR 33.3%

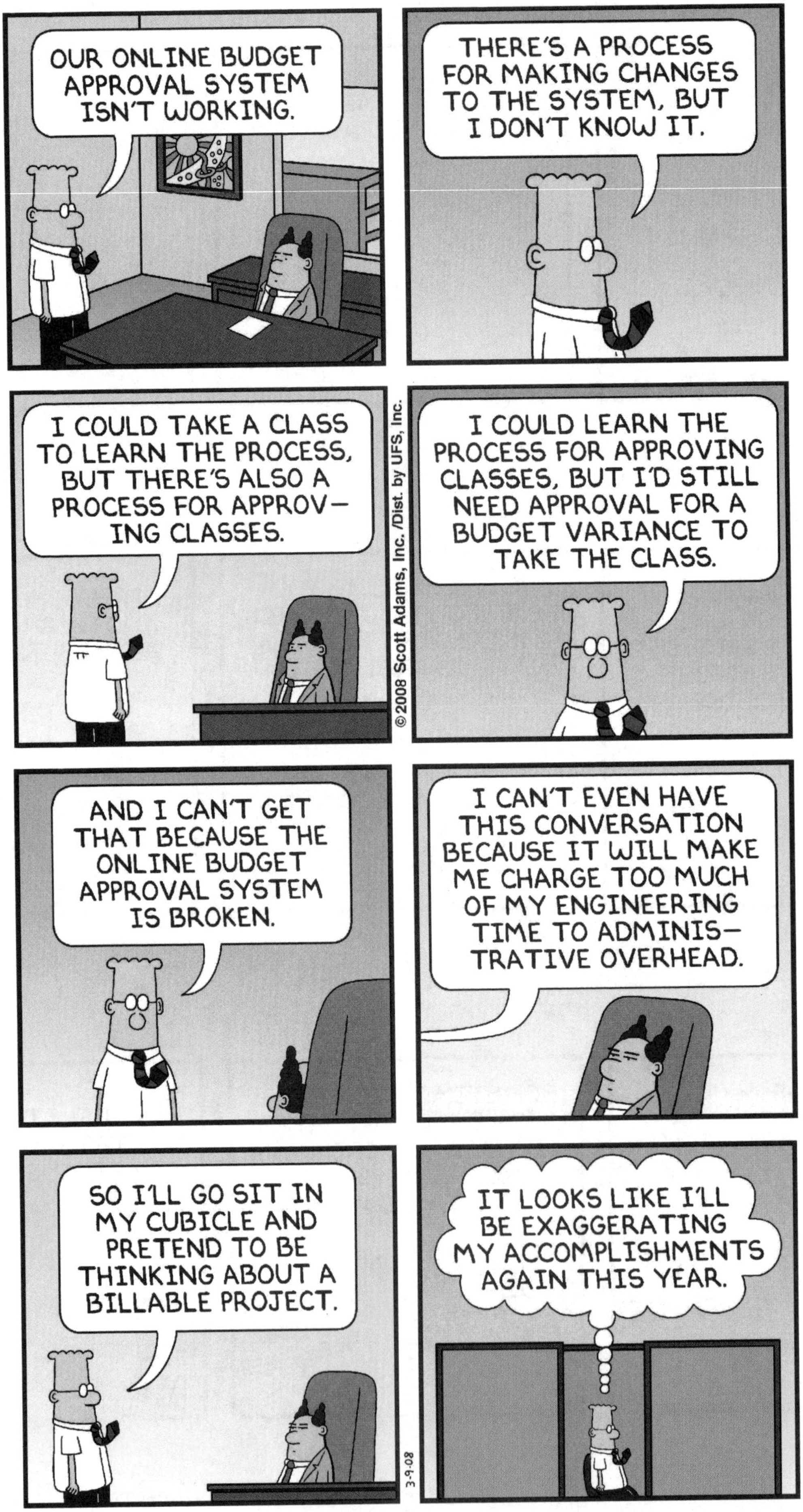
OUR ONLINE BUDGET APPROVAL SYSTEM ISN'T WORKING.
THERE'S A PROCESS FOR MAKING CHANGES TO THE SYSTEM, BUT I DON'T KNOW IT.
I COULD TAKE A CLASS TO LEARN THE PROCESS, BUT THERE'S ALSO A PROCESS FOR APPROV-ING CLASSES.
©2008 Scott Adams, Inc. /Dist. by UFS, Inc.
I COULD LEARN THE PROCESS FOR APPROVING CLASSES, BUT I'D STILL NEED APPROVAL FOR A BUDGET VARIANCE TO TAKE THE CLASS.
AND I CAN'T GET THAT BECAUSE THE ONLINE BUDGET APPROVAL SYSTEM IS BROKEN.
I CAN'T EVEN HAVE THIS CONVERSATION BECAUSE IT WILL MAKE ME CHARGE TOO MUCH OF MY ENGINEERING TIME TO ADMINIS-TRATIVE OVERHEAD.
SO I'LL GO SIT IN MY CUBICLE AND PRETEND TO BE THINKING ABOUT A BILLABLE PROJECT.
3-9-08
IT LOOKS LIKE I'LL BE EXAGGERATING MY ACCOMPLISHMENTS AGAIN THIS YEAR.

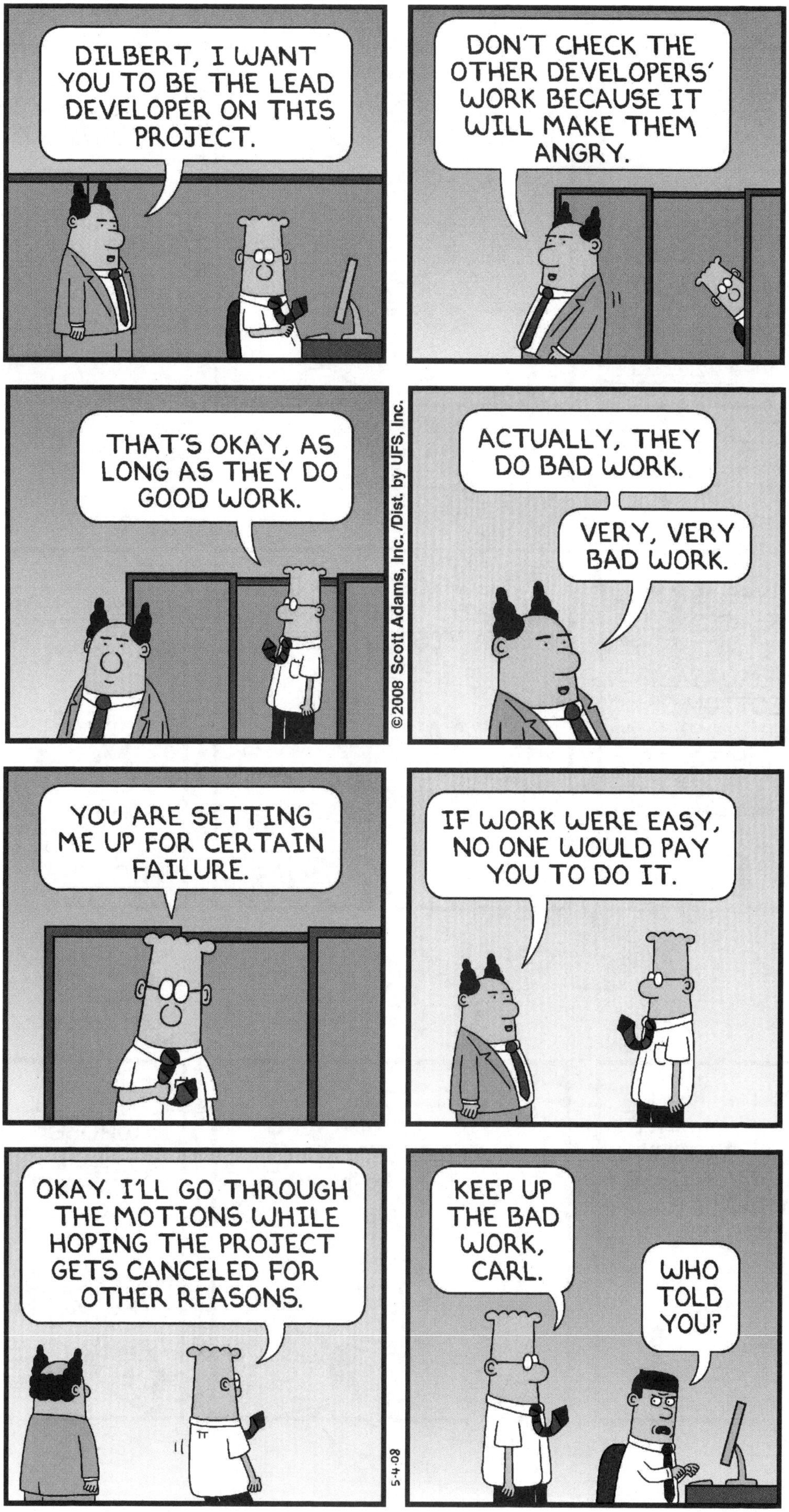
DILBERT, I WANT YOU TO BE THE LEAD DEVELOPER ON THIS PROJECT.
DON'T CHECK THE OTHER DEVELOPERS' WORK BECAUSE IT WILL MAKE THEM ANGRY.
THAT'S OKAY, AS LONG AS THEY DO GOOD WORK.
ACTUALLY, THEY DO BAD WORK.
VERY, VERY BAD WORK.
©2008 Scott Adams, Inc. /Dist. by UFS, Inc.
YOU ARE SETTING ME UP FOR CERTAIN FAILURE.
IF WORK WERE EASY, NO ONE WOULD PAY YOU TO DO IT.
OKAY. I'LL GO THROUGH THE MOTIONS WHILE HOPING THE PROJECT GETS CANCELED FOR OTHER REASONS.
5-4-08
KEEP UP THE BAD WORK, CARL.
WHO TOLD YOU?

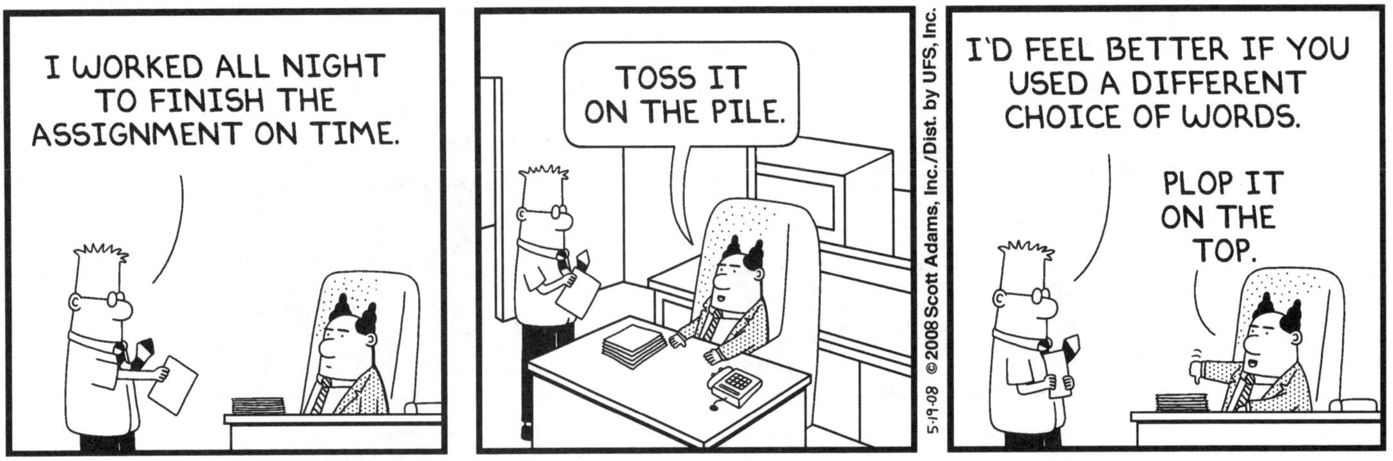
I WORKED ALL NIGHT TO FINISH THE ASSIGNMENT ON TIME.
TOSS IT ON THE PILE.
5-19-08 ©2008 Scott Adams, Inc./Dist. by UFS, Inc.
I'D FEEL BETTER IF YOU USED A DIFFERENT CHOICE OF WORDS.
PLOP IT ON THE TOP.

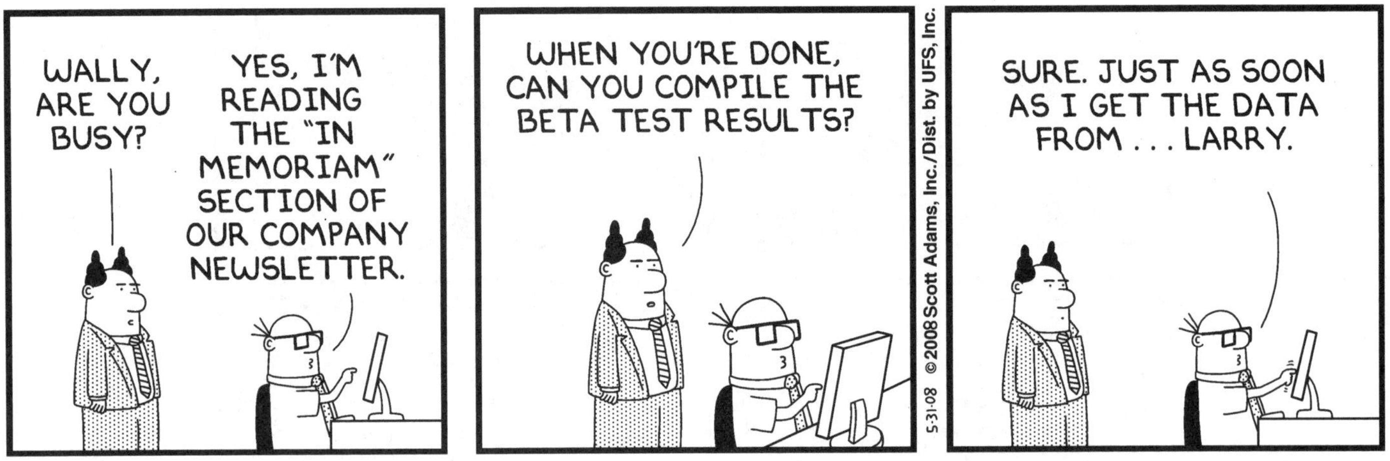
WALLY, ARE YOU BUSY?
YES, I'M READING THE "IN MEMORIAM" SECTION OF OUR COMPANY NEWSLETTER.
WHEN YOU'RE DONE, CAN YOU COMPILE THE BETA TEST RESULTS?
5-31-08 ©2008 Scott Adams, Inc./Dist. by UFS, Inc.
SURE. JUST AS SOON AS I GET THE DATA FROM . . . LARRY.

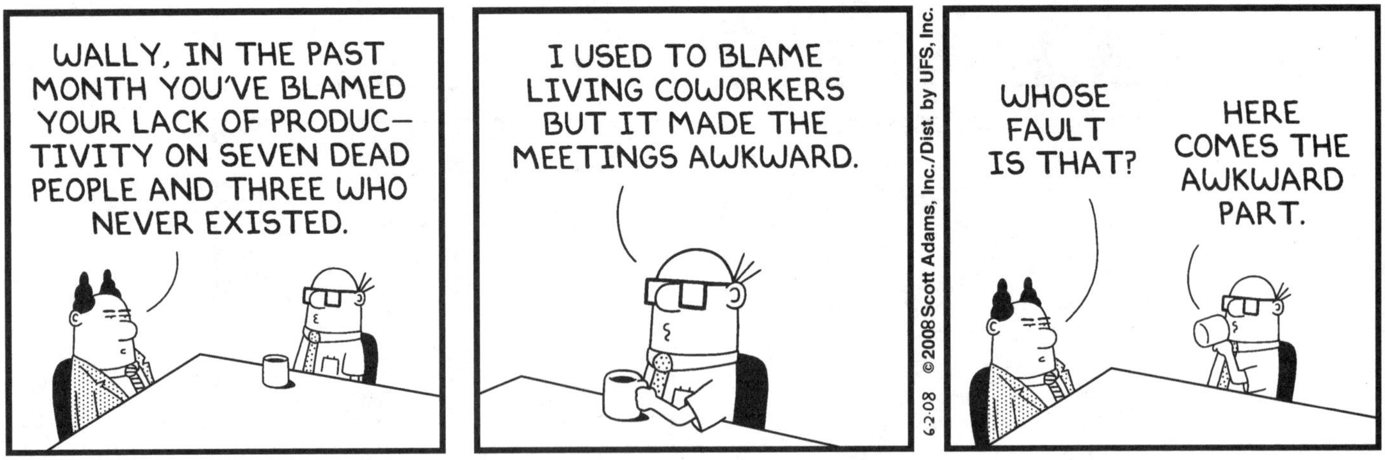
WALLY, IN THE PAST MONTH YOU'VE BLAMED YOUR LACK OF PRODUC-TIVITY ON SEVEN DEAD PEOPLE AND THREE WHO NEVER EXISTED.
I USED TO BLAME LIVING COWORKERS BUT IT MADE THE MEETINGS AWKWARD.
6-2-08 ©2008 Scott Adams, Inc./Dist. by UFS, Inc.
WHOSE FAULT IS THAT?
HERE COMES THE AWKWARD PART.

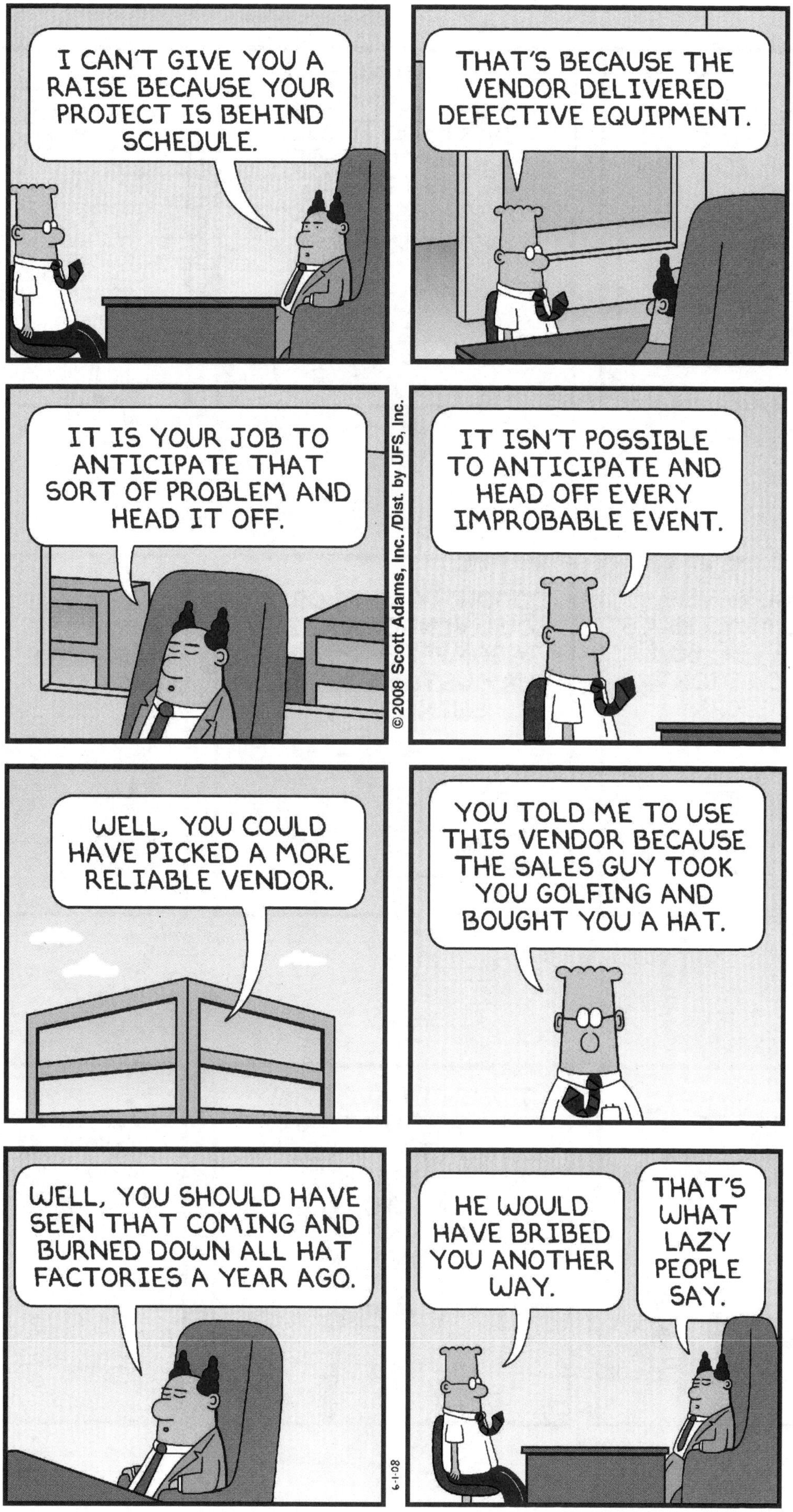
I CAN'T GIVE YOU A RAISE BECAUSE YOUR PROJECT IS BEHIND SCHEDULE.
THAT'S BECAUSE THE VENDOR DELIVERED DEFECTIVE EQUIPMENT.
IT IS YOUR JOB TO ANTICIPATE THAT SORT OF PROBLEM AND HEAD IT OFF.
IT ISN'T POSSIBLE TO ANTICIPATE AND HEAD OFF EVERY IMPROBABLE EVENT.
WELL, YOU COULD HAVE PICKED A MORE RELIABLE VENDOR.
YOU TOLD ME TO USE THIS VENDOR BECAUSE THE SALES GUY TOOK YOU GOLFING AND BOUGHT YOU A HAT.
WELL, YOU SHOULD HAVE SEEN THAT COMING AND BURNED DOWN ALL HAT FACTORIES A YEAR AGO.
HE WOULD HAVE BRIBED YOU ANOTHER WAY.
THAT'S WHAT LAZY PEOPLE SAY.
©2008 Scott Adams, Inc./Dist. by UFS, Inc.
6-1-08

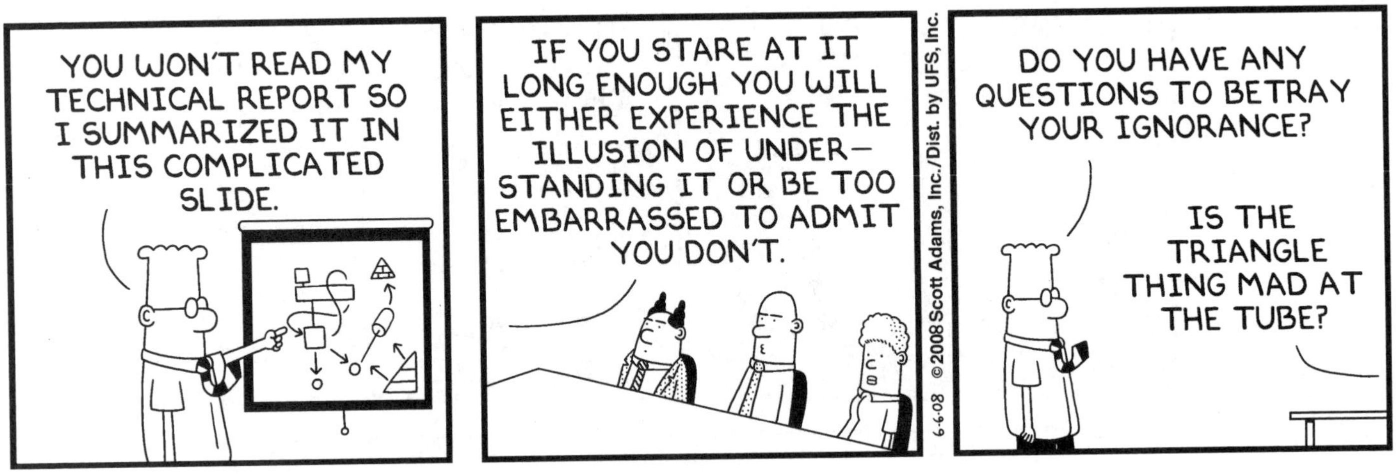
YOU WON'T READ MY TECHNICAL REPORT SO I SUMMARIZED IT IN THIS COMPLICATED SLIDE.
IF YOU STARE AT IT LONG ENOUGH YOU WILL EITHER EXPERIENCE THE ILLUSION OF UNDER–STANDING IT OR BE TOO EMBARRASSED TO ADMIT YOU DON'T.
6-6-08 ©2008 Scott Adams, Inc./Dist. by UFS, Inc.
DO YOU HAVE ANY QUESTIONS TO BETRAY YOUR IGNORANCE?
IS THE TRIANGLE THING MAD AT THE TUBE?

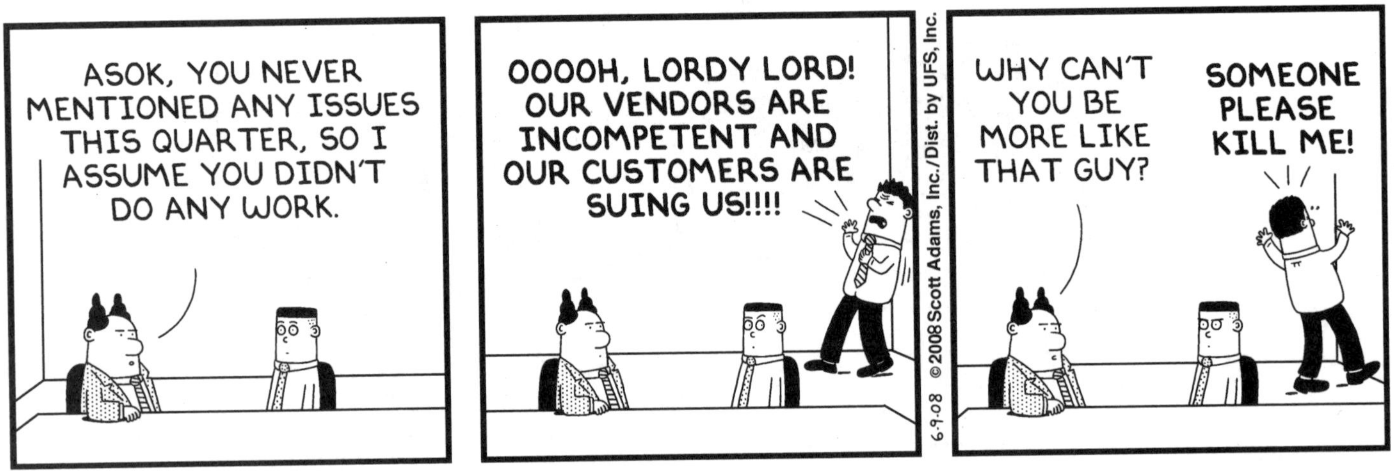
ASOK, YOU NEVER MENTIONED ANY ISSUES THIS QUARTER, SO I ASSUME YOU DIDN'T DO ANY WORK.
OOOOH, LORDY LORD! OUR VENDORS ARE INCOMPETENT AND OUR CUSTOMERS ARE SUING US!!!!
6-9-08 ©2008 Scott Adams, Inc./Dist. by UFS, Inc.
WHY CAN'T YOU BE MORE LIKE THAT GUY?
SOMEONE PLEASE KILL ME!

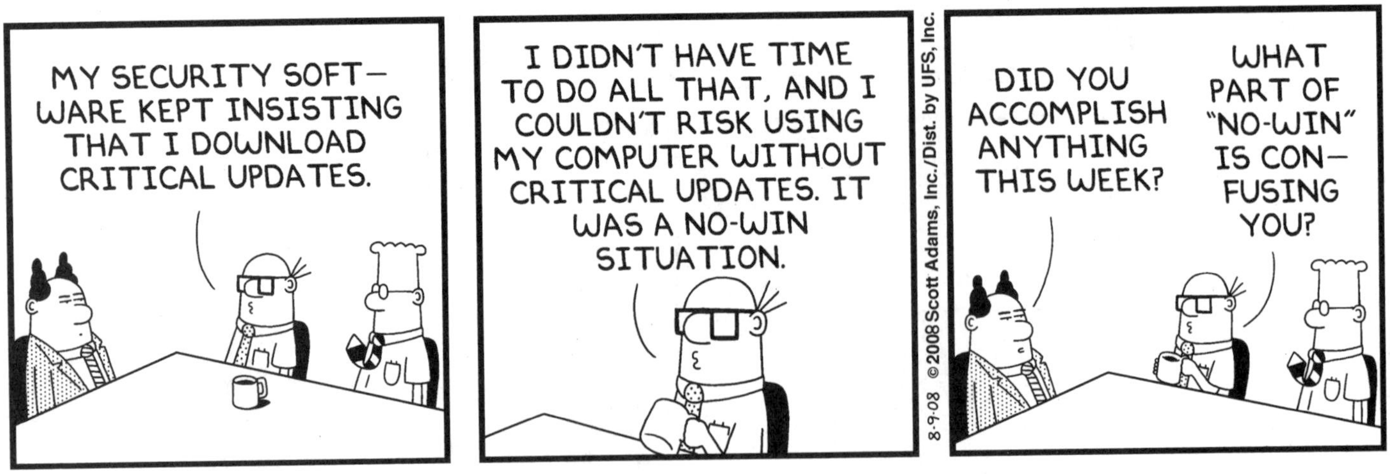
MY SECURITY SOFT–WARE KEPT INSISTING THAT I DOWNLOAD CRITICAL UPDATES.
I DIDN'T HAVE TIME TO DO ALL THAT, AND I COULDN'T RISK USING MY COMPUTER WITHOUT CRITICAL UPDATES. IT WAS A NO-WIN SITUATION.
8-9-08 ©2008 Scott Adams, Inc./Dist. by UFS, Inc.
DID YOU ACCOMPLISH ANYTHING THIS WEEK?
WHAT PART OF "NO-WIN" IS CON–FUSING YOU?

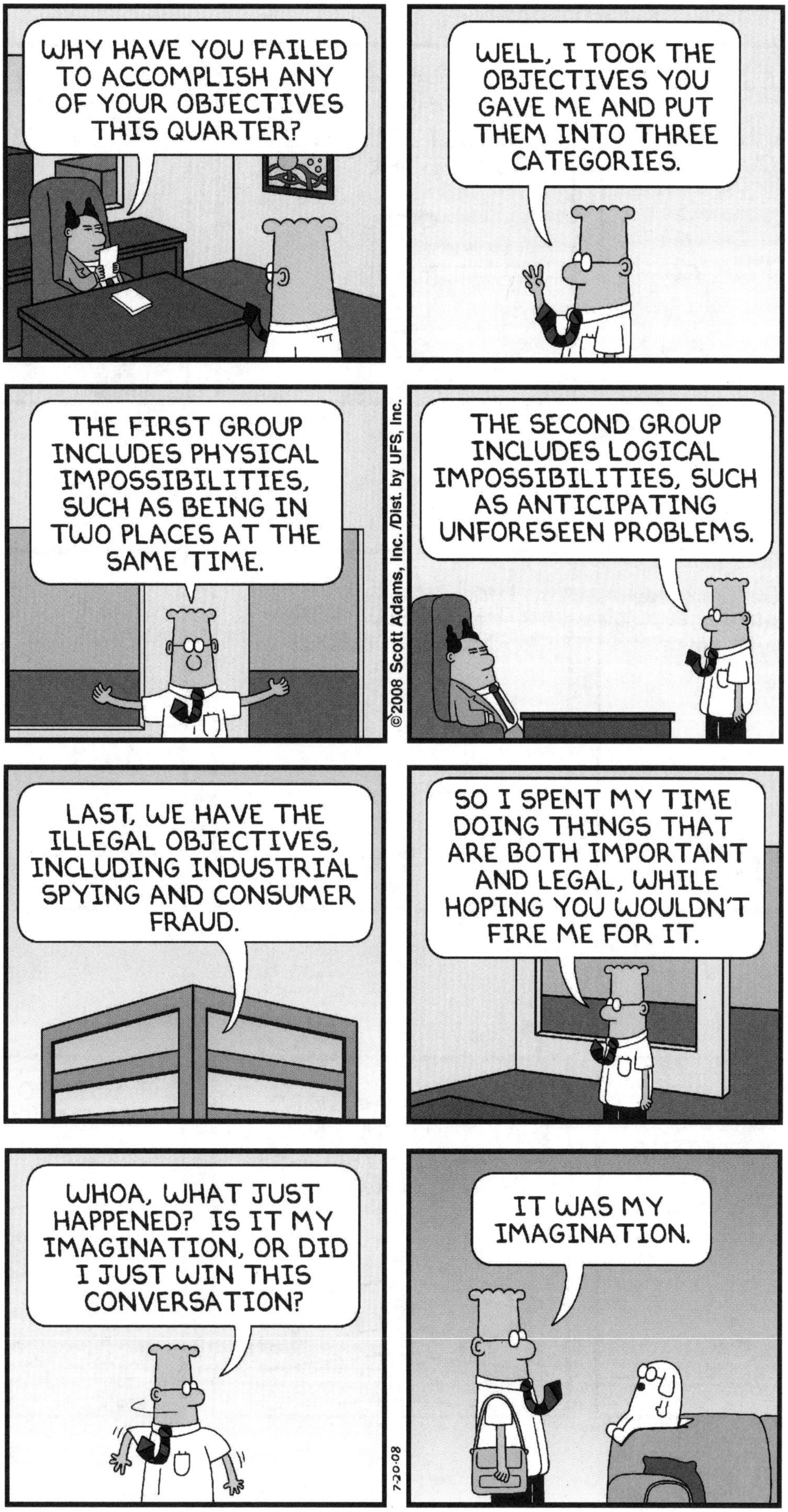
WHY HAVE YOU FAILED TO ACCOMPLISH ANY OF YOUR OBJECTIVES THIS QUARTER?
WELL, I TOOK THE OBJECTIVES YOU GAVE ME AND PUT THEM INTO THREE CATEGORIES.
THE FIRST GROUP INCLUDES PHYSICAL IMPOSSIBILITIES, SUCH AS BEING IN TWO PLACES AT THE SAME TIME.
©2008 Scott Adams, Inc./Dist. by UFS, Inc.
THE SECOND GROUP INCLUDES LOGICAL IMPOSSIBILITIES, SUCH AS ANTICIPATING UNFORESEEN PROBLEMS.
LAST, WE HAVE THE ILLEGAL OBJECTIVES, INCLUDING INDUSTRIAL SPYING AND CONSUMER FRAUD.
SO I SPENT MY TIME DOING THINGS THAT ARE BOTH IMPORTANT AND LEGAL, WHILE HOPING YOU WOULDN'T FIRE ME FOR IT.
WHOA, WHAT JUST HAPPENED? IS IT MY IMAGINATION, OR DID I JUST WIN THIS CONVERSATION?
7-20-08
IT WAS MY IMAGINATION.

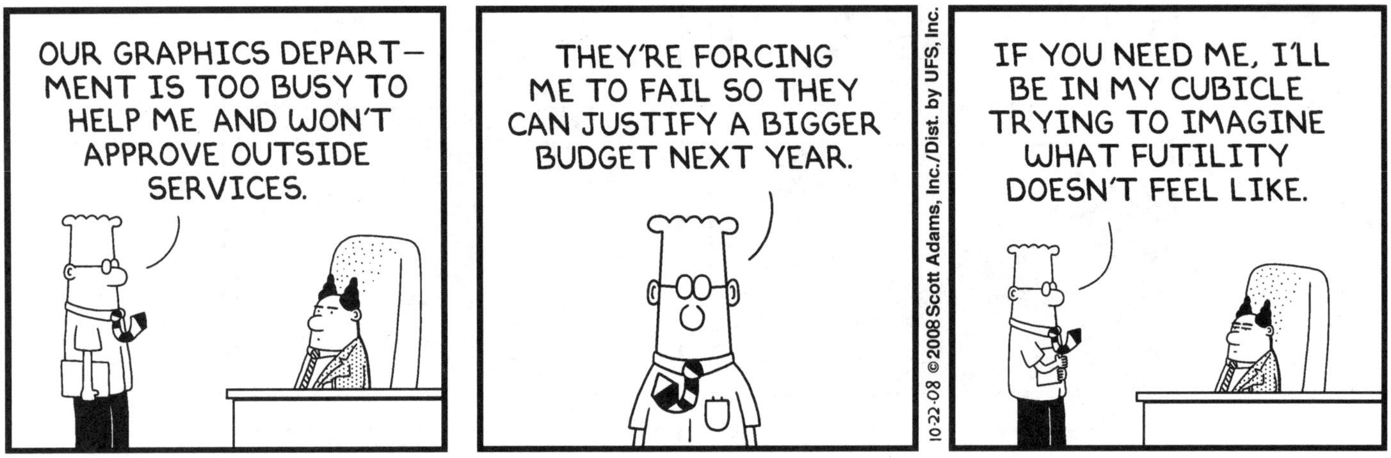
OUR GRAPHICS DEPARTMENT IS TOO BUSY TO HELP ME AND WON'T APPROVE OUTSIDE SERVICES.
THEY'RE FORCING ME TO FAIL SO THEY CAN JUSTIFY A BIGGER BUDGET NEXT YEAR.
IF YOU NEED ME, I'LL BE IN MY CUBICLE TRYING TO IMAGINE WHAT FUTILITY DOESN'T FEEL LIKE.
10-22-08 © 2008 Scott Adams, Inc./Dist. by UFS, Inc.

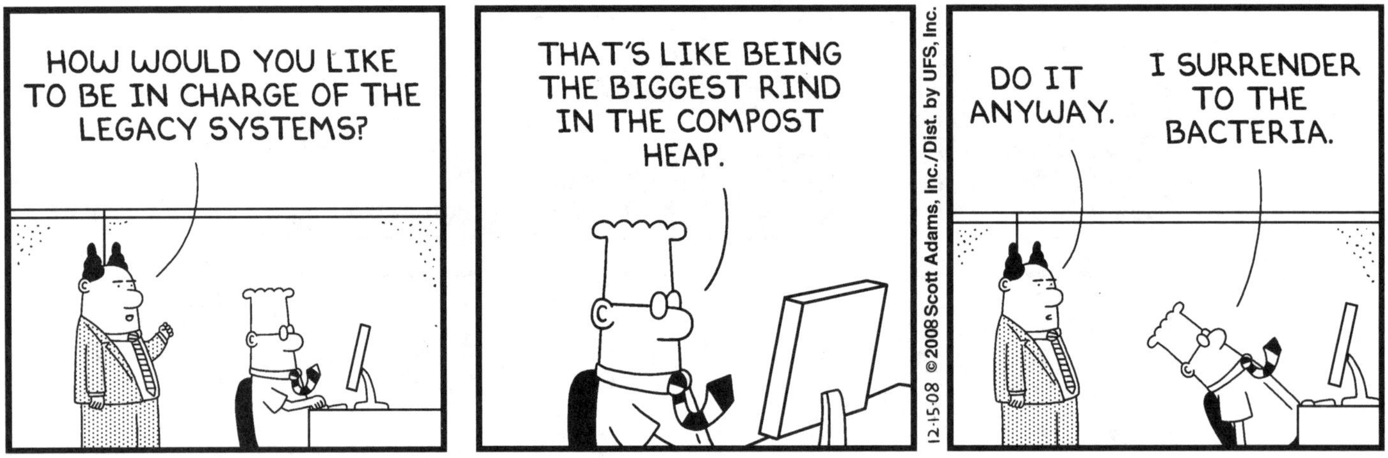
HOW WOULD YOU LIKE TO BE IN CHARGE OF THE LEGACY SYSTEMS?
THAT'S LIKE BEING THE BIGGEST RIND IN THE COMPOST HEAP.
DO IT ANYWAY.
I SURRENDER TO THE BACTERIA.
12-15-08 © 2008 Scott Adams, Inc./Dist. by UFS, Inc.

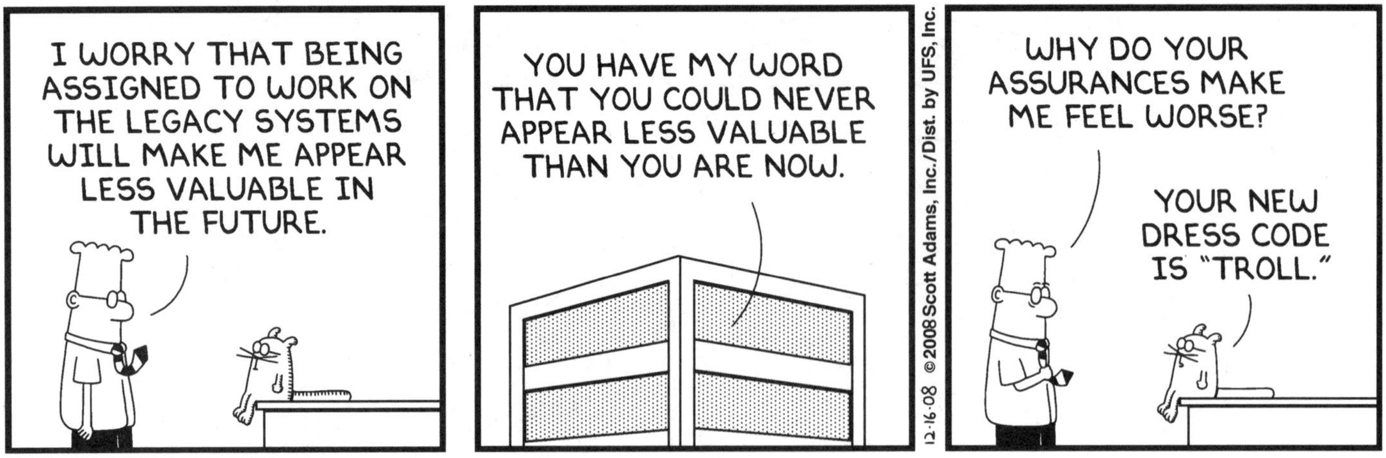
I WORRY THAT BEING ASSIGNED TO WORK ON THE LEGACY SYSTEMS WILL MAKE ME APPEAR LESS VALUABLE IN THE FUTURE.
YOU HAVE MY WORD THAT YOU COULD NEVER APPEAR LESS VALUABLE THAN YOU ARE NOW.
WHY DO YOUR ASSURANCES MAKE ME FEEL WORSE?
YOUR NEW DRESS CODE IS "TROLL."
12-16-08 © 2008 Scott Adams, Inc./Dist. by UFS, Inc.

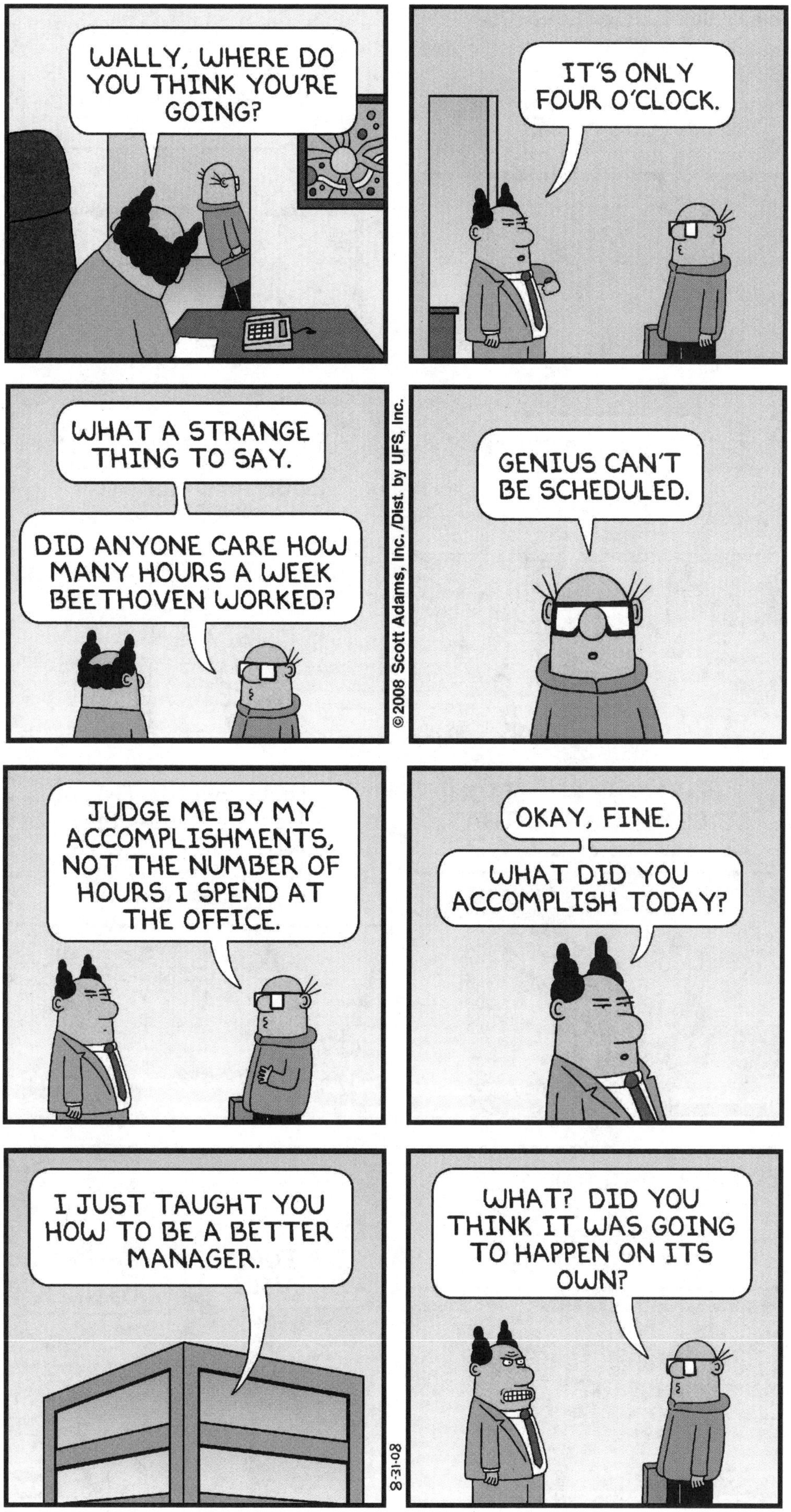
WALLY, WHERE DO YOU THINK YOU'RE GOING?
IT'S ONLY FOUR O'CLOCK.
WHAT A STRANGE THING TO SAY.
DID ANYONE CARE HOW MANY HOURS A WEEK BEETHOVEN WORKED?
©2008 Scott Adams, Inc./Dist. by UFS, Inc.
GENIUS CAN'T BE SCHEDULED.
JUDGE ME BY MY ACCOMPLISHMENTS, NOT THE NUMBER OF HOURS I SPEND AT THE OFFICE.
OKAY, FINE.
WHAT DID YOU ACCOMPLISH TODAY?
I JUST TAUGHT YOU HOW TO BE A BETTER MANAGER.
8-31-08
WHAT? DID YOU THINK IT WAS GOING TO HAPPEN ON ITS OWN?

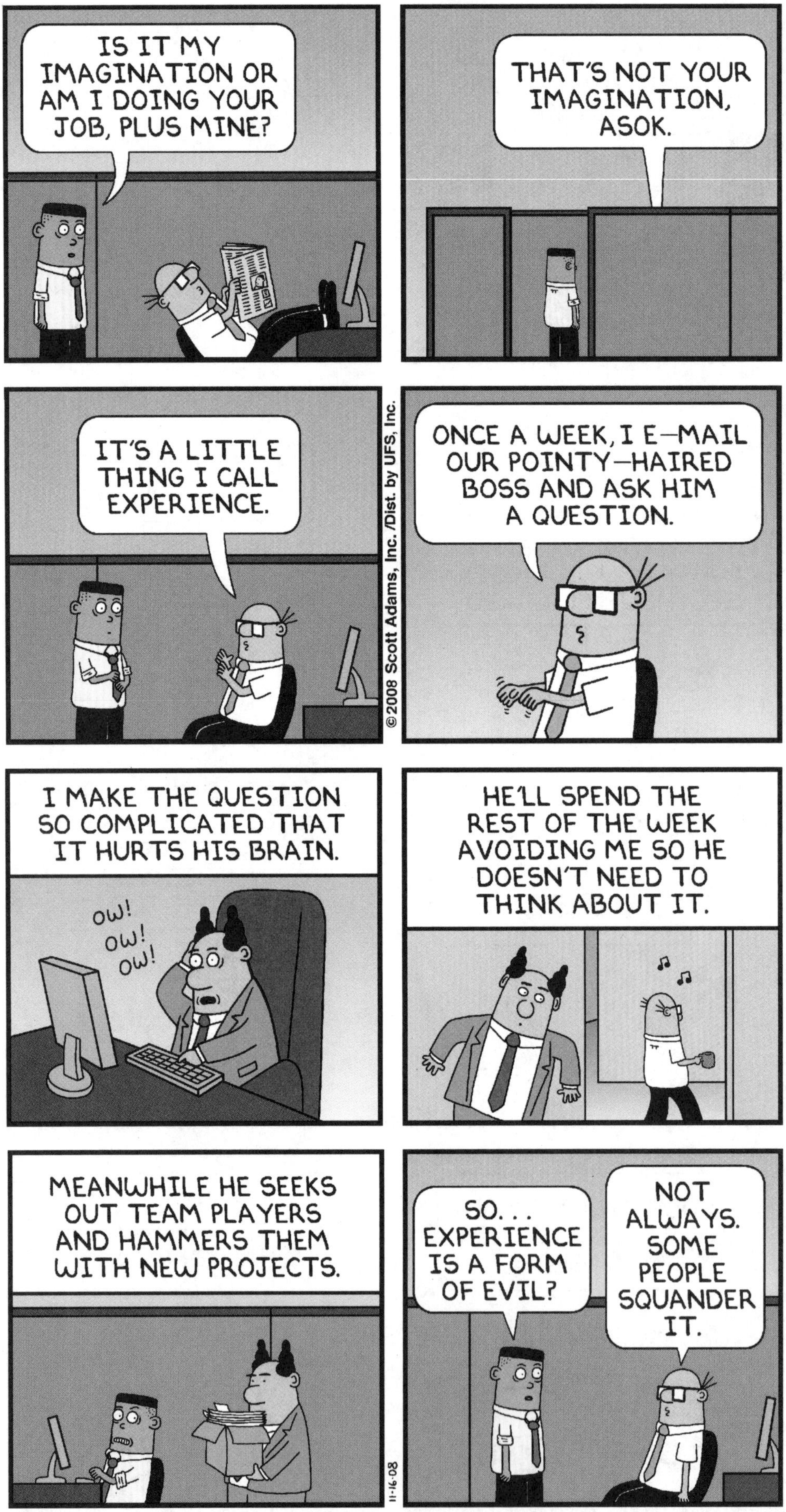
IS IT MY IMAGINATION OR AM I DOING YOUR JOB, PLUS MINE?
THAT'S NOT YOUR IMAGINATION, ASOK.
IT'S A LITTLE THING I CALL EXPERIENCE.
©2008 Scott Adams, Inc./Dist. by UFS, Inc.
ONCE A WEEK, I E-MAIL OUR POINTY-HAIRED BOSS AND ASK HIM A QUESTION.
I MAKE THE QUESTION SO COMPLICATED THAT IT HURTS HIS BRAIN.
OW! OW! OW!
HE'LL SPEND THE REST OF THE WEEK AVOIDING ME SO HE DOESN'T NEED TO THINK ABOUT IT.
MEANWHILE HE SEEKS OUT TEAM PLAYERS AND HAMMERS THEM WITH NEW PROJECTS.
11-16-08
SO. . . EXPERIENCE IS A FORM OF EVIL?
NOT ALWAYS. SOME PEOPLE SQUANDER IT.

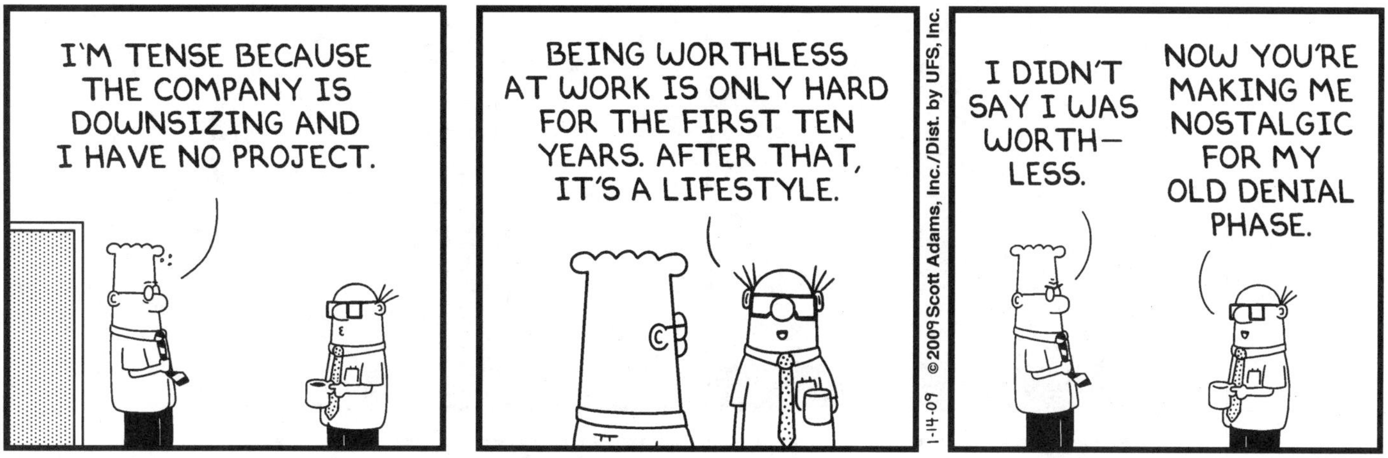
I'M TENSE BECAUSE THE COMPANY IS DOWNSIZING AND I HAVE NO PROJECT.
BEING WORTHLESS AT WORK IS ONLY HARD FOR THE FIRST TEN YEARS. AFTER THAT, IT'S A LIFESTYLE.
1-14-09 © 2009 Scott Adams, Inc./Dist. by UFS, Inc.
I DIDN'T SAY I WAS WORTH-LESS.
NOW YOU'RE MAKING ME NOSTALGIC FOR MY OLD DENIAL PHASE.

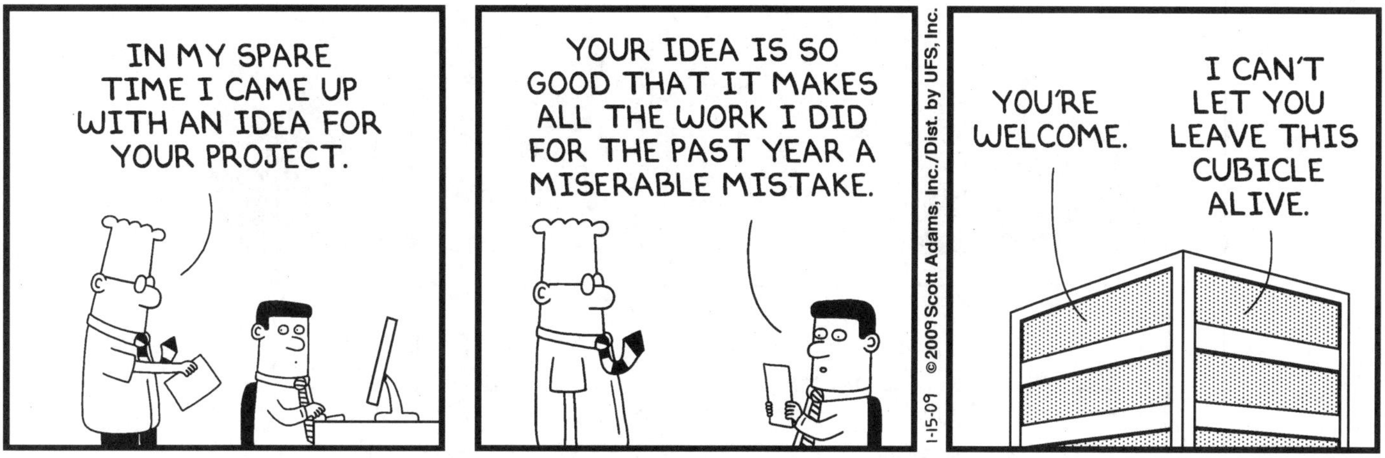
IN MY SPARE TIME I CAME UP WITH AN IDEA FOR YOUR PROJECT.
YOUR IDEA IS SO GOOD THAT IT MAKES ALL THE WORK I DID FOR THE PAST YEAR A MISERABLE MISTAKE.
1-15-09 © 2009 Scott Adams, Inc./Dist. by UFS, Inc.
YOU'RE WELCOME.
I CAN'T LET YOU LEAVE THIS CUBICLE ALIVE.

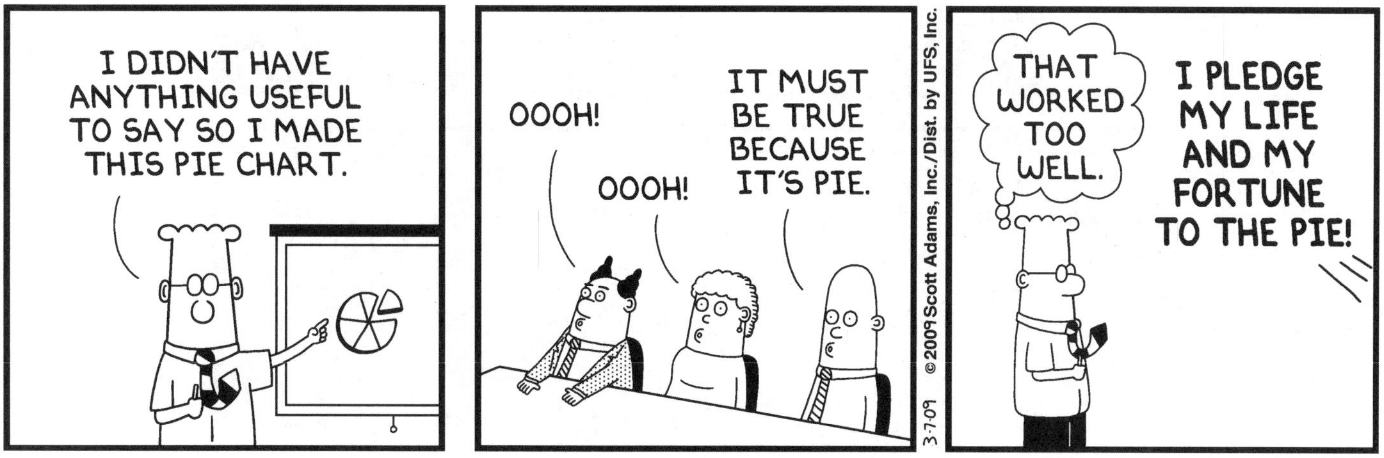
I DIDN'T HAVE ANYTHING USEFUL TO SAY SO I MADE THIS PIE CHART.
OOOH!
OOOH!
IT MUST BE TRUE BECAUSE IT'S PIE.
3-7-09 © 2009 Scott Adams, Inc./Dist. by UFS, Inc.
THAT WORKED TOO WELL.
I PLEDGE MY LIFE AND MY FORTUNE TO THE PIE!

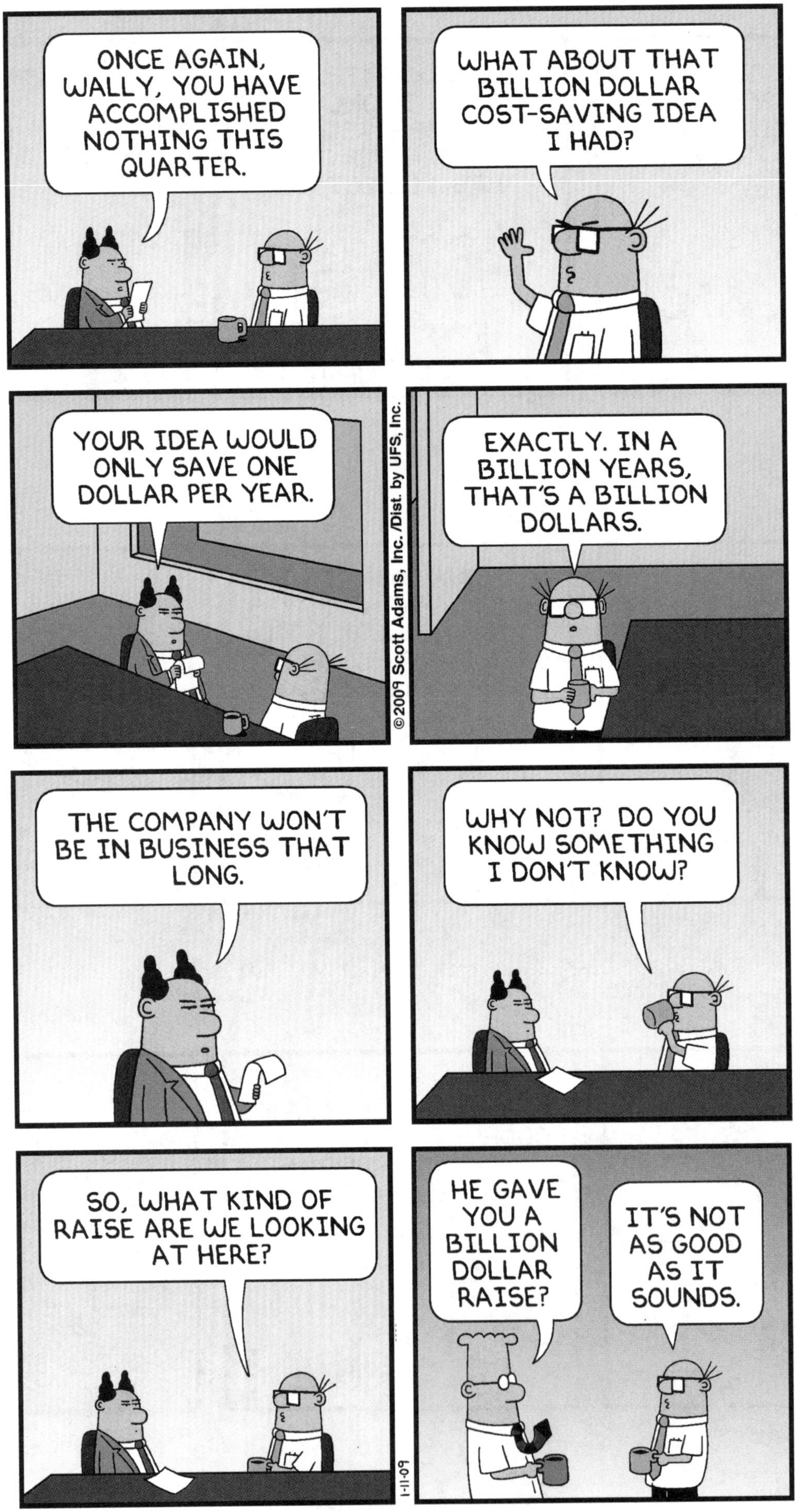
ONCE AGAIN, WALLY, YOU HAVE ACCOMPLISHED NOTHING THIS QUARTER.
WHAT ABOUT THAT BILLION DOLLAR COST-SAVING IDEA I HAD?
YOUR IDEA WOULD ONLY SAVE ONE DOLLAR PER YEAR.
EXACTLY. IN A BILLION YEARS, THAT'S A BILLION DOLLARS.
THE COMPANY WON'T BE IN BUSINESS THAT LONG.
WHY NOT? DO YOU KNOW SOMETHING I DON'T KNOW?
SO, WHAT KIND OF RAISE ARE WE LOOKING AT HERE?
HE GAVE YOU A BILLION DOLLAR RAISE?
IT'S NOT AS GOOD AS IT SOUNDS.
©2009 Scott Adams, Inc./Dist. by UFS, Inc.
1-11-09

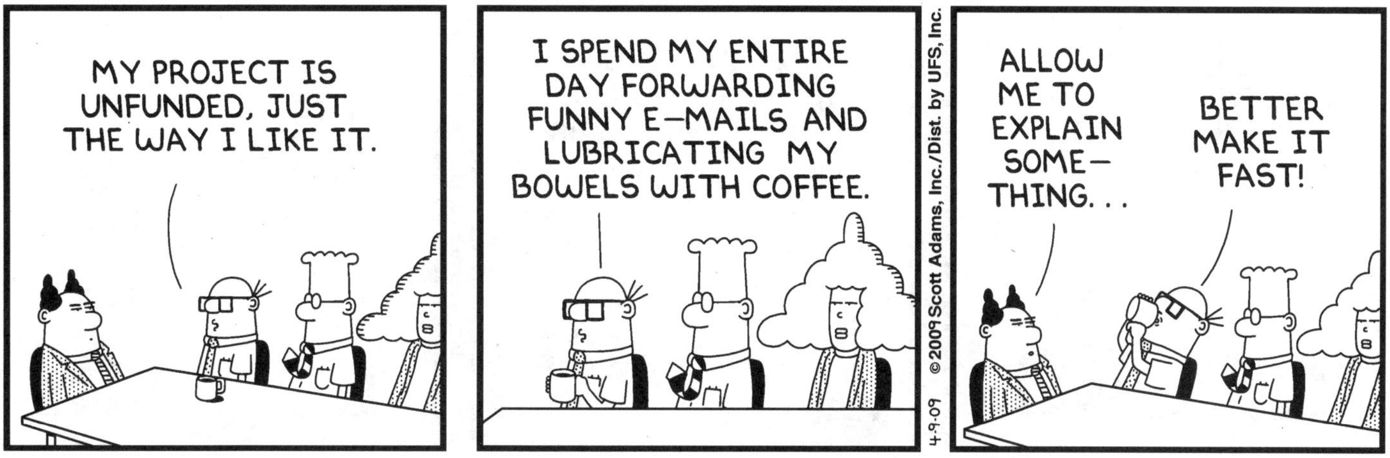
MY PROJECT IS UNFUNDED, JUST THE WAY I LIKE IT.
I SPEND MY ENTIRE DAY FORWARDING FUNNY E-MAILS AND LUBRICATING MY BOWELS WITH COFFEE.
4-9-09 ©2009 Scott Adams, Inc./Dist. by UFS, Inc.
ALLOW ME TO EXPLAIN SOME-THING. . .
BETTER MAKE IT FAST!

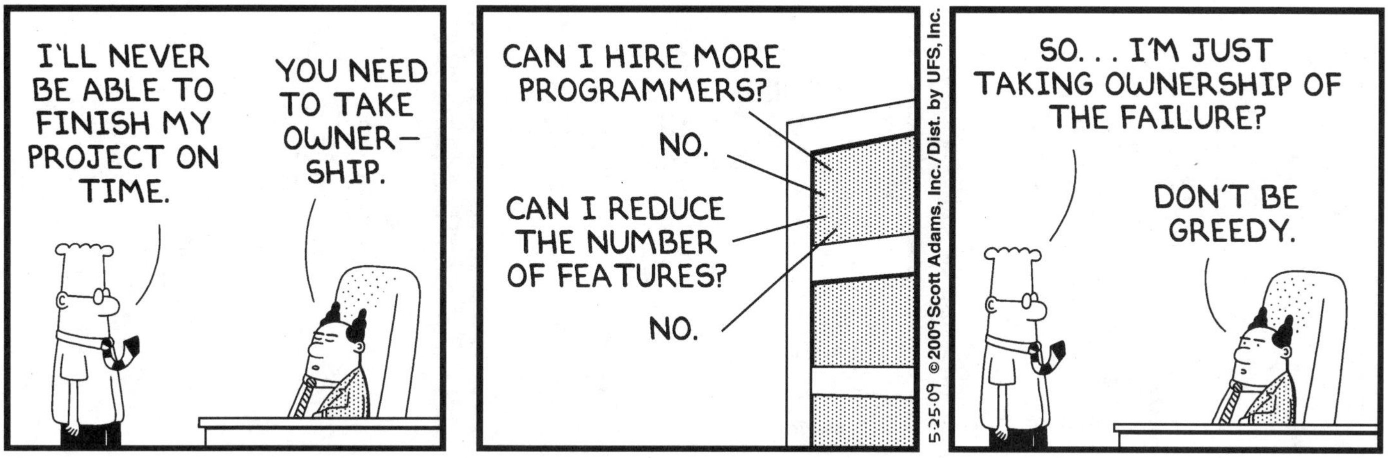
I'LL NEVER BE ABLE TO FINISH MY PROJECT ON TIME.
YOU NEED TO TAKE OWNER-SHIP.
CAN I HIRE MORE PROGRAMMERS?
NO.
CAN I REDUCE THE NUMBER OF FEATURES?
NO.
5-25-09 ©2009 Scott Adams, Inc./Dist. by UFS, Inc.
SO. . . I'M JUST TAKING OWNERSHIP OF THE FAILURE?
DON'T BE GREEDY.

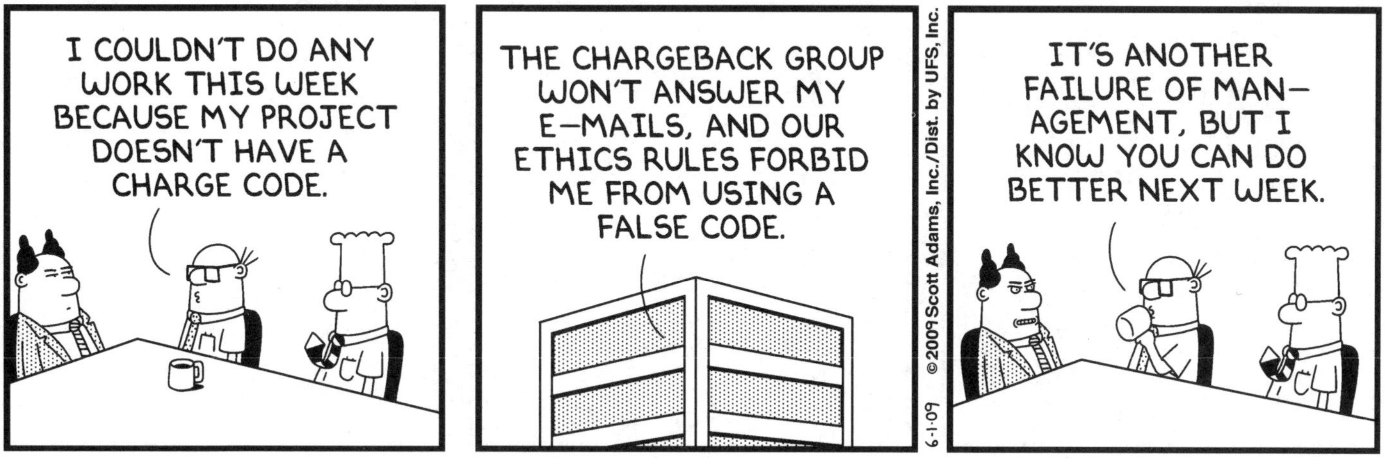
I COULDN'T DO ANY WORK THIS WEEK BECAUSE MY PROJECT DOESN'T HAVE A CHARGE CODE.
THE CHARGEBACK GROUP WON'T ANSWER MY E-MAILS, AND OUR ETHICS RULES FORBID ME FROM USING A FALSE CODE.
6-1-09 ©2009 Scott Adams, Inc./Dist. by UFS, Inc.
IT'S ANOTHER FAILURE OF MAN-AGEMENT, BUT I KNOW YOU CAN DO BETTER NEXT WEEK.

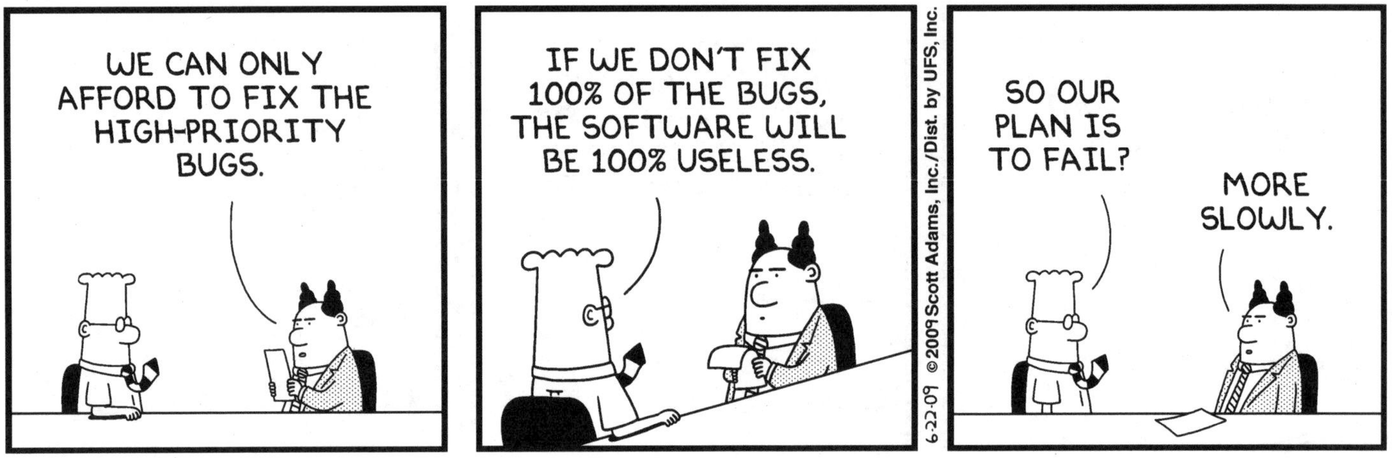
WE CAN ONLY AFFORD TO FIX THE HIGH-PRIORITY BUGS.
IF WE DON'T FIX 100% OF THE BUGS, THE SOFTWARE WILL BE 100% USELESS.
SO OUR PLAN IS TO FAIL?
MORE SLOWLY.
6-22-09 © 2009 Scott Adams, Inc./Dist. by UFS, Inc.

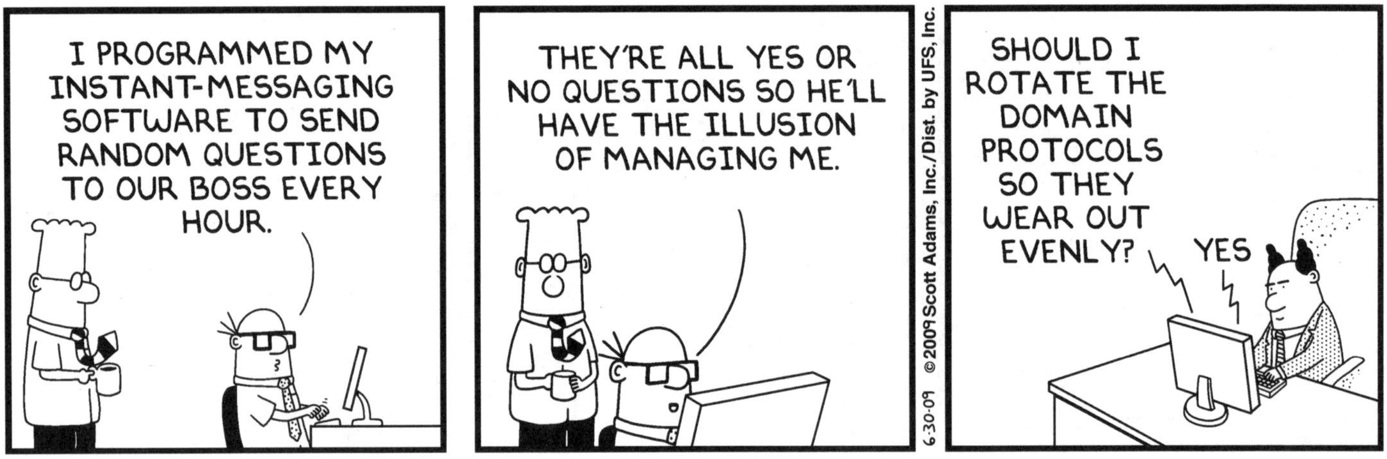
I PROGRAMMED MY INSTANT-MESSAGING SOFTWARE TO SEND RANDOM QUESTIONS TO OUR BOSS EVERY HOUR.
THEY'RE ALL YES OR NO QUESTIONS SO HE'LL HAVE THE ILLUSION OF MANAGING ME.
SHOULD I ROTATE THE DOMAIN PROTOCOLS SO THEY WEAR OUT EVENLY?
YES
6-30-09 © 2009 Scott Adams, Inc./Dist. by UFS, Inc.

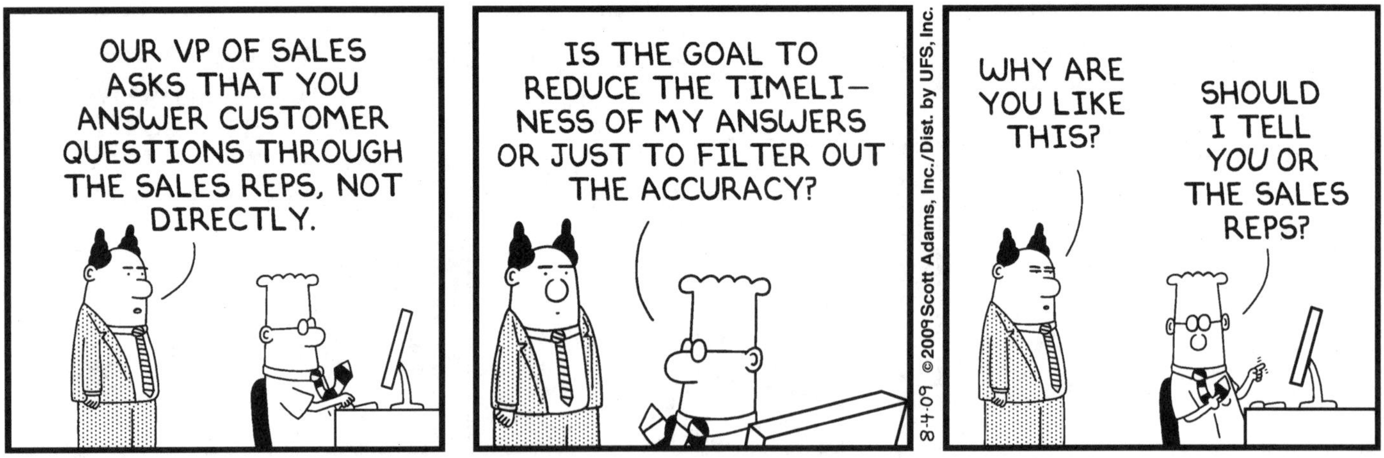
OUR VP OF SALES ASKS THAT YOU ANSWER CUSTOMER QUESTIONS THROUGH THE SALES REPS, NOT DIRECTLY.
IS THE GOAL TO REDUCE THE TIMELI-NESS OF MY ANSWERS OR JUST TO FILTER OUT THE ACCURACY?
WHY ARE YOU LIKE THIS?
SHOULD I TELL *YOU* OR THE SALES REPS?
8-4-09 © 2009 Scott Adams, Inc./Dist. by UFS, Inc.

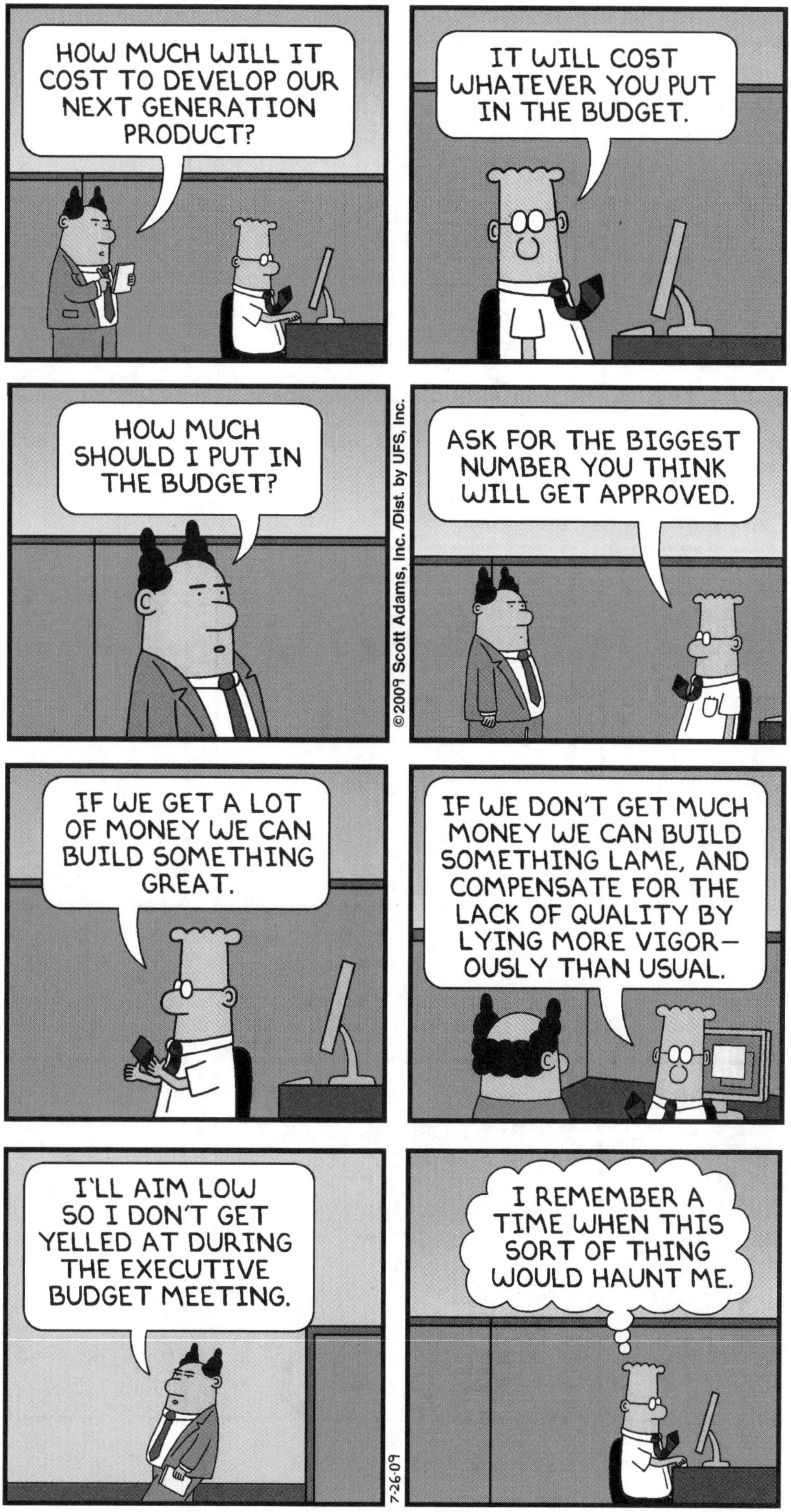
HOW MUCH WILL IT COST TO DEVELOP OUR NEXT GENERATION PRODUCT?
IT WILL COST WHATEVER YOU PUT IN THE BUDGET.
HOW MUCH SHOULD I PUT IN THE BUDGET?
ASK FOR THE BIGGEST NUMBER YOU THINK WILL GET APPROVED.
IF WE GET A LOT OF MONEY WE CAN BUILD SOMETHING GREAT.
IF WE DON'T GET MUCH MONEY WE CAN BUILD SOMETHING LAME, AND COMPENSATE FOR THE LACK OF QUALITY BY LYING MORE VIGOR-OUSLY THAN USUAL.
I'LL AIM LOW SO I DON'T GET YELLED AT DURING THE EXECUTIVE BUDGET MEETING.
I REMEMBER A TIME WHEN THIS SORT OF THING WOULD HAUNT ME.
©2009 Scott Adams, Inc./Dist. by UFS, Inc.
7-26-09

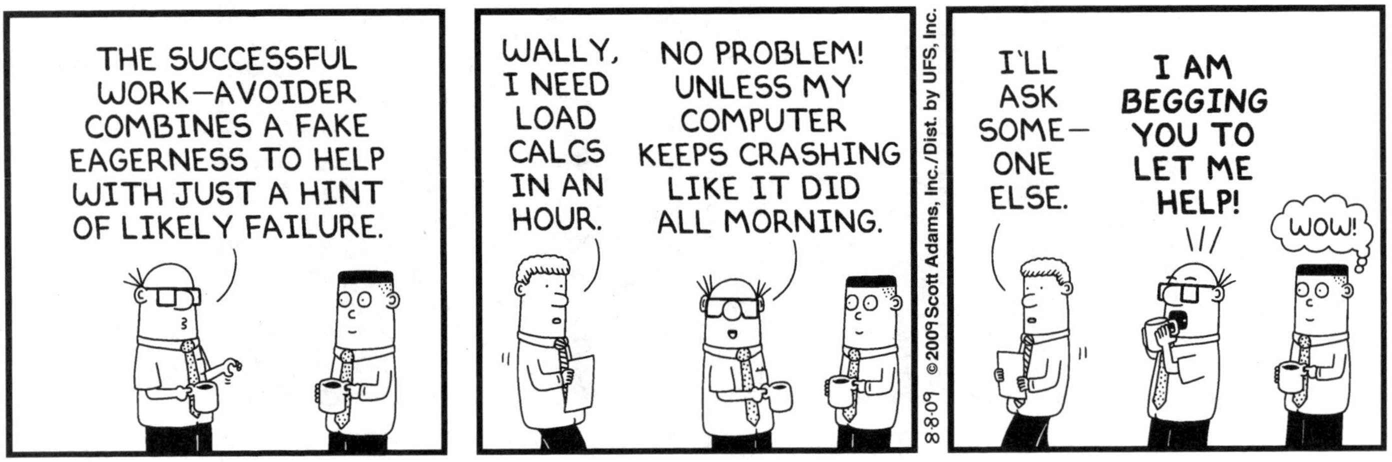
THE SUCCESSFUL WORK—AVOIDER COMBINES A FAKE EAGERNESS TO HELP WITH JUST A HINT OF LIKELY FAILURE.
WALLY, I NEED LOAD CALCS IN AN HOUR.
NO PROBLEM! UNLESS MY COMPUTER KEEPS CRASHING LIKE IT DID ALL MORNING.
8-8-09 © 2009 Scott Adams, Inc./Dist. by UFS, Inc.
I'LL ASK SOME—ONE ELSE.
I AM BEGGING YOU TO LET ME HELP!
WOW!

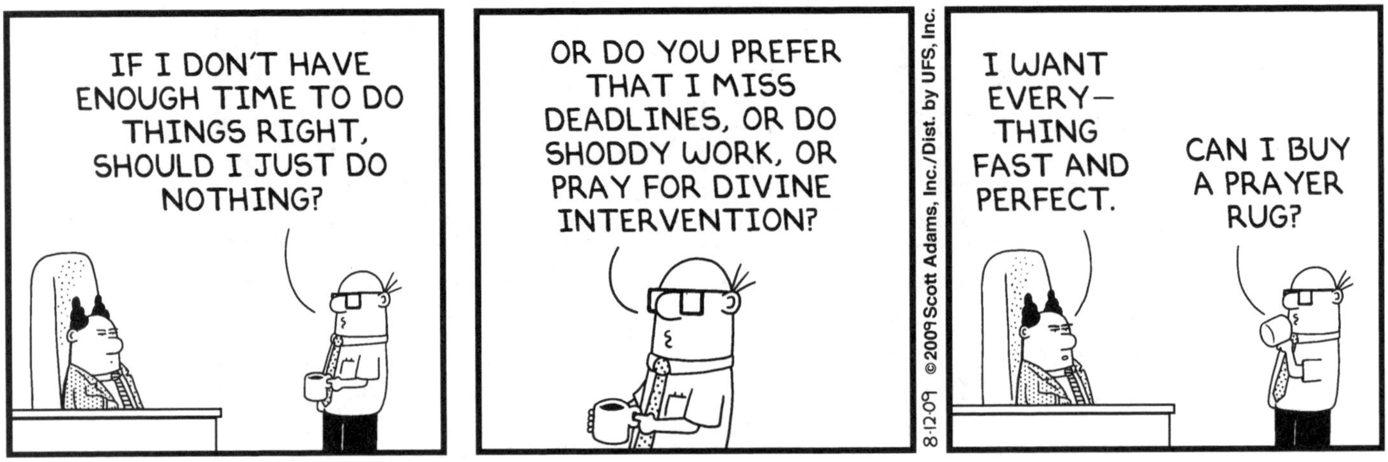
IF I DON'T HAVE ENOUGH TIME TO DO THINGS RIGHT, SHOULD I JUST DO NOTHING?
OR DO YOU PREFER THAT I MISS DEADLINES, OR DO SHODDY WORK, OR PRAY FOR DIVINE INTERVENTION?
8-12-09 © 2009 Scott Adams, Inc./Dist. by UFS, Inc.
I WANT EVERY—THING FAST AND PERFECT.
CAN I BUY A PRAYER RUG?

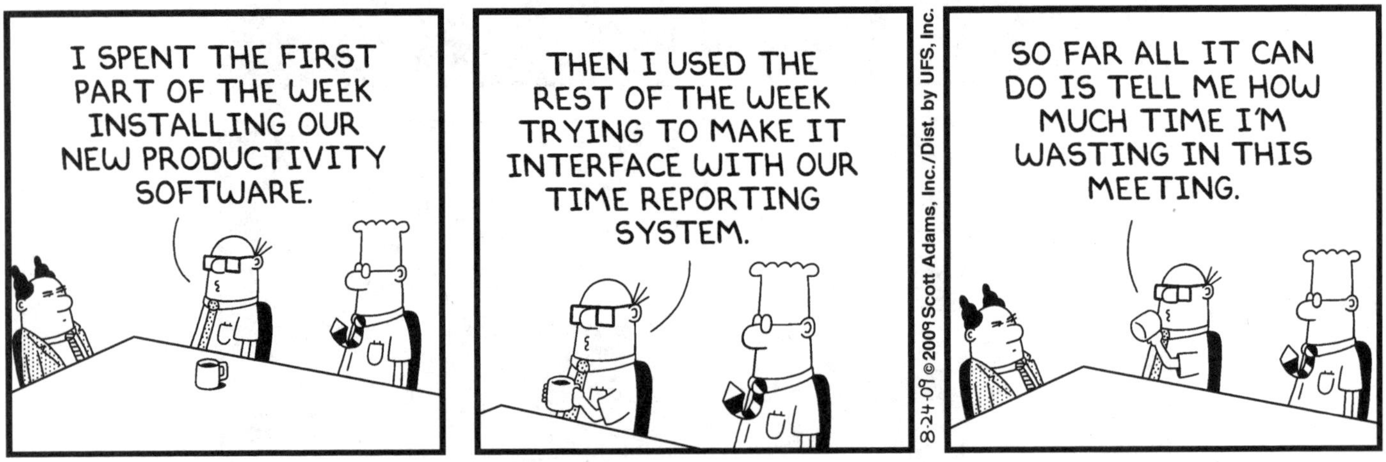
I SPENT THE FIRST PART OF THE WEEK INSTALLING OUR NEW PRODUCTIVITY SOFTWARE.
THEN I USED THE REST OF THE WEEK TRYING TO MAKE IT INTERFACE WITH OUR TIME REPORTING SYSTEM.
8-24-09 © 2009 Scott Adams, Inc./Dist. by UFS, Inc.
SO FAR ALL IT CAN DO IS TELL ME HOW MUCH TIME I'M WASTING IN THIS MEETING.

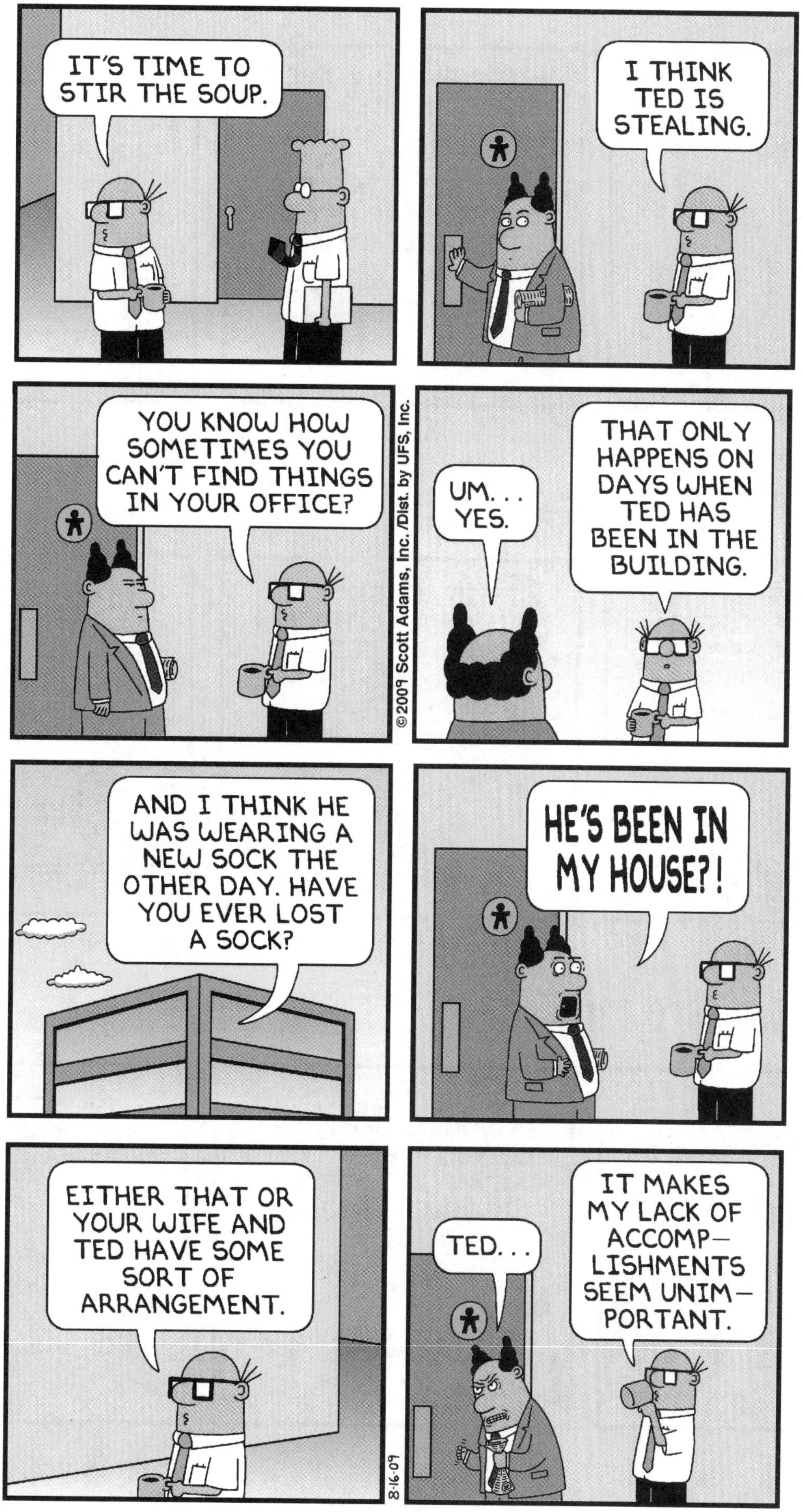
IT'S TIME TO STIR THE SOUP.
I THINK TED IS STEALING.
YOU KNOW HOW SOMETIMES YOU CAN'T FIND THINGS IN YOUR OFFICE?
UM... YES.
THAT ONLY HAPPENS ON DAYS WHEN TED HAS BEEN IN THE BUILDING.
©2009 Scott Adams, Inc. /Dist. by UFS, Inc.
AND I THINK HE WAS WEARING A NEW SOCK THE OTHER DAY. HAVE YOU EVER LOST A SOCK?
HE'S BEEN IN MY HOUSE?!
EITHER THAT OR YOUR WIFE AND TED HAVE SOME SORT OF ARRANGEMENT.
8-16-09
TED...
IT MAKES MY LACK OF ACCOMP-LISHMENTS SEEM UNIM-PORTANT.

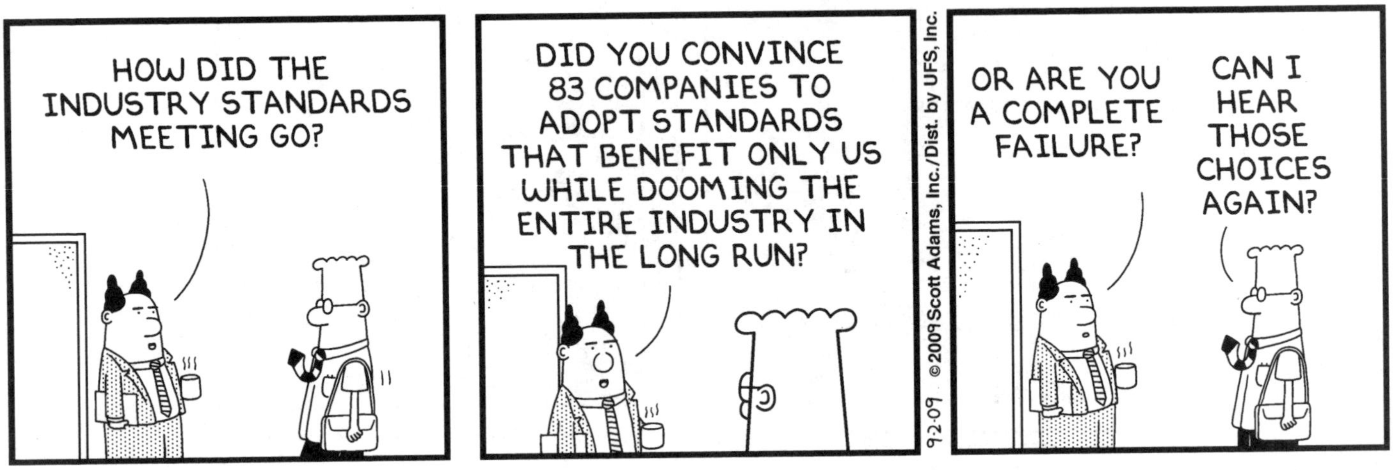
HOW DID THE INDUSTRY STANDARDS MEETING GO?
DID YOU CONVINCE 83 COMPANIES TO ADOPT STANDARDS THAT BENEFIT ONLY US WHILE DOOMING THE ENTIRE INDUSTRY IN THE LONG RUN?
OR ARE YOU A COMPLETE FAILURE?
CAN I HEAR THOSE CHOICES AGAIN?
9-2-09 ©2009 Scott Adams, Inc./Dist. by UFS, Inc.

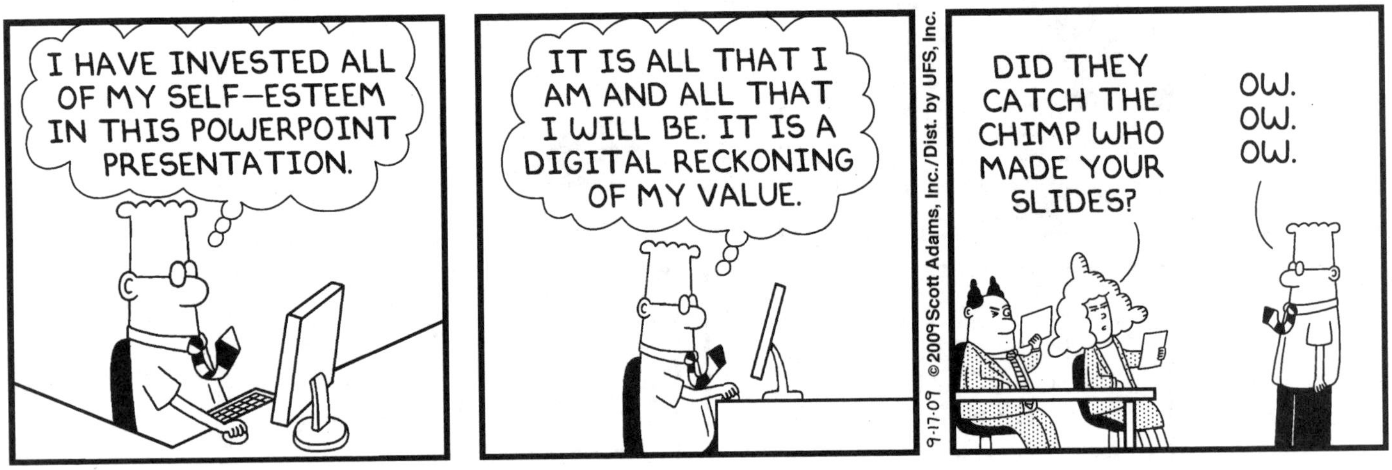
I HAVE INVESTED ALL OF MY SELF—ESTEEM IN THIS POWERPOINT PRESENTATION.
IT IS ALL THAT I AM AND ALL THAT I WILL BE. IT IS A DIGITAL RECKONING OF MY VALUE.
DID THEY CATCH THE CHIMP WHO MADE YOUR SLIDES?
OW. OW. OW.
9-17-09 ©2009 Scott Adams, Inc./Dist. by UFS, Inc.

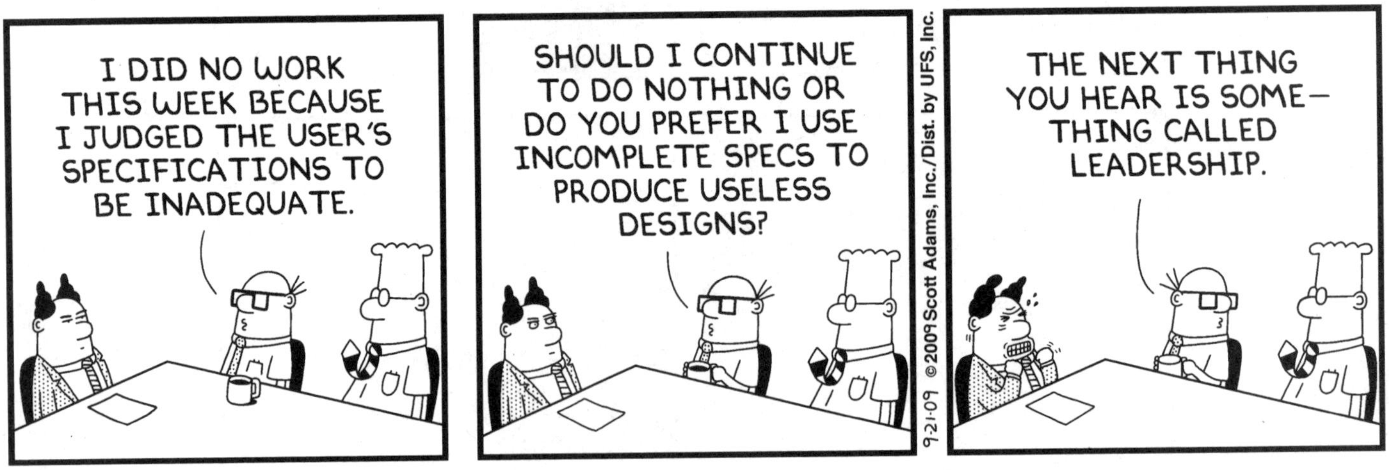
I DID NO WORK THIS WEEK BECAUSE I JUDGED THE USER'S SPECIFICATIONS TO BE INADEQUATE.
SHOULD I CONTINUE TO DO NOTHING OR DO YOU PREFER I USE INCOMPLETE SPECS TO PRODUCE USELESS DESIGNS?
THE NEXT THING YOU HEAR IS SOME—THING CALLED LEADERSHIP.
9-21-09 ©2009 Scott Adams, Inc./Dist. by UFS, Inc.

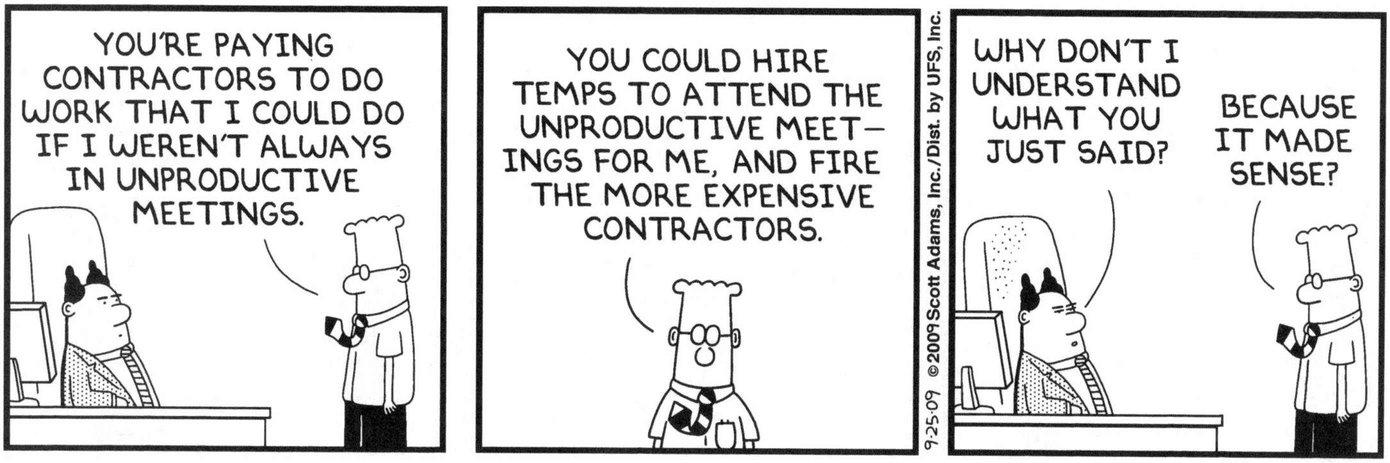
YOU'RE PAYING CONTRACTORS TO DO WORK THAT I COULD DO IF I WEREN'T ALWAYS IN UNPRODUCTIVE MEETINGS.
YOU COULD HIRE TEMPS TO ATTEND THE UNPRODUCTIVE MEET-INGS FOR ME, AND FIRE THE MORE EXPENSIVE CONTRACTORS.
9-25-09 © 2009 Scott Adams, Inc./Dist. by UFS, Inc.
WHY DON'T I UNDERSTAND WHAT YOU JUST SAID?
BECAUSE IT MADE SENSE?

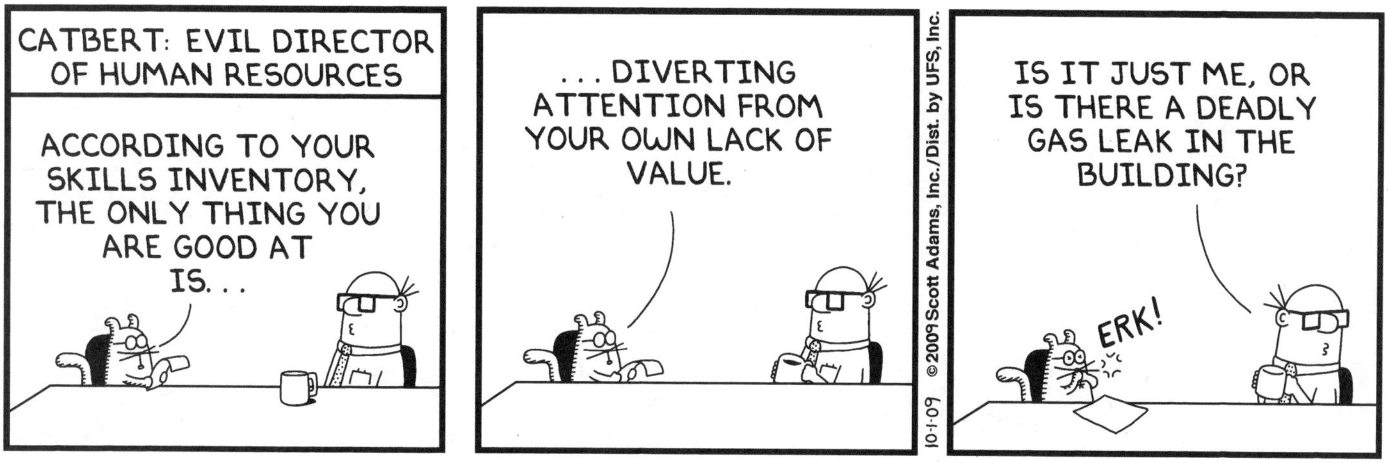
CATBERT: EVIL DIRECTOR OF HUMAN RESOURCES
ACCORDING TO YOUR SKILLS INVENTORY, THE ONLY THING YOU ARE GOOD AT IS...
...DIVERTING ATTENTION FROM YOUR OWN LACK OF VALUE.
10-1-09 © 2009 Scott Adams, Inc./Dist. by UFS, Inc.
IS IT JUST ME, OR IS THERE A DEADLY GAS LEAK IN THE BUILDING?
ERK!

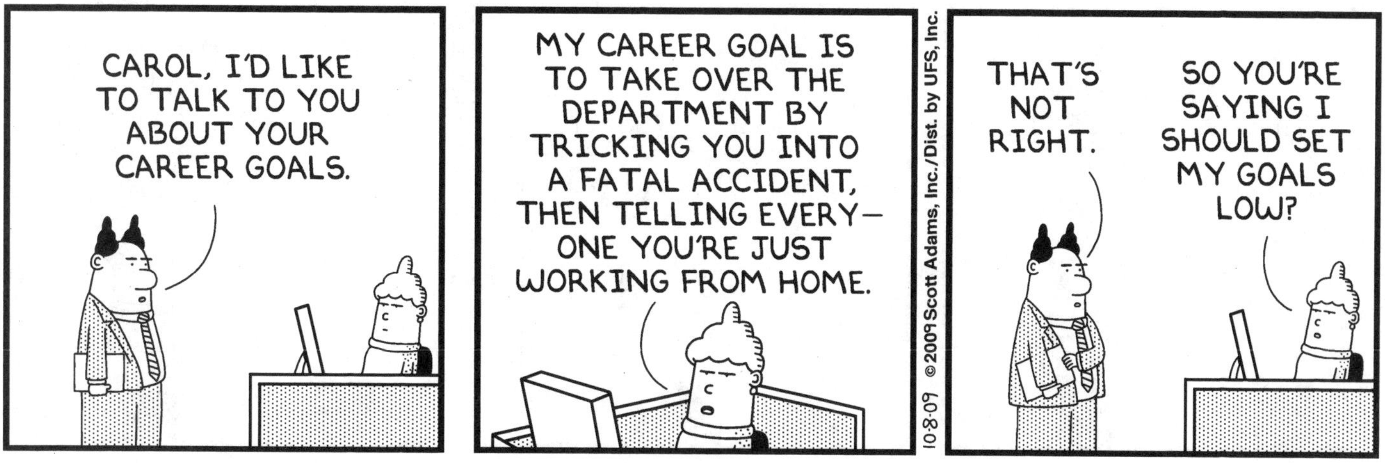
CAROL, I'D LIKE TO TALK TO YOU ABOUT YOUR CAREER GOALS.
MY CAREER GOAL IS TO TAKE OVER THE DEPARTMENT BY TRICKING YOU INTO A FATAL ACCIDENT, THEN TELLING EVERY-ONE YOU'RE JUST WORKING FROM HOME.
10-8-09 © 2009 Scott Adams, Inc./Dist. by UFS, Inc.
THAT'S NOT RIGHT.
SO YOU'RE SAYING I SHOULD SET MY GOALS LOW?

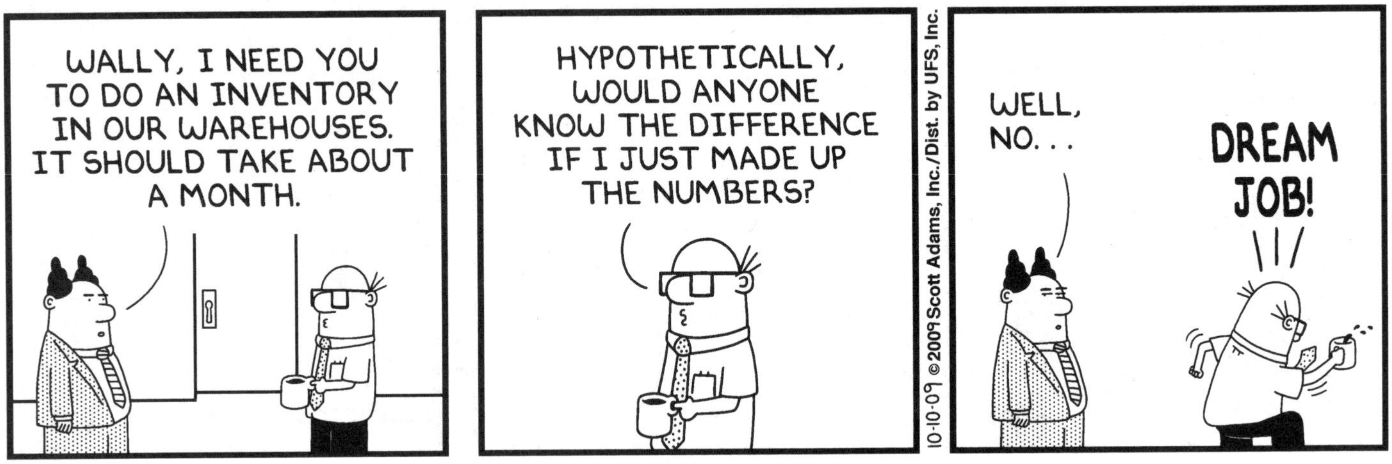

WALLY, I NEED YOU TO DO AN INVENTORY IN OUR WAREHOUSES. IT SHOULD TAKE ABOUT A MONTH.
HYPOTHETICALLY, WOULD ANYONE KNOW THE DIFFERENCE IF I JUST MADE UP THE NUMBERS?
10-10-09 © 2009 Scott Adams, Inc./Dist. by UFS, Inc.
WELL, NO. . .
DREAM JOB!

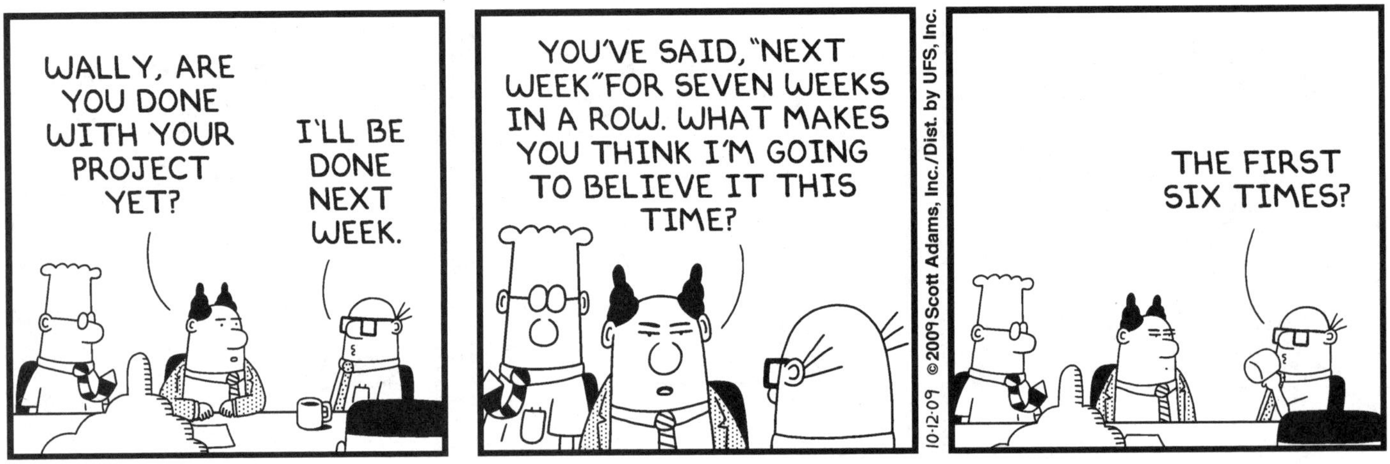

WALLY, ARE YOU DONE WITH YOUR PROJECT YET?
I'LL BE DONE NEXT WEEK.
YOU'VE SAID, "NEXT WEEK" FOR SEVEN WEEKS IN A ROW. WHAT MAKES YOU THINK I'M GOING TO BELIEVE IT THIS TIME?
10-12-09 © 2009 Scott Adams, Inc./Dist. by UFS, Inc.
THE FIRST SIX TIMES?

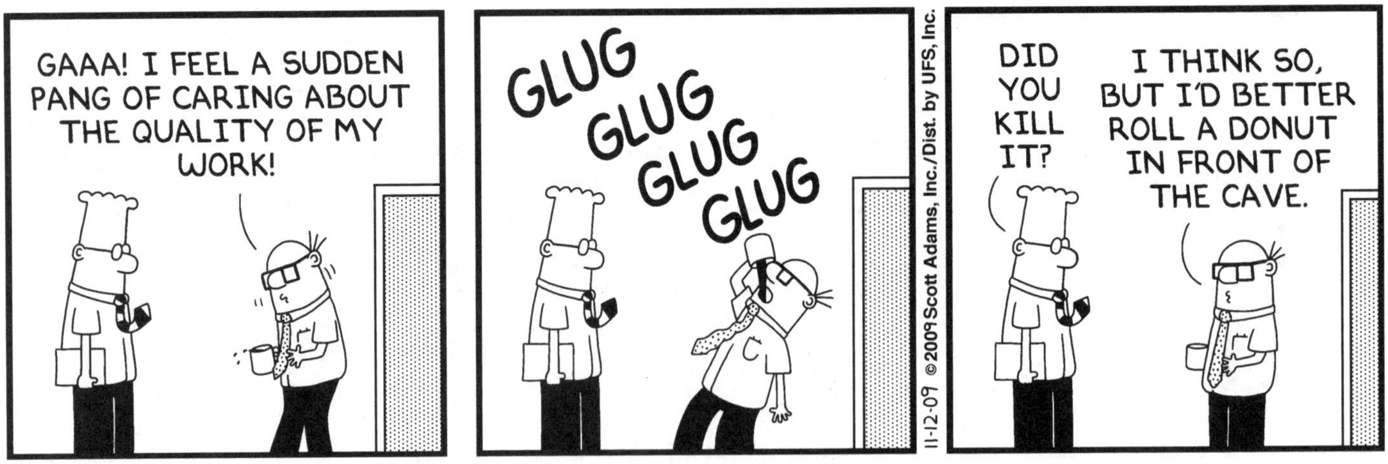

GAAA! I FEEL A SUDDEN PANG OF CARING ABOUT THE QUALITY OF MY WORK!
GLUG
GLUG
GLUG
GLUG
11-12-09 © 2009 Scott Adams, Inc./Dist. by UFS, Inc.
DID YOU KILL IT?
I THINK SO, BUT I'D BETTER ROLL A DONUT IN FRONT OF THE CAVE.

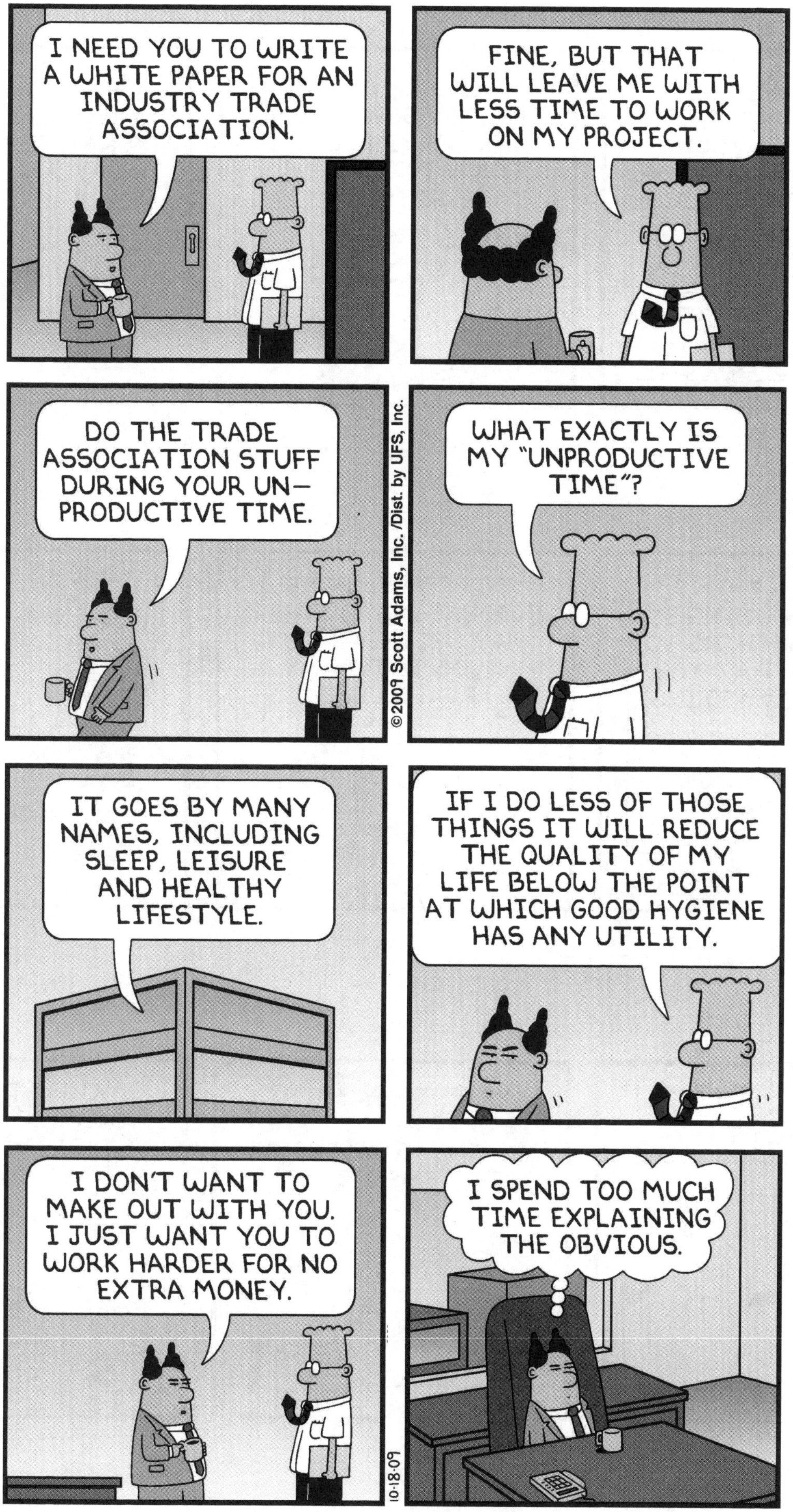
I NEED YOU TO WRITE A WHITE PAPER FOR AN INDUSTRY TRADE ASSOCIATION.
FINE, BUT THAT WILL LEAVE ME WITH LESS TIME TO WORK ON MY PROJECT.
DO THE TRADE ASSOCIATION STUFF DURING YOUR UN-PRODUCTIVE TIME.
WHAT EXACTLY IS MY "UNPRODUCTIVE TIME"?
IT GOES BY MANY NAMES, INCLUDING SLEEP, LEISURE AND HEALTHY LIFESTYLE.
IF I DO LESS OF THOSE THINGS IT WILL REDUCE THE QUALITY OF MY LIFE BELOW THE POINT AT WHICH GOOD HYGIENE HAS ANY UTILITY.
I DON'T WANT TO MAKE OUT WITH YOU. I JUST WANT YOU TO WORK HARDER FOR NO EXTRA MONEY.
I SPEND TOO MUCH TIME EXPLAINING THE OBVIOUS.
©2009 Scott Adams, Inc. /Dist. by UFS, Inc.
10-18-09

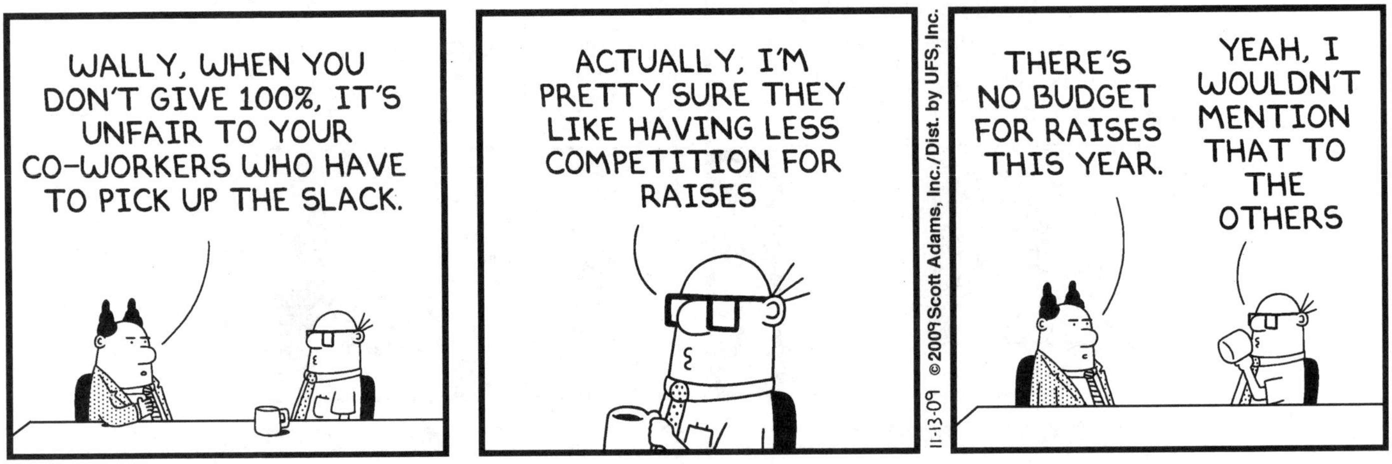
WALLY, WHEN YOU DON'T GIVE 100%, IT'S UNFAIR TO YOUR CO-WORKERS WHO HAVE TO PICK UP THE SLACK.
ACTUALLY, I'M PRETTY SURE THEY LIKE HAVING LESS COMPETITION FOR RAISES
THERE'S NO BUDGET FOR RAISES THIS YEAR.
YEAH, I WOULDN'T MENTION THAT TO THE OTHERS
11-13-09 ©2009 Scott Adams, Inc./Dist. by UFS, Inc.

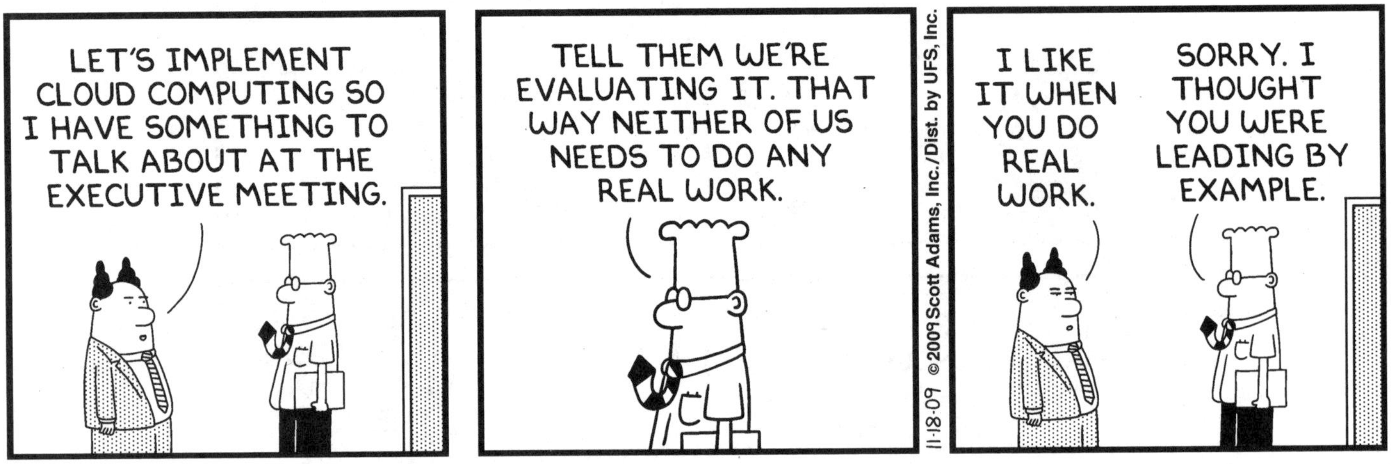
LET'S IMPLEMENT CLOUD COMPUTING SO I HAVE SOMETHING TO TALK ABOUT AT THE EXECUTIVE MEETING.
TELL THEM WE'RE EVALUATING IT. THAT WAY NEITHER OF US NEEDS TO DO ANY REAL WORK.
I LIKE IT WHEN YOU DO REAL WORK.
SORRY. I THOUGHT YOU WERE LEADING BY EXAMPLE.
11-18-09 ©2009 Scott Adams, Inc./Dist. by UFS, Inc.

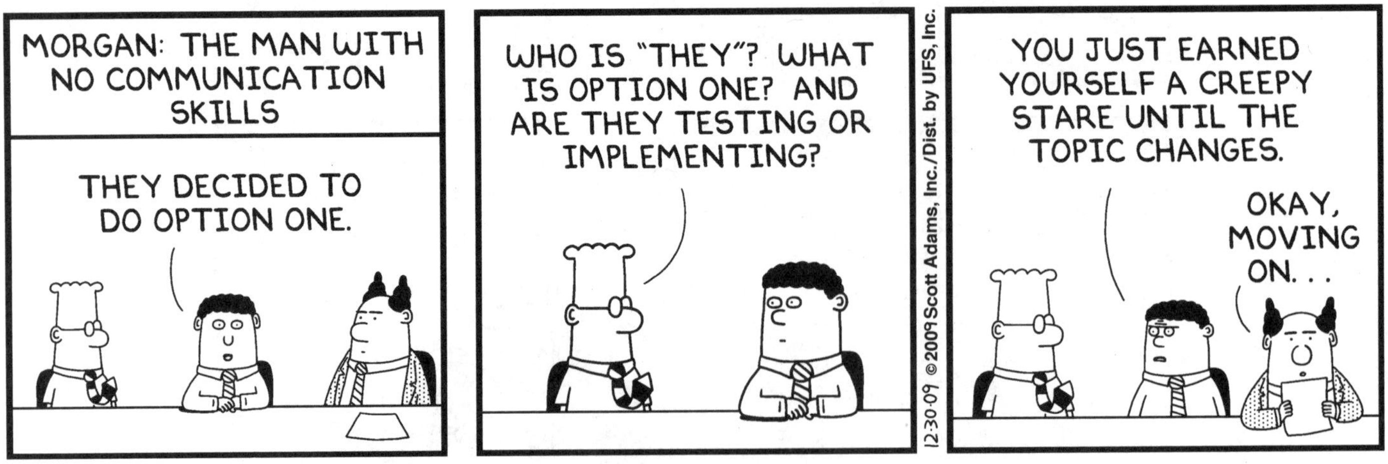
MORGAN: THE MAN WITH NO COMMUNICATION SKILLS
THEY DECIDED TO DO OPTION ONE.
WHO IS "THEY"? WHAT IS OPTION ONE? AND ARE THEY TESTING OR IMPLEMENTING?
YOU JUST EARNED YOURSELF A CREEPY STARE UNTIL THE TOPIC CHANGES.
OKAY, MOVING ON. . .
12-30-09 ©2009 Scott Adams, Inc./Dist. by UFS, Inc.

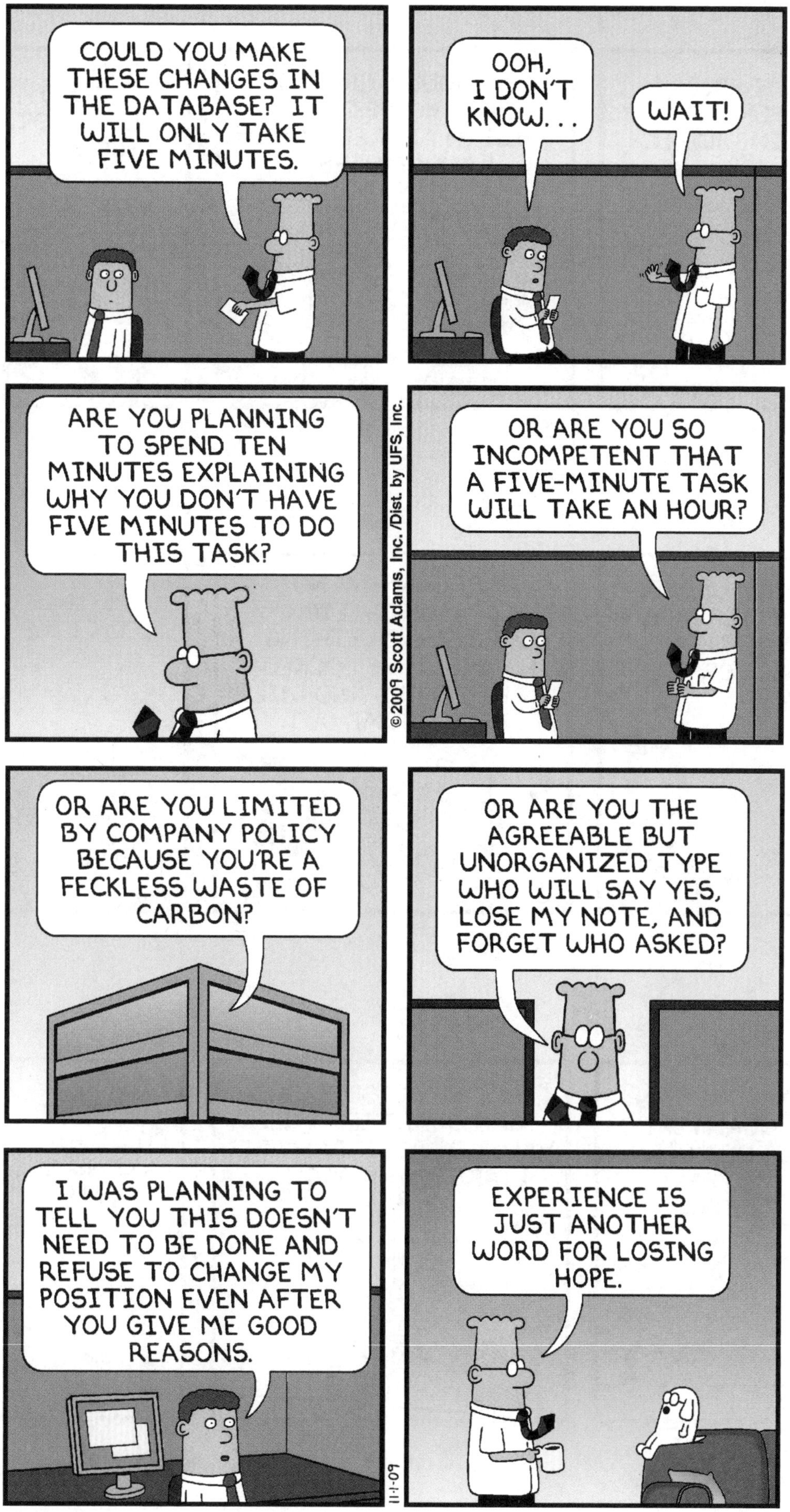
COULD YOU MAKE THESE CHANGES IN THE DATABASE? IT WILL ONLY TAKE FIVE MINUTES.
OOH, I DON'T KNOW. . .
WAIT!
ARE YOU PLANNING TO SPEND TEN MINUTES EXPLAINING WHY YOU DON'T HAVE FIVE MINUTES TO DO THIS TASK?
©2009 Scott Adams, Inc./Dist. by UFS, Inc.
OR ARE YOU SO INCOMPETENT THAT A FIVE-MINUTE TASK WILL TAKE AN HOUR?
OR ARE YOU LIMITED BY COMPANY POLICY BECAUSE YOU'RE A FECKLESS WASTE OF CARBON?
OR ARE YOU THE AGREEABLE BUT UNORGANIZED TYPE WHO WILL SAY YES, LOSE MY NOTE, AND FORGET WHO ASKED?
I WAS PLANNING TO TELL YOU THIS DOESN'T NEED TO BE DONE AND REFUSE TO CHANGE MY POSITION EVEN AFTER YOU GIVE ME GOOD REASONS.
11-1-09
EXPERIENCE IS JUST ANOTHER WORD FOR LOSING HOPE.

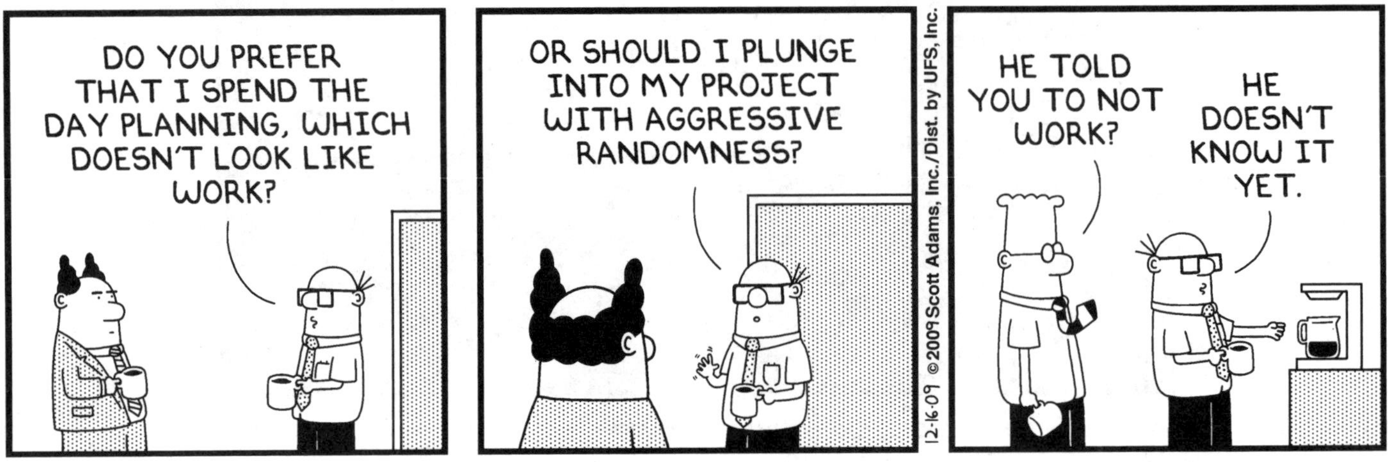
DO YOU PREFER THAT I SPEND THE DAY PLANNING, WHICH DOESN'T LOOK LIKE WORK?
OR SHOULD I PLUNGE INTO MY PROJECT WITH AGGRESSIVE RANDOMNESS?
12-16-09 ©2009 Scott Adams, Inc./Dist. by UFS, Inc.
HE TOLD YOU TO NOT WORK?
HE DOESN'T KNOW IT YET.

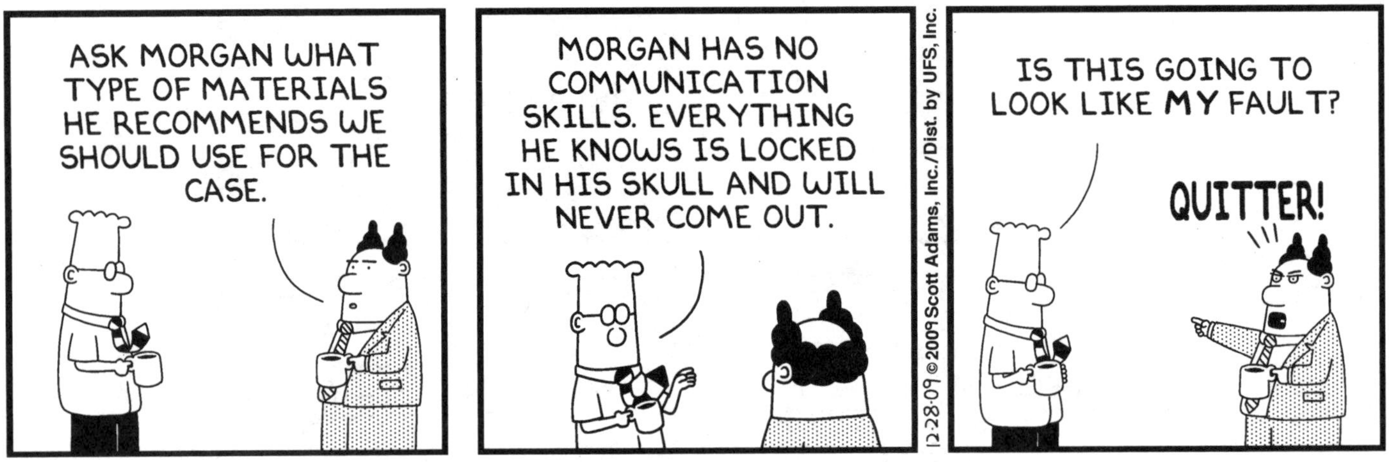
ASK MORGAN WHAT TYPE OF MATERIALS HE RECOMMENDS WE SHOULD USE FOR THE CASE.
MORGAN HAS NO COMMUNICATION SKILLS. EVERYTHING HE KNOWS IS LOCKED IN HIS SKULL AND WILL NEVER COME OUT.
12-28-09 ©2009 Scott Adams, Inc./Dist. by UFS, Inc.
IS THIS GOING TO LOOK LIKE MY FAULT?
QUITTER!

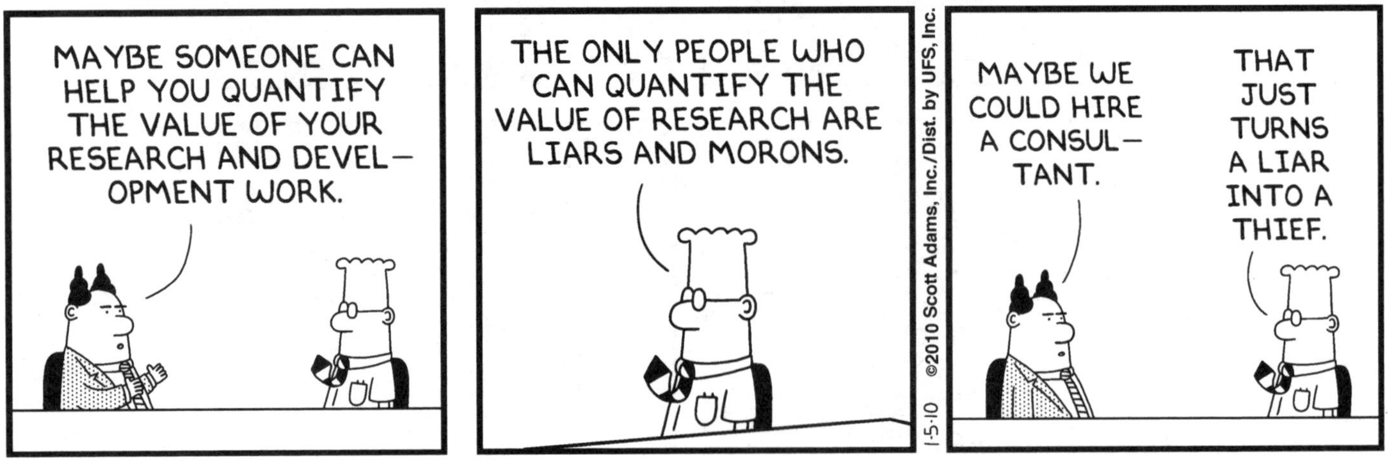
MAYBE SOMEONE CAN HELP YOU QUANTIFY THE VALUE OF YOUR RESEARCH AND DEVEL-OPMENT WORK.
THE ONLY PEOPLE WHO CAN QUANTIFY THE VALUE OF RESEARCH ARE LIARS AND MORONS.
1-5-10 ©2010 Scott Adams, Inc./Dist. by UFS, Inc.
MAYBE WE COULD HIRE A CONSUL-TANT.
THAT JUST TURNS A LIAR INTO A THIEF.

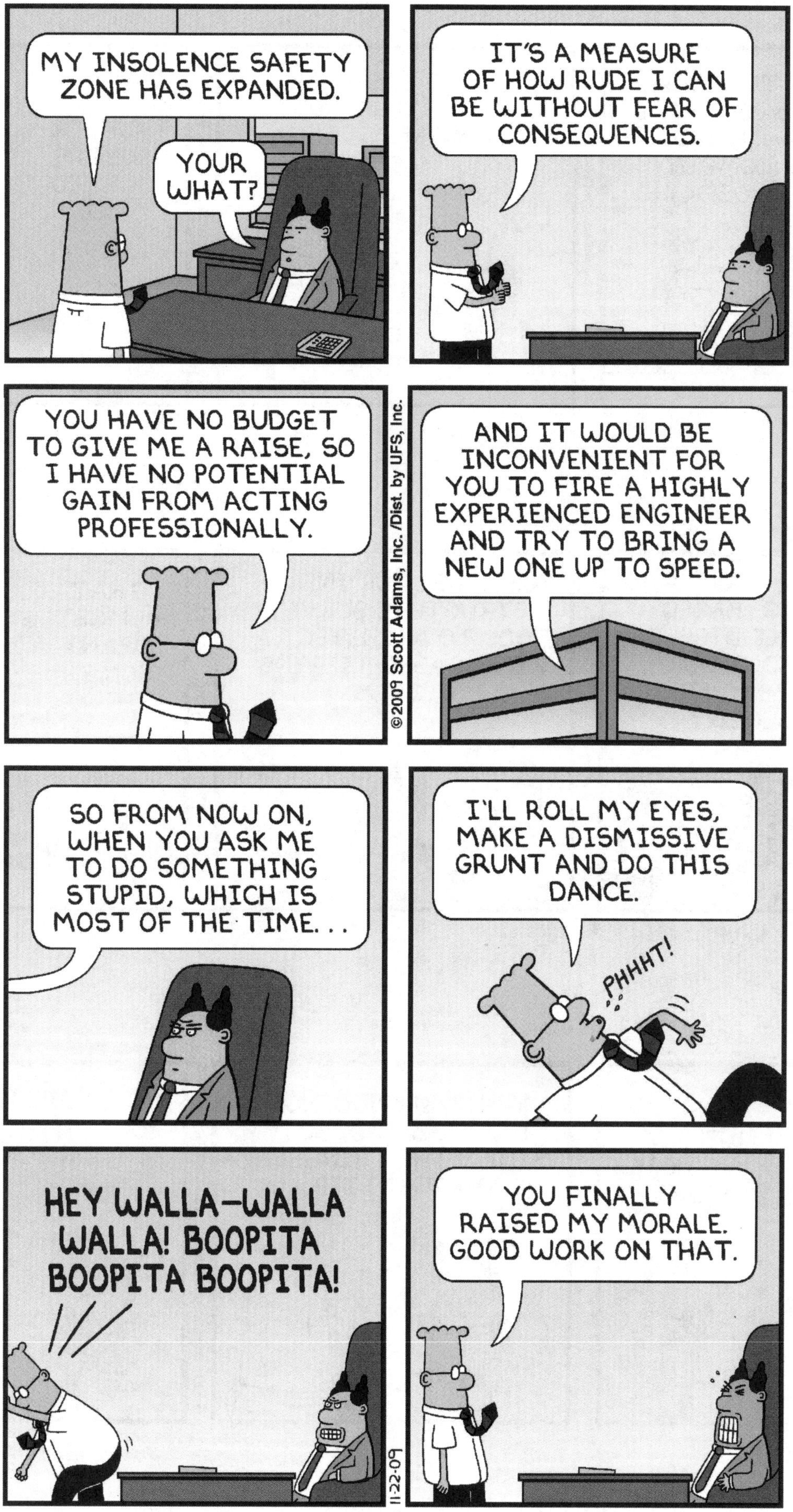
MY INSOLENCE SAFETY ZONE HAS EXPANDED.
YOUR WHAT?
IT'S A MEASURE OF HOW RUDE I CAN BE WITHOUT FEAR OF CONSEQUENCES.
YOU HAVE NO BUDGET TO GIVE ME A RAISE, SO I HAVE NO POTENTIAL GAIN FROM ACTING PROFESSIONALLY.
©2009 Scott Adams, Inc. /Dist. by UFS, Inc.
AND IT WOULD BE INCONVENIENT FOR YOU TO FIRE A HIGHLY EXPERIENCED ENGINEER AND TRY TO BRING A NEW ONE UP TO SPEED.
SO FROM NOW ON, WHEN YOU ASK ME TO DO SOMETHING STUPID, WHICH IS MOST OF THE TIME...
I'LL ROLL MY EYES, MAKE A DISMISSIVE GRUNT AND DO THIS DANCE.
PHHHT!
HEY WALLA-WALLA WALLA! BOOPITA BOOPITA BOOPITA!
11-22-09
YOU FINALLY RAISED MY MORALE. GOOD WORK ON THAT.

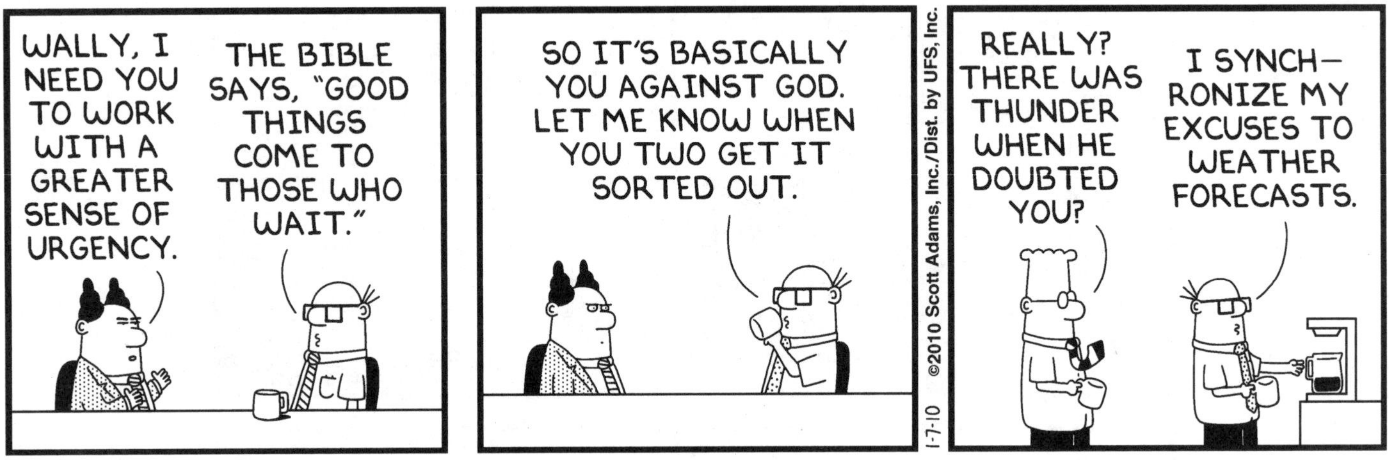
WALLY, I NEED YOU TO WORK WITH A GREATER SENSE OF URGENCY.
THE BIBLE SAYS, "GOOD THINGS COME TO THOSE WHO WAIT."
SO IT'S BASICALLY YOU AGAINST GOD. LET ME KNOW WHEN YOU TWO GET IT SORTED OUT.
1-7-10 ©2010 Scott Adams, Inc./Dist. by UFS, Inc.
REALLY? THERE WAS THUNDER WHEN HE DOUBTED YOU?
I SYNCH-RONIZE MY EXCUSES TO WEATHER FORECASTS.

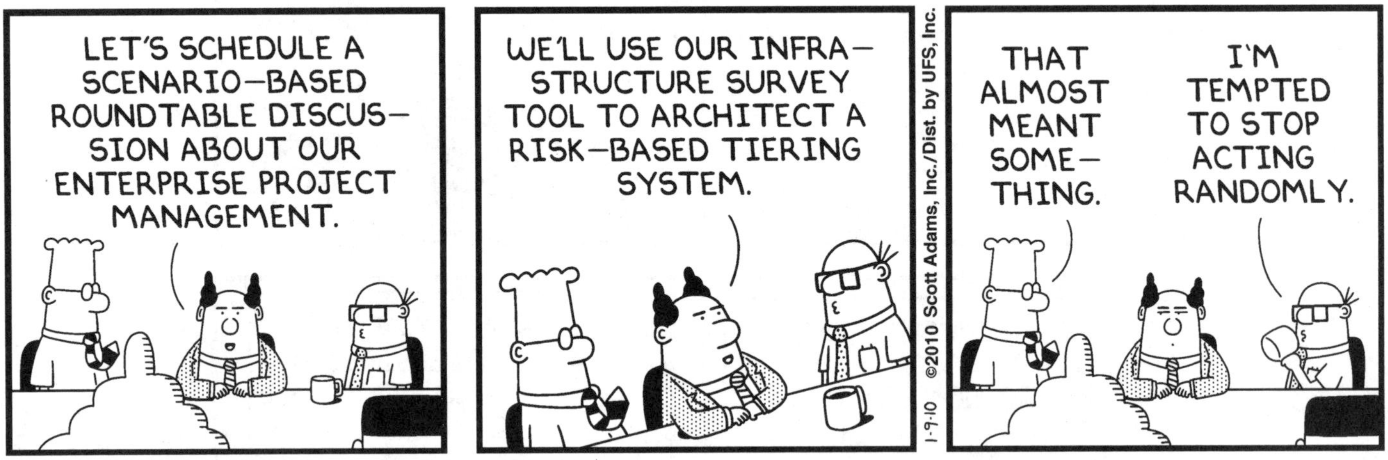
LET'S SCHEDULE A SCENARIO-BASED ROUNDTABLE DISCUS-SION ABOUT OUR ENTERPRISE PROJECT MANAGEMENT.
WE'LL USE OUR INFRA-STRUCTURE SURVEY TOOL TO ARCHITECT A RISK-BASED TIERING SYSTEM.
1-9-10 ©2010 Scott Adams, Inc./Dist. by UFS, Inc.
THAT ALMOST MEANT SOME-THING.
I'M TEMPTED TO STOP ACTING RANDOMLY.

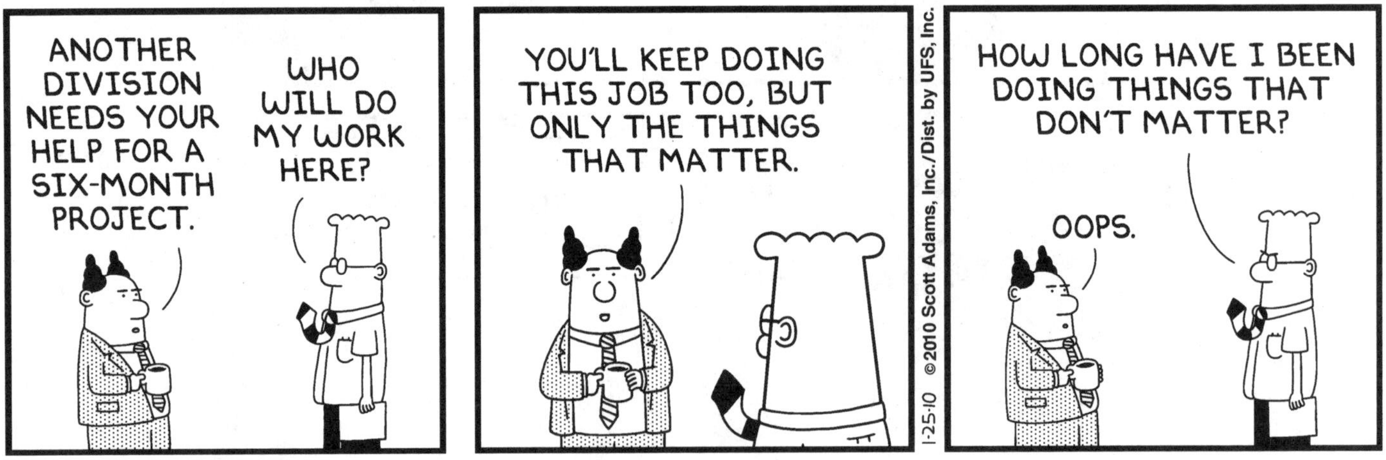
ANOTHER DIVISION NEEDS YOUR HELP FOR A SIX-MONTH PROJECT.
WHO WILL DO MY WORK HERE?
YOU'LL KEEP DOING THIS JOB TOO, BUT ONLY THE THINGS THAT MATTER.
1-25-10 ©2010 Scott Adams, Inc./Dist. by UFS, Inc.
HOW LONG HAVE I BEEN DOING THINGS THAT DON'T MATTER?
OOPS.

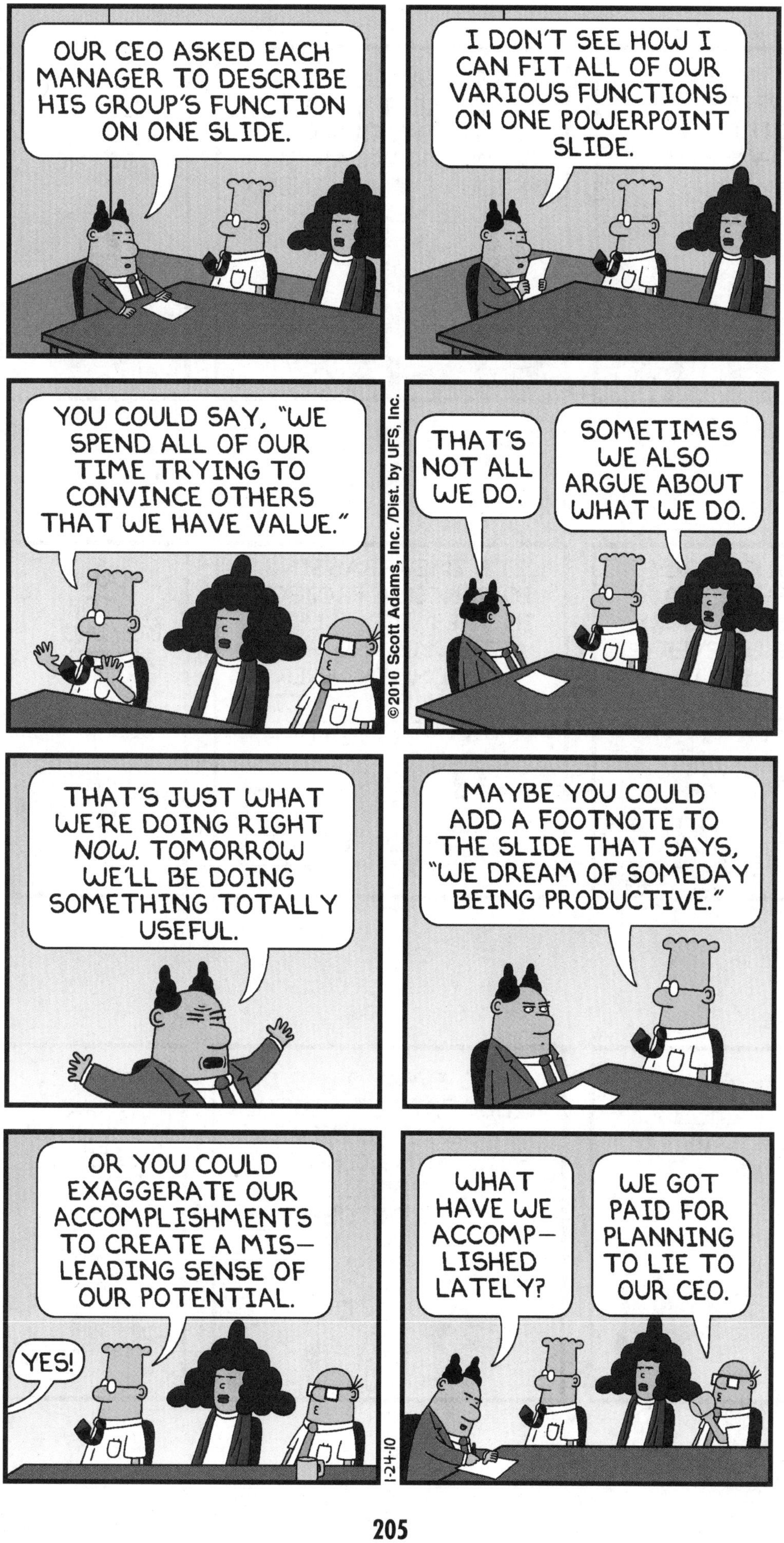
OUR CEO ASKED EACH MANAGER TO DESCRIBE HIS GROUP'S FUNCTION ON ONE SLIDE.
I DON'T SEE HOW I CAN FIT ALL OF OUR VARIOUS FUNCTIONS ON ONE POWERPOINT SLIDE.
YOU COULD SAY, "WE SPEND ALL OF OUR TIME TRYING TO CONVINCE OTHERS THAT WE HAVE VALUE."
©2010 Scott Adams, Inc./Dist. by UFS, Inc.
THAT'S NOT ALL WE DO.
SOMETIMES WE ALSO ARGUE ABOUT WHAT WE DO.
THAT'S JUST WHAT WE'RE DOING RIGHT *NOW*. TOMORROW WE'LL BE DOING SOMETHING TOTALLY USEFUL.
MAYBE YOU COULD ADD A FOOTNOTE TO THE SLIDE THAT SAYS, "WE DREAM OF SOMEDAY BEING PRODUCTIVE."
OR YOU COULD EXAGGERATE OUR ACCOMPLISHMENTS TO CREATE A MIS-LEADING SENSE OF OUR POTENTIAL.
YES!
1-24-10
WHAT HAVE WE ACCOMP-LISHED LATELY?
WE GOT PAID FOR PLANNING TO LIE TO OUR CEO.

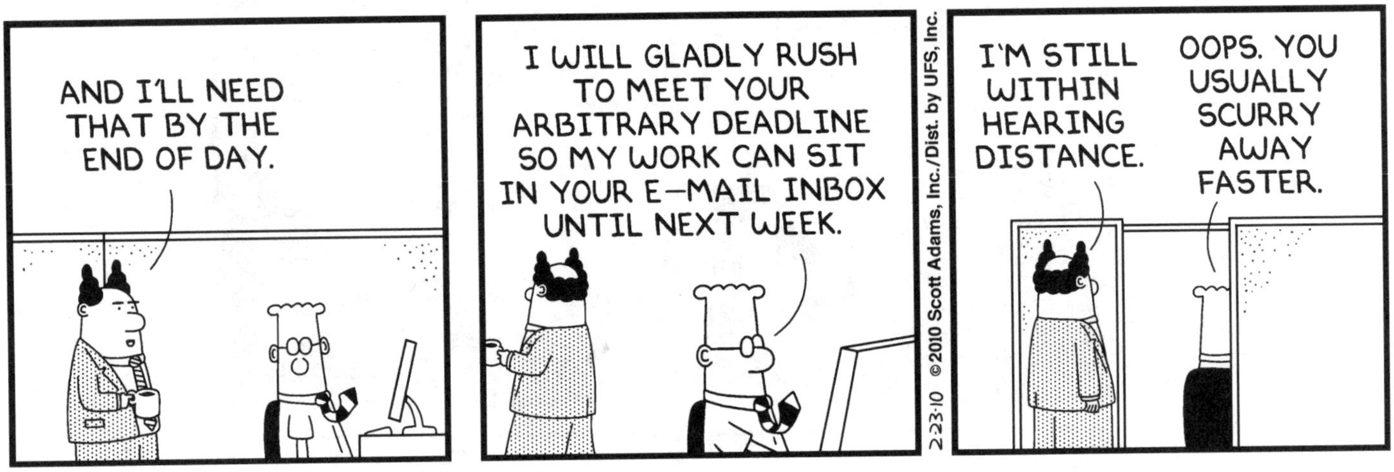
AND I'LL NEED THAT BY THE END OF DAY.
I WILL GLADLY RUSH TO MEET YOUR ARBITRARY DEADLINE SO MY WORK CAN SIT IN YOUR E-MAIL INBOX UNTIL NEXT WEEK.
2-23-10 ©2010 Scott Adams, Inc./Dist. by UFS, Inc.
I'M STILL WITHIN HEARING DISTANCE.
OOPS. YOU USUALLY SCURRY AWAY FASTER.

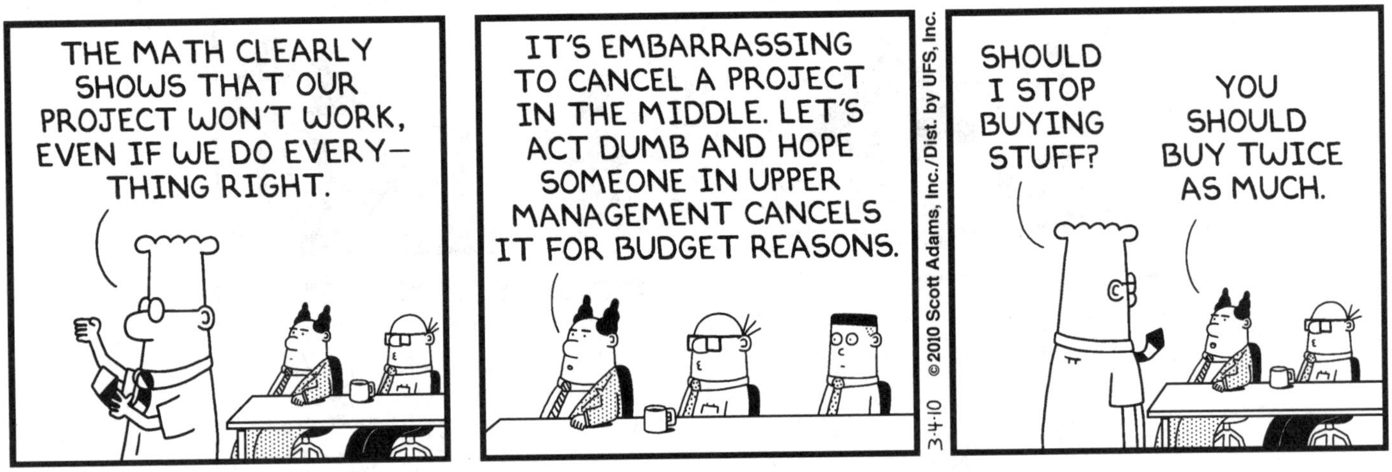
THE MATH CLEARLY SHOWS THAT OUR PROJECT WON'T WORK, EVEN IF WE DO EVERY-THING RIGHT.
IT'S EMBARRASSING TO CANCEL A PROJECT IN THE MIDDLE. LET'S ACT DUMB AND HOPE SOMEONE IN UPPER MANAGEMENT CANCELS IT FOR BUDGET REASONS.
3-4-10 ©2010 Scott Adams, Inc./Dist. by UFS, Inc.
SHOULD I STOP BUYING STUFF?
YOU SHOULD BUY TWICE AS MUCH.

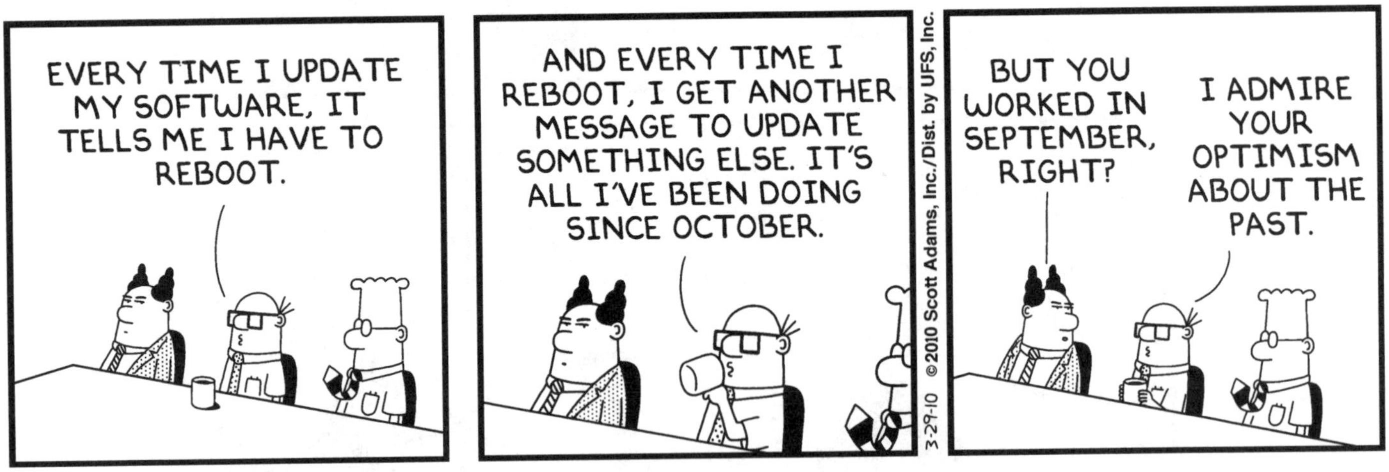
EVERY TIME I UPDATE MY SOFTWARE, IT TELLS ME I HAVE TO REBOOT.
AND EVERY TIME I REBOOT, I GET ANOTHER MESSAGE TO UPDATE SOMETHING ELSE. IT'S ALL I'VE BEEN DOING SINCE OCTOBER.
3-29-10 ©2010 Scott Adams, Inc./Dist. by UFS, Inc.
BUT YOU WORKED IN SEPTEMBER, RIGHT?
I ADMIRE YOUR OPTIMISM ABOUT THE PAST.

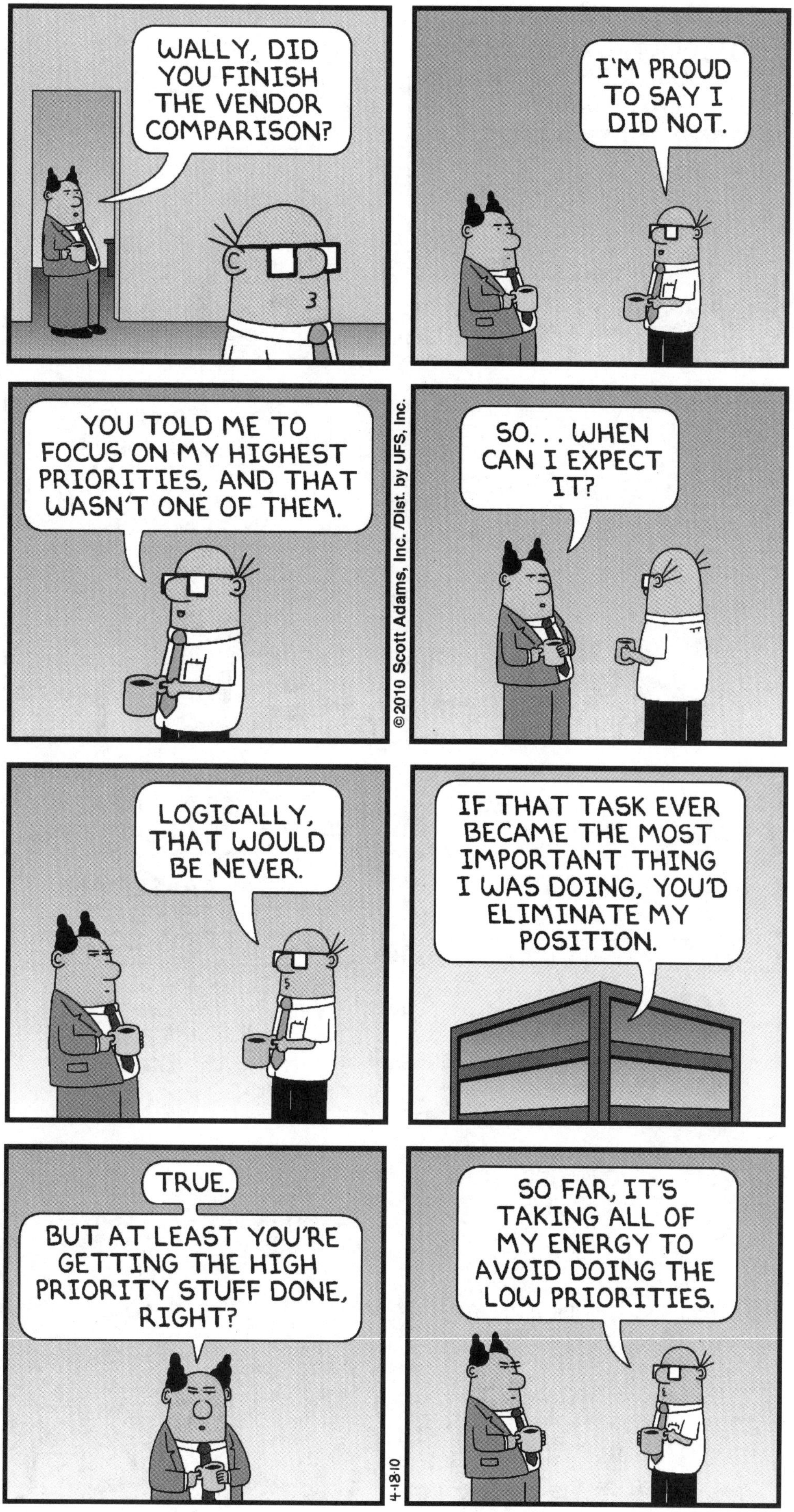
WALLY, DID YOU FINISH THE VENDOR COMPARISON?
I'M PROUD TO SAY I DID NOT.
YOU TOLD ME TO FOCUS ON MY HIGHEST PRIORITIES, AND THAT WASN'T ONE OF THEM.
SO. . . WHEN CAN I EXPECT IT?
LOGICALLY, THAT WOULD BE NEVER.
IF THAT TASK EVER BECAME THE MOST IMPORTANT THING I WAS DOING, YOU'D ELIMINATE MY POSITION.
TRUE.
BUT AT LEAST YOU'RE GETTING THE HIGH PRIORITY STUFF DONE, RIGHT?
SO FAR, IT'S TAKING ALL OF MY ENERGY TO AVOID DOING THE LOW PRIORITIES.
©2010 Scott Adams, Inc./Dist. by UFS, Inc.
4-18-10

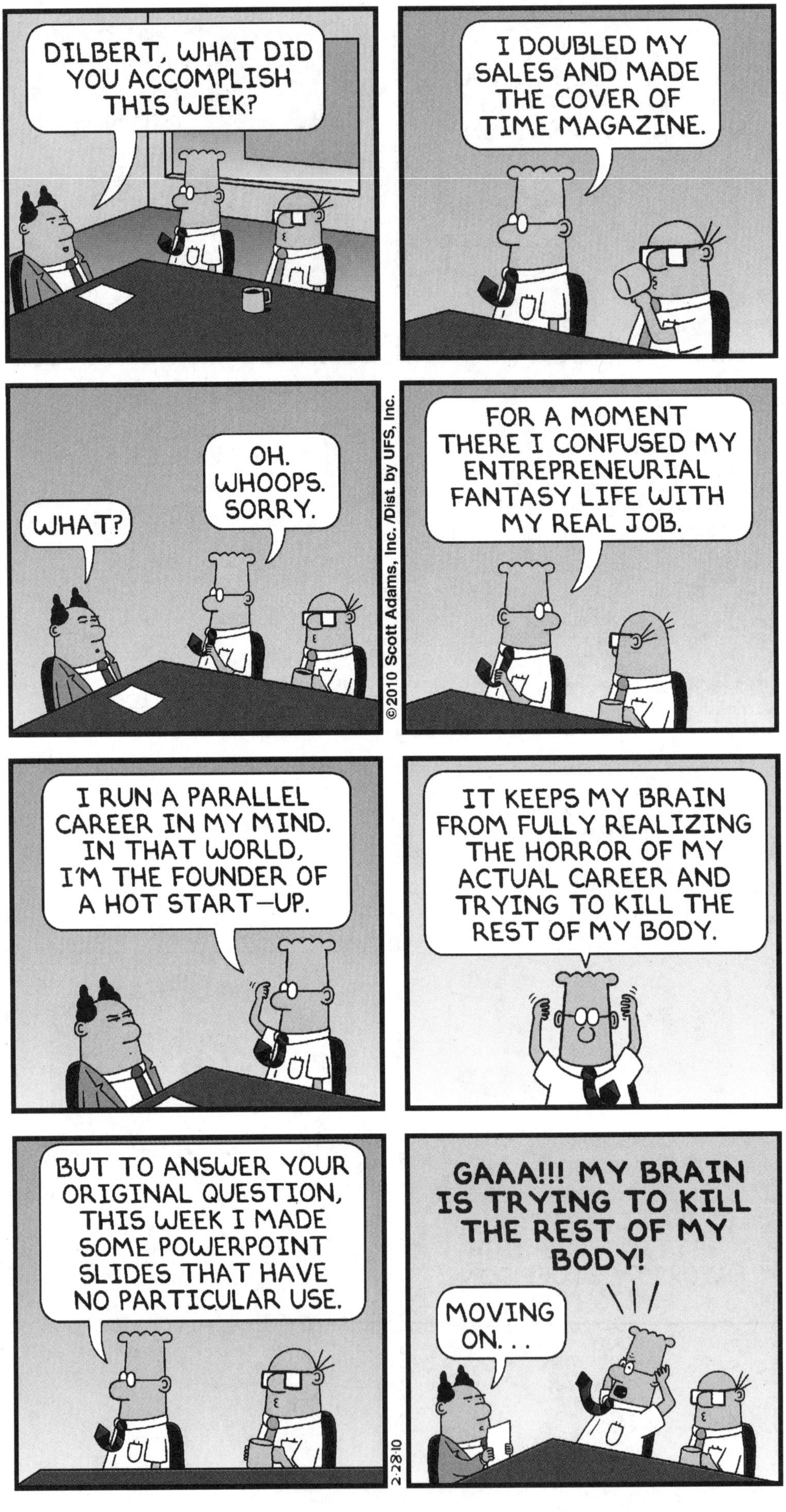
DILBERT, WHAT DID YOU ACCOMPLISH THIS WEEK?
I DOUBLED MY SALES AND MADE THE COVER OF TIME MAGAZINE.
WHAT?
OH. WHOOPS. SORRY.
FOR A MOMENT THERE I CONFUSED MY ENTREPRENEURIAL FANTASY LIFE WITH MY REAL JOB.
I RUN A PARALLEL CAREER IN MY MIND. IN THAT WORLD, I'M THE FOUNDER OF A HOT START-UP.
IT KEEPS MY BRAIN FROM FULLY REALIZING THE HORROR OF MY ACTUAL CAREER AND TRYING TO KILL THE REST OF MY BODY.
BUT TO ANSWER YOUR ORIGINAL QUESTION, THIS WEEK I MADE SOME POWERPOINT SLIDES THAT HAVE NO PARTICULAR USE.
GAAA!!! MY BRAIN IS TRYING TO KILL THE REST OF MY BODY!
MOVING ON...
©2010 Scott Adams, Inc./Dist. by UFS, Inc.
2-28-10